# INTERNATIONAL INSTITUTIONAL REFORM

The Foundation The Hague Joint Conferences on International Law gratefully acknowledges the indispensable and structural financial support of the Gemeente Den Haag (Municipality of The Hague).

The Foundation wishes to thank the sponsors of the Seventh Hague Joint Conference:

De Brauw Blackstone Westbroek
Clifford Chance
Freshfields Bruckhaus Deringer
Gemeente Den Haag
H.T.M. Personenvervoer N.V.
Koninklijke K.P.N. N.V.
Ministerie van Buitenlandse Zaken
Ministerie van Economische Zaken
Ministerie van Justitie
Provincie Zuid Holland
Shell International B.V.
Stichting Fonds voor de Geld- en Effectenhandel
Stichting Levi Lassen

FOUNDATION THE HAGUE JOINT CONFERENCES
ON INTERNATIONAL LAW

# INTERNATIONAL INSTITUTIONAL REFORM

Proceedings of the Seventh Hague Joint Conference held in
The Hague, The Netherlands
30 June – 2 July 2005

Edited by:

AGATA FIJALKOWSKI

T·M·C·ASSER PRESS
The Hague

Published by T.M.C.ASSER PRESS
P.O.Box 16163, 2500 BD The Hague, The Netherlands
www.asserpress.nl

T.M.C.ASSER PRESS English language books are distributed exclusively by:

Cambridge University Press, The Edinburgh Building, Shaftesbury Road,
Cambridge CB2 2RU, UK,
or
for customers in the USA, Canada and Mexico:
Cambridge University Press, 100 Brook Hill Drive, West Nyack, NY 10994-2133, USA
www.cambridge.org

ISBN 978-90-6704-250-5



The Foundation Hague Joint Conferences on International Law was founded in 1999. Its objective is to further the study of issues of international law through activities organised in the city of The Hague, the Netherlands. The Foundation aims to achieve this objective by means of seminars, conferences, scientific meetings and all other activities that may contribute to the Foundation's objective.

The organizations that have set up the Foundation Hague Joint Conferences on International Law are:

1. The Nederlandse Vereniging voor Internationaal Recht (Netherlands Society of International Law);
2. The Stichting Promotie Den Haag en Omstreken/VVV;
3. The American Society of International Law;
4. Stichting T.M.C. Asser Instituut, Institute for Private and Public International Law, International Commercial Arbitration and European Law.

# Preface

*International Institutional Reform* was the theme of the 2005 Hague Joint Conference – the seventh in a series of collaborations led by the American Society of International Law (ASIL) and the Nederlandse Vereniging voor Internationaal Recht (NVIR). Ably developed by Conference Co-Chairs Lucy F. Reed (ASIL) and Menno Kamminga (NVIR), twelve panels, four plenary sessions and sixty-six panelists tackled issues related to the reform debates that seem to be a part of virtually every international institution today. However, as these pages will demonstrate, a thoughtful examination of these discussions provided an occasion to appreciate the progress and development of forms of cooperation that would have been unthinkable even a decade ago when these joint conferences first began.

This gathering in The Hague in 2005 was also special because it marked the eve of ASIL's Centennial celebration in 2006. As ASIL's younger sister by five years, NVIR was pleased to be among the first to congratulate ASIL on reaching this milestone. As we opened this seventh joint conference in the Peace Palace, we reflected on The Hague's role as the world's legal capital and the extensive ties that ASIL members have had with this historic city and with their Dutch colleagues. We further reflected on the international character of the ASIL's membership that included many of the non-US participants at this joint conference.

Though we opened our meeting in the Peace Palace, we met in the shadow of the war in Iraq. Our first Joint Conference was also convened in the shadow of war following Iraq's invasion of Kuwait in 1990. A luncheon address was abruptly cancelled in 1995 when the minister of government who was to make the address was called away to deal with what we have come to know as the Srebrenica crisis. These are sober reminders that our deliberations are not academic ones, but address fundamental issues of global governance. The premise of the Joint Conference program was to create an opportunity for transatlantic and international discussion of contemporary issues in international law. The energetic attendance at the meeting reminded us of the many well-placed and informed individuals who together can play an important role in developing wise and enduring policies for the future.

We would like to close on a note of sincere gratitude to the Board of the Foundation, led by Mr Rein-Jan Hoekstra of the Council of State, and the Asser Institute, led by its Director Frans Nelissen, for having organized this event so well once again. Equally, we are much indebted to our colleagues Lucy Reed and Menno Kamminga, the two Conference Co-Chairs who, through genuine transatlantic cooperation, organized a topical, interesting and coherent program. The continued support on the part of the staff of the American Society of International Law is much appreciated. We further gratefully acknowledge the support of the Municipality of The Hague. We warmly thank the Municipality of The Hague and the other sponsors and contributors who helped to ensure a secure financial base for the Seventh Hague Joint Conference.

As we write these words, we are already planning our next Hague Joint Conference and look forward to seeing you in The Hague in 2007.

JAMES H. CARTER
*President*
*American Society of International Law*

NICO SCHRIJVER
*President*
*Netherlands Society of International Law*

The Hague, September 2006

# Message from the Program Committee Co-chairs

We chose 'international institutional reform' as the theme for the Seventh Hague Joint Conference on Contemporary Issues of International Law because institutional questions often do not seem to receive the attention they deserve, because presentation of the UN Secretary-General's High Level Panel report on Threats, Challenges and Change offers a perfect opportunity to discuss badly needed reform of the United Nations, and because The Hague offers the perfect setting for a discussion of institutional issues.

We and our fellow (and much appreciated) program committee members – Niels Blokker, Susan Karamanian, Erika de Wet and Ralph Wilde – were pleasantly surprised by the overwhelming response to our call for papers and proposals. The program you have in front of you is our attempt to create a challenging mix of items proposed in response to our invitation and items we ourselves identified as crucial. We have also tried to invite as chairs and panelists an exciting and international mix of established authorities and upcoming talent, practitioners and academics, international institution insiders and 'users', women and men. If we have not always managed to meet these objectives it has not been for want of trying.

The conference is addressing a very wide range of international institutions. We hope that participants will take the opportunity to learn about institutions less familiar to them and to allow plenty of cross-fertilization to occur. We also ask participants to apply the discipline to stick to the conference theme – while panels may have to begin by analyzing the substantive challenges facing the international community, the emphasis of presentations and discussions should be on the institutional reform needed to ensure proper and effective responses to these challenges.

Some of the thematic questions we aim to air: Are international institutions that were for the most part created in the 20th century suited to deal with the challenges of the 21st century? What is the self-reforming or self-cleansing power of international organizations? How much can be managed by relying on the implied powers doctrine? Which international institutions have been particularly successful in achieving their objectives and why? Which institutions have proven failures and ought to be scrapped forthwith?

As the Nederlandse Vereniging voor International Recht congratulates the American Society of International Law on its first century of expanding the boundaries of international law, we encourage you to think big. We encourage you to think beyond reforms that may seem realistic today. We wish you a stimulating conference!

Menno T. Kamminga and Lucy Reed
Program Committee Co-chairs

# Editor's Note

It has been aptly observed that international law inspires both hope and fear. In the preface to this publication, Professor Nico Schrijver is right to draw inspiration from international law, and identifying the important role that national, transatlantic and international discussions play in creating successful policies and provoking further reflection.

The theme of the Seventh Hague Joint Conference was 'International Institutional Reform'. The Conference demonstrates successful collaboration between the American Society of International Law (ASIL) and the Nederlandse Vereniging voor Internationaal Recht (NVIR). The Conference Co-Chairs, Lucy F. Reed (ASIL) and Menno Kamminga (NVIR), played a critical role in the Conference's success.

The meeting was a great achievement, and important evidence of this fact is reflected in these pages. Panels dealt with a wide range of topical subjects and many participants provided innovative and insightful suggestions concerning reforms. The energy, enthusiasm and passion were positive signs of the creativity and innovation among international law scholars and practitioners.

It was a great privilege to edit this book, and come into contact with such a wise and well-informed group of persons. The themes between panels reflect the main questions that international law faces as concerns the reform of institutions that carry great authority, and reflect long-standing tradition and far-reaching effect.

The Board of the Foundation, in particular Mr Rein-Jan Hoekstra of the Council of State, and the Asser Institute, in particular its Director Frans Nelissen, deserve thanks for organising another successful meeting. Lucy Reed and Menno Kamminga, as the two Conference Co-Chairs, brought together an illustrious group of scholars and practitioners to participate in a carefully planned programme. The American Society of International Law's support is appreciated as is the support on the part of the Municipality of The Hague.

It also has been such a great pleasure to work with former colleagues from the Asser Institute. Those involved were professional, enthusiastic, and committed to publishing a work that properly reflected the achievement of the 2006 meeting. Special appreciation is extended to Mieke Eijdenberg, Marjolijn Bastiaans, Hans Ouwerkerk, and Lyske de Vries.

Lancaster, September 2006

Dr Agata Fijalkowski
*Lecturer-in-Law*
Lancaster University, United Kingdom

# Table of Contents

# Opening of the Conference

by His Excellency Bernard Bot
Minister of Foreign Affairs of the Kingdom of the Netherlands

## The Reform of International Organisations

### Introduction

Excellencies, distinguished guests, ladies and gentlemen,

It is a great pleasure for me, even at this early hour, to open this Joint Conference on Contemporary Issues of International Law. My compliments to the American Society of International Law and the Nederlandse Vereniging voor Internationaal Recht for organising the seventh conference in this series. In our fast-moving times we cannot do without meetings like this one, which bring together international lawyers, scholars and practitioners from so many countries and such diverse backgrounds. This is the perfect forum for discussing the implications of global changes for international law, and for considering how international law can help us meet the challenges that come with change.

### International Institutional Reform

Yes, **change** will be our topic today, for the central theme of this conference is international institutional reform. Your co-chairs, Professor Kamminga and Ms Reed, deserve recognition for choosing that theme and, in particular, for preparing a thematically cohesive programme that should lead to constructive discussion. They mentioned three reasons for their choice. First, "because institutional questions often do not seem to receive the attention they deserve". Second, because the presentation of the UN Secretary-General's report "In larger freedom" offers "a perfect opportunity to discuss badly needed reform of the United Nations". And third, "because The Hague offers the perfect setting for a discussion of institutional issues".

I hardly need to expand on the role of The Hague, because it is so clearly the ideal location for this event. Former UN Secretary-General Boutros Boutros-Ghali called the Hague "the legal capital of the world". And the city's claim to that title has grown even stronger since the International Criminal Court opened its doors here, exactly three years ago today. Within a relatively short time, a multitude of States have become parties to the Rome Statute. I very much hope that many more will soon follow, and make the International Criminal Court a truly universal institution. The ICC, and the many other organisations that make The Hague the world's legal capital, have brought a large number of international lawyers to this city. Not only to the judicial and legal institutions, but also to embassies. A number of those lawyers are here today. I invite them to take active part in the discussions and share their experiences with us.

## The Importance of Institutional Questions

But now let me return to the other two reasons that our co-chairs mentioned for choosing the theme of international institutional reform. The first is that institutional questions do not always receive the attention they deserve. Such questions are all too often associated with technical details of the work of international organisations, such as provisions defining a quorum, or the procedures that an organisation must follow to become party to a treaty. But institutional questions can also be ***fundamental*** to the work of international organisations. One person who, decades ago, recognised the importance of institutions for international cooperation was Jean Monnet. He was the intellectual father of the European Coal and Steel Community, and inspired the "Community method" of cooperation within all three of the original European Communities.

Jean Monnet had an extraordinary career. At first, he followed in his father's footsteps as a cognac merchant, doing business all over the world. After the First World War he became Deputy Secretary-General of the League of Nations. In that role, he discovered both the potential and the pitfalls of intergovernmental cooperation. He came to realise that many States tend to focus too narrowly on their own short-term interests. That attitude makes the classical, intergovernmental method of decision-making very slow and ineffective. Monnet therefore proposed the creation of institutions to which States could attribute decision-making powers for the common good. As he wrote in his memoirs: "Nothing is possible without men: nothing is lasting without institutions.... But men pass away; others will take our place. We cannot bequeath them our personal experience. That will die with us. But we can leave them institutions. The life of institutions is longer than that of men: if they are well built, they can accumulate and hand on the wisdom of succeeding generations." Monnet's wise words make it clear why international institutions are so essential.

His ideas were put into practice in the 1950 Declaration by the French foreign minister Robert Schuman. Faced with Cold War tensions and the threat of new friction between Germany and France, Schuman aimed to safeguard world peace by means of, as he said at the time, "creative efforts proportionate to the dangers which threaten it". The measures he proposed in his Declaration formed the basis for the Treaty establishing the Coal and Steel Community. In essence, those measures were exactly what Monnet had proposed;. namely, attributing unprecedented powers to independent institutions. The scope of this "Community method" was later extended, when two other European Communities were created.

I firmly believe that Schuman chose the ***right*** method. Of course, like so many things, the process of European integration has its ups and downs. But during my ten years in Brussels as Permanent Representative of the Netherlands, I saw that Monnet's model has proved its value. A few years ago, Philippe de Schoutheete, who was my Belgian counterpart on the Committee of Permanent Representatives, wrote that this model has played an essential role in making the Communities ***action-oriented***. It overcomes the inefficiency of the traditional method of decision-making used in the League of Nations, as well as the Council of Europe, which was created shortly before Schuman's declaration.

So it makes sense for us to ask whether the EU's experience could be useful to other regional or global organisations. In my view it is. Although we cannot simply transplant that experience directly into other regional and global frameworks, I believe that its lessons are valuable. In fact, we ***must*** heed those lessons, especially in the types of cases mentioned in the Schuman Declaration, where today's world requires efforts proportionate to the dangers which threaten it.

One main difference between the EU and other international organisations is the role of independent **institutions**. Among the core characteristics of the three original European Communities, inspired by the ideas of Jean Monnet, was the extraordinary attribution of unprecedented powers to independent institutions. In general, states have been – and still are – reluctant to grant extensive powers to international organisations. They have done so only in a few exceptional cases. One of the best examples is the UN Security Council.

It is remarkable that in 1945, the makers of the United Nations endowed the Security Council with such impressive powers. However, it is not hard to understand their reasons. As the opening words of the UN Charter tell us, the peoples of the United Nations were determined to save succeeding generations from the scourge of war. At the end of the Second World War, it was generally believed that the measures taken in response to the First World War had proven inadequate. The UN's founding fathers therefore agreed to provisions that read almost like Jean Monnet *avant la lettre*. Article 24, paragraph 1 of the UN Charter states, "In order to ensure prompt and effective action by the United Nations, its Members confer on the Security Council primary responsibility for the maintenance of international peace and security, and agree that in carrying out its duties under this responsibility the Security Council acts on their behalf." In short, the Members confer responsibility on the Security Council, and the Security Council acts on their behalf – this is a striking example of giving up powers to a higher authority, in the common interest.

Of course, the institutions of the European Communities, which were created in the 1950s, differ in important ways from the Security Council. For instance, many of them are composed of independent individuals, who do not represent the Member States. This possibility was not really considered for the Security Council. It was generally agreed that its members should be representatives of States, not independent experts. As you probably know, the crucial issue at the 1945 San Francisco negotiations was permanent representation of the five great powers of the period on the Council, along with veto power for those five states.

Naturally, the Security Council is an exceptional case. The vast majority of international organisations have not been endowed with such far-reaching powers. And often that's just fine, because in many cases, we do not need highly supranational institutions. It is often sufficient for organisations to serve as meeting places where Members can exchange information, carry out consultations and coordinate policies, and where secretariats simply facilitate that process and provide services. In each individual case, we must decide whether this is adequate or whether it may be necessary to go a step further. And when it is in our common interest to go further, we must do so.

At times, a clear ***long***-term perspective is vital. That may sound rather idealistic, but it is in our common interest. And, I should add, it is in our national interest as well. The Netherlands, with the world's fourteenth largest economy, understands that in a time of cross-border threats and opportunities, its own wealth and security cannot be separated from the wealth and security of other states.

## Reforming International Organisations

Ladies and gentlemen,

Keeping the importance of multilateralism in mind, we should be prepared to take bold steps whenever necessary, and we should be able to decide when the time is ripe to reform international organisations. That brings me to yet another reason that the topic of this conference is such a timely one: now is the time to reform a ***number*** of international institutions. I therefore applaud your decision to take a ***broad*** perspective and concentrate not only on reform of the United Nations, but also on other cases, ranging from institutional reform of the EU and regional human rights courts to less well-known organisations such as the International Organisation of Vine and Wine. Before I discuss UN reform, let me first make some brief remarks on the reform of international organisations in general.

My first point relates to the ***constitutional*** characteristics of treaties that create international organisations. If well-drafted, such treaties lay down a durable framework of substantive rules and institutional structures. A framework that can last not just a few months, but for a much longer period. That is not an easy task in a rapidly changing world. The substantive rules have to be sufficiently broad to be useful in the long run, but at the same time they must be specific enough to guide the practice of member states. A case in point is the UN Charter's rules on the use of force. More specifically, the prohibition against the threat or use of **armed** force, with two exceptions: self-defence and Security Council authorisation. Since this substantive framework was established in 1945, it has been tested in practice many times, and there is not much support for changing it. Even the most recent reform proposals recommended leaving the Charter's rules on the use of force unchanged.

However, it is not so much the **substantive** rules that distinguish constitutions of international organisations from other treaties. Instead, their most defining characteristic is the institutional **framework** that they set up. As the International Court of Justice held in 1996, the object of such constitutions is "to create new subjects of law endowed with a certain autonomy, to which the parties entrust the task of realizing common goals." This is certainly the most important method of enabling international organisations to perform their functions. States grant powers to an organisation, and by exercising those powers the organisation aims to "realize goals that are common to the Member States", to quote the Court once again.

For example, the drafters of the UN Charter could not foresee what kinds of security threats UN Members would face sixty years later. If they had included a list of security threats in the Charter, it is unlikely that they would have mentioned terrorism, poverty, deadly infectious disease and environmental degradation. But in our own day, the UN Secretary-General has emphasised all those threats in his report "In larger freedom". The drafters of the Charter wisely left it to the Security Council to determine whether or not a threat to the peace exists in concrete cases, and what measures should be taken.

A wide variety of techniques have been developed to enable international organisations to respond to practical needs. They include implied powers, teleological interpretation, and *effet utile*. Without a doubt, these techniques are necessary and useful. But there is a limit to what they are capable of. That is especially true in the international legal order, which is not as strong as most national legal orders, and in which the role of courts is much more limited. Member States of an international organisation will sooner or later disagree about the course the organisation should take. Some may favour a dynamic role, while others may criticise what is sometimes referred to as 'mission creep'. At such moments it may become necessary to consider reforming the organisation.

## UN Reform

Ladies and gentlemen,

Reform of international organisations – this summer, that phrase inevitably brings to mind the proposals for institutional reform of the United Nations. In September, leaders from all over the world will convene in New York to discuss UN reform. This reform initiative is unprecedented. A frank, worldwide debate is already under way, based on the recommendations of the UN Secretary-General and the reports of the High-level Panel on Threats, Challenges and Change and the UN Millennium Project Team.

The Secretary-General has said that the UN is at a crossroads. I agree. The challenge is now to decide which signposts we will follow, and how to avoid detours and roadblocks. Our common destination is clear: we want to arrive at a multilateral system that is fully equipped to face ***today's*** challenges and ***tomorrow's***.

Gradually, we are all waking up to the fact that in a globalised world, national interests and the common interest have become two sides of the same coin. In this new world, there is a new rule: cross-border challenges ***demand*** cross-border responses. Global warming and rising sea levels, poverty and AIDS – they threaten us regardless of nationality, ethnicity or religion. As do terrorism and the spread of weapons of mass destruction. Security, development and respect for human rights are inextricably linked. The debate and the decisions on UN reform will largely determine whether or not mankind's only truly global political institution will be able to adapt to this rapidly changing world. In the coming months we will have to determine what route will lead us to a UN that is *more effective and more legitimate.*

Let me briefly discuss some of the signposts we find at the crossroads where we are now. And I will explain why, in my view, those signposts point us towards establishing a Human Rights Council and a Peacebuilding Commission, as well as reforming the Economic and Social Council and the Security Council.

The need for institutional reform is very clear in the case of the Human Rights Commission. Most states agree that its sessions are politicised and that it is selective in its work. The Secretary-General has put forward a bold and praiseworthy recommendation to replace the Human Rights Commission with a Human Rights Council.

The Netherlands believes that this new Council could have several major advantages. It could sit permanently, instead of six weeks a year; it could respond immediately in a crisis; and it would allow dialogue and constructive mutual criticism to take place at a high political level. We have a strong preference for making this new Council a principal organ of the UN, on an equal footing with the Security Council and the Economic and Social Council. That would perfectly reflect the fundamental triangle of development, security and human rights, with human rights no less important than development or peace and security.

There are still issues to be debated; for instance, the mandate of the proposed Council, its size and composition, and its relationships with other UN institutions. In addition, effective "mainstreaming" of human rights will remain crucial within all UN bodies. And we should preserve the constructive achievements of the Human Rights Commission, by maintaining the active participation of non-governmental organisations and the system of Special Rapporteurs. However, now is the time to choose the right direction; the exact characteristics of the Human Rights Council can be worked out later.

## Peacebuilding Commission

The Netherlands is also a strong supporter of establishing a Peacebuilding Commission, as the Secretary-General has proposed The Commission's mandate should primarily cover the transition between the end of conflict and the resumption of sustainable development activities, encompassing whatever period may be necessary. While the Commission should not categorically exclude ***conflict prevention*** activities, it should focus on ***post-conflict peacebuilding*** activities. There are already enough UN mechanisms focused on conflict prevention. In connection with this point, our government is in favour of strengthening the Secretary-General's conflict prevention capacity: In the first stages of peacebuilding, the new Commission should start by assisting with the work of the Security Council. Its reports should also be made available to other bodies in the UN system; in particular, the Economic and Social Council, specialised agencies, funds and programmes.

The Dutch government considers it essential for the international financial institutions to become actively involved in the Peacebuilding Commission, each in accordance with its own activities and objectives. The Secretary-General is currently conducting discussions on this topic, and we look forward to the results. It also seems appropriate for non-governmental organisations to become involved in the Commission's work.

The functions of the Peacebuilding Commission should be advisory, including exchange of information, coordination, strategic planning and mobilisation of adequate resources. It will be important for the Commission to have adequate ***funding***, preferably from mandatory contributions.

## ECOSOC

Reform of the Economic and Social Council remains a difficult challenge. That Council has the potential to play a more central role in monitoring progress towards the Millennium Development Goals. I am in favour of reforming ECOSOC so that it can fulfil that potential, with effective monitoring of the Millennium Development Goals by means of peer reviews.

ECOSOC should also be promoting and monitoring the integrated follow-up to UN summits from the perspective of sustainable development, because the issues associated with Cairo, Beijing, Copenhagen, Johannesburg and Monterrey are complementary to each other.

In addition, there is potential to increase efficiency, reduce overlap and cut transaction costs and bureaucracy, by decreasing the large number of ECOSOC commissions and carrying out further streamlining.

Finally, the agenda for ECOSOC should be more politically focused, so that it captures more attention at a higher political level. In short, more robust efforts are necessary to achieve meaningful reform and revitalisation of ECOSOC.

### Security Council

Reform of the Security Council has been on the international political agenda for years, but it is such a politically charged subject that discussions have been in permanent deadlock. The fact that the High-Level Panel was unable to propose just one model, but felt compelled to propose two alternatives, demonstrates once again how deeply UN members are split on this issue. Still, the Panel's proposals did form the starting point for renewed and intense debate, and the issue has caught the attention of the public and national parliaments – including our own, here in the Netherlands. We have seen alternative proposals emerge, such as the "green" and "blue" models, as well as the "G4 proposal". Basically, the disagreement comes down to the issue of whether the Council should be enlarged to include more permanent members, and if so, how many?

From the outset of this debate, the Netherlands has underlined the importance of a representative and ***legitimate*** Council. Accordingly, we are strongly in favour of harnessing the momentum already generated in the debate on Security Council reform, and we would welcome a decision on this matter, preferably before the September summit.

A second element we stress is the need for an ***effective*** Council, which can take on the many challenges of today's complex world. For that reason, we strongly object to extending veto power to new permanent members.

And I would like to make a third point, without denying the importance of equitable geographical distribution. We also need to look at other, non-geographical criteria to determine whether a country is eligible for a seat on the Security Council – whether permanent or non-permanent. We need to take into account what a country actually contributes to the work of the UN; for example, its support for peace operations, financial contributions, promotion of human rights, and development assistance.

You might ask what overall Dutch position emerges from these basic principles. Do we believe there should be new permanent members? Do we support Brazil, Germany, Japan and India, the countries that have joined forces as the G4? On this issue, I would say that we sympathise with their ambitions, and we are ***also*** sympathetic to the ***African*** campaign to be represented by two permanent members. However, we do not believe the current reform should be set in stone. The world might look very different ten or fifteen years from now. That's why the Netherlands' support for new permanent members has one condition attached. We should all have the opportunity to take stock of developments in ten to fifteen years' time. That would also encourage the new permanent members to live up to the expectations that come with their new status. After all, their position would be under review in a decade or so. This proposal might even be acceptable to countries that ***oppose*** the notion of new permanent members.

In September the whole world will judge how we review and reform the workings of the United Nations. The proposals on the table reflect a profound understanding that the international community cannot do without adequate international institutions, and they are full of sensible plans for reform. It is now up to the Member States to take action. The Netherlands will participate in whatever way it can.

## Conclusion

Ladies and gentlemen,

For the UN and for any other international organisation, eventually the time comes to reflect on the need to adapt its structures and amend its constitution. At such moments, it is important to recall the importance of effective international institutions. They are crucial components of the international legal order, which we depend on in many ways, and which we must develop further. Let me conclude by returning to Jean Monnet, who rightly emphasised that "nothing is lasting without institutions.... If they are well built, they can accumulate and hand on the wisdom of succeeding generations."

I wish you a successful and inspiring conference. Thank you.

# Reformability: Why (and How) Are Some International Organizations Able to Reform Themselves and Others Not?

The panel was convened by its Chair, Menno Kamminga*

## Remarks by Gian Luca Burci**

### Institutional adaptation without reform: the actors and challenges of globalization

One of the most interesting phenomena since the end of the Cold War is the degree to which 'traditional' international organizations have adapted to deeply changing political and factual circumstances, without formally amending their own constitutional structures or functions. They have relied on the general and flexible nature of their constitutive instruments and on political processes to assume roles that could have hardly been foreseeable at the moment of their establishment.

The World Health Organization (WHO) offers a good example of such 'adaptation without reform', having substantially developed its normative, policy-making and operational functions, sometimes on the basis of decisions of its governing bodies, and at other times on the initiative of its Secretariat, but without changing its overall legal framework. Firstly, what are the reasons that have caused and steered this process of development and adaptation? They are certainly diverse and sometimes antagonistic, but all are facets of the process of globalization in its overall complexity. The following challenges and developments may better illustrate the pressures and increasing competition faced by WHO in its role as the only global public health agency:

- The relative decline of governments as the main providers of medical and health care services domestically, and as the only legitimate authorities setting health rules and policies internationally. Market mechanisms and corporate interests have assumed a primary role in defining global health governance;
- The dark side of the pervasiveness of market and corporate values in the public health field is the failure of the market to adequately address the so-called 'neglected diseases', i.e., those disproportionately affecting poor countries and which do not offer prospects of sufficient financial returns for pharmaceutical companies. This imbalance is captured in the notion of the '10/90 divide': only 10 per

* Professor of International Law, Maastricht University, the Netherlands.

** Legal Counsel, World Health Organization. The opinions expressed are those of the author and do not necessarily reflect those of the World Health Organization.

cent of investments is destined to the research and development of medicines for diseases affecting 90 per cent of humankind;

- The increasing speed and ease in the international movement of goods and persons, together with profound social and economic changes in developing countries, has facilitated the emergence or re-emergence of infectious diseases at an unprecedented pace. The capacity of such diseases to destabilize entire regions or even the whole international community, dramatically confirmed by the SARS outbreak of 2003 and the current fear of a new influenza pandemic, has challenged existing regimes of intergovernmental cooperation and accepted notions of national sovereignty;
- In a globalizing and increasingly interdependent world, health has clearly emerged as a cross-cutting issue, interacting with areas of international relations and law such as trade, intellectual property, environmental protection, human rights, arms control and the fight against international terrorism. The WHO has not actively participated in the establishment of the respective legal regimes, and has somehow found itself at the margin of political debates and normative developments;
- Finally, globalization is also reflected in the explosion of information technology and the increasing speed and availability of information. The WHO has, on occasion, relied on the internet not only or so much for information purposes, but rather as an important operational tool, allowing it to provide guidance that could reach directly individuals and other non-state actors besides governments.

Why then, faced with such developments and challenges, has the WHO not enacted more formal and substantial institutional changes? The reasons are manifold. Firstly, the history of the UN system shows consistently the reluctance of Member States to open constitutions of international organizations to formal amendments, except for increasing the membership of executive bodies. Secondly, and more specifically to the WHO, there has been a reluctance to codify and regulate activities of the Organization that may impact and affect the international pharmaceutical market and the interests of major corporate actors. Thirdly, the Secretariat of a technical agency such as WHO arguably enjoys more 'freedom of manoeuvre' *vis-à-vis* its governing bodies than, for example, the Secretariat of a political organization such as the UN. This relatively broader authority has allowed the WHO Secretariat to change and adapt its operational activities incrementally without the involvement of its policy-making organs, while arguably remaining within the limits of its existing mandates.

Concerning some key examples of 'adaptation without reform', I would like to focus on two developments that have substantially changed the way WHO implements two of its core functions, namely, addressing neglected diseases of poor countries; and preventing and controlling the international spread of infectious diseases.

I have mentioned before the historical failure of market mechanisms alone to tackle the yawning gap between the morbidity and mortality caused by infectious diseases in developing countries and the research and pharmaceutical resources spent on them. Indeed, while basic research often takes place in university or public laboratories, both the development of new medicines and clinical trials for promising candidate drugs (two crucial steps in the manufacturing of medicines) are largely left to pharmaceutical companies on the basis of financial or commercial considerations. The scarce financial attractiveness of neglected diseases explains why, for example, out of more than one thousand patents filed in the pharmaceutical area between the mid-1970s and the mid 1990s, only 13 related exclusively to tropical diseases.

In the light of this situation, the WHO has developed, since the 1970s, mechanisms for collaboration with the private industry, for example by supporting clinical trials of medicines under development or by licensing to private companies intellectual property rights on certain compounds as a 'push' factor to encourage them to develop new medicines for neglected disease. The role played by the WHO in this connection is particularly visible in the area of tropical diseases, such as onchocerciasis, leishmaniasis and hemorrhagic fevers.

At the same time, however, there have recently been efforts by many public and private actors to develop innovative mechanisms to generate additional and much needed financial resources as well as to try to correct the inadequacies of the market. The initiatives taken in this direction have been labelled 'public-private partnerships', i.e., long-term collaborative mechanisms to address a specific public health problem, encompassing a diverse array of partners both private and public, with an agreed division of labour and contribution of resources. Most of these partnerships are not established as separate international agencies or private law entities; they are rather unincorporated groups of stakeholders, and are normally 'hosted' by an existing international organization which provides their secretariat. The WHO has been particularly proactive, hosting more than 20 such initiatives of which it is also a member.

To give an example of the diversity of models and approaches characterizing the recent proliferation of health partnerships, brief mention should be made of the Global Alliance on Vaccine and Immunization (GAVI) and of the Medicines for Malaria Venture (MMV). The GAVI was launched in 2000 thanks to an initial grant from the Gates Foundation, its main objective being improving access to sustainable immunization services in developing countries. The members of GAVI encompass foundations, governments of donor and recipient countries, NGOs, vaccine manufacturers and international bodies including WHO. An interesting element in the GAVI, as well as in many other partnerships, is their degree of self-organization; for example, membership in the GAVI's Board – its steering body – is left to the various 'constituencies' that compose it and that decide which among their members will represent that particular group on the Board. The GAVI's resources come from foundations, donor governments and financial institutions (e.g., the World Bank) and are dispensed either as grants or in the form of vaccine procurement through UNICEF, which also provides the GAVI's secretariat. In order to attract corporate donations, the members of GAVI also have established a separate Vaccine Fund in the United States as a charity with tax-deductible status; it is the Fund that formally decides which projects to finance based on the Board's recommendation. The philosophy is that of a performance-based programme, where emphasis is placed on national donor coordination and monitoring of progress and outcomes. The WHO assists recipient countries from a technical point of view and monitors implementation on behalf of the GAVI.

The MMV is one of the very few partnerships to have been incorporated, in this case as a Swiss foundation. It operates more like a virtual R&D company (albeit non-for-profit) than a public funding agency, hence the need for a separate legal personality. The MMV is run by a management team and funded from a variety of sources, including, again, the Gates Foundation, the WHO and several donor countries. The WHO is also *ex officio* member of its Board. The MMV focuses on the discovery and commercialization of new anti-malarial drugs, funding projects by large pharmaceutical companies on a competitive basis. To ensure some control over the development of candidate drugs, it uses intellectual property rights by securing downstream rights to develop compounds, either in the form of patent ownerships or through a free licence on candidate drugs. The balance between ensuring a return for participating companies and the affordability of new drugs revolves among other things around the nature of the funds made available to the MMV and its non-for-profit nature.

The main challenges for the WHO as a member and host of several partnerships derive from the tendency of the latter to develop forms of self-governance that accentuate their 'separateness' from the hosting organization and their intention to control both programmatic and administrative processes. The very fact of their establishment in a way indicates that the WHO's efforts in a particular area have not been successful or have not been enough, and that coordination and resource mobilization among a broad group of stakeholders is necessary to tackle a particular health problem. The WHO Secretariat thus feels an understandable pressure in being an active member and possibly a host of partnerships. At the same time, however, their proliferation has led to a situation where a growing proportion of the Secretariat works in support of external groups and programmes rather than for the WHO as such, and under some form of control or oversight by those groups. This has created tensions between the need to adapt to operate in a changing environment, on the one hand, and doubts about the constitutionality and sustainability of such arrangements, on the other hand.

The second example of successful adaptation without reform concerns the important role of the WHO in leading and coordinating international efforts to prevent and control the spread of infectious diseases. This is one of the core areas of the WHO's constitutional mandate, and to a certain extent the WHO has been established to centralize disease control functions that used to be exercised by a number of international sanitary bureaus. Also from a normative point of view, the WHO has exercised regulatory powers that were supposed to replace the largely ineffective sanitary conventions from the 1850s onwards. Particular mention should be made in this connection of the International Health Regulations (IHR), an international instrument akin to a treaty adopted by the WHO's Health Assembly and binding for all Member States that do not object to it within a certain period from its adoption. The IHR currently in force, adopted in 1951 and revised in 1969, have largely become irrelevant since they were based on a number of principles and assumptions that did not prove adequate to either ensure international control of epidemics or to reassure states against over-reactions by other countries. A grave flaw of the IHR was their being based on a list of named diseases, in particular in view of the emergence of new diseases at an unprecedented pace since the late 1980s. The IHR were also based on the concept of maximum measures that states could impose when faced with a particular health risk; that concept is not in keeping with the science-based approach embedded in WTO agreements such as those on Sanitary and Phytosanitary measures and on Technical Barriers to Trade.

As a consequence of the progressive marginalization of the IHR as a tool for disease control, the WHO Secretariat developed and successfully implemented in practice since the mid-1990s an operational approach to disease surveillance and control based on a few innovative ideas. Firstly, experience showed that governments are either unable or reluctant to verify and disclose disease outbreaks on their territory.

Most relevant information comes to WHO from third parties, whether they are international agencies, NGOs, or even individuals in the countries concerned. The WHO Secretariat relies on such information to then ask the governments concerned to verify their correctness, and holds them accountable if they do not through the possibility of making public the information available. The government of Canada has even developed a web crawler called GPHIN (Global Public Health Intelligence Network) which sweeps the web seeking keywords that can reveal unusual pathogenic events. The raw information is then elaborated by the WHO Secretariat for any necessary follow-up. It was precisely though GPHIN that the WHO was alerted in November 2002 to an outbreak of atypical influenza in the Chinese province of Guandong, which later proved to be the beginning of the SARS epidemic. Through this approach, the WHO Secretariat has quietly discarded the assumption that an international secretariat may only rely on information provided by Member States for subsequent action.

Secondly, the WHO has coordinated, and participates in, networks of experts and collaborating institutions that provide the scientific expertise and operational capacities that its secretariat sometimes lacks. Prominent among them in the field of infectious diseases is the Global Outbreak Alert and Response Network (GOARN), which encompasses almost 100 national and international agencies and research institutes. The interesting aspects of GOARN and other similar networks is their degree of self-organization and governance. They are based on flexible and non-binding arrangements which define their operational principles and rules, are 'hosted' and supported by the WHO and comprise both public and international agencies and NGOs. From the latter point of view, it is striking how self-organized networks of heterogeneous partners, often working through virtual means (e-mail, videoconferences), may play a crucial role in developing technical and normative guidance for the whole international community, once again replacing traditional international mechanisms for the provision of expert advice.

Thirdly, the WHO has successfully used modern information technology – in particular the internet – to disseminate information, guidance and advice concerning particular disease outbreaks. This approach, which has not been challenged as such as exceeding the authority of the Secretariat, has allowed the WHO to bypass, if necessary, governments as the irreplaceable interface between an international organization and individuals or other non-state actors. The WHO has been able to reach directly through the internet economic and public health operators and even individuals, thus making it more difficult for governments to exercise control over available information.

The most visible and dramatic exercise by the WHO of the operational approaches just described has taken place in response to the SARS epidemic. While remaining within its constitutional mandate but nonetheless in the absence of a specific legal framework adopted by the WHO's Assembly, the WHO Secretariat has successfully overcome China's initial lack of collaboration in disclosing the extent of the SARS epidemic and in taking aggressive control measures by relying on all available information to bring pressure on the government. The WHO has used its internet site as an electronic platform to provide much needed centralized information on the epidemiological and clinical developments of the epidemic as well as on the breakthroughs concerning its nature and available treatments. Most importantly, it has provided electronically much needed advice to governments and non-state actors, including clear advice against travelling to certain affected areas. The impact of such formally non-binding guidance has been dramatic; it has allowed public health authorities to focus their prevention and control activities and arguably reduced the possibility of international spread of the disease. Equally impressive has been the willingness of sovereign states to accept or acquiesce to such unprecedented exercise of authority from an international secretariat.

In this case, law-making has followed developments in practice. The World Health Assembly, in 2003, launched an intergovernmental process to revise the IHR which led to the formal adoption of a radically revised instrument in May 2005. The revised IHR will enter into force in 2007 and to a certain extent codify what the WHO Secretariat has already utilized in practice for a number of years.

## Remarks by Peter Van den Bossche*

### Radical Overhaul or Pragmatic Change? The Need and Scope for Reform of Decision-making in the World Trade Organization

#### 1. Introduction

In 2005, the World Trade Organization (WTO) celebrates its $10^{th}$ anniversary.[1] While the WTO is thus still a young organisation, the issue of its reform is already the subject of much debate. In recent years the functioning of the WTO has been severely criticized by opponents as well as by partisans of economic globalisation and trade liberalisation. The opponents have argued that the WTO is 'pathologically secretive, conspiratorial and unaccountable to sovereign states and their electorate'.[2] Partisans of economic globalisation and trade liberalisation have openly questioned whether the current institutions and procedures of the WTO are adequate to fulfil its mission of managing and regulating economic globalisation. After the unsuccessful Ministerial Conference in Cancún in September 2003, the then EC Trade Commissioner and now newly elected WTO Director General Pascal Lamy characterised the WTO as 'a medieval organisation' and called for careful reflection and consultation on the reform of the WTO's institutional structure and procedures.[3] Earlier, in June of that year, WTO Director-General Supachai Panitchpakdi requested a group of eight eminent

* Professor of International Economic Law and Head of the Department of International and European Law, Maastricht University; former Counsellor and Acting Director, WTO Appellate Body Secretariat, Geneva. The author thanks Iveta Alexovičová, Bertram Boie, Sergey Ripinsky and Jill Roche for their able assistance. For a detailed description of the institutions and procedures of the World Trade Organization, see P. Van den Bossche, *The Law and Policy of the World Trade Organization: Text, Cases and Materials* (Cambridge University Press, 2005), pp. 77-172. See also P. Van den Bossche and Iveta Alexovičová, 'Effective Global Economic Governance by the World Trade Organization', *Journal of International Economic Law,* 2005.

persons, under the chairmanship of former GATT/WTO Director-General Peter Sutherland, to study and clarify the institutional challenges that the WTO faced and to consider how the WTO could be reinforced and equipped to meet these challenges.[4] According to Dr. Supachai, at the time the WTO was established there was 'too little serious thinking on whether the institutional design and practice that had served the GATT [the WTO's *de facto* predecessor] so well would do the same for the WTO.'[5]

## 2. The Sutherland Report on the Future of the WTO

In January of 2005, Sutherland's group of eminent persons, referred to as the Consultative Board, presented to the WTO Director-General a report entitled *The Future of the WTO: Addressing Institutional Challenges in the New Millennium,* commonly referred to as the 'Sutherland Report'.[6] This 85-page report starts with a spirited but balanced argument for liberalizing trade and the role of the WTO therein (Chapter I); a sharp condemnation of the current erosion of the core WTO principle of non-discrimination as a result of the proliferation of preferential trade arrangements (Chapter II); and a thoughtful analysis on national sovereignty and WTO membership, concluding that in committing to WTO disciplines, governments are recapturing a degree of 'sovereignty' lost through the process of economic globalisation (Chapter III). The remainder of the report addresses specific institutional issues, including coherence and coordination with intergovernmental organisations (Chapter IV); transparency and dialogue with civil society (Chapter V); dispute settlement (Chapter VI); decision-making (Chapter VII); the institutional structure (Chapter VIII); and the role of the Director-General and the Secretariat (Chapter IX). In the Conclusions section, the Report recapitulates the principal recommendations of the Consultative Board. Overall, the reactions to the Sutherland Report to date have been positive, although to different degrees. According to Steve Charnovitz of the George Washington University Law School, the Report is 'stellar' and makes 'several important recommendations'; Patrick Messerlin of the Institut d'Etudes Politiques de Paris called the Report 'highly commendable'.[7] Some commentators, however, have been more critical. For example, while recognizing that the Report 'offers a truly thoughtful and interesting analysis', Joost Pauwelyn of Duke University Law School considers the Report 'largely a defence of the status quo by WTO insiders' and therefore a 'missed opportunity'.[8]

## 3. Focus of this Contribution

As reflected in the Sutherland Report, the institutional and procedural problems facing the WTO are multiple and complex. This contribution cannot, and does not, address all of these problems. Instead, it focuses on only one problem, namely the problem of decision-making in the WTO.

The general perception of decision-making in the WTO is often quite negative.[9] However, the WTO's record in terms of decisions made over the past decade is arguably not as bad as frequently suggested. The WTO was able to agree, for example, on the accession of China,[10] on further liberalization of trade in financial services and basic telecommunication services,[11] on the waiver of TRIPS obligations to give developing countries access to essential medicines such as those for HIV and malaria,[12] on certain rules regarding the recognition of the equivalence of SPS measures,[13] and, of course, on the start of the Doha Development Round negotiations.[14] On the other hand, the highly public failures of the 1999 Seattle and 2003 Cancún Sessions of the Ministerial Conference, the relatively small number of decisions made and the lack of progress in the on-going Doha negotiations can be seen as clear evidence of the problems relating to decision-making in the WTO. Moreover, the 'overburdening' of the WTO dispute settlement system as well as the proliferation of regional trade arrangements are attributed to the deficient functioning of the WTO decision-making process.

This contribution will examine the need and scope for reform of decision-making in the WTO. In this examination, the Sutherland Report will obviously be of particular relevance. As decision-making is problematic in many international organisations, the findings of this paper may also be relevant to organisations other than the WTO.

## 4. WTO Agreement Rules on Decision-making

The normal decision-making procedure for WTO bodies is set out in Article IX:1 of the *WTO Agreement*, which states:

> 'The WTO shall continue the practice of decision-making by consensus followed under GATT 1947. Except as otherwise provided, where a decision cannot be arrived at by consensus, the matter at issue shall be decided by voting. At meetings of the Ministerial Conference and the General Council, each Member of the WTO shall have one vote, ... Decisions of the Ministerial Conference and the General Council shall be taken by a majority of the votes cast, unless otherwise provided in this Agreement or in the relevant Multilateral Trade Agreement.'

Pursuant to Article IX:1, Members first try to reach decisions *by consensus*. Footnote 1 to Article IX defines consensus decision-making as follows:

> 'The body concerned shall be deemed to have decided by consensus on a matter submitted for its consideration, if no Member, present at the meeting when the decision is taken, *formally* objects to the proposed decision.' [Emphasis added]

If consensus cannot be achieved, Article IX:1 provides for voting on a one-country/one-vote basis.[15] Under the normal procedure, decisions are then taken by a majority of the votes cast. Additionally, the *WTO Agreement* sets out a number of special decision-making procedures which deviate from the normal procedure. Under these special procedures, decisions are either to be taken by consensus (with no resort to voting allowed)[16] or by a majority other than a simple majority of the votes cast. The latter is the case, for example, for the decisions on accession, which, pursuant to Article XII:2 of the *WTO Agreement*, are taken by a two-thirds majority of WTO Members if consensus cannot be achieved. Similarly, Article IX:3 of the *WTO Agreement* specifies that decisions on waivers are taken by a three-fourths majority of WTO Members if consensus cannot be reached within 90 days.[17] According to Article IX:2 of the *WTO*

*Agreement* a three-fourths majority of WTO Members is also necessary for decisions on the interpretation of WTO provisions.[18]

## 5. The Troublesome Practice of Consensus Decision-making

While the *WTO Agreement* provides, as a rule, for decision-making by majority vote when consensus cannot be achieved, in practice it is exceptional for WTO bodies to take decisions by voting. In fact, decisions are virtually always taken by consensus. If consensus cannot be achieved, no decision is taken even if this results in harmful political paralysis.

In recent years, the prevailing practice of consensus decision-making has been repeatedly questioned. After the failure of the Cancún Session of the Ministerial Conference in September 2003, the *Financial Times* reported on the frustration of the European Communities with the consensus requirement as follows:

> 'Mr Lamy also expanded on his calls for a sweeping overhaul of the way in which the 146-strong WTO operates, and promised that the EU would come up with a set of reform proposals. His comments made clear that he is primarily concerned with the body's consensus-driven approach. "I think it's above dispute that the principle of the permanent sit-in of 146 trade ministers in order to take a number of very detailed decisions . . . is a theory that visibly does not work," he said. A Commission official said Mr Lamy was not yet in a position to come up with a set of rounded proposals but that they were likely to address the WTO's most obvious shortfalls. "Everything needs to be done by consensus. Even the agenda needs to be decided by consensus. And the powers of the WTO director-general are very limited," the official said. "All that is incredibly complicated with 146 members".'[19]

The Sutherland Report also raises the question of the appropriateness and effectiveness of consensus decision-making in the WTO.[20]

Consensus decision-making entails that a decision is only taken when *no* Member formally objects to the proposed decision. Consensus decision-making therefore gives every Member *veto power*. It is obvious that in an organisation such as the WTO, composed at present of 148 Members with very different interests, decision-making by consensus is thus necessarily a troublesome process. This is even more so now that developing country Members, as a result of much-enhanced training and technical assistance programmes, have 'many more effective negotiators with the capacity to make a mark'.[21] Should the WTO steer away from the practice of consensus decision-making and welcome decision-making by majority vote in order to avoid political paralysis and to safeguard the effectiveness and relevance of the organisation? Is there scope and support for a reform in this direction?

## 6. Advantages of Consensus Decision-making

While troublesome, decision-making by consensus has a number of advantages that the alternative, decision-making by majority vote, does not possess to the same extent. Firstly, decision-making by consensus is – as former WTO Director-General Mike Moore stated shortly after the dismal failure of the 1999 Seattle Session of the Ministerial Conference – a 'fundamental democratic guarantee'.[22] It cannot be disputed that decisions taken by consensus, i.e., 'collectively', have *greater* 'democratic legitimacy' than decisions taken by majority vote.[23] For an organisation often accused of being 'undemocratic', this is a significant bonus. Secondly, consensus decision-making gives small and poor WTO Members a degree of influence in the decision-making process that they would not have if decisions were made by majority vote. As even the weakest and poorest WTO Members can block decisions, powerful Members must spend time persuading them of the merits of proposed decisions.[24] Consensus decision-making gives many WTO Members leverage which they would not have otherwise. Thirdly, decision-making by consensus is a useful device to ensure that only decisions that have a good chance of being implemented are adopted because only those decisions to which there is no major opposition within Members are agreed upon.[25] It is clear that a decision which a Member considers to be incompatible with its vital economic interests, but which is nevertheless forced upon it by a majority vote, will give rise to major implementation problems. Fourthly, consensus decision-making, unlike decision-making by majority vote, ensures that decisions made by the WTO are not out of touch with economic and political reality. Given the fact that developing country Members account for three-quarters of the membership of the WTO, these Members could prevail on any issue which is submitted to a vote, provided that they vote as a bloc. However, developing country Members account for less than 30 per cent of world trade, while developed country Members account for more than 70 per cent. Decision-making by majority voting on a one-country/one-vote basis thus risks alienating developed country Members from the WTO and rendering it ineffective and redundant as a forum for negotiation of new rules on trade. Decision-making by consensus does not carry that risk. While decision-making by *weighted* vote also would not carry the risk of producing decisions out of touch with economic and political reality (provided the votes are properly weighted), decision-making by weighted vote would not have the other advantages of consensus decision-making discussed above. Moreover, reaching agreement on the criteria to be taken into account in determining the weight of the vote of Members (share of world trade, population, degree of market openness, GDP, etc.) is likely to trigger a never-ending debate.[26] The vast majority of WTO Members is currently not willing even to consider decision-making by weighted vote as an alternative to consensus decision-making.

## 7. Limited Scope for Decision-making by Majority Vote

In view of the advantages of consensus decision-making over decision-making by majority vote, it may seem sensible to continue the current practice of consensus decision-making. The Sutherland Report states that 'voting is rarely, if ever, a wise alternative' to consensus decision-making.[27] However, in my opinion, this is an overstatement. In deciding on the appropriateness of decision-making by majority vote or by consensus, it is useful to distinguish between different types of decisions made in the WTO. For some types of decisions, such as decisions on 'housekeeping' matters or decisions that do not affect the rights and obligations of Members (e.g., the adoption of the agenda of meetings or the appointment of the WTO Director-General), decision-making by majority vote is totally appropriate and should be promoted. As the

*WTO Agreement* already allows for decision-making by majority voting if consensus cannot be achieved, there is no need to amend the rules on decision-making; only the practice has to be changed. However, for decisions regarding the application and interpretation of existing WTO rules and, obviously, for decisions by which new rules are created, the continuation of the current practice of consensus decision-making is, for the reasons discussed above, the best course of action.[28]

## 8. Facilitation of Consensus Decision-making

Albeit the best course of action, continuing the current practice of consensus decision-making brings with it the apparent risks of paralysis in the WTO rule-making bodies and a subsequent flight to other forums (regional trade arrangements) or mechanisms (dispute settlement). To mitigate these risks, consensus decision-making has to be facilitated. This 'facilitation' can take various forms.

Firstly, as suggested in the Sutherland Report, it may be useful to require a Member blocking the adoption of a broadly supported measure to declare in writing that the proposed measure negatively affects a *specific* vital national interest and is therefore unacceptable.[29] In other words, Members should justify the use of their 'veto power'. At present, Members often block consensus decision-making not because a vital national interest is at stake, but because they wish to avoid 'giv[ing] an advantage "to the other side"', 'to increase or maintain their nuisance value', or 'simply for leverage or out of spite'.[30] An example of the latter was the blocking of the decision on the extension of the ACP waiver in the period before the 2001 Doha Session of the Ministerial Conference.[31] It can be argued that requiring Members to explain in writing why they block consensus will make it politically more difficult for them to do so in the absence of compelling reasons. At first, this requirement can be introduced in an informal, pragmatic manner and without change to the *WTO Agreement*. It could be provided for in the Working Procedures of the WTO bodies concerned. After a few years, should this requirement prove to be an effective manner to facilitate consensus decision-making, a formal amendment of the *WTO Agreement* could be considered.

Secondly, consensus decision-making may also be facilitated by allowing for 'variable geometry in WTO commitments'.[32] At present, all WTO agreements, except two, apply to all Members. Consensus decision-making would be facilitated if the WTO abandoned in specific cases the ambition to conclude a multilateral agreement (binding upon all Members) and aim for a plurilateral agreement (binding upon only a group of 'willing' Members). Allowing 'the willing to move forward' provides welcome opportunities for experimentation and innovation appropriate in an organisation of 148 Members where it is not tenable that 'one size fits all'.[33] It is obvious that this would result in 'splintering' the multilateral trading system, with different rights and obligations applying to different Members. However, to some degree this is already the case and will become even more so, if the proliferation of regional trade arrangements continues. Nothing in the *WTO Agreement* prevents negotiation of plurilateral agreements within the WTO. Perhaps this flexibility is currently not sufficiently exploited.

Thirdly, consensus decision-making may be facilitated by providing, as the Sutherland Report states, 'new levels of political engagement and high-level consultative machinery that would serve to give direction and drive to negotiation processes'.[34] To this end, the Sutherland Report suggests that the Ministerial Conference meet annually (instead of bi-annually) and that senior trade-policy makers in state capitals should meet in Geneva more frequently, such as every three to six months in the context of General Council meetings.[35] Giving effect to these suggestions would not require an amendment of the *WTO Agreement.* It would 'only' require a change of practice. The Sutherland Report also suggests the establishment of a senior-level consultative body with a restricted membership (maximum 30) to 'discuss the political/economic environment as well as current dossiers'.[36] As diplomats in Geneva often lack the power and flexibility to take decisions on even the most humdrum issues, a select group of senior trade officials from the capitals may help to break deadlocks and make negotiations move forward. Reaching agreement on which Members will be represented (permanently or not) on this consultative body will obviously be a major challenge but the rules on the representation in the executive bodies of the World Bank and the IMF could be a useful source of inspiration.

## 9. Conclusion

In recent years, the current practice of consensus decision-making in the WTO has been under severe criticism. Both its appropriateness and effectiveness in an international organisation of 148 Members with very different interests have been questioned. It is undisputed that consensus decision-making brings with it the apparent risks of paralysis in the WTO rule-making bodies and a subsequent flight to other forums (regional trade arrangements) or mechanisms (dispute settlement). Nevertheless, there is little, if any, support among Members for a radical overhaul of decision-making in the WTO. This lack of support for substantial reform reflects an awareness among Members of the advantages of consensus decision-making over alternative decision-making procedures, and, in particular, over decision-making by majority vote. While troublesome, consensus decision-making may be the lesser of two evils. The lack of support for substantial reform is arguably also due to the fact that Members realize that a debate on alternatives (such as decision-making by weighted vote) would be highly divisive and most likely without result. The Sutherland Report of January 2005 bears witness of this reality. To the regret of some observers, the Report does not propose any *substantial* changes to WTO decision-making procedures. In fact, it does not propose radical reform to any of the WTO's institutions or procedures. As stated in the Report, such proposals for radical reform could not 'have commanded the degree of support necessary for them to be effected'.[37] The Report explicitly restraints itself to 'realizable reforms'.[38]

At present, and in the foreseeable future, the best way to address the problems relating to consensus decision-making in the WTO is through modest, pragmatic solutions and remedies. The *WTO Agreement* provides for a significant degree of institutional flexibility. This flexibility must be used to allow the new institutions and procedures for which there is a need to emerge in a pragmatic and gradual manner. Once tried and proven effective, the new institutions and procedures may be further worked out and, if useful, formally established. In the period between 1948 and 1995, the pragmatism with regard to institutions and procedures displayed by the GATT, the

WTO's *de facto* predecessor, has served the multilateral trading system well. Such pragmatism would also serve the WTO.

## Notes

[1] The WTO was established on 1 January 1995 by the 1994 *Marrakesh Agreement Establishing the World Trade Organization* (the '*WTO Agreement*'), available at: <http://www.wto.org/english/docs_e/legal_e/legal_e.htm#wtoagreement>, visited on 9 June 2005; or *Legal Texts: The Results of the Uruguay Round of Multilateral Trade Negotiations* (WTO/Cambridge University Press, 1999), 492 p.

[2] As reported by G. de Jonquières, 'Prime target for protests', *Financial Times*, 24 September 1999.

[3] Pascal Lamy, Press conference statement on the World Trade Organisation's 5th Ministerial Conference in Cancún, 14 September 2003. Available at: <http://www.eurunion.org/news/press/2003/2003057.htm>, visited on 10 September 2005.

[4] Report by the Consultative Board to the Director-General Supachai Panitchpakdi, *The Future of the WTO: Addressing Institutional Challenges in the New Millennium* (WTO, 2005), p. 2. Available at: <http://www.wto.org/english/thewto_e/10anniv_e/future_wto_e.htm>, visited on 9 September 2005. Subsequently referred to as the 'Sutherland Report'. In addition to Peter Sutherland (Chairman, BP plc & Goldman Sachs International), the group of eminent persons included Jagdish Bhagwati (University Professor, Columbia University); Kwesi Botchwey (former Minister of Finance, Ghana); Niall FitzGerald (Chairman, Reuters); Koichi Hamada (Professor of Economics, Yale University); John H. Jackson (University Professor of Law, Georgetown University); Celso Lafer (former Minister of Foreign Relations, Brazil); and Thierry de Montbrial (President, French Institute of International Relations).

[5] Sutherland Report, p. 2.

[6] See <http://www.wto.org/english/thewto_e/10anniv_e/10anniv_e.htm#future>, visited on 9 June 2005.

[7] S. Charnovitz, 'A Close Look at a Few Points', *Journal of International Economic Law*, 2005, p. 311; and P. Messerlin, 'Three Variations on "The Future of the WTO"', *Journal of International Economic Law*, 2005, p. 299.

[8] J. Pauwelyn, 'The Sutherland Report: A Missed Opportunity for Genuine Debate on Trade, Globalization and Reforming the WTO', *Journal of International Economic Law*, 2005, pp. 329-330.

[9] See, for example, R. Blackhurst and D. Hartridge, 'Improving The Capacity Of WTO Institutions To Fulfill Their Mandate', *Journal of International Economic Law,* 2005, p. 705; Amitra Narlikar, 'WTO Decision Making and Developing Countries', South Centre Trade-Related Agenda, Development and Equity (T.R.A.D.E.), Working Paper No. 11, November 2001. Available at: <www.southcentre.org/publications/wtodecis/workingpapers11.pdf>, visited 9 September 2005.

[10] China Accession Protocol, WT/ACC/CHN/49, dated 1 October 2001.

[11] Second Protocol to the General Agreement on Trade in Services, S/L/11, dated 24 July 1995 and Fifth Protocol to the General Agreement on Trade in Services, S/L/45, dated 3 December 1997 (on financial services); Fourth Protocol to the General Agreement on Trade in Services, S/L/20, dated 30 April 1996 (on basic telecommunication services).

[12] General Council, *Implementation of Paragraph 6 of the Doha Declaration on the TRIPS Agreement and Public Health*, WT/L/540, dated 2 September 2003.

[13] Committee on Sanitary and Phytosanitary Measures, *Decision on the Implementation of Article 4 of the Agreement on the Application of Sanitary and Phytosanitary Measures*, G/SPS/19, dated 24 October 2001.

[14] Doha Ministerial Declaration of 14 November 2001, WT/MIN(01)/DEC/1, dated 20 November 2001.

[15] Note that Article IX:1 of the *WTO Agreement* provides in relevant part: 'Where the European Communities exercise their right to vote, they shall have a number of votes equal to the number of their member States which are Members of the WTO'.

[16] Pursuant to footnote 3 of Article IX of the *WTO Agreement* and Article 2.4 of the WTO Dispute Settlement Understanding, all decisions taken by the Dispute Settlement Body must be taken by consensus. Note, however, that key decisions, such as the decision on the establishment of a panel and the decision to adopt a panel and/or Appellate Body report are taken by *reserve* consensus (see P. Van den Bossche, *The Law and Policy of the World Trade Organization* (Cambridge University Press, 2005), 229 p.).

[17] Note that decisions by the Dispute Settlement Body and decisions by the SPS Committee must always be taken by consensus.

[18] Note that Article IX:2 of the *WTO Agreement* does not require Members to first attempt to reach consensus.
[19] T. Buck, 'EU may rethink multilateral trade role', *Financial Times*, 16 September 2003.
[20] Sutherland Report, pp. 63-65.
[21] Ibid., p. 62.
[22] M. Moore, *Back on Track for Trade and Development*, Keynote address at the UNCTAD X, Bangkok, 16 February 2000. Available at: <www.wto.org/english/news_e/spmm_e/spmm24_e.htm>, visited on 30 August 2004.
[23] See P. Van den Bossche, *The Law and Policy of the World Trade Organization* (Cambridge University Press, 2005), 148 p. See also Sutherland Report, p. 63.
[24] Sutherland Report, p. 63.
[25] P. Van den Bossche and I. Alexovičová, 'Effective Global Economic Governance by the WTO', *Journal of International Economic Law*, 2005.
[26] For a discussion on WTO decision-making by weighted vote, see T. Cottier and T. Satoko, 'The Balance of Power in WTO Decision-Making: Towards Weighted Voting in Legislative Response', *Aussenwirtschaft*, 2003), p. 171.
[27] Sutherland Report, p. 64.
[28] P. Van den Bossche and I. Alexovičová, 'Effective Global Economic Governance by the WTO', *Journal of International Economic Law*, 2005.
[29] Sutherland Report, p. 64.
[30] P.J. Kuijper, Do Parallels with Other International Organizations Help?, *International Organizations Law Review*, 2005, p. 191.
[31] Ibid.
[32] Sutherland Report, p. 65.
[33] Ibid.
[34] Sutherland Report, p. 69.
[35] Ibid., pp. 69-70.
[36] Ibid., p. 71.
[37] Sutherland Report, p. 5.
[38] Ibid.

# Remarks by Edward Kwakwa*

## International Institutional Reform: The Case of the World Intellectual Property Organization

### 1. Introduction

The World Intellectual Property Organization (WIPO) is a specialized agency of the United Nations whose principal mandate is to promote the protection of intellectual property worldwide. While WIPO is somewhat younger than the World Health Organization (WHO), it is much older than the World Trade Organization (WTO). Unlike WHO and WTO, however, WIPO has an important non-state constituency: the private sector. This is because WIPO is mandated to provide commercial services to

* Legal Counsel, World Intellectual Property Organization (WIPO). The views expressed here are those of the author; they do not necessarily reflect the views of WIPO.

end-users. These services include the registration systems for patents, trademarks and industrial designs, and a fully functional Arbitration and Mediation Center for the resolution of intellectual property disputes between private parties. As a result, WIPO's budget is also unique among UN-system agencies, in that WIPO is largely self-financing and relies on Member States for less than 10 per cent of its annual budget. The Organization currently has 183 Member States, a Secretariat of some 1,400, and an annual budget of about CHF 265 million.

The WIPO is a constitutionally complex Organization. This complexity results from the fact that, in the past several decades, new treaties in different areas of intellectual property have been progressively adopted, each establishing a legally separate Union of States, usually with its own administrative organ of Member States and its own budget. Those separate Unions have been linked by their common interest in intellectual property, and by a common Secretariat that administers the treaties establishing the Unions. There are currently 23 such treaties that are administered by WIPO.[1]

This paper will briefly discuss the challenges facing the WIPO in terms of international institutional reform, and how WIPO has responded to those challenges. Section 2 and 3 of the paper will describe the processes of constitutional reform and extra-constitutional reform at WIPO. Section 4 will discuss the increasing role and participation of non-governmental organizations (NGOs) in intellectual property (IP) norm-making and policy formulation, and section 5 will discuss the challenge of 'development' in the area of intellectual property, while section 6 deals with the impact of rapid advances in technology on IP norm-making at WIPO. Section 7 ends with some concluding observations.

## 2. Constitutional Reform

In October 2003, the Member States of WIPO adopted certain amendments to all the WIPO-administered treaties. The amendments are aimed at simplifying the Organization's complicated governance structure and formalizing certain practices that, while at variance with the textual formulation of the WIPO-administered treaties, have been followed in practice in the last few years. The amendments are in three main areas, namely (i) the abolition of the WIPO Conference,[2] (ii) the formalization of the unitary contribution system and changes in contribution classes,[3] and (iii) a change in the periodicity of the ordinary sessions of the WIPO General Assembly and the other Assemblies of the Unions administered by WIPO.[4] This is nothing radical or exceptional in the scheme of international organization practice. The amendments, however, will only enter into force one month after written notifications of acceptance have been received by the Director-General of WIPO from three-fourths of the Member States of WIPO in accordance with the relevant provisions of the WIPO-administered treaties. The total number of WIPO Member States when the amendments were adopted stood at 179. This means that 135 acceptances are needed for entry into force of the amendments. As of 1 September 2005, however, only eight such acceptances had been received. The implication is quite clear that the amendments are unlikely to enter into force in the next several years. The inordinate amount of time required for the entry into force of constitutional reform measures dictated the need for other measures that would take effect more quickly.

## 3. Extra-Constitutional Reform

In certain respects, WIPO's complicated governance structure has been simplified without any constitutional amendments. This has included the adoption of resolutions by WIPO's General Assembly and other Bodies to adopt practices that are at variance with the textual formulation of the WIPO-administered treaties. In some cases, treaty bodies have simply passed a resolution to wish themselves out of existence, notwithstanding the relevant treaty language establishing them. For example, in September 2000, two of the Organization's Governing Bodies passed resolutions in which they unanimously decided not to meet in future, and also requested that the Director-General of WIPO not convene them.[5] Another three of the Governing Bodies each resolved to dissolve themselves that same year.[6] The WIPO's Secretariat proposed these extra-constitutional measures because of the immediacy of their impact and in view of the very long timelines associated with the constitutional measures described above. Some international law scholars would probably describe this practice at WIPO as being unconstitutional or outside the framework of recognized canons of international treaty law. One must, however, take into account the fact that these resolutions were passed by the same States that are party to the treaties in question. They were unanimously adopted at a time when the States Parties to the treaties felt the need to take urgent action in order to safeguard the integrity of the very treaty to which they were parties. Recognizing that formal constitutional amendments would take an inordinate amount of time to enter into force, they passed mere resolutions which have ended up having the same effect as formal constitutional amendments would have had. There is no reason why these resolutions cannot be regarded as legally valid, even if they were adopted by extra-constitutional means.

## 4. The Increasing Role and Participation of NGOs

The WIPO Convention, which dates back to 1967, only envisaged cooperation with, and participation by *international* NGOs in the work of WIPO.[7] In the last few years, however, there has been a proliferation of interest in WIPO's work not only by international NGOs, but also by *national* NGOs. In response to this, the Governing Bodies of WIPO accepted the Secretariat's recommendation that a proposed set of guidelines should be followed in deciding whether to also accredit national NGOs with permanent observer status.[8] The WIPO Convention was not amended for this purpose. This could therefore be seen as another extra-constitutional measure to stay abreast with the changing times.

A second issue associated with the increasing participation of NGOs relates to the speed with which the deliberations of WIPO meetings are posted on the internet. Under the Organization's rules of procedure, reports on the work accomplished at the meetings are only adopted by the Member States at the end of the meeting, after the

Secretariat has presented a formal report of the proceedings.[9] In the last year in particular, however, the admission of several new NGOs has created some new issues for the Secretariat as well as the Member States. What most of the NGOs do in practice is that they attend the meetings and post reports almost simultaneously on the Internet as the meetings are going on. So Member State Delegations are now put in a position where their statements and positions on any matter are reported to the outside world almost *verbatim*, even before those Delegations have made formal reports to their capitals on the outcome of the WIPO meeting. This has created some problems that are yet to be resolved.

A third issue is the changing nature of the participants in international legal regulation. I will use the internet as an illustrative example. As we all know, under traditional international law, only States were regarded as competent participants in norm making. In today's knowledge-based economy, however, that has changed dramatically. In the particular example of the Internet, perhaps the most active player is the entity known as the Internet Corporation for Assigned Names and Numbers (ICANN). In 1998, ICANN was formed in response to a suggestion by the United States Government that the private sector create such a body to assume responsibility for certain administrative and technical aspects of the Domain Name system, the Internet address space allocation and root server system management functions. As stated in its articles of incorporation, ICANN is a non-profit public interest corporation organized under the California Non-profit Public Benefit Corporation Law.[10]

In its relatively short period of existence, however, ICANN has had a significant impact in the area of the governance of the Internet Domain Name system. Among others, it has introduced several new generic Top Level Domains (gTLDs) into the Domain Name system.[11] More significantly, ICANN adopted a proposal by WIPO, an intergovernmental organization with 183 Member States, to establish the Uniform Domain Name Dispute Resolution Policy (UDRP),[12] a mechanism which has resulted in the implementation of a successful administrative system for resolving domain name disputes involving trademarks and a system of best practices for domain name registration authorities, designed to avoid such disputes.[13] The UDRP is now used worldwide and has, in effect, set clear standards for the resolution of intellectual property disputes in cyberspace. I mention the example of ICANN to illustrate the point that NGOs are now playing an increasingly significant role in norm-making and legal regulation in intellectual property and challenging the traditional paradigms of international legal regulation.

## 5. The Challenge of 'Development'

There have been increasing calls for the WIPO to change course and to incorporate economic, social and cultural development within its mission, instead of pushing for stronger forms of intellectual property rights. The WIPO has been accused by some of being out of step with the United Nations system and of not taking into account the needs and concerns of developing countries. As a result, some critics have actually called for the amendment of the constituent document establishing the Organization with a view to changing the objectives of the Organization to include explicit language on the development dimension of intellectual property. Other related proposals include the establishment of a committee on intellectual property and technology transfer, and a proposal to consider the elaboration of a Treaty on Access to Knowledge and Technology. These proposals have been debated in the context of an Intergovernmental Intersessional Working Group that met three times in 2005, and whose report is scheduled to be discussed in the General Assembly of WIPO in September.[14] The debate over the establishment of a development agenda in WIPO has been described as 'a disagreement' that 'reflects the fundamental philosophical difference between developed and developing countries.' According to this view, the majority of the developed countries take the position that the 'WIPO has always addressed development issues and that intellectual property rights have driven innovation', while the majority of the developing countries 'see development issues being reduced to technical assistance and say intellectual property rights sometimes limit innovation in their countries'.[15] The issue of development is likely to remain on the agenda not only of the WIPO, but also of several other organizations, in the years to come. Apart from the importance of development as a subject, it is recalled that the majority of WIPO's 183 Member States, as well indeed as the majority of the WTO's 148 Members, are developing countries. These countries naturally are interested in ensuring that discussions in trade and intellectual property, in particular, take into account the needs of the less fortunate members of the international community.

At the WIPO, we have tried to incorporate the issue of development more effectively in intellectual property discussions and in the Organization's overall activities, without at the same time compromising the Organization's mandate or ignoring the interests of WIPO's other very important constituency, the private sector/industry.

## 6. Supplementing the Traditional Means of Norm Making

Another major challenge at the WIPO is that of rapid advances in technology. An organization's ability to reflect and respond to the changing needs and demands of its constituents by adapting rapid and effective means of rule-making is one of its most important features. This ability is particularly important in the field of intellectual property, a technology-driven area of law.

The practice at the WIPO is different from that of the WHO, where they have only recently resorted to treaty-making. Indeed, several other intergovernmental organizations have traditionally used various forms of soft law mechanisms. Examples of this include declarations and decisions of international organizations (including certain widely supported and generally accepted resolutions or declarations of the UN General Assembly), the express authority granted by the Convention on International Civil Aviation (the Chicago Convention) to the Council of the International Civil Aviation Organization (ICAO) to adopt international standards and recommended practices,[16] and the WHO framework under which the Health Assembly is authorized to adopt, by simple majority, regulations that are binding on all Member States, except those that notify the WHO Director-General of reservations or rejection of the regulations within a specified time.[17]

At the WIPO, rules concerning intellectual property have traditionally been adopted by the treaty method. As a result of the rapid advances in technology, however, traditional treaty-making processes are now unsuited to the realities of intellectual property law. As is well-known, the treaty-making process is slow and time-consuming. And treaties are normally binding only on those States that ratify or accede to them. The treaty-making method will normally be delayed further by the fact that both international and domestic requirements need to be fulfilled before a treaty comes into force in the States concerned.

Intellectual property is one of the most rapidly growing and probably one of the more controversial areas in the practice of law today, both nationally and internationally. This naturally raises the potential for an increasing number of international disputes involving various forms of intellectual property. It is thus imperative that intellectual property law remains current, responding to today's fast-paced technological developments. In order to ensure the WIPO's continued relevance, viability and legitimacy, the Organization has had to adapt its traditional rule-making processes by adopting more rapid, transparent, effective and politically acceptable means of norm creation.

In 1999, the Assemblies of Member States of the WIPO adopted a Resolution Concerning Provisions on the Protection of Well-Known Marks.[18] In 2000, WIPO's Assemblies of Member States approved a Recommendation Concerning Trademark Licenses.[19] And again in 2001, the Assemblies of Member States of WIPO adopted a Recommendation Concerning Provisions on the Protection of Marks, and Other Industrial Property Rights in Signs, on the Internet.[20]

The Resolution and Recommendations listed above are all part of the new soft law initiatives at WIPO. While the use of such soft law techniques is nothing new in the United Nations and most other intergovernmental organizations, as described above, it is a relatively new development at WIPO. The WIPO Secretariat's decision to introduce such initiatives as a means of advancing the development of intellectual property law is in large measure a direct example of institutional reform aimed at maintaining the relevance of the Organization.

As I have described elsewhere, the legal value of newly created norms generally depends on the content of those norms and the procedure through which they were adopted. In general, such norms would seem to be of greater precedential value if they: address matters of importance to States; are codifications, reaffirmations or clarifications of certain generally-accepted or widely-recognized norms; are adopted by consensus, by unanimity or by an overwhelming majority of the concerned Member States; and are adopted through a process of transparent and extensive consultations and negotiations.[21]

To the extent that the Resolutions and Recommendations are carefully negotiated, taking into account the real status, rights and interests of concerned States and other actors on the international scene, and insofar as they contain reasonable and practical provisions for implementation, we believe that they invariably may be regarded as binding instruments. To be sure, the Resolution and Recommendations passed to date are already exercising a real influence on national law and practice, as several States have adopted domestic legislation aimed at incorporating the essence of the Resolution and Recommendations within their laws and practices. This may in part be attributable to their subject matter and the conditions in which they were adopted. In particular, they went through a long process of negotiation and extensive but informal consultations, and thus embody a fairly representative view of the Member States of WIPO.

Such soft law also has the advantage of greater flexibility as a means of keeping up with rapidly changing developments. Soft law instruments are easier to adopt than treaties, and yet they may be applied immediately by States. In any event, it is our expectation that some of these Resolutions and Recommendations could be adopted initially as a first step towards negotiation and conclusion of legally binding obligations, thus providing a basis for a treaty regime. It is hoped that such a supplementary means of norm-creation will allow WIPO to promulgate norms more efficiently and with greater precision than could be done by the traditional treaty-making method. The challenge, as we see it, is how best to make WIPO and intellectual property norms more effective and more relevant in an attempt to increase universal compliance with fundamental intellectual property norms while also exercising greater selectivity in the production of new standards.

## 7. Conclusion

The process of institutional reform is one that must perforce be taken seriously by any organization, as it goes to the very existence of the organization in question.

This paper has sketched in brief fashion some of the challenges facing the World Intellectual Property Organization and the efforts it has made to address those challenges. The WIPO seems to have done quite well, thus far, in addressing institutional challenges with which it is faced, and this has enabled the Organization to maintain its relevance, viability and legitimacy.

## Notes

1 For a more detailed description of the governance structure of WIPO, see generally 'The Governance Structure of WIPO' (World Intellectual Property Organization, Doc. A/32/INF/2, 20 February 1998, reproduced at: <www.wipo.int/documents/en/document/govbody/wo_gb_ab/pdf/a32-inf2.pdf> (last visited 1 September 2005)).

2 Whereas the WIPO General Assembly consists of all the States which are members of WIPO and are also member of either the Berne Union (for the Protection of Literary and Artistic Works) or the Paris Union (for the Protection of Industrial Property), the WIPO Conference is composed of all the WIPO Member States, whether or not they are member also of either the Paris or Berne Unions. In practice, however, the Conference always meets at the same time and in the same room as the WIPO General Assembly, and the only discernible difference in the proceedings is the difference in the Presiding Officer. According to WIPO's Rules of Procedure, the General Assembly has precedence over the Conference.

3 In 1993, the WIPO Conference and the Assemblies of the Paris and Berne Unions adopted the unitary contribution system in replacement of the multiple contribution system provided for in the WIPO Convention and other WIPO-administered treaties. Under this unitary contribution system, a State party to any of WIPO's contribution treaties would pay a single contribution, regardless of the number of WIPO treaties to which it was party. The unitary system was adopted on a provisional basis, on the understanding that, if it worked well in practice, the relevant WIPO treaties would subsequently be amended to reflect the new practice. The changes in contribution classes were also adopted in 1989, 1991 and 1993, also on the understanding that the relevant WIPO treaties would later be amended to bring them in line with the new practice.

4 The texts of the WIPO treaties provide that ordinary sessions of the Assemblies of Member States should take place on a biennial basis. In actual practice, however, the Assemblies have met on a yearly basis, alternating between ordinary sessions and what are referred to as extraordinary sessions.

[5] These were the Paris Union Conference of Representatives and the Lisbon Union Council. See WIPO Doc. A/35/15, at para. 134, reproduced at: <www.wipo.int/documents/en/document/govbody/wo_gb_ab/doc/a35_15.doc>.

[6] These were the Berne Union Conference of Representatives, the Hague Union Conference of representatives and the Nice Union Conference of Representatives. See ibid., at para. 136.

[7] See Art. 3(i) of the Convention Establishing the World Intellectual Property Organization, 14 July 1967, 21 UST 1770, 828 *UNTS* 3 (last amended 28 September 1979) (providing that the objectives of WIPO are to promote the protection of intellectual property throughout the world through cooperation among States 'and, where appropriate, in collaboration with any other international organization').

[8] The said Guidelines were adopted by the Member States of WIPO at their annual meetings in September 2002. See WIPO Doc. A/37/14, at para. 316. Since then as many as 13 national NGOs have been admitted to permanent observer status in WIPO. Another 18 are likely to be admitted at the September 2005 meetings of the Member States.

[9] See Rule 44, WIPO General Rules of Procedure (WIPO Publication 399 (FE) Rev. 3), Geneva, 1998 (providing that '[a]t the end of every session the Secretariat shall submit to the assembly a draft report on the work accomplished', and '[a]fter the session, the report adopted by the assembly shall be transmitted by the Director General to the States and organizations invited to the session').

[10] See ICANN's Articles of Incorporation, at: <http:www.icann.org/general/articles/htm>.

[11] These include: .aero, .biz, .coop, .info, .museum, .name and .pro.

[12] As explained in the Report of the Second WIPO Internet Domain Name Process, however, the UDRP 'does not seek to regulate the whole universe of the interface between trademarks and domain names, but only to implement the lowest common denominator of internationally agreed and accepted principles concerning the abuse of trademarks. The exercise was less about legislation than about the efficient application of existing law in a multijurisdictional and cross-territorial space' and the Second WIPO Internet Domain Name Process involves more difficult questions that have far-reaching implications for the manner in which the international community creates law in this completely new area. See WIPO, *The Recognition of Rights and the Use of Names in the Internet Domain Name System: Report of the Second WIPO Internet Domain Name Process* (3 September 2001), para. 66, reprinted at: <http://wipo2.wipo.int>.

[13] In its first year of operation alone, the UDRP of WIPO received some 2,000 cases. Several of these cases were submitted by well-known celebrities, including Julia Roberts, Bruce Springsteen, Venus and Serena Williams, Isabelle Adjani and Madonna, as well as major corporations, including Microsoft Corporation, General Electric Company and Nokia Corporation.

[14] The decision by WIPO Member States to consider the agenda item on the establishment of a development agenda for WIPO has been described by Joseph Stiglitz as being 'as important as the World Trade Organization's decision that the current round of trade negotiations be devoted to development'. See Joseph Stiglitz, 'Intellectual Property Rights and Wrongs', *Daily Times*, 23August 2005 (reprinted at: <www.dailytimes.com.pk/print.asp?page=story_16-8-2005_pg5_12&ndate=8/23/20…> (last visited 31August 2005).

[15] See William New, 'Officials in Stalemate on Global Development Reform', *Technology Daily*, 25 July 2005.

[16] Convention on International Civil Aviation, 7 December 1944, Art. 54(1), 15 *UNTS* 295 (amended 28 October 1990).

[17] *The World Health Organization, Basic Documents* 7 (47th edn. 1998).

[18] The Resolution was aimed at clarifying and supplementing existing international protection of well-known marks, under the Paris Convention and the TRIPS Agreement. In particular, it contains a list of factors to help determine whether a mark is well known in a territory. See WIPO Doc. A/34/13 (4 August 1999), reprinted at:<http://www.wipo.int/news/en/index.html? wipo_content_frame=/news/en/conferences.html>.

[19] The Recommendation seeks to simplify and harmonize procedures relating to the recordal of trademark licenses. In that connection, it sets out a maximum list of indications and elements that may be required by national or regional authorities when presented with a request for recordal, cancellation or amendment of the recordal of a license. See WIPO Doc. A/35/10 (26 July 2000), reprinted at: <http://www.wipo.int/news/en/index.html?wipo_content_frame=/news/en/conferences.html>.

[20] The Recommendation seeks to make all rights in distinctive signs that are of a territorial nature Internet-compatible, particularly, trademarks, trade names and geographical indications. See WIPO Doc. A/36/8 (18 June 2001), reprinted at: <http://www.wipo.int/news/en/index.html?wipo_content_frame=/news/en/conferences.html>.

[21] See generally Edward Kwakwa, 'Some Comments on Rulemaking at the World Intellectual Property Organization', 12 *Duke Journal of Comparative & International Law* (2002), pp.179, 191-193.

## Discussion

M. Kamminga: You will agree that these have been fascinating presentations from true insiders in the work of international organizations. It is obvious that there are some common patterns in these three presentations. First of all, there is a tendency towards gradual reform, rather than spectacular reform of international institutions. Secondly, those reforms take place on an extra-constitutional basis. There is a clear preference for going ahead pragmatically, without achieving constitutional changes. Quite often, these pragmatic changes appear to contradict constitutional provisions, but people do not seem to mind, as long as the work gets done. Thirdly, the private sector is becoming increasingly involved in the work of these intergovernmental organizations. These are the common threads I found in these interventions, and I would like now to give the floor to you for questions and comments.

H. Schermers:* Mr Burci's last point was the relation with private sources and I have a question concerning financing. Normally in private household you have an income and you decide your budget on that basis. In international organizations, the opposite happens: you have some functions and programme to fulfill and the budget is decided on that basis; Member States will provide the necessary financial resources to cover that budget. The problem is that, if private sources give further money to fulfill the programme, Member States will be relieved from part of their financial contribution. However, the net contribution will remain the same, the programme will remain the same, the only difference will be that the financial burden is shifted, but the activities remain the same without any real difference. I could imagine that that could be overcome by keeping certain projects outside the normal budget, if you get private sources. I would like to know more in detail from Mr Burci whether there are some techniques to get private money to finance extra activities, in order to avoid that the only benefit goes to the Member States without any advantage for the organization.

G. Burci: This is a crucial question I did not have the time to address in my presentation. WHO is not going as far as WIPO, but it is going in the same direction. For the biennium 2006-2007, 30 per cent of our financial resources comes from the regular budget financed by the Member States, 70 per cent comes from extra-budgetary contributions, including a significant part in private contributions from corporations [....] Secondly, as far as private sources are concerned, we try to avoid sheer money donations in order to avoid potential conflicts of interest. But we try to engage companies in most elaborate programmes. For example, where the company donates the drug, the company will help us in clinical trials, to monitor the impact of that particular drug, strengthening the distribution in different countries. In conclusion, it is not only the dollar-bill, but also the way we try to link contributions and programmatic engagements by the private sector.

P. Van den Bossche: On the involvement of private actors in the financing of international organizations, the WTO is perhaps an example of an organization where

* University of Leiden.

such model did not work. Former Director-General Mike Moore in 2000 invited private companies to help develop certain capacity-building programmes of the WTO. That was very controversial among Member States. At the end, few companies accepted the invitation to provide money for these programmes. We do not have at WTO generous benefactors, but when a Member State undertakes to organize a Ministerial Conference, as it was the case in the Seattle Conference, the local business will provide most of the money for the organization of that conference. At any rate, eventually Seattle did not turn out to be a success for the WTO.

P. Sieger:* First of all, I would like to thank the three panelists for the very interesting presentations. My point concerns the private-public partnership model to which Mr Burci has referred previously. I wonder whether this model does not raise some serious questions concerning the status of these international organizations under international law. International organizations have been granted privileges and immunities because they are equated to States. If international organizations are increasingly doing things which private corporations could do, or actually do things together with private corporations, one should question whether privileges and immunities, in particular legal immunities, do or should apply. For us it is a very practical question because we are the host State. I take the example of Mr Burci, the GAVI example he has mentioned before, to ask what happens if, for instance, some individual or organization claims that WHO acted wrongly and presents a claim against WHO. So far the organization has been protected by legal immunities, but should that be still the case in the future, considering the extent to which these international organizations act as private companies or in concert with private companies?

E. Kwakwa: Thank you for the question. We go a long way in trying to avoid private donations. Even from the perspective of Member States, some years ago we proposed to eliminate Member States contributions, since we get more than sufficient money from the services we provide. The Member States refused that, as that it is clearly a form of control they do not want to renounce. As to the privileges and immunities, I am sure you will agree that WIPO has been a very good international organization in avoiding abuses of its legal immunities. In our case, we are in a difficult situation since most of our services are arguably commercial services. As a result of that when individuals sue us, we do not immediately jump on our immunities, especially when you take the Patent Corporation Treaty. We take 70 per cent of our budget from that function and we realize that if we invoked immunities anytime a private partner has a legal dispute with us, we would end-up being in a situation where the private sector would stop using these services. The same applies with the Arbitration and Mediation Centre. While we have those immunities, we prefer to often waive them, in order not to lose the trust of the private sector from which we make most of our money. The system has built-in check and balances, and while we are generally entitled to those immunities, we also have a duty under the relevant conventions to waive those immunities and we systematically do that.

G. Burci: You raise a very important point. The first part to your point is whether we are starting to act as a private corporation. Secondly, through these new hybrid structures, we are hosting actors which are external to the organization. For instance,

* Swiss Ministry of Foreign Affairs.

in the case of the Partnership Secretariat, are the people working there part of the organizations? Which legal status do they have? I do not think that in the WHO we are going in the direction of WIPO, as we do not offer commercial services. Whereas there has been a clear policy to continue to operate as a public agency, at the same time that we have to interact with the corporate world in more complex and articulate ways. The problem is common to the whole UN, as many agencies are pushed towards activities which are no more those typical of a public agency, but they belong more to for-profit organizations. In this legal environment, it is difficult to invoke a restrictive theory of sovereign immunity for international organizations. I remember that a few years ago the hot topic among legal advisors was that donors like the World Bank or the EU were forcing technical agencies to bid for projects, for example for consulting services together with private companies. UNIDO had to bid for World Bank projects to consult on industrial development alongside private companies. That made the private companies furious, as international organizations not only could rely on their non-profit nature, but also could shield behind all kinds of legal immunities and privileges. On the other hand, questions were raised whether the immunities would cover this kind of activities, where the international organizations were acting in a different capacity. These are problems that are still unsolved today. We have to ask ourselves how far we can go in that direction, before reaching the breaking point of losing our identity. I do not think that in the case of WHO we have reached that point. I hope we have managed to always meet the consensus of the host countries and avoid partnerships where we would lose sight of our original mission.'

I. ALEXOVICOVA:* I have a short question on extra-constitutional measures which were mentioned by Mr Kwakwa. I think that extra-constitutional is another word for anti-constitutional, especially for those measures which are against the intentions and purpose of the treaty. What are the reactions of Member States to those measures, especially those who voted against them?

K. YOCHEVA:** I have a similar question to the one just made. With regard to extra-constitutional changes, can those changes be considered an indication of a customary process initiated by the international organization, as opposed to customary process initiated by States?

E. KWAKWA: I would not call these changes unconstitutional. These measures have been taken by the Member States themselves by resolution or formal constitutional amendment. In other words, where you have a governing body and all the members of that governing body, notwithstanding the treaty language, adopt a resolution that goes against the treaty language, we cannot see that as unconstitutional. I guess that in response to that, you could argue that these resolutions are not legally binding. However, these resolutions become legally binding when they find their way into domestic legislation and that has been the case in many extra-constitutional measures. Do these measures establish custom? Yes, I would say that that is the case, at least as practice is concerned. According to the WIPO Treaty, a unitary contribution system was originally envisaged whereby every state would pay a contribution according to the number of treaties it had joined. The practice shows that, since 1993, the contribution system has been changed, so that every Member States pays only one

* University of Maastricht.

** New Bulgarian University.

contribution amount, regardless of the number of treaties it has joined. When the reform was adopted in 1993, Member States decided to see how the system would work and then possibly approve formal constitutional amendments. It was in practice for 10 years and it was only in 2003 that, given the success of the new system, we decided to adopt those amendments. It turns out that those formal measures will take at least 10 years to legally come into force. Pendent that, States have decided to adopt a resolution to the effect that the amendments will enter into force immediately for those Member States accepting the resolution. We can conclude that that is indeed binding custom, in the same way as GA resolutions can create custom.

G. BURCI: How do Member States react? First of all, some of these extra-constitutional measures have been pushed by Member States as a result of their reluctance to undertake formal amendments to the constitution. In other cases, for instance in response to our practice related to infectious disease, States have acquiesced or have not properly thought about the political implications of what we were doing, until we had a major episode like the SARS. There is a variety of behaviours according to the particular political context and moment. It is difficult to say whether this practice contributes to the strengthening of customary international law. Certainly, it relies on a long tradition of teleological interpretations of treaty constitutive instruments that has characterized the life of most international organizations and their organs.

M. BRUS:* I would like to go back to Peter Van den Bossche's paper and I would like to make two comments. One relates to his position that consensus decision-making carries more legitimacy than other forms of decision-making. I would not agree with that position, given the lack of transparency in what leads to consensus decision-making, which is normally behind-the-scenes exercise of power. Sometimes majority decision-making can be more legitimate than consensus decision-making. The other one is more related to the conclusion that it is particularly difficult to change the procedures of decision-making in the WTO. I would have liked to see in the analysis further exploration of the reason why it is so difficult to change those procedures at this moment. Why is it difficult? Who blocks the changes on decision-making and for what reasons? Who benefits from the *status quo*? Which groups of States would lose some of their power or benefits when we changed these rules? What can we do to offset the losses by some groups in the system, by benefits which are created within the WTO, by having a different decision-making system? Which brings me to my final point, which is that, if the aim is to change the rules, the paper should have looked more at cross-institutional reforms, considering other institutions participating in the system of world economic governance. Reform in the WTO will not be possible if other institutions, such as the World Bank, the IMF and OSCE, are not changed too. The conclusion that change is not possible for political reasons, does not really answer these fundamental questions, that should be at the heart of every attempt to bring about progress and to resist attempts to destroy the system through pluralist or bilateralist policies.

P. VAN DEN BOSSCHE: Let me take the questions in the order you raise them. As far as legitimacy is concerned, with particular regard to consensus decision-making, I think that, if a decision is taken by consensus, it means that it is acceptable to everybody or, put it in another way, that it is not unacceptable to anybody. You refer to

* University of Leiden.

what happens behind the scenes in terms of pressure on certain members to join the consensus. But you should bear in mind that that would also happen if there was decision-making by voting. In conclusion, I stand by my opinion that decision-making taken by consensus is more legitimate than decision-making by voting. Secondly, one of your questions is who benefits most from the *status quo*. On the basis of my experience and research, I have come to the conclusion that everybody benefits from the *status quo*, both the rich and powerful, and the weak and poor, for the reasons that I explained in the paper. On the last point, about the limitations implicit in looking at institutional reform in the WTO in isolation, I would definitely agree with that; on the other hand, it is already so ambitious to look at institutional reform in the WTO alone, that I had to limit myself.

M. ANDEM:* I just have a general question to make. Thirty-one years ago a declaration on the NIEO was adopted by the General Assembly unanimously. If one goes through paragraphs 1 to 7, you will realize that it deals with all the existing problems facing the nations of the world, such as inequality, injustices. The economic basis of the world today is not balanced at all. There are a lot of problems going on today, and without looking at the basic problems, reform is not sufficient. If one goes through the history of the UN, one must realize that those founding fathers had good intentions. There are certain obligations to make this world a safe place to live for everybody, whether rich or poor. I think that the inequalities and injustices are continuing today, and I believe that reforms should serve to solve these problems. We need a new NIEO, otherwise things will only get worst. We need to have strong foundations; otherwise the whole structure will collapse. That means that we have to start building again. I come from the developing world, my country is an oil-producing country, but normal people are not getting any benefit, they only get pollution. How can we make them to participate to economic and social development? Through justice.

G. BURCI: I may agree with all that. On the other hand, the idea of NIEO must have had its own shortcomings, if it more or less fizzled out. But I agree that reform must be a means to an end, otherwise it becomes a pure power game. I hope I expanded on how certain reforms in the WHO are instrumental to responding to the needs of Member States, in particular those of developing countries. I hope that that there is and will be substance to our reforms, even without creating a major ideological structure like that of a world economic order.

*Reporter:* E. Milano**

* University of Lapland.

** University of Maastricht.

# Has the Time Come for a Permanent War Damage Compensation Commission

The panel was convened by its Chair, Liesbeth Zegveld*

## Remarks by Norbert Wühler**

No paper received.

## Remarks by John Crook***

> 'The establishment of ad hoc post-conflict mechanisms for the consideration of claims by victims of war easily raises the accusation of victors' justice. The question must be considered whether, just as the ad hoc war crimes tribunals prepared the ground for the International Criminal Court, experience with the ad hoc war damage compensation commissions established so far points the way towards a permanent war damage compensation mechanism.'

### Contemporary Mass Claims Programmes

The last two decades have seen the creation of several important mass claims institutions aimed at providing compensation or other kinds of relief following large-scale human tragedies.

In some ways, this is not a new phenomenon. Scores of mass claims commissions and tribunals were created in the 19th and early 20th century to sort through the aftermath of wars and insurrections. Two things are new with these more recent institutions, however. First is the sheer magnitude of modern programs and the associated technological innovations that make them possible. Second is the way in which these institutions are addressing new types of individual claims.

I have been involved in creating or operating some of these programs, and I believe that properly conceived mass claims programs can sometimes significantly contribute to effective post-conflict programs of reconstruction and reconciliation. By far the largest of these new institutions is the UN Compensation Commission, which has processed over 2.6 million claims arising from the invasion of Kuwait in 1990, and paid out over $18.8 billion in compensation. The overwhelming majority of these

* Böhler Franken Koppen en De Feijter.

** International Organization for Migration.

*** Commission Eritrea Ethiopia Claims Commission. The original manuscript of this contribution was not received. The following text has been derived from the tapes on which the conference sessions were recorded.

were claims by individuals, mostly poor people from developing countries whose lives were disrupted by the invasion and war. You will hear more about the UNCC from Norbert Wühler, with whom I had the pleasure of working at the Iran-US Claims Tribunal in the 1980's and at the United Nations Compensation Commission in the 1990's.

Several other important mass claims processes have been created since the UNCC. All of them have utilized some of the mass claims processing machinery and techniques pioneered by the UNCC, although the extent of 'borrowing' has varied. These processes are varied and complex, and can be mentioned here only briefly. Many of them do not directly address post-conflict situations, but all of them have contributed to the store of experience bearing on the design and operation of mass claims systems. These processes include:

- The Claims Resolution Tribunal for Dormant Bank Accounts in Switzerland, a process created in 1996 that expanded significantly after a US court approved $1.25 billion lump sum settlement of US litigation claiming that Swiss banks wrongfully retained victims' accounts and benefited from financial transactions with the Nazis.

- A process addressing claims against major German firms that used forced and slave labor during the Nazi era. Following extensive negotiations involving companies, claimants and other interested parties, the German Government and major German companies created a 10 billion DM compensation fund.

- France and Austria both created processes to address claims by Jews and others injured during the Nazi era.

- A process has been created to address claims relating to insurance policies covering persons who died under Nazi persecution.

- An extensive process operated to address claims to real property by Bosnians driven from their homes during the Balkan wars of the early 1990s. It concluded in 2003, after issuing over 311,000 final and binding decisions. A similar mechanism is operating in Kosovo. About 29,000 claims were filed there; as of February 2005, over 23,000 have been resolved, and the process should end this year. The Iraqi authorities are working on a similar commission to address property displacements under the prior regime, particularly in Kurdish areas.

These experiences resonate in other situations involving large-scale violations of international humanitarian law and human rights. In October 2004, Security Council Resolution 1566 created a Security Council working group to consider 'an international fund to compensate victims of terrorist acts and their families.' The February 2005 report of the UN Commission of Inquiry on Darfur also recommended a compensation commission. A number of large-scale claims processes have been established to address historic injustices at the national level. Other similar national and international programs are readily conceivable.

There have also been related normative developments. The much-maligned UN Commission on Human Rights this spring adopted (with 40 affirmative votes and 13 abstentions) a set of 'Basic principles and guidelines on the right to a remedy and reparation for victims of gross violations of international human rights law and serious violations of international humanitarian law.' There has also been some interesting recent state practice. The Congress of the United States, not normally a hotbed of international legal innovation, included in a recent supplemental spending bill 20 million dollars to assist families and communities inadvertently harmed by US military operations in Afghanistan and Iraq.

## The Eritrea-Ethiopia Claims Commission

I myself am involved as a commissioner in another much smaller claims process set-up to address the aftermath of the war between Eritrea and Ethiopia between May 1998 and June 2000. As part of the Parties' December 12, 2000 agreement to bring the war to a final conclusion, they agreed on an unusual step. In Article 5 of the December 12 Agreement, they agreed to create an arbitral commission to decide through binding arbitration claims for all loss, damage or injury by one Government or its nationals, or certain other persons, against the other Government that are related to the earlier conflict between them and result from "violations of international humanitarian law, including the 1949 Geneva Conventions, or other violations of international law.'

This body is separate from the distinguished commission the Parties established to determine their boundary under the chairmanship of Sir Elihu Lauterpacht. It is a quite separate body set-up to resolve through binding arbitration a broad array of claims for violations of international humanitarian law and other international law related to the war and its immediate aftermath. The commission has its seat here in The Hague. It is far more modest in scale and resources than the UN's war crimes tribunals or the International Criminal Court. Its relatively modest costs are borne by Eritrea and Ethiopia themselves. The Permanent Court of Arbitration provides important logistical support, and a capable PCA attorney serves as Commission Registrar. While the process has received little public notice, the parties and the Commission have worked diligently over the last four years to decide the merits of a challenging docket. The Commission held its final hearings in April on the merits of the last group of the parties' claims. The parties and the Commission now are consulting regarding the liability stage of the proceedings.

The Commission process is still underway, and there are of course limits about what I can say about it. The Commission has issued three sets of awards on the merits of the Parties' claims. All of these awards are public and are available on the PCA website (<www.pca-cpa.org>). The Commission's awards also have been, or soon will be, published in *International Legal Materials*. The awards contain much information about the structure of the process, the nature of the claims, and the parties' very different perceptions of what happened during the war.

The first pair of awards addressed the two Parties' claims that their prisoners of war were mistreated. The second addressed complex claims that the two side's military forces abused civilians, engaged in indiscriminate or otherwise unlawful military operations, or otherwise violated international humanitarian law in the Central Front of the war. In the third pair of awards, issued in December 2004, the Commission addressed extensive claims that civilians were mistreated in areas away from the fighting fronts. The fourth and final set of claims, heard at the end of April 2005, include claims related to the conduct of air and ground operations, for closures of ports, for claimed violations of diplomatic law, and several other matters.

## A Universal Mechanism?

Based on my past activities, you might think that I would enthusiastically support the concept of some sort of universal mechanism created to address claims for war damage. However, I believe that the concept of a universal 'one-size fits all' mechanism raises a number of difficult questions requiring very critical scrutiny. It is not at all clear to me now that the concept of a universal permanent mechanism ultimately is workable or desirable.

## What is the Objective?

The threshold question concerns the whole purpose of any claims enterprise. Is the objective to seek to compensate those who may have suffered legal injury as the result of armed conflict, or to compensate the potentially far larger group who suffered injury in fact as the result of war?

The question must be asked, because of the exceptional legal character of large-scale armed conflict. The truth is that under the *jus in bello*, the law regulating the conduct of armed conflict, death and destruction related to armed conflict often may not be illegal. In the context of an armed conflict, the death or wounding of civilians on either sides, or the destruction of their property, will not necessarily result in responsibility for breach of the *jus in bello* under the law of state responsibility. Further, internal displacement of persons fleeing to avoid armed conflict often may not be unlawful.

Nevertheless, all of those who have been injured by war, or the families of the dead, or those who have been displaced or lost their homes or livelihoods, require support to rebuild their lives. The law of state responsibility may allocate responsibility under the *jus in bello* for some of these injuries, but not for many others. This seems to me a narrow and perhaps unsatisfactory approach to addressing the totality of the human consequences of war. And, as I will suggest below, determining state responsibility for breaches of the *jus in bello* can be a difficult, expensive and uncertain process.

For completeness, it would be useful if I could say something about the legal theory underlying the UN Compensation Commission, in the establishment of which I had some part in the early 1990's. However, the Eritrea-Ethiopia Commission is now deliberating claims involving legal issues that involve questions related to the legal foundations of the UNCC. In the circumstances, it would not be appropriate for me to comment on this issue.

## The Problems of Finding the Facts

The fact that wartime injury is not necessarily illegal leads to a further set of questions. Is a claims procedure seeking to apply the law of state responsibility the best way to address the destructive outcomes of war?

My experience indicates the need for caution here. We all know that legal proceedings can be slow and expensive. They also offer limited tools for determining complex, disputed and obscure events associated with large-scale armed conflict. The types of mass claims institutions I cited at the beginning cannot solve this problem. These institutions do not deal well with disputed or complicated facts. To operate most effectively, mass claims programs require that (a) large numbers of similarly situated people have suffered similar injuries, (b) some body has made an authoritative judgment that these injuries entitle the victims to compensation, and (c) there is an underlying political consensus and adequate resources to pay for claims processing and to provide compensation. These factors often will not exist at the end of a conflict. As the attention required to determine the facts affecting each individual claimant increases, delays and costs increase, and the potential benefits of speed and economy diminish. There is a relentless trade-off between mass claims processing and individual assessment.

Without violating the confidentiality of our processes, I believe that study of the Eritrea- Ethiopia Claims Commission's awards would suggest the following regarding the problems of finding facts.

First, the awards make clear that wars can be extraordinarily complex events, and can lead to large numbers of claims. Creating a process to marshal these, and to provide for their orderly consideration, is a challenge. In any case, time and the determined efforts of highly skilled people are required.

The awards also illustrate how it can be very difficult to determine crucial facts required to assess application of the *jus in bello*, even in a process where both parties participate actively, there are large amounts of testimonial evidence and the Commission is able to actively question counsel and witnesses. The fog, confusion and complexity of war are familiar. The difficulties of determining the facts are multiplied by all states' tendency to hold closely to their own understandings of events.

The application of international humanitarian law usually involves judgments that are based on facts – were specific uses of force proportionate, were feasible precautions taken, and the like. Assessment requires understanding of the terrain, the positions and makeup of opposing forces, the available weaponry, and other military considerations that may be extremely difficult – or impossible – to reconstruct on a large scale in a hearing room long after the event. Given these difficulties, the 'default mechanism' for resolving important issues may depend on who bears the burden of proof on a particular issue.

## Where Will the Resources Come From?

A third set of questions involves an unedifying but absolutely essential subject – money. Mr. Willie Sutton, a noted American bank robber, was once asked why he robbed banks. 'Because that's where the money is', he said. To be more than a gesture, a compensation process needs to provide meaningful compensation. This is where I have difficulty with the suggested analogy between the International Criminal Court ('ICC') and other international criminal courts, and what we can call here the International War Claims Commission.

A secure source of funding, perhaps in very large amounts, is essential for any credible compensation process. There is little justice in raising claimants' expectations, and collecting their claims, if the process cannot be completed and compensation paid. This extends not only to payments to victims, but also to the costs of running the claims program. Programs to address tens or hundreds of thousands of claims cannot be done 'on the cheap'. The UNCC had a peak staff of over 375. The Bosnian real property commission employed 400. Serious programs cannot be done without a serious commitment of people and resources and a serious commitment of funding.

The ICC and its predecessors, the International Criminal Tribunal for the Former Yugoslavia and the corresponding tribunal for Rwanda, address the individual criminal responsibility of a comparatively small number of senior individuals allegedly responsible for particularly serious crimes. The objective is to put those found guilty in jail. Jailing a few dozen convicted individuals is something the international community can accomplish. Nevertheless, it bears recalling that the international criminal courts ultimately depend upon the willingness of national authorities to incarcerate convicted prisoners.

The objective of a compensation exercise would be different. It would transfer resources to injured persons, in some amount related to their injuries as measured by the international law of damages or in some other way. There is little point in launching such a process if there are no resources to transfer.

Where will those resources come from? Norbert Wühler will tell you where the UNCC got money to pay claims. Some have criticized the UNCC as 'victor's justice', and I detect a hint of this criticism in the program describing our panel. But what are the alternatives? Will former enemies, both of which may have been economically devastated, voluntarily provide compensation? Will that body called 'the international community' be asked to bankroll the enterprise voluntarily, as it has been asked to provide jail cells for convicted defendants from The Hague or Arusha?

Or will there be some outside mechanism to extract reparations from a party found to have violated the *jus in bello,* by sanctions or even by force if necessary?

## Foundations of the Process

This brings us to a final set of questions, concerning the political and legal foundations of any future global compensation process. Will it be created and enforced pursuant to treaty? How many of the countries potentially facing armed conflicts of some kind will support and adhere to such a treaty? States like, say, the United States, Russia, and Israel? Consider the large-scale armed conflicts now going on or recently concluded – how many of the belligerents are likely to voluntarily participate in such a tribunal?

Will the parties to such a treaty be prepared to attempt to enforce compliance against the states that do not adhere? Or is participation to be compelled, pursuant to the Chapter VII powers of the Security Council? Will the Security Council have the stomach for another UNCC, often affecting countries with far fewer resources than were available to Iraq, or in cases where ultimate responsibility for the initiation of hostilities may be far less clear?

Concluding Thoughts

For these and other reasons, I believe it is fair to question whether a universal, 'one-size-fits-all' institution is likely to be effective.

There will indeed be situations where a post-war mechanism to address claims can be very useful. I believe that Eritrea and Ethiopia acted wisely in deciding to create the Eritrea-Ethiopia commission. The parties' continued active support and participation in the arbitration process over more than four years suggest to me that both governments see the process as useful as they work to redefine their relationship following a costly war. Will such a mechanism provide corresponding benefits in other situations? My answer would probably be, 'it all depends'.

I suspect, although I do not know, that one element of Eritrea's and Ethiopia's continued commitment to the Commission and support for its work is a sense that the process 'belongs' to them and has not been imposed by some outside agency. The Commission was created as the result of political decisions taken by both of the parties. The parties selected four of the five commissioners, and the Commission's chair was chosen by agreement among the four party-appointed members.

During my career, I have worked with other institutions created and maintained by somewhat similar agreements between former adversaries: the Iran-US Claims Tribunal, created by agreement between Iran and the United States at the end of the 1979-81 hostage crisis, and the Multinational Force and Observers, the peacekeeping force in the Sinai Desert created by agreement between Egypt and Israel to support Israel's withdrawal from the Sinai. In each of these very different settings, I believe that the concept of 'ownership' by the participating states was important in the continued viability of the institution. Some say this invites 'politics' and is a bad thing. My experience leads me to a different conclusion.

## Remarks by Rainer Hofmann*

No paper received.

* University of Kiel.

# Remarks by Avril McDonald*

## The International Victims Reparations Agency: Helping Victims to Help Themselves

### 1. The Need to Provide Reparations for Victims of Serious International Crimes

Persons who are victims of serious international crimes, particularly, war crimes, crimes against humanity and genocide, are persons whose lives have been grievously damaged or destroyed. They have often lost all that is nearest and dearest to them. They may have lost family members and loved ones because of the armed conflict or repression and its attendant violations of the law, as well as their health, their home and most important possessions, their ability to sustain future employment or education, and even their future prospect of happiness.

For a victim of a serious crime, nothing can turn back the clock. The worst cannot be undone. Still, there are ways that the international community could respond to the needs of such victims in a more sustained and systematic way than heretofore that could assist them in rebuilding their lives.

While victims of serious violations of international humanitarian law are not a homogeneous group of people, and all individuals will have specific needs, many victims share a similar set of needs.[1] Foremost amongst the needs expressed by victims of crimes is a need for justice.[2] What constitutes justice finds different expression in different people but often expresses itself in a desire for prosecution of the perpetrator and to receive reparations, especially compensation. While the former has been the subject of considerable activity over the past decade, the latter is only belatedly receiving international attention.

In recent years, relative to past performance,[3] a lot of time, effort and money have been invested in prosecuting persons the persons whose actions wreak such havoc and misfortune for others, in the expectation or at least hope that the pursuit of international criminal justice can restore some equilibrium to a chaotic, bewildering and lawless situation; can express the judgment of the international community and its institutions that criminal acts against individuals even in the fog of war cannot and will not be tolerated; and can return a measure of security and peace to a war-affected country. In fact, the pursuit of criminal justice at both international and national levels has been a central plank of the international community's newfound political resolve to contribute to peace and security in transitional societies in ways that do not involve the use of force. A desire to contribute to international peace and security in the Balkans was one of the main justifications for establishing the International Criminal Tribunal for the Former Yugoslavia (ICTY) under Chapter VII of the UN Charter.[4] The Preamble of the Rome Statute establishing the International Criminal Court

* Dr Avril McDonald is Head of the Section of International Humanitarian Law and International Criminal Law at the TMC Asser Institute for International Law, The Hague and Managing Editor of the *Yearbook of International Humanitarian Law*.

(ICC) recognises that such grave crimes as those included under its jurisdiction 'threaten the peace, security and well-being of the world'.[5] The establishment of international criminal courts is believed to contribute to international and national peace and security by prosecuting persons suspected of the worse crimes, by removing the guilty from society through their imprisonment, as well as by exerting a deterrent effect. The Preamble of the Rome Statute expresses the Court's determination 'to put an end to impunity for the perpetrators of these crimes and thus to contribute to the prevention of these crimes'.

This long overdue public acceptance by the international community of the link between impunity and international peace and security, and the recent focus by the international community on combating impunity by prosecuting the perpetrators of the most serious crimes, is to be commended, even if the deterrent effect of criminal prosecutions have yet to be really felt and are in any event hard to measure. The extent to which the investment in international criminal justice represents value for money is also difficult to gauge. Clearly, it cannot be evaluated according to the same criteria as national criminal justice models, given that it has much more broad and diffuse purposes. Certainly, if an international court such as the ICTY was only to be measured in terms of its outputs it would not be considered efficient. Together, the ICTY and its sister Tribunal in Rwanda have cost the international community almost two billion dollars since their creation in 1993 and 1994,[6] and by the time they wrap up proceedings it will be considerably more. Yet in the scheme of things they have only prosecuted a handful of persons, and in many cases, the process and sentences have seemed inadequate from a victim's perspective. Moreover, the restoration of peace and security in the regions has come about mainly through political and military rather than judicial means. Still, the importance of criminal prosecutions at the international level cannot be underestimated. Criminal prosecutions for international crimes by either international or national courts are a vital part of any transitional policy for a post conflict state, although it is regrettable that, to date, victims' participation in these processes has been very limited. Where possible, prosecutions should preferably be undertaken at the national level, although experience has shown that often they need to be stimulated by either the establishment of an international court or with the encouragement, including through assistance in national institution building, of international organisations or third states.

It is clear that victims of international crimes consider criminal justice, usually meaning the prosecution of the perpetrator, to be an essential element of justice. But it is not the only element. Victims of international crimes have many other needs and rights which are not currently being met. For all the money that has been spent on prosecuting the perpetrators, the victims of the conflicts in the Balkans and the genocide in Rwanda, for example, have received almost no reparations from either the perpetrators or the state[7] and many of them have been unable to return to their homes.

Just as the investment of copious financial resources in international criminal justice is considered, or at least hoped to, have a positive knock on impact on international peace and security, so too the investment, or lack of it, in victims of international crimes, can affect the extent to which they consider themselves to be stakeholders in transitional processes. To the extent that they do not, this could have repercussions for international peace and security. It is only lately being recognised that assisting victims of mass violations in a concrete way, through the provision of reparations, for example, is not only necessary in helping them to rebuild their lives it is also an essential element of any serious attempt to achieve justice and security that is meaningful to victims.[8] Foremost amongst victims' needs and rights are a need and right to reparations, especially compensation; a right to return home and to reclaim their property; a need to participate in any judicial or administrative processes involving their rights or interests; and a need for information.

The ICC fortunately recognises a much more active role for victims than the earlier *ad hoc* Tribunals by allowing them the possibility to participate in the processes and the hearings of the Court. Victims have a general right to participate in the proceedings.[9] In addition, numerous provisions of the Statute establish the possibility for victims to participate in various ways, from petitioning the Court[10] to making a claim for reparations. The Statute also provides for the possibility for victims to receive reparations through the machinery of the Court itself, from a convicted person (Art. 75) and through the Trust Fund (Art. 79).

The ICC might be considered as the answer to the prayers of victims of serious international crimes. Yet it will hardly begin to address the problem of reparations for victims of serious international crimes. It is a model of criminal justice and a catalyst for national action rather than a mechanism for dealing in any kind of systematic way with international crimes and their victims. Because of its limited financial resources, the Court will only be able to deal with a handful of situations, and within them, to prosecute only a small number of crimes. Only those victims who are directly affected by a crime being prosecuted by the Court will be able to claim reparations, and even then, only those in cases where there is a successful prosecution. Some more may benefit through the Trust Fund. However, the majority of violations of international humanitarian law that are experienced by victims will never be adjudicated by the ICC, and most victims will never have an opportunity to be heard or represented in The Hague.

The ICC Statute envisages that states have the primary duty for prosecuting suspects under the principle of complementarity,[11] but the complementarity principle does not speak to states' and perpetrators' obligations *vis-à-vis* victims at the national level, in particular, the question of reparations. States that have implemented the ICC Statute into their national law have generally not addressed the question of victims' rights in relation to international crimes.

States clearly need assistance in understanding the importance of developing victim-centred processes in responding to international crime and in adjusting their criminal and civil judicial processes to take better account of victims. They also need to ensure that mechanisms are in place to compensate victims and to otherwise assist them with financial and other needs. But the geography of armed conflict today means that the most needy victims live in those states where there is the least possibility that they will be able to have those needs addressed. In particular, it is unlikely that they will receive reparations, either from the state or the perpetrator. How can the international community respond to their needs?

## 2. The Merits of Establishing a Permanent International Claims Commission

In order to provide other possibilities beside the ICC for victims who cannot access it, various other mechanisms could be envisioned. The members of the panel were asked in particular to consider the merits of a permanent war damage commission.

### 2.1 A brief historical overview of the international claims commissions following armed conflicts

The establishment of claims tribunals as part of a peace settlement has a rich history. There are many examples of peace treaties providing for the possibility of individuals affected by war to make claims directly against states other than their own, as well as against the nationals of other states. The Treaty of Versailles,[12] by its Articles 232, 296, 297, 304 and 305, and the corresponding articles of the other peace treaties signed after the First World War, authorised nationals of the Allied and Associated Powers to claim compensation in respect of damages caused by extraordinary war measures on Germany's part (Art. 297(e) Versailles); and they provided for the institution of mixed arbitral tribunals.[13] 'Before these tribunals individual citizens of the victor states could bring claims against nationals and governments of the defeated states. The tribunals dealt with a large number of claims and functioned for about ten years'.[14] Almost always, claims had to be directly against states, rather than against individuals.[15]

A number of bilateral treaties have also permitted individuals to bring claims against states by establishing mixed claims commissions.[16] Article 5 of the German-Polish Convention of 15 May 1922, regarding Upper Silesia, authorised private individuals to bring a suit before an international court against a state which had violated certain interests of individuals protected by the Convention.[17] An Agreement of 10 August 1922 between the US and Germany, entered into pursuant to the 1921 Treaty of Berlin, established a Mixed Claims Commission to hear claims by US citizens against Germany for damage to property, rights and interests in Germany, other claims for injury to persons or property as a consequence of war and debts due to American citizens by the German Government or German nationals. A French-Mexican Claims Commission was established in 1924 by a Convention between France and Mexico to receive claims by French nationals in respect of injuries suffered during the revolutionary activities in Mexico from 1910 to 1920.

Indeed, more than 80 mixed arbitral tribunals and claims commissions have been created following armed conflicts and revolutions,[18] with the first being the US-Great Britain Commission established under the Jay Treaty of 1794[19] and among the most recent examples being the Iran-US Claims Tribunal established by the Algerian Accords of 19 January 1981 and still operating[20] and the Eritrea-Ethiopia Claims Committee, established pursuant to the Agreement between the Government of the Federal Democratic Republic of Ethiopia and the Government of the State of Eritrea of 12 December 2000. The latter's mandate is

> 'to decide through binding arbitration all claims for loss, damage or injury by one Government against the other, and by nationals (including both natural and juridical persons) of one party

> against the Government of the other party or entities owned or controlled by the other party that are (a) related to the conflict that was the subject of the Framework Agreement, the Modalities for its Implementation and the Cessation of Hostilities Agreement,[21] and (b) result from violations of international humanitarian law, including the 1949 Geneva Conventions, or other violations of international law.'

The direct reference to violations of international humanitarian law as a basis for claims by individuals is significant, as it is the first of its kind. However, claims must be submitted through states, which can make claims on their own behalf and behalf of their nationals (natural and juridical persons).

In recent years, with the notable exceptions of those established by Iran-US and Eritrea-Ethiopia, claims commissions have fallen out of favour as a means of dispute resolution for several reasons. In the first place, modern conflicts generally do not lend themselves to international claims commissions to resolve disputes. The fact that there are far fewer situations of international armed conflict means that their applicability is limited. The least that has been required to establish a claims commission has been the existence of two states. Furthermore, according to one commentator, '[t]he decline in the number of international claims tribunals in the past forty years has been linked to the demise of diplomatic protection and the espousal by States of claims.'[22]

A serious problem with claims commissions, as with many other forms of dispute settlement, is that they usually only allow the nationals of the victor state to make claims. Violations of the law and damage committed by the victor states have historically not been the subject of claims. In principle, the legal obligation is on both sides, but in practice, only the winning side has had to pay compensation. In this respect, the Eritrea-Ethiopia Claims Commission is unusual, as the nationals of both sides can submit claims through their states. Its establishment shows the potential utility of claims commissions as a means of making remedies available to victims where there is no clear winner or loser in an armed conflict.

An advantage of claims commissions is the fact that they can allow individuals to directly participate in the claims process. For individuals with access to a claims commission, either directly or through their government, there is a high probability of getting an award.

In conclusion, one can say that the concept of international claims by individuals for violations of international law sustained during an armed conflict, including violations of international humanitarian law, is recognised by international law, both by multilateral and bilateral treaties. Particularly during the nineteenth and early-twentieth centuries, international claims commissions were created to resolve claims arising out of armed conflicts.

## 2.2 The merits of a permanent international claims commission

The panel was asked to consider the merits of building on this concept and establishing a permanent war damage commission. This begs the question of what is meant by such a term. The nomenclature suggests that it would be only concerned with war related damage. The term damage suggests that such a commission might settle claims based on damage, rather than wrongdoing.

If one were to go to the trouble of establishing a permanent claims commission, it would at least be useful to consider whether other victims of international crimes, such as victims of crimes against humanity or genocide, or their relatives, should not also benefit from such a mechanism. Although there is something to be said for the establishment of a separate and distinct war crimes commission to benefit victims of war crimes, a permanent claims commission, which could adjudicate claims regarding all the core crimes, rather than just war crimes, also presents advantages which should also be assessed.

It could be argued that a war damage commission or some kind of international claims commission would address the problems of lack of competence and resources at the national level. But despite the significant successes of many of the national claims commissions that have been established to deal generally with violations of international law committed during international armed conflicts, transposing at the international level in a permanent manner what has proven successful in a number of *ad hoc* cases at the national level may prove neither advisable nor workable, at least in the short-term, pending greater understanding of the tremendous complexity of the challenges that the enterprise would involve.

Many questions would have to be resolved before such any permanent claims commission could be established. Determining the victim pool, and the basis for claims, would be difficult, and should surely be influenced by the financial wherewithal of the institution. Should only victims of crimes (which would be somewhat unfair for those who could not prove the existence of a crime and especially an international crime) be allowed to file claims? Even here, the potential pool would be potentially large. If one was to broaden the potential group of claimants to include anyone who could show that they had suffered damage as result of an international crime without having to prove the existence of the crime, one sees the possibly limited resources being stretched even further. Add in all war-affected victims, or all victims of crimes against humanity, or genocide, and their relatives, and the resources of the claims commission would have to be considerable in order to make it worth victims' time and effort to bring a claim before it.

This raises the question of who would fund such an initiative. The existing claims commissions, in particularly the United Nations Compensation Fund, have had relatively deep pockets and a specific and mandated source of funding.

In order to justify establishing an international claims commission it would have to have a substantial, continuous, steady, guaranteed source of funding. Before any serious efforts would be made to establish a permanent claims commission, it would be necessary to establish whether the necessary funding would be available. Such costs will be considerable, if it were to make a meaningful contribution. The administrative costs alone would be expensive, given that, if national claims commissions are anything to go by, running a claims commission is a hugely complex administrative task.

While establishing a permanent claims commission, whatever its remit, has some merits, the practical difficulties bedevilling such an enterprise would not be easy to overcome in the short-term. However, if a reliable and continuous source of funding could be identified, the idea should be actively pursued.

## 3. The International Victims Reparations Agency

Rather than trying to respond to the needs of only some victims – those that are fortunate enough to get to hear about any permanent claims commission and who could actually bring a successful claim, in the absence of such a body being established – a more immediate, realistic, feasible and useful solution might be to create a mechanism that could help to develop and strengthen existing national and international competence, resources and information for victims of international crimes. What is needed as a practical matter is not so much a variant on a national or internationalised mechanism for assessing claims transposed to the international level but a mechanism that can be quickly and easily implemented to oversee and help build and coordinate national and international capacity in the area of victims' rights and help develop, coordinate and finance worthy projects. The proposed mechanism is what might be called the International Victims Reparations Agency.

### 3.1 The International Victims Reparations Agency's function and purpose

Essentially, the International Victims Reparations Agency would be a facilitator. It would serve as

- a capacity builder;
- a consultancy;
- a coordinator;
- a clearing house and channel for information.

Its main purposes would be:

- Assisting states and other national and international providers in building their capacity to address victims' needs at the national and international levels;
- Developing understanding of those needs;
- Assisting victims in knowing their rights and in accessing available services, both at the national and international levels.

### 3.2 The legal basis of the International Victims Reparations Agency

Such a mechanism could be established in various ways. One theoretical possibility would be a multilateral treaty, although this does seem a remote and unrealistic prospect. Another option would be a bilateral treaty. For this, all that would be necessary would be the agreement of two or more states (cf., IOM).

If the enthusiasm and political will could be summoned, such a body could also be established, viz. various UN organs, including by the UN Security Council, the General Assembly or by the Secretary General, as a sub organ of the Secretariat. Technically, it might be possible to establish such a facility as part of or connected with the ICC, the Assembly of States Parties or the Trust Fund. If international or bilateral agreement and support would not forthcoming to create such a body by treaty, it could be established in the short-term as an independent foundation or non-governmental organisation. Still, some political support would be highly desirable and probably necessary in terms of funding, etc. The private sector could also be a possible source of funding.

## 3.3 The International Victims Reparations Agency's mandate

### 3.3.1 *General and ongoing functions*

In setting itself up and defining its priorities, part of the main initial work of the International Victims Reparations Agency would involve mapping and evaluating existing services, including legal, administrative, medical, psychological, etc., that exist at the national and international levels that are or might be available to crime victims, in particular victims of international crimes. It would also be important to identify the legal and other reforms necessary to establish a system of compensation and other means of reparations for victims of international crimes and other essential services for victims within priority states, and for responding to the specific needs of victims of war and other forms of mass trauma in particular cases. The Agency would also include as a major part of its work conducting, coordinating, prioritising and publicising research on the needs of victims of international crimes; establishing and maintaining a worldwide network of victim service providers and services; coordinating with other international initiatives on victims, including the ICC Trust Fund, the UN Fund for Torture Victims, national claims commissions, and so on.

### 3.3.2 *Functions addressed to states and NGOs*

The Agency would provide several specific services to governmental and non-governmental clients, including expert advice on capacity-building at the national and international levels, legal advice on introducing domestic legislation to provide for victims' compensation and other necessary reforms to the criminal and criminal procedural codes and civil law; providing advice on coordination of services and networking at the national and international levels; and providing technical support and advice at the national level, for example, in information technology, including database construction, etc.

### 3.3.3 *Functions addressed to victims*

A major part of the client base of the International Victims Reparations Agency would naturally be victims. An effective Outreach program would thus be an essential requisite. It would have several aspects:

*Informing victims as to their rights and available services.* The International Victims Reparations Agency should, in coordination with national agencies, help to fund and develop national information campaigns to ensure that as many victims as possible know their legal rights and what services are available to them
*Communicating* with all the necessary actors, in particular, victims groups and decision-makers
*Information clearing house*: One of the International Victims Reparations Agency's most useful functions would be to serve as a depository of information and virtual

information clearing house and one stop shop for victims. A user friendly and interactive website, which would include a database of all national legislation concerning victims' rights, would be essential.

### 3.4 Funding of the International Victims Reparations Agency

While funds would have to be found for the International Victims Reparations Agency, the cost would be nowhere near as much as for a permanent international claims commission or a war damage commission and are within reach. The essential feature of the International Victims Reparations Agency is that it would provide and coordinate expertise and know-how, and its main fixed cost would be the wages of its staff, who would mainly be lawyers; persons with special expertise in victims' issues; psychologists; communications specialists; technical specialists; and fund-raising experts. Where necessary, the International Victims Reparations Agency could hire national experts on short-term contracts. Ideally, some money should be available for projects.

Depending on how the International Victims Reparations Agency was established, funding for the agency could conceivably come from various sources; States' Parties, UN Member States, individual contributions from states; the private sector, etc. The agency itself could take a dynamic approach to fundraising.

### 3.5 The virtues of the International Victims Reparations Agency

- It is an achievable and relatively uncomplicated solution for a pressing problem;
- The idea is predicated on the fact that what is really missing and most urgently required is the legal and institutional infrastructure at the level of states to address the needs of victims of international crimes;
- As the agency is geared to capacity building, it would helps to build sustainable and accessible mechanisms at the national level;
- The International Victims Reparations Agency would help to promote and coordinate victims' issues at the international law;
- It would be relatively cheap and easy to establish;
- It is geared to assisting the maximum number of victims and service providers;
- The International Victims Reparations Agency would follow a local and bottom up approach and in doing so take account of and help develop the existing legal, administrative and other apparatuses in a way that complements existing mechanisms;
- Its creation would not in any way interfere with the potential establishment of (any other) treaty-based international institution(s), such as a permanent international claims commission or even an international civil court.

## 4. Conclusion

The International Victims Reparations Agency would fulfil a role that is not currently being served but that is needed. Victims of international crimes need the help of the international community in attaining reparations for the crimes they have suffered, but they need it in a way that is meaningful for them. It is unrealistic to expect most victims of international crimes to be able to bring a claim before any future permanent war damage or international claims commission or to appear before the International Criminal Court. What victims need is something that will smooth the way for them in their quest for justice, and that means in most cases at the national level. The International Victims Reparations Agency's main goal would ultimately be to make it possible and easier for victims of international crimes to access some form of reparations at the national level. While this may not always be monetary compensation, victims' needs can also be addressed in other ways that are meaningful, useful and necessary. Developing a clear picture of what is currently the situation for victims of international crimes at the national level, and then helping states and international and national providers to better meet victims' needs and victims to help themselves would be a positive start and would have a far more concrete and positive impact on the lives of victims of international crimes than the establishment of an international claims commission in some western capital far removed from the lives of the majority of victims of the most serious international crimes.

## Notes

[1] Summarising the work of victimisation experts, Stauffer and Hamber list the basic needs of a victim as:

- To be able to speak and be heard in a 'safe-space';
- To know that what happened to them was wrong and that their emotions are legitimate;
- To experience both real and symbolic restitution;
- To be given a chance to tell their story/the truth;
- To be empowered, as power has been taken from them by force.

C. Stauffer and B. Hamber, 'Putting a Face on the Past: Survivor-Offender Mediation and the Truth and Reconciliation Commission'. Paper presented at the Centre for the Study of Violence and Reconciliation, Johanesburg, Seminar No. 1, 1996. Quoted in *Torture Survivors' Perceptions of Reparation: Preliminary Survey* (London, The Redress Trust 2001).

Zehr has identified the five main needs of victims as being:

- To be awarded compensation/restitution;
- To receive 'answers';
- To speak the truth about what has happened to them;
- To receive guarantees of non-repetition;
- To be actively involved in the judicial process.

H. Zehr, *Changing Lenses: A New Focus for Crime and Justice* (New York, Herald Press 1990).

[2] According to one survey, '[m]any of the "gatekeepers" interviewed remarked that the main "want" expressed by survivors [of torture] is often an unfocussed desire for "justice". There has, however, been little exploration of what this word means to the survivor.' *Torture Survivors' Perceptions of Reparation,* ibid., p. 60. Cohen states that 'the act of reparation is symbolically extremely important – and may be more effective than individual punishment in meeting the victims' need for recognition of their dignity'. S. Cohen, 'State Crimes of Previous Regimes: Knowledge, Accountability, and the Policing of the Past', 20 *Law and Social Inquiry* (1995) pp. 7-50 at 24. Summerfield has written that: 'Some torture victims seek psychological help but all of them want social justice. ... Allied to this is the vital question of official reparation for human rights crimes. Victims may better become survivors if some part of the legacy of the past is addressed ... Justice, even if long delayed, is reparative ... to assist both distressed individuals and distressed societies ... to endorse the link between psychological recovery and societal reparation and justice.' D. Summerfield, Addressing Human responses to war and atrocity: major themes for health workers, Medical Foundation for the Care of Victims of Torture, 1993, quoted in B. Bowring, 'Redress for Survivors of Torture', in C. Joyner (ed.), *Reining in Impunity for International Crimes and Serious Violations of Fundamental Human Rights: Proceedings of the Siracusa Conference 17-21 September 1998* (Paris, Association Internationale de Droit Pénal 1998) pp. 431 at 432-433.

[3] Following the conclusion of the Nuremburg and Tokyo Trials, no trials before an international or

internationalised criminal jurisdiction occurred for almost 50 years, until the establishment of the ICTY.

[4] Pursuant to Security Council Resolution 827 (1993), adopted by the SC on 25 May 1993.

[5] U.N. Doc. A/CONF.183/9*. Available online at: <http://www.un.org/law/icc/statute/romefra.htm>. Reprinted in A. Cassese, P. Gaeta and John R.W.D. Jones, *The Rome Statute of the International Criminal Court: A Commentary,* Vol. III, Materials (Oxford, Oxford University Press 2002).

[6] Details of the ICTY's budget can be found at: <http://www.un.org/icty/glance/index.htm>. For information about the ICTR's budget, go to: <http://www.ictr.org>.

[7] See I. Bottigliero, *Redress for Victims of Crimes under International Law* (Leiden, Martinus Nijhoff Publishers 2004) pp. 1-4 and generally for a comprehensive analysis of victims' failure to attain redress in most cases.

[8] In his Report on the rule of law and transitional justice in conflict and post-conflict societies, the UN Secretary-General noted that: 'Whatever mode of transitional justice is adopted and however reparations programmes are conceived to accompany them, both the demands of justice and the dictates of peace require that something is done to compensate victims. Indeed, the judges of the tribunals for Yugoslavia and Rwanda have themselves recognized this and have suggested that the United Nations consider creating a special mechanism for reparations that would function alongside the tribunals.' S/2004/616, 23 August 2004, para. 55.

[9] Art. 68(3) is a general clause regarding victims' participation. It provides:
'Where the personal interests of the victims are affected, the Court shall permit their views and concerns to be presented and considered at stages of the proceedings determined to be appropriate by the Court and in a manner which is not prejudicial to or inconsistent with the rights of the accused and a fair and impartial trial. Such views and concerns may be presented by the legal representatives of the victims where the Court considers it appropriate, in accordance with the Rules of Procedure and Evidence.'

[10] See Arts. 15(3) and 19(3), and Rules 89, 90, 91, 92 and 93, in particular.

[11] Preamble, Art. 17 ICC Statute.

[12] Treaty of Versailles, 28 June 1919, 1 Bevans 43. Art. 232 of the Treaty of Versailles provided that '... The Allied and Associated Government require and Germany undertakes that she will make compensation for all damage done to the civilian population of the Allied and Associated Powers and to their property during the period of belligerence of each as an Allied or Associated Powers and to their property during the period of belligerency of each as an Allied or Associated Power against Germany by such aggression by land by sea and from the air ... '

[13] H. Kelsen, *General Theory of Law and State* (Cambridge, Mass., Harvard University Press 1949) p. 347.

[14] I. Brownlie, *Principles of Public International Law,* 4th edn. (Oxford, Clarendon Press 1990) p. 584.

[15] 'Claims were almost always directed against the respondent state, and not its nationals. International claims tribunals were never intended to directly vindicate the rights of private parties, nor to serve as an alternative to domestic court litigation. If claimants could not prove that the cause of their injuries was the result of an action imputable to the respondent state, the claim would be disallowed. Very few claims settlement instruments elaborated on this point, with the consequence that individual tribunals were often confronted with thorny issues of state attribution.' D.J. Bederman, 'The Glorious Past and Uncertain Future of International Claims Tribunals', in M.W. Janis (ed.), *International Courts for the Twenty-First Century* (Dordrecht, Martinus Nijhoff 1992) p. 172.

[16] R.B. Lillich, 'Lump Sum Agreements,' in 8 *Encyclopedia of Public International Law* (Amsterdam/New York/Oxford, North-Holland 1985) p. 368.

[17] Kelsen, *supra* n. 13, p. 348.

[18] Bederman, *supra* n. 15, pp. 189-192.

[19] *The Jay Treaty. Treaty of Amity, Commerce, and Navigation, signed at London, 19 November 1794, with additional article.* In Miller (ed.), *Treaties and Other International Acts of the United States of* America, Vol. 2, Documents 1-4, 1776-1818 (Washington, Government Printing Office 1931).

[20] Algerian Accords (Declaration of the Government of the Democratic and Popular Republic of Algeria Concerning the Settlement of Claims by the Government of the United States of America and the Government of the Islamic Republic of Iran, 75 *AJIL* (1981) p. 422 / 20 *ILM* (1981) p. 230. The work of the Iran-US Claims Tribunal has stimulated an extensive literature. See, *inter alia,* J. Collier and V. Lowe, *The Settlement of Disputes in International Law: Institutions and Procedures* (Oxford, Oxford University Press 1999) p. 78.

[21] Of 18 June 2000.

[22] Bederman, *supra* n. 15, p. 176.

## Discussion

This Panel considered the question whether, as the *ad hoc* war crimes tribunals prepared the ground for the International Criminal Court, experience with the several *ad hoc* war damage compensation commissions has paved the way towards a permanent war damage compensation mechanism.

John Crook points out that although there is room for some steps forward, one should not be too ambitious. Two developments can be recognized with regard to the more recent claims commissions. First, there is the sheer magnitude of modern programs, made possible by, amongst others, technological innovations. Second, in contradiction to their predecessors who tended to be more State-centered, modern institutions focus more on individual claims. Crook believes that properly conceived mass claims programs can sometimes significantly contribute to effective post-conflict programs of reconstruction and reconciliation. *Ad hoc* systems however seem to be more equipped to fulfill this job than an eventual permanent equivalent. Crook argues that the creation of a universal mechanism raises a number of difficult questions regarding the workability and desirability of such system. First, what is the objective? The question must be asked because of the exceptional legal character of large-scale armed conflicts. In the context of armed conflict, atrocities committed do not always result in responsibility for breach of the *ius in bello* under the law of State Responsibility. It is thus unsatisfactory to link the right to compensation to the question whether the *ius in bello* has been breached. Also, in cases where there has not been breach of the *ius in bello,* victims of the atrocities of war should be deemed to have the right to rebuild their lives. A second problem that needs to be addressed is the problem of *fact finding* in the context of armed conflict, since wartime injury is not necessarily illegal. One should question whether a claims procedure seeking to apply the law of State Responsibility is the best way to address the destructive outcomes of war in this respect. A third question that must be asked is where the resources should come from. To be more than a gesture, a compensation process needs to provide meaningful compensation. Also, funding is needed for setting-up a permanent commission. Crook considers that a certain notice of ownership of the procedure is indispensable, taking the Ethiopia Eritrea Claims Commission, which has been set-up as part of a bilateral agreement by the parties, as an example. The concept of ownership in this context contributed in an important manner to the viability of this institution. This experience is another reason for being not too supportive of an eventual permanent commission.

Norbert Wühler finds that setting-up a permanent war crimes compensation commission could lead to more consistent practice, since it would create its own case law. However, setting-up such organ would entail many difficulties, whereby the greatest challenge would be the funding; it is important to note that for such commission to be credible, sufficient funding is needed. As does Crook, Wühler foresees difficulties in defining the legal framework. 'War' is a legal term, and it is often not easy to distinguish whether from a legal point of view a 'war' exists. As a result of this, it will be difficult to distinguish between the claimants. Then there are the logistical problems. If the commission would settle, for example, in The Hague, having generalized jurisdiction, it would have to judge upon all kinds of claims arising from all kinds of conflicts, in all kinds of languages. It would be an impossible operation. Therefore,

Wühler proposes to set-up a Permanent Standing Facility, that is, a Secretariat, that can recruit staff, create infrastructure, provide information to claimants, collect background information, design rules of procedure, provide computer support, etc. This Facility could help establish compensation mechanisms after conflicts in a quick way if the need arises. The Facility should be set-up within the context of the United Nations, whereby the International Organization for Migration would be a good host. Another good option would be to place this Facility under supervision of the Permanent Court of Arbitration.

AVRIL MCDONALD agrees with the first two speakers that the idea of setting-up a permanent compensation commission is unfeasible. Although there is a need for reform of the current system of *ad hoc* commissions, there are more disadvantages than advantages in setting-up a permanent compensation commission. The problem of funding is only one issue here. One should also realize that it would be difficult to gain enough political support for a permanent institution. Another issue is the material scope of such institution: which victims would be able to make claims, and with respect to which crimes? And should the practice of the commission be fault or non-fault based? Then there is the fact that one can not expect most victims of international crimes to be able to bring a claim before an international institution. Victims need assistance in their quest for reparation, but in most cases this reparation is most likely to be found at the national level. Thus, instead of transplanting a traditional national claims commission to the international level, McDonald proposes to set-up a mechanism that can help build and coordinate national capacity in the area of victim's rights. This International Victims Reparations Agency could have the status of a Non-Governmental Organization of Foundation with UN Observer Status, for which the political support of only a few States would be enough. The Agency would function as a capacity builder, assisting victims in finding the available service and providing advice to States. It would furthermore fulfill a coordinating role, functioning as a center of expertise.

In conclusion, none of the speakers are very supportive of the idea of setting-up a permanent war crimes compensation commission. All three speakers envisage problems in the creation of such a system. By far the most mentioned issue in this respect is the *funding* of a permanent institution. The speakers agree that in order to be credible, any such commission must have sufficient resources. Additionally, the speakers mention the logistical problems that setting-up a permanent institution will entail. The speakers furthermore foresee difficulties in defining the legal framework for a permanent commission. McDonald stipulates that defining the material scope will be a great challenge. Crook points out that it is unsatisfactory to link the right to compensation to the question whether the *ius in bello* has been breached. The problem of *fact finding* should also be taken into account, since wartime injury is not always illegal. Wühler argues that it is often difficult to distinguish whether from a legal point of view in a particular conflict a *war* existed, which distinction is indispensable in order to identify which victims may file requests.

All speakers present alternatives for a permanent compensation commission. Crook mentions that in order to be successful, a compensation mechanism must bear a notion of ownership, since in the past, mechanisms have proved to be more successful if the parties were involved in their setting-up. Wühler suggests that a Permanent

Standing Facility should be set-up, which could function as a Secretariat for all future compensation mechanisms. McDonald proposes the installation of an International Victims Reparations Agency, which, functioning as a center of expertise, could help victims to help themselves.

*Reporter*: Els Dinjens*

* Ministry of Justice of the Netherlands.

# THE EXPANDING POWERS OF THE SECURITY COUNCIL

The panel was convened by its Chair, Erika de Wet*

## INTRODUCTORY REMARKS BY ERIKA DE WET

The panel concerns the legislative powers of the Security Council and the delegation of specific powers to the sanctions committees. The focus of the discussion is on the institutional dimensions of the expanding powers of the Security Council.

When referring to legislative powers we refer to broad, vague and abstract norms that are found in Resolutions 1373 relating to the financing of international terrorism, 1540 that concerns the proliferation of weapons of mass destruction. Questions discussed in this panel concern the following: Did the Security Council, by adopting these resolutions, remain within the limits of the UN ? Is the issuing of these resolutions in accordance with basic principles of treaty interpretation?

Furthermore, did states consent to these measures, during the negotiations leading up to the adoption of these resolutions? Seemingly, states have acquiesced in these measures. Does this have an impact on the legality of the way in which the Security Council acted? Even if we determine that the Security Council remained within the bounds of legality by issuing these resolutions, can they be seen as legitimate? What is the political authority of these measures, if we perceive that the Security Council does not represent the interests of the international community but mainly those of the US as the international hegemonic power?

Thus we see that the Security Council issues Resolutions that contain broad sanctions – Resolutions 1373 and 1540 are examples of this. However, these broad sanctions contain enough leeway for states to implement the sanctions in a way that facilitates due process. Alongside these broad sanctions, the Security Council also has started with targeted sanctions. These targeted sanctions pose specific problems of their own and they are the second problem that is related to the way in which the Security Council uses its powers.

Targeted sanctions cross the bounds between what is within the public realm and that which is considered in the private realm. They are directed at those individuals that seem responsible for terrorist actions, condemning and punishing individuals directly. The sanctions committees identify which individuals and are seen as responsible and can authorise the freezing of their assets. The problematic aspect is that these individuals do not have recourse to a court of law and thus the demands of due process are not taken into account by these sanctions.

* Professor of International Constitutional Law, University of Amsterdam.

## Remarks by Björn Elberling*

## The *Ultra Vires*-Character of Legislative Action by the Security Council

### 1. Development of the Security Council towards a World Legislature

Since the inception of the United Nations, and especially since the end of the Cold War, the Security Council has developed an ever broader understanding of its powers under Chapter VII of the UN Charter: It has held an ever increasing variety of concrete situations to constitute a threat to the peace in the sense of Article 39, thus increasing the scope of its executive functions.[1] It has, in several instances, decided upon the legal consequences of certain acts, thus exercising what may be deemed a quasi-judicial function.[2] Finally, and most importantly in this context, it has also in the last years implemented several measures of a legislative nature.[3]

This process began when the Council started considering, without reference to any particular situation or conflict, certain problems of concern to the international community. Among topics discussed in such 'thematic resolutions' were the protection of civilians in international conflicts or the spread of HIV/AIDS, but also certain methods employed by terrorist groups. However, in this context the Council has never invoked its Chapter VII powers to lay down obligations for states.[4]

This changed with Resolution 1373 (2001). Reacting to the terrorist attacks of 11 September, the Council determined 'that such acts, like any act of international terrorism, constitute a threat to international peace and security', thus referring to terrorist acts (also) in the abstract. The Council then imposed on all states duties to 'prevent and suppress the financing of terrorist acts', *inter alia*, by criminalizing conduct aimed at financing or supporting terrorist acts. These duties were not dependant on the continuance of the threat posed by the Al Qaeda network or otherwise linked to the concrete situation, in other words: The Council laid down norms of general and abstract applicability.

The Council again dealt with abstract dangers in Resolution 1422 (2002). By exempting certain 'acts or omissions relating to a United Nations established or authorized operation' from the jurisdiction of the International Criminal Court although no ICC investigation was imminent, the Council in effect held the abstract possibility of investigation to be a threat to the peace. And – at least if one holds the view that this general exemption, which was extended for another 12 months by Resolution 1487 (2003), was not covered by Article 16 of the Rome Statute[5] – the Council in effect changed the applicability of that Statute, thus participating indirectly in the creation of norms of general applicability.

* Research Fellow, Walther Schücking Institute for International Law, University of Kiel, Germany. This contribution is largely based on Andreas Zimmermann/Björn Elberling, 'Grenzen der Legislativbefugnisse des Sicherheitsrats, Resolution 1540 und abstrakte Bedrohungen des Weltfriedens', *Vereinte Nationen* (*VN*), Vol. 52 (2004), pp. 71-77.

The final step was marked by Resolution 1540 (2004). Here, the Council again identified an abstract danger – the proliferation of weapons of mass destruction to non-state actors – as a threat to the peace, and it again laid down general and abstract obligations for all states to refrain from assisting non-state actors in acquiring weapons of mass destruction, to criminalize behavior of non-state actors aimed at acquiring such weapons, etc. And while Resolution 1373, already referring to terrorist acts in the abstract, had still also been a reaction to a particular attack, Resolution 1540 dealt with the problem of proliferation *only* in the abstract.

These resolutions represent an unprecedented new development: The Council has started legislating for the entire international community. That this is a remarkable development was also acknowledged by several state representatives in the context of Council negotiations, and many scholars and state representatives seem to agree that the Council should only resort to such resolutions in situations where the cumbersome mechanisms of treaty or customary law do not function fast enough to close dangerous gaps in international law.[6]

## 2. Course of the Presentation

Contrary to this assertion, I will argue that the Council should not exercise legislative functions at all – not only because legislative resolutions are *ultra vires* according to the UN Charter, but also because they have wider implications going to the core of international law as we know it.

I will first show why, based on a systematic interpretation of Articles 39, 41 of the Charter, the legality of Security Council Resolutions dealing with abstract problems and/or laying down norms of general and abstract applicability is indeed questionable. I will then refer to arguments brought forward in favor of the legality of legislative Council action in the context of an evolutive interpretation of the Charter. Finally, I will try to show why even such an evolutive interpretation does not support the Council's legislative powers and what broader implications for the international system such powers would have.

I proceed from three basic assumptions: First, while the Security Council possesses a margin of appreciation in the application of Chapter VII, it is bound by international law at least insofar as it must keep within the boundaries of its powers as proscribed in the UN Charter.[7] Second, while there is a presumption of legality for Council resolutions, this presumption is rebuttable, especially in situations where the competence of the Council – or even that of the United Nations – to adopt a measure is in doubt.[8] Third, legislative resolutions which may not be based on Chapter VII do not find a valid basis in Article 25 of the Charter, either. Even leaving aside for the moment the question whether the Council may base binding decisions on Article 25 at all, a systematic interpretation shows that this cannot be the case for decisions on topics that fall within the ambit of Chapter VII – otherwise, any legal limits to Chapter VII powers would be devoid of any practical effect.

## 3. Systematic and Historical Arguments why Legislative Resolutions are *ultra vires*

Determining whether the Security Council may enact legislative resolutions can be done by interpreting two norms of the UN Charter: First, does the term 'threat to the peace' in Article 39 of the UN Charter also encompass abstract dangers? Second, are norms of general and abstract applicability among the non-forceful measures which the Council may apply under Article 41?

A systematic interpretation of the phrase 'threat to the peace' in Article 39 should first take into account the immediate surrounding: Both other terms used in Article 39 – 'breach of the peace', 'act of aggression' – clearly refer to concrete situations. In the same vein, Article 40 authorizes the Council to 'call upon the parties concerned' to adopt certain behavior – it seems hard to refer to a state as party to an abstract problem. Finally, Articles 33 and 34, which deal with situations not (yet) reaching the threshold of Chapter VII, also refer to a 'dispute' or 'situation', *concrete* situations also. The same is true of Article 32 on the participation of a 'party to a dispute under consideration by the Security Council' in the Council discussions.

An interpretation of Article 41 leads to a similar conclusion: While the list of measures under this article is not exhaustive, this does not mean that any non-forcible measure is *per se* permissible under Article 41: The list contains only measures dealing with concrete situations, not norms of general and abstract applicability. This is a clear indication that, for other measures to be covered by Article 41, they should resemble the listed ones at least in this regard. And in fact, other measures based on Article 41, such as the establishment of the *ad hoc* Tribunals for Rwanda and the former Yugoslavia, did conform to this requirement.

Finally, one should regard the distribution of competences within the UN system: While there is no true legislative organ within this system, the organ that comes closest to such a function is the General Assembly – among its tasks, according to Article 13 paragraph 1 lit. a of the Charter, is the progressive development of international law, a task it discharges with the assistance of the International Law Commission. Nowhere in the Charter is an equivalent task conferred on the Security Council.

This interpretation of the Charter as not granting legislative powers to the Council also is confirmed by the *travaux préparatoires*: The role of the Security Council, as perceived by the UN founders, was limited to dealing with concrete crises only. In fact, the Security Council was not even supposed to resolve such crises through the application of international law, but only to stabilize them so that a solution could be found by other peaceful means.[9]

## 4. Arguments for Legislative Powers of the Security Council

Two arguments are brought forward for the view that the Council may nevertheless exercise legislative functions, both based on the assertion that as the founding instrument of an international organization and the *de facto* constitution of the international system, the UN Charter must be considered a 'living instrument' and interpreted in an evolutive manner. Such evolutive interpretation links arguments concerning the object and purpose or *effet utile* of Charter norms with arguments from subsequent practice.[10]

The first argument concerns the object and purpose of Articles 39 and 41: Given that the Security Council is charged with keeping the peace, defined as (at least) the absence of large-scale violence, and given the development of ever changing threats to the peace, such as the 'globalization of violence'[11] with the attendant dangers posed by non-state actors possessing weapons of mass destruction and willing to use them, the Council must be allowed to adapt its functions to these threats.[12]

This argument is enforced by reference to the unanimous adoption of Resolutions 1373 and 1540 and the support which several states not members of the Council declared for these resolutions before or after their passage. Such agreement may constitute subsequent practice of states in the interpretation of Articles 39, 41 UN Charter, a fact to be taken into account in the interpretation of the Charter according to the customary rule codified in Article 31 paragraph 3 lit. b of the Vienna Convention on the Law of Treaties.[13]

## 5. Reply

These arguments in favor of legislative Council powers can be answered in two ways: First, by questioning their actual basis, such as the amount of practice in support of legislative Council functions or the suitability of the Council for this role; second, and more importantly, by inquiring into the boundaries of evolutive interpretation in general.

### 5.1 Extent of state practice in support of legislative powers

Concerning the argument derived from subsequent practice, one may ask what practice actually exists in support of legislative Council powers. In this regard, it should first be noted that the practice of the organ Security Council as such does not provide sufficient support for an evolutive reading of the Charter, but that such organ practice must be accepted by the UN membership in general.[14] And whether there has been such acceptance is open to doubt:

First of all, despite some assertions to the contrary, state reports to the Committees established under Resolutions 1373 and 1540 cannot necessarily be seen as an implicit acceptance of the Council's competence to adopt these resolutions: Such reports might be an acceptance only of the *goal* of combating terrorism, not of the *means* by which the Council has tried to reach this goal. Of the many statements in context of the so-called war against terrorism one should carefully distinguish statements that refer to the goal of combating terrorism, from those that also refer to the means, namely legislative action by the Council to further this Goal. Only the latter statement may – in my view – be taken to support legislative powers of the Council. And while there is some such support, especially in the discussion after the adoption of Resolution 1540, there were also quite a number of critical statements.

Some reports, in fact, served totally different aims, such as propaganda – the first report of Iraq to the Counter Terrorism Committee established under Resolution 1373, for example, stated that Iraq was one of the chief victims of state-sponsored terrorism emanating from the United States.[15] Furthermore, state abidance by the terms of Resolutions 1373 and 1540 may also be motivated by the fear that the Council's lack of competence to adopt these resolutions might not keep the Council – or even other states acting unilaterally[16] – from enforcing them.

Finally, the debates in the context of the adoption of legislative resolutions do not show widespread acceptance of the Council's legislative powers, either.[17] As shown by *Roberto Lavalle,* the debate before the adoption of Resolution 1373 was practically non-existent and thus cannot show any measure of state support.[18] Resolutions 1422 and 1487 met with widespread protest[19] which led to Resolution 1487 not being renewed when it expired. And in the debate on Resolution 1540, many delegations stated doubts concerning the Council's competence;[20] even proponents of the resolution stated that it was clearly an exceptional measure.[21]

## 5.2 Suitability of the Security Council for legislative action

Furthermore, one may question whether the Council is suitable for the exercise of legislative functions. The Council, first of all, is not a very transparent organ, as can be seen, *inter alia,* in the process leading to the adoption of Resolutions 1373 and 1540, which to a large part consisted of secret negotiations of the permanent members.[22] Second, and most importantly, it is not a very democratic or representative institution, especially given the veto-power of its five permanent members representing only part of the world community.

Both facts may be ascribed to 'the single-minded purpose to establish a causally effective centre of international power'.[23] In the words of *Vera Gowlland-Debbas:* 'The mandatory decisions of the Security Council under Chapter VII [...] are *the outcome of political considerations, not legal reasoning,* and nor are its proceedings subject to judicial procedures. That its reactions to events can neither be automatic *nor impartial* is an intended result of the way its competence and powers are delimited in the Charter.'[24] In other words, while composition and procedure of the Council might be appropriate for an executive organ which needs to react quickly and forcefully to emerging crises, they are far from acceptable for a world legislature. In this context, the fact that even the General Assembly, which through the representation of all Member States most closely approximates the ideal of a legislative body, does not have true legislative powers should give pause to those who would grant such powers to the far less representative and intransparent Security Council.[25]

On the other hand, it also seems questionable whether granting legislative powers to the Council would actually do the international community much good. It is true that there are several pressing concerns for the world community and that some of these concerns may also correlate with gaps in international law. However, one may legitimately ask whether such problems will likely be solved by legislative Council action. The problem of disarmament, for example – not in the sense of non-proliferation to non-state actors, but in the sense of reduction of state arsenals – was only inserted into Resolution 1540 after pressure on the permanent Council members by other states,[26] and such references to disarmament as are contained in the resolution do not have any binding effect. And it is even more questionable whether the devastation of the environment or problems typically affecting developing countries such as poverty and infectious disease[27] will be tackled in an effective manner by a Security

Council in which developed states reluctant to enter into binding treaties on environmental matters are equipped with veto power.

Thus, neither from the viewpoint of procedure nor from that of likely material outcomes does the Council seem suitable for the role of world legislature.

### 5.3 Limits to an evolutive interpretation of the Charter – wider implications of Security Council legislative powers

Furthermore, one should also consider the boundaries of evolutive interpretation in general: No evolutive interpretation may be taken to such an extreme that it radically changes the whole system to be interpreted.[28] And this is indeed what Resolutions 1373 and 1540 do.

As seen above, the United Nations system does not contain a true legislative organ. This is because of the principle that every norm of international law is based, at least in principle, upon the consent of all states bound by it – no state is to be bound by a rule of international law if it did not have at least the opportunity to influence the development of that norm.[29] This necessitates the absence of a central law-making organ, even if this means that certain very desirable norms do not come into existence. In other words, international law very much values input legitimacy over output legitimacy. Arguments for legislative powers of the Security Council do the exact opposite. And finally, as seen above, the actual output will be limited to problems the solution of which does not clash with other political goals of the permanent Council members.

It is true that there is some movement towards more 'democratic' decision-making, in that before the adoption of Resolution 1540, the Council at least allowed all states to express their views. Still, such improvements fall far short of the requirements of state consent that international law requires. In fact, any method of creating norms of international law which does not – at least formally – grant some actual influence to every state involved would mean giving up the legislative equality of states, part of the principle of sovereign equality and thus part and parcel of the international system.[30]

It is also true that the strict reliance on state consent seems to be more and more supplanted by reference to values or interests of the international community as a whole. However, whatever one may think of such value-based or 'constitutional' approaches in general, it seems clear that the responsibility for those interests of the international community should rest with the community as such, not be laid into the hands of an oligarchy of five permanent and between four and ten elected Council members.

## 6. Conclusion

In conclusion, the discharge of legislative powers by the Security Council not only violates the UN Charter, it also calls into question one basic foundation of international law, the sovereign equality of states, by denying the importance of input legitimacy in favor of output legitimacy – an output legitimacy moreover which, at the end of the day, is rather questionable.

In the end, one can only hope that in the future, Security Council members will keep in mind the warning that *Sir Gerald Fitzmaurice* issued already 1971 in the

Namibia Case: 'It was to keep the peace, not to change the world order, that the Security Council was set-up'.[31]

## NOTES

1 Cf., Jochen Abr. Frowein/Nico Krisch, Art. 39, mn. 16 et seq., in Bruno Simma (ed.), *The Charter of the United Nations: A Commentary*, 2nd edn. (2002).

2 Catherine Denis, 'Le Pouvoir normatif du Conseil de sécurité des Nations unies: Portée et limites', 2004, Chapter 2, gives a detailed overview, concluding that in such instances the Counsel acts '*tel un juge*' (para. 115).

3 For a more detailed view, see Denis, *supra* n. 2, Chapter 3. Resolutions 827 (1993) and 955 (1994), establishing the *ad hoc* criminal tribunals for the Former Yugoslavia and Rwanda, might also be deemed legislative in the sense that the establishment of judicial bodies is usually the role of the legislature. However, they do not concern the competence of the Council to legislate in the sense of producing norms of general and abstract applicability.

4 On 'thematic resolutions' in general, see Denis, *supra* n. 2, paras. 118-130; on the earlier anti-terrorist resolutions, id., paras. 171-181.

5 See Andreas Zimmermann, 'Acting under Chapter VII (...)' – Resolution 1422 and Possible Limits of the Powers of the Security Council, in Jochen Abr. Frowein (ed.), 'Verhandeln für den Frieden', *Liber Amicorum Tono Eitel* (2003), pp. 253, 264.

6 See, e.g., Stefan Talmon, 'The Security Council as World Legislature', 99 *AJIL* (2005), p. 175, as well as the statements by the representatives of Namibia, Nigeria, Kuwait, South Korea and Switzerland in UN Doc. S/PV.4950 and Resumption 1 (2004).

7 Susan Lamb, 'Legal Limits to United Nations Security Council Powers', in Guy S. Goodwin-Gill, et al. (eds.), *The Reality of International Law – Essays in Honour of Ian Brownlie* (1999), pp. 361, 365; ICTY, *Prosecutor* v. *Tadic*, IT-94-1-AR72, Decision on the Defence Motion for Interlocutory Appeal on Jurisdiction, 2 October 1995, reprinted in 35 *ILM* (1996), pp. 32, 42. On further limits to the Security Council's Chapter VII powers see Erika de Wet, The Chapter VII Powers of the Security Council, 2004.

8 Cf., ICJ, *Certain Expenses of the United Nations (Article 17, paragraph 2, of the Charter)*, Advisory Opinion of 20 July 1962, *ICJ Reports* 1962, pp. 150, 168 (referring to situations where 'it is agreed that the action in question is *within the scope of the functions of the Organization*' [emphasis added]). See also Derek Bowett, 'The Impact of Security Council Decisions on Dispute Settlement Procedures', 5 *EJIL* (1994), pp. 89, 101.

9 Cf., Statement of the US Representative, UNCIO, Vol. VI, p. 29; Statement of the US and UK governments, UNCIO, Vol. XII, p. 162; Report of the Sub-Committee on the Spanish Question, UN Doc. S/75 (1946), paras. 18-22. For further references see Denis, *supra* n. 2, paras. 368-370.

10 Georg Ress, Interpretation, mn. pp. 1-2, 19-22, 26 et seq., in Simma, *supra* n. 1.

11 See Thomas Bruha/Christian J. Tams, 'Die Vereinten Nationen und das Völkerrecht', 22 *Aus Politik und Zeitgeschichte* (2005), pp. 32, 34-35.

12 Jurij Daniel Aston, 'Sekundärgesetzgebung internationaler Organisationen zwischen mitgliedsstaatlicher Souveränität und Gemeinschaftsdisziplin' (2005), pp. 102-104, 111-112.

13 Talmon, see *supra* n. 6, p. 180; Markus Wagner, 'Die wirtschaftlichen Maßnahmen des Sicherheitsrates nach dem 11. September 2001 – Von Wirtschaftssanktionen zu Wirtschaftsgesetzgebung?', 63 *ZaöRV* (2003), pp. 879, 911-912.

14 ICJ, *Certain Expenses*, see *supra* n. 8, pp. 182, 192 (Sep. Op. Sir Percy Spender); Id., *Legal Consequences for States of the Continued Presence of South Africa in Namibia (South West Africa) notwithstanding Security Council Resolution 276 (1970)*, Advisory Opinion of 21 June 1971, *ICJ Reports* 1971, pp. 16, 22; T.O. Elias, 'The Modern Law of Treaties' (1974), pp. 76-77.

15 UN Doc. S/2001/1291.

16 On this danger see, e.g., José E. Alvarez, 'International Organizations as Law-makers' (2005), p. 212. See also Wolff Heintschel von Heinegg, 'The United Nations Convention on the Law of the Sea and Maritime Security Operations', forthcoming in *GYIL*, who uses the terms of Resolution 1540 to justify the unilateral interdiction of ships on the High Sea as a countermeasure short of self-defence.

17 On several statements voicing concern over a legislative role already with regard to the *ad hoc* tribunals and 'thematic resolutions', see Denis, *supra* n. 2, paras. 416-423.

[18] Roberto Lavalle, 'Constitutional Aspects of the Processes that Led to the Adoption of Resolutions 1373 and 1540 and Their Sequel', see following contribution of this panel. See also Jasper Finke/Christiane Wandscher, 'Terrorismusbekämpfung jenseits militärischer Gewalt', *VN*, Vol. 49 (2001) pp.168, 171.
[19] See only Letter from the Representatives of Brazil, Canada, New Zealand and South Africa to the President of the Security Council, 12 July 2002, UN Doc. S/2002/754. For further statements, see Denis, *supra* n. 2, para. 440.
[20] Statements by the representatives of Pakistan, India, Cuba, Indonesia, Iran, Mexico, Nepal and Namibia in UN Doc. S/PV.4950 and Resumption 1 (2004).
[21] Statements of the representatives of the Philippines, Algeria, Korea and Switzerland, id.
[22] Lavalle, *supra* n. 18.
[23] Martti Koskenniemi, 'The Police in the Temple – Order, Justice and the UN: A Dialectal View', 6 *EJIL* (1995), pp. 325, 338.
[24] Vera Gowlland-Debbas, 'The Functions of the United Nations Security Council in the International Legal System', in Michael Byers (ed.), *The Role of Law in International Politics* (2000) pp. 277, 287 (emphasis added).
[25] To avoid any misunderstandings on this point: This is not an argument for (majority) legislation in the General Assembly. However, *if* one were to grant legislative powers to the UN, the Assembly would be the more proper body for this role.
[26] See the Statement of the Indian representative, *supra* n. 20.
[27] Cf., 'A more secure world: Our shared responsibility – Report of the High-level Panel on Threats, Challenges and Change' (2004), paras. 44 et seq.
[28] Ian Sinclair, *The Vienna Convention on the Law of Treaties* (1984), 2nd edn., p.138.
[29] Gerry Simpson, Great *Powers and Outlaw States – Unequal Sovereigns in the International Legal Order* (2004), p. 28, with further references.
[30] On this principle, see id., pp. 48-53.
[31] ICJ, *Namibia, supra* n. 14, para. 215 (Diss. Op. Sir Gerald Fitzmaurice).

## Remarks by Roberto Lavalle*

## Constitutional Aspects of the Processes that Led to the Adoption of Resolutions 1373 and 1540 and Their Sequel

### 1. Introduction and Scope of Treatment

Although, Guatemala was not on the Security Council (the Council) at the relevant times (nor indeed at any other), it would hardly have provided the present author with information concerning the negotiations leading to either of the resolutions dealt with here. Thus the present author has no knowledge about the negotiations that led to the adoption of Resolution 1373, which, like those concerning Resolution 1540, were private, and do not appear to have been reported in the press or anywhere else. Regarding the negotiations that led to the adoption of Resolution 1540, the information that can be provided hardly extends beyond what is known to the public.[1]

Those deficiencies do not, however, prevent the present author from making a meaningful contribution to the panel's debates. For the panel should focus not on the

* The present author is a member of Guatemala's permanent mission to the United Nations. The opinions expressed in this paper and the present author's participation in the panel are in a purely personal capacity.

details of the negotiations proper but on the possible relationship between them and the constitutional aspects of Resolutions 1373 and 1540.[2]

From this perspective, it is not the negotiations which went on within the Council that are interesting: in addition to not being part of the official records (which precludes their use as means of interpretation), they would not, if what is unofficially known about them is true, be of any constitutional significance.

It has been pointed out, and can be regarded as a practical necessity, that 'the Council would be well advised to legislate only to the extent that reflects the general will of the member states.'[3]

This necessarily involves a process of consultation between the states on the Council and the others. Since that process can lead to changes in the draft resolution concerned,[4] it can be viewed as being in the nature of or akin to negotiations – all the more so since the process may result in a general or majority acceptance of the draft resolution by the membership at large. This acceptance may be express or implicit.

Such acceptance can also take place *ex post* facto, i.e., after the adoption of a legislative resolution of the Council. This will occur if all or a majority of the United Nations members fulfill the obligations the resolution seeks to lay on them, thereby implicitly accepting them. As the present author has been asked to comment on the negotiations leading to the two resolutions in question, *ex post* facto acceptance is in principle beyond his task. However, whatever the nature or effect of either type of acceptance may be, one of the two can supply the lack of, complement, or (if advance acceptance is deficient) confirm the other, *ex post* facto acceptance cannot be ignored.

In theory, advance acceptance need not be implicit. Indeed, the ideal way for it to be expressed is by a decision of the principal organ of the United Nations that, being composed of all its members, is the most representative. This is, of course, the General Assembly.

Thus, the perfect way for the Council to legislate for the international community as a whole would be a two-stage one.[5] The General Assembly would first, preferably by consensus, adopt a resolution declaring that a situation exists which creates a worldwide, albeit abstract, threat to international peace and security and specifying actions to be taken by all states in response to it. By such a resolution the Council would be asked to declare, under Article 39 of the Charter, the existence of the threat and then, acting under Article 41 (or, as it is wont, under Chapter VII as a whole), render those actions binding on all states.

Since all the members of the Council are represented in the Assembly, it is highly likely, and virtually certain if the Assembly's resolution is adopted by consensus, that the Council would do the Assembly's bidding.

The process would be akin to the dual one by which democratic States normally enact statutes. The action of the Assembly and that of the Council would correspond, respectively, to the passage of a bill by the legislative branch of a state, while the subsequent sanction by the Council of the General Assembly's action would correspond to the acceptance of the bill by the executive branch.

This procedure is as unorthodox as unprecedented. But it does not appear unconstitutional: the Assembly would be acting under Article 10 and the Council under Articles 39 and 41 of the Charter.

It is doubtful that this hypothetical process for adopting international legislation would be politically workable. It would, in particular, be unrealistic to think that it could have been used for the adoption of Resolutions 1373 or 1540.

The process would, however, be ideal as regards the *democratic* enactment of worldwide legislation. For, if we disregard the privileged position that the 15 members of both the Assembly and the Council would occupy, the process (hereinafter: 'the parliamentary paradigm'), would, in line with paragraph 1 of Article 2 of the Charter, ensure to all United Nations members absolutely the same opportunities of opining on the proposed legislation and bringing their individual influence to bear on it. The process would bring together the United Nations organ that is representative of the international community but lacks authority in the area concerned, with the United Nations organ that is vested with such authority but is not representative of that community.

It may be noted that the 'parliamentary paradigm' would give some meaning to a Charter provision that, legally, makes no sense otherwise.[6] The provision is the second sentence (beginning with '... and agree') of paragraph 1 of Article 24: were the parliamentary paradigm to be applied, one could consider that, albeit not in a strictly legal sense, the Council would be acting 'on... behalf' of the United Nations members.

The parliamentary paradigm provides a template for assessing, from the viewpoint of basic democratic principles, the processes by which Resolutions 1373 and 1540 were adopted.

## 2. Analysis and Assessment of the Negotiating Processes that Led to the Adoption of Resolutions 1373 and 1540

From the perspective of our 'parliamentary paradigm', the process by which Resolution 1373 was adopted is most defective. Since it lasted 'just over 48 hours' and involved negotiations in which only the five permanent members of the Council participated,[7] it would appear that the resolution received no advance acceptance.[8] Arguments exist, though, for the opposite view. As observed by Szasz, the binding portions of Resolution 1373 'were not ... invented by the Council' but corresponded, if somewhat loosely, to provisions of prior General Assembly resolutions, for example those in the International Convention for the Suppression of the Financing of Terrorism, adopted by the General Assembly it in 1999.[9] Moreover, having been adopted barely over two weeks after 11 September, when deep sympathy for the United States was universal, no opposition to it was realistically imaginable.[10] And that non-members of the Council had no meaningful opportunity to express their views on the text and, even less, seek to have any amendments made to the corresponding proposal (adopted without changes). Thus, such advance acceptance of Resolution 1373 by the international community as might be implicit in the attendant circumstances is a far cry from the 'parliamentary paradigm'. Accordingly the general acceptance that Resolution 1373 appears to enjoy is far more in the nature of an *ex post* facto than an advance one.[11]

Compliance with the rules Resolution 1373 sought to impose on states, while not as wide and thorough as it could be, seems sufficient to have produced general *ex post* facto acceptance of the resolution. One can therefore maintain that defective advance acceptance of Resolution 1373 has been cured by a less imperfect *ex post* facto one, or that the general acceptance is of a hybrid nature, partly advance and partly *ex post* facto.

The process that led to Resolution 1540 was, fittingly, initiated when, on 23 September, 2003, President Bush stated before the General Assembly that '[b]ecause proliferators [of weapons of mass destruction] will use any route or channel… open to them, we need the broadest possible cooperation to stop them', adding that he was asking the Council to adopt a 'new anti-proliferation resolution' calling 'on all Members of the United Nations to criminalize the proliferation of weapons of mass destruction, to enact strict export controls… and secure all… sensitive materials within their own borders.'[12] Later at the same meeting, speaking on behalf of the European Union, Prime Minister Berlusconi supported Bush by saying that '[w]e cannot allow'… such 'weapons… to end up in the hands of terrorists or regimes that represent a threat to world peace.'[13]

These statements make clear the intention that the Council should adopt measures of a legislative nature and that Bush's initiative was backed by the European Union.

It is often thought that a regular feature of the off-the-record process by which the Council agrees on draft resolutions it later formally adopts is that they are first negotiated exclusively among the permanent members and that only once they have agreed on a text is it communicated to the ten elective members (who may feel more or less constrained to approve it). It may be that as a rule this is not what happens.

But in the case of Resolution 1540 this exclusionary process was actually applied. And it was only after some five months of negotiations involving solely the permanent members that, once they had agreed on a text, the door was opened, on 23 March 2004, to the non-permanent members.[14] This marked the start of a second stage of the negotiations, consisting only of private meetings within the Council.

A third, more democratic but not yet public stage began on 6 April, when the sponsors of the draft resolution met with the 113 members of the Non-Aligned Movement and also, at about the same time, those of the European Union, the OSCE and the Commonwealth of Independent States. The number of states not members of the Council or of any of these three groups being small, this third stage, although fragmented, was not too far from what can be regarded as general negotiations. The fourth, fully universal and democratic stage, extended from a public meeting of the Council on 22 April, to its final public meeting on 28 April, at which Resolution 1540 was unanimously adopted.[15]

If this four-stage process is compared to the 'parliamentary paradigm', one can consider that up to a point there was a fairly general acceptance of the terms of the resolution (in the sense that, although it was strongly criticized, no state said that it would not comply with it).[16] It is clear, however, that while the democratic deficit of this process, in which fairly ample, if unequal, opportunity to make their case was given to states not on the Council, was far less serious than that inherent in the adoption of Resolution 1373, the process nevertheless falls very considerably short of that paradigm.

Compliance with Resolution 1540 appears, as of this writing (21 May 2005), to be somewhat sketchy: only 117 of the members of the United Nations, or 61 per cent of them, have replied to the request for information contained in the resolution.[17]

### 3. Opportunity that Existed for Bringing the Process of Adoption of Resolution 1540 into Considerable Conformity With The 'Parliamentary Paradigm'

It is of some constitutional interest to note that in the case of Resolution 1540 a way was open that could have smoothly led to at least an approximation to the 'parliamentary paradigm'.

On 22 November 2002, the General Assembly adopted, on the report of its First Committee and without a vote, a resolution addressing essentially the same subject as Resolution 1540. By this resolution, numbered 57/83 and entitled 'Measures to prevent Terrorist from acquiring Weapons of Mass Destruction', the Assembly urged all Member States to take and strengthen national measures within the scope of its title, also inviting those states to inform the Secretary-General, 'on a voluntary basis' (an obviously unnecessary qualification), of the measures taken in that regard, adding that the information was to be reported to the Assembly. This resolution was not adopted under any one of the more specific sub-items of item 66, i.e., 'general and complete disarmament'.

At its 58th session, the Assembly dealt with the subject that is the title of Resolution 57/83 in a more specific context, that subject having become a sub-item (sub-item 'w') of item 74, i.e., 'general and complete disarmament'. In connection with that sub-item the Assembly adopted, on 8 December 2003, again on the report of its First Committee and without a vote, Resolution 58/48, which has the same title as Resolution 57/83 and repeats the appeal to states contained in the latter, reiterating its invitation to them to inform the Secretary-General of their action pursuant thereto, which information was to be reported to it.

Interestingly enough, barely over two weeks before, on 23 September, President Bush made his above-quoted speech, the United States submitted to the Secretary General, pursuant to the request contained in Resolution 57/83, a comprehensive account of its relevant activities (but, curiously, without giving the slightest hint of the initiative that President Bush would be launching that same month at the Assembly).[18]

Thus, the groundwork had been laid for placing the US initiative within the prior action by the Assembly which has been noted and which, by submitting the information mentioned, the United States appeared to have countenanced. President Bush could, accordingly, have said, when addressing the Assembly on 23 September, that his initiative would build on its ongoing work to prevent terrorists from acquiring weapons of mass destruction, thus paving the way for a process approximating the parliamentary paradigm.

### 4. Constitutional Significance of Such Acceptances as Resolutions 1373 and 1540 May Have Received From the International Community

The present writer remains of the view previously maintained by him that the Charter should be interpreted in an evolutionary manner and that accordingly Resolutions 1373 and 1540 should not be deemed intrinsically unconstitutional.

This view is based, however, exclusively on the relevant provisions of Chapter VII of the Charter (i.e., Arts. 39 and 41), without regard for the question whether any kind of acceptance, at any time, by the general membership of the United Nations of a legislative resolution of the Council is necessary for the resolution to be deemed constitutional.

This question will now be discussed. But, it must first be observed that since, as has been noted, such acceptance is of great practical usefulness, if not, to borrow the characterization in the statement by Costa Rica cited in note 3, 'essential', it is somewhat unrealistic to distinguish, in connection with the matter, between constitutionality and practicality (effectiveness), since non-observance is tantamount to rendering the Council's action impracticable (or ineffective).

Coming now to the question posed, the case will first be addressed where there has been no advance acceptance of a legislative resolution of the Council. Can one maintain that in such a case the resolution will be constitutional only if it is accepted *ex post* facto, i.e., if those of its provisions meant to be mandatory are complied with by all or a sizable majority of states?

An affirmative answer to this question leads to uncertainties and anomalies.

Pending *ex post* facto acceptance the resolution would be in a legal limbo. And it would be very difficult to determine the precise time as from which, a sufficiently large number of states having complied with it, the resolution has become, simultaneously, both binding and constitutionally valid. For there will be serious doubt about precisely how many states must have complied with it in order for that transformation to have come about. And what if compliance by some of the states that have taken action pursuant to the resolution amounts to less than full or proper compliance? How far will this affect the attainment of that threshold? An additional difficulty arises from the unreasonableness of considering that attainment of the threshold can be postponed indefinitely, which implies that it should be subject to a time limit. But how could the time limit be precisely determined? Moreover, pending the transformation, compliance by any state will have been on a purely voluntary basis, which is paradoxical.

It is submitted that these uncertainties and anomalies, which mirror some of the problems inherent in the formation of customary international law, rule out a persuasive case for considering that a legislative resolution of the Council which does not enjoy (or does not enjoy enough) advance acceptance will be constitutional only if it is accepted *ex post* facto by all or a sizable majority of Member States.

It should be noted, finally, that, far from it being possible to rely on either a textual analysis of the Charter or any consideration based on its spirit to support the contention that a legislative resolution of the Council depends for its validity on the position taken on it, in advance or *ex post* facto, by either the General Assembly or the membership of the United Nations at large, it is the contrary that is the case: in its Articles 4(2), 5, 6 and 97, second sentence, the Charter provides for actions that the General Assembly may take only upon the recommendation of the Council.

An entirely different point not devoid of constitutional interest may, finally, be noted. By pursuing, as it has,[19] the path initiated by Resolution 57/83 and continued by Resolution 58/48, the General Assembly has not allowed the Council's adoption of Resolution 1540 to preclude it from also dealing with the subject-matter of that resolution.

## Notes

1 The statements made at the Council's two public meetings on Resolution 1540, while of considerable constitutional interest, involve no interaction and accordingly cannot be regarded as negotiations. They do, however, provide insights into the actual negotiations, which, entirely in private, went on earlier. For the records of the two meetings see UN Docs. S/PV.4950 and S/PV.4950 (Resumption 1)

2 What follows, presupposes, of course, that the resolutions are not *ab initio* and incurably unconstitutional.

3 Stefan Talmon, The Security Council as World Legislature, 99 *AJIL* (2005), p. 175, at p. 193. According to the late Paul Szasz, the Council should legislate 'only to the extent that [in so doing] it reflects the general will of the world community.' 96 *AJIL* (2002), p. 901, at p. 905. Cf., also the last sentence of the statement by Costa Rica quoted by Talmon, at pp. 187-188.

4 To be sure, non-members of the Council may not themselves submit proposals to it; but if one of them is aware of what is going on in the Council it probably could, in many if not most cases, persuade a Council member to do so, particularly if the non-member has won the support of other non-members.

5 Cf., Matthew Happold, 'Security Council resolution 1373 and the Constitution of the United Nations', 16 *LJIL* (2003), p. 593, at p. 608.

6 Hans Kelsen, 'The Law of the United Nations', A Critical Analysis of Its Fundamental Problems (1950), p. 280.

7 Talmon, *supra* n. 3, at p. 187. (his statement that 'non-members of the council were not present' is somewhat misleading: the meeting was held in public and any one of them could have requested, and probably would have been given, the floor.)

8 As shown by the record of the meeting at which Resolution 1373 was adopted, no state not a member of the Council took the floor and there was no discussion or debate whatsoever. (Cf., UN Doc. S/PV.4385.)

9 Szasz, *supra* n. 3, pp. 902, 903 and 905. (It may be noted that, as pointed out by Jurij Daniel Aston, 'Die Bekämpfung abstrakter Gefahren für den Weltfrieden durch legislative Maßnahmen des Sicherheitsrates – resolution 1373 (2001) im Kontext', at pp. 262-263, and notes 26 and 27, 62/1-2 *ZaÖRV* (2002), there is less than complete concordance between the obligations laid on states by that Convention and the corresponding provisions of Resolution 1373. Moreover when Resolution 1373 was adopted, the Convention was not in force, only four states having taken full action to become parties to it.)

10 Cf., Markus Wagner, 'Die Witschaftlichen Maßnamen des Sicherheitsrates nach dem 11.September 2001 im völkerrechtlichen Kontext – Von Wirtshafssanktionen zur Wirtshaftsgesetzgebung?', 63 *ZaÖRV* (2003), p. 879, note 185, at p. 912. It appears that the United States took care to make hay while the sun was shining!

11 On the wide compliance by states with their obligations under Resolution 1373, see Wagner, *supra* n. 10, at p. 912, and Talmon, *supra* n. 3, at p. 177 [note 30] and pp. 191-2.)

12 Cf., UN Doc. A/58/PV.7, at 13.

13 Cf., UN Doc. A/58/PV.7, at 32.

14 What the present author knows about this initial stage of the negotiations that is not in the public domain comes only from the texts of seven altogether informal draft resolutions confidentially provided to him by colleagues from other missions, the first one dating from November 2003, and from an article in the *Washington Post* (Column Lynch, Weapon Transfers Targeted, 29 April 2004, at A21) according to which the United States secured China's support by dropping a provision authorizing the interdiction on the high seas of foreign vessels suspected of carrying weapons of mass destruction. (None of the seven informal draft resolutions mentioned contains any such provision.)

15 For the records of these meetings see n. 1 *supra*. In the interval between them, certain amendments (by two developing nonpermanent members of the Council) were accepted by the sponsors of the draft resolution (i.e., most probably, the members which sponsored that draft resolution, issued on 28 April [UN Doc. S/2004/326], namely the permanent members minus China plus the Philippines, Romania and Spain). Of those amendments (not issued as official documents) the only ones of some objective significance called for adding two preambular paragraphs, i.e., the fourth and thirteenth preambular paragraphs of the definitive text. The official text of the draft resolution, adopted without changes on 28 April, came out only on that day. Thus the reader of the [verbatim!] record of the two-part 22 April meeting cannot, from the official records alone, know exactly what was being discussed. This glaring defect, which could have been so easily remedied, is a shocking example of the insufficient transparency characterizing the work of the Council.

16 This does not necessarily mean that all states considered the resolution binding: any one of them could have regarded it as unconstitutional but nevertheless decided to take the measures it mandates because it considers them well-advised.

[17] Cf., UN Docs. S/AC.44/2004 (02)/1 to S/AC.44/2004 (02)/117. (Almost all the countries that have not complied are, however, small developing ones.)

[18] Cf., UN Doc. A/58/208/Add. 1, starting at 9.

[19] Cf., Assembly Resolution 59/80 of 3 December 2004, adopted, on the report of the First Committee and without a vote, under sub-item (r) of agenda item 65, entitled, respectively, 'Measures to prevent terrorists from acquiring weapons of mass destruction' and 'General and complete disarmament'. Except that in its preamble it takes note of some developments occurring in the meantime, including Council Resolution 1540 (on which it makes no comment), Resolution 59/80 is a carbon copy of its immediate predecessor, Resolution 58/48. The fact that Resolution 59/80 (whose consistency with Charter Article 12[2] may be open to doubt) was adopted by both the First Committee and the plenary without a vote shows that the members of the Council have no objection to the Assembly pursuing the parallel track to Resolution 1540 initiated by Resolution 57/83.

## Remarks by Shirley V. Scott*

## UN Security Council Resolution 1540 and Political Legitimacy

International law is a vital medium for debate on political action; the language of law functions as an effective mechanism by which to defend and/or oppose the policies and/or actions of international actors. But there is a major limitation on its utility, which was all too apparent in relation to the use of force during the Kosovo crisis and, I would suggest, is apparent in inverse form, in debate on UN Security Council Resolution 1540 (2004). Put simply, international law provides for the categorisation of actions as inside or outside the law, legal or illegal. Illegal behaviour is presumed bad; hence, legal action is readily assumed good – or at least acceptable. This leaves lawyers with the dilemma of how to express support for a political act that is most readily interpreted as lying outside the law (the situation experienced by many lawyers in NATO States during the Kosovo crisis) or how to use their persuasive rhetoric to oppose a political action that is most readily interpreted as lying within the law. This latter scenario, I would suggest, is what we are seeing with Resolution 1540 (although please note that I would not presume to comment on the political views of my colleagues on this panel). It seems to me that it is because many do not like the resolution and its implications for international law but do not find the legal case against it sufficiently strong, that discussion is frequently being framed in terms of legitimacy – and often *political* legitimacy at that!

In Resolution 1540 (2004) the Council drew on its Chapter VII powers to decide that states were not to support efforts of non-state actors to access nuclear, chemical, or biological weapons and their means of delivery, that states were to legislate at a national level to prohibit non-state access to these weapons, and that states were to adopt and enforce effective domestic controls to develop and maintain appropriate effective measures to account for and secure such items in production, use, storage or transport; develop and maintain appropriate effective physical protection measures; develop and maintain appropriate border controls and law enforcement efforts to prevent the illicit trafficking in such items and establish, develop, review and maintain effective national

* Senior Lecturer in International Relations, University of New South Wales.

export and trans-shipment controls over such items. Resolution 1540 also established a committee for a period of no more than two years, to receive reports from states. The Council stopped short of using its Chapter VII powers to require states to report to the Committee, but states were 'called' to make their first report within six months of the adoption of the resolution.

## UNSCR 1540 as Legislation

The principal reason why we are considering the legitimacy of UNSCR 1540 is that it has given rise to claims that the Security Council has through this and other resolutions usurped a legislative role. Conventional wisdom held that there was no body at an international level comparable to a domestic legislature. Weapons of mass destruction had been managed via multilateral treaty. And yet, beginning with Resolution 1373 of 28 September 2001, and continuing with Resolutions 1422 and 1487 on the International Criminal Court, and 1540 on WMD, the Security Council has taken on a legislative role; that is, it has used its Chapter VII powers 'to order all States to take or to refrain from specified actions in a context not limited to disciplining a particular country.'[1] The Council has become increasingly bold in this role; while Resolution 1373 drew on prior resolutions of the General Assembly that had been adopted unanimously or by overwhelming majorities, including the International Convention for the Suppression of the Financing of Terrorism,[2] there was no equivalent Assembly precedent for 1540.

The implications for international law and for world politics of the Security Council assuming an active legislative role are considerable. To challenge consent as the basis for the legal obligations of States is to challenge legal positivism as the foundation of the international legal order. It is also to challenge sources jurisprudence, which has long held that treaties and custom are the prime sources of international law. And yet the arguments in favour of 1540 as falling within the authority of the Council seem strong, even if the founders had not originally envisaged that the Council would play such a role, and despite the fact that the Council did not play that role during its first half century. I am not even so sure that the resolution is so qualitatively different to a 'standard' resolution; while to an observer 1540 might appear to be addressing an abstract danger as opposed to a particular situation or conflict, I do not think that the United States, as the chief architect of the resolution, saw the 'threat to the peace' posed by the transfer of WMD material to non-state actors as anything but a very real and concrete threat as evidenced by the activities of the A.Q. Khan nuclear trafficking network. Indeed, the Council found that that the possession of WMD by non-state actors constituted a threat to the peace sufficiently far-reaching for it to decide that all states should act to mitigate that threat.

The real legal problem caused by 1540 is not, I would suggest, that as to its legality, but that of locating the legal limits on the exercise of the Council's legislative-like function. As Szasz explained in response to 1373 (2001), the 'basic legal limitation on the legislative capacity of the Security Council is evidently that its exercise must relate to the maintenance of international peace and security';[3] he went on to say that the potentially binding nature of such a decision 'is clearest when taken under Charter Chapter VII upon a determination by the Council that there exists a threat to the peace, breach of the peace, or act of aggression.'[4] Beyond this there appear to be no obvious legal limitations on the authority of the Council to legislate. Here, I would suggest, is the real reason why the word 'legitimacy' is cropping up so frequently in debate on the subject. If one accepts the legality of the Council's legislative role, is one left to accept whatever the Council wishes to legislate in the name of international peace and security?

## The Source of the Security Council's Political Legitimacy

It is in pulling back from consideration of this uncomfortable legal question that one might choose to assess the *political* legitimacy of the resolution and to explore whether this offers an alternative standard against which to measure 1540 and the limits on the exercise by the Council of a legislative function. The Council is inequitable in terms of membership, voting structure, and the powers it wields. Contrary to some rhetoric we hear in the context of Security Council reform, democracy has never been the source of its legitimacy. I would propose that, in political terms, the key to its legitimacy despite the absence of equity, has been necessity. The prior experience of each of the dominant post World War Two powers with the League was the prime shaper of the composition and procedure of the Security Council, and it was out of necessity – the simple fact of having little choice – that other states accepted the Council largely in the form that had been negotiated by the great powers. The veto at the heart of the working of the Security Council is obviously not an exercise in democracy; it stems from the reality of power politics and the horrors of world war; the obligation of Members to 'accept and carry out the decisions of the Security Council' similarly stems from the perceived necessity to avoid, wherever possible, further war.

To nominate 'necessity' as the basis of the political legitimacy of Security Council action, is, however, to beg the question of 'necessary for what?' and while the Charter offers some guide – most obviously in Article 24(1), political legitimacy is a broader concept than legal legitimacy and may not equate exactly with the terms of the Charter. I would therefore like to propose the 'Evatt' test of political necessity as it relates to the function of the Council within the United Nations system. Dr Herb Vere Evatt played an active role at San Francisco, particularly in relation to the veto, which he did not want applicable to Chapter VI responsibilities. Evatt went on to become President of the General Assembly in 1948-49. The opening of the General Assembly in New York on 5 April 1949 had been overshadowed by the signing on the previous day of the North Atlantic Treaty. Questions were being asked as to whether the United Nations would still matter, perhaps not an unreasonable question given that even the opening of the General Assembly was postponed at the last minute because Dean Acheson was still busy dealing with NATO matters. Finally, four hours and twenty minutes late, Dr Evatt was able to open the Assembly, reminding members of the fact that under the Charter all obligations must be subordinated to and in accordance with those of the Charter. Dr Evatt called Members to give 'unfaltering steady support for the UN and its objectives'. And here we have the statement of purpose, a basis on which to determine the necessity of Council action:

> 'By so doing what we shall be trying to achieve is simply this: the heartfelt desires of the ordi-

nary man and woman everywhere. What do they desire? Not very much; just peace and justice and decent standards of living, for themselves perhaps, but mainly for their children.'[5]

It is thus the job of the Security Council to ensure the peace and justice that are the precursors to ordinary people going about their daily lives. Its structure, procedure, and the exercise of its powers enjoy political legitimacy to the extent that they are *necessary* to ensure this peace and security. The same test of political necessity relates, I would suggest, to both process and substance. WMD readily relates to security. While it might have been necessary to tighten national controls to prevent the transfer of weapons of mass destruction to non-state actors, was it necessary that this be achieved via an executive order of the Security Council? Or was Resolution 1540 simply the imposition of US policy wishes on the rest of the world? It was inevitable that the United States, as the world's greatest military power, should have been the dominant influence on a resolution pertaining to weapons of mass destruction. According to the United States, Resolution 1540 *was* necessary; there simply had not been time to engage in a process of lengthy multilateral treaty negotiations.

## Legitimacy as Determined by Beholder

Here, however, is the crunch. Legitimacy is ultimately a matter of perception. Even if Resolution 1540 were accepted as legal and even if it fitted every criteria of political legitimacy that had ever been proffered, this would amount to nil if, in the eyes of the people of the world, it were regarded as illegitimate. Without direct access to the necessary intelligence, it is ultimately very difficult for most people to judge whether the objectives of 1540 could not have been pursued equally successfully by other means, such as multilateral treaty negotiations. (Here it should be noted that the Chemical Weapons Convention and Biological Weapons Convention both have provisions requiring parties to exercise effective control over materials and technology of relevance to those instruments.[6]) Acceptance that 1540 was truly necessary involves a degree of trust in the Council, and in the United States in particular. And trust in the United States, its foreign policy motives, methods, and use of intelligence, is in short supply. Question-marks over the legitimacy of 1540 may well have more to do with actions and policies of the United States not immediately connected to this resolution, than to the resolution itself. I will nominate two in particular.

First is the rhetoric and actions of the United States within the principal WMD regimes: the Nuclear Non-Proliferation Treaty, the Biological Weapons Convention, and the Chemical Weapons Convention. The NPT was viewed by the United States as a treaty designed primarily to halt the horizontal spread of nuclear weapons. For much of the rest of the world, however, and particularly for those with the capacity to develop nuclear weapons but who were choosing to forego that option, the Treaty was as much about disarmament as about non-proliferation. By Article VI, parties to the Treaty undertook 'to pursue negotiations in good faith on effective measures relating to cessation of the nuclear arms race at an early date and to nuclear disarmament, and on a Treaty on general and complete disarmament under strict and effective international control.' The United States maintains that it has done this, pointing both to numerical reductions in weapons and delivery systems and to the fact that, in comparison with its predecessors, the 2001 Nuclear Posture Review places far less reliance on nuclear weapons to meet US defence policy goals.[7]

Critics challenge the United States claim to have complied in good faith with Article VI, citing as prime evidence the US-imposed limbo into which the Comprehensive Test Ban Treaty has been placed, despite the commitments made by the nuclear weapon states at the time of the indefinite extension of the NPT in 1995; as well as the US treatment of the Fissile Material Cut-Off Treaty. More generally, the Bush administration's nuclear policy choices appear driven by a desire to 'keep all options open' to develop new types of weapons,[8] while at the same time emphasizing the need for non-nuclear weapon states to accept the stringent limitations the NPT imposes on their future policy choices. The United States seems to want to 'rub the noses' of other countries in the inequity that, perhaps out of necessity, was built into the NPT, and has in recent years appeared a less than willing and enthusiastic supporter of the BWC and CWC.

The second action of the United States – and the United Kingdom – that may well have had ramifications for the perceived political legitimacy of Resolution 1540 is, I would suggest, the spurious justification for the 2003 use of force against Iraq. Here the meaning of Resolution 1441 and previous resolutions were stretched almost beyond recognition to justify invasion of another country, at a time when the perceived US political interest in invading Iraq was all too apparent. The fact that the United States was prepared to contort the language of Resolution 1441 to pass off the invasion as the enforcement of Security Council resolutions raises reasonable concerns as to the uses to which 1540 might one day be put, and the way in which its wording might one day be interpreted, while the fact that it became apparent that the US administration may not be fully trustworthy in its use of intelligence on weapons of mass destruction makes it that much more difficult not to question the US justification for the resolution.

## Conclusions

Political legitimacy rests in the eyes of the beholder. The United States has been willing to expose the vulnerability of international law to political manipulation. It is therefore not surprising that actions which might otherwise have been accepted as both legal and necessary for the good of the international community have aroused suspicions. The power of the Security Council is ultimately indistinguishable from the power of its permanent members. Similarly, when doing as the United States wills it to, the legitimacy of the Security Council cannot ultimately be distinguished from the perceived legitimacy of US foreign policy – particularly as it relates to international law. While Resolution 1540 might have constituted 'clever' politics, the United States would do well to bear in mind that a legislating Council, limited only by what can be justified as responding to a threat to the peace, would, absent political legitimacy, constitute a very severe provocation for many participants in the international system, of both the state and non-state varieties.

NOTES

1 Paul C. Szasz, 'The Security Council Starts Legislating', 96 *AJIL* (2002), pp. 901-905 at p. 901.
2 Ibid., pp. 901-905 at pp. 902-903.
3 Ibid., pp. 901-905 at p. 904.
4 Ibid., pp. 901-905 at p. 901.
5 Quoted in John MacLaurin, *The United Nations and Power Politics* (London, George Allen & Unwin 1951) at pp. 29-30.
6 Malik Azhar Ellahi, Presentation at the Workshop on UN Security Council Resolution 1540 as it Pertains to Biological Weapons, 3 December 2004. University of the Pacific McGeorge School of Law, at: <http://www.mcgeorge.edu/resolution_1540/develop_1540_and_its_goals_ellahi.htm>, accessed 7 June 2005.
7 'U.S. Implementation of NPT Article VI', 24 May 2005. US State Department Press Release. Ambassador Jackie W. Sanders, Special Representative of the President for the Non-proliferation of Nuclear Weapons Statement to the 2005 Review Conference of the Treaty on the Non-proliferation of Nuclear Weapons, New York, 20 May 2005, at: <http://www.scoop.co.nz/stories/WO0505/S00351.htm>.
8 See 'The International Security Value of the Nuclear Test Ban Treaty', at: <http://www.armscontrol.org/factsheets/ctbtissue.asp>.

# REMARKS BY ELIZABETH WILMSHURST*

## THE SECURITY COUNCIL, SANCTIONS AND SANCTIONS COMMITTEES

The Security Council has moved from imposing comprehensive economic sanctions on whole countries or whole trade sectors to targeting sanctions against particular persons or groups of persons. The move is welcome on humanitarian grounds; targeted sanctions do not affect large numbers of innocent people in the way that comprehensive measures did. But it has necessitated the making of quasi-judicial determinations by the Security Council's sanctions committees as to which people come within the target categories. The problems associated with this have been extensively discussed in the literature. Two recent Resolutions, 1572 (2004) on Cote d'Ivoire, and Resolution 1591 (2005) on Sudan, illustrate these problems particularly vividly.

### A BRIEF HISTORY OF SANCTIONS

Until the sanctions regime on Iraq, the Council had imposed economic measures only in respect of Southern Rhodesia[1] (a wide-ranging sanctions regime) and South Africa[2] (an arms embargo). The early 1990s were activist years for the Council and economic sanctions came to be a much used tool in the Council's peace and security mandate. The sanctions imposed were generally of a comprehensive nature, in that they applied to the whole territory of the targeted country, even if they did not apply across the whole range of economic and commercial activity. The import/export ban imposed on

* International Law Programme, Chatham House; formerly a deputy legal adviser at the UK Foreign and Commonwealth Office, and legal adviser from 1994 to 1997 at the UK Permanent Mission to the United Nations in New York.

products originating in or destined for Iraq[3] is a good example of a comprehensive measure; a similar ban was imposed in relation to trade with the Federal Republic of Yugoslavia (Serbia and Montenegro) in 1992.[4] Assets freezes on all commercial enterprises in Iraq and in the FRY were imposed by the same resolutions. Although humanitarian exemptions were provided for, these comprehensive measures could have a harmful effect on the local economy. The provisions of Article 50 of the Charter which had been intended to alleviate impacts on third parties were ineffective. The move towards 'smart sanctions' followed various international initiatives,[5] which called for sanctions to be targeted against political leaders rather than a whole country, so that, as the people most responsible for the actions threatening peace and security, they would have the greatest incentive for the cessation of those activities; and the measures would not harm the innocent population.

## Role of Sanctions Committees

While a committee had been set-up by the resolutions imposing measures against Southern Rhodesia, its role was only to monitor the implementation of the sanctions and to seek information. It was the series of resolutions on Iraq that gave the first substantial powers to a sanctions committee. The '661 committee' had to deal with requests for authorisation of exemptions, and later with the oil for food regime. The huge amount of work it dealt with showed up both the possibilities and the limitations of conferring these roles on a small group of Council member representatives – most of the work being left to those with the most resources – and a small Secretariat staff. It also highlighted one of the difficulties of committee procedures; sanctions committees work by consensus and thus confer an effective veto on fifteen members, rather than just five.

With the introduction in 1997 of targeted sanctions against UNITA in Angola[6] and the leaders of the military coup in Sierra Leone,[7] the relevant sanctions committees were given the responsibility of listing persons coming within categories identified by the Council as the intended targets for sanctions. The targets were the members of the regime or organisation concerned (and adult members of their families); the criteria for listing were therefore relatively specific, although that did not remove the need for judgments to be made in particular cases by the relevant committees.

The committee established by Resolution 1267 (1999) was given novel tasks. The resolution imposed a flight ban and an assets freeze on members of the Taliban; by that resolution and a later one[8] the sanctions committee was given the following principal functions: to designate the persons or entities who were sufficiently closely connected with the Taliban to have their flights banned or their assets frozen; to grant exemptions from the flight ban and to authorise the release of funds, both on the basis of humanitarian need; to designate what parts of Afghanistan were under Taliban control for the purpose of implementing an arms embargo and banning military assistance; and to authorise exemptions from the arms ban in humanitarian cases. With Resolution 1390 (2002) the sanctions lost their link with Afghanistan and became geographically open-ended: the '1267 committee' now had to include in the list it kept for the purpose of the sanctions 'Usama bin Laden, members of the Al-Qaida organisation and the Taliban and other individuals, groups, undertakings and entities associated with them.' Since Al Qaeda is a very loose organisation, if it can properly be called an organisation at all, the committee had and has a very wide discretion as to who should be listed and consequently who should be subject to sanctions; the phrase 'persons associated with them' carries with it additional matter for judgment.

Concerns about the work of the sanctions committees in implementing targeted sanctions have been frequently voiced, and may indeed have been in the minds of the legal advisers who drafted the resolutions concerned. Is it a proper role of the Council – or committees – to judge which individuals are responsible for specified acts, with consequences for use of their property and their freedom of movement? And if such decisions are to be taken, should there not be a reliable and fair procedure put in place to assist with the decision-making?

## Recent Resolutions

Resolution 1572 (2004) on Cote d'Ivoire and Resolution 1591 (2005) on Sudan introduce sanctions regimes which are very similar to each other. We discuss here the later one, but many of the points made could apply also to the resolution on Cote d'Ivoire.

Resolution 1591 (2005) is one of the measures which the Security Council is using to try to stop the conflict in Darfur; it seeks compliance by the Government of Sudan and the militias with the earlier demands of the Council. For some time sanctions had been called for, but the negotiation was difficult and the resolution was adopted with three abstentions, of which two were by permanent members. The resolution strengthens the arms embargo and imposes a travel ban and an assets freeze. But the extraordinary aspect of it for the purposes of this paper is the description of the categories of person against whom the measures are targeted. They are those who are designated by the sanctions committee because they 'impede the peace process, constitute a threat to stability in Darfur and the region, commit violations of international humanitarian or human rights law or other atrocities, violate the measures [imposing an arms embargo] or are responsible for offensive military overflights' in Darfur.

## Quasi-judicial Powers

The committee set-up by the resolution will thus have the function of determining responsibility for breaches of the law, as well as for violations of the Council's resolutions. It will have to make decisions on whether an individual is responsible for human rights abuses or breaches of humanitarian law, with consequent application of sanctions. On its face the resolution may require the committee to interpret international law and judge whether an individual has committed the alleged violation.

It need scarcely be said that sanctions committees are not best placed to exercise judicial functions. The '1591 committee' has the distinguished Greek Permanent Representative to the UN as chairman; the others attending the committees are likely to be first secretaries from the missions in New York. But with the best will in the world, no sanctions committee is competent to make determinations as to the responsibility of individuals for criminal acts, even where, as here, they have the benefit of a Panel of

Experts set-up to assist them, and the advantage of the report of the United Nations International Commission of Inquiry.[9]

Two days after adopting Resolution 1591 (2005) and after protracted negotiations, the Council adopted a resolution[10] referring the situation in Sudan to the International Criminal Court. Having decided that persons responsible for atrocities should be listed by the committee and subjected to sanctions, the Council then decided to hand to an internationally recognised judicial body the responsibility for bringing the same people to justice.

The ICC Prosecutor has opened an investigation. Various questions arise about the possible relationship between the committee and the Court. The Prosecutor will have to seek evidence which can be used in court. The information used by the committee will presumably not be of the same high standard. If a person on the committee's list is subsequently indicted by the ICC it will of course be irrelevant to the Prosecutor's case that the person is on the committee's list as being responsible for a breach of international humanitarian law. The principle of *ne bis in idem* will not apply to prevent the Court from trying the case.

Will the committee and the ICC investigators be able to be of any practical assistance to each other in their different tasks? Although the committee is unlikely to have information of an evidentiary nature, it or its Panel of Experts might be able to assist the Court with information which could lead to further investigation. But will the Court be able to share any information with the committee or will that breach confidentiality? The Court has the power to request States Parties to order the temporary freezing of assets for the purpose of eventual forfeiture.[11] Will the Court encourage the committee to list its own suspects, so as to attract the mandatory Security Council measures on assets freezes, valid in every country, not just in the territory of States Parties to the ICC Statute?

The criticisms once made about the Council's establishment of the two *ad hoc* Tribunals have largely died away. It is agreed that the Council in those instances was able to delegate to bodies created by it judicial powers which it could not have exercised itself. It was able to do so because it set-up proper judicial institutions and procedures.[12] It would be an exaggeration to claim that the Council was trying by Resolution 1591 (2005) to confer on the committee similar powers to those of the *ad hoc* Tribunals, particularly when it then referred the whole situation to the ICC; but the resolution does have the appearance of the Council delegating to its sanctions committee a judicial function, without judicial procedures or powers.

## Wide Discretion Delegated to the Committee

In addition to breaches of international criminal law, the '1591 committee' has also to determine which people impede the peace process or constitute a threat to stability in Darfur and the region, and it has to authorise exemptions which would further the objectives of the Council's resolutions. These are less than clear criteria for taking decisions on what can be severe restrictions on a person's property rights and freedom of movement.[13]

Since the committee has the same membership as the Security Council, the problem is not so much in the *delegation* of the powers as in the vagueness and breadth of the description of the persons targeted and the correspondingly wide discretion given to the committee in assessing who should come within the specified category.

The categories of persons targeted by sanctions are becoming more and more loosely formulated by the Council, with consequent wider powers for the sanctions committees. When the Council was targeting only countries (and their populations) there was no need for the Council or committee to judge between individuals. Whatever criticisms can be made of comprehensive sanctions, they did not raise the problems of difficulty of identification.

When targeted sanctions were first introduced, the targets were the members of the government or regime concerned; the people concerned were fairly easy to identify and this gave less discretion to a committee than the '1267' series of resolutions or Resolution 1591 (2005). Even where the circle of persons includes those *associated* with a regime, the basis on which the committee makes its decisions is much clearer. Resolutions that give wide discretion are bound to be vulnerable to criticism, both in terms of the decision made by the sanctions committees and in terms of the procedures used.

It is interesting to note that one of the earliest sanctions resolutions (Resolution 253 (1968) on Southern Rhodesia), also gave wide discretion in determining who was a targeted person: a travel ban was imposed on those persons whom states had reason to believe had furthered or encouraged the unlawful actions of the illegal regime, were likely to do so, or were encouraging activities 'calculated to evade' a sanctions measure. But the sanctions committee was not given the task of making these determinations; that was left to states, and states were free to establish their own procedures for assessing who fell within the categories described.

## Procedures

Resolution 1591 (2005) starkly raises the problem of what procedures sanctions committees should use to make their decisions. The committee will be undertaking a task which would normally be done, though for different purposes, by judges and prosecutors. The very broad description of the persons against whom sanctions are targeted would give even a court of law difficulty in judging what the description was intended to cover, and whether a particular person fell within it. Individual rights will be affected by the committee's decisions. But unless this committee departs from the practice of its predecessors, there will be no opportunity for allegations by one or other member of the Council to be weighed against defences, explanations or simple denials by the person alleged to have committed the violations concerned; no representations to the committee are possible except through the mouth of a government.

It has been some time now since the concerns about committees' lack of procedures have been voiced. Proposals have been made for improvement. The *Stockholm process* recommended that persons and entities listed as targets for financial sanctions and travel bans should be given due process rights by the Council, including the right to be informed of the reasons behind the imposition of sanctions and to view the evidence, the right to be heard in defence, and the right to obtain a review. The suggestion was made that the Security Council consider the creation of an independent body to monitor the observance of due process rights.

The '1267 committee' has improved its procedures but not to the extent of addressing sufficiently the concerns about lack of due process.[14] The UN high-level panel, reporting in December 2004,[15] recommended that sanctions committees should establish procedures to review the cases of those claiming to have been incorrectly placed or retained on the lists of those targeted. Since then, in Resolution 1617 (2005) the Council has decided that states should provide to the '1267 committee' a statement of case describing the basis of any proposal to add a name to the committee's list, that the statement could be used by the committee in responding to queries from Member States about people included on the list, and that information from it might be released to other parties with the prior consent of the designating state. A useful step, but nowhere near the review process suggested by the high-level panel and others.

## The Powers of the Council

What are the arguments that can be made in support of the current practice of the Council?

Overriding all else, it is the objective of the Council to maintain and restore international peace and security; nothing should be allowed to be an obstacle to the fulfilment of this objective. The drafters of the Charter even avoided subjecting the Council's Chapter VII decisions to the requirements of international law: the wording of Article 1.1 of the Charter makes clear that it is only Chapter VI decisions that must be in conformity with 'the principles of justice and international law'.

As regards the quasi-judicial functions under discussion, the argument is made that in taking decisions with regard to the application of sanctions to specific persons, the Council is not doing anything qualitatively different from making its determinations under the Charter on the existence of a threat to international peace and security. In the exercise of its peace and security responsibilities, the Council frequently holds states and non-state actors responsible for a conflict, breach of a ceasefire, and other actions against the peace. These determinations may of course be the precursor to the imposition of sanctions or the authorisation of the use of force. The decisions taken under Resolution 1591 (2005) will be for the purposes only of the imposition of sanctions; they are not intended for any legal proceeding and cannot truly be classed as judicial. The sanctions are only temporary and the assets are frozen, not appropriated.

The breadth of discretion given to the committees results from the move to targeted sanctions. This development may go beyond what was originally contemplated in the Charter.[16] But it does not serve to the advantage of the international community to be too formalistic about the constitutional rules of the Charter. Over the years there have been many interpretations of the Charter which would not have been contemplated by the original negotiators but which have been hallowed by practice and generally accepted: obvious examples are the avoidance of the veto effect of an abstention by permanent members of the Council, the invention of Chapter VI and a half peacekeeping missions, the stretching of the concept of international peace and security, the creation of the *ad hoc* Tribunals. The move away from the imposition of measures on whole populations of states and territorial entities is another example of creative development, in this case to meet humanitarian objectives. The Council is reflecting a development in international law and practice to directly affect non-state actors.

As regards the lack of due process, the argument is made that it is difficult to devise procedures which would satisfy the concerns while meeting the requirement to restore peace and security. Allowing states themselves to designate targeted persons in accordance with Council criteria would mean that universality of targeting would be lost; the effectiveness of the sanctions would depend even more than it does now upon the efficiency and willingness of states. Developing an international mechanism to review the evidence against an individual would require states with intelligence evidence to trust it to an international body, something that states are notoriously unwilling to do.

Finally, the alternatives to targeted sanctions are unattractive. Comprehensive sanctions have been tried and rejected on humanitarian grounds, and use of force must be a last resort.

## Conclusions

These points have all been used to support the present practice, and all have some degree of validity. But none of them provides a justification for the grant to a political organ of the function of determining responsibility for violations of international law. And nothing justifies the continuing lack of effective procedures or mechanisms of some kind to allow those who have been wrongly targeted by sanctions to defend themselves.

But does this mean that Resolutions 1572 (2004) and 1591 (2005) are therefore unlawful and invalid? This is a large discussion. The Security Council has only such powers as have been given it by the Charter. But Chapter VII uses expansive terminology and these two resolutions have not so far attracted much negative comment or criticism. As regards the lack of due process procedures, Chapter VII must be read subject to the requirement in Article 24.2 that the Council must act in accordance with the purposes and principles of the United Nations. That provision attracts the reference in Article 1 that one of the purposes of the UN is to promote and encourage respect for human rights and fundamental freedoms. But does this very general wording mean that a particular Council measure which does not incorporate human rights procedural measures is *invalid*? And does not Article 103 of the Charter trump all other treaties, including those parts of human rights treaties that do not constitute *ius cogens*?

In my view we need to be cautious before we designate Council measures as unlawful. Some arguments made by academics would render a large number of existing Chapter VII resolutions invalid. I am not sure that this adds to the credibility of international law or international lawyers when, in the real world, governments are on the whole accepting those measures as law, and either complying with them or making legal arguments – specious or not – as to why they are not complying. On the other hand, if the Council continues to give such extraordinary powers to its sanctions committees it risks losing its own credibility. It will also tempt *national* courts[17] confronted by an apparent clash between Security Council measures (and Art. 103 of the Charter) on the one hand and human rights obligations on the other to prefer the latter, either on the ground (justified or not) that due process rights have attained the status of *ius cogens* or that a dynamic approach must be adopted to the interpretation of the Charter so as to invalidate measures which contravene human rights.

## Notes

1 Resolutions 232 (1966) and 253 (1968).

2 Resolution 418 (1977).

3 In Resolution 661 (1991).

4 In Resolution 757 (1992).

5 For example, the five permanent members of the Security Council wrote to the President of the Council in 1995 saying that further sanctions regimes should be 'directed to minimize unintended adverse side effects of sanctions on the most vulnerable segments of targeted countries'. The *Interlaken Process, the Bonn-Berlin Process* and the *Stockholm Process* made recommendations with regard to various aspects of the implementation of targeted sanctions.

6 In Resolution 1127 (1997), following the oil embargo imposed by Resolution 864 (1993) which did not require a list to be compiled by the sanctions committee.

7 In Resolution 1132 (1997).

8 Resolution 1333 (2000).

9 Established by Resolution 1564 (2004). Although the committee may not, perhaps, be given the list of those whom the Commission considered responsible for theatrocities in Darfur.

10 Resolution 1593 (2005).

11 Art. 93.1(k) of the Statute of the ICC.

12 See the *Tadic* Appeals Chamber decision of 2 October 1995.

13 A later example of a similarly wide discretion can be found in Resolution 1596 (2005) on the Democratic Republic of Congo. The travel ban imposed by the resolution does not apply where the committee decides that an exemption would further the objectives of the resolutions on the DRC.

14 At the Security Council meeting on 20 July 2005 the Chairman of the committee pointed out that 'many Member States have argued that the Committee should further improve procedures for listing and delisting names....During my visits to selected States, and through reports to the Committee, it has become very clear that more is expected from the Committee in terms of the quality of information used for identification.' Speaking in the same debate in her capacity as representative of Denmark, she went further in underlining the need for due process in the committee's functions. 'A way forward in this respect could be to establish a review mechanism that would consider individual petitions for delisting from individuals and entities affected... After having considered a complaint, the review mechanism would submit a recommendation to the Committee. The Committee would endorse or dismiss the recommendation, thus keeping decision-making within the realm of the Security Council. This mechanism would also act as a filter in cases that are deemed unfounded and consequently do not merit consideration in the Committee.' (S/PV.5229)

15 'A more secure world: our shared responsibility' Report of the Secretary-General's High-level Panel on Threats, Challenges and Change, at para. 152.

16 The predecessor to Art. 41 of the Charter is Art. 16, para. 1 of the Covenant of the League of Nations, which required all members to break off trade or financial relations with states which had gone to war in breach of the Covenant and to stop commercial and other arrangements between the nationals of that state and theirs. Art. 50 of the UN Charter also implies that economic measures are to be taken against states.

17 A number of cases on issues such as these have been submitted to the European Court of First Instance, including Aden (T-306/01); Kadi (T-315/01); Othman (R-308/01); OMPI (T-228/02); PKK and FNL (T-229/02); Ayadi (T-253/02); Al-Aqsa (T-327/03); Hassan (T-49/04); Aydar and others (T-253/04); Selmani (T-299/04).

# Discussion

Erika de Wet, posing a question to Elberling: Have you sufficiently considered the presumption of legality? Whatever our doubts of Council measures are, the Council acts under the presumption of legality, which means that States have to act very quickly and indicate that they are nor in agreement with a resolution.

Elberling responding to Erika de Wet: I consider it necessary to distinguish between council measures that are possibly *ultra vires* for formal and for material reasons. A formal reason would for example be when there is a problem of competence. A material reason when for instance humanitarian law was violated. Especially in cases where the competence of an organ or even of the United Nations in case of legislative actions is in doubt this presumption is indeed rebuttable, the question of course then is how should it be rebutted. This goes together with the question whether state acquiescence make these measures legal over time. The only way that these measures can become legal through state acquiescence is if this acquiescence is unanimous.

Erika de Wet, posing a question to Lavalle: What do the reactions of states to Resolutions 1373 and 1540 tell us? States had to report back to the Council and implement certain measures. From the reports of states it has appeared that states do not comply fully and implement the resolutions only up to a point. Can we draw any legal conclusions from the fact that States do not fully comply with the resolutions? Are there patterns of non-implementation? Would that imply that States do not regard those aspects of the resolutions as binding? Or is it simply a matter of incompetence or unwillingness?

Lavalle responding to Erika de Wet: The question of how states comply with measures enjoined on them by the Council by means of so called international legislation. This question must be separate from the lawfulness of those provisions. Except in one case, namely when the Council asks states to take actions that are incompatible with treaties or with general international law because then Article 103 would come into play and of course it would come into play only if council resolutions are constitutional. We will never have complete compliance with the Council resolutions, but however, even incomplete compliance is better than nothing. I think, except in the exceptional case when Article 103 comes into play, compliance is an extra-constitutional matter. One wonders whether this whole matter of compliance can really be regarded as legal.

Erika de Wet, posing a question to Wilmshurst: Do you see a role for national courts in providing due process for various individuals and private entities finding themselves on sanctions lists convicted of violations of international law and having all their assets frozen?

Wilmshurst responding to Erika de Wet: The question whether Security Council Resolutions should be upheld because of a lack of due process rights is no before national courts and the European Court of Justice and decisions are going to come out there. The question is what those decisions should be. When you regard the matter as an international lawyer you may say that Article 103 trumps. Whether or not that will happen depends on the particular domestic or European legal order concerned; it will really depend on what the domestic legal order dictates. I understand that in the UK we have got an upcoming case where Article 103 of the UN Charter will be set against

Article 5 of the European Convention on Human Rights, except that it is not in a sanctions context.

I do not think it will be a bad thing at all if the Security Council was a little bit troubled by the fact that national courts were sniffing around and getting interested in this area, whether their decisions were in accordance with international law or not. Because I do believe that it is time that the Security Council was able to devise some mechanism, which is better than the present in safeguarding the rights of individuals, especially concerning the freezing of suspected terrorists assets. At the moment there really is not a satisfactory way for people who are suspected of terrorist actions to make representations, it always has to be through the mouth of governments.

S. MURPHY,* posing a question to ELBERLING: In your presentation you seem to indicate that the General Assembly might be more appropriate than the Security Council for legislative action. As between the two it seems that the Security Council is the organ that has been provided an ability to issue decisions that bind states in a somewhat wide-ranging manner as opposed to the General Assembly, which cannot do that except in respect to some very limited functions such as adopting the UN budget. That would seem to suggest that the Security Council, if there is going to be a legislator, is the better organ.

Furthermore, you seemed to imply that the General Assembly was perhaps the more democratic or more representative organ, and I can see that in terms of each state being represented in the General Assembly. But in today's world of human rights one might think that popular representation is a better gage and when you think of Luxemburg having one vote and China having one vote, given the disparity in their populations, and given that the membership of the Security Council by and large, no matter how it is composed, year after year, does represent somewhere around the half of the worlds population, I just wonder whether it is really correct to be assuming that the General Assembly is the more representative body if you were to legislate.

ELBERLING, responding to MURPHY: You pose the question if we give any organ legislative power, what can they do with it. In answer to this question we will say that the Security Council can do a lot more with a legislative power than could the General Assembly. However, rather we should ask the question if we want to give any organ a legislative power, which organ is best suited for this function, for instance in terms of democracy. If one were to give any organ such power than it should rather be the general Assembly than the Security Council (although this would not be a perfect solution either).

Regarding the representation of actual people. If we consider the manner in which international law usually comes into existence, at least in theory, every single human being is being represented in the law-making process. This would probably still be the case if one were to give legislative powers to the general assembly, as then such norms could not come into existence by simple majority of states. Representation of half of the world's population in the Security Council is not enough.

* John Washington University.

G. Hafner,* posing a question to Wilmshurst: We are facing an absence of any opposition to resolutions of the Security Council such as 1591, despite the problem it creates. What does this absence of opposition mean? Does it mean that the states agreed only to this resolution or does it open the way to implied powers of the Security Council on which the Security Council in later instances could rely?

Wilmshurst responding to Hafner: Legally it does not matter whether there was opposition to Resolution 1591 or not. I can only answer that it depends on the question whether the Council will continue to act like that in the future and it already has acted twice.

Chris Harland,* making a general remark: I would like to remark that Resolutions 1540 and 1373 strike me slightly more like making treaties than legislating. The provisions requiring criminal sanctions placed in the domestic legal order. It is a little like what you see in the Chemical Weapons Convention and the Biological Weapons Convention and it is up to each state to define the elements of crime and to impose what level of sanctions will be required.

Elberling responding to the remark of Harland:

My response concerns whether Council measures are really legislation, or whether they were not more treaty based. I think the way the panel used the term legislation not to indicate norms that are applicable directly in any national legal order, rather as norms that are applicable in the international legal order. And that would usually be done by setting-up a treaty or by contributing to international customary law.

Harland posing a question to Lavalle: Was there much consultation on Resolution 1540? How did states perceive this consultation?

Lavalle responding to Harland:

The answer is that yes, indeed, consultations were held in advance of the adoption of Resolution 1540. The consultation were held in particularly with the Non-Aligned Movement and consultations were also held with the OSCE and with the European Union and what is particularly important is that a public meeting was held at which every member of the UN had the opportunity to be heard and to express his or her opinion. Of course such consultation is a good thing.

However, what applies here is the adage 'the proof of the pudding is in the eating'. What is really important is what happens after the resolution is adopted, whether states comply and how far they comply.

Harland posing a question to the panel: What should a conscientious national judge do faced with a conflict between Article 103 of the UN Charter and human rights instruments? I refer to a situation where the conflict does not involve *jus cogens* norms and assuming that we are talking about a judge in a monist state in which international law is directly applied. Are there tools open to judges, in the context of international law to solve such a conflict?

Wilmshurst responding to Harland:

(What should a conscientious national judge do faced with a conflict between Article 103 of the UN Charter and human rights instruments?)

* University of Vienna.

** ICRC.

I would find this problem very difficult and I would not like to judge in such a case. The formal answer would be that Article 103 trumps even human rights treaties, unless you are talking about *jus cogens*.

MARY ELLEN O'CONNELL,* posing a question to LAVALLE:

Won't the determination whether a resolution is recommendatory or mandatory depend on whether non-compliance will be sanctioned? Does the Security Council intend to sanction non-compliance with Resolutions 1373 and 1540?

LAVALLE responding to O'CONNELL (but not to her question): I would like to answer to the question what the Council would do to states that did not comply with one of its resolutions. The answer is that the Security Council, if it believes that such action is a threat to international peace and security can indeed take action against that state.

I would like to add that compliance with Resolution 1540 is at this moment far from satisfactory. As of yesterday only a 119 countries have replied and many of these replies are far from satisfactory. Whereas compliance with Resolution 1373 I think has been by and large quite satisfactory.

MARY ELLEN O'CONNELL, posing a question to WILMSHURST:

Is it not peremptory to dismiss the application of sanction to a whole country on the basis of human rights considerations? Is it not possible to design sanctions regimes that are more targeted but in terms of the whole country and obviate some of the problems that we are hearing about. I am wondering whether we did not move a bit too quickly away from the old model in light of the Iraq sanctions to this new model, which obviously is raising serious concerns.

WILMSHURST responding to O'CONNELL:

Sanctions targeted against the leaders of a state are still targeted sanctions. Arms embargos against a whole country are still being imposed and those are what I call comprehensive sanctions but against a particular trade sector. I agree entirely that the Council has gone two far in adopting categories of persons targeted by sanctions, which are far too wide, which give far too much discretion to sanctions committees and therefore give rise to this sort of question we are raising. I do think it would be possible in particular cases for them to define their categories more narrowly even though leaving it as targeted.

HANS CORELL,** making a general remark: One should be very careful to name resolutions by the Security Council unlawful. I think they are acting in a very distinct manner. I do not for a minute believe that the General Assembly should assume some role as a legislator. It is much better to confine this to the Security Council. Before Resolution 1373 was adopted I was asked whether there were any limits for the Security Council or can they act just as they think fit in a particular situation. And basically I said that there are no precise limits and I think it is the acceptance of the membership of the organisation that is the ultimate judge here. If the Council transgresses that limit then of course they risk destroying not only itself but also the organisation as such.

CORELL posing a question to WILMSHURST: My question concerns Article 103. If you say that the Council can develop Chapter VII and adopt resolutions of the kind

* Ohio State University.

** Former Legal Counsel of the UN.

they have including directing themselves against individuals, is it not true than that the rules on human rights can be developed as they have been by member states in treaties when they clash what does Article 103 say? If you look at Article 6 of the European Convention, for example, doesn't it say that an individual has the right of access to court in case their civil rights and obligations are in jeopardy? I would like to ask Ms Wilmshurst whether there is an opening in article 103 to look at the outflows of other elements when you balance this?

Would it be possible to have also at the international level some institution that can address individual complaints, if they have been listed for example, because not all individuals might have access to courts at the national level as we have in Europe for example?

WILMSHURST responding to CORREL: Concerning your question about Article 103 in relation to Article 6 of the ECHR I have already given the answer that Article 103 should theoretically trump. But I believe very firmly that the Security Council should try a little harder to develop an international mechanism of some kind to allow people who have been wrongly accused of being terrorist to have some recourse to complain to the Sanctions Committee other than by finding a government through whose mouth they have to speak.

H. SCHERMERS,* posing a question to the panel: I am of the opinion that world legislation is badly needed. I am also of the opinion that neither the Security Council nor the General Assembly really represents the world population. Of course the Security Council can adopt resolutions with legislative provisions whenever they please. The question is whether these provisions are legally permitted. However, even if they are not legally permitted they can be very effective as long as states comply with them.

The real question than comes to the supervision of possible legislative measures of the Security Council. Is there any judicial or any other supervision over them? In international law the practice is that any state that does not like a certain decision declares it illegal and the states that like it comply with it. Now the suggestion of Ms Wilmshurst is to give more authority to national courts rather than international politicians to decide on the legality and I think that would be a step forward. But none the less it would be very chaotic because one state judge would declare himself incompetent to do this, not all judges are willing to comply international law, Furthermore, another judge would decide one way, another the other way.

A well functioning system would need some international supervision. The international Court of Justice should have the power to declare legislative measures of the Security Council void if they are illegal. As a lawyer I would accept this.

However, the basic question is do we want to place the law above politics, or political supervision above the law. There are people who say, no, politics is much more flexible politics is able to adapt to recent developments, whereas law always looks backwards, is based on previous periods, so there should not be control by courts but there should be supervision by a political organ. These arguments favour placing the Security Council above the International Court of Justice and giving them the freedom to legislate.

* Emiritus Professor Leiden University.

Another possibility would be to supervise legislative power by a human rights organ in the sense that legislation would be void only if it violates human rights.

LAVALLE on the representativeness of the Security Council, responding to MURPHY AND SCHERMERS: One must take into account that the membership of the Security Council rotates and that this has considerable influence on the representativeness of the Council.

ELBERLING on the representativeness of the Security Council, responding to MURPHY AND SCHERMERS: No matter how large a part of the world population is represented in the Security Council one should not forget the veto power of the permanent five.

Considering the legislative powers of the Security Council the question is do the end really justify the means? I think in this regard what really goes to the core of international law, the ends do not justify the needs.

N. BLOKKER,* posing a question to the panel: Concerning the topics that have been discussed today very little can be found in the recent reform documents, namely the High Level Panel Report and the Secretary General Report of March 2005. I wonder what conclusions I should draw from this, is this a missed opportunity, or is our discussion more an academic debate?

WILMSHURST responding to BLOKKER: The High-Level Panel report and the Secretary General's report 'In larger freedom' both deal with the matter of targeted sanctions and problems of due process. For example, the High-Level Panel report mentions humanitarian exemption and further procedures for sanctions committees to ensure that people who should not be listed are not listed. In the General Assembly this has not been universally welcomed and the US has advised to be cautious in revising sanctions mechanisms less the process be overly complicated; The US do not favour creating a quasi-judicial process. For that reason I am not sure whether the High Level Panel Report will be able to change much.

SCOTT making a comment: Regarding the meaning of the sparse discussion by states on the legality of the legislative provisions of Security Council resolutions, one has to take into account that this is perhaps caused by pragmatism. I guess it would be in the interests of those who wish to use this mechanism not to force the issue of the legality and of the extent of the powers of the Security Council, but rather to use this mechanism in a pragmatic way as perceived political needs arise.

## FINAL REMARKS BY ERIKA DE WET

I would like to make one last comment on creative judging by national courts. A variety of national courts, the Swiss Supreme Court, the French *Court du Cassation* and the Belgium Court, have recently issued decisions pertaining to international organisations. In these decisions they determined that the denial of due process to an individual affected by a decision of an international organisation, constitutes denial of justice, which violates a fundamental norm of the international public order. Two cases con-

* Dutch Foreign Ministry, Leiden University.

cerned the denial of immunities by International Organisations; the other case concerned the transferral of somebody from Switzerland to the Rwanda Tribunal couple of years ago. A creative judge could argue that due process, access to court, as a fundamental norm of the international public order, comes very close to *jus cogens.*

*Reporter:* Geranne Lautenbach*

* University of Amsterdam, the Netherlands.

# The Role of International Institutions in Territorial Administration and Post-Conflict Justice

The panel was convened by its Chair, Ralph Wilde*

## Introductory Remarks by Ralph Wilde

### Direct international involvement in domestic criminal law processes

One recent innovation in the regime of international criminal justice has been the direct involvement of international actors in the operation of criminal justice processes situated within the territory to which they relate.

Various institutions operating or planned in Cambodia, East Timor, Bosnia and Herzegovina, Sierra Leone and Kosovo have a mixture of international and local elements, for example criminal tribunals with a bench comprising both local jurists and international experts.

This represents a new phase in international criminal institutions: after the shift from the situation-specific regime of *ad hoc* international tribunals to the potentially all-encompassing ICC, we have a return to the situation-specific paradigm, but with key differences. In particular, these institutions:

- operate in the territory to which they relate;
- have a mixture of international and local elements;
- are more diverse in the crimes covered, sometimes including so-called 'ordinary' or 'non-international' crimes; and
- are more diverse in the manner in which they operate, sometimes involving alternative non-criminal processes such as truth commissions.

These developments raise a number of important legal and policy issues. For example:

- Why were 'mixed,' locally-based processes introduced, instead of greater international support for processes operated exclusively by local actors or the international tribunal model? Are these reasons supportable? Who decides what type, if any, of international involvement there should be, and what is and should be the role of the local population in making such a decision?

* Reader, Law Faculty, University College London, University of London.

- What are the relative merits of these processes when compared with the alternatives?
- What legal authority is provided for them?
- What is their legal status? The Special Tribunal for Sierra Leone determined in the *Charles Taylor* case that because of the nature of the involvement of the Security Council in the Tribunal, for the purposes of the law on state immunity it was an 'international' tribunal like the *ad hoc* international criminal tribunals. Was this correct? Does it hold true for other 'mixed' processes?
- What obligations of cooperation, if any, do local, foreign and other international actors on the ground, from the host government to peacekeeping troops, have in relation to such institutions, and are these adequate?
- What practical challenges are faced by these processes, and to what extent are the mandates, funding, expertise and support provided for them adequate to meet these challenges?

Clearly it is not possible today to address fully these and other important issues.[1] Instead we will focus on three different case studies – certain processes in Bosnia and Herzegovina, East Timor and Sierra Leone – by way of considering in detail specific examples of the more general phenomenon. We are very fortunate to have three speakers who have direct hands-on experience of the particular process they will be talking about.

## Note

1 See, e.g., *Internationalized Criminal Courts,* Cesare P.R. Romano, André Nollkaemper and Jann K. Kleffner (eds), 2004.

# Remarks by Fidelma Donlon*

## The Court of Bosnia and Herzegovina War Crimes and Organized Crime Chambers and the Registry for War Crimes and Organized Crime

### 1. Introduction

In the context of ongoing judicial reform in Bosnia and Herzegovina (BiH) and the desire of the International Criminal Tribunal for the Former Yugoslavia (ICTY) to re-

* Deputy Registrar of the Court of Bosnia and Herzegovina, War Crimes and Organized Crime Chambers. The author is the former Head of the Criminal Institutions and Prosecutorial Reform Unit (CIPRU) of the Office of the High Representative. In coordination with the BiH government CIPRU managed the establishment of the Court of Bosnia and Herzegovina and the restructuring of the BiH Prosecution system since 2002.

turn cases for trial to a suitable Court in BiH (as a critical element of the ICTY Completion Strategy),[1] the ICTY and the Office of the High Representative[2] (OHR) finalized Joint Conclusions on the domestic prosecution of war crimes cases in BiH.[3] The expert group recommended the establishment of Specialized Chambers (the War Crimes Chambers) within the Court of BiH, a Specialized War Crimes Department in the Prosecutor's Office of BiH and the Registry for War Crimes. It was agreed that persons indicted for serious violations of international humanitarian law and other grave violations of human rights under the Criminal Code of BiH,[4] as well as the transfer of cases from the ICTY under Rule *11 bis*[5] would be prosecuted before the Court of BiH. The purpose of the Project was to provide the justice sector institutions of BiH with the tools and capacity to ensure international standards in the prosecution and trial of those cases.

Subsequently, the joint conclusions were presented and agreed with the BiH authorities, and in advance of the War Crimes donors' conference held in October 2003 a detailed project proposal and budget were prepared and submitted to donor countries. The project proposal reflected the gradual phasing out of the international component from the Court and the Prosecutor's Office over the course of a five year period. At that conference the donors pledged 16.1 million Euros for the first two years of the War Crimes Chamber Project with the expectation that additional funding would later be forthcoming.

## 2. Institutional and Legal Framework

The Registry of the War Crimes Chamber of the Court of BiH and the Special Department of the Prosecutor's Office was established by an international agreement and domestic legislation to enable the provision of management and administrative support for prosecution and trial of violations of international humanitarian law and other grave abuses of human rights and organized crime indictments confirmed by the Court of BiH.[6] The policy of the Registry is that the proper role of the international community in this process is and should be to empower the people and institutions of Bosnia and Herzegovina with the necessary management and technical tools and financial and material resources which can give them the capacity to carry out the task of bringing to justice perpetrators of crimes of this magnitude. Only the support and commitment of the people of Bosnia and Herzegovina can ensure the viability of the Court of BiH. The Registry is providing, with the funds available, both the necessary physical infrastructure and the expert legal and administrative assistance to ensure that the Court and Prosecutors Office of BiH is able to meet both the expectations of the BiH citizens and the standards required by the international community.[7]

The Registry is organized as follows to ensure that the core functions of the Court and Prosecutors Office of BiH are satisfactorily serviced by the project:

a. Administration Division;
b. Court Management Section;
c. Judicial Support Section;
d. Prosecution Support Section;
e. Criminal Defence Support Section;

f. Detention Unit;
g. Information Technology Management Section;
h. International Protocol Section;
i. Security Section;
j. Victim and Witness Support Section;
k. Public Information and Outreach Section;
l. Legal Counsel Office.

Structures have been built in the Court and Prosecutors Office which give nationals the leading role in how the institutions function. National staff are recruited at all levels to help manage the Registry from the very beginning of the process in order to ensure a seamless transition to national professionals over the five year project period.

The War Crimes Section of the Court of BiH is established by domestic legislation.[8] The War Crimes Section will have at least eight and up to twelve trial chambers and an Appellate Division. During the initial period, each of the trial and appeal panels may be comprised of two international judges and one national judge. The panels will, in due course, evolve into panels with a majority of national judges and will finally be exclusively composed of national judges near the end of a five year period.

Likewise, the Special Department of the Prosecutor's Office is established by domestic legislation.[9] The Prosecutor's Office is fully staffed with national Heads of teams, supported by both national and international personnel. The Department will evolve over the five year period into a department composed exclusively of national prosecutors.

The applicable procedural and substantive criminal laws are the Criminal Procedure Code of BiH,[10] the Criminal Code of BiH[11] and the Law on the Transfer of cases from the ICTY to the Prosecutor's Office of BiH and the use of evidence collected by the ICTY in proceedings before the Court of BiH.[12]

## 3. Methodology and Implementation Plan

The language of the Court is Bosnian, Serbian and Croatian. No national personnel are required to be fluent in any language other than Bosnian, Croatian or Serbian.

The project contemplates the following six phases:

| | |
|---|---|
| **Phase I:** | Planning Phase – start of project to August 2004. |
| **Phase II:** | Development Phase –September to December 2004. |
| **Phase III:** | Implementation Phase – January 2005 to August 2005. |
| **Phase IV:** | Management Transition Phase – August 2005 to August 2006. |
| **Phase V:** | International Judges and Prosecutors Transition Phase – August 2006 to December 2007. |
| **Phase VI:** | Completion of Transition Phase – January 2008 to August 2009. |

**Phase I**

During this phase, planning for the five year project was undertaken by OHR and a provisional budget was presented to and accepted by the Donors' Conference. Reconstruction plans for the Court building and premises of the Prosecutor's Office were commenced. The package of laws establishing the authority and mandate of the Registry was prepared, completed and submitted for BiH Parliamentary adoption. A Project Director was appointed in June of 2004 and the Project Director in turn organized and led the OHR team in preparing the final plan for implementation of the Project. Expert personnel were recruited to prepare detailed plans for each component part of the core functions of the Registry and the Court of BiH.

**Phase II**

The project team developed the capacity to implement the institutional plan by staffing the core functions and setting-up the management structure for the Registry in coordination with the President of the Court and the Chief Prosecutor of BiH. In addition, the team managed the design and construction of a new BiH Detention Unit. The package of laws establishing the War Crimes Chamber was adopted by the BiH Parliament and the international agreement establishing the Registry was signed by the High Representative and the BiH Presidency. All the procedures and protocols of the Registry were in place by 31 December 2004 to ensure that war crimes judicial proceedings could start in January 2005.

**Phase III**

The Registry commenced independent operations and began to exercise its functions in respect of the war crimes cases and Rule *11 bis* referrals as of January 2005. On 9 March 2005 the War Crimes Chamber of the Court of Bosnia and Herzegovina and the Special War Crimes Department of the Prosecutors Office of Bosnia and Herzegovina were inaugurated. On the same day the Official dedication and transfer of the Detention Unit to the Ministry of Justice occurred after the adoption by the BiH Parliament, in regular session, of the Law of Bosnia and Herzegovina on the Execution of Criminal Sanctions, Detention and other Measures. The staff of the Detention Unit are under the budget and administration of the Ministry of Justice of Bosnia and Herzegovina and work together with an international advisor from the Registry. They have completed an intensive preliminary training program conducted by the Council of Europe and a Joint Entity Prison Training Team.

The Registry has signed a Memorandum of Understanding on Cooperation in the area of Witness Protection and Witness Support with the BiH State Police Force (SIPA). In order to establish and maintain the operational capacity of the SIPA Witness Protection Department the Registry provides technical and material assistance to the SIPA Department. Training projects, methodology and the operational plan for implementation of all witness protection measures to be carried out by SIPA in the short- and long-term are jointly developed with the Registry and all activities are now being coordinated by an international witness protection advisor and a senior SIPA police inspector.

The Witness Support Office commenced operations in the Court of Bosnia and Herzegovina. The office is responsible for logistical operations and administration matters relative to witnesses appearing in cases before the War Crimes Chamber. Staff provide appropriate psychological support and assistance to witnesses before, during and after trial.

The process of recruiting, appointing, and assigning War Crimes judges and clerks to fixed Panels was completed in May 2005. Qualified Judges have been appointed by the High Representative on the joint recommendation of the President of the Court of Bosnia and Herzegovina, the High Judicial and Prosecutorial Council and the Registrar. The Presiding Judge for the War Crimes panels will be a national judge.

The formal public announcement of the Strategy and prosecution mandate in respect to War Crimes indictments in the Court of Bosnia and Herzegovina was announced by the Chief Prosecutor of BiH. The indictments for approximately 200 very sensitive cases will begin to be presented to the Court by early June. The Prosecutor's Office has selected the cases after a thorough review of all pending investigations which had been marked with a positive rating by the ICTY Rules of the Road process. The Prosecutor's Office is fully staffed with national Heads of teams, supported by both national and international personnel. Communications with the Office of the Prosecutor at the ICTY have been further developed to ensure the smooth transfer of evidence to the Prosecutors Office of Bosnia and Herzegovina. In October 2005, approximately seven 11-Bis cases were pending referral to the Court of BiH from The ICTY.

The Criminal Defense Section of the Registry of the Court of Bosnia and Herzegovina is established and works to provide administrative and legal support to individual defense advocates. The Section has started training Bosnian lawyers in the new elements of the Law of Bosnia and Herzegovina, War Crimes Law, advocacy, and other relevant areas of Law so as to ensure the highest standards of representation in War Crimes Cases.

The Information and Communication Technology Department fully supports all aspects of the Court, the Prosecutors Office and the Registry. The Department has been working with the ICTY to take advantage of the lessons learned by the Tribunal and to enhance systems in the Court. The Electronic Disclosure Suite which contains the majority of the documentary evidence in the ICTY will be delivered to the Registry for use by the Court, the Prosecutor, and the Defense in the preparation and trial of cases indicted in the Court of Bosnia and Herzegovina.

The Public Information and Outreach Section has held intensive training seminars in cooperation with outside partners for reporters of Bosnian and regional media which will be reporting on war crimes trials held at the Court of Bosnia and Herzegovina. The Section is actively engaged in communication with victim groups from all three peoples in Bosnia and Herzegovina. The aim of this communication is to provide information on the work of the Court, the process of transfer of cases from ICTY and opportunities for their engagement in the process.

On 17 May 2005 the ICTY Referral Bench issued the Decision under Rule *11 bis* for the referral of the case of Radovan Stankovic from the International Criminal Tribunal for the Former Yugoslavia to the Court of Bosnia and Herzegovina for trial. The Referral Bench noted that it 'is satisfied that the laws applicable to proceedings against the Accused in Bosnia and Herzegovina provide an adequate basis to ensure compliance with the requirement for a fair trial.' In September 2005 Radovan Stankovic was transferred to BiH and is now detained in the high security detention unit on the grounds of the Court of BiH.

**Phase IV**

The War Crimes Chamber Project will complete the transfer of responsibility for management of each of the core functions of the Registry to domestic professionals. The transfer will be effected over the course of eighteen months from the commencement of the War Crimes Chamber proceedings in January 2005.

**Phase V**

The configuration of the panels of the War Crimes Chamber will change from mixed trial chambers comprising two internationals and one national judge to panels with one international judge and two national judges.

**Phase VI**

The remaining international judges and prosecutors will (subject to completion of the trials in which they are participating) leave at the beginning of this phase, resulting in the War Crimes Chamber and the Special Department in the Prosecutor's Office being comprised entirely of national personnel.

## 4. The Role of Internationals in the Prosecution of War Crimes in Bosnia and Herzegovina

The project is designed to build domestic capacity for the prosecution of *war crimes* that will meet international standards of fair trial. The Registry uses international financial contributions, domestic appropriations, non-governmental contributions, and in-kind donations to meet its resource requirements. International professionals assist the project in the management functions and as judges and prosecutors in mixed panels of judges and prosecution teams. The international professionals assist in the establishment of the capacity of the Registry, the recruitment of qualified national professionals as counterparts capable of managing that capacity, and training and transferring skills to those domestic counterparts. No long-term (more than one year) contracts are available to internationals outside the financial accountability functions. Short-term consultants are utilized in place of staff positions wherever possible.

During the initial phase of the project a transition strategy and timelines were incorporated into the business plan for the War Crimes Chamber of the Court and Prosecutor's Office of BiH and the Registry rather than preparing the transition plan at a later stage. A major objective of the Registry is to introduce international professional support to the management and litigation functions of the Court and Prosecutor's Office over the course of the five year project. A secondary goal of the Project is to gradually phase out the international component, as outlined above, from the Registry after the first twenty-four months of the project by transferring authority and title to national professionals. International judicial and prosecutorial support will be gradually phased out of the project over the course of the second twenty-four months. It is contemplated that the final year of the project will be completed with an entirely national staff for the judicial panels and prosecutorial personnel. The ultimate absorption of the War Crime Chamber's capacity into the justice system of Bosnia and Herzegovina and its national funding system is essential to the mandate of the project.

Owing to the skill and commitment of the President of the Court of BiH and her staff, the Chief Prosecutor and his teams and the Minister of Justice of BiH the transition strategy is ahead of scheduled timelines. A large number of staff already work under the direct supervision and control of national professionals. The Court of BiH has approximately 43 war crimes files in various phases of proceedings, including the 'Kravice Warehouse' case involving ten suspects involved in the murder of approximately 1,000 men/boys in the Srebrenica area in 1995.

The design and goals of the BiH war crimes project can be exported to other post-conflict or transition states. The number and transition timelines of international professionals and their role in the justice sector institutions in the country will vary depending on the given environment, however, the critical goal is to build domestic capacity from the initial project phase and transition at a time when it can be sustained.

## Notes

1 The ICTY strategy for completing investigations by the end of 2004, all trial activities at first instance by end 2008, and all of its work in 2010 (ICTY Completion Strategy) (S/2002/678), by concentrating on the prosecution and trial of the most senior leaders suspected of being most responsible for crimes within the ICTY's jurisdiction and transferring cases involving those who may not bear this level of responsibility to competent national jurisdictions, as appropriate, as well as the strengthening of the capacity of such jurisdictions.

2 The OHR was created under the General Framework Agreement for Peace in BiH (Dayton Peace Agreement) of 14 December 1995 to oversee implementation of the civilian aspects of the Peace Agreement.

3 Joint Conclusions of ICTY and OHR regarding domestic prosecution of war crimes in Bosnia and Herzegovina, The Hague, 21 February 2003. The Peace Implementation Council Steering Board (session of 21 November 2002) proposed that ICTY and OHR develop a common plan to enable the effective prosecution of war crimes cases in BiH.

4 Chapter 17 of the Criminal Code of BiH, *Official Gazette 3/03.*

5 Rule *11 bis* of ICTY Rules of Procedure and Evidence.

6 Agreement between the High Representative for BiH and the BiH Presidency on the establishment of the Registry – *Official Gazette of BiH – International Agreements 12/04,* Law on Amendments to the Law on Court of BiH – *Official Gazette of BiH 61/04,* Law on Amendments to the Law on Prosecutors Office of BiH – *Official Gazette of BiH 61/04.*

7 See, for further details, The Registry Project Implementation Report, Sarajevo October 2004.

8 Law on Amendments to the Law on Court of BiH – *Official Gazette of BiH 61/04.*

9 Law on Amendments to the Law on Prosecutors Office of BiH – *Official Gazette of BiH 61/04.*

10 *Official Gazette BiH- 3/03.*

11 *Official Gazette BiH* – 3/03.

12 *Official Gazette BiH – 61/04.*

## Remarks by Erica Harper*

## The Challenge of Judicial Rehabilitation under UN Auspices: Reconciling Legal-Cultural Incompatibilities

The past decade has witnessed a growing expectation by the international community that peacekeeping operations include 'justice packages'.[1] Such packages promote democratic institution building, the rule of law, judicial independence, and a policing and legal culture based upon internationally recognised principles. As was seen during the UN missions in Kosovo and Timor Leste in 1999, these interventions can comprise direct legal rehabilitation and administration responsibilities. In other situations, for example El Salvador, Haiti, Liberia, Sierra Leone, Guatemala and Cote d'Ivoire, justice-related activities have been more limited.[2]

The Report of the Secretary General on *The Rule of Law and Transitional Justice in Conflict and Post-Conflict Societies* (23 August 2004)[3] makes strategic and operational recommendations for improving the way in which the UN undertakes the challenge of reconstructing collapsed or dysfunctional legal systems in conflict and post-conflict states. It advocates a move away from foreign conceived solutions and pre-formulated legal models. Instead, the UN should develop more integrated approaches to judicial rehabilitation which identify, empower and develop local legal capacity. By vesting leadership and decision-making in local stakeholders, UN missions should assist national constituencies develop their own reform agendas and actions plans for transitional justice. Such strategies would more accurately reflect domestic needs, aspirations, and the society's unique legal culture, socio-economics and traditions. This will enhance the likelihood of successful judicial reformation as well as long-term peace and stability.[4]

At the same time, UN rule of law activities must continue to promote laws and policies that are consistent with modern human rights doctrines, international jurisprudence, and the principles enshrined in the UN Charter.[5]

Herein lies a fundamental challenge to modern peacekeeping. Experience has shown that effective and sustainable judicial rehabilitation is contingent upon strategies which respond to local needs, protect cultural traditions and prioritize national participation. Strategies fulfilling such criteria, however, are not always consistent with the standards and doctrines that the UN is legally and politically obliged to uphold. This will be particularly the case in societies with underdeveloped or non-existent legal infrastructures, that have a legacy of human rights abuse, impunity and discrimination, and that have no experience with democratic governance, an independent judiciary or the rule of law.

* Erica Harper (B.Com, LL.B. Hons) is a doctoral candidate at the Faculty of Law at the University of Melbourne, Australia. This article draws upon the author's field experience in East Timor with the United Nations (2001-2002), and a research program directed by the author (2002-2004) which investigated the effects of UN judicial reconstruction and administration on rural populations in East Timor. Ms Harper currently works at the UN High Commissioner for Refugees in Geneva.

This paper focuses upon how such disparities have, and will continue to impact upon the development of a viable legal framework in UN peacekeeping operations. Through an examination of the UN mission in East Timor,[6] it is shown that the transitional administration was unable to preserve important socio-legal customs where they were deemed to abrogate internationally accepted principles of law. Similarly, officials felt obliged to replaced 'dysfunctional' (although widely accepted) legal rules with international investigation methodology and trial procedures. The results were widespread popular dissatisfaction, a rejection of the introduced legal framework, and a marked increase in extralegal dispute resolution. Most of these problems could not have been resolved or avoided. They were the result of disparities between two distinct legal cultures, neither of which had room to compromise. In each of these situations a commitment to UN objectives and principles made an agenda driven by local needs, aspirations and customs, impossible to achieve. This dilemma will continue to frustrate the viability and sustainability of law reform activities conducted under UN auspices.[7]

## 1. The Scope of the Law

One of the first problems confronting the UN Transitional Administration in East Timor (UNTAET) was the inconsistencies between the introduced law and local norms concerning jurisdiction. The resulting discord had the potential to cause a myriad of problems. Most were avoided because the introduced legal system's lack of capacity meant that only the most serious offences could be resolved judicially. In the case of domestic violence and sexual assault offences, however, the population's strong and consistent desire to uphold the traditional jurisdictional distinction, was met with an equally strong push by the international community to maintain the rule of law.[8]

In East Timorese legal culture gender crimes fell under the jurisdiction of traditional law. However the most recent changes in western attitudes to gender crimes had not yet touched Timorese society. In some cases what would be regarded as a serious gender issue in developed countries, was seen as part of everyday life by the East Timorese. When sanctions were applied, they were mild, and seemed to be unduly supportive of male perpetrators.[9]

> 'If the incident is reported directly to the *selcom* [traditional leader] it will be resolved traditionally. Generally she will be sent back to her husband. Sometimes the husband gets a punishment, but if the *selcom* believes the wife misbehaved maybe he won't.'[10]

This situation attracted criticism from human rights and women's advocacy organisations throughout the transitional period. Such groups argued that the non-judicial resolution of such crimes violated basic human rights and that UNTAET had a responsibility to remedy the situation.[11]

In response, and in an effort to avoid further international criticism, UNTAET undertook to ensure that gender crimes were resolved according to law. Such measures included education campaigns and intervention by district human rights officers and civilian police (Civpol).

These efforts were largely ineffective. The laws continued to be rejected and the reality of the transitional period was that many, perhaps the majority of rape and domestic violence cases were resolved traditionally.[12] There were several reasons for this. First, the formal legal system was difficult to access, slow, time-consuming and costly. Respondents claimed that the time taken to resolve rape and domestic violence matters at court would cause a protracted state of intra-village conflict and non-reconciliation. The counselling and punishment delivered under traditional law, however, was immediate, making it a more effective method of resolving disputes and preventing further marital disharmony.[13]

Second, the courts, unlike the traditional system, failed to accommodate the important social and practical issues that gender crimes created. For example, in the case of a rape, prosecution did not account for the fact that because the woman had lost her virginity she may not be able to marry. As a result, she would have to largely provide for herself and any children resulting from the attack, for most of her adult life. Traditional law did take account of such consequences, either through financial compensation or by requiring that the perpetrator wed the victim.[14]

A final reason was that in Timorese legal culture, domestic violence and sexual assault were not considered to be matters worthy of judicial intervention. As 'non criminal' offences, they were to be resolved by traditional means, and to seek a resolution outside this structure was seen as a studied rejection of custom.[15]

> 'In East Timorese culture only certain types of criminals go to the police. Now under international law, every criminal has to go to the police, even where it is a family dispute, and this is no good for East Timor.'[16]

Given this situation, what, if anything could UNTAET have done to prevent the population's rejection of the law? As a UN organisation, UNTAET was bound to promote laws and policies that were consistent with modern human rights doctrines and international jurisprudence.[17] De-criminalising gender crimes or officially sanctioning their traditional resolution was not a viable option.

Responding to the issues that discouraged formal resolution was equally problematic. UNTAET would have first had to resolve the socio-economic realities that rendered formal adjudication so inappropriate. Phrased another way, if the transitional administration was to require that East Timor deal with gender crimes in the same way as western legal cultures, East Timorese society would need to take on the (relatively recent) changes, that in western societies have made the formal processing of such crimes possible. UNTAET would have had to create a modern welfare state, and an environment in which gender-neutral employment opportunities ensured that women were not financially dependant on a male breadwinner.

UNTAET would have also had to modify the way in which the East Timorese conceptualised gender crimes. Such an exercise would have been problematic from both ethical and operational perspectives. It could be argued, for example, that attempts to change the belief patterns intrinsic to East Timorese legal culture to a more 'advanced' or 'correct' set of values, amounted to cultural imperialism. Even if such ethical quandaries could have been resolved, it may have been impossible to modify such deeply entrenched norms. As UNTAET discovered, neither civic education campaigns nor directives by different elements within the international community could reverse hundreds of years of cultural indoctrination.

## 2. Introduced Procedure and Methodology

UNTAET also encountered resistance to the judicial procedures and investigation methodology imported as part of the interim legal framework. For example, a major constraint in the resolution of cases involving international crime was that investigators and prosecutors were often unable to gather sufficient evidence. Much physical evidence could not be located or had been destroyed, either purposefully or due to lengthy exposure in tropical conditions.[18] Prosecutors also had difficulty obtaining sufficient eyewitness evidence. This was primarily due to the nature of the crimes perpetrated. Most witnesses had been killed, and of those that did survive many were reluctant to give evidence. Scantly acknowledged post-traumatic stress disorders, a legitimate fear of reprisal, and the population's general mistrust of the judicial system and international workers were all contributing factors.

Finally while many militia, members of the Indonesian armed forces, police and civilian administration staff would have been able to provide evidence, most had fled to West Timor. Investigators' efforts to interview or compel testimony from such persons were largely frustrated by lack of cooperation by either the witnesses themselves or the Indonesian government.

Interestingly, the indigenous population did not conceptualise this problem in the same way as the UN legal teams. For them, the primary factor preventing the trial of suspected criminals was not insufficient evidence, but rather the evidentiary requirements of the introduced law. Some did not understand why the courts needed specific types of evidence. Those who did understand the court's requirements saw this as a flaw in the transitional legal system or in international law:

> 'The problem with this justice system is that it needs strong proof like witnesses. If there are no witnesses Civpol won't investigate as they say there is not complete evidence. It's not fair.'[19]

Clearly, what authorities saw as a defect of circumstance, the population saw as a flaw in the legal system. The real issue was hence a disparity between what the population expected and how the legal system actually operated.

This is not to say that the two positions were equally valid, and that the solution lay in appointing politically minded individuals to find some sort of 'middle ground'. In terms of western legal practice and modern scientific rationalism, the East Timorese method of determining guilt and innocence was seriously flawed. Perhaps these flaws are most succinctly explained by drawing on what is known in science as the 'Groupthink' hypothesis. The groupthink concept began its life in military psychology, and has been used to provide explanations for some of history's most destructive and incomprehensible military blunders, the most recent being inaccurate intelligence on weapons of mass destruction in Iraq. Groupthink is a well documented form of dysfunctional decision-making in which group members make decisions based on their affiliative needs rather than a logical analysis of the situation. When groupthink is operating, the decision made by the group is not the decision that the majority of the individuals would have made if they had been allowed to consider the issues free from the influence of peer pressures.[20]

The groupthink concept provides a plausible explanation for the development of a legal tradition in East Timor where outcomes were not based solely upon fact but also on shared emotions such as vengeance, fear or domination. The result was an entrenched ethic of group-based, leader-driven decision-making when justice issues were being dealt with. One consequence was the marginalisation of other forms of evidence such as eyewitness and physical. Guilt was determined by a shared sense of knowing rather than an objectively applied process such as the production of evidence sufficient to meet the burden of proof.

The introduced legal model did not share this philosophy. The law required that persons accused of serious crimes be tried in court pursuant to pre-determined rules and conditions. Where a person deemed guilty by the population could not be prosecuted because of lack of evidence, the population's facile explanation was that it was based on a 'technicality'. Not only was this result seen as highly unjust, but the whole legal system was deemed to have failed. The central problem therefore, was obviously not UNTAET's inability to gather evidence. The authorities were trying to deal with two fundamentally different concepts of justice.

As a problem borne out of differences in legal culture, there was little that the transitional administration could have done to satisfy all of the indigenous population's needs. UNTAET was bound to introduce a legal model that applied internationally accepted criminal trial principles. Recognising hearsay, a defective and unjust form of legal reasoning, might have been illegal[21] as well as politically untenable.

Nor, it is argued, could the transitional administration have altered the situation in any meaningful way. It was not part of the transitional government's mandate to impose a 'more advanced' culture upon the existing one, even when the 'more advanced' viewpoint was supported by scientific research. Further, experience has shown that cultural change takes place slowly, and is almost always initiated from within society.

## 3. Facilitating Cultural Imperatives

A final problem encountered during the UNTAET period was that the introduced system of law prevented, or otherwise frustrated the realisation of cultural imperatives. Certain locally held beliefs, rituals and customs were perceived by the transitional administration to be discriminatory or inconsistent with basic standards of human rights. The outlawing of such customary practices had serious social ramifications, the most salient example being the administration's attempts to prevent traditional reconciliation ceremonies.

Under traditional law, disputes in East Timor were resolved through a hierarchy of five problem solving fora. After a solution was agreed upon by all parties, a reconciliation ceremony would be held. The importance of reconciliation was found to be closely related to how the East Timorese conceptualised wrongs. Wrongs were not looked upon in terms of the actual injury or loss sustained. Instead, they were conceived in terms of the perpetrator's lack of respect for the victim. The gravity of the incident or the magnitude of the loss was largely immaterial: 'He could steal twenty cows or one chicken, it is the same wrong, it says "I do not respect you".'[22]

As such, simply compensating a victim for their loss, or 'righting the wrong', was insufficient to resolve a conflict. What the victim ultimately looked for was a symbol of the perpetrator's regret, one which showed that the perpetrator respected the victim and had accepted responsibility for their wrong. These needs were satisfied particularly through the perpetrator's provision of alcohol and/or animals to be consumed at the ceremony. Providing nourishment was perceived as evidence to the victim, the community and to the ancestors, that the perpetrator had committed a wrong, had acknowledged that wrong and had restored the victim's respect.

The ceremony also had religious significance. It was believed that the ceremony broke down the barriers separating the present life and the afterlife, providing the living with a unique opportunity to connect with their ancestors. The ceremony was thus a collective act of contrition, symbolising the community's regret for displeasing their ancestors, a request for forgiveness and a rekindling of clan-ancestral unity.[23]

The reconciliation ceremony, however, was not incorporated into the interim legal model. As a result, the formal legal process was insufficient to fully resolve disputes. Moreover, from a cultural perspective, the process was considered profane. So unacceptable was this situation that communities simply held their own reconciliation ceremonies, tweaking the introduced legal model to make it compatible with their own legal and cultural needs.

For some of the lawyers within the transitional administration, this constituted a profound problem. Based on concerns that reconciliation ceremonies amounted to 'double jeopardy', steps were taken to ensure that such practices either did not take place, or were conducted in a manner that did not abrogate international legal standards.[24]

> 'We have a way to get peace that works for us, but the UNTAET human rights officer said that now there is a different system and we cannot do a reconciliation ceremony.'[25]

The double jeopardy issue arose because of the animals and/or alcohol that the perpetrator provided for the reconciliation ceremony. UNTAET lawyers believed that this 'fine' constituted a double punishment (a sanction in addition to that imposed at the judicial level) and hence violated the principle of *ne bis in idem*.

However moves to prevent reconciliation ceremonies were aggressively opposed. For the East Timorese, their need for reconciliation outweighed the injustice of double punishment. It was not even clear that the population saw this as an injustice. Most importantly, the power of the reconciliation ceremony in East Timorese society was so great that any steps taken by the traditional authority to eliminate or regulate reconciliation ceremonies proved largely ineffective.

## 4. Conclusion

From the East Timor experience it is clear that a major stumbling block to developing a sustainable and popularly acceptable legal system, was the lack of compatibility between the legal values and norms inherent in East Timorese legal culture, and those the UN was required to apply.

A further important observation is that where problems were rooted in value and norm incompatibility, these problems were difficult to either avoid or resolve. Many believed that the administration was legally compelled to uphold international law, and feared the political repercussions that a tolerance of domestic norms might have attracted. Others felt that creating a legal culture based on democratic ideals and human rights was more important than a culturally sensitive approach to judicial rehabilitation, even if this was inconsistent with local desires. Such rationale was well founded. UNTAET did come under aggressive and well-publicised criticism when it was perceived to be 'overlooking' the traditional resolution of gender crimes. There was also a strong argument that had officials condoned reconciliation ceremonies, or not applied modern rules of evidence, they would have abrogated UNTAET Regulation 1999/1.

The alternate option – modifying the values of the East Timorese so as to correspond more closely with those imported – was equally problematic. Active attempts to displace a population's beliefs with those from another legal culture would have generated a multitude of ethical and political ramifications. Not the least of these would have been accusations of paternalism and cultural imperialism. Further, it has been argued that many such values were so deeply entrenched and played such important social, spiritual and economic roles in Timorese society, that any attempt to displace them would have been ineffective.

The critical point is that even if it had been UNTAET's intention, constructing a justice system that reflected local aspirations and concerns was not a legal or political possibility. This is likely to be the case in other UN operations. It is therefore unclear how the recommendations contained in the Secretary General's Report are to be implemented. Specifically, if peacekeeping operations are to apply a locally-driven approach to judicial rehabilitation, how will UN authorities resolve incompatibilities between what local populations want, and the principles enshrined in international jurisprudence?

It is unlikely that the UN will relax its standards and tolerate practices and behaviours that are inconsistent with the very standards it is mandated to protect. At the same time, the societies in which judicial rehabilitation is most likely to be necessary will continue to have legal cultures, belief structures and/or economic realities that make a 'UN'ese' legal model inappropriate or ineffective.

Does this mean that where there is incompatibility in terms of legal principles introduced, and such incompatibility cannot be resolved due to mandatory, ethical or feasibility restrictions, that transitional jurisprudential modelling is destined to fail? Not necessarily so. In certain cases there will be solutions that respond to the needs of the population whilst still allowing a UN body to remain within its legal and geopolitical boundaries.

For example in East Timor, UNTAET might have eliminated some of the economic barriers to the judicial resolution of gender crimes by allowing the courts to impose monetary sanctions, hence providing victims with what communities regarded as necessary compensation. Similarly, UNTAET could have removed the double jeopardy aspect of traditional reconciliation ceremonies by incorporating the 'fine' payable by the perpetrator into the sanction imposed by the court.[26] Without explicitly supporting or opposing the system, courts could have acknowledged the reality of traditional dispute resolution. Judges could have taken into account traditional sanctions already imposed, and the administration could have encouraged indigenous leaders to take account of punishments effected at the formal level.[27]

Of course, some problems would have remained. Dominant legal values relating to the nature of evidence, proof and investigatory standards were the result of centuries of occupation and will perhaps take generations to be reversed. Despite this, UNTAET could not have arrested or convicted persons simply because the population 'believed' they were guilty. Likewise, the construction of an operational welfare state and an economic environment where women could obtain financial independence might have facilitated the formal resolution of gender crimes. The creation of such an environment, however, would have taken far longer than UNTAET's 32 months in power. Problems such as these may be the inevitable concomitants of exercises in post-conflict judicial administration.

In conclusion, the UN's recent experiences in designing, constructing and applying justice systems in post-conflict states provide important insights into the nature of transitional jurisprudential modelling, the problems that might arise, and whether or not solutions exist. It is clear, for example, that judicial rehabilitation will be most successful and sustainable where it responds to local needs, protects cultural traditions and prioritizes national decision-making. The Secretary General acknowledged as much in his Report on *The Rule of Law and Transitional Justice in Conflict and Post-Conflict Societies.* It is also evident that the primary impediment to such an approach will be incompatibilities between the UN's own legal culture and that of the states it is trying to assist. Until this anomaly is resolved, peacekeeping missions will continue to find themselves confined by their own rules, and unable to deliver a measure of justice that is completely acceptable to a population.

This is not to say that the Report's recommendations are not useful. The East Timor example plainly illustrates why the UN must look to national constituencies and the population at large when deciding upon the mix of legal mechanisms that will best suit the nature of the conflict, the existing legal culture, and the society's political and socio-economic context. More effective local consultation, empowerment and capacity building constitute important first steps to realising these goals. Where such an agenda is blocked by the UN's institutional mandate, new strategies should be developed that allow transitional administrations – legally, ethically and politically – to respond to the unique needs of the target society. Such an approach will involve a thorough examination of each administration's obligations, and more concentrated efforts in identifying and understanding the essential elements of the domestic legal tradition. Finally, when local needs or expectations cannot be met, authorities must look to how a population is most likely to respond. Will the situation beget revenge crimes, or will discontent dissipate over time? Again, this will be a function of the legal culture in question. What is certain, however, is that future transitional administrations will have to become more generally aware of issues relating to legal-cultural disparity, and be prepared to act in response as they materialise.

## Notes

1 J.C. Beauvais, 'Benevolent Despotism: A Critique of UN State-Building in East Timor', 33 *New York U J of Intl Law and Politics* (2001), pp. 1101, 1148-1150.
2 UNSC, 'Report of the Secretary General on the Rule of Law and Transitional Justice in Conflict and Post-Conflict Societies', (2004) UN Doc S/2004/616 [11].
3 Ibid.
4 Ibid. [15-18].
5 Ibid. [9-10].
6 Note that this paper will use the county name 'East Timor' as opposed 'Timor Leste' in the interests of enhanced readability.
7 For more information on UNTAET and its legal mandate see UNSC Res. 1272 (25 October 1999) UN Doc. S/RES/1272 [1]-[3]; UNGA, 'Report of the Panel on United Nations Peace Operations', UN GAOR 55th Session UN Doc. A/55/305–S/2000/809 [79]-[80].
8 Under the domestic legal culture, there was a distinction drawn between 'criminal' and 'non-criminal' offences. 'Non-criminal' offences (including domestic violence, minor theft, physical assault, land and property disputes, marital and dowry disputes, and sexual assault) fell within the jurisdiction of traditional law. 'Criminal' disputes (including arson, political crimes, murder and intent to murder) were considered to be the formal legal system's responsibility.
9 UNTAET Human Rights Unit (Report) (20 June 2001) 8; letter from Deputy Chief of Operations Civpol Headquarters to Civpol Community Policing Headquarters (12 February 2001) 5-6.
10 E. Harper, interview with East Timorese civilian (Covalima, East Timor 23 August 2003). Note that identities have been withheld in all references to interviews conducted by the author pending publication of Ph.D. dissertation, research under which was conducted subject to ethics and confidentiality agreements.
11 E. Harper, interview with expatriate UNTAET employee (Dili, East Timor 18 June 2003); Amnesty International, *East Timor: Justice Past, Present and Future* (Report) (July 2001) AI-Index ASA 57/001/2001; 40-41.
12 E. Harper, interview with expatriate civilian police officer (Covalima, East Timor 22 June 2003); letter from Deputy Chief of Operations Civpol Headquarters to Civpol Community Policing Headquarters (12 February 2001).
13 Letter from Deputy Chief of Operations Civpol Headquarters to Civpol Community Policing Headquarters (12 February 2001) 5.
14 E. Harper, interview with East Timorese civilian (Covalima, East Timor 23 August 2003). Prosecuting perpetrators of domestic violence often had similar unintended ramifications. As one village leader explained, when the perpetrator of such crimes is arrested and removed from the village there are 'serious consequences that the police just do not see'. In the short-term the victim suffers because her husband has been arrested or is in jail. In the long-term (because when the perpetrator returns to the village he will most likely take another wife) she will have no one to support her or her family. With no operational welfare system the victim and her children become the communal responsibility of the village. The result is resentment of, and hostility towards the victim and her children, social disunity and widespread confusion regarding the logic of the formal legal process. E. Harper, interview with East Timorese traditional leader (Covalima, East Timor 12 August 2003).
15 E. Harper, interview with East Timorese traditional leader (Covalima, East Timor 7 July 2003); UNTAET (n. 9) 8; Letter from Deputy Chief of Operations Civpol Headquarters to Civpol Community Policing Headquarters (12 February 2001) 5; Amnesty International (n. 11) 40-41.
16 E. Harper, interview with East Timorese traditional leader (Covalima, East Timor 2 June 2003).
17 Under UNTAET Regulation 1999/1 (1999) ss 2-3, the laws applied in East Timor could not conflict with internationally recognised human rights standards and all staff were obliged to observe such standards.
18 E. Harper, interview with expatriate UNTAET employee (Covalima, East Timor 10 May 2003). UNGA, 'Question of East Timor', UN GAOR 54th Session UN Doc. A/54/726, S/2000/59 [134].
19 E. Harper, interview with East Timorese civilian (Covalima, East Timor 6 July 2003).
20 C.V. Ford, *Lies Lies, Lies: The Psychology of Deceit* (American Psychiatric Press Inc 1996) pp. 258-260.
21 UNTAET (n. 17).
22 E. Harper, interview with East Timorese civilian (Covalima, East Timor 17 August 2003).
23 For more information on traditional law in East Timor, see D.C.B. Soares, 'A Brief Overview of the Role of Customary Law in East Timor' (paper presented at Symposium on East Timor, Indonesia and the Region, Lisbon 2001) 39; letter from Judicial Affairs Officer Manatuto to Member of Cabinet in Charge of Justice (24 September 2000); Diocesan Justice and Peace Commission, *Grass-Root Reconciliation Process in the Aileu Parish*

(Report) (2001); M. Angelina, Kadalak Sulimutuk Institute, *Community Based Pastoral Reconciliation* (Report) (2000); S. Ospina and T. Hohe, UNTAET Political Affairs Unit, *Traditional Power Structures and the Community Empowerment and Local Governance Project* (Report) (2001) 58-65; A.B. Da Silva, Kadalak Sulimutuk Institute, *Nahe Biti and Popular Demand for Justice* (Report) (2000).

24 See, e.g., Art. 14.7 of *The International Covenant on Civil and Political Rights* (1966); E. Harper, interview with expatriate UNTAET employee (Covalima, East Timor 11 July 2003).

25 Interview with Alias ET-TRAD (Covalima, East Timor 6 July 2003).

26 This certainly would have been possible in civil cases where damages are awarded, and may have been possible in certain criminal cases. A problem would have remained when the accused had been found innocent, but it could be argued that what happened after that was not a matter for the court.

27 UNTAET could have followed the lead of other western jurisdictions facing this issue. For example in the Northern Territory, Australia, courts have been increasingly empowered to take into account punishments that have or will be imposed upon indigenous suspects under Aboriginal law. D. Mearns, Australian Legal Resources International, *Looking Both Ways: Models for Justice in East Timor* (Report) (2002) 16; Northern Territory Law Reform Committee, *Report on Aboriginal Customary Law* (Report of the Committee of Inquiry into Aboriginal Customary Law) (2003).

# Remarks by William A. Schabas*

## The Sierra Leone Truth and Reconciliation Commission and the Special Court for Sierra Leone

Truth and reconciliation commissions have become one of the standard options on the palette of transitional justice alternatives. They stand as something of a half-way house between extreme approaches towards accountability for past atrocities and other human rights violations. The truth and reconciliation commission does not 'forgive and forget', because it is predicated on public truth-telling, but nor does it insist upon rigorous prosecution by criminal justice mechanisms. The South African model is probably the best known, although it had some atypical features, such as the power to recommend amnesty to perpetrators who made full confession of their deeds.[1]

The Sierra Leone Truth and Reconciliation Commission was established in July 2002. It presented its final report to the President of Sierra Leone on 5 October 2004. The actual operations of the Commission, consisting of both private and public encounters with victims and perpetrators, public hearings on thematic issues, and other research and investigation took only about eight months, however. The report provided Sierra Leone with a detailed narrative of the country's history, with a focus on the brutal civil war of the 1990s, analysis of various dimensions of political, economic and social life with a view to understanding the causes of the conflict, and a series of findings and recommendations.

Perhaps the most distinctive feature of post-conflict justice in Sierra Leone has been the parallel existence of an international criminal justice mechanism, the Special

* Professor of Human Rights Law, National University of Ireland, Galway, and Director, Irish Centre for Human Rights; <william.schabas@nuigalway.ie>. The author was a member of the Sierra Leone Truth and Reconciliation Commission. This article is written in his private capacity and does not necessarily reflect the views of the other commissioners or of the Commission.

Court for Sierra Leone. Traditionally, truth and reconciliation commissions have been viewed as an alternative to criminal justice that, sometimes only in an informal manner, obviates or at the very least suspends prosecutions. In Sierra Leone, the two institutions operated contemporaneously. This unprecedented experiment revealed some of the tensions that may exist between the two approaches. Yet it also demonstrated the feasibility of the simultaneous operation of an international court and a truth commission. The Sierra Leone experience may help us understand that post-conflict justice requires a complex mix of complementary therapies, rather than a unique choice of one approach from a list of essentially incompatible alternatives.

## Creation and Mandate of the Truth and Reconciliation Commission

Sierra Leone's civil war began on 23 March 1991, when forces styling themselves the Revolutionary United Front (RUF) raided the town of Bombali, which is near the northern border with Liberia. The declared objective of the RUF was to overthrow the corrupt and tyrannical government of Joseph Saidu Momoh and the All People's Congress (APC), which had ruled Sierra Leone since the late 1960s. The events that day were little more than a skirmish, but they heralded the beginning of a decade of violence that devastated the country. If the aims of the RUF might have been shared by many in Sierra Leone, who were frustrated by years of dictatorship, and by the descending spiral of poverty and underdevelopment that characterised the country since its independence from British colonialism in 1961, the war soon lost the veneer of any legitimate aspirations. Not only the RUF, but also both its allies and opponents, indulged in tactics of the utmost brutality.[2]

A promising attempt to resolve the conflict, reached at Abidjan, Côte d'Ivoire in late 1996, and brokered by various international actors including the United Nations,[3] soon broke down and conflict resumed. The climactic conclusion was a devastating attack on the capital in January 1999, chillingly labelled 'Operation No Living Thing'. With Freetown in ruins, the government sued for peace. The formal beginning of the end of the conflict was the *Lomé Peace Agreement* of 7 July 1999, between the Government of Sierra Leone and the Revolutionary United Front of Sierra Leone.[4] The agreement provided a controversial amnesty, sometimes also referred to as a pardon or reprieve, for perpetrators of atrocities on all sides of the conflict.[5] The Special Representative of the Secretary-General of the United Nations, Francis Okelo, formulated a reservation to the amnesty provision, insisting that it could not apply to crimes against humanity and war crimes.[6]

The *Lomé Peace Agreement* pledged the establishment of a Truth and Reconciliation Commission (TRC), to be set-up within ninety days. Although efforts were soon directed to this task,[7] legislation for the purpose was not adopted by Sierra Leone's Parliament until 22 February 2000.[8] Pursuant to section 6(1) of the *Truth and Reconciliation Commission Act 2000*, the Sierra Leone TRC was established

> 'to create an impartial historical record of violations and abuses of human rights and international humanitarian law related to the armed conflict in Sierra Leone, from the beginning of the Conflict in 1991 to the signing of the *Lomé Peace Agreement*; to address impunity, to respond to

> the needs of the victims, to promote healing and reconciliation and to prevent a repetition of the violations and abuses suffered'.

Although a national institution, the TRC had an international dimension because of the participation of the Special Representative of the Secretary-General for Sierra Leone and the High Commissioner for Human Rights in its establishment.[9] Virtually all of the financing for the Commission came from international donors, with the Office of the High Commissioner assuming the responsibility for fund-raising. Initially budgeted at $10 million,[10] poor donor response resulted in a reduction to less than $7 million. In the end, the TRC received approximately $4 million, a disappointing result that seems to indicate an indifference to its mission, despite grand statements to the contrary.[11]

The work of the TRC consisted of two principal phases. The first, described as the 'statement taking phase', began in December 2002. Approximately seventy 'statement takers' were recruited throughout the country. Most were drawn from various sectors of civil society, such as NGOs and religious institutions. Attention was paid to ensuring that a significant percentage of the statement takers were women. Fluency in local languages was one of the main criteria in the hiring of statement takers. The statement taking proceeded until March 2003. Approximately 7,000 statements, mainly from victims but with a not unsubstantial number of perpetrators, were compiled. The statements were analysed in order to identify 'window cases', that is, representative statements that served to illustrate important aspects of the conflict. All of the statements were also coded and entered into a computerised data base for the purpose of statistical analysis.

The second phase, known as the 'hearings phase', began in April 2003 and continued until early August 2003, concluding with a rather unsatisfactory performance by President Tejan Kabbah. In contrast with all of the other leaders of various factions in the conflict, Kabbah refused to acknowledge any responsibility or to apologise to the people of Sierra Leone for his own role in the conflict. It was an unfortunate ending to the process, and a bad omen for the follow-up to the work of the Commission

Many of the hearings brought together victims and perpetrators for what were often quite dramatic exchanges, and the occasional public reconciliation. These hearings were held throughout the country, often in isolated towns that were only accessible by helicopter. Other hearings focused on thematic issues, such as the media, the legal profession, governance and corruption. In parallel with these quite public activities, the Commission also undertook a more discrete programme of research and investigation. Here it was terribly handicapped by poor resources. This part of the Commission's work is a story of missed opportunities, although the existing staff performed honourable and produced results of good quality.

The final phase of the Commission's work, namely the drafting of the report, took more than a year. The Commission spent more time writing up its results than it did in the operational phase of its mandate. The delays were partly the result of staffing shortages, and also the consequence of an overly ambitious vision of the report. It was decided that the report should be several volumes in length, perhaps so as to match that of the South African Commission. A shorter and more succinct report would have been far more accessible to Sierra Leoneans, and yet could have covered all of the essentials.

## The TRC and the Special Court

Perhaps the most distinctive aspect of the Sierra Leone transitional justice programme was the parallel existence of a truth and reconciliation commission and an international criminal tribunal.[12] This was not part of a master plan, but rather the result of circumstances subsequent to the decision to establish the TRC. A renewal of fighting in May 2000 stalled the creation of the TRC, but also revived debate about the legitimacy of the amnesty. The Government of Sierra Leone reassessed its position with respect to the amnesty, and requested that the United Nations establish a special tribunal. On 14 August 2000, the Security Council supported the creation of a court to try 'persons who bear the greatest responsibility' for serious violations of international humanitarian law and the laws of Sierra Leone, and mandated the Secretary-General to negotiate an agreement with the government of Sierra Leone to this effect.[13] Like the TRC, this too took some time to materialise, and it was only in January 2002 that the United Nations and the Government of Sierra Leone reached formal agreement on the project.[14] In April 2002, the *Special Court Agreement (Ratification) Act 2002* was adopted to enable the effective operation of the Court and to implement Sierra Leone's commitments under the agreement with the United Nations.

The Special Court is an international organisation in its own right, created by treaty between the Government of Sierra Leone and the United Nations.[15] Institutionally, it largely resembles the *ad hoc* Tribunals for the former Yugoslavia and Rwanda, although the latter were created by the Security Council and are therefore blessed with the international enforcement powers that this entails. Like the TRC, the Special Court is funded by voluntary contributions from international donors, and its budget has also been scaled down from an amount that originally exceeded $100 million to about $56 million over three years. There is no prescribed life-span for the Court, but it is not expected that trials will continue much beyond the three-year period. While the Special Court may deliver 'truth-seeking', 'catharsis', 'expiation of guilt' and so on, its mission is essentially punitive:

> 'to prosecute persons who bear the greatest responsibility for serious violations of international humanitarian law and Sierra Leonean law committed in the territory of Sierra Leone since 30 November 1996, including those leaders who, in committing such crimes, have threatened the establishment of and implementation of the peace process in Sierra Leone'.[16]

In a letter to the Security Council in 2001, as the Court's legal framework was still being negotiated, Kofi Annan said that 'care must be taken to ensure that the Special Court for Sierra Leone and the Truth and Reconciliation Commission will operate in a complementary and mutually supportive manner, fully respectful of their distinct but related functions'.[17] Once it became clear that the two institutions would operate in parallel, there was intense speculation about how they might interact. Those who were suspicious of truth commissions and oriented towards criminal prosecution, saw the opportunity to marginalise the TRC, subordinating it to the Court as a kind of investigative arm or grand jury. For example, Amnesty International wrote that the TRC's 'contribution to ending impunity is likely to be extremely weak or non-existent'. Furthermore, it recommended that

> 'the government of Sierra Leone and the international community should acknowledge that, while the TRC may be able to make an important contribution to establishing the truth about human rights abuses and understanding the nature of the conflict in Sierra Leone, it should not be a substitute for prosecuting those responsible for serious crimes under international law'.[18]

Those who favoured restorative justice approaches responded by insisting upon the relevance of a strong and dynamic TRC as a complement to prosecution.

In addition to UN-sponsored meetings, some international NGOs developed some rather elaborate proposals on the type of provisions that might be governed by a relationship agreement. Although there was consideration of the possibility of joint or common efforts at witness protection, translation and public awareness, most of the reflection on how the two bodies might cooperate tended to dwell on what was called 'information sharing', something the December expert meeting had agreed was a 'difficult issue'.

In the result, there was never any agreement between the two bodies, nor was there any information sharing. Neither institution showed any interest in cooperation. Both seemed to value polite, neighbourly relations, and nothing more. The Prosecutor of the Special Court, David Crane, very helpfully declared that he was not interested in seeking information from the TRC, a move that may have reassured some perpetrators who were concerned that any information they might provide to the Commission would be used to build a case against them at the Special Court.

After the TRC had concluded its public hearings, in August 2003, some detainees of the Special Court asked to give public testimony to the TRC. Even more surprisingly, the Prosecutor then opposed the initiatives taken by the TRC with a view to facilitating such public hearings. A ruling by the Court's President, Geoffrey Robertson, allowed defendants to appear before the Commission, but did not authorise a public hearing.[19] Deprived of the platform they had been seeking, the defendants ultimately refused to cooperate with the TRC. Unfortunately, the tensions generated by this litigation left a sour taste in relations between the TRC and the Special Court. In reality, it was little more than an incident in what had been an essentially serene relationship.

The issue of testimony by Special Court detainees might have been addressed from the standpoint of a division of labour between the two institutions. There had been suggestions that the TRC would, in effect, concern itself with the 'small fish' while the Court focussed on the 'big fish'. There was certainly no doubt that the Court's mandate was confined to 'those who bear the greatest responsibility', something spelled out explicitly in Article 1 of its Statute. During establishment of the Court, the Security Council had stressed that it would be preferable for juvenile offenders to be dealt with by the TRC, perhaps suggesting that the Council understood the relationship between the two bodies as involving some sort of identification of distinct spheres of interest.[20] But in pursuing the testimony of alleged offenders being held in custody by the Special Court, the Commission demonstrated that it considered even the 'big fish' to fall within its own terms of reference. Indeed, how could it be otherwise, given that the TRC was tasked with preparing an historical record of the conflict, something that necessarily involved a consideration of the role of the principal participants.

## CONCLUSION

Observers in the field continue to report that people in Sierra Leone are confused about the distinctions between the two bodies. This is presented as a problem, for which the solution proposed is further campaigns of sensitisation. Yet confusion about the mandates and functions of these two bodies would seem to be not only inevitable but quite natural and understandable. After all, most European law students have trouble explaining the distinctions between the European Court of Human Rights and the European Court of Justice. The average citizen of the United States would be challenged to distinguish between the Chief Justice of the Supreme Court and the Attorney-General. Who can really expect uneducated, illiterate peasants in the countryside of Sierra Leone to do better? Perhaps the 'confusion' about the two bodies is proof of success, not failure. To the extent that the people of Sierra Leone understand that the two bodies exist, and that they have some shared objectives, such as accountability for human rights violations, then the message has been delivered and 'sensitisation' achieved.

Sierra Leone has provided the evolving discipline of transitional justice with a laboratory in which to examine how the two bodies, special 'internationalised' courts and truth commissions, relate to each other. As experience has now shown, much of the speculation about potential problems and relationships proved to be somewhat wide of the mark. The relevance of this work to other post-conflict justice situations cannot be underestimated. Virtually everywhere, the two concepts have their promoters, although they are often presented in the alternative. Sierra Leone demonstrated that the relationship is rather more synergistic than many might have thought. The complexities of the matter are well illustrated in the saga of attempts to establish a truth commission for Bosnia and Herzegovina, and the evolving view of the International Criminal Tribunal for the former Yugoslavia from one of virtual opposition[21] to one that might be characterised as benign tolerance.[22] These issues are likely to be at the top of the agenda of the Prosecutor of the new International Criminal Court as he wrestles with the adequacy of domestic responses to atrocity in assessing the potential admissibility of cases under Article 17 of the Rome Statute.[23] Perhaps the unfolding practice in Sierra Leone will convince him of the usefulness of a genuinely complementary approach, by which international prosecution co-exists with alternative accountability mechanisms, rather than the context of antagonism and confrontation that many observers expect.

Although there had been some discussion within Sierra Leone about the importance of a truth commission prior to its establishment, the idea was obviously borrowed from elsewhere. It seems open to question whether Sierra Leone would have organised a truth commission had this not been promoted and encouraged by the 'international community'. If the United Nations had insisted that Sierra Leone contribute a reasonable proportion of the costs of the venture, it would probably never have seen the light of day. Sierra Leone is an extremely poor country, and it could never have been expected to shoulder a large part of the expense of a truth commission. Still, the insignificant participation in the TRC's funding by Sierra Leone and by Sierra Leoneans can only have affected negatively the sense of ownership. Sierra Leone is a graveyard to wonderful international initiatives, established by generous funders, which are left abandoned and decaying when the foreign support concludes. Why should the TRC be any different?

With the presentation of its report, the Commission formally went out of existence. The *Truth and Reconciliation Act 2000* provided for follow-up mechanisms, to ensure that the recommendations are implemented. It seems likely that the real successor of the Commission may be the new Human Rights Commission, which will be a permanent institution. The Truth and Reconciliation Commission has fulfilled its general objectives, and it seems likely that the Special Court will do the same. The problem is not with the viability of the transitional justice institutions, but with the limited nature of the overall transition within Sierra Leone. A useful comparison can be made with South Africa, where the transitional justice institutions were part of a much broader social transformation, driven by an extremely dynamic civil society. Sierra Leone lags far behind South Africa in this respect. And this sad conclusion inevitably limits the potential of the Sierra Leone Truth and Reconciliation Commission to influence the future of this troubled country.

## Notes

1 Alex Boraine, *A Country Unmasked* (Oxford, Oxford University Press 2000).

2 See, for background: Paul Richards, *Fighting for the Rain Forest: War, Youth and Resources in Sierra Leone* (Portsmouth, N.H., Heinemann, 1996; Oxford, James Currey 1998).

3 Peace Agreement between the Government of the Republic of Sierra Leone and the Revolutionary United Front of Sierra Leone (RUF), 30 November 1996.

4 For discussion of the legal status of the agreement, see *Prosecutor* v. *Kallon* et al. (Case Nos. SCSL-2004-15 and 16-AR72(E)), Decision on Challenge to Jurisdiction (Lomé Accord Amnesty), 13 March 2004.

5 *Peace Agreement between the Government of Sierra Leone and the Revolutionary United Front of Sierra Leone*, Lomé, 7 July 1999, Art. IX. See K. Gallagher, 'No Justice, No Peace: The Legalities and Realities of Amnesty in Sierra Leone', (2000) 23 *T. Jefferson L. Rev.* 149; Daniel Macaluso, 'Absolute and Free Pardon: The Effect of the Amnesty Provision in the Lome Peace Agreement on the Jurisdiction of the Special Court for Sierra Leone', (2001) 27 *Brooklyn J. Int'l L.* 347.

6 UN Doc. S/1999/836.

7 Richard Bennett, 'The Evolution of the Sierra Leone Truth and Reconciliation Commission', in *Truth and Reconciliation in Sierra Leone*, UNAMSIL: Freetown, 2001, pp. 37-51.

8 *Truth and Reconciliation Commission Act 2000*, Supplement to the Sierra Leone Gazette Vol. CXXXI, No. 9.

9 *Truth and Reconciliation Commission Act 2000*, s. 3.

10 'Fourteenth report of the Secretary-General on the United Nations Mission in Sierra Leone', S/2002/679, para. 27.

11 As a result of inadequate financial resources, many of the activities that had been planned have had to be scaled down or simply eliminated. The TRC did not have the robust team of internationally-qualified researchers and investigators, with vehicles, travel funds and other appropriate resources, that had been planned and expected. Because of funding and cash flow issues, salaries were often left unpaid for unacceptably long periods, with obvious consequences in terms of employee morale.

12 For more detailed discussion of the relationship between the two bodies, see William A. Schabas, 'The Relationship Between Truth Commissions and International Courts: The Case of Sierra Leone', (2003) 25 *Human Rights Quarterly* 1035; William A. Schabas, 'A Synergistic Relationship: The Sierra Leone Truth and Reconciliation Commission and the Special Court for Sierra Leone', in William A. Schabas and Shane Darcy (eds.), *Truth Commissions and Courts, The Tension Between Criminal Justice and the Search for Truth* (Dordrecht: Kluwer Academic Publishing 2004), pp. 3-54; Abdul Tejan-Cole, 'The Complementary and Conflicting Relationship Between the Special Court for Sierra Leone and the Truth and Reconciliation Commission', (2003) 6 *Yale Human Rights & Development Law Journal* 139.

13 UN Doc. S/RES/2000/1315. On the Court, there is now a considerable literature: Micaela Frulli, 'The

Special Court for Sierra Leone: Some Preliminary Comments', (2000) 11 *Eur. J. Int'l L.* 857; Robert Cryer, 'A 'special court' for Sierra Leone?', (2001) 50 *Int'l & Comp. L. Q.* 435; Suzannah Linton, 'Cambodia, East Timor and Sierra Leone: Experiments in International Justice', (2001) 12 *Crim. L. Forum* 185; Avril McDonald, 'Sierra Leone's Shoestring Special Court', (2002) 84 *Int'l Rev. Red Cross* 121; S. Beresford & A.S. Muller, 'The Special Court for Sierra Leone: An Initial Comment', (2001) 14 *Leiden J. Int'l L.* 635; Melron C. Nicol-Wilson, 'Accountability for Human Rights Abuses: The United Nations' Special Court for Sierra Leone', [2001] *Australian Int'l L.J.* 159; Celina Schocken, 'The Special Court for Sierra Leone: Overview and Recommendations', (2002) 20 *Berkeley J. Int'l L.* 436; Abdul Tejan Cole, 'The Special Court for Sierra Leone', (2002) 14 *Interights Bulletin* 37-39; J. Cerone, 'The Special Court for Sierra Leone: Establishing a New Approach to International Criminal Justice', (2002) 8 *ILSA J. Int'l & Comp. L.* 379; Nicole Fritz and Alison Smith, 'Current Apathy for Coming Anarchy: Building the Special Court for Sierra Leone, (2001) 25 *Fordham Int'l L.J.* 391; C. Denis, 'Le Tribunal special pour la Sierra Leone – Quelques discussions', [2001] *Revue belge de droit international* 236; Marissa Miraldi, 'Overcoming Obstacles of Justice: The Special Court of Sierra Leone', (2003) 19 *N.Y.L. Sch. J. Hum. Rts.* 849; D.M. Amann, 'Calling Children to Account: The Proposal for a Juvenile Chamber in the Special Court for Sierra Leone', (2002) 29 *Pepp. L. Rev.* 167.

14 The establishment of the Court is discussed in some detail in *Prosecutor* v. *Kallon* et al. (Case Nos. SCSL-2004-15, 16 and 17-AR72-E), Decision on Constitutionality and Lack of Jurisdiction, 13 March 2004.

15 *Agreement between the United Nations and the Government of Sierra Leone on the Establishment of a Special Court for Sierra Leone*, Freetown, 16 January 2002.

16 Ibid., Art. I(1).

17 'Letter dated 12 January 2001 from the Secretary-General addressed to the President of the Security Council', UN Doc. S/2001/40, para. 9.

18 'Sierra Leone: Renewed Commitment to End Impunity', AI index: AFR 51/007/2001, 24 September 2001.

19 *Prosecutor* v. *Norman* (Case No. SCSL-2003-08-PT), Decision on Appeal by the Truth and Reconciliation Commission for Sierra Leone ('TRC' or 'The Commission') and Chief Samuel Hinga Norman JP Against the Decision of His Lordship, Mr Justice Bankole Thompson Delivered on 30 October 2003 to Deny the TRC's Request to Hold a Public Hearing With Chief Samuel Hinga Norman JP, 28 November 2003.

20 'Letter dated 22 December 2000 from the President of the Security Council to the Secretary-General', UN Doc. S/2000/1234, p. 1.

21 'Fifth annual report of the International Tribunal for the Prosecution of Persons Responsible for Serious Violations of International Humanitarian Law Committed in the Territory of the Former Yugoslavia since 1991', 27 July 1998, UN Doc. A/53/219 - S/1998/737, annex, para. 225.

22 See, for example, the speech of then-President Claude Jorda of 12 May 2001 delivered in Sarajevo, of which the full text is contained in the Press release of 17 May 2001, JL/P.I.S./591-e, available at <www.un.org/icty>, under 'Latest developments', in the folder 'Archived Press Releases'.

23 *Rome Statute of the International Criminal Court*, UN Doc. A/CONF.183/9. The parameters of prosecutorial discretion in this area are set out in Art. 53 of the *Statute*. For an overview of the *Statute*, see William A. Schabas, *Introduction to the International Criminal Court*, 2nd edn. (Cambridge, Cambridge University Press 2003).

## Discussion

Kathleen Paisley:* Question for all: Ms. Harper said it would have been illegitimate for the UN to restrict its scope to international crimes. This seems counter-intuitive to me. Why should the UN not restrict itself to the most serious issues and leave other issues, like gender crimes, to the domestic system? Why take on everything and therefore potentially fail or not do as well as one could with respect to certain issues?

Rumu Sarkar:** Question for Schabas: The Lomé Peace agreement granted am-

* Brussels based lawyer.

** General Counsel Overseas Basing Commission, Washington D.C.

nesty in Sierra Leone. Why was that done as matter of law and did that have the tendency to moot out the work of the Truth and Reconciliation Commission and the Special Court?

JAN ERIK WETZEL:* Comment to Schabas: Maybe the distinction between judicial institutions (SC-SL) and non-judicial institutions (TRC) needs to be clear where no national justice system exists and basic functions of the rule of law still have to be explained.

Question for Harper: What is your experience of the cooperation between the TRC and judicial institutions in East Timor, especially since the UN is now investigating whether they should to do both in Burundi?

THE PANEL:

HARPER: The UN had to set-up both an ordinary crime structure and a serious crime structure. The serious crime structure dealt with international crimes that were committed before the administration was established. The UN also had to set-up a domestic legal structure that was assumed would eventually become East Timor's national judiciary. To remove something as political as gender-crimes from the domestic criminal code would not have been politically feasible.

Also, the domestic system must not be confused with the traditional system. The former was regulated by the UNTAET whilst the latter was not. Because the traditional system was disconnected from the formal legal structure, it came under a lot of criticism from both East Timorese and International groups. Politically, this issue was therefore one that had to be dealt with by UNTAET.

SCHABAS: I was asked about the Lomé Peace agreement. In 1999, the president and the democratically elected government were very much on the defensive militarily. The general feeling as peace negotiations developed was that granting amnesty was a condition for concluding a peace agreement. We addressed this in the report of the Truth Commission and we concluded that we were not in a position to second-guess whether it was a condition for peace or not. We also said that if this was necessary to make peace, that it was absolutely legitimate to do so. This was a controversial view: the Special Court has held in one of its judgments that the amnesty is illegal. Not just unwise, not just imprudent: illegal.

The Special Representative of the Secretary General, who was present at the Lomé peace agreement, allegedly appended a note to the agreement, saying that the UN could not agree to a peace agreement that included a grant of amnesty for War Crimes, Crimes Against Humanity and Genocide. We have tried to find this note but it does not seem to exist.

Since it is in UN-reports that this was done, let us however assume that it was. I have always felt this was this a bit of a cheap shot by the Secretary General. I understand the position taken in the UN on amnesties, although I do not entirely agree with it. But to say that you do not agree with the peace agreement when you are not actually a party to it, what are you then actually saying? Are you saying they should keep fighting? If the Secretary General would have been really consistent, that is what he should have said. But from the Security Counsel Resolution that was adopted fol-

* Doctorate Student, University of Cologne.

lowing the peace agreement, it is clear that the UN supported the peace-agreement. That is why it is a bit of a cheap shot: you would not have had the peace agreement without the amnesty.

I have a question for Donlon and Wilde:
It is about the Rule 11bis referrals to the Court in Bosnia and Herzegovina. I believe there is one case now that has been decided: Stankovic. It has been more than two years now since he has been arrested in Bosnia and sent to The Hague. He has been sitting in jail now for all this time waiting to be tried in The Hague and now they send him back to be tried in Bosnia after all. If I were his lawyer, I would be preparing my application to the European Court of Human Rights now for violation of Art. 5 and Art. 6 of the European Convention. We have not had any litigation testing the ICTY before the ECHR yet. There have been some cases but they did not go anywhere, but now you have someone that can legitimately say that Bosnia, not the ICTY, is violating his rights by first sending him to The Hague and then taking him back.

DONLON: In the initial application before the ICTY-referral bench, the Stankovic-defense did prompt a discussion on the issue that their client had surrendered with the intent to be tried before the ICTY, rather than the State Court in Bosnia and Herzegovina. However, this focused on the fact that he had surrendered voluntarily instead of being apprehended and that it was therefore his decision to be tried by the ICTY. The panel did not support the argument that Bosnia had violated his rights by initially transferring him to The Hague and then returning him back. The point in relation to spending two and a half years in detention in The Hague and now being transferred back to a domestic jurisdiction is well taken. On appeal, it may well be raised by his new defense counsel. But upon return to Bosnia and confirmation of the indictment, the national legislation kicks in, in terms of timelines and foreign detention. The time spent in detention in The Hague can be taken into account in sentencing but not in his detention upon arrival.

WILDE: When precisely was he transferred from Bosnia to The Hague? Because Bosnia did not ratify the European Convention until the middle of 2002, so there may be an issue as well about whether the obligations apply. This feeds in to the broader issue of the degree of international scrutiny of these processes and the degree to which these individuals have redress, either domestically or internationally. An interesting thing about the Balkans is that for a long period of time, International Human Rights Law, and particularly the European Convention, did not apply there. Now when they do apply, there are further questions because of the privileges and immunities afforded to the international actors involved in these processes.

DANA SHAHRAM:* Question for Harper: Your presentation reminded us of keeping in mind cultural, social, economic and religious factors when considering international interventions. These factors affect how people react to the law and also how their communities enforce the law. From your study of East Timor, can you give some examples of how they have affected the length, severity and nature of the sentences given by the East Timor Court?

* University of Maastricht.

LAURA DICKINSON:* Question for all: One question raised by all the presentations is whether hybrid Courts that have domestic and international participation have an enhanced form of legitimacy over purely international institutions. If legitimacy derives from consent and involvement of the population affected by the institution, you could argue that a hybrid court, provided that it has that participatory quality, has greater legitimacy. Since in practice, most international courts have not had that much domestic participation, I am curious, given your involvement in these hybrid institutions, whether you see them as possessing that kind of enhanced legitimacy or the potential for it.

UNKNOWN PARTICIPANT:** Question for Schabas: I generally agree with you on the advantages of Truth Commissions. However, there is the obligation of States to prosecute international crimes. In relation to missing persons, from the perspective of the relatives, there is however also what we call in the Americas 'the right to truth'. Some people say: 'I would rather forget about punishment of the perpetrator if I can know where my relative is.' A Truth Commission could be more effective for that purpose, but there is also this obligation of the state to prosecute. Which of the two should prevail?

UNKNOWN PARTICIPANT:*** Comment: The European Convention on Human Rights has applied in Bosnia and Herzegovina since the Dayton Agreement, so it has applied for years, whether they ratified or not…

Access to the Court is of course an entirely different matter. The convention was in fact applied by the Human Rights Commission.

In a way, the wrong question was being asked. One of the issues that really needs to be looked at is: why are international institutions considered to be not bound by Human Rights Principles? As far as I can see, the international institutions have absolutely no respect for the rights of the defense, the right to liberty and in some instances the right to a fair trial, Stankovic is an example of this.

Question for all: On the fair trial front: The ICTY Prosecutor does not release to the defense files saying there is not enough evidence to sustain a prosecution against person X. If this person returns to his home country and is brought up on charges for War Crimes, the defense will need those files, but the ICTY will refuse to hand them over. I would like your comments on that.

BILL THOMAS:**** Question for Harper: There have been insistent reports in the press that members of the High Commission for Refugees are violating Human Rights themselves. Are those reports to be believed? Is there any reason to believe that the activities of the Commission are being blocked where activity is necessary?

THE PANEL:

WILDE: When I said the European Convention did not apply to Bosnia, I was referring to the *treaty* applying to the *State* of Bosnia. As a matter of domestic law, of course, you are right, the law of the European Convention applied internally. There was however no international obligation and therefore no redress.

* University of Connecticut School of Law.

** LL.M. Student, Leiden University.

*** Former member Human Rights Commission.

**** Dutch lawyer.

HARPER: The East Timor Truth Commission received quite a good press; I seem to be one of the only people that have a few criticisms about it. The Truth Commission was set-up after the serious crimes tribunal was established. This was done because it was clear that there was no way that the tribunal would be able to come close to prosecuting or even investigating all the registered cases registered.

However, the way it was done was like trying to fix something that was not broken. I have used the analogy that East Timor had scraped its knee and they put a band-aid on its ankle. The crimes that the Truth Commission was able to deal with were not the crimes that the East Timorese wanted to go to court. One of the main examples was the burning-cases. The East Timorese really wanted those to be dealt with by the court, not the Truth Commission. A perpetrator might only have burnt five houses, but in East Timor, that can be an entire village. So some very significant crimes were insufficiently dealt with by the Truth Commission. For the small crimes the Truth Commission could deal with, the people preferred to use their domestic reconciliation mechanisms. Therefore, there was a lot of effort and money spent on something while the population continued to use their own methods.

SCHABAS: In reaction to Laura Dickinson, on the legitimacy of hybrid institutions:

The Truth Commission in Sierra Leone was essentially a Sierra Leonian operation. The other two international commissioners were Africans, I was often the only non-African in the whole institution. It was essentially an indigenous operation, except for the money, all of which came from Geneva. There was no contribution from the people or the government of Sierra Leone. I think that was a fatal flaw. As a result, while there was a lot of national participation, there was no national ownership of the Commission. I think the results of the work will be limited for that reason. When we ran out of money last year, all the national staff went home. Thus, the heavy lifting on finishing the report was done over the internet by the small international staff and the members of the commission.

In answer to the question on reconciling the duty to prosecute with the search for truth:

Firstly, we were a Truth Commission that did not do much in terms of the 'micro truth', like the South African Commission did. Most people we interviewed could not identify the perpetrators, so we were not able to.

Secondly, the duty to prosecute is not an absolute duty, it is subject to limitations. That is the flaw in the argument that amnesties are prohibited in international law, which is based on the idea that there is an absolute duty to prosecute. I believe that the duty to prosecute must be balanced against other imperatives, such as the right to peace. Also, nobody disagrees that the duty to prosecute is limited by recourses. When the UN said there was a duty to prosecute in Sierra Leone, it was not a duty to prosecute everyone; it was a duty that was limited to ten people. The duty was limited because the international community only wanted to spend 60 million on the project. How can it be that the duty to prosecute is limited by recourses, while it cannot be limited by other needs, like the right to peace?

One final comment on the ICTY and the issues of due process: I will not say I agree with everything the questioner said about it, but I certainly agree with the spirit of it. I believe the Milosevic trial is becoming one of the uglier episodes in international due process – the Nuremberg trial actually compares rather well to what is happening to Milosevic. Therefore, I think that it will be good if we can find a way to get the

European Court of Human Rights to indirectly assess what the ICTY is doing. It would be good for the judges of the ICTY to realize that they are being scrutinized by the European Court of Human Rights. Until recently, I do not think they do.

DONLON: In reaction to the points Schabas has raised in relation to the Truth Commission's funding: The Bosnian institutions are all in place by virtue of national legislation, all of which has been adopted in through national parliamentary procedures. That is an achievement, but the point on funding is valid, because a way to cripple them from the national side is not to pay for them. The strategy that we have employed to deal with this is that the second international donor conference will take place in the autumn of 2005. Learning from previous lessons in Bosnia and elsewhere, where the political cosmetic commitment has been provided but the financial commitment has not, we are working with the national government to develop a long term funding strategy requiring their commitment parallel to the donor conference.

Wilde thanks the panelists and the audience.

*Reporter:* Maarten van der Vlugt*

* University of Amsterdam, the Netherlands.

# The United States and International Organizations

The panel was convened by its Chair, Gerhard Hafner*

## Introductory Remarks by Gerhard Hafner

In this panel, we are faced, on the other hand, with what is more or less the only remaining superpower of the world – the United States, and on the other hand, with international organizations, which are a necessary tool of present international relations, and without which States cannot live together.

International organizations can be used for different purposes, though they cannot be used by individual States for their own national interest. Against this background, we are going to shed some light on the relations between the United States and international organizations: for example, how the United States cooperates or does not cooperate with international organizations, the latter because of a difference of policies; what is the consequence of such disharmony of policies, and so on.

I think this is really an important issue, worthy dealing with, and I am very grateful to the organizers of this meeting for taking it up. Importantly, we have very competent people to deal with the issue.

* Professor of International Law, University of Vienna; former member of the International Law Commission.

## Remarks by Michael J. Matheson*

### The United States and International Organizations: A US Perspective

I have been asked to provide a 'US perspective' on this topic, particularly with respect to the possibility of US withdrawal from an organization or other US actions designed to bring about its reform. Needless to say, I will not attempt to speak for the US Government, but I will try to look at the subject from the point of view of what I see to be the interests of the United States.

#### 1. Some Basic Points

Let me start with a few basic points that may seem obvious but that can easily be forgotten in the current political climate.

*First,* there is, or should be, a strong common interest of the United States on the one hand, and of international organizations and their supporters on the other, in cooperative rather than antagonistic relationships. This has never been more clear than in the post-Cold War period, where the United States successfully resorted again and again in the 1990s to the UN Security Council and the institutions created by it, whereas the decline of such cooperative action in the past few years has been a significant impediment to US policy and has often marginalized international institutions.

When changes are desirable, as they often are, the United States should actively pursue them, but wherever possible should do so in a manner that minimizes disruption to the organization and preserves the long-term position of the United States in the organization. At the same time, international organizations and their supporters should make every effort to accept reasonable change, and to resist the temptation to oppose US initiatives merely to minimize or counterbalance US influence.

*Second,* it is inevitable that major states will exercise special rights and influence in international organizations commensurate with their resources and influence in the world generally, and their special interests and responsibilities in the context of particular organizations, and there is nothing wrong with this. This is not at all limited to the United States: for example, Europe enjoys an even greater measure of disproportionate representation and rights in various international institutions.

The objective of reform should not be to attempt to eliminate these differences; rather, the structures and procedures of an organization should appropriately reflect the differences in the interests, capabilities and contributions of its members. Again, this is not limited to the United States: it makes sense, for example, to realign the membership of the Security Council to take account of changes that have occurred over the years in the relative importance and contributions of other UN members.

* International Law Commission, former Acting Legal Adviser, US State Department.

*Third,* the character of changes proposed by the United States may affect the role it can effectively play in pursuing them. In some cases, the United States has proposed reforms that, generally speaking, are consistent with any rational approach toward the effective functioning of an international organization, such as greater financial accountability, more efficient use of resources, increased transparency, and greater flexibility in administration.

On the other hand, the US Government has sometimes pressed for changes under the rubric of reform that reflect particular political positions of the United States which may or may not be shared in principle by the international community as a whole, such as the position of Israel or the composition of UN organs. There is nothing wrong with this, but it would not be realistic to expect that other members of international organizations would necessarily give the same sort of deference to US positions.

## 2. Alternative United States Strategies

*Next,* let me turn to a brief consideration of the alternative strategies that the United States has used in pursuing such changes.

*First,* and most commonly, the United States has pursued reform from within – that is, remaining an active member of the organization in question and seeking change through its normal rules and procedures. For example, this is the current strategy of the United States with respect to reform of the UN system, where the US Government is pursuing a variety of objectives, including greater financial accountability, more efficient use of resources, increased transparency, consolidation and rationalization of programs, and greater flexibility in administration. But the United States is not threatening to withdraw or limit its financial contributions to secure its objectives.

Nonetheless, as you may know, this position is currently under challenge in the US Congress, where a sweeping piece of legislation has been proposed that would require the withholding of 50 per cent of the assessed contributions of the United States until a long list of specific changes have been effected. To its credit, the Bush Administration has taken the position that, while it shares many of the objectives of this proposal, the threat to withhold assessed contributions would be counterproductive and damaging to US influence and interests within the UN, including its interests in producing meaningful reform.

*Second,* from time to time the United States has declined from the outset to participate in an international organization or treaty regime but at the same time has actively pursued changes in its structures or policies with the intent of participating fully when those changes were made. A good example of this is the UN Convention on the Law of the Sea and its various organs, where the United States originally voted in favor of the Convention, but did not become a party because of concerns about the regime for seabed mineral resources. However, the United States (and other like-minded governments) actively pursued changes through a multilateral negotiating process that resulted in adoption of an Implementing Agreement in 1994 that adequately met US objections. The Clinton Administration then submitted the Convention and the Implementing Agreement to the US Senate for its advice and consent. Regrettably, the Senate has not yet acted, but the Bush Administration is also actively supporting US adherence, so that one may still be hopeful of a positive result. For present purposes, the point is that the United States used its non-participation as a means of securing change, but always with the intent to resolve matters on a multilateral basis and to adhere to the regime when specific objectives were met.

*Third,* on occasion the United States has withdrawn from an international organization or regime to which it had originally adhered, with the objective of returning when changes were made. One notable example of this was the US withdrawal from and subsequent return to the ILO, which Mr. Martin has already described. Another was the US withdrawal from UNESCO in 1984 due to various objections that included the alleged politicization of the organization's agenda, its alleged hostility to a free press, and alleged deficiencies in financial responsibility and organizational management. But changes were made in the management, leadership and policies of the organization, and the United States eventually responded favorably by rejoining UNESCO in 2003. During this period, the United States continued its involvement in UNESCO in various ways, including through voluntary financial contributions and participation in subsidiary bodies.

*Fourth,* on occasion the United States has withdrawn from or refused to participate in an international organization or treaty regime, not in pursuit of a positive agenda for change, but rather in outright opposition to the organization or regime. A prominent example of this was the campaign by the United States, following the start of the Bush Administration, against the International Criminal Court.

David Scheffer will be discussing this at some length, so I will not attempt to go into any detail at this point. Let me only note that this is, in my view, a good example of a situation in which the United States and the organization in question have serious mutual interests in a non-antagonistic relationship, even if the United States does not, for the time being, adhere to the Statute of the Court or agree to submit its personnel to the Court's jurisdiction.

Specifically, the Court is likely to need the support and influence of the Security Council, and the United States in particular, to carry out effective prosecutions in situations where the states in question may be uncooperative or refuse to consent to the Court's jurisdiction. At the same time, situations will arise in which the United States will strongly desire to see international prosecution of non-US persons but the Court may be the only practical alternative for such prosecution. In such a case, it would be sensible for the United States, as in the recent case of Darfur, not to prevent the Security Council from referring the situation to the Court, and even better, to give financial and forms of support to help the prosecution effort succeed.

## 3. Issues Presented by Different Strategies

*Finally,* let me turn briefly to the issues that are presented from the US point of view by these various strategies for pursuing reform.

*First* is the question of whether US withdrawal or non-participation would violate its international legal obligations. Of course, nothing obliges the United States to adhere to a treaty regime or to join an international organization; and once a member, there are usually lawful means of withdrawing. On the other hand, the requirement to pay assessed contributions is a legal obligation, and its violation by the United States would make it more difficult to oppose similar actions by other states in pursuit of their own objectives.

*Second* is the question of whether such withdrawal or non-participation is more effective than working for change from within in accordance with the normal procedures. I think that this question cannot be answered in the abstract. To be sure, the threat of US non-participation can be a powerful stimulant for change in some circumstances, given the fact that most organizations would suffer substantially from the withholding of US financial contributions, US political support, and US participation in the organization's activities. On the other hand, US non-participation can be counter-productive in that it removes the United States from the organization's decision-making process, may raise doubts in the minds of other members as to whether there is any point in accommodating US concerns, and may put the debate about reform in an adversarial posture that is not conducive to reasonable negotiation. Further, during the period of its non-participation, the United States is less likely to be able to influence the actions of the organization on other issues that were not involved in the decision to withdraw or not participate, and it may not be possible to recoup such damage after the United States joins or returns.

*Third* is the question of whether US withdrawal or non-participation will cause damage to the organization or regime that will not be in the long-term interests of the United States. In most of these cases, the United States has important interests that may be served by the organization, and it will not be in US interests to cripple that organization for the purpose of reforming it. This was certainly the case with respect to the law-of-the-sea regime and UNESCO; and pursuing a strategy of non-participation or non-contribution to the point of causing the collapse of such an institution, or substantially impairing its ability to function, would not serve US interests in the long run.

Even where the United States follows a strategy of withdrawal or non-participation, there are usually ways to do so that cause less damage to US interests in the organization. For example, the United States continued to make voluntary contributions to UNESCO and to take part in certain of its activities; and it stressed its acceptance and support of the great majority of the provisions of the Law of the Sea Convention. As I have already suggested, the same is, in my view, true for the ICC as well, even if the United States does not at this time adhere to the Statute of the Court or agree to subject US personnel to the Court's jurisdiction.

*Fourth* is the question of whether withdrawal or non-participation will cause undue damage to the eventual position of the United States within an organization, even after desired changes are made and US participation resumes. Other members may be chastened by the experience and be more attentive to US interests; or on the other hand they may resent US conduct and be less willing to accommodate the United States, and they may take measures to prevent it from exercising such leverage in the future.

*Fifth* is the question of whether US withdrawal or non-participation will harm interests of the United States in other areas. For example, US actions concerning the International Criminal Court may damage bilateral relationships with important states and might interfere with the creation of peacekeeping missions of importance to the United States.

There are no absolute answers to any of these questions, but clearly the United States needs, if only from the point of view of advancing its own interests and objectives, to take a measured approach in pursuing reform of international organizations that does not unduly rely on confrontation and unilateral action.

## Remarks by Georg Nolte*

## The United States and International Organizations: A European Perspective

### 1. Introduction

After the rejection of the European Constitutional Treaty in two popular referenda, it is particularly difficult to respond to an invitation to articulate 'a European perspective' with respect to such a broad and divisive issue such as 'The United States and International Organizations'. And it is, of course, impossible to write a short piece on this topic without doing injustice to the specifics.

Foot, MacFarlane and Mastanduno have concluded that the US attitude towards international organizations is characterized by an 'instrumental multilateralism'.[1] This term is sufficiently wide and ambiguous to encompass both present and past US policies with respect to International Organizations. The term even presupposes a substantial degree of US unilateralism. At the most abstract level 'instrumental multilateralism' would seem to mean that the given capacity of international organizations to continuously and successfully fulfill their functions, as they are understood by the US government, is much more important for the United States than their mere existence as fora, procedures, and repositories of common values. Given the European experience, both within Europe and *vis-à-vis* much of the rest of the world, the emphasis would probably be set differently from 'a European perspective'.

### 2. Basic Elements of the US Role with Respect to International Organizations

Three well-known basic elements contribute to a specific relationship of the United States with international organizations. These elements are power (1), exceptionalism (2), and the US domestic system of powers (3).

#### 2.1 **Power**

The United States is currently the most powerful state on the globe. It is not so important how powerful the United States actually is in overall terms, or in any given

* Professor of International Law, University of Munich.

area, and how long this position of power will last.[2] It is more important that in most political systems the most powerful actor is the focal point for important interactions and that this actor will provide impulses for the development of new rules. While such impulses can be more self-interested or more in the common interest, this distinction collapses from the point of view of the most powerful actor. In the international institutional context examples for this are the history of the crises over the withholding of UN dues by the United States,[3] as well as the role of the United States in the institutionalized effort to combat terrorism, in particular the US role in the Counter-Terrorism Committee of the Security Council.[4] Of course, the specific role of the most powerful actor can be more aggressive or more defensive, depending on whether less powerful actors undertake successful counter-balancing efforts.

### 2.2 Exceptionalism

While power as such already tends to create a bias in favor of an instrumental view of international institutions it does not yet predetermine the particular mode, or flavor, of its exercise. The exercise of power can be more heavy-handed, as in the case of the former Soviet Union, or more subtle, as mostly in the case of the former British Empire. In addition, the justification for the exercise of a special role in world affairs is typically not expressed in terms of 'because we have the power' but rather in the exceptionalist terms of 'because we have a mission'.[5] In the US case, such a sense of mission is first identified in the Declaration of Independence, then in the Monroe doctrine in its various forms, to Wilson's Fourteen Points, the Atlantic Charter and, as its latest manifestation, the Bush-Doctrine of 2002. Perhaps the particular flavor of the American variant of the exceptionalism of the powerful even consists in its expression and rationalization in the language of law. And it is probably this assumption which makes the recent American light-handedness in dealing with international law and institutions so worrisome for many Europeans. It should, however, be recognized that law and institutions are, and have always been, only one element of the American exceptionalism and that international institutions have always sometimes played a larger and sometimes a smaller role in US policy.[6] While substantive legal norms can be stretched and bended when needs for changes to the law are being perceived, international institutions can be inherently less flexible and more fragile. The evolution of the US position during the Rome negotiations in 1998 on the ICC Statute has been a significant indicator for the relative loss of importance of law and institutional design for US policy.[7] In Rome, David Scheffer, the head of the US delegation, ultimately explained the US position by saying:

> 'The U.S. has special responsibilities and special exposure to political controversy over our action. We are called upon to act, sometimes at great risk, far more than any other nation. This is a reality in the international system'.[8]

### 2.3 Domestic system of separation of powers

The third fundamental set of facts which affects the relationship of the United States to international organizations lies in the specific US constitutional system of separation of powers.[9] This aspect concerns the possibility – well-known since the rejection of the Covenant of the League of Nations – that the US Senate does not ratify a treaty (as with the rejection in 1998 of the Comprehensive Test Ban Treaty) and the difficulties of US governments to obtain authorizations or appropriations from Congress without unrelated strings attached. However, the differences between the US presidential system and European parliamentary systems with respect to the political space for the executive should not be overestimated. It may be that, in Europe, popular referenda will in the future play a role that is, to a certain extent, functionally equivalent to that of the US Senate.

## 3. Europe's Role from a US Perspective

Can there be 'a European perspective' which appropriately takes these three basic elements into account? As it is somewhat ambitious to answer this question directly, I prefer to tackle it through the mirror of the following question: How is the *European* attitude with respect to our question perceived by and in the United States? Three widespread perceptions can be identified.

### 3.1 'Tying Gulliver to the ground'

Many in the United States hold the view that European states attempt to use international institutions 'to tie Gulliver to the ground'.[10] The two most prominent examples given are, first, the resistance within the UN system by France and Germany, based on the opinion of the vast majority of Europeans, towards the Iraq war, and, second, the ICC project where European states were leading a large group of like-minded states, ultimately against the United States. Both examples are, however, misleading. In the case of Iraq a substantial number of European states expressed support for a US policy which has been – kindly – interpreted by those states as an effort to finally implement decisions taken by an international institution. The ICC project, on the other hand, was pursued by most like-minded states not primarily out of anti-hegemonic motives, but rather out of a strong sense of purpose,[11] of a kind that could equally emanate from the United States. Thus, these two examples suggest that if there is a European inclination of using international institutions 'to tie Gulliver to the ground' this inclination is often either not a dominant motive or not sufficiently widespread to become 'European' in a strong sense. As far as there have indeed been European efforts to constrain the United States by way of international institutions they would seem to have been pursued for substantive policy reasons and not out of an empty resentment of power.

### 3.2 Accomodationism

A second perception in the United States is that European states tend to use international organizations to engage and accomodate problematical actors, rather than to put the necessary pressure on them in order 'to solve the problem'.[12] According to this point of view, such a European attitude was already visible during the Cold War, not only in the field of trade relations, but also in institutional dealings with the developing world, such as in the case of the Law of the Sea Convention. Today this European attitude is seen to manifest itself in dealings with formerly so-called rogue states, such as Iran and North Korea, where Europeans defend institutionalized approaches to the problem through IAEA, while the United States remains sceptical and openly toys with other options.[13] It is an open question whether US unilateralism would contribute to a solution of such problems or whether the 'European' patience, inclusiveness, diplomacy would more likely lead to face-saving and sustainable solutions.

### 3.3 **Analogizing international organizations to states**

A third perception in the United States of a particular 'European' perspective on international organizations is legally more sophisticated. It is based on the perception that, in Europe, international organizations, such as the EU and the UN, are considered to be more than just functional instruments designed to fulfill a particular narrow purpose. While European legal theorists hesitate to openly claim that these organizations should be analogized to states, many do ascribe them constitutional qualities.[14] Even concepts such as 'multi-level system' or 'multi-level democracy', which pretend to keep a distance from the state, ultimately reveal themselves as being fed by holistic conceptions which often have their roots in an imagined order with state-like qualities. It is possible that such theoretical perspectives do not merely represent a speculative *avant-garde*, but are rather the self-conscious tips of a largely unconscious European conception of a desirable quasi-state-like order in the international realm. If this is true it may explain why the exit option, the decision to leave an international organization, represents a higher hurdle for almost all European governments than for the United States.

## 4. Preliminary Conclusion

These three perceptions may be true, false, or they may possess a kernel of truth. In any case they do not contradict the hypothesis that US and European perspectives on international organizations are based on a commonly accepted recognition of certain basic elements, in particular on an asymmetrical power relationship. Different, but not necessarily contradictory conclusions can be drawn from this point of departure, depending on the respective view of the roles of the United States and other states in global affairs. If they are seen as being complementary they offer themselves to be translated into a division of labour between the United States on the one hand and European states on the other. One example of such a division of labour could be the 'good cop – bad cop' approach of the western states as a whole towards Iran – potentially going nuclear.

## 5. Recent Developments

Are there new developments which call these assumptions into question? There are three candidates.

### 5.1 Coalitions of the Willing

The first candidate is what has been called 'Coalitions of the Willing'. This concept is not restricted to the loose association of states which in 2003 attacked and occupied Iraq under the leadership of the United States. It has also been applied to other informal cooperative regimes such as the Proliferation Security Initiative, the Financial Action Task Force, or the Global Fund to fight Aids, Malaria and Tuberculosis.[15] It is characteristic of such regimes that a limited number of participating states pursue their aims 'below the radar screen' of international law.[16] Such regimes are not entirely new and they can be conceived as being merely variations of informal government networks whose appearance can be expected in a time of globalization and the need of increased speed and cooperation.[17] In another sense, however, such informal regimes can also be conceived as instruments of choice for a hegemonic power that does not wish to be constrained in the pursuit of its goals by formal institutions with their tendency towards inclusiveness.[18] If we concentrate on this second aspect of some of the modern Coalitions of the Willing it will strike us as significant that the European states most often support such US-inspired regimes which sidestep, and perhaps even undermine, more formally established international organizations.

### 5.2 The goal of establishing Europe as a global player

The second candidate has to do with the fact that European states have proclaimed the goal of establishing Europe as a more cohesive global player which should 'strive for multilateral solutions within the framework of the United Nations' (Art. III-292 of the European Constitutional Treaty). This is another sign that the EU tends to prefer institutionalized forms of cooperation. While the European Constitutional Treaty is perhaps politically dead, it is nevertheless rather safe to say that the proclamation in the Preamble of the Constitutional Treaty according to which 'the Union will be led by the principles which were essential for its own development' expresses a renewed preference for such institutionalized relations on the basis of substantive equality.

### 5.3 The fragmentation of the developing world

A third development which may affect the relationship between the United States and international organizations is the increasing differentiation of the developing world, in particular in the trade area.[19] Certain states, such as China, India and Brazil, see themselves as emerging powers in their own right and not so much anymore as leaders of a group called 'The Third World', non-aligned or developing countries. The states of the former 'Third World' are increasingly split between those with emerging economies and those without the necessary good governance.

## 6. Possible Future Scenarios for the Role of International Organizations

What are the possible consequences of these recent developments for the relationship between the United States and International Organizations? Are they likely to modify the US attitude and policies of 'instrumental multilateralism'?

### 6.1 Shadows of the past?

One possible scenario is that formal international organizations will continue to lose part of their functions to more informal regimes, just as some domestic administrations have lost many of their powers due to the fact that their bureaucratic ways were considered to be inefficient. The emergence of so-called Coalitions of the Willing may be a sign for such a development. The constitutional crisis currently prevents Europe from projecting its own administrative and political ways onto the international level. The fragmentation of the developing world presents opportunities for the strongest state, the United States, to select its partners and thereby to act in *its* own preferred ways. All this would mean fewer incentives for the United States to pursue its goals through formal international institutions which would then tend to become 'shadows of the past'.

### 6.2 A renaissance of the diplomatic clearing house?

A different scenario could emerge if Coalitions of the Willing were only a transient phenomenon, typically bound to be institutionalized or formalized in a foreseeable time-frame, and if the aspirations certain emerging powers, such a China and India – and perhaps even Europe – would gain more real political weight. Such a development would increase the demands for more formally negotiated solutions, as it happens today within the WTO. Although such a renaissance of international organizations as diplomatic clearing houses does not appear likely in the short-term it is a real possibility in the medium or long-term, at least in certain areas.

### 6.3 Catalysts for legitimacy and stigma?

Only formal international organizations, not informal government networks, can fulfill the function of attributing international legitimacy, or stigma, on to a particular state or activity. To European eyes, the United States has a particularly strong tendency to use international organizations for that purpose. While there is a widespread scepticism in Europe towards expressions such as 'rogue states' or 'war on terror', and a resistance towards sanctifying such terminology through their use by international organizations, it is likely that the function of international organizations to attribute legitimacy and stigma will become more important in the future – and even if a tendency towards a renaissance of the diplomatic clearing house emerges. Here, the particular flavor of US policy tends to coincide with the general interest in establishing a system of common values in a globalized world.

## 7. Conclusion: Towards a More Symmetrical Equilibrium?

At the moment it is unlikely that attempts by the EU and other states will be successful to modify the US attitude, or practice, of treating international organizations merely as one of several possible instruments of foreign policy, and not as values in themselves which provide transparency, legitimacy, and a voice to smaller powers. It is possible, however, that there will be a movement in the medium- or long-term towards more symmetrical forms of equilibrium, which would in turn give rise to more formal and/ or more substantive forms of cooperation *within* international organizations.

## Notes

[1] Rosemary Foot, S. Neil MacFarlane, and Michael Mastanduno, 'Conclusion: Instrumental Multilateralism in US Foreign Policy', in Rosemary Foot, S. Neil MacFarlane, and Michael Mastanduno (eds.), *US Hegemony and International Organizations* (Oxford, Oxford University Press 2003) p. 273.

[2] For a description and a critical analysis see, e.g., Michael Mann, 'The First Failed Empire of the 21st Century', 30 *Review of International Studies* (2004), pp. 631-653.

[3] Francesco Francioni, 'Multilateralism à la Carte: The Limits to Unilateral Withholdings of Assessed Contributions to the UN Budget', 11 *EJIL* (2000), pp. 43-59.

[4] Eric Rosand, 'Security Council Resolution 1373, the Counter-Terrorism Committee, and the Fight against Terrorism', 97 *AJIL* (2003), pp. 333-341; Edward J. Flynn, 'Counter-Terrorism and Human Rights', *European Human Rights Law Review* (2005), pp. 29-49.

[5] Harold Hongju Koh, 'On American Exceptionalism', 55 *Stanford Law Review* (2003), pp. 1479-1527; Peter J. Spiro, 'The New Sovereigntists', 79 *Foreign Affairs* (2000), pp. 9-15; T. Jeremy Gunn, 'American Exceptionalism and Globalist Double Standards', 41 *Columbia Journal of Transnational Law*, pp. 137-152.

[6] Nico Krisch, 'Weak as Constraint, Strong as Tool: The Place of International Law in U.S. Foreign Policy', in David M. Malone and Yuen Foong Khong (eds.), *Unilateralism & U.S. Foreign Policy* (Boulder, Rienner 2003) pp. 41-70.

[7] Georg Nolte, 'The United States and the International Criminal Court', in David M. Malone and Yuen Foong Khong (eds.), *Unilateralism & U.S. Foreign Policy* (Boulder, Rienner 2003) pp. 71-93.

[8] David Scheffer, 'The U.S. and the International Criminal Court', 93 *AJIL* (1999), pp. 12-21, at p. 12.

[9] Martin S. Flaherty, 'The Future and Past of U. S. Foreign Relations Law', 67 *Law and Contemporary Problems* (2004), pp. 169-193; Curtis A. Bradley & Jack L. Goldsmith, 'Foreign Relations Law', *Cases and Materials* (New York, Aspen 2003); Thomas Franck and Michael Glennon, *Foreign Relations and National Security Law*, 2nd edn. (St. Paul, West 1993).

[10] Robert Kagan, *Of Paradise and Power – America and Europe in the New World Order* (New York, Knopf 2003).

[11] See Nolte, *supra* n. 7, at pp. 86-90.

[12] See Edward C. Luck, 'The United States, International Organizations, and the Quest for Legitimacy', in Steward Patrick and Shepard Forman (eds.), *Multilateralism & U.S. Foreign Policy* (Boulder, Rienner 2002) pp. 47-75, at p. 55.

[13] 'Iran vows not to yield as Western leaders split', *International Herald Tribune*, 15 August 2005, at p. 1.

[14] Armin von Bogdandy (ed.), *Principles of European Constitutional Law*, (Oxford, Hart 2005); Bardo Fassbender, 'The United Nations Charter as Constitution of the International Community', 36 *Columbia Journal of Transnational Law* (1998), pp. 529-619; Jochen Abr. Frowein, 'Konstitutionalisierung des Völkerrechts', in *Völkerrecht und Internationales Privatrecht in einem sich globalisierenden internationalen System* (Berichte der deutschen Gesellschaft für Völkerrecht) (2000) pp. 427-447; Anne Orford, 'The Destiny of International Law', 17 *LJIL* (2004), pp. 441-476, at pp. 445-452.

[15] Stewart Patrick, 'Beyond Coalitions of the Willing', 17 *Ethics & International Affairs* (2003), pp. 37-54; White House Press Release, Principles for the Proliferation Security Initiative, at: <http://www.state.gov/t/np/rls/prsrl/23809.htm> (last visited 16 August 2005); Michael Byers, 'Policing the High Seas: The Proliferation Security Initiative', 98 *AJIL* (2004), pp. 526-543; The Global Fund to Fight AIDS, Malaria and Tuberculosis, at: <http://www.theglobalfund.org/en/> (last visited 16 August 2005).

[16] Eyal Benvenisti, 'Coalitions of the Willing and the Evolution of International Law', in Christian Calliess, Georg Nolte & Tobias Stoll (eds.), *Coalitions of the Willing*, to be published in 2006 (manuscript on file with the author).

[17] Anne-Marie Slaughter, *A New World Order* (2004); id., 'Global Government Networks, Global Information Agencies, and Disaggregated Democracy', 24 *Michigan Journal of International Law* (2003), pp. 1041-1075.

[18] Krisch, *supra* n. 6, at pp. 59-60.

[19] Marc L. Busch, 'Developing Countries and General Agreement on Tariffs and Trade', 37 *Journal of*

*World Trade* (2003), pp. 719-735; Basudeb Guha-Khasnobis (ed.), *The WTO, Developing Countries and the Doha Development Agenda*, (London, Palgrave Macmillan 2004).

## Remarks by David Scheffer*

### How Reform Initiatives Can Bridge The Gulf Between The United States and The International Criminal Court

I see my primary task here today as one of foresight: what pragmatic institutional reforms might be pursued in coming years to bridge the gulf between the US Government and the International Criminal Court and strengthen that international institution in the process? Bearing in mind that the forthcoming 2009 review conference of the Rome Statute of the International Criminal Court offers an opportunity for amendments to the Rome Statute, there also are other initiatives that could be undertaken soon and which fall short of formally amending the treaty.

I will make several proposals today with a perspective that is often misunderstood by some scholars, commentators, and politicians who view US policy as one long continuum of opposition to the ICC. The Clinton Administration, for which I worked, strongly supported the establishment of an international criminal court and President Clinton called for that goal to be met by the end of the 20th century. Although the United States objected to certain provisions of the final draft of the Rome Statute presented at the Rome Conference on 16 July 1998, we worked very hard thereafter in 1999 and 2000 to address our remaining concerns about the Rome Statute. After the US delegation to the UN talks satisfied some of those concerns in the Rules of Procedure and Evidence and the Elements of Crimes, and joined the consensus vote on them in June 2000, we obtained encouraging informal support from key governments for further US proposals for other supplemental documents that were scheduled for negotiation in 2001. President Clinton authorized the signing of the Rome Statute by the US Government on 31 December 2000. We thought, at the time, that we were presenting the Bush Administration with the strongest possible negotiating opportunity for 2001 as a signatory state to the Rome Statute. But you know the rest of the story: the Bush Administration abandoned the UN negotiations forthwith and entirely and in May 2002 sent a letter to the United Nations effectively nullifying the US signature on the treaty. The American Service Members Protection Act of 2002, which the Clinton Administration has vigorously opposed when it was first introduced in the summer of 2000, was adopted with strong Bush Administration support. An aggressive campaign, led by John Bolton, to compel other governments to sign purported Article 98(2) non-surrender agreements with Washington have widened the gulf between the United States and the ICC, as well as certain foreign governments, in recent years. A largely destructive American relationship with the ICC has only added to the

* Visiting Professor, Northwestern University Law School (2005-2006); Former U.S. Ambassador at Large for War Crimes Issues (1997-2001).

overall tension between the Bush Administration and many international treaties and institutions. Nonetheless, the American abstention on the vote for UN Security Council Resolution 1593 of 31 March 2005, which I and others had been urging since early 2004, permitted the referral of the Darfur situation to the ICC and may have signaled a slight shift in policy, one that should be nurtured carefully by other governments interested in US engagement.

I believe strongly in a constructive US relationship with the ICC, one that ultimately can lead to repeal of the non-cooperation provisions of the American Service Members Protection Act and to an American posture that is not so fearful of, or intimidated by, the workings of the ICC. There are several reform initiatives that could be taken, I will argue, that would have a profound effect on the viability of the ICC and of America's role in its future development.

A great deal of America's standing and effectiveness at the United Nations flows from its commitment, or lack thereof, to broadly-accepted international treaty regimes. That is particularly true of the permanent International Criminal Court. Often overlooked in the American debate about the ICC is the simple reality that the effective and fair operation of the ICC can go a long way towards dispelling concerns over whether it will seek to influence, by threat of investigation and indictment, the foreign policy choices of major military powers, particularly against newly emerging threats. The UN Security Council could play a very constructive role, assuming the United States has the wisdom to permit it. There are several initiatives, some involving the Security Council and others engaging other bodies, that could be undertaken so as to diminish US Government concerns about the ICC and strengthen the relevancy and efficiency of the ICC.

## 1. Non-amendment Reforms

The first category of reforms I want to discuss are ones that would not require any amendment to the Rome Statute, but some would involve amendments to the Rules of Procedure and Evidence. These are proposals that could be acted upon within a short period of time provided the necessary diplomatic initiatives and political will existed.

### 1.1 **Article 98(2) agreements**

In the May 2005 issue of the Journal of International Criminal Justice, I present what I firmly believe is the proper interpretation of Article 98(2) of the Rome Statute, an interpretation that is at odds with the Bush Administration's reading and implementation of that provision of the Rome Statute through the signing of 100 flawed bilateral non-surrender agreements with foreign governments. In short, Article 98(2) only covers those agreements of bilateral or multilateral character between or among nations (whether party or non-party to the Rome Statute) and/or international organizations (such as the ICC or the United Nations) that provide for non-surrender to the ICC of a nation's military or official personnel and related civilian component sent abroad on official mission by such nation. The agreements were not intended to cover individuals acting abroad in a private capacity or independently for foreign government or international organization purposes. The bilateral non-surrender agreements negotiated by the current US administration are intended to cover not only current or former government officials, government employees (including contractors), and military personnel, but also all US nationals, including those acting in a strictly private or non-US capacity (such as businessmen, international civil servants, non-governmental organization staffers, tourists, journalists, and mercenaries). It will be up to primarily the ICC judges, not the US Government or its treaty partners or anyone else, to interpret the application of these bilateral non-surrender agreements under Article 98(2) of the Rome Statute and if they are flawed, their enforceability before the Court will be problematic, to say the least.

How can a solution emerge from this unnecessary mess? I would propose that existing bilateral non-surrender agreements could be rectified with a US public declaration confirming that the reference to 'nationals' in such agreements will be interpreted by the US Government to mean the US civilian component of a military deployment. New or amended agreements negotiated by the United States with foreign governments should limit the scope of application to official and military personnel of the 'sending State', and to cover them for actions they undertook in their official capacity. Thus, former officials and personnel would be covered for actions they took while in the service of the sending State, such as the United States. Private contractors may qualify for coverage only to the extent that they can be described as persons of the sending State, are directly contracted by the US Government to undertake duties in the foreign jurisdiction in connection with an official mission, and are held accountable (including criminal responsibility) before US courts for their performance. But in order to ensure that impunity for atrocity crimes would not be the end result of the bilateral agreement, the 'sending State' should commit itself in the Article 98(2) agreement to full investigation and, if warranted, prosecution of persons of the 'sending State' who are suspected of committing such crimes, particularly if arrest warrants against such persons have been issued by the ICC. The European Union has sought (so far without success) a similar assurance as a pre-condition to any of its members entering into an Article 98(2) agreement with the United States. Such a provision would greatly facilitate a State Party's compliance with the Article 98(2) agreement by permitting it to point to an effective exercise of complementarity by the sending State.

The Bush Administration also should issue a declaration that designates all US SOFAs and SOMAs covering US personnel as Article 98(2) agreements to the extent that their terms (which can vary) require criminal jurisdiction to be allocated in a specific manner between the parties to such agreements and such criminal jurisdiction covers the atrocity crimes within the jurisdiction of the ICC. The bottom line of such a declaration must be that a suspect of an atrocity crime will be investigated and, if merited, prosecuted before a competent court of law pursuant to the procedures of the SOFA or SOMA. Such a presidential declaration would not be regarded as credible if it sought to shield individuals from any investigation whatsoever of atrocity crimes by simply designating SOFAs and SOMAs as Article 98(2) agreements.

This 'fix' for the Article 98(2) non-surrender agreements would strengthen their enforceability and encourage European Union governments in particular to consider signing such agreements with the United States. While many, including many experts in this audience, would regard this as an imperfect procedure undermining the reach of the ICC's jurisdiction, it would provide a wide range of enforceable non-surrender protection for US official and military personnel (active and retired) and hence diminish American concerns about the Court's future intentions. That can be an important contribution to a fresh overall policy of US engagement with the ICC in coming years.

### 1.2 Temporal jurisdiction

It is probably heresy to most international lawyers engaged with the study and practice of the ICC to suggest that within the temporal jurisdiction of the ICC lies a simple formula for resolving the concerns of non-party States and, if ignored would lead to efforts to prohibit national cooperation with the Court (witness the American Service Members Protection Act) and to inhibit some major countries from joining the ICC due to the exposure of their nationals while in non-party status, a contingency that is politically unacceptable. A misinterpretation of the Court's temporal jurisdiction poisons the well for signature and ratification of the Rome Statute by governments whose participation could prove so important to the universal application of the Rome Statute.

I will not recite here my interpretation of Articles 126(2), 11(2), 121(5), 24, 22(1), 12 and 13 of the Rome Statute that leads me to conclude that the temporal jurisdiction of the Court commences, except under circumstances of UN Security Council referral or State consent, for the nationals of a non-party State on the date 60 days following the filing of that State's instrument of ratification, pursuant to Article 126(2). That argument is well developed by me elsewhere. Suffice it to say here that so many complex formulas for reform of the ICC in order to address US concerns and the concerns of other major nations such as India, China, Japan, Indonesia, Russia, Pakistan, and Egypt would be simplified with a proper interpretation of the Rome Statute and its jurisdictional reach over non-party nationals. An honest appreciation of the ICC's temporal jurisdiction would create robust political dynamics to fully empower the Court to investigate the most serious atrocity crimes and their perpetrators.

For example, in exchange for an agreed interpretation of the Rome Statute of this character, the permanent members of the UN Security Council (consisting of three non-Party States (the United States, China, and Russia) and two States Parties (France and the United Kingdom) to the Rome Statute) could inform the Assembly of States Parties that where circumstances become compelling enough to require that the ICC have jurisdiction over non-party State nationals, due to such State's (or such individuals' particular) threat to international peace and security giving rise to alleged violations of ICC crimes, they would act as speedily and as favorably as possible to approve a Chapter VII enforcement resolution that refers the situation to the ICC and thus eliminates any doubts about the ICC's jurisdiction over the suspects. The recent referral of the Darfur situation to the ICC is encouraging in this respect. While such a temporal jurisdiction initiative would require considerable diplomacy to accomplish, the benefit of doing so in accordance with a correct interpretation of the ICC's temporal jurisdiction would liberate the United States, China, Russia and other major States to support and join the Rome Statute far sooner and with a greater sense of integrity. Such an initiative would achieve the jurisdiction of the ICC over the nationals of such major states more effectively and expeditiously than will reliance on a popular but illogical application of temporal jurisdiction.

The Assembly of States Parties of the ICC could adopt an interpretation of the court's temporal jurisdiction as an amendment to the ICC Rules of Procedure and Evidence that would dispel concerns by existing non-States Parties, particularly the United States, the People's Republic of China, Russia, Indonesia, Japan, and India, that seek certainty of interpretation of the reach of the Court's jurisdiction. This could be a relatively painless procedure by the Assembly of States Parties that would vastly improve cooperation and participation in the treaty regime by major world powers which remain non-party States in significant part because of continued confusion over the ICC's temporal jurisdiction.

### 1.3 Amendments to US federal criminal and military law

Ironically, many of the States that have ratified the Rome Statute and enacted implementing legislation that modernizes their criminal and in some cases military codes and aligns them with the crimes of the Rome Statute are now more insulated from the jurisdiction of the ICC than is the United States as a non-party State. That is because the US federal criminal and military codes are out-dated and demonstrate fundamental gaps between US law and the atrocity law falling within the jurisdiction of the ICC. If those gaps could be filled with amendments to US Code Title 18 (criminal) and Title 10 (military), then the United States would be far better positioned to exercise complementarity with the ICC than is currently the case. Improving the complementarity rights of the United States would be a significant confidence-building step for US officials and scholars concerned about the ICC's review of US investigations and prosecutions. That exercise in modernizing Titles 10 and 18 of the US Code and aligning US law with Articles 5-8 of the Rome Statute is far too detailed to relay in a discussion of this character. But the objective deserves some explanation to a foreign audience, because this exercise alone would greatly ease concern in the United States about whether the exercise of complementarity in fact would be the safeguard from ICC prosecution of American suspects that it purports to be. I want to provide a preview of what might be possible before the US Congress.

First, there is a wealth of experience now recorded in other major jurisdictions, including the ICC implementing legislation in the United Kingdom, Germany, France, Canada, and Australia, that can assist with a modernizing exercise in the United States. So there is much to draw upon regarding how the crimes of the ICC have been incorporated in other national legal systems.

Title 18 of the US Code does not codify crimes against humanity as such. The combined definitional and juridical elements required for a crime against humanity in the Rome Statute and Elements of Crimes simply do not exist in US federal law, and some of the Rome Statute's crimes against humanity – such as the crime of apartheid or the crime of extermination or of persecution – do not exist as such in the federal criminal code. Title 18 should be amended to ensure that the full range of crimes against humanity and their constituent elements, including the requirement that the individual crime be committed as part of 'a widespread or systematic attack directed against any civilian population', are properly recited therein. The federal genocide statute (18 USC §1091) does not permit prosecution of an alien for genocide committed outside US territory, even if the alien is a resident of or otherwise present in the United States. Title 18 should be amended to enable such prosecution in US courts. The federal war crimes statute (18 USC §2441) requires a broader jurisdiction to include perpetrators or victims who are not necessarily US nationals or members of the US military, including perhaps the opportunity whereby if the alleged alien perpetrator is present on US territory, then he or she can be prosecuted. If only the alien victim of the war crime is on US territory, he or she could not seek relief unless the alleged alien perpetrator also appears on US territory. Further, the federal war crimes statute should be amended to include the war crimes under international customary law that are reflected in Article 8 of the Rome Statute – only some of which are covered by the existing federal law.

I recently asked one of my graduate law students, an experienced active duty Air Force JAG officer, to research Title 10 of the US Code and advise me whether it satisfactorily enables US military courts to fully prosecute all Article 8 war crimes under the Rome Statute. She discovered that the Uniform Code of Military Justice, found in Title 10 of the US Code, is inadequate to the task of prosecuting military personnel for most of the specific war crimes in Article 8 of the Rome Statute. As she wrote in her thesis:

> 'Title 18 war crimes have never been fully integrated into Title 10. This makes the UCMJ incomplete and ill-suited to address war crimes. Offenders indeed may end up with criminal records and go to jail, but they avoid the stigma of being labeled a war criminal...War crimes should receive a prominent placement within or near the articles of the UCMJ that directly address the conduct of military members during war. Congress should align the provisions of Title 10 directly with the relevant provisions of Title 18 by incorporating a new article in Title 10 for that purpose. By so aligning Title 10 with Title 18, Congress would create and maintain a distinction between war crimes and common crimes within the UCMJ. Making this same distinction within Title 10 prosecutions is important in promoting uniformity within our domestic system of criminal laws. Why should civilians be subject to greater punishment than military members for the same conduct, especially when the underlying conventions that Title 18 implemented primarily address the conduct of the armed forces?
>
> Second, adding a war crimes article to the UCMJ will encourage greater uniformity in prosecuting war crimes within the U.S. military justice system. Once statutory provisions define war crimes within Title 10, military authorities may be more likely to charge serious battlefield misconduct as what it is: a war crime. Third, such an amendment could yield greater uniformity in the range of available maximum punishments. Although the convening authority has the discretion to decide which charges are referred to trial, adding a new article aimed at war crimes can encourage the development of the practice of distinguishing between war crimes and common crimes in courts-martial. As cases arising out of the Abu Ghraib scandal show, the maximum punishment will vary greatly on the offenses charged. Charging crimes under a new UCMJ war crimes article will have the added effect of providing a more consistent range of punishments when the cases are presented to the military judge or court-martial panel for sentencing.
>
> Finally, adding the substance of the war crimes act would balance statutory military law and the use of military commissions in a manner consistent with military custom and the intent of the UCMJ drafters. Traditionally, military commissions were used for U.S. service members only for offenses, with the exception of spying and aiding the enemy, that were not covered by the soldier's code. Although military commissions have not been used to try American forces since the UCMJ was enacted, this option remains available. Adding a new war crimes UCMJ article would thus weigh against trying the U.S. service member by a military commission for violations of the Geneva Conventions.'

## 1.4 Double complementarity

The ICC Assembly of States Parties also could amend the ICC Rules of Procedure and Evidence so as to implement a procedure of *double complementarity*, namely a procedure that would ensure the initial transfer of ICC suspects to their national jurisdictions that are willing to investigate and, if merited, prosecute them under the complementarity procedures of the ICC Statute. Governments need to be assured, through the procedural workings of the ICC, that a claim of national jurisdiction over an individual which is invoked as part of a government's right, under ICC Statute Article 18, to investigate and prosecute individuals within its jurisdiction will mean the following: Where a State Party to the ICC decides not to investigate or prosecute an individual who is subject to its national jurisdiction for commission of an ICC crime, then that State Party would agree to transfer the individual to a requesting government (regardless of whether it is a State Party to the ICC) that properly invokes the complementarity privileges of Article 18 of the ICC Statute with the intention of investigating and, if merited, prosecuting the individual in its national courts for the ICC crime(s) in question.

Such *procedural* complementarity, incorporated in the ICC Rules of Procedure and Evidence and ensuring the transfer of the individual to, in most cases, his or her own national jurisdiction, would assure all governments that their implementation of *substantive* complementarity before national courts will be achievable. In the event, for example, a non-State Party fails to follow through with credible investigation and prosecution of an individual transferred to its jurisdiction and then fails (as would be its right as a non-State Party) to heed the ICC's request to voluntarily transfer such individual to the ICC, the new rule could provide for termination of any State Party's obligation to transfer anyone to that non-party State as part of any implementation of Article 18 of the ICC Statute and the new double complementarity procedure. In contrast, a State Party that invokes Article 18 of the ICC Statute and achieves custody of a suspect would be required to transfer such individual within its custody to the ICC in accordance with Articles 89 and 90 of the ICC Statute in the event complementarity fails and the ICC requests the transfer.

## 1.5 Strengthened admissibility review

During the negotiations of 2000 concerning supplemental documentation to the Rome Statute, the US delegation developed a proposal that gained considerable informal support among other governments. The proposal was to ensure that just prior to any surrender of a suspect to the ICC, there would be a review of the admissibility of the case by the judges, using their Article 19(1) power to initiate such a review. This would ensure that if there were developments in a national court system between the time when the suspect was first identified by the ICC and the time of a surrender request by the Court, the judges would take those developments into account to determine whether that national jurisdiction had fulfilled its complementarity responsibilities. For the United States, such a procedure established by amendment to the Rules of Procedure and Evidence, would provide much greater assurance that good faith efforts of investigation and, if merited, prosecution of a suspect in US courts following any Article 18 procedure of complementarity and prior to actual surrender to the

Court would be honored by the ICC judges as a consequence of this Article 19(1) admissibility review on the eve of surrender.

This strengthened admissibility review could be established by amending the Rules of Procedure and Evidence with wording of the following character:

> 'Unless there has been a referral to the Court pursuant to article 13(b) of the Statute, the Court shall determine on its own motion pursuant to article 19(1) the admissibility of a case in accordance with article 17 when there is a request for the surrender of a suspect who is charged in such case with a crime that occurred outside the territory of the suspect's State of nationality.'

### 1.6 **Security Council referral to the ICC**

ICC Statute Article 13(b) invites the Security Council to refer atrocity situations to the ICC for investigation and prosecution, and that referral power can be executed on terms set forth in the relevant Council resolution. Such application of the Security Council's referral power should enable the Security Council, using its UN Charter Chapter VII enforcement authority, to limit or qualify the personal, subject-matter, territorial, or temporal jurisdiction of the ICC, as well as the scope of complementarity, with respect to the specific situation being referred to the Court. Simultaneously, the Security Council's invocation of Chapter VII authority can enhance greatly the powers of investigation of the Court and broaden the Court's reach over designated non-party States to the ICC and the nationals of such non-party States. These measures of control over the scope of the ICC's investigative and ultimately prosecutorial powers in atrocity situations referred by the Security Council should be recognized by the US Government and other permanent members of the Council as remarkable opportunities to use accountability under international criminal law in the most constructive possible way to help maintain or restore international peace and security.

Security Council Resolution 1593 referring the Darfar situation to the ICC reflects some of what the Council can accomplish in this respect. The resolution includes an explicit exemption from the ICC's jurisdiction, stating that

> 'nationals, current or former officials or personnel from a contributing State outside Sudan which is not a party to the Rome Statute of the International Criminal Court shall be subject to the exclusive jurisdiction of that contributing State for all alleged acts or omissions arising out of or related to operations in Sudan established or authorized by the Council or the African Union, unless such exclusive jurisdiction has been expressly waived by that contributing State.'

While this exemption from the jurisdiction of the ICC was an unattractive feature of the resolution in the eyes of many Court supporters, including myself, it does demonstrate that the United States can ensure adequate safeguards for its own personnel through a Security Council referral in order to achieve the objective of bringing foreign perpetrators of atrocities occurring outside the United States to justice.

### 1.7 **The Security Council's power to block the ICC**

ICC Statute Article 16 empowers the Security Council to block the ICC from acting during particularly sensitive security challenges with much calibrated use of the Council's enforcement power under the UN Charter. This power of blockage is potentially a very potent instrument of leverage on the ICC by the Security Council. Even the threat of a Security Council resolution invoking Article 16 authority could deeply influence the choices the ICC Prosecutor makes in the exercise of his powers. The United States already has toyed with Article 16 in achieving adoption of Security Council Resolutions 1422 (2002) and 1487 (2003), albeit for purposes never intended by the negotiators of the ICC. If the United States turned its attention to a more constructive use of Article 16 in the future, using it sparingly and for persuasive purpose in agreement with other members of the Security Council with respect to particular situations, then it could become a safeguard of considerable utility.

## 2. Amendments to the Rome Statute

### 2.1 Amendment to make the crime of aggression actionable

There remains a high probability that an effort will be made at the 2009 Review Conference of the ICC Statute to amend the subject-matter jurisdiction of the Court so as to establish a trigger mechanism and definition for the crime of aggression, and thus to make it an actionable crime before the Court. It would be folly for the United States to remain disengaged in the on-going negotiations by the Assembly of States Parties over how, for purposes of individual criminal responsibility, the crime of aggression will be enforced by the ICC. (Even as a non-party State, the United States can participate as an observer in such negotiations.)

If there is any ICC crime that might be used for political purposes against the United States in the future, it is the crime of aggression due to America's global military commitments and often bold and controversial use of its armed forces on or over foreign territory. A proper trigger procedure and definition for the crime of aggression would dispel concerns that the ICC might be manipulated by governments or the ICC prosecutor to thwart legitimate uses of military force to confront threats to international peace and security. As a no-show in the negotiations, the United States may have only itself to blame if the trigger mechanism and definition of the crime of aggression that emerge for consideration at the 2009 review conference prove unacceptable.

### 2.2 Amendment to the ICC Statute to criminalize UN corruption and sexual abuse

In addition to the crime of aggression, crimes of terrorism and drug crimes are expected to be seriously considered for amendment to the ICC Statute at the 2009 Review Conference. While these initiatives may be all the review conference can absorb regarding the ICC's subject-matter jurisdiction, effort should be made to consider using the ICC to investigate and prosecute officials charged with the most egregious types of corruption and sexual abuse within the UN system, including its specialized agencies, related organizations, and peace operations. In light of the recent investigation into the Oil-for-Food Program for Iraq and sexual abuse investigations of the UN peacekeeping operation in the Democratic Republic of the Congo, there is a strong case to be made that the United Nations needs access to an independent criminal court before which to bring UN administrators charged with corruption or UN peacekeeping personnel charged with sexual assault. The requirements of sufficient gravity and importance to the international community that limit the range of crimes already in the ICC Statute also would need to be retained in some fashion for these additional categories of crimes. Otherwise, the ICC would be overwhelmed with investigating and prosecuting relatively low-level individuals for relatively low-impact crimes. Some criteria for the targets of investigation and the magnitude of the crimes at issue would have to be established. Given Washington's investigative focus on both UN corruption and peacekeeping sexual abuse, the US Government should find such subject matter jurisdiction a very attractive feature of the ICC and one worth cooperating with and perhaps participating in.

## 3. Declarations and Understandings to a US Ratification of the Rome Statute

If some of the reform initiatives introduced above can be realized, and the United States achieves the political will to ratify or accede to the Rome Statute, then it is entirely predictable that the US Senate would push as close to the cliff of reservations – not permitted under the Statute – as possible in order to assure the sufficient two-thirds vote required in that body for approval of a treaty. Various governments that already have ratified the Rome Statute have employed declarations and understandings of occasional bold character. One can easily imagine what the United States might draw upon to frame its own declarations and understandings. For example, Australia confirmed a far-reaching declaration regarding complementarity, requiring that

> 'no person will be surrendered to the Court by Australia until it has had the full opportunity to investigate or prosecute any alleged crimes. For this purpose, the procedure under Australian law supplementing the Statute of the Court provides that no person can be surrendered to the Court unless the Australian Attorney-General issues a certificate allowing surrender. Australian law also provides that no person can be arrested pursuant to an arrest warrant issued by the Court without a certificate from the Attorney General.'

The Australian declaration further states

> 'its understanding that the offences in Articles 6, 7 and 8 will be interpreted and applied in a way that accords with the way they are implemented in Australian domestic law.'

Colombia included in its declaration the requirement that

> 'Concerning Article 17(3), Colombia declares that the use of the word "otherwise" with respect to the determination of the State's ability to investigate or prosecute a case refers to the obvious absence of objective conditions necessary to conduct the trial.'

Colombia's declaration further requires that

> 'none of the provisions of the Rome Statute alters the domestic law applied by the Colombian judicial authorities in exercise of their domestic jurisdiction within the territory of the Republic of Colombia.'

Both Colombia and France invoked their right under Article 124 of the Rome Statute to exempt their nationals from investigation by the ICC for Article 8 war crimes for a period of seven years following ratification. France also addresses several specific issues arising under Article 8 with interpretative declarations that one could easily envisage the United States employing. One such interpretation relates to Article 8(2)(b) and France's view that it

> 'relates solely to conventional weapons and does not prohibit the use of nuclear weapons nor impair the other rules of international law applicable to other weapons necessary to the exercise by France of its inherent right of self-defense…'

Some of the constitutional concerns raised by American commentators could be addressed in a US interpretative declaration which in part clarifies that no action taken by the United States under the Rome Statute shall be taken in violation of the US Constitution. While this may prove controversial, it has become a standard declaration in US ratifications of international treaties and in practice should mean very little if anything to the cooperative relationship between the United States and the ICC.

## Remarks by Jack Martin*

## The United States and the ILO

Default, withdrawal and return 1970-1980

In November 1975, the United States gave notice of withdrawal from the International Labour Organization (ILO). In November 1977 its withdrawal took effect – the first time that the United States had withdrawn from an Organization of the United Nations system. In February 1980, 27 months later, it returned to the ILO. This paper gives a brief account of the events leading up to US withdrawal and its subsequent return.

### The Background

#### 1. **A brief introduction to the ILO**

Created in 1919 as part of the Treaty of Versailles to promote universal peace through social justice by improving working conditions and defending labour rights throughout the world, the ILO was the only part of the League of Nations machinery to have survived the Second World War. After the war it became a specialized agency of the UN. Two distinctive features of the ILO are emphasized here, because they have a particular relevance to the events described in this paper:

* Former Assistant Director-General, ILO. Any views or opinions expressed in this paper are those of the author, not of the International Labour Office. It should also be emphasized that this paper neither contains nor implies any comment on the present state of US-ILO relations.

- Its *tripartite structure*, which gives representatives of employers and workers an equal voice with those of governments in ILO organs – a structure which was intended to demonstrate that social problems are best dealt with by free negotiation among different interests rather than by revolution and class warfare. The main policy-making organs of the ILO are the *International Labour Conference* which meets annually and consists of tripartite delegations from all Member States; and the *Governing Body* which today consists of 56 persons: 28 representing governments (of which 10 States of chief industrial importance, while the remaining 18 governments are selected by government delegates to the Conference), 14 representing employers and 14 representing workers, elected respectively by employers' and workers' delegates to the Conference.[1] Tripartism implies that each of the three groups should enjoy complete autonomy in determining its position on particular issues – employers and workers representatives are entitled to act and vote independently of governments (and of each other), and they are generally expected to respect group discipline in casting their votes.
- Its *standard-setting activities and supervisory machinery*, which have always been the backbone of the ILO's work. Standards take the form of Conventions that are legally binding on States that ratify them, and Recommendations that are intended to provide guidance to national policy but create no legally binding commitments. These instruments are adopted by the International Labour Conference. There is an elaborate machinery for *supervising compliance with ratified Conventions*: governments are required to submit reports on the steps they have taken to bring national legislation and practice into line with the provisions of ratified Conventions; these reports are examined by a Committee of independent experts, which in turn reports to a Committee of the International Labour Conference each year. The Conference has the possibility of singling out States which have seriously and persistently failed to fulfill their obligations in regard to ILO standards for special mention. The ILO Constitution also provides for a *complaints procedure* under which a complaint may be filed against a member concerning the non-observance of any Convention which it has ratified,[2] and special procedures exist for the examination of complaints submitted by trade unions (or employers) relating to violations of *freedom of association*. Following the accession to membership of large numbers of developing countries, the ILO also became an important *technical cooperation* agency, providing assistance to such countries in developing skills, promoting employment and creating the institutions and conditions for implementing policies consistent with ILO standards.

## 2. The United States and the ILO – an uneasy relationship

Although the United States had played a special role in the creation of the ILO,[3] it did not become a member until 1934 (and it never became a member of the League of Nations to which the ILO was constitutionally linked). Since then, relations between the United States and the ILO have had many ups and downs. They started to become especially problematic when the USSR re-entered the ILO in 1954.[4] The main contentious issue that then arose was the position of employers' and workers' representatives from communist countries in their respective groups at ILO meetings. They invariably voted as instructed by their governments – i.e., they followed the Party line, rather than the positions of their groups. The reaction of the employers' group was to exclude representatives of communist countries from their meetings; no 'employer' representative from a communist country was ever elected by the group to the ILO Governing Body or to Committees of the Conference. The situation in the workers' group was different in the sense that communist worker delegates were not systematically excluded, but the communist trade union movement had very little influence over the formulation of worker group policies and positions.

Thus, the ILO, perhaps more than any other UN organization, became a battleground in the cold war. The USSR and other communist countries complained of discrimination, and pressed for changes in the ILO's structures and procedures in order that they may be fully represented in all three groups. Employers and workers were determined to oppose any change that would threaten the autonomy of their respective groups. The United States became increasingly concerned at the undermining of tripartism, and at the growth of communist propaganda and influence, in ILO organs. The United States was not, of course, alone; its concern was shared by many other (particularly OECD) countries. But even the countries most sympathetic to the United States considered that the UN and its specialized agencies, including the ILO, should include all political and economic systems; and that attempts should be made to reconcile the essence of the ILO's unique tripartite structure with the no less compelling need for the ILO to be universal in membership and in action. The United States (government, employers and workers) seemed to be less convinced that it was either possible or necessary to reconcile these two objectives in the ILO.

New dimensions were added to this difficult problem with the accession to independence and to ILO membership of large numbers of developing countries in the early 1960s. There was great frustration among these new States when they found that, though numerous, they could have only a marginal effect on ILO policy-making. They soon discovered, for instance, that the real decision-making power was concentrated in the Governing Body, where the main industrial powers were dominant, rather than in the International Labour Conference where the combined voting power of developing and communist countries outweighed that of market economy countries.[5] They also felt that the employers' and workers' groups were dominated by Western interests. With the support of communist countries they demanded changes to ILO structures and procedures. And their frustrations were compounded when they found that amendments to the ILO Constitution that would be required to make such changes possible had to be adopted by a two-thirds majority at the Conference, and then ratified by two-thirds of the Member States, *including five of the ten States of chief industrial importance.*[6]

Thus, developing and communist countries frequently voted together, and the United States and its allies found themselves outvoted on a number of sensitive issues at the International Labour Conference. This was, of course, also happening in other international organizations, including especially the UN itself. But the ILO was different: it was tripartite, and it was not only the US Government, but even more so US employers and workers, who were incensed at this state of affairs.

Until 1970, the ILO had an American Director-General, David Morse, who managed to calm down US concerns at these developments in the ILO. Morse resigned in May 1970 after 22 years of service. Without his restraining influence the stage was set for a major confrontation.

DEFAULT

The incident that triggered off the crisis was the decision taken by the newly elected Director-General, Wilfred Jenks, in June 1970 (within a few weeks of his election), to appoint a Soviet national to a post of Assistant Director-General. In any other organization, this event would have passed almost unnoticed; every other UN organization at that time had at least one national of a communist country in a senior position, without this having any disruptive effect on the functioning of the organization. But as soon as news of this appointment reached Washington, George Meany, President of the US trade union movement (AFL-CIO) and a militant anti-communist, took the initiative of bringing the matter before the Appropriations Sub-Committee of the House of Representatives (whose Chairman, John Rooney, was a close political friend of his). For Meany this appointment was 'the last straw' in a long sequence of events since 1954 that had led to a strengthening of communist influence in the ILO. The US employers' representative in the ILO Governing Body supported Meany, and the Sub-Committee recommended the withholding of the US contribution to the ILO for 1970. This recommendation was supported by the Senate Sub-Committee, and Congress deleted the contribution to the ILO from the appropriations for 1970.

The US Administration was not party to Meany's initiative, and it lost control of the situation. Its embarrassment was made quite clear in the testimony of the State Department to Congress:

> 'The United States has undertaken a legal duty to pay the share of the budget voted by the ILO Conference, and we would be in violation of that obligation if we did not make our full payment. ... failure to pay our obligatory assessment would seriously weaken the ability of the United States to exert influence in the Organization.'[7]

The ILO was plunged into a major financial crisis, as the US contribution amounted to 25 per cent of the Organization's regular budget. At first, it was expected that the crisis would be short-lived – US government representatives in the ILO Governing Body and elsewhere constantly reaffirmed that the United States recognized its obligation to pay its contribution in full. But the crisis was not short-lived. Ignoring a proposal by the Administration, Congress voted in 1971 not to restore the 1970 arrears or to provide for any payment at all of the 1971 contribution to the ILO; draconian measures had to be adopted by the ILO to deal with a critical financial situation: e.g., postponement of virtually all meetings, complete freeze on recruitment. The Director-General was also given authority to borrow in order to meet commitments, and many staff members contributed to a voluntary fund. But significantly, no Member State responded to an appeal by the Director-General to contribute to an emergency fund to assist the ILO. Even the closest allies of the United States were appalled at the failure of the United States to meet its financial obligations, and were not prepared to let it off the hook.

The embarrassment of the US Administration at this state of affairs was such that President Nixon himself felt obliged to state at the end of 1971:

> 'It is simply not consistent with our national dignity to attempt to maintain influence and membership in the ILO if we are not prepared to pay our dues. The Administration will there-

fore have no choice but to give notice of withdrawal from the ILO unless Congress sees fit to provide our assessed contributions to that Organization.'[8]

In 1972 the United States would have lost the right to vote if it did not resume payment of its dues.[9] For the next five years therefore it paid enough to maintain the right to vote, although it remained in arrears. But the threat of withdrawal loomed larger and larger.

## Towards Withdrawal

The threat was taken seriously by the friends and allies of the United States in all three groups, and they tried to dissuade socialist and developing countries from provoking the US any further, as did the Director-General (Wilfred Jenks) himself. But to little avail. The next stage of the crisis was provoked by the situation in the Middle East, which has poisoned the atmosphere in the ILO ever since. At the 1973 session of the Conference, a resolution had made its way through Committee condemning 'the policy of racial discrimination and violation of trade union rights which the Israeli authorities are pursuing against the Arab peoples', and inviting the Governing Body to set-up a Committee to investigate 'Israel's persistent violations of trade union freedoms and discriminatory practices against Arab workers.' In his speech of reply to the Conference, Jenks warned that 'for the ILO first to condemn and then to call for an inquiry to confirm such a condemnation would be to offend the principle of due process on which all our work relating to the implementation of Conventions rests.'[10] The resolution failed to be adopted for lack of quorum, to the fury of Arab delegations who withdrew their support from the Director-General. The United States praised the Director-General's stand, but this did not prevent him from continuing to be subjected to pressure and even abuse in Washington. The strains and pressures to which he was subjected from all sides led to his sudden death in October 1973. Francis Blanchard of France was elected to succeed him.

The new Director-General did not have an easier time than his predecessor. The 1974 session of the Conference was a particularly black one for the United States. It adopted a resolution on Israel very similar to that which had failed to be adopted in 1973. Another blow to the United States in 1974 was the failure of the Conference to adopt the report of its Committee on the Application of Conventions and Recommendations which, *inter alia*, singled out the Soviet Union for practices which violated the Convention on forced labour which it had ratified. An unholy alliance of Communist countries and right-wing dictatorships in Latin America (which were also singled out in the report for non-respect of ratified Conventions) succeeded in getting enough support to prevent the Committee's report from being adopted.

The fateful moment came at the 1975 session of the Conference when it amended its Standing Orders to enable observer status to be granted to the PLO.[11] In this the ILO Conference was only following the lead of the General Assembly of the UN (as specialized agencies normally do on political matters); but it was too much for George Meany who, with the support of the employers, called on the US Government to withdraw from the ILO. The letter giving notice of withdrawal, signed by Secretary of State Henry Kissinger, was received by the Director-General on 6 November 1975.[12]

WITHDRAWAL

The Kissinger letter made it clear that the United States considered the ILO to have been falling back on 'four matters of fundamental concern':

- erosion of tripartism;
- an appallingly selective concern for human rights;
- disregard of due process;
- increasing politicization of the Organization.

Even those most sympathetic to the United States position could not fully support it on all these 'four matters of concern'. For instance, it was difficult to see how tripartism was being 'eroded' – employer and worker groups continued to play their role in ILO organs in complete autonomy. The allegation of 'an appallingly selective concern for human rights' implied that the ILO's supervisory bodies were quick to condemn certain countries friendly to the United States (e.g., Chile, Argentina, Turkey) for the violation of workers' rights, while communist countries were 'granted immunity'. But this ignored the fact that the ILO's Committee of independent experts had year after year addressed strong criticism to the USSR and other communist countries for violation of the most basic ILO standards, including those on freedom of association and forced labour. The communist countries were thus constantly under pressure, even though they were generally able to secure enough votes to prevent a formal condemnation by the Conference. Moreover, the United States would have been on stronger ground if it had itself ratified the relevant ILO Conventions; in fact it was among the very few countries not to have ratified any of the ILO's basic human rights Conventions.[13]

Nevertheless, the United States certainly had every reason to be concerned at a country being condemned by Conference resolutions without due process; and it was this issue that led to US withdrawal. Attempts by Arab countries at the 1977 Conference to condemn Israel for violation of ILO Convention No. 111 on discrimination in employment and occupation were defeated in the Conference Committee on Application of Conventions – a victory for Israel and the United States; but the report of the Committee failed (as in 1974) to be adopted by the Conference. A further blow was the failure of the Conference to adopt an amendment to its Standing Orders which aimed to prevent resolutions condemning a State for violation of ratified Conventions without due process coming before the Conference. These two developments destroyed all hopes of the United States remaining in the Organization.

President Carter took the decision to confirm the withdrawal of the United States effective 6 November 1977. The only good news was that the US had to pay up all its arrears of contributions before leaving!

During the two year notice period, the Director-General had had a contingency plan prepared for dealing with the financial consequences, so that within two weeks of the US withdrawal the Governing Body had before it detailed proposals for reductions of expenditure and of programme in the 1978-79 budgetary period. The package of reductions ultimately approved by the Governing Body amounted to $36.6 million (21.7 per cent of the approved budget). It naturally involved some very painful cuts (e.g., in publications, research, meetings), and difficult decisions had to be taken (particularly concerning staff reductions, reorganization and restructuring the Office). But special care was taken not to impair the effectiveness of the ILO's standard-setting activities or its capacity to provide technical cooperation for developing countries; indeed the ILO succeeded in attracting increased amounts of extra-budgetary funds from UNDP and elsewhere for its technical cooperation programmes. Moreover, in contrast to the period when the United States had been in default, voluntary contributions were received from numerous governments and other bodies around the world to help the Organization over its difficulties.

Even more significant, no other Member State followed the US out of the ILO. Some circles in the US had thought that the work of the ILO (and its tripartite structure) could be transferred to some other Organizations less subjected to communist influence – such as OECD or the Organization of American States. But this initiative received no support at all. The ILO survived, although weakened, and carried on with its work.

On the other hand, US withdrawal did have a sobering effect on the remaining membership. Sessions of the Governing Body and the International Labour Conference were more businesslike (no provocative political resolutions were adopted in 1978 or 1979). Paradoxically, too, the United States started taking more interest in the substantive work of the ILO than when it had been a member. A Presidential Committee was established to follow developments in the ILO, and US Government representation in the ILO (in an observer capacity) was upgraded.

## Return

The decision to return to the Organization was taken by President Carter in February 1980. Compared with the drama of withdrawal, the return of the United States was almost an anti-climax, and the reasons for its return after such a brief absence were not altogether clear (and are no clearer today). US spokesmen justified the decision by claiming that withdrawal had forced the ILO to change its ways. Nobody wished to contradict them at the time, but it was difficult to see in what way the ILO had changed. The Soviet ADG whose appointment had triggered off the crisis in 1970 was still in post; the PLO continued to enjoy observer status at the Conference; no significant progress had been made on any of the four 'matters of fundamental concern' identified in the Kissinger letter. One innovation introduced during the absence of the United States was intended to go some way towards addressing US concerns: an amendment to the Conference Standing Orders was adopted in 1979, which introduced the possibility of vote by secret ballot – in the hope that this would encourage delegates to vote according to their conscience rather than to instructions. But any illusions that this would prevent 'political' resolutions from being adopted were dashed at the Conference in 1980 – immediately after the return of the United States – when a resolution concerning Israel was adopted after a vote ... by secret ballot!

## Consequences

The ILO emerged from the crisis with its reputation, if anything, enhanced. Much of the credit for this should go to Director-General Blanchard who had very skilfully and responsibly handled a situation which could have been terminal for the Organization. The crisis had indeed resulted in a sizeable reduction in the resources available to the Organization (the level of the budget was not restored to its former level when the United States returned), but this forced the ILO to concentrate on its main priorities and to undertake some streamlining of its structures and procedures.

The events that precipitated the crisis were in many respects peculiar to the ILO, because of its tripartite structure. But the fury of the United States against the ILO was fuelled by the treatment it was receiving in other Organizations – especially in the General Assembly of the UN where on one critical issue after another the United States found itself in a humiliating minority. The ILO was in a sense a useful scapegoat, and withdrawal from the ILO was meant to send a signal to the rest of the UN system. Perhaps, however, US policy-makers realized soon after withdrawal that they had made a mistake in picking on the ILO, and in allowing policy to be dictated by the whims of one George Meany.

Today, some 30 years later, the ILO crisis is all but forgotten – a product of the Cold War, with little relevance to today's world. Perhaps its most serious long-term consequence is that it created a *precedent* for using financial pressure and withdrawal (or the threat of withdrawal) to attempt to achieve certain aims in international organizations – a precedent that has since been followed by the United States (and by other countries) in various organizations. On the other hand, the most important lesson that should have been learned (but does not appear to have been learned) from these events is that such aggressive methods can be quite counter-productive. It is difficult to see how the United States benefited from using these tactics against the ILO. It isolated itself from its allies (including the world trade union movement and employers' circles), it tarnished its reputation for financial integrity, it flouted international law, and it also underestimated the potentially important role that the ILO – for all its imperfections – could play in the promotion and defence of workers' rights, tripartism and democracy, a role that it was to play with much success a few years later in upholding trade union rights in Poland. The United States was able to achieve its objectives much more effectively when it resumed membership and constructive participation in the ILO than when it brandished threats and exerted financial pressure against it.

## Notes

1 Prior to 1974 it consisted of 24 governments (including 10 States of chief industrial importance), 12 employers and 12 workers.

2 Such complaints may be filed by another State which is party to the same Convention; by a delegate or delegates to the Conference; or by the Governing Body of its own motion.

3 Samuel Gompers, president of the American Federation of Labor, was Chairman of the Commission on International Labour Legislation, which led to the creation of the ILO, at the Peace Conference in 1919.

4 The Soviet Union had first joined the ILO in 1934, and ceased to be a member of the League of Nations

and the ILO in 1939. When it rejoined in 1954 it was followed shortly afterwards by Byelorussia and Ukraine. Other communist countries, such as Albania, Bulgaria, Czechoslovakia, Hungary, Poland and Yugoslavia were already members of the Organization.

5 For instance, it was (and still is) the Governing Body, not the Conference, that appoints the Director-General, fixes the agenda of all ILO meetings (including that of the Conference itself), supervises all ILO activities and in fact determines the size and content of the ILO's programme and budget before it is transmitted to the Conference for final adoption.

6 Since for this reason constitutional changes could not be adopted by a mere majority vote at the Conference, a Committee on Structure was set-up to attempt to reach a consensus on these contentious issues. Various Committees and Working Parties on structure continued to meet in different forms over the years. Initially they were just fruitless 'talking shops', with each side standing on its position. But as the years went by, concessions were made on all sides, and in 1986 a package of Constitutional reforms was put to the Conference as an Instrument for the Amendment of the Constitution and adopted. But by then the heat had gone out of the debate; the Instrument has still today not received the required number of ratifications to enter into force.

7 Congressional Record, Senate, 24 August 1970: S14106.

8 Richard M. Nixon, Report to the Congress, *United States Foreign Policy for the 1970s* (Washington DC, Government Printing Office 1971), p. 214.

9 The ILO Constitution provides that a Member State whose arrears in the payment of its contributions equal or exceed the amount of the contributions due for the preceding two full years shall lose the right to vote.

10 International Labour Conference, 58th Session, Geneva, 1973: *Record of Proceedings* (Geneva, ILO 1973), p. 707.

11 The wording of the new provision of the Standing Orders made it possible for 'liberation movements recognized by the Organization of African Unity or the League of Arab States' to be represented by observers at the Conference.

12 The ILO Constitution provides for a period of notice of two years before withdrawal can take effect.

13 It has since (in 1991) ratified one such Convention – the Abolition of Forced Labour Convention, 1957 (No. 105).

## Comments by Gerhard Hafner

Thank you very much for your presentations. Mr Matheson has been able to give us a full picture of all facets of the possible relations and attitudes of the United States towards international organizations, and I am grateful Professor Nolte has in his presentation also tried to identify those ways in which there can be cooperation between the United States and the European States. Mr Scheffer has brought forward ways of reconciling the United States with the ICC, so that the ICC can be seen as a positive value in the development of international law. With regard to Mr Martin's presentation on the ILO, it may be asked whether the activity of the United States in the second phase of its participation in the ILO was useful because it had earlier withdrawn, and so there was always the threat at the ILO that it may withdraw again.

## Discussion

Susan Karamanian:* I have a question for Professor Scheffer. What sorts of declarations and understandings are you looking at, in relation to other nations?

David Scheffer: I did try to put those in considerable detail in my paper. I would say the easiest declaration that could be applied, would be that which Colombia

* LL.M Student, George Washington University.

and France invoke, which is the Article 124 declaration – that for a seven year period, the Article 8 war crimes would not be available for prosecution against the United States. That would really be the easiest declaration to invoke since the Statute very clearly entitles States to invoke that.

Of course, if you approach the discussion with the strong view that you do not like Article 124, and therefore no one should sign on to it, then I would not know where we would go from there. What I am trying to suggest are options that are available, which do not violate the Rome Statute whatsoever, and can be used very constructively to try to bring some of the remaining major powers on board the ICC Statute. In this regard, I am not just talking about the United States, but also some other major powers like India, Pakistan, China, and Russia. I must also mention one other declaration – now common in US treaties – the one where we tack on to the end of a treaty that nothing in it will be interpreted or applied in direct contravention to the US Constitution. Though it is sort of a standard clause now in U.S treaties, it is something I can imagine, if the treaty went before the US Senate, that senators would not insist it be added as a declaration.

HANS CORELL:* I must say I found this panel very refreshing. I have an observation on the contributions. I lived through 10 years in the UN, in the middle of which the United States did not pay its contributions and my US colleague, who was then Head of Administration and I and others simply sweated it through, though it was devastating. I think that if this was done to change the organization, it was the worst medicine you could give because it actually prevented us from engaging in reform work. Therefore in this regard, I could not agree more with the speakers.

My question is actually for DAVID SCHEFFER, and it is on something you touched upon – the way the US participation in the drafting of the ICC Statute ended up. I had been following the process and found it a sad development. I am sure, nevertheless that we will see the United States a member of the ICC, as it has indeed become a member of other treaties, only that it is taking more time (and sometimes States need more time for reflection)

My question relates to this latter point: do you think that a declaration of this kind, in other words, where you make a general reference to your constitution, is valid under international law? I am asking this because when I tried the same thing while defending my country before the Court of Human Rights in Strasbourg, I saw a faint smile on the faces of the judges and the explanation for that smile came later in the judgement, where it stated that you can never do that. You cannot in an international setting make such a reservation because if you agree to an international agreement, then you will have to swallow that pill – lock, stock and barrel. And reservations to the Rome Statute, as you know, are not permitted.

DAVID SCHEFFER: You have raised an excellent point and I do think there is a lot of value to it. I do not think it would be possible as a reservation to the treaty to clear the trump of the US Constitution in all cases where there might be a conflict, as a matter of international law. I guess where I would argue from a lawyer's perspective that there could be a distinction drawn, is when a State steps forward and attaches

* Former Legal Counsel of the United Nations and the Secretary General's Representative at the Rome Conference.

such a caveat as a declaration, as opposed to a reservation to the treaty. In that case, it opens itself up to the criticism of other States that it may ultimately act in a manner which would violate its commitment to the Statute, that it will thus be in violation of international law if it did so, but that because it is so classified as a declaration to the treaty, it can stand as a legal declaration to the treaty until such time as that violation actually takes place. In the latter case, the performance of the party will be judged under international law, regardless of the fact that the State may insist that it is going to ensure it stays in compliance with its domestic law, including its constitution (here I am referring to the classic American contrast between compliance with domestic law v. international law, the later in time principles applied in determining when statutory law trumps treaty law, etc.)

I would say however – though I qualify it by expressing deep recognition and respect for the efforts undertaken by so many governments, including France, to literally amend their constitution, in order to be able to ratify the ICC Statute – that amending the US Constitution would not be considered a realistic option in the United States for this purpose. On the other hand, I think that we need to respect the efforts made by other governments in this regard, and hence make effort to structure our relations with the Court as much as possible in a way that also enables us to remain in compliance with our Constitution. This on its own, raises a big issue which we will not get into now, in other words the issue of whether the existing Rome Statute, if we were to be a party to it today, is a violation of the US Constitution. I would argue no very strongly, but you have to understand that the critics, including those in the Bush Administration, would argue that it is a violation of the US Constitution.

GERHARD HAFNER: On the issue of declarations, I would mention that there was opposition to one declaration and it was then declared to be a reservation.

GIAN LUCA BURCI:* I have a question for Mr. MATHESON, especially in view of his previous role as legal adviser to the US State Department. The question came to my mind as I was listening to Mr. Corell mentioning the occasional US withdrawal and non-payment of contributions. It is my understanding that maybe not in all cases, but certainly in some cases of US withdrawal from an international organization, for example in the case of UNIDO, the US has left behind a sizeable amount of its assessed contributions unpaid when it withdrew. Now, obviously, the United States has an obligation under the constitutions of the various organizations to pay its assessed contributions in full and in time. So I would argue that there would be an obligation of the withdrawing State to pay up its arrears before it withdraws. I wonder whether there has been any sort of analysis at the State Department or at the academic level that you know of, where this was somehow seen as a violation of a US obligation under those constitutions, and provision made for the later repayment of those arrears. I ask because I remember distinctly the then legal adviser of UNIDO, being somehow desperate because the organization had been left with a sizeable financial hole, without a clear legal remedy of how to get that money back.

MICHAEL J. MATHESON: Now, I do not recall any analysis on that particular point, in relation to that particular agreement. I would imagine one would have to look at

* World Health Organization.

the specifics of the statute and regulations of the organization in question, and make a judgment as to what was required as part of the withdrawal process. I am sorry I do not know about this specific case of UNIDO. But I think the concern you have raised is a perfectly legitimate one.

JACK MARTIN: In the case of the ILO, when the United States withdrew, they did pay up all the arrears of contributions they owed and they recognised that they had that obligation.

MARY ELLEN O'CONNELL:* I respect profoundly Hans Corell and Mr. Martin's point that withholding dues is a bad policy and can be very bad for an organization. I am wondering whether it is entirely true that withholding dues is in all cases unlawful as both Mr Martin and Professor Matheson said. I could imagine the argument that those organizations that do not have an alternative internal means of enforcing their constitutions, leave members with no other option than to withhold dues in the face of a clear violation of the organization's constitutional document; in other words, as a countermeasure in response to an unlawful action, in order to enforce the law of the organization. Some organizations are established in such a way that countermeasures are the only option available to States in terms of enforcement. I will appreciate your comment on this issue.

MICHAEL J. MATHESON: I do not believe that I said that withholding dues was unlawful in all circumstances. What I said was that the requirement to pay assessed contributions is an international obligation of the State, and that there may be circumstances under which such withholding might have some justification. For example, there is always the question of actions which are plainly *ultra vires* for an organization, and in this regard one would have to look at the specific rules and procedures of an organization. What I do say is that the kind of arbitrary withholdings that you see in this congressional proposal are not lawful and that the obligation to pay is indeed an obligation, not simply a political commitment as has sometimes been suggested.

JACK MARTIN: The emphasis must always be on the word 'assessed'. Assessed contributions have to be paid. It is illegal to withhold assessed contributions. Where questions can arise concerns voluntary contributions. In cases where the United States and others have withheld contributions that they had pledged, for instance to the UN Fund for Population Activities (UNFPA) because of alleged birth control activities in China, their actions are not so much illegal as they are sending a political signal. But if you are contributing to a budget that has been assessed, then I do not think that there can be any doubt it would be illegal to withhold such contributions.

DAVID SCHEFFER: Just on this point of assessments. Just to say that I am working with some others on a third edition of a casebook on the law of international organizations and we have just been looking at this. The best that you can really come up with is that there is no effective remedy to deal with the normally illegal act of withholding your assessed contributions as you withdraw from an organization. In other words, where you take your remedy in terms of trying to enforce that payment of assessments is rather uncertain in international law. But where you can recoup your leverage is if that State wishes to rejoin the organization. Obviously, your negotiating leverage with that State is to insist that there be an arrearage payment made in other for it to resume

* Ohio State University.

its membership in the organization. But then the question of whether or not that leverage is actually applied as a negotiating tool is a political one that only plays out on a case-by-case basis.

E. VAN VLASTUIN:* I have a question for Mr. SCHEFFER. If I listen carefully to the conclusion of your speech, you see it as possible that the gap between the US Administration and the ICC will be breached. But do you also see it as likely that this will happen?

DAVID SCHEFFER: I think it is very difficult to see it happening while the so-called 'War on Terror' is in full steam, because there are just too many issues related to the ICC that will play out in Washington policy-making as to why we would want to subject ourselves to that risk when we are waging a very controversial and legally challenged war against terrorists on so many different fronts around the world. So I think this is a reality we have to step up to – that it is going to be difficult to get there while all of these other issues that have so dominated the news, that is those regarding the challenges to the legality of US military and intelligence operations around the world, are out there. But I do think that ultimately, and over the long term – as Hans Corell noted – the benefits of the ICC such as its performance, its professionalism, the fact that it indeed will become in some respects an indispensable organization to the United States, the latter being said with all seriousness, will ultimately have an impact and we might see sixty-six senators begin to move in the desired direction.

## CONCLUDING REMARKS BY GERHARD HAFNER

Thank you very much. I think we have come to the end of this panel. First of all, I want to thank the panellists who showed us a very broad spectrum of international organizations and the relations of the United States towards them – from the ILO to the ICC, and including other general comments on the issue. I will also pay tribute to the reporter who took note of all this. I thank everyone who took part in this discussion. My thanks also go to the organizers of this conference.

*Reporter*: Nwamaka Okany**

* Reporter, Reformatorisch Dagblad, the Netherlands.

** Ph.D candidate, University of Amsterdam Center for International Law.

# Institutional Reform and the European Union

The panel was convened by its Chair, Ramses Wessel*

## Introductory remarks by Ramses Wessel

After welcoming the audience to this panel Mr. Wessel expressed his gratefulness to the organisers of the conference for including a panel on the institutional reform of the European Union. In his opinion this issue is a very important one in the context of International Institutional Reform, because usually there is too much distinction made between the EU and International Law, whereas the EU is certainly one of the most important International Organisations.

Having the current development of the EU-Constitution in mind,[1] Mr. Wessel mentioned the reasons for European Institutional Reform: namely the accession of ten new Member States to the organisation in 2004; as a result to this the new neighbourhood policies of the EU, as well as the development of the EU towards consolidating its external relations.

### Note

1 The referendums about the ratification of the Constitution of the European Union in France and the Netherlands in May 2005 turned out in a serious crisis of the EU, because the people voted against the European Constitution and therefore stopped the ratification process for the time being.

## Remarks by Jan Wouters**

### Making the European Union a Global Actor? Reform of the External Relations Machinery under the EU Constitution

In December 2001, the European Council adopted the Laeken Declaration, which, *inter alia*, expressed the ambition to 'develop the Union into a stabilizing force and

* Professor of the Law of the European Union and other International Organisations, University of Twente.
** Professor of International Law and the Law of International Organizations, Leuven University; *Of Counsel*, Linklaters De Bandt, Brussels. The author would like to thank Mr. Dominic Coppens, Research Assistant at the Institute for International Law, Leuven University, for his assistance in the preparation of this contribution.

a model in the new, multipolar world'.[1] Three-and-a-half years later, however, the momentum of the Declaration seems to have been lost. In this contribution it will be submitted that the Treaty establishing a Constitution for Europe ('Constitution'),[2] which resulted from the European Convention set-up by the Laeken Declaration and the Intergovernmental Conference ('IGC') that followed it, does not entirely fulfil the grand ambitions of the Declaration as far as the EU's external relations are concerned. Following an overview of the general elements that make up the Union's external action in the Constitution, specific attention will be paid to the main changes proposed by the Constitution for the EU's external relations machinery, i.e., the Union Minister for Foreign Affairs ('UMFA'), the European External Action Service ('EEAS') and the Common Foreign and Security Policy ('CFSP').

## General Framework for External Action

One of the principal underlying aims of the Constitution was to provide the EU with an instrument for making it a global political actor apart from, and in coherence with, its economic external relations. The Constitution makes a vital step in this regard, by formally abolishing the 'pillar' structure which was introduced by the Maastricht Treaty in 1992. It merges the EU and EC Treaties as well as the different pillars and brings together the different aspects of the Union's external policies under Title III of Part III, 'the Union's External Action'. Consequently, at least in theory, there should be no difference in whether the EU's external action deals with economic or political matters. The Union is endowed with legal personality (Art. I-7). Under the current Treaties, only the European Community has been granted legal personality explicitly and enjoys international legal personality. It can be argued, though, that the Union is implicitly provided with legal personality, especially since the Treaty of Nice. However this may be, the Constitution places beyond doubt that the Union is able to conclude agreements on the international forum.

The Constitution also clusters the objectives of the EU's external action currently divided over different domains. Article I-3(4) describes them as follows:

> 'In its relations with the wider world, the Union shall uphold and promote its values and interests. It shall contribute to peace, security, the sustainable development of the Earth, solidarity and mutual respect among peoples, free and fair trade, eradication of poverty and the protection of human rights, in particular the rights of the child, as well as to the strict observance and the development of international law, including respect for the principles of the United Nations Charter.'

These objectives are elaborated upon further in Article III-292, which in paragraph 2 lists eight specific objectives that, according to paragraph 3, should be respected and pursued in developing and implementing the different areas of the Union's external action. Such a common set of goals is a prerequisite for a coherent external policy. It requires, for example, that the Common Commercial Policy (CCP) not only pursues trade-related objectives as stated in Article 133 EC Treaty, but takes into account and even contributes to other dimensions, such as human rights and sustainable development.

However, the Constitution only lists the different objectives. It does not link them to one another; nor does it offer a mechanism for prioritizing or resolving (potential) conflicts between the different objectives.

The Council and the Commission, assisted by the UMFA, are responsible for ensuring consistency between the different areas of the Union's external action and between these and the internal action (Art. III-292(3)). Moreover, pursuant to Article I-28(4), the UMFA must ensure the consistency of the Union's external action.[3] Yet, which tools they employ to fulfil this task remains the key question. A first such an instrument is placed in the hands of the European Council, which can adopt European decisions on strategic interests and objectives along the entire spectrum of the Union's external action. Unlike the common strategies under the current Treaty on European Union ('TEU'), these decisions are not restricted to the CFSP's domain. This means that the European Council's role in the Union's external action is increased, but also that it can contribute to ensuring consistency in this field of action – and presumably at a more authoritative level than the Commission and Council.

## Union Minister for Foreign Affairs

Many consider the creation of the position of Union Minister for Foreign Affairs to be one of the Constitution's most important innovations. The UMFA should serve to bridge the dual aspects of the Union's external policy, namely (i) the institutional tension between the Commission and the Council in the first (Community) pillar, in which the Member States' influence is often tempered by decision-making based on qualified majority voting ('QMV') and (ii) the substantive tension between the external aspects of the first pillar, traditionally with a primary focus on the economic sphere, on the one hand, and the CFSP, focusing on political areas, on the other. This second source of tension also has an institutional dimension of a vertical nature (*Commission* v. *Member States*) since the Member States remain the main players through the unanimity requirements in the Council and European Council in the area of CFSP. In order to transcend this duality, the Constitution introduces the position of the dual-role UMFA. The UMFA has a double hat in the sense that he combines the functions of High Representative for the CFSP[4] (Council) and Commissioner for External Relations (Commission).

The UMFA's dual nature and mandate is reflected in the conditions of appointment, the institutional position and the range of competences. First, the UMFA is appointed by the European Council, acting by QMV, with the agreement of the President of the Commission (Art. I-28(1)). The same procedure can be used to end the mandate of the UMFA. However, since the UMFA also wears a 'communitarian hat', the European Parliament has an indirect say in his/her appointment, since the Commission as a body is subject to a vote of consent by the European Parliament.[5] Likewise, the European Parliament may vote a censure motion on the Commission resulting in the resignation of the Members of the Commission as a body and the UMFA 'in the duties that he or she carries out in the Commission'.[6] In this case, the UMFA retains his/her position in the Council until the appointment of a new Commission. Moreover, the President of the Commission can request that the UMFA, like all other

Members of the Commission, resign, but in the UMFA's case this should be done 'in accordance with the procedure set out in Article I-28(1)' – which implies that the European Council must also agree.

Second, the UMFA's institutional position mirrors its double hat. On the one hand, the UMFA will preside over the Foreign Affairs Council, which is one of the configurations of the Council.[7] In addition, the UMFA will take part in the work of the European Council (I-21(2)). He will thus have a more privileged position in the European Council than the Ministers or the Commissioners, who may assist the European Council upon invitation by the European Council. This being said, the UMFA is not a 'member' of the Council or European Council and he does not have a voting right.[8] On the other hand, the UMFA will also be one of the Vice-Presidents of the Commission. He will be a full member of the Commission[9] and shall accordingly take part in the latter's decision-making process.

Third, the UMFA's competences and responsibilities encompass the different fields of the Union's external action. A detailed overview of all different tasks and instruments falls outside the reach of this contribution. In general, in the field of CFSP, they range from preparation (through the right of initiative), management and implementation (including, to some extent, the oversight of Member States' implementation[10]) to the EU's external representation with third countries, in international organizations and at international conferences.[11] For example, the UMFA shall be asked by Member States that sit on the Security Council, to defend the Union's position therein.[12] Obviously, this presupposes a common position and thus a European decision that still requires in principle unanimity; in other words, the UMFA's introduction does not as such reduce the power and competences of Member States sitting on the Security Council. The UMFA should become the single voice of the Union in the world. However, even within the domain of the CFSP, the UMFA will not entirely fulfil Kissinger's request for a 'single European telephone number', since the President of the European Council will, pursuant to Article I-22, 'at his or her level and in that capacity', ensure the Union's external representation 'without prejudice to the powers of the Union Minister for Foreign Affairs'. This vague description might suggest that the President of the European Council is supposed to meet with Heads of State and Government of third countries. One may wonder whether the Constitution did not create a new type of rivalry in this way. Within the Commission, the UMFA disposes of a broad range of duties since he shall be responsible for tasks incumbent on the Commission in external relations and for coordination of other aspects of the Union's external policy.[13] The UMFA should therefore not only build a bridge between the Commission and the Council (and European Council) but also between the various Commissioners responsible for different aspects of the external policies.

The UMFA's dual functions call for double loyalty, as a Member of the Commission, subject to its collegiate nature, and as President of the Foreign Affairs Council. Theoretically, this loyalty is defined by Article I-28(4), which declares that in exercising his responsibilities within the Commission, and only for these responsibilities, the UMFA shall be bound by Commission procedures to the extent that this is consistent with his role in the CFSP field and position in the Council. However, in practice, it remains to be seen how 'the UMFA will be able to ride two horses at once'.[14] The suspicion that the UMFA might become a Trojan horse for the Commission may have some merit. This is because the UMFA is strongly linked to the Council and the European Council and therefore to the intergovernmental approach (e.g., the UMFA's appointment and resignation). However, the President of the Commission's competence to order the UMFA's resignation, albeit with the European Council's approval, might prove a useful instrument in preventing this 'Trojan effect'.

The main reason why in practice, the UMFA position might not be able to meet high expectations, is that the Constitution does not sufficiently neutralise the duality within the Union's external policy to enable it to execute its dual functions. First, the UMFA's position does not alter the dividing lines between the Commission and the Council concerning external relations. The implementation of the EEAS cannot leave this sensitive relationship untouched. Second, although the pillar structure is formally abandoned, the CFSP upholds a specific position in the Constitution and the UMFA is not equipped with a powerful instrument within the CFSP to bring coherence among the different domains of the Union's external action. Both aspects will be examined below.

## European External Action Service

Somewhat hidden in Article III-296(III), the Constitution calls for the establishment of a 'European External Action Service' to assist the UMFA in the fulfilment of his mandate. This provision's place in the Constitution is not entirely fortunate since it is part of the CFSP Chapter. Nevertheless, the EEAS should bridge the different components of the Union's external action and should therefore at least be brought under the Chapter on the Union's external action having a general application. Moreover, this provision grossly understates the difficulties in working out an EEAS. The precise reach, structure and incorporation are totally left open. The importance and sensitivity of the subject can be deduced from the complex decision-making process to set-up the EEAS. It will be established by a European decision of the Council reached by unanimity.[15] The Council must act on a proposal of the UMFA after consulting the European Parliament and after obtaining the Commission's consent. Interestingly, the preparatory work was not made dependent on the Constitution's ratification and entry into force but had to start, pursuant to a declaration attached to the Constitution,[16] as soon as it was signed (29 October 2004), by the Secretary-General of the Council, the High Representative for the CFSP, the Commission and the Member States.

The Constitution merely prescribes that the EEAS will encompass 'the officials from relevant departments of the General Secretariat of the Council and of the Commission as well as staff seconded from national diplomatic services of Member States.'[17] The departments that might be 'relevant' and the EEAS's institutional position are left undecided. The entire spectrum thus still remains open as to who will serve in the EEAS.

On 1 March 2005, Solana and Barroso jointly presented an issues paper on the EEAS that was intended to serve as the basis for initial discussions with Member States in the context of preparing a joint progress report.[18] The Solana-Barroso issues paper presents a rather minimalist model with an emphasis on the roles of the UMFA and EEAS in the domain of the CFSP. The European Parliament has expressed the concern that the EEAS would not have an institutional link with the Commission: in a resolution on 26 May 2005 it stressed that the form the EEAS takes is 'extremely important' in light of the objective of bringing more coherence in the Union's external relations.[19] The resolution reminds the Commission that a decision to set-up an EEAS cannot be taken without its agreement and calls on the Commission to put its full weight behind the objective of preserving and further developing the Community model in the field of the Union's external relations. To this end 'the EEAS should be incorporated, in organizational and budgetary terms, in the Commission's staff.'

In the meantime, the Solana-Barroso issues paper was discussed with Member States. This resulted in a joint progress report of Solana and Barroso[20] that was planned to be presented at the European Council summit on 16-17 June 2005 but was dropped from the agenda because of the ratification failures in France and the Netherlands. It was felt that it would send out a wrong signal if the European leaders discussed the Constitution's content. For the moment, there is no plan to put the report on the agenda in the near future. The joint progress report reveals a consensus among Member States on some general points. For example, they appear to share the view of the Solana-Barroso issues paper on the 'sui generis' nature of the EEAS, which would mean that it would not be a new 'institution', but a service under the authority of the UMFA, with close links to both the Council and Commission. Moreover, Member States emphasized that the purpose of the EEAS is to assist the UMFA in his various functions, including that of Vice-President of the Commission, and that it should have the means to fulfil these functions. However, Member States seem to hold divergent opinions on the equipment that is required to that end. Their views encompass the entire spectrum ranging from a very minimalist model to a rather maximalist version. Concerning the Council's preparatory bodies, many Member States stress that those in the area of external relations and dealing with current first pillar matters should still be chaired by the rotating Presidency. On the other hand, a majority of Member States appears to be supportive of the Solana-Barroso issues paper's idea to bring groups dealing with pure CFSP or working closely with the Political and Security Committee under the chairmanship of a member of the EEAS. As to groups with mixed competences, the feeling among the Member States seemed to be that the decision should be taken on an *ad hoc* basis. Lastly, there seems to exist a broad consensus that the current Commission delegations should become, as 'Union Delegations', an integral part of the EEAS. A majority of Member States appears to support even the idea, raised by the Solana-Barroso issues paper, to confer on the Union Delegations additional tasks such as consular protection and visas.

In general, the preparatory work seems to highlight the roles of the UMFA and the EEAS in the field of the CFSP, resulting in a minimalist version of the EEAS. While this may be a realistic option, it might not be able to bring cohesion between the CFSP and the other external action fields of the Union. The European Parliament preference for incorporating the EEAS within the Commission will probably not be followed if the main domain of the UMFA, backed by the EEAS, is the CFSP.

## Common Foreign and Security Policy

Although the pillar structure is formally abandoned by the Constitution, the CFSP's particular position still resonates within the Constitution. It is, first, far from clear what competence the CFSP constitutes under the Constitution. Article I-12 lists the different categories of competences: exclusive, shared, or 'supportive, coordinative or supplementary'. Nonetheless, the CFSP is mentioned separately in paragraph 4 of this Article. Therefore, some argue that the CFSP constitutes a kind of 'sui generis' competence. Others, however, classify it under the shared competences, since this forms the residual category.

Second, the special nature of CFSP is corroborated by the fact that the decision-making process in this area still remains strongly intergovernmental in nature. Decision-making by unanimity within the Council remains the point of departure,[21] in spite of a Franco-German initiative that proposed QMV as a general rule. Moreover, the exceptions whereby the Council can decide by QMV are not fundamentally broadened. One circumstance is added:

> 'when adopting a European decision defining a Union action or position, on a proposal which the Union Minister for Foreign Affairs has presented following a specific request to him or her from the European Council, made on its own initiative or that of the Minister.'

Yet, a cautious reading reveals that the UMFA cannot independently open the door for decision-making by QMV in the Council. Some countries had strongly argued for this possibility but it was followed neither by the Convention nor by the IGC. Consequently, the fundamental structure is identical to the other general exceptions:[22] the starting point remains a decision by the European Council, taken by unanimity.[23] The individual Member States thus preserve the chance to block decision-making by QMV. However, it cannot be excluded that this exception might generate a considerable QMV extension in practice, since a skilful UMFA, backed by a well-documented EEAS, could take initiatives demanding the European Council requesting him or her to make a proposal to the Council that can subsequently be adopted by QMV. This 'specific request' of the European Council might in practice pass a broad and open mandate on to the UMFA. Nevertheless, even when a decision is reached by QMV in the Council, Member States can still invoke the 'national interest' exception, which the Constitution leaves unabridged.[24] Innovative is the specific bridging clause ('*passerelle*') that enables the European Council to extend, by unanimity, the scope of QMV in the field of CFSP.[25] Thus, the Constitution brings in a dynamic element in the CFSP by which the unanimity rule can be gradually restricted without needing to follow the procedure of treaty revision each time. Enhanced cooperation between some Member States also tempers the unanimity requirements and can have a dynamic effect insofar as the other Member States are not left behind once and for all. Therefore, it might be welcomed that the Constitution extends the opportunity for enhanced cooperation to the entire spectrum of CFSP. However, this extension is compensated for by strengthening the authorization requirement that requires the Council to act by unanimity, in contrast with the current situation, which merely requires QMV in the Council.[26] Moreover, Member States that enter into enhanced cooperation can decide, by unanimity, to switch to decision-making by QMV.[27] This turns enhanced cooperation, in fact, into a double instrument of flexibility: a group of Member States can strengthen cooperation and agree thereby to decide by QMV in their field of enhanced cooperation.

Apart from the principle of unanimity in the Council and European Council, the marginal role of the other institutions also highlights the intergovernmental nature of the CFSP domain. The Commission has even lost its autonomous right of initiative in the field of CFSP, since it is confined under the Constitution to support proposals submitted by the UMFA.[28] Furthermore, the European Parliament's position has not been strengthened[29] and the Court of Justice's jurisdiction remains, in principle excluded.[30]

The European Security and Defence Policy ('ESDP') forms an integral part of the CFSP.[31] If the CFSP can still be labelled strongly intergovernmental, then the ESDP forms the 'hyperintergovernmental' part of it. The principle of unanimity in the Council applies without exception, and this cannot even be altered by the European Council because the aforementioned *passerelle* is not applicable in the field of ESDP.[32]

The Constitution broadens the reach of the ESDP by widening the so-called 'Petersberg tasks' to include joint disarmament, military advice and assistance tasks, conflict prevention and post-conflict stabilisation.[33] In addition, the Constitution introduces a mutual defence clause[34] and a solidarity clause.[35] Nevertheless, the most important innovations in this field arguably lie in the instruments which the Constitution provides to Member States willing to strengthen cooperation. First, a group of Member States, which are willing and capable to carry out such a task can be entrusted by the Council to implement a Petersberg task.[36] Second, the legal basis is laid for a European Defence Agency.[37] Third, Member States which fulfil higher criteria for military capabilities and which are willing to make more binding commitments, can establish a so-called 'structured cooperation'. Fourth, the Constitution introduces the opportunity for enhanced cooperation in the field of ESDP, which should be authorized by the Council acting by unanimity.[38]

## Conclusion

The Constitution is a necessary but not a sufficient step to make the Union a powerful global actor. On the one hand, the Constitution's provisions on external action are inadequate to transform the Union into a strong political actor at the international level. For that purpose, the CFSP is still too intergovernmental and the institutional and decision-making duality in the external action field is too deep seated. Although the birth of a dual-functioning UMFA can soften the CFSP's intergovernmental nature and form an institutional bridge between the Council and the Commission, and a substantive bridge between the CFSP and the other external action fields, the tools at his/her disposal could be just too weak to fulfil these high expectations. For example, the UMFA is unable to unlock the Council's unanimity principle and to open the gate for decision by QMV. Admittedly, in practice, a skilful UMFA might demand the European Council to request him or her to make a proposal that can subsequently be adopted by QMV. Another weakness is that the design of the EEAS, which has to touch inevitably on the underlying duality, is left totally open in the Constitution. The preparatory work shows that the construction of this vital instrument for the UMFA will not be an easy task.

On the other hand, the Constitution seems to be a necessary condition for the Union to become not just an economic but also a political global actor. Some important innovations (such as the dismantling of the pillar structure and the introduction of a double hatted UMFA) do require a revision of the current Treaties. The same holds for important procedural provisions, such as the general and specific bridging clauses and the extended enhanced cooperation clause, that make the Constitution a dynamic document. They provide the Union with a more flexible institutional framework that can more easily be adapted to further European integration.

## Notes

1 Laeken Declaration on the Future of the European Union, annexed to the Presidency Conclusions of the European Council summit, 14-15 December 2001, section II.

2 Treaty establishing a Constitution for Europe, signed at Rome 29 October 2004, *OJ* 2004, C310.

3 Note the difference between Art. III-292(3) and Art. I-28(8), which is one of the inconsistencies of the Constitution.

4 Currently Javier Solana. Mr. Solana is set to become the first UMFA once that position is created (decided by the Council meeting, at the level of Heads of State or Government, on 29 June 2004).

5 Art. I-27(2).

6 Art. I-27(8).

7 Art. I-28(3), I-21(3).

8 Art. I-21(2), I-23(2).

9 Art. I-26(5)(6).

10 See Art. III-294(2).

11 See Art. III-296 and III-325(3).

12 Art. III-305(2).

13 Art. I-28(4).

14 C. Hill, 'A Foreign Minister without a Foreign Ministry – or with too many?', 1 *CFSP Forum* (2003), p. 2.

15 Art. III-296(3) *juncto* Art. III-300(1).

16 Declaration on Art. III-296 (No. 24).

17 Art. III-296(3).

18 Issues Paper on the European External Action Service, 1 March 2005, SN 1508/05.

19 European Parliament resolution on the institutional aspects of the European External Action Service, adopted on 26 May 2005.

20 Joint Progress Report to the European Council by the Secretary General/High Representative and the Commission, 9 June 2005, 9956/05.

21 Art. I-40(6) and III-300(1).

22 With the exception of the European decision concerning the appointment of a special representative (Art. III-300(2)d).

23 Unanimity is the general rule for decision-making by the European Council in the field of CFSP (Art. I-40(6)).

24 The UMFA can play a mediating role. If no solution is found, the Council can by QMV 'kick up' the decision to the European Council which shall decide by unanimity (Art. III-300(2)).

25 This specific bridging clause (Art. III-300(3)) differs from the general bridging clause (Art. IV-444(1)), since the former does not require the consent of the European Parliament and does not provide for the involvement of the national parliaments.

26 Compare Art. 27c EC Treaty and Art. 419(2).

27 This specific bridging clause can be found in Art. II-422.

28 Compare Art. 22(1) TEU and Art. III-299(1) Constitution.

29 Compare Art. 21 TEU and Art. I-40(7) and I-41(8) Constitution.

30 Art. III-376. It provides for two exceptions: the Court shall have competence to monitor the delineation between CFSP and other fields of the Union's external action (III-308) and reviewing the legality of European decisions providing for restrictive measures against natural or legal persons (Part III, Title V, Chapter II).

31 Art. I-41.

32 Art. I-41(4) and III-300(4).

33 Compare Art. 17(2) TEU and Art. III-309(1) Constitution.

[34] Art. I-41(7).
[35] Art. I-43 and III-329.
[36] Art. III-310.
[37] Art. I-41(3) and III-311(2).
[38] Art. III-419(2) and III-420(2). The specific bridging clause between Member States engaging in enhanced cooperation can however not be used (Art. III-422(3)).

## Remarks by Jan Klabbers*

### Is there a need for institutional reform?

Whether there is a need for institutional reform in the EU is something I am not sure of. I tend to think that the EU is very good at institutional reform; it has been doing little else for the last two decades. The Single European Act, the Maastricht Treaty and the Human Rights Charter are only some examples. Quite a bit of institutional reform has been taking place, and of course now, that everyone is thinking of the current crisis of the EU, there is again a 'reflex' to engage in some institutional reform.

One of the obvious attractions of talking about institutional reform is that it is the sort of thing to do when nothing else seems possible anymore. It also has the attraction of lending itself as a wonderful substitute for a more substantive debate. For example: If you know you cannot reach agreement on employment policies, then perhaps you should say that the EP and the national parliaments should talk more along these lines, or that decision-making procedures ought to be amended. In short, institutional reform is what we resort to when substantive agreement remains out of reach.

And of course institutional reform has the attraction (more seriously) of tapping into purposiveness, or idea that law and legal institutions generally need to have a purpose. This taps into sentiments often associated with social democracy, and presupposes the malleability of society.

There are however two reasons to suggest that institutions are only half the story. The other half is the style of politics, the style of leadership if you will. The way government is conducted may be much more important than the precise checks and balances that may be laid down in a legal document.

Additionally, in the particular case of the EU, institutional reform might miss the point a bit. Institutional reform might be useful for enhancing the efficiency of an institution or an organisation, but it is perhaps less useful for enhancing legitimacy. And this is the most important issue at the moment: the gap between Europe's leadership and the people of Europe.

That is not a very novel observation as such, but what is perhaps slightly novel is my prescription: instead of focusing on institutional reform, the EU should rather concentrate on educational reform. Not with a view to educating the people, but with a view to educating its leadership!

* Professor of International Organizations Law, University of Helsinki. The original manuscript of this contribution was not received. The following text has been derived from the tapes on which the conference sessions were recorded.

My argument draws on two notions developed by the British political philosopher Michael Oakeshott. He called himself a conservative (this might give you an idea as to where I stand …) and made a distinction between two forms of association. One he called *universitas*, which is a purposive organisation – a number of people banding together in order to achieve a common goal; a common purpose or a set of common purposes.

Against that he recognises what he referred to as *societas*, which stands for a group of people who just happen to live together without having a common purpose; the bonds between them merely consists of respect for an agreed set of rules, but that is it. They leave each other alone and do not feel that they have a common goal to accomplish.

What is striking about the EU's Constitution (excusez: Draft Treaty establishing a Constitution) is that it is still highly purposive in nature. The preamble, e.g., contains a wonderful list of objectives, and this ambition is carried out throughout the whole document. All these objectives show that the creators of the constitutional document felt a great urge to justify the existence of the EU, and, moreover, felt the urgent need to justify it in terms of having a purpose.

In the drafters' eyes, the EU cannot simply exist. Instead, its existence still needs to be justified, and needs to find justification in some purpose or other (a bunch of purposes, in fact, not always easily reconcilable with one another). That is what is curious if you think of the past 50 years in Europe. Compare it to Botswana, or Canada for example! They do not have to justify themselves either! No one asks what Canada's purpose is, or why there is a Botswana. So why, after 50 years of European integration, does the EU still feel it has to justify its existence by pointing to the purpose it serves?

It may sound strange, but Europeans should, for once perhaps, become a bit more arrogant. The EU's leadership (not usually reluctant to show arrogance) should stop thinking in terms of self-justification and should rather just accept that the EU is there and that the people who rejected the Constitution may have voted like this simply because they were not content with some of the policies that are embedded in it. Europe's people (the French and the Dutch at least) seem to have intuitively grasped that Europe needs no further justification, when they treated the draft constitution as a political document to be accepted or rejected. It is about time for Europe's leadership to learn the same lesson.

## Remarks by Rutger Wissels*

### The European Union and its neighbourhood-policies

During the past decades the European Union has developed more and more policies concerning their neighbours and in particular those neighbours like for example the

* Director, European Neighbourhood Policy Co-ordination, Directorate-General for External Relations, European Commission. The original manuscript of this contribution was not received. The following text has been derived from the tapes on which the conference sessions were recorded.

Ukraine, Moldova, Syria or Morocco, which are not going to become members of the EU.

In this respect the EU has become a 'change-agent' in his neighbourhood. This development has got several reasons.

First of all the European Union has got a vital interest in stable and prosperous neighbours, just like any other country does.

Secondly the EU also has clear defensive interests, primarily concerning migration flows, organised crime, fighting terrorism as well as proliferation of weapons of mass destruction or environmental hazards.

Thirdly the EU has got offensive interests, thinking of fostering trade or the securisation of energy-supply, which will even get more important in the near future.

The European Union is an untidy organisation, but it does work. And it has already proved to be effective in stabilizing its neighbours.

After 11 September 2001, which was a threat to our civilization, and the ongoing political and economic crisis people have become afraid of the threats in a globalised world. The result is that the EU has become scapegoat and victim at the same time. It has learned to use its 'gravitational-pool' as you may call it, by working with, rather than against its gravity. By its neighbours it is seen as a free and open society and indeed all of them would like to join the EU. For decades we have cleverly used this situation by telling them: If they want to join the European Union, they have to abide by its rules. In practice we have been able to inforce this process, starting with the accession of Greece more than 25 years ago.

We have used the enlargement and accession process of the organisation for becoming a political as well as economic award for good behaviour. Therefore we consolidated democracy and prosperity.

Looking for example at the situation in the western Balkans you can easily see that these states are far away from meeting membership conditions, since there is still a large incongruency between ethnicity and state borders. No rearrangement of state-borders will probably ever solve the potential for conflict in this region.

Nevertheless one can also easily detect that the prospect of accession to the EU is probably the only trick to resolve this problem. By using the gravitational-pool of the EU we are able to even integrate these countries into our sphere and to push them up.

Of course the enlargement of the European Union does have limits, and we have gone pretty far over the past years and are continuing further while trying to stabilize internal processes. But we can still use our gravitational pool beyond the countries in the accession pipeline.

This exactly is the idea of the new neighbourhood policy: using the tools we have developed in recent enlargement processes. These tools help countries to get ready for the often rather high demands for functioning as an EU Member State.

In practice we apply quite a number of these tools to countries beyond the accession pipeline and have already experienced that even though we are not offering accession, we are able to develop good cooperation and positive economic as well as political developments in a number of these countries.

Examples for the functioning of the new neighbourhood policy are Tunisia and Ukraine, which both have started to constructively work on their problems as a result to the neighbourhood policy.

Therefore there are quite a number of useful stabilizing effects through the use of the gravitational pool without offering membership.

Even though we have never really defined the borders of the EU, we have given a few hints in the past – thinking of the rejected application of Morocco in 1987. Nevertheless this constructive uncertainty about where the borders of the EU lie, remains the best choice. The major debate on the case of Turkey has already been conducted and will undoubtly continue and intensify over the coming period.

Even in this respect there is an interesting phenomenon: quite a number of observers of the situation in Turkey see that there is an effect there. In recent years there has been major political reform in Turkey, which was induced by the wish to join the EU and by the demands the EU has on Turkey in order to even start accession negotiations.

There has been an effect of 'Europeanisation' in terms of the functioning of the democracy in these countries and according to many observers this democracy has become irreversible. So if, in the case of Turkey, it would never become a member of the EU, the positive effects and reforms made so far will remain.

In the system of the EU we rule by law and not by force. We do not have a big standing army, we rather work with 'soft' power.

We do have 80.000 pages of legislation rather than a large army, navy or airforce, but these 80.000 pages do work in this stabilizing process.

It is true that over our history we have lurched from crisis to crisis, but we have always come out stronger and also larger than before in the past 50 years.

The current crisis in the process of constitutionalisation is really serious, but in my opinion we will still come out stronger and probably again larger in the end!

## Remarks by Pieter Van Nuffel*

### Mixed agreements in the EU's external relations

So-called 'mixed agreements' are agreements concluded with third countries by the EC and its Member States. Such agreements have to be ratified by all Contracting Parties, which means today that such an agreement needs to be ratified by 26 parties on the one side (the EC and 25 Member States) and of course the third country on the other side.

The practice of concluding mixed agreements was set-up, to overcome difficulties created by the division of competence between the EC and its Member States. Although in theory it might be envisaged that the Community acts alone, as soon as it is established that the Community has power to act on the subject matter of the agreement (it is only a matter of political will to do so), the Member States insist that the EC only becomes active on the international field if it has exclusive competence.

* Legal Advisor, Legal Service, European Commission. The original manuscript of this contribution was not received. The following text has been derived from the tapes on which the conference sessions were recorded.

Therefore there is in external relations a big difference between having exclusive competence and simply having competence.

The EC can receive exclusive competence explicitly by the treaties. This is for example the case for commercial policy.

Further, it follows from the 'AETR'-case law of the European Court of Justice that the EC has exclusive competence where it has already internally adopted common rules which would be affected if the Member States would undertake obligations individually or collectively with third countries.

With the development of internal Community law – and as consequence the extension of the area of exclusive competence – recourse to mixed agreements diminished. However, in the past decade, we see an important increase in mixed agreements, because the European Union organises more and more the whole of its relations with third countries in a single framework, often an association or cooperation agreement. For example, our relations with the countries of the new neighbourhood policy, which Rutger Wissels introduced earlier, are usually based on mixed agreements. Indeed, they concern all kinds of topics: trade policy, environmental policy, energy and also political dialogue, some of which are exclusive EC competence, some others not.

Mixed agreements may be an inventive way to avoid difficult discussions on competence, they are not without creating themselves other problems.

Indeed, the most important problem is that a mixed agreement (and in principle any later modification of the agreement) needs ratification by so many parties. This procedure takes a long time and therefore the EU's external relations tend to be slowed down by its complicated internal procedures.

One example, which shows the weight of this problem, is the Stabilisation and Association Agreement with Croatia. The agreement was signed on 29 October 2001 and eventually entered into force on 1 February 2005. And this was at a time when it only had to be concluded by 15 Member States, the EC and Croatia!

Now we are 25 Member States and there will be more to come. Ratification by so many Member States usually means going through national parliaments, in many Member States even through two chambers in the national parliaments, and in some Member States even through the regional parliaments, like for example in Belgium.

Of course, I would welcome a greater involvement of national parliaments in European matters, as provided for in the European Constitution, but one has to be aware that in the case of mixed agreements the role of national parliaments is purely and only to rubber-stamp. And I have no knowledge of national parliaments really discussing the substance of a mixed agreement before approving it.

This procedure is not a very intelligent way of organising the EU's external relations; there is some potential for reform in this matter.

Indeed, for the national parliaments the procedure only means bureaucratic work that has to be done. Another negative influence of mixed agreements on Europe is that it introduces the necessity of reaching unanimity, where agreements concluded by the Community would often be decided by qualified majority in the Council.

But I did not only want to speak about the negative characteristics of mixed agreements. We also have reached some improvements in the past years.

The first thing I wanted you to know is that, luckily, it is accepted that when mixed agreements need to be modified, this is, in cases where the EC has exclusive competence over the subject-matter of the modification, possible by a protocol, which is only concluded by the EC (and not its Member States). So if we want to change the trade-provisions in such an agreement it can be done by a Protocol to be concluded between the Community and the third country. The Member States only participate in this process by their presence in the Council. This is important, because modifications of mixed agreements usually concern matters which are within the Community's exclusive competence.

This set-up makes life much easier once a mixed agreement is concluded.

In some cases, the same result can be achieved, when the associational council is empowered to modify some of its provisions.

The second kind of remedy is the provisional application of some provisions. More and more it is agreed in agreements with third countries that parts of the agreement, especially the trade parts, will be applied from a certain date, often immediately, that is from the day of signature – even though the entry into force would take place years later.

It means that the Council, when deciding to sign an agreement on behalf of the EC, decides at the same time that parts of the agreement will be provisionally applied by the EC, pending its entry into force after ratification by all Contracting Parties. The other parts of the agreement, which include in particular the institutional set-up of the agreement or those on the political dialogue with the third country, will only be applied from its entry into force.

The third development I want to introduce is the following: In the accession treaty of the ten new Member States to the EU (as well as in that on accession by Romania and Bulgaria), the Council has been empowered to conclude on behalf of the Member States all the protocols necessary to modify the mixed agreements, to take into account the fact that the Community does no longer consist of 15, but of 25 Member States. As a consequence, these protocols have only to be ratified by the Council, acting on behalf of the EC and acting on behalf of the Member States, and by the third country. It is a way of avoiding the need to go through ratification procedures for all these protocols in all Member States.

Beyond the actual, limited, remedies to the problems raised by the recourse to mixed agreements, we should think about further reaching solutions. One would be that Member States change their attitude about the competence question – not so much in theory, but more in practice – and try to limit the figure of mixed agreements to these only cases where part of the agreement falls within the exclusive competence of the Member States, leaving the Community to conclude international agreements where the whole subject-matter falls within exclusive or mixed Community competence. But that would require acceptance by the Member States to change the present practice of mixed agreements.

Another response – at least in theory – might be to replace in some cases the current EC/Member States mixity with a new type of mixity: 'first pillar' with the 'second pillar' (CFSP). This would be possible where the provisions which give an agreement a mixed nature concern foreign and security policy aspects.

In such cases, one might envisage that, from our side, the Council concludes the agreement on behalf of the EC (first pillar) and of the EU (second pillar). The legal basis would be the relevant provision of the EC-Treaty and Article 24 of the Treaty on European Union.

For the time being, however, both the Commission and the Council legal services are very reluctant to consider such a construction; it would indeed replace a complex but well-chartered situation with a situation, the complexities of which are still to a large extent unknown.

This leaves me where I started. The only real solution might be the adoption of the Constitution, in the framework of which (although basically the division of competence has not been changed in this area) the last construction I envisaged, mixed first- and second pillar agreements, would be much more easily realised.

## Discussion

Eddy Fonyódy:* asked Mr. Wissels, if he senses a change in the attitude towards enlargement within the European Union and, if so, how this effect will affect the accession of states to the Union, like for example Romania, Bulgaria or even Turkey.

Rutger Wissels answered that at least in a formal sense there is no suspension of the enlargement process. The accession of Bulgaria and Romania will proceed as planned, since the treaties have already been signed and consequently both countries will join the European Union either in 2007, or if they do not meet the criteria one year later.

But of course there is a change in the climate towards accession, which might affect others in the accession pipeline. Again, formally the procedures go on, but taking for example the situation in Germany into account, where the opposition (which has a clear view against the accession of Turkey as a full Member State) is likely to win the elections in September of this year, the practical consequences of the current crisis are impossible to predict.

So as an answer to the question Mr. Wissels concluded that – yes, there is a change in the attitude, but right now one cannot say how long this will last and what exact consequences it will have.

Joost van Iersel:** First of all he pointed out the reasons for the current need for a new constitution in the European Union. In his view there is no European peoples who identify themselves with the European Union. Therefore the EU has to rationalize its objectives every time a reform is made and every time the EU has to explain to the peoples what it is all about. Hence the EU is bound to make progress in order to bring the EU in a further stage and this progress necessarily has to be manifested by treaty changes. He asks to discuss the issue of the current need for a constitutional change in the EU.

Jan Klabbers answered, that he agrees that if there are changes, for example from unanimity to QMV, these changes may have to be explained to people, but he does not think that the EU has to justify its very existence. Of course also in his view the details need explanation and justification, but the very existence of the organisation as a whole does not need that anymore. In his sense one has to differ precisely between these two different levels of justification.

* Brussels.

** Member of the European Economic and Social Committee.

A.A.H. VAN HOEK:* remarked that the speakers of this panel all pointed out that in order to improve the powers and effectiveness of the EU the role and powers of the Member States have to be minimized. Concerning this she asked, if it is not time to rethink some of the elements of the AETR-Doctrine and to give the Member States the powers to act if this makes sense from the point of national interests and if it does not hurt European interests.

PETER VAN NUFFEL: answered that in his view the level a decision for example on issues of private international law is taken on, namely the European or the national level, does not bring either of the levels closer to the citizen. His argument for treating at least parts of private international law at the European level is that it gives for the countries concerned leverage in congresses like the Hague Conference on Private International Law. Secondly, if all decisions are taken on the national levels citizens are confronted with different solutions for the same kind of question. This might rather bring confusion than identification.

CATHERINE BRÖLMANN:** asked, if there is not a difference between the territoriality and the functionality of the European Union and if the EU as a territorial entity is really becoming a confederation, or if it does not go back to the level of the nation states.

JAN KLABBERS: answered that he does not think that one can pigeonhole the EU in either of the two principles of territoriality and functionality. In his view it might be more interesting to think of alternatives, instead of trying to catch the EU by its territoriality. He also thinks that the EU has outgrown its functionality basis and, much as he dislikes the phrase has become an organisation *sui generis*. Therefore one has to 'think outside the box', to unhappily use another cliché, since the EU cannot be pushed in either of the two categories: it does not replace the nation-state, but to suggest it owes its existence to its capacity to fulfil a few useful functions does not seem very plausible anymore either.

KATHLEEN PAISLEY:*** asked, if the panellists agree that the text of the Constitution is far too long, complex and too hard to understand for the people and if it should not have been reduced to about thirty Articles in order to make it easier for the people to identify themselves with the EU.

JAN WOUTERS: answered that he would go along with the critique about the European Constitution. During the works on the Constitution there has been a moment in which part I of the text was conceived as a form of 'Mini-Constitution', referring to the idea of Valéry Giscard D'Éstaing of a 'pocket-constitution', which the European citizens could carry close to their hearts. But after all even part I of the Constitution does not have a title, nor does it say what it stands for and it consists of 60 Articles, which are hard to understand for someone who does not know EU-law. In this respect the constitutional exercise has not been managed very well in his view. Further on he argued that the EU might do a good exercise if it tried to translate the Constitution in a more plain language which the people could identify themselves with.

*Reporter:* Wibke Helene Franz****

* Professor of Law at the University of Tilburg.

** University of Amsterdam.

*** Practitioner, Brussels.

**** Ph.D. student, University of Twente.

# UN-Reform: What Follow-Up to the High Level Panel Report and the Recommendations by the Secretary-General?

The panel was convened by its Chair, Niels Blokker*

## Remarks by Lord David Hannay**

### Collective Security and the Use of Force

I have been asked to focus my remarks today on the third part of the report of the High-level Panel on Threats, Challenges and Change – the section dealing with Collective Security and the Use of Force – and I will in fact just do that. But, before turning to that subject, I think it would be useful to situate it in the wider framework of the report as a whole and to look at it, as we, the authors of the report did, as only one part, albeit an exceptionally important one, of the overall picture; and to make one or two wider remarks.

First it is really important to start, as we did, with an analysis of the threats which face the international community at the outset of the 21th century. They are quite different in their nature and their number from those we faced in the second half of the 20th century. Not everything has changed since the end of the Cold War removed the immediate threat of a catastrophic war between two superpowers and the daily reality of proxy wars between their satellites around the world which were ruled off-limits to the UN; but most things have. We still do have a number of long-festering disputes – in Palestine, in Kashmir and in Korea to mention the best known – which have the potential to damage the fabric of international relations if we do not address them more purposefully and effectively than we have done in the past. But the new threats we face – from international terrorism, from the proliferation of weapons of mass destruction, from the failure of states, from organised crime, from extremes of poverty and pandemic diseases, from environmental degradation – are in many cases ones we would not have classified as security threats at all some years ago. And yet the inter-connections between these different threats, and the way in which – partly as a result of the phenomenon of globalisation – they impact on all corners of the

* Netherlands Ministry of Foreign Affairs and Leiden University.
** Former Permanent Representative of the United Kingdom to the UN.

world, mean that addressing only a shortened agenda or giving some portion of the agenda absolute priority, is simply not going to produce the sort of collective and coherent response that is required if those threats are to be prevented or mastered. This rationale, linking security and development issues, may sound banal but it is quite fundamental in its implications; and it is completely different from the kind of 'grand bargain' under which the richer countries are supposed to produce more resources for the poorer and the latter are then supposed to agree to security policies which will help the richer ones protect themselves.

Then, secondly, it is important to recognise that the use of force is not at the heart of our analysis, although it remains an important aspect of it. At the heart of the analysis is the need to develop effective policies of prevention, at which the international community has so far been relatively unsuccessful. These policies of prevention will in many cases not require the use of force at all, indeed one of the main reasons for their development is to avoid, or at least sharply to reduce, the need for any subsequent use of force. In the struggle against international terrorism, the use of military force, as it was deployed, quite legitimately in my view, against Taliban, is likely to remain the exception that proves the rule, if only because the fate of the Taliban was so salutary. Nor is military force an element in the fight against poverty or pandemic diseases or organised crime; and it only becomes so in the context of state failure if one fails to prevent the failure of the state in question in the first place. In the case of the proliferation of weapons of mass destruction the possible use of force bristles with drawbacks; and the case for measures of non-military prevention which must address the security fears that drive proliferation as well as the technical symptoms of it, is a compelling if complex one.

That said, we were no more able to duck the issue of the use of force than were the founding fathers of the UN when they sat down to write the Charter in 1945. Their noble objective may have been to 'banish the scourge of war for succeeding generations'; but they had no illusions that that could be achieved if the international community was not prepared to contemplate, and indeed to use, force in certain well defined circumstances. Hence Chapter VII of the Charter, for many years virtually inoperative as a result of the Cold War, since then more used, but often in a rather haphazard, unsystematic and inequitable sort of way. The background against which we worked was one in which twice in recent years, in Kosovo and in Iraq in 2003, it had proved impossible to take collective decisions authorising the use of force even when mandatory Security Council resolutions were being flouted; and on a number of occasions, most notably in Bosnia and Rwanda and also while we were working in Darfur, it had proved impossible to muster the will and the resources to prevent the most appalling abuses of international humanitarian law. Add to that, the clear evidence that some of the new threats which faced the international community, raised the hugely sensitive issues of the pre-emptive and the preventive use of force, and it was clear that there was plenty of matter for reflection.

From the outset there was no doubt in any of our minds that, far from emerging from the Cold War into the sunlit uplands of that 'new international order' so unwisely proclaimed by the father of the present President of the United States, the world was in face drifting through a period of disorder of unpredictable duration, whose elements could threaten our security and prosperity, less directly perhaps, but more insidiously than the Cold War had done. This disorder had not only led to extensive recourse to the use of force in every corner of the world, but also sometimes now by non-state actors as well as states. More positive, however, was the evidence during this period that, to a far greater extent than during the Cold War, states were looking to the UN for an effective response, preventive if possible but prepared to contemplate the use of force if not, to these new challenges. Our efforts were directed to enlarging the scope of that recourse to the Security Council, making the Council's response more predictable and thus more potentially deterrent. What we never had any illusion we could or should be doing was to produce a kind of push-button certainty for the handling of each and every crisis which came along; nor that we were in the business of writing binding legal rules in international law which would have that objective. It is perfectly possible and legitimate to argue that the world would be a better place if such certainty and such rules existed. But we were determined to come forward with approaches across the board which could be realised in the here and now, not just at some putative moment in the future.

We began by considering carefully the arguments that have arisen over the use of the inherent (not conferred) right of self-defence set out in Article 51 of the UN Charter. Some pressed us to make these provisions, or at least their interpretation, more restrictive, others to make them more expansive. We noted that, under customary international law, Article 51 is normally considered to encompass the taking of pre-emptive action if a threat is clear and imminent. We did not consider, however, that it extended to cases where the object of the action was preventive against a threat that was not clear and imminent. We concluded that any re-writing of Article 51 was neither necessary, nor desirable, nor practicable.

We were clear, however, that the terms of Chapter VII of the Charter do not preclude collective action to deal preventively with a threat which is not yet imminent. I would underline here the word collective. The wording of the Charter, which talks of determining the existence of a threat to international peace and security before any authorisation of measures involving coercion, has the potential for considerable flexibility in its activation. Action could well be, in the first instance, of a non-military kind. That is why we devoted some thought and a number of our recommendations to how best to make non-military sanctions better targeted and more effective. And, when the issue of the use of force can no longer be avoided, we recommended – and the Secretary-General has firmly endorsed this recommendation – that the Security Council should undertake to operate within a set of guidelines dealing with the seriousness of the threat, proper purpose, last resort, proportional means and the balance of consequences. Every individual instance of authorising the use of force would still need to be debated and decided on its merits in the Security Council.

And then we had to consider probably the most sensitive area of all, instances where the Charter's very sweeping preclusion of any actions which intrude on the sovereignty of Member States had been used, abused rather, in recent years to provide cover for genocide, ethnic cleansing and other massive breaches of international humanitarian law. Clearly what has come to be called the responsibility to protect human security falls on the first instance on the state in question and an increasing proportion of states do fulfil that obligation. But, where a state is either unable or unwilling to fulfil it, we considered that responsibility shifts to the international community as a whole, acting collectively. That is a rather different concept from the so-called 'right of intervention' which has been much talked about; but it has aroused some of the same concerns. It is not in fact a completely novel thought, it was drawn from the Axworthy/Evans/Sahnoun report; it is one which inspired the Genocide Convention although that instrument contains no prescription or procedures for the action to be taken in the event of a breach of the convention; and it also underpins the jurisprudence of the International Tribunals on the former Yugoslavia and Rwanda and of the newly established International Criminal Court. We are under no illusion that it will prove easy or straightforward to apply; but we do believe that it represents the direction in which the international community needs to move if it is not to lose credibility and support for its activities.

The debate over these crucial issues of the use of force should not blind us, however, to the fact that peacekeeping and post-conflict peace-building remain for the UN its daily bread and butter issues, but not ones at which its record is beyond reproach or improvement. Many of the recommendations of the excellent Brahimi report on peacekeeping remain either unimplemented or only partially implemented; and yet the demand for UN peacekeeping is on the rise again, in Africa particularly. We recommend that the funds for disarmament and demobilisation, crucial tasks for almost every peacekeeping mission but frequently left neglected and only partially funded, should be met, in future, from assessed contributions. We argued for much closer cooperation between the UN and regional and sub-regional organisations in matters relating to conflict prevention and peacekeeping. We proposed a ten year capacity-building programme for the African Union and acceptance of the fact that, when the UN turns to an organisation like the African Union for help, it should back it with training, with logistics and, again, with assessed contributions; and we argued for the conclusion of framework agreements between the UN and regional and sub-regional organisations to facilitate these objectives. The Secretary-General is already moving ahead on that last front. And we can see, in the case of Darfur, just how much a more systematic and more integrated approach to cooperation between the UN and regional and sub-regional organizations is needed, in place of the present well-meaning but inadequate *ad hoc* improvisations.

Post-conflict peace building is widely recognised as a yawning gap in the UN's armoury. Countries – Haiti is an example – momentarily attract the attention of the Security Council – but are then left to drift back towards the abyss. No systematic attempt is made to organise the international community's resources to help a country get back on its feet, to provide the support it needs over a sustained period of time. To fill that gap we have proposed the establishment of a Peace-building Commission, supported within the Secretariat by a Peace-building Bureau staffed by people with field experience. The Peace-building Commission would bring together the efforts of the Security Council and the Economic and Social Council, of the International Financial Institutions (the World Bank and the IMF), of the main donors and troop contributors and of the relevant regional organizations and banks. The aim would be to achieve a coherence and continuity which has so far been lacking. Support for this proposal appears gratifyingly strong, especially from the European Union. The challenge now is take the necessary decisions at the Summit in September and to avoid the usual reductive process in New York which so often leads to most worthy proposals being voided of most of their substance.

As the panel debated all these issues we were only too well aware of the wider debate raging over the supposed choice between multilateralism and unilateralism, as if these two doctrines were each an alternative do-all solution to the threats and challenges which face the international community. And yet, the further we went in our work, the less convincing we found any such crude juxtaposition of the alternatives. Hard choices do have to be made; and sometimes these are indeed between options that can broadly be classified under these two headings. But few if any serious practitioners of international relations, be they politicians, diplomats or military, believe that any country, acting alone, can find fully effective responses to all the threats and challenges of today's world; and few if any believe that every one of them can be handled by multilateral action alone. This is not a titanic struggle between the supporters of world governance on the one hand and of the nation state on the other. What is at issue is now to harness the joint efforts of states and of multilateral institutions so that they are mutually reinforcing; and how to decide collectively what should be done when a state steps over the limits of acceptable behaviour as defined its international obligations and when it fails egregiously to fulfil its responsibility to protect all of its own citizens.

These are the questions that will be on the table for decision in New York this September; and to which I believe we must encourage our governments to find effective and equitable solutions.

## Remarks by Karel van Kesteren*

## Reform of the Un Security Council

The debate on UN Security Council (hereinafter: SC) reform has been going on for more then ten years now. In the '90s the 'Razali Plan' (expansion with 9 new seats, 5 permanent and 4 non-permanent, no new vetos) got considerable support, but led to nothing. The High Level Panel established by the UNSG proposed two alternatives for an expanded SC of 24 members: one with and one without new permanent members. An innovation in both models was the replacement of the current regional electoral groups: Africa, Asia, Latin America and the Caribbean (GRULAC), Western European and Others Group (WEOG) and Eastern Europe, by four new groups: Africa, Asia, Americas and Europe.

In the ensuing debates, the traditional controversy around the subject persisted. On the one hand those who favour expansion with new permanent members (and some additional non-permanent seats), on the other hand those who do not want additional permanent seats and favour expansion with non-permanent seats only, either of the existing sort (two year seats, without option for immediate re-election), or with variations (seats of a duration of three or four years, option of immediate re-election,

* Director, United Nations and International Financial Institutions Department, Dutch Ministry of Foreign Affairs. The views expressed are those of the author and not necessarily those of the Dutch government. The original manuscript of this contribution was not received. The following text has been derived from the tapes on which the conference sessions were recorded.

designation of SC members by their respective electoral/regional groups). The core members of the first group are Japan, Germany, India and Brasil (the G-4), themselves candidates for new permanent seats. Prominent countries in the second group are Italy, Pakistan, Mexico, South Korea and Argentina. This group calls itself the 'Uniting for Consensus' group (UfC).

In his recommendations to the UN membership of March 2005, Secretary-General Kofi Annan did not make a choice between the two HLP models and explicitly left open the possibility of 'any other viable proposal in terms of size and balance that have emerged on the basis of either model'. He furthermore expressed a preference for a decision to be taken before the September summit, preferably by consensus, 'but if they (i.e., the Member States) are unable to reach consensus this must not become an excuse for postponing action'. In other words: take a decision, if need be by a vote.

There is much that speaks in favour of the SG's view. If again the UN membership fails to reform the SC, the image of the UN as an impotent talking shop will be confirmed in the eyes of the public. And a continued deadlock will seriously jeopardize the Summit. Furthermore, everyone agrees that the SC must be adapted to the present-day world so as to be seen as a legitimate and representative body, capable of taking the far-reaching decisions needed to ward off old and new threats in the 21st century (including, yes, legislative measures if need be). The status quo is no option. Others, however, argue that in view of the sharp divisions among the UN membership more time is needed to come to a decision. In this approach, the SC item should be set aside so as not to influence negatively the other issues before the Summit. Pushing through now is what would sour the Summit atmosphere.

Changing the composition of the SC implies amending the UN Charter, which requires an affirmative vote of by two third majority in the UNGA (i.e., 128 states) plus ratification by two thirds including the P-5.

The G-4 have proposed a draft 'framework resolution', aimed at expanding the SC to 25 members, by adding 6 permanent seats (2x Africa, 2x Asia, 1x GRULAC, 1x WEOG) and 4 non-permanent seats (1 each for Africa, Asia, Eastern Europe and GRULAC). (In all proposals the current electoral groups are retained). New permanent members would in practice not have the right to veto. The draft also contains provisions about improvement of working methods and about a review of the new provisions 15 years after their entry into force.

The G-4 intention is to table this draft resolution at the end of June and to have a vote on it by mid-July. After that, elections would have to take place to select the new permanent members and the relevant Charter amendments would have to be adopted. The G-4 emphasize that there is no real alternative to their proposal: while they are on their way to a two-thirds majority, the UfC group is supported by a much smaller share of UN members. They insist that if one wants a SC reform, their plan is the only game in town.

But there are serious stumbleblocks on the path of the G-4, such as:

- Securing the necessary 128 votes. It is still not clear whether this level of support indeed exists.
- Strong opposition by China against a permanent seat for Japan.
- The position of the US, which has said it wants "two or so" additional permanent seats and "two or three additional non-permanent seats", in other words: expansion

of the SC to 19 or 20 members.
- The two African permanent seats. An African summit meeting in the beginning of July is supposed to select the two African countries for those seats, but in view of the number of candidates (among which South-Africa, Nigeria, Egypt, Senegal, Libya) one wonders what the outcome will be.

It is impossible to predict the course of events until the Summit. Adoption of the G-4 proposal? Continuation of the stalemate, that is to say: no reform? What makes events even more unpredictable is the amendments that can be expected when it comes to voting on the G-4 draft, including possibly so-called 'killer amendments'.

The ideal outcome would be that still a compromise formula could be found that can count on the backing of, at least, a broad majority of UN members. A key element of such a formula could be the review clause. If this clause was beefed up, in such a way that the whole question could be looked at again in, say, 15 years time, the arrangements to be decided upon would have a less absolute character, which could facilitate decision-making. If a compromise formula is still possible, the President of the UNGA will have to play a key role in brokering it.

## Remarks by Nico Schrijver*

## Collective Security and the Use of Force: Reviewing the Kofi Annan Criteria[1]

### Introduction

In recent years, there appears to be a reappraisal of the use of force in international relations. Increasingly there are calls for more "robust" action in an early stage of a conflict, implicating the use of force and running the risk of blurring the distinction between peace-keeping and peace-enforcement. The "pre-emptive (and preventive) strike" doctrine, as advanced by President Bush in his *National Security Strategy* of September 2002, is also based on the assumption that the use of force can be effective in facing the "new" threats and the "Axis of Evil". Furthermore, some calls are made for the recognition of "pro-democratic intervention". However, quite apart from the issue of the lack of a clear basis in international law so far little evidence appears to be available as to the effectiveness of the resort to the use of force for containing, let alone preventing or solving conflicts and domestic strife. To let the fences of Article 2 (4) down may well have very serious consequences. Frequently, there is either too little or much delayed reaction paid to the peaceful methods of dispute settlement as an alternative. Nevertheless, and as also envisaged under the UN Charter, the use of force can under certain circumstances be instrumental in restoring or maintaining international peace and security.

* Professor of Public International Law, University of Leiden, The Netherlands. President of the Netherlands Society of International Law.

From this perspective it is highly interesting to take note of what Secretary-General Kofi Annan writes on the use of force in his report *In Larger Freedom*.[2] This contribution briefly assesses the merits of the criteria for the use of force put forward in the Secretary-General's report, by reference to the state of the art of contemporary international law in this field.

## 1. The Annan Report in Brief

Kofi Annan adopts the comprehensive, integral concept of security as proposed by the High-level Panel: "any event or process that leads to large-scale death or lessening of life chances and undermines States as the basic unit of the international system is a threat to international peace and security". Such threat to peace can emanate from a variety of sources, not only from interstate war, internal conflict and terrorism, but also from economic and social threats, including extreme poverty, infectious diseases and environmental degradation and transnational organized crime. Of course, a strategy of prevention and a solid collective security system are the best ways of promoting the maintenance of peace and security. However, the Secretary-General does not exclude the use of military force as an ultimate remedium to maintain or restore international peace and security.

With regard to the use of force, Kofi Annan identifies three problem areas on which widely diverging ideas exist: (1) **pre-emptive action** against imminent threats; (2) **preventive action** against latent threats; and (3) **protective action** on behalf of citizens in other states threatened with genocide or other similar international crimes.

## 2. The UN Charter and the Use of Force

Before discussing each of them, I would like to briefly recall the basic rules of the UN Charter. The basic rule is, of course, the prohibition of the use of force in Article 2, paragraph 4 – perhaps the most important provision of the Charter. There are two main Charter exceptions to it: collective military action authorized by the UN Security Council (Art. 42) and the right of self-defence (Art. 51). It is also important to recall the primary responsibility of the Security Council for the maintenance of peace and security (Art. 24 of the Charter), a function which is also explicitly recorded in Article 51 on self-defence.

## 3. Pre-emptive Action

In reviewing the first problem area identified by Kofi Annan, that is that of pre-emptive action, we should first of all realize that, obviously, the right of self-defence as codified in Article 51 stems from a different period. Only inter-State wars were contemplated in 1945. However, the exact interpretation of Article 51 is not cast in iron but can evolve over time. In the post-September 11$^{th}$ world strong indications exist that Article 51 could also extend to armed attacks by non-State entities. Moreover, based on the *Caroline criteria*, but dating back to the period of 1837-1841, it also encompasses self-defence against identifiable imminent attacks. During the incident with the *Caroline* US Secretary of State Daniel Webster made a classical attempt to define and to limit anticipatory self-defence. In response to wider claims by the British, he stated that such a right arises only when there is: "a necessity of self-defence, ... , instant, overwhelming, leaving no choice of means and no moment for deliberation". This is widely recognized as reflecting customary international law. The use of the words "inherent right" in Article 51 (in the French text of the Charter "*droit naturel*") may well incorporate these criteria, subject of course to the requirements of Article 51 such as immediate reporting to the Security Council and suspension of the right of self-defence as soon as the Council takes collective measures. Hence, I agree with the high-level panel and the Secretary-General that there is no need to amend or rewrite Article 51 from the perspective of pre-emptive action. States invoking the right of self-defence should, of course, be aware of and respect the supervisory role of the Security Council with respect to the exercise of the right of self-defence. For the Charter provides that this rights applies "until the Security Council has taken measures necessary to maintain international peace and security". Apart from the text, the position of Article 51 in Chapter VII provides another indication that it is part and parcel of the collective security system as envisaged in 1945.

## 4. Preventive Action

Turning to the second problem area, that of preventive action against latent threats, in the view of the Secretary-General this should be the responsibility of the UN Security Council. With the wider interpretation of the concept of "threat to peace" (Art. 39), the Council has ample power and opportunity to address such threats and to take collective action. Often, responses of a non-military nature under Article 41 UN Charter will be the proper response. However, in view of bitter lessons learned – Rwanda, former Yugoslavia, Sierra Leon, Darfur – as well as in view of the advancement in military operations the use of force in an early stage of a conflict as part of collective action to prevent or contain a conflict should not be excluded. With the advancement in military operations, I refer to current trends in crisis management and programmes for tailor-made, swift, small-scale military operations through rapid deployment forces and also just early deployment of forces in an early phase of a conflict such as practiced in Macedonia. Reference can be made to the Standing High Readiness Brigade (SHIRBRIG), a pool of national commitments to the UN Stand-by Arrangements System (UNSAS). However, in all these cases of preventive action only the Security Council has currently the authority and discretion to decide so. Its decisions can, of course, include to mandate regional organizations to take action or to authorize so-called coalitions of the able and willing, such as the multinational forces in Afghanistan and East-Timor.

## 5. Protective Action and the Emergence of the Principle of the Responsibility to Protect

Taking up the third problem area as identified by Annan, that of protective action, this problem area is closely related to the doctrine of humanitarian intervention, a doctrine which is slippery and controversial. Obviously, it is first of all the responsibility of the Security Council to address such situations and to respond timely, decisively and adequately, with non-military or military measures. The recent referral by the Council of the situation in Darfur to the International Criminal Court is an encouraging, additional collective measure, next to conventional Article 41 measures such as diplomatic or economic sanctions. Kofi Annan's response to the question what to do in case the Council does not act is, in my view, clear and appealing: "The task is not to find alternatives to the Security Council as a source of authority but to make it work better". However, in practice cases may occur in which the Council continues to be deeply divided and paralyzed while a man-made humanitarian emergency unfolds itself. There is a growing body of consensus that in such a humanitarian emergency, with a State unable or unwilling to protect its citizens, third States have a right, if not a duty to take protective action, if necessary unilateral military action, with the purpose of bringing mass and flagrant violations of human rights to a halt. This is closely related to the emergence of the principle of the "responsibility to protect", which takes as a starting point the security and the fates of citizens rather than the security and sovereignty of States. If this concept were to be adopted as a fundamental principle of international law, that would of course be quite a revolutionary change in international law. It is much too early to say so and there is much reason to emphasize as much as possible the primary responsibility of the State itself and to invest in promoting the exercise of "responsible sovereignty" in a rule of law-based society. However, there is an encouraging trend towards a secondary responsibility incumbent upon third States or the international community as a whole for the fate of citizens, world citizens, wherever they live.

## 6. Kofi Annan's Five Criteria

Having reviewed these three problem areas, I now would like to discuss the criteria for the use of force. Building on the report Responsibility to Protect of the International Commission on Intervention and State Sovereignty and the report of his own High-level Panel, the Secretary-General proposes to record five criteria which the Security Council should take into account for determining the (in)appropriateness of the use of force in a particular situation:

first, the seriousness of the threat. This is closely related to the classical principle of "necessity", which features prominently in the Caroline criteria and customary international law. Furthermore, is relevant to recall the considerable body of practice of the Security Council under Article 39 that a threat to peace and security does not only arise from movement of troops, from fighting between armies but also from flagrant and mass violations of human rights and mass flow of refugees;

second, the requirement of the proper purpose of the proposed military action. The sole purpose should be halting of aggression, the spread of weapons of mass destruction, the serious mass and flagrant violation of human rights. Under current international law it can not extend to toppling a dictator, and cannot be launched for pursuing a so-called pro-democratic military intervention;

third, Kofi Annan mentions as a requirement to assess whether means short of the use of force are a plausible alternative to halt the threat. In my view, there is reason to rethink whether the taking of military measures should always be a matter of last resort. For we have learnt too often that the United Nations intervened much too late; earlier mention was made concerning advancements in the techniques of military operations;

However, this makes of course also the fourth criterion relevant: the proportionality of the military option to the threat at hand, a classical criterion well-established in customary international law;

This certainly applies also to the fifth criterion which is not always taken closely at heart if I refer to the Iraqi Freedom operation: that is the reasonable chance of success. This is a somewhat newer criterion, namely that of effectiveness which to a certain extent is an offspring of the principle of proportionality.

Kofi Annan puts rightly forward that a common view of the Council on the sensitive matter of criteria for the use of force would not only potentially enhance its effectiveness, but would also add transparency to its deliberations and make its decisions more likely to be respected, by both Governments and world public opinion.

In sum, I am of the opinion that the five criteria as proposed by Annan, with the caveats made, are sensible ones. I would welcome it if they were to be laid down in a text. Unfortunately, I noted that they have disappeared from the current Draft Outcome document. Obviously, it is a very sensitive topic.

## 7. Is the Security Council the Proper Body to Record Criteria for the Use of Force?

Lastly, I would like to raise an institutional issue. The Secretary-General recommends the Security Council to adopt a resolution setting out these principles and expressing its intention to be guided by them when deciding whether to authorize or mandate the use of force. One could argue that institutionally it is the task of the General Assembly rather than the Security Council to adopt such standard-setting resolutions. And let us not forget that in the past the General Assembly has done very useful standard-setting work in this respect in the spirit of Article 13 of the UN Charter to promote the progressive development of international law and its codification. Reference may be made to the Non-Intervention Declaration (1966), the Friendly Relations Declaration (1970), the Definition of Aggression (1974) and the Declaration on the Non-Use of Force (1987). However, in the light of the (albeit somewhat controversial) trend towards a quasi-legislative role of the Council and in view of the great importance to involve and commit the United States to the maximum extent possible, Annan's proposal to seek endorsement of these criteria by the Council has considerable merits.

NOTES

1 This contribution builds on other recent publications by the author, including: N.J. Schrijver, 'Responding to International Terrorism: Moving the frontiers of international law for "Enduring Freedom"?', 48 *Netherlands International Law Review* (2001) pp. 271-291; 'September 11th and Challenges to International Law', in J. Boulden and T.G. Weiss, eds., *Terrorism and the UN: Before and After September 11* (Bloomington, Indiana University Press 2004) pp. 55-73; 'Article 2, paragraphe 4', in J.-P. Cot and A. Pellet, eds., *La Charte des Nations Unies. Commentaire article par article*, Vol. I, 3rd edn. (Paris, Economica 2005) pp. 437-467; and N.M. Blokker and N.J. Schrijver, eds., *The Security Council and the Use of Force. Theory and Reality – A Need for Change?* (Leiden, Nijhoff 2005).

2 See *In Larger Freedom: Towards Development, Security and Human Rights for All*, Report of the Secretary-General, UN Doc. A/59/2005, paras. 122-126.

## DISCUSSION

NIELS BLOKKER: Ladies and Gentlemen, we had somewhat long introductions, but I think it was very interesting this afternoon. Now it is your turn; it is now question time. Let me particularly encourage students that are present here, to ask questions that they may have. Who could I give the floor to?

ERIKA DE WET:* I would like to make three brief comments, which I hope are quite provocative. First of all, there have been several high-level panels over the years, which suggested extensive changes, but nothing has come of that in the last 50 years. Lord Hannay, why should we take this High-level Panel any more seriously than any of the previous ones? Secondly, Mr Van Kesteren, it seems to me – and I am deliberately articulating this rather radically – that enlarging the Security Council without addressing the issue of the veto, might make the Council slightly more representative, but will not lead to any more efficient decision-making. I realize that it will be politically difficult to get any changes in this regard, but it leaves me rather pessimistic as to whether this is going to lead to any results. Thirdly, Nico Schrijver, regarding the criteria for the use of force, it seems to me that the problem is not about whether the Council is using force excessively or disproportionally when it resorts to force, but about getting the Council to use force in the first place. The issues that should have been addressed – and which are largely left undealt with – are those issues that keep countries from intervening when they should be doing so, for example in Zimbabwe and Darfur.

LORD DAVID HANNAY: Why should we take the High-level Panel report more seriously than previous such reports? I think for two reasons. One of them lacks a certain modesty: because I think this is a slightly better report than many that the United Nations had over the years. The less immodest reason is because the state of the United Nations demands measures of reform, and not just reform of institutions, but also reform of its policies. We have seen over the past few years that what we currently have in a whole range of policy areas is inadequate, for example with regard to counter-proliferation, the handling of state failure, and the use of force. In my experience – I have done about thirty or more speaking engagements since the beginning of the year– there is a great deal of interest in all this, much more so than previously, much more

* University of Amsterdam.

so than when UN reform just meant fiddling about with the institutions. Now, why do I assert that the High-level Panel Report is a better one than some of its predecessors? Because of we astuted what I call 'blue sky thinking'. We did not go for hugely ambitious ideas that we knew before we started would never be realized, e.g., an UN Rapid Reaction Force, or the setting-up of an economic and social security council, or the abolition of veto. All these are ideas that have figured in various UN reports and they are of course dead on arrival. I would challenge anyone to go through the 101 recommendations we made and tell me one single one that is not practical, and capable of being applied within a few months, if the will could be summoned up to do it. Now that is a pretty big 'if' and therefore this report may end up gathering dust like the other ones in the UN's library, but it should not.

KAREL VAN KESTEREN: In fact it is not gathering dust, as it is translated to a large extend into the draft Outcome Document for the Summit in September. That is a big difference. With regard to the question about the veto, let me make myself clear: when I spoke about the veto, I only spoke about it in the context of the framework resolution of the G4. It only related to the new permanent members of the Security Council. There is nothing in the proposals that are now on the table that refers to the veto powers of the current permanent members. It was also not among the recommendations of the High-level Panel, as this would not be a viable proposition. The question now is whether we should give veto power to possibly new permanent members of the Security Council. The answer of the vast majority of Member States, including the Netherlands, is negative, because if you have a Security Council with eleven veto powers you can be pretty sure that no decision can be taken.

Will an enlarged Security Council be more efficient? I think it will be more representative and more legitimate, and that is very important. It could even be more efficient in some situations. Take for example the situation of Darfur. It could be easier in a bigger Council to isolate the individual opponent of badly needed action. Thus the enlargement could result in more efficiency. However, we do not know it for sure. The Netherlands would like to try it out for 10 to 12 years. Then we could re-evaluate and decide whether to make the Council smaller or bigger, if need be.

NICO SCHRIJVER: In the view of Professor De Wet it would not be a matter of first priority to formulate criteria for the use of force, but rather to getting the Council to decide, including resorting to the use of force if necessary. With due respect, I hold to a different view. There is quite an extensive practice during the last 15 years of the Council authorizing the use of force. It all started with Resolution 678 when the Council authorized the use all necessary means to get Iraq out of Kuwait. Quite a number of these authorization resolutions have been adopted. They were addressed to coalitions or individual countries. Secondly, we can also note that in response to the disasters in Somalia, Rwanda, and Srebrenica, the use of force is more often part of a so-called 'more robust mandate' of UN Peacekeeping operations. On these scores there is quite some practice of the Security Council resorting the use of force, at least in the last 15 years more than in the previous 45 years. So to a certain extend it would make sense if the Council would formulate a common view as to the criteria for the resort to the use of force. These criteria would build upon the 'Caroline criteria', but would not be exactly the same. I believe that such criteria would add more 'transparency' to the deliberations of the Council. This would increase the respect for the decisions of the Council and they would be important in preventing unilateralism, the bypassing of the Council and making it irrelevant, as we have seen in the question of Iraq in recent years.

NIELS BLOKKER: Thank you very much. We have a few more questions here. I see that my encouragement to students has helped. I see Matthijs Geneste, and then we will take some other questions at the same time.

MATTHIJS GENESTE:* We have to ask ourselves the question whether we would like to have a Council dealing with security issues, or do we want some kind of representative world government? For the sake of the maintenance of international peace and security one would need the largest players on the world stage in your Council. Most of these players are already in the Council. In order to keep the Security Council an effective organ I would actually urge not to enlarge the Council to 25 members. It is already hard to make decisions in the current composition. I would like to hear the opinion of the Panel on this issue.

BIBI VAN GINKEL:** A question for Lord Hannay: I was somewhat disappointed that the High-level Panel report did not comment on the expanding powers of the Security Council, especially the legislative and quasi-judicial powers. Could you please comment on that?

SUSAN BREAU:*** As a Canadian I am complimented that it was mentioned that the Canadians developed the concept of 'responsibility to protect'. However, it was actually proposed prior to that in a Dutch report on humanitarian intervention. Given the fact that it has been developed over several years, how likely is it that the international community will accept the 'responsibility to protect'? Is the concept that revolutionary or has its time come?

ROBERTO LAVALLE:**** In my view the criteria for the authorization of the use of force by the Security Council, contained in the *In Larger Freedom* report do not tie in with the Council's practice and are not realistic. The recommendations disregard the recent authorizations by the Council for UN Peace-keeping operations which allow use force proactively (i.e., not just self-defence) whenever this is necessary for the fulfilment of the mandates, and thus leaving the use of force entirely to the discretion of those forces. More important, for the Council to have an idea as to the likelihood of success of the use of force, it would be necessary that states provide the Council precise information as to how they will proceed (or change plans during the action to adapt to changing circumstances). When the Council has not received any of such reports, it has thus issued, so to speak, a 'blanc cheque' regarding the use of force. However, it cannot be expected that the Council should act as a commander-in-chief, which would be necessary to assess the chances to success.

NIELS BLOKKER: Before we go on, let us try to have answers from the panellists on these four groups of questions.

LORD DAVID HANNAY: I am afraid I am going to duck about the question about the Security Council, because I applied one rule in the last 6 months and that is: never on a public platform to depart from the even-handedness of the Security Council's offer of two alternative ways of enlarging it. I do not think it is helpful to go away from that.

* Leiden University.

** Utrecht University.

*** British Institute of International and Comparative Law.

**** Permanent Mission of Guatemala to the UN.

On the subject of legislative powers, we indeed did not refer to actions like Resolution 1540 with regard to nuclear matters. It was quite contentious within the panel and we did not think it made sense to try to produce a unified view of that, particularly since the Council had actually used these powers. However, there are some references to the potential use of it in a reference to the need to make the Additional Protocol of the International Atomic Energy Agency the 'the gold standard' for applying nuclear safeguards. You could read into that, in my view, the possibility that if people not hasten a bit faster towards all signing up to the Protocol, it could very well be that the Security Council will one day make the Additional Protocol mandatory.

With regard to the concept of 'responsibility to protect', I do think that it is actually a huge step when a concept like this, moves from various non-governmental, or quasi-governmental reports and seminar discussion into the centre stage of actual decision-making at the United Nations, which is what now happened. If it were to be endorsed by a resolution of the General Assembly and by a resolution of the Security Council, that would also be a huge step forward. Of course, we all need to be fairly cautious about this, firstly because it may not happen, but secondly because even when that happened, you would still have to actually apply it. I think myself that – and here I depart totally from the Panel's thinking, because we did never go that far – there would have to be a development of practice in this matter, which would be extremely important. I do not think that the Council would, just like that, 'cold' authorize an intervention, naming the 'responsibility to protect'. I think it is far more likely that the Council would in the first instance tell the state in question that it had the responsibility to protect and demand that it fulfil that responsibility. If they did that under Chapter VII, I think it would be a pretty clear warning that something, a great deal nastier, might come down the road quite soon. It would not be in the first instance an authorization to use military action. However, that is just me, as an old ambassador, sort of musing of what might happen. I think there is a huge journey before the 'responsibility to protect' becomes real, and I think we have taken quite a long step down the road on that journey, but by no means the last of it.

As to the use of force, we did not say anything about the use of force to protect the mandate in a peacekeeping operation, because it is now so firmly embedded in so many resolutions of the Security Council that I think we did not believe it necessary to say anything more about it. It is clearly understood, that in the very fraught circumstances of modern peacekeeping missions where you are often dealing with non-state actors, and spoilers who are not states, you really do have to have a fairly robust mandate. However, that is frankly a long way away from the authorization to use force of which we were talking.

Finally, I would really contest the view that Resolution 678, which authorized the use of force to remove the Iraqi troops from Kuwait, did not fit the 5 criteria. Frankly, I think it fit the 5 criteria admirably. I think we scored just about as close to 100 per cent as you could. The 5 criteria of course did not exist at that time, or were not being put forward, but I think it shows that you can do it. For example, the fact that the coalition forces stopped at the Iraqi frontier, once they had expelled all the Iraqi troops from Kuwait was an excellent example of proportionality. So I do not agree, frankly, that that was not. And that shows how these 5 criteria could be extremely useful to the Security Council, if they were given a more formal meaning than they have now. I do say again, as I said in my introductory words, we were not, and are not, trying to write international law. These criteria will not become international law. That is absolutely out. If you try to do that, you will get nothing. But they could become something that is quite important in terms of international practice.

KAREL VAN KESTEREN: I wholeheartedly agree with what Lord Hannay said in his last remarks. We are talking here also about my point of view. We are not talking about codifying international law; we are talking about international politics and practices.

With regard to the question on the criteria, I would like to say that I am convinced that those criteria will not be formally adopted by the Summit in September. Because there are two groups that are against it. You have the big countries that say 'we do not want our hands to be tied to that extend' and a big group of developing countries that do not want it, as they see it as a guideline for military intervention. There is also another argument of those people that point out that formal guidelines may shift the discussion away from the merits of the case to the words of the guidelines. I see a point there from a practical point of view. Take the case of Darfur, where you saw this happening to a certain extend. People started talking mainly about whether the Genocide Convention was applicable, whether the situation fit the definition of genocide.

The Canadians have contributed enormously to the concept of 'responsibility to protect'. The Dutch discussions were about humanitarian intervention, which is a very dangerous wording, as it is not about intervention. The Canadians changed it into 'responsibility to protect', which is in the first place a responsibility of a state to protect its own citizens. When the state fails to do so, because it is unable or unwilling to do so, then there is a responsibility for the international community. That is not a responsibility to take 'military action', but to take 'action', which can be for example sending advisors or observers, or applying sanctions. Perhaps, in the last resort – if there is no other option – you can consider the military option and the use of force. Please make that difference. Otherwise you will set the debate on the wrong footing and then the discussion will be about military intervention and the rules for military intervention and that is not what the concept of 'responsibility to protect' is about. I am fairly optimistic about the adoption of the concept. However, the principle has to be defined very clearly. A lot of developing countries are afraid that this indeed is an open door to military intervention at any moment. So we are currently in the process of trying to define and state clearly that we are talking about situations of genocide, mass violations of human rights and ethnic cleansing, etc. Everyone already accepts the concept in this regard. Take the case of Darfur. I hear no-one say that the international community should not talk about Darfur, because it is an internal affair of Sudan. And that is the difference; it shows that the whole international community already accepted the idea that this situation is a legitimate concern for the international community, and that is exactly what the 'responsibility to protect' is about.

NICO SCHRIJVER. I will try to be brief in my response to these very interesting questions. With regard to the question of Matthijs Geneste, I would like to say that it is of course everybody's guess what the ideal composition of the Security Council is from the point of view of effectiveness. At a first glance you may say 15 is better than 21, 22 or 25. But in view of the fact that the Council is widely seen as not to being any longer a representative body, in view of the fact that this affects its legitimacy of its decisions, and in view of the fact that it is very difficult to get members out of the Council, it is unavoidable to look for expansion of the Council in order to improve its effectiveness. Personally, I am very much in favour of Model B, with semi-permanent seats. I also note that the Secretary-General departs a bit from the High-level Panel report in suggesting that next to Models A and B other viable options may also be discussed.

With respect to the question on the responsibility to protect you could indeed argue that by way of human rights obligations there is to a certain extend already a 'responsibility to protect'. However, I argued that it goes much further. The 'responsibility to protect' may mean, that you take as a starting point the life, the security, the fate of citizens, rather than the peace and security of national states and regions. In my view, that would be quite a revolutionary change in international law.

Karel van Kesteren referred to the 'responsibility to protect' as a 'principle'. Well, 'principles' do form the basis of international law. Sometimes they are emerging; sometimes they are already firmly established. Of course the concept of 'responsibility to protect' is at the moment not an issue that lends itself to be codified in the form of a treaty. We would first need more and more resolutions, and more and more reports. You can note that a new *opinio iuris communis* is growing, as to the emergence of the concept of 'responsibility to protect', and that in a number of situations it is already practiced.

Lastly, Mr. Lavalle, I do agree with Lord Hannay, that Resolution 678 got a successful follow-up in practice. The basic purpose of this resolution was to restore Kuwait in its sovereignty, in its territorial integrity, and for that purpose to get the Iraqi army out of Kuwait. I also take issue with his remarks that the criteria as proposed by Kofi Annan are not realistic. I think they provide a very useful list of criteria. I do believe, even when Karel van Kesteren is right in his somewhat pessimistic assessment that they will not be adopted, that they play an important role. They have gained a lot of authority in the extremely interesting High-level Panel report. They are endorsed by a Secretary-General, who has an enormous political stature. It would be helpful to record the criteria in a more formal instrument, but even if this will not happen, they are still very much on the table and hopefully in the back of the minds of decision-makers, and certainly of international lawyers.

NIELS BLOKKER: Thank you very much, Nico. Ladies and Gentlemen, we ran out of time but I think we have just time for two more, short, last questions.

PETER BAEHR:* Would the panel as such consider bringing down the number of members of the Security Council, rather than expanding it? Peter van Walsum, former ambassador of the Netherlands, also proposed this. In this context, I would also like to remind you that in the proposals for the so-called Human Rights Council as compared to the present Commission on Human Rights, which counts 53 members, the Secretary-General has suggested that there should be fewer members in the Human Rights Council in order to make it more effective and decisive.

SIR MICHAEL WOOD:** My first question is about the 'responsibility to protect'; I am not sure whether to call it a concept or a principle or an emerging norm or a catch phrase. Is the Responsibility to protect intended to be some new legal responsibility, and if so, who is the bearer of this new obligation? Or are we essentially referring to a moral responsibility? My second question: is it implicit in the 'responsibility to pro-

* University Utrecht.

** Foreign & Commonwealth Office, UK.

tect' that individual states may in certain circumstances have the right to use force, or are we talking exclusively about the Security Council.

LORD DAVID HANNAY: I really do think that the idea of reducing the numbers of members of the Security Council falls absolutely smack into that category of what I call 'blue sky proposals' which ensure that something is dead on arrival. I am not saying that it would not be a good idea. There are many wonderful ideas around, but I think it is best at this stage to limit the discussion to proposals that might actually be achieved. In the context of the huge expansion of the membership of the United Nations and given the fact that the idea of having a group of a limited number of states which has the power to declare or authorize the declaration of war is such as absolutely astonishing concept (which arrived in 1945), it would be seen a bit offensive by many countries around the world to limit further the number of members states who participate in those decisions. It might rouse a real storm of protest, even if the case for it was a case of effectiveness.

With regard to Michael Wood's question about the 'responsibility to protect', I think I am going to duck a little bit. Saying whether it is a moral or a legal issue? I think it is an issue of legitimacy, really. It clearly is a major step away from Article 2(7) of the UN Charter. There are those who argue that Article 2(7) should never have been in the Charter and this opened the door to massive abuse. The second of those propositions, I think is almost impossible to refute. Since what has been put forward is not a legal text, and it is not suggested that it should amend the Charter, I think one has to say that it is not a fully legal proposal. However, it is not a purely moral proposal, based on purely moral grounds, either. It is actually intended to influence policy. In the way the panel has put it forward, it is a collective decision that has to occur, if country A or B proves itself unwilling or unable to provide the human security for all its citizens, that is the duty of every government to provide. Am I saying that therefore it is inconceivable that the 'responsibility to protect' could be used by an individual government without Security Council legitimisation? Well, it is quite interesting to note that three times – long before the 'responsibility to protect' was ever invented – something very like the 'responsibility to protect' was exercised, namely in the case of Tanzania's action in Uganda, in the case of India's action in Bangladesh and in the case of action in Cambodia. The interesting thing was that each of the 3 countries that exercised it, swore blind that that was not what they were doing, because they were terrified of the concept. Quite a lot of Bangladeshis and Ugandans and Cambodians are alive today because it was done (which does not prove it was necessarily a good thing to do). Anyway, my answer to this question is: what we were thinking about, clearly was that the 'responsibility to protect' resides with individual governments is and that it is transferred to the international community in the form of the Security Council if they fail to exercise it.

KAREL VAN KESTEREN: Just a short remark to professor Baehr about the size of the Security Council. I agree with Lord Hannay that under the present circumstances it is absolutely impossible; it is not realistic and not conceivable. In the long run it might be. The idea of the Dutch government – despite of the outcome of the recent referendum – still is a common EU presence in the Security Council. I could imagine in the long run a process of regionalisation by which a smaller Security Council could be legitimate in the sense that the individual members represent blocks of countries or regions that would be much more integrated than today. However, that is something for the future. This is again a reason not to make decisions or changes for the rest of eternity, but to take into account that the world changes. We should change the Council's size and composition for a limited number of years, so we take steps into the direction of reducing the size, if the geopolitical realities of that moment warrant it.

NICO SCHRIJVER: I will briefly response to professor Baehr's questions. I do not think it is very helpful to suggest that the Security Council should become smaller. To reduce the Council as a whole back from 15 to the original 11 simply will not fly. As to the Human Rights Council, I find it very interesting to note that on this point Kofi Annan departs in a very interesting way from the High-level Panel. The High-level Panel proposed to have an universal membership for the UN Commission on Human Rights, and Kofi Annan comes with the proposal to dismantle totally the UN Commission on Human Rights and to establish a small size Human Rights Council of 18-27 members. I believe that is a very relevant proposal, because it would upgrade the discussions on concerns on human rights to the same level as we deal with security issues in the Security Council, and economic and social issues in the Economic and Social Council.

As to Sir Michael Wood's question on the 'responsibility to protect', I believe it is more than a moral principle. We already discussed that to a certain extend it has some footing in international law, especially in human rights law. There is an international obligation incumbent on states to respect the human rights of its own citizens. I do believe that the formulation of Article 2(7) of the Charter is flexible enough to accommodate it, because it prevents intervention of the UN in matters, which are essentially in the domestic jurisdiction of a state. Of course the word 'essentially' can be interpreted according to the state of the art in the field of international law, including human rights law. I also do believe that first of all the 'responsibility to protect' as a principle, as an emerging norm, should be addressed to the UN Security Council. It should be taken as an incentive to act timely, decisively, and adequately. Thus from that point of view it is first of all the Security Council that is the bearer of the duty. However, the Security Council could fail to exercise its primary responsibility. Take the example of northern Iraq, where 4 states, including your own, and including the Dutch government, took military action in a swift, military operation to stop the mass flow of refugees, to stop Saddam Hussein going into northern Iraq, to provide an opening for humanitarian relief. I believe this is an example of an adequate response to the emerging norm of the 'responsibility to protect'.

NIELS BLOKKER: Ladies and Gentlemen, I think we can go for hours, but we will not. I would like to thank the people who have asked questions, but mainly I would like to thank the panellists for giving such interesting presentations and such good answers to the questions that have been asked. Thank you very much.

*Reporter:* Geert-Jan van den Hoek*

* Ministry of Foreign Affairs of the Netherlands.

# The Interplay Between National, Regional and International Courts: Fragmentation or Figmentation?

The panel was convened by its Chair: Hannah Buxbaum*

## Introductory remarks by Hannah Buxbaum

Hannah Buxbaum introduced the panel entitled 'The Interplay between National, Regional and International Courts: Fragmentation or Figmentation' by emphasizing that the goal of the panellists was to address the interplay between national, regional and international courts in a broad sense. Thus, the panel would focus not only on the jurisdictional conflicts arising between courts at different levels, but also the political issues these conflicts present to States and the international system. Professor Buxbaum stated that in doing so, the intention of the panel was to identify possible reforms to the way in which judicial resources are deployed globally.

In addressing this topic, Professor Buxbaum noted that the panel presentations would proceed in the following order. First, Gareth Davies, would focus on the regional level by speaking on the relationship between European national courts and the European Court of Justice ('ECJ'). Second, Ronald Goodman, would examine overlapping and competing jurisdictions between international arbitral tribunals and national courts with regard to international investment disputes. Third, Hannah Buxbaum herself would address the potential for national courts to deal with certain transnational economic harms. Finally, William Burke-White, would consider the legal and political influence of international criminal tribunals on national governments and domestic courts.

* Professor of Law, Indiana University School of Law at Bloomington.

## Remarks by Gareth Davies*

## Reforming the Relationship Between National and European Courts

### 1. Introduction

The preliminary reference procedure found in Article 234 EC provides that the task of ensuring Community law is respected in the Member States is shared between the European Court of Justice and national courts. The national courts send questions of interpretation of the Treaties and associated legislation to the ECJ, and then apply the answers that they receive to the cases before them.

Unfortunately, this procedure is in severe difficulties. The time taken to answer references is approaching two years, and it is accepted that it is likely to rise further. Enlargement may lead to an extra dramatic growth, as new courts, unfamiliar with Community law, increase the number and diversity of references.

This puts the effectiveness of Community law in jeopardy, partly by preventing the timely use of the correct principles of law in national courts, but also by strongly discouraging national courts from referring questions at all. Given the enormous extra time and cost that references add to the case, it is understandable that national judges are sometimes reluctant to refer. This raises the risk of non-uniformity of Community law, as judges in at least some Member States increasingly prefer to rely on their own interpretations, rather than seeking them from the ECJ.

As a result, reform has been considered an urgent priority for some years now. However, proposals have focussed almost exclusively on improving the institutional structure and operation of the Community courts – more money, more judges, less judges per case, specialized chambers, and so on. This paper suggests that this strategy is unlikely to be successful (and indeed, until now, despite some of these reforms being implemented, there has not been any dent in the growing delays). The problem is not located in the organisation of the Community court system, but rather in the relationship between the two levels of courts, and in the way that the ECJ manages that relationship. It is this that needs to be reformed.

The problem lies in the way the ECJ understands the division of functions between national and Community courts, and in particular the distinction between 'interpretation' (for the ECJ) and 'application' (for the national court). Essentially, it tends to treat – albeit with occasional deviations from this view – every application of a Community rule as involving a new interpretation.[1]

This approach is understandable. As a matter of principle, it can be argued that each application of a rule fleshes out its meaning and so in a sense 'interprets' it. More importantly, the ECJ's approach gives it a deep involvement in the national caseload, and enables it to steer the use and development of Community law. This prevents divergent understandings of the law from arising. It can also be useful for national judges, who may value clear and concrete guidance with deciding their case, and will not

* Lecturer in European Law, University of Groningen.

appreciate being told that it raises no new interpretative issues, and so they should just apply existing case law. They want an answer.

However, there are considerable disadvantages to the ECJ's approach. It potentially results in an unmanageable workload, and it alienates and infantilises the national legal system. The workload problem arises because if each application is an interpretation then the ECJ will potentially receive references in all national cases involving Community law. They all become suitable for reference. This is clearly, even with the most well-funded and efficient Community court system an unsustainable position. The infantilisation occurs because in any case involving Community law the national judge is reduced to mechanically applying the answer she receives from the ECJ. It is as if the national judiciary has no intelligent role to play in Community law. Clearly, this will not help with the long-term integration of Community rules into the national legal system.

In short, the ECJ's approach is a centralising one, in which it maintains a very broad interpretative monopoly. This has enabled it to exert a powerful influence on the EU's legal development, but it cannot represent a viable approach indefinitely. At some point it must re-interpret its relationship with the national courts to give them a more autonomous and contributory role.

This can be partly achieved by interpreting 'interpretation' more narrowly, so that a new interpretation arises only where a genuinely analytically new point is raised. Then in most cases the national courts can just apply existing principles to the facts before them. Centralisation would be reduced. However, another approach may be, paradoxically, to move towards more hierarchy. At the moment, the relationship between national and Community courts is formally one of cooperation. However, in practice, this means that where Community law is relevant the national courts are entirely sidelined, except as enforcers of the ECJ's word. By contrast, were the reference procedure to be replaced by an appeal on cassation to the ECJ, then there would be a greater role for national courts to provide their own complete interpretations of Community rules, with the possibility for the ECJ to supervise these on cassation, in order to maintain uniformity. As a genuine supreme court of Community law, the ECJ would lose no status or power, but would be less taxed by a need to interpret every single mundane case.

This paper follows the above argument. The following section outlines the way that the Court understands the division of functions between it and national courts, and why it does so. Subsequent sections then consider the major problems arising from the Court's approach. Finally, an alternative, cassation, is considered.

## 2. Interpretation and Application

The Treaty provides that where national judges are faced with a case in which it is necessary for a question of Community law to be answered they may refer that question to the Court of Justice.[2] If they are the final court, beyond which no appeal in the case is possible, then they must do so – subject to very narrow exceptions.[3] The national court is then obliged to apply the answer that it receives to the case before it.

The Court of Justice emphasises the labour-sharing character of this process, rather than any element of hierarchy. While it is true that it has the last word on the

Community law point, by contrast, it has no competence or jurisdiction to interpret the national laws involved in the case, nor to apply the Community law to the facts.[4] These functions are exclusively for national courts. By working together, national and Community judges provide the pieces necessary to solve the case.

The conventional description of the division of functions is that the Court of Justice interprets Community law, and the national judge applies that interpretation. However, while clear at first glance, it is apparent upon consideration that the line between these two functions is far from clear. Examples are the best way of illustrating this.

In one of the most famous – and important – Community law cases, *Cassis de Dijon*,[5] the referring German Court asked whether a German rule requiring fruit wine sold in Germany to have a minimum alcohol content was a measure equivalent to a quantitative restriction on imports, contrary to Article 28. The question was raised because French Cassis typically had a lower percentage of alcohol, and the German rule therefore prevented it from being imported and sold in Germany.

The Court of Justice found that such a national product standard would indeed be prohibited unless it was necessary to protect some important public interest, such as consumer protection. The important part of this, which has been the core of free movement law and of the internal market ever since, was the requirement of necessity, which is part of the principle of proportionality. The Court was deciding that product standards must be proportionate, if they were to be enforceable against imports.

The Court then went on to decide that the German rule was disproportionate, because although it aimed to protect the consumer, which was legitimate, that aim could be achieved by less burdensome means, such as a labelling requirement. In deciding this, was the Court interpreting Community law, or in reality applying to the facts?

One view is that the question whether a given rule is in fact necessary to achieve its ends is part of what interpretation is. Each fact set raises a new question, and each *ratio decidendi* is a new interpretation. Interpretation, on this view, is something that is done through application, through considering specific instances. This might be called a very common law view. It has the advantage of practicality – clearly it is through use of a rule in particular situations that one understands what it really means. However, it has the disadvantage that it renders the Court's distinction between interpretation and application nugatory.

A different view is that the Court began by interpreting the law on goods. Its finding that the application of national product standards to imports was only permissible if the standards were proportionate was a true interpretation of Article 28 EC. However, in then examining whether the German rule was in fact necessary, and in reaching the conclusion that labels would protect consumers just as well, it was delving into facts, drawing conclusions about them, and essentially applying its interpretation to the case – that is to say, transgressing the boundary to its competences which it had laid down itself.

The Court is variable. Often it pronounces that whether a particular rule is proportionate is a matter for the national court. However, more often it essentially decides such questions itself.[6] Not only does it do this where proportionality is in issue – which arises in free movement, sex discrimination, and other contexts – but with other principles too. When is a violation of Community law by a Member State 'sufficiently serious' to incur liability? When does interpretation of a particular national rule to comply with an unimplemented directive go beyond the compulsory 'so far as possible' test?

What all of these have in common is that they are 'mixed' principles, whose use and meaning involves both law and fact. An interpretation of them out of context has only limited explanatory power. Hence the Court dives into the facts – unless of course it is one of those complicated or politically sensitive cases where it chooses not to and refers to the division of functions between courts to explain this.[7]

This gives a clue to the main reason why the Court takes the approach it does. It wishes to provide maximum assistance to national judges – who often ask very concrete questions, and so perhaps expect concrete answers – and it wants to provide answers that make sure that the national judge cannot subsequently get it wrong. Merely handing down abstract principles to be applied would still leave room for a great deal of delinquency and divergence. What one judge may find to be necessary and proportionate to protect consumers, another may not. The Court of Justice is keeping control in the interests of the uniformity of Community law.[8]

However, there is another approach possible. A greater degree of control over outcomes could also be reached through more detailed and precise abstract principles, and more explanation of the procedural steps that a national judge must follow. In *Cassis* the Court could have explained the steps involved in assessing proportionality, and how the relevant interests which may arise should be balanced against each other. This would both assist the national judges in applying the Community law principles, and limit their capacity for highly divergent applications.[9] It is notable that the Court does not generally provide such explanations. While there is some expansion of what is 'sufficiently serious' to be found in the case law, one may search in vain for a thorough and useful explanation of how a national judge should apply proportionality.

Therefore, the wide view of the function of the Court should not be taken as a given, even less so since it seems to go against the natural reading of both the Treaty and the division of functions as the Court explains it. In the light of that, it is worth focussing on some of the considerable problems that it causes.

## 3. Workload

On a narrow view of interpretation, there will probably never again be a need to refer a case concerning free movement law. The principles are now quite clear. All national standards must be justified and proportionate, and there are a few other rules as well, but essentially the law is in place. It just remains to apply it to the situations which occur.

On the view which the Court seems to take, the position is dramatically different. Every new fact set requires a new interpretation, and therefore justifies a reference. Potentially, almost every case in a national court where Community law is involved may generate a question for Luxembourg.[10] Only where the Court has already pronounced on identical facts or where the answer is so dazzlingly obvious that there is in fact nothing to seriously think about – rather narrow limitations – is this not the case.[11] Certainly, every case where a 'mixed norm' is involved is appropriate for the Court of Justice, but these are famously ubiquitous in Community law.

It is clear that no institutional reform will ever create a Court of Justice capable of dealing with references from every national case involving Community law. It must therefore hope that national judges exercise their discretion not to refer – and the increasing slowness of answering questions is no doubt an effective deterrent here – or it must change its approach to its own function. Since it shows no sign of doing the latter, the future of the Community judicial system currently rests on the former. This hardly seems desirable.

## 4. Infantilising Supreme Courts

A peculiarity of the reference procedure is that while lower judges may refer questions, final judges must. Unlike their lower brethren, supreme courts are prohibited in all circumstances from deciding any question of Community law themselves. Even the narrow *CILFIT* exceptions do not change this, since these may be understood as describing circumstances where there is really nothing to decide.

The reason for this rule is clear and understandable. While if lower judges decide the law themselves and get it wrong there is still room for appeal, if the final court is allowed to decide Community law points, and it gets them wrong, then incorrect interpretations of Community law will be entrenched in national systems. Final courts are too powerful to be allowed to play freely, and so they must automatically refer all the Community law questions which are necessary for the cases before them.

This must be frustrating for senior judges, the cream of their national profession. They will never, for the rest of their career, be permitted to think intelligently about any question of Community law, at least within the context of their work. However, this is mitigated somewhat if interpretation is interpreted narrowly. Then at least they can decide whether a measure is proportionate, sufficiently serious, and so on. Unfortunately, since the Court of Justice regularly answers such questions they are clearly within its jurisdiction, and so must also be referred. Matters of Community law should, if national courts obey the Court of Justice and the Treaty, simply slip through the supreme courts without touching the sides.

It is difficult to imagine national supreme courts accepting this humiliation, particularly in a time when references take so long. Nor is it good for Community law itself. If this is to become properly integrated into national legal systems, and properly used by national judges, then supreme courts clearly have an important role to play. Within the nation they have more authority and day-to-day influence than the Court of Justice, and are well-placed to create a culture of good use of Community law, either through example or pronouncement. Unfortunately not only is this role blocked by the simple fact that they are not allowed to use that law themselves, but any motivation they may have to encourage its integration by other means must be significantly reduced.

In fact there seems to be evidence that supreme courts are rebelling against the Court of Justice, and refusing to refer when they are in fact obliged to. This is of two sorts – on the one hand, anecdotal evidence from practicing lawyers and judges is that in several Member States, including the Netherlands and the UK, there have been cases where Community law points were not referred to the Court of Justice but should have been. This should be straightforward to empirically establish, and its extent, and would be a worthwhile research project, but is beyond the scope of this paper. Secondly, a recent case against Italy, brought by the Commission, as a result of the failure of its judges to refer,[12] and the famous *Köbler* case,[13] in which the Court of Justice outlined that such failure may occur state liability, suggest that there is an awareness within Community institutions that delinquent supreme courts are an increasing threat to the integrity and function of Community law. These two cases seem to suggest the emergence of a policy to enforce the obligation to refer, presumably based on an awareness of growing failure to do so. On reason for this divergence between supreme courts and Community law must be the infantilising approach taken to them by the Court of Justice.

Perhaps more alarming still is the question of pure principle. Supreme courts have largely accepted that in principle they are obliged to obey the Treaty and the Court of Justice. In not doing so they are setting aside the law for reasons of mixed practicality and pride. It is very worrying when a dysfunctional system reaches the point that it causes the highest judges in a country to deliberately disobey the law. The respect of the population for the legal system and the popular assumption that judges may be trusted in their function are both called into question.

## 5. The Confusion of Lower Courts

One of the claims most often made in defence of the Court's concrete answers is that this is just a reaction to the way that national judges ask their questions, and that they expect an answer to these. If they ask whether a national rule is disproportionate, they will be unhappy if they are not told.

This is a very weak defence. There is no doubt that the Court of Justice is responsible for interpreting the scope and nature of the preliminary reference system, and if national judges have the idea that they may or should refer questions of proportionality then this is because the Court has always treated such questions as appropriate and answered them, and so given the impression that they are indeed ones of interpretation. The corollary is that if the Court were to indicate to national judges that they should apply proportionality themselves, instead of asking it to do so, they would presumably take this advice and reduce the number of references. The argument that the nature of answers is led by the nature of the questions is an abdication of responsibility. The questions are part of the procedure too, and so it is for the Court to indicate what sorts of questions should be sent.

At the moment the Court sends wildly mixed messages. For the hard-headed national judge who has no desire to refer support can be found in the cases stating that only a national judge can assess a national rule. For the nervous judge who is inclined towards 'if in doubt, ask' there are also the majority of cases where the court embraces application. How can a poor national judge who is neither nervous nor stubborn but simply wishes to do the legally correct thing be expected to find his way?

It is very likely that one reaction of national judges will be irritation, and a tendency to rebel. Cooperation with the Court of Justice and use of Community law in national courts are both hindered if national judges perceive these to involve imprecise and unprincipled decision-making. Perhaps even worse, from the Community law perspective at least, is that reactions are likely to vary considerably, both from judge to judge and from land to land. Whereas the judicial culture of one land may lead judges to tend to go for non-referral, in another land the culture may be more deferential and referral rates may be much higher.[14] Since there is evidence that the Court of Justice does not always take the same view of proportionality as national judges do,[15] which court makes the decision affects the substantive outcome of the case. Thus differences in referral rates will lead to non-uniformity of Community law. Avoiding such non-uniformity is one of the major reasons why the reference procedure exists.

Moreover, such diversity will not be easy to see. To know whether Community law is really going off the rails and being misapplied or not applied in national courts, which simply fail to refer questions involving mixed norms, will require national research on this question. While that is no doubt being done to some extent, it will be a significant challenge for the central Community authorities to monitor what is going on. One has to ask whether perhaps there is a better way, which avoids these problems in the first place.

## 6. A Possible Solution

The founding myth of the preliminary reference procedure is that there is no hierarchy involved. Of course in reality, on the point of Community law, there is a clear and absolute hierarchy. There may be cooperation in reaching a result in the case, but not in interpreting the Treaty and secondary legislation.

Why not then move to a system of cassation, whereby national judges, even final judges, would decide the interpretation of Community law themselves but parties could appeal to the Court of Justice on the grounds that Community law had been misinterpreted? This would refer the case back to the national court for redecision if this was so. This would enable national judges of all levels to use Community law fully, to integrate it into their thinking and judging,[16] while still enabling the possibility of control of uniformity. If there was a right to appeal, then there would also be less problems resulting from a national judicial refusal to play the game.

Appeal could be possible from any level, or only from final courts – encouraging higher national courts to supervise the interpretation of Community law by lower ones. The disadvantage of this latter would be that it would create a long chain of appeals before a case was finally settled. However, that is true already, where a litigant may go to the Supreme Court and then have to wait for a reference.

Perhaps appeals would result in more cases, and so a greater workload. However, if appeal was only from a final court then this would not be so, yet the conventional hierarchical structure would train and discipline lower judges so that a consistent approach to using the law was present throughout the system; indeed, Community law would be using the approach and mechanism for consistency that national legal systems use, a hierarchy of appeals.

The argument against appeals is that national judges, particularly final judges, do not wish to be overturned by the Court of Justice. This might offend their dignity. The current system, by not allowing them to speak about Community law avoids this risk. However, since the hierarchy of Community law authority is already real and effective, one may wonder whether preserving a myth of cooperation, and the delicate sensibilities of supreme courts, is enough reason to justify a process that otherwise does not work well.

## Notes

1 The argument in this paper draws heavily on Davies, 'The Division of Powers Between the European Court of Justice and National Courts', ConWEB working paper No.3/2004, available at: <http://les1.man.ac.uk/conweb>. Considerably more detail on the points raised here and discussion of a large number of cases can be found in that paper.

2 Art. 234 EC; Art. III-369 of the Constitution.

3 See Case 283/81 *CILFIT* [1982] ECR 3415.

4 See Case 6/64 *Costa* v. *Enel* [1964] ECR 585; Case C-320 *Staatsecretaris van Financien* v. *Shipping and Forwarding Enterprise Safe BV* [1990] ECR I-285; Case 13/68 *Salgoil Spa* v. Ministero *per il Commercio con l'Estero* [1968] ECR 453.

5 Case 120/78 *Cassis de Dijon* [1979] ECR ù649.

6 See Rasmusson, 'Remedying the crumbling EC judicial system', 37 *CMLRev.* (2000), p.1071 at p. 1101 for some quantitative discussion of this; Pager, 'Strictness v discretion: the ECJ's variable vision of gender equality', 51 *AJCompLaw* (2003), pp. 553-608; Cohen, 'The European preliminary reference and US Supreme Court review of state court judgments: a study in comparative judicial federalism', 44 *AJCompLaw* (1996), p. 421; Craig and de Burca, *EU Law*, 3rd edn. (Oxford, Oxford University Press 2003) at pp. 472-473.

7 See de Burca, 'The principle of proportionality and its application in EC law', *YEL* (Oxford, Oxford University Press 1993).

8 See Tridimas, 'Knocking on heaven's door: fragmentation, efficiency and defiance in the preliminary reference procedure', 40 *CMLRev.* (2004), p. 9 at p. 24.

9 Jarvis, *Application of EC Law by National Courts: Free Movement of Goods* (Oxford, Clarenden Press 1998) at pp. 206-207.

10 See Rasmussen, *supra* n. 6, at p. 1108; AG Jacobs in Case C-338/95 *Wiener* [1997] ECR I-6495.

11 See *CILFIT*, *supra* n. 3.

12 Case C-129/00 *Commission* v. *Italy*, judgment of 9 December 2003.

13 Case C-224/01 *Köbler* [2003] ECR I-10239.

14 See Tridimas, *supra* n. 8, at p. 17 and pp. 37-38.

15 Jarvis, *supra* n. 9, at pp. 220-221.

16 See Weiler's notion of 'compliance pull' in his 'Journey to an unknown destination: a retrospective and prospective of the ECJ in the arena of political integration', 31 *JCMS* (1993), p. 417 at p. 422.

# Remarks by Ronald Goodman*

## Overlapping Jurisdictions in International Commerce

Mr. Goodman introduced his presentation by stating that he would address meddling courts and competing arbitral tribunals. He disclosed from the outset that he was personally not much in favor of international institutional reform in this area.

In addressing this topic, Mr. Goodman began with a few examples, the first being the '*KBC v. Pertamina* tragic comedy'. Once upon a time, there was contract between

* Partner at the Washington D.C. office of the law firm Winston & Strong and former member of staff of the Iran-US Claims Tribunal in The Hague. The original manuscript of this contribution was not received. The following text has been derived from the tapes on which the conference sessions were recorded.

Pertamina, a wholly owned energy company of the government of Indonesia, and KBC, a Cayman Islands private power development company, to build and operate electric power generation facilities in Indonesia. Indonesia suspended the project in the aftermath of the Asian financial crisis and KBC initiated arbitration proceedings in Switzerland relying upon a contractual arbitration clause. An award was eventually issued in favour of KBC. Pertamina unsuccessfully sought annulment of the award in Swiss courts. Thus, KBC brought enforcement actions in several jurisdictions around the world where Pertamina had assets including in the state of Texas in the United States (US). A US federal District Court confirmed the award. Pertamina then brought an action before the Central District Court of Jakarta seeking to annul the award and to enjoin KBC from enforcing the award anywhere in the world. In response, the federal District Court in Texas issued its own preliminary injunction barring Pertamina from pursuing the Indonesian annulment action and barring the enforcement of the Indonesian court's injunction anywhere in the world. Pertamina then appealed to the US 5th Circuit Court of Appeals. The Indonesian court converted its preliminary injunction to a permanent one backed by a fine of $500,000 per day for non-compliance. The Jakarta court also eventually annulled the award.

Mr. Goodman noted that series of tit-for-tat actions between courts as represented in the *KBC* case, in order to prevent the jurisdiction of other courts or arbitral tribunals, have been widely criticized. They have been discussed in a recent book by Judge Stephen Schwebel wherein he argues that these kinds of injunctions may be potentially in violation of the 1958 New York Convention on the Recognition and Enforcement of Foreign Arbitral Awards and other treaty provisions such as those of International Centre for the Settlement of Investment Disputes (ICSID); may constitute a denial of justice; and may be an arbitrary confiscation of an alien's contractual right.

Turning back to the *KBC* case, Mr. Goodman stated that after careful analysis of the international legal framework pertaining to the enforcement of arbitral awards, the US 5th Circuit Court of Appeals concluded that the US District Court's grant of a preliminary injunction barring Pertamina from pursuing its annulment action in Indonesia was an abuse of discretion. The court explained that although concerned about the propriety of the Indonesian suit, nevertheless, international comity weighed heavily against granting an injunction involving the judicial system of a foreign sovereign.

In addition to the *KBC* case, Mr. Goodman noted that there are other cases involving similar anti-suit injunctions, some of them more complicated than others, for example, *SGS v. Pakistan*, where there were three possibly four overlapping jurisdictions with a series of injunctions going back and forth. Nevertheless, eventually, the ICSID tribunal was able to proceed and issued an award.

Mr. Goodman pointed out that in the European Community there is a kind of solution in place to deal with these types of complex cases involving competing jurisdictions. European Council (EC) Regulation 44/2001 attempts to set-up *ex ante* rules on jurisdiction that would avoid multiple courts claiming jurisdiction over the same matter. Where a case comes within the jurisdiction of multiple courts, the regulation requires the dismissal of all actions except the one first seized. In a recent case, *Turner* v. *Grovit*, the ECJ considered the compatibility of this framework with the longstanding common law practice of granting anti-suit injunctions. In that case, an English court had attempted to enjoin a Spanish court proceeding that it believed was solely initiated in order to intimidate and exert pressure on one of the parties in a related proceeding in England. The ECJ ruled, however, that the English court's attempt was incorrect and inconsistent with the Brussels Convention on which EC Regulation 44/2001 was based and thus, the English court's anti-suit injunction could not be allowed.

Within these examples of cases involving competing jurisdictions, Mr. Goodman stated that one could also find examples of cases where there were overlapping jurisdictions. The 'Stockholm/London Syndrome' arose out of two arbitrations against the Czech Republic. One was in Stockholm under the Dutch/Czech bilateral investment treat ('BIT') brought by CME, a Dutch company controlled by a US minority shareholder by the name of Ronald Lauder. The other was in London, brought 6 months earlier, under the US/Czech BIT by Ronald Lauder himself as an individual investor. Both arbitrations involved precisely the same set of facts and the same complaints about actions by the Czech Republic. In both cases, liability was found. However, in London it was found only under one ground because the tribunal had a problem with causation. The arbitral tribunal found that Ronald Lauder's damages were not a result of actions by the Czech Republic. On the other hand, the Stockholm tribunal had no such difficulty and awarded CME approximately $270 million. These cases call to mind others in which there is yet unrealized potential for differing results, not necessarily conflicting, from overlapping jurisdictions. For example, the cases against Argentina involving claims brought by unrelated minority shareholders and claims brought both by a foreign company and its 100 per cent owned intermediary company, which itself directly owns the Argentine company, and may be considered as an asset and also a foreign investor under the definition in the BIT. There are also cases demonstrating opposing or differing interpretations of treaty and contractual rights.

From these cases, Mr. Goodman posited that one may be able to ascertain the so-called malaise resulting from various competing jurisdictions over the same case. However, he queried whether these cases really indicate that international institutional reform is necessary. In *KBC v. Pertamina*, the US 5$^{th}$ Circuit Court seemed to have gotten it right in the end. The Stockholm/London cases of conflicting results indicate that the arbitral tribunals seemed to be not that far a part, if at all, on the standards of law to be applied. Furthermore, the Czech Republic repeatedly declined CME's offer to structure the proceedings to avoid conflicting results through either consolidation of the cases or to have the same arbitrators in both cases or to have a kind of *lis pendens.* Thus, Mr. Goodman queried, one must ask whether these cases, in fact, demonstrate different conclusions on developing areas of international law and practice requiring some kind of institutional reform or whether they are, instead, evidence of lively and continuing debate, increasingly transparent in the investment sector, on important and complex issues.

Mr. Goodman noted that the harm that is of most concern from these kinds of cases is that of inconsistency arising from tribunals at the same level coming to opposing conclusions of law or opposing appreciation of the facts. In addition, there is the inconsistency resulting from 'extreme consistency' where two tribunals come to exactly the same result and award the claimant the same amount of money twice. Another feared harm is that of multiplicity of proceedings resulting in disorderliness, inappropriate assertion of jurisdictions, and a lack of finality.

Mr. Goodman suggested that perhaps traditional remedies to these 'harms' such as *lis pendens*, where the strictures under that doctrine were relaxed somewhat, should be examined more closely. In addition, there is the doctrine of *res judicata*, 'fork in the road' clauses in treaties, anti-abusive forum shopping clauses, provisions in national legislation such as *forum non conveniens,* and, as previously noted, regional regulations such as EC 44/2001. Where governments are exorcised about competing jurisdictions, they may collaborate with other government with which they have signed BITs and exchange notes as to the interpretation of the treaty to have, if they wish, more restrictive interpretations of their treaties. Finally, transparency is a remedy which may lead to an avoidance of competing and conflicting results. Mr. Goodman stated that in his view, in light of these possible remedies, he was not so sure institutional reform in the investment area was entirely necessary. He did concede that perhaps, the argument could be made that institutional reform is required because these competing cases have the potential for resulting in awards of billions of dollars at the expense of the taxpayer. However, Mr. Goodman noted that many of these competing and overlapping cases in the investment area have come out right in the end. Mr. Goodman concluded by stating that perhaps patience before rushing to reform is something to be considered more closely in these cases.

## Remarks by Hannah L. Buxbaum*

### Global Wrongs, Local Remedies: the Role of National Tribunals in Addressing Global Harms

Within the global judicial arena, jurisdictional and political complexity arises in part from the ever-increasing overlap among multiple layers of tribunals. It also arises, more generally, from the fracturing of the concept of territorial sovereignty that has traditionally delimited the role of courts on the international stage. Globalization, by challenging that concept, has caused a rethinking of how even national judicial resources can be mobilized in order to help remedy certain transnational harms. In the United States, for instance, advocates have used the Alien Tort Claims Act (ATCA) to bring human rights violations by individuals and corporations before domestic courts.[1] Such cases fall under the rubric of transnational public law litigation,[2] a form of domestic civil litigation in which courts apply international law norms in order to secure remedies for violations of those norms that are not otherwise available. Many commentators have praised such a use of national courts as a step toward a new understanding of judging as a global process. Consider the following, from an academic proponent of ATCA claims:

> Ultimately, the torture cases give us a glimpse into the imperatives of a future in which law – including private law – is increasingly cosmopolitan. Here, as the torture cases and the surrounding debates reveal, the limitations of the traditional conception of binding law come to

* Professor of Law, Indiana University School of Law at Bloomington. This paper is part of a larger project on transnational regulatory litigation: see Hannah L. Buxbaum, 'Transnational Regulatory Litigation', 46 *Va. J. Int'l L.* (2006) p. 251. I am grateful for research support from the Alexander von Humboldt Foundation, and for helpful comments and questions from participants in the conference.

seem pressing to judges and others faced with a world where legal problems are profoundly multi-jurisdictional in nature. The task of the advocate, the judge, and the law-maker no longer seems adequately captured – if it ever was – by the notion of discrete mutually exclusive spheres of binding law, conjoined through a set of rules premised on conflict and choice. And indeed, what the torture cases show is a subtle, yet distinct, move away from this model and towards a more multi-faceted integrative understanding of sources and a broader persuasive approach to authority.[3]

Others have criticized ATCA claims, on both legal and political grounds, as an untoward arrogation of judicial authority by U.S. courts over cases insufficiently connected with the United States. In a brief filed in the U.S. Supreme Court last term, the European Commission stated that

in order to respect the authority of States and organizations, like the European Community, exercising their authority to regulate activities occurring on their own territory, and hence to preserve harmonious international relations, States must respect the limits imposed by international law on the authority of any individual State to apply its laws beyond its own territory.[4]

These reactions are not simply far apart in terms of viewpoint, but illustrate two completely different narratives that can be used to discuss these cases – one that takes territorial sovereignty as its starting point, and one that reaches toward a more global and perhaps also more pragmatic vision of how national courts might assist in addressing global harms. The tension between these narratives arises from two sometimes incompatible priorities: one the one hand, the need to observe the jurisdictional norms that order the exercise of authority within the international community; on the other, the need for enhanced enforcement of global substantive norms in regulating cross-border conduct. Understanding that tension is important to clarifying the role that national courts might play in the future, and to recognizing the potential political limits of such a role.

Although the debate surrounding the proper role for national courts has centered on human rights litigation, the use of domestic civil actions to address global harm is developing in other areas as well. This paper suggests that it can be traced in certain categories of claims brought in U.S. courts under domestic regulatory law, which it refers to as transnational regulatory litigation. These claims are grounded even more firmly in the national level than ATCA claims, as they involve litigation not only in a national forum, but under national rather than international law. Despite this important difference, though, they present similar questions about the viability of the international jurisdictional framework and the possible evolution of national courts as an institution that might play a meaningful role in combating global harms. Further, they are subject to the same criticism: that, especially while conducted exclusively in U.S. courts,[5] such litigation may operate as a hegemonic institution. It is therefore important to take this kind of economic litigation into account when considering the phenomenon of judicial globalization.

This paper discusses two examples of transnational regulatory litigation, one involving claims brought against international price-fixing cartels and the other involving claims arising out of securities fraud. It outlines the dominant narrative used to analyze (and decide) such cases, which is based on notions of territorial jurisdiction. It then argues that the global nature of the harms addressed in these cases suggests an alternative narrative, one that envisions a broader role for national courts in combating certain challenges to global economic welfare. The paper does not conclude that the jurisdiction of national courts over these cases is necessarily justified. Rather, it argues that the debate over the jurisdictional and political conflict that necessarily attends such claims might be more profitably situated outside the classic framework of territorial sovereignty.

* * *

In a series of cases culminating in one heard by the Supreme Court,[6] foreign plaintiffs brought private actions in U.S. courts, pursuant to U.S. antitrust law, for damages caused by the activities of price-fixing cartels.[7] Each of the cartels in question had affected multiple markets, including U.S. markets. The foreign plaintiffs, however, sought compensation for damages arising out of purchase transactions that had taken place outside the United States. The cases therefore raised the question whether U.S. antitrust law extended to global conduct whose effect was felt in foreign transactions. The plaintiffs in these cases focused on the global nature of the cartel arrangements. In the case heard by the Supreme Court, for instance, which addressed a cartel operating in the bulk vitamin market, the plaintiffs stated that the success of the cartel depended on keeping vitamin prices worldwide in equilibrium. They argued that the defendants had fixed prices in the United States and then used those prices as a benchmark for prices in other markets, thereby linking the harm caused in one jurisdiction with market impact in others. Their starting point, in other words, was that the cartel had pursued a global strategy to cause global harm. The plaintiffs then pointed out that the regulatory standard at issue – embodied in rules condemning hard-core price fixing – is shared by virtually every antitrust system. In this respect, they noted, the case was unlike the more common cases in which the application of domestic law in litigation involving cross-border elements creates a substantive conflict with the law of another jurisdiction. Given the shared norm against hard-core price-fixing, the plaintiffs argued, there was no such conflict and therefore no reason not to permit recovery by foreign as well as domestic purchasers. The plaintiffs in the vitamins case and the other global cartel cases further argued that U.S. jurisdiction over the claims of foreign purchasers would enhance global competition regulation by compensating for insufficient regulation in other countries,[8] which otherwise would leave the conduct underdeterred on a global basis. They therefore invoked the application of U.S. law to enforce a shared regulatory standard for the benefit of the global market.

A second class of transnational regulatory cases arises out of cross-border securities fraud. Like the global cartel cases, these involve claims of foreign purchasers for damages suffered in transactions occurring outside the United States – here, purchases of securities, on foreign exchanges, at prices artificially inflated by fraudulent misrepresentations. One such case[9] involved a Netherlands corporation with securities listed on both U.S. and foreign exchanges. Officers of the company were alleged to have made misrepresentations in filings with the U.S. Securities and Exchange Commission and also in a variety of press releases, public statements and news articles that were published both in the United States and elsewhere. The plaintiff group, which included purchasers who had bought their shares on foreign exchanges as well as some who had purchased on the U.S. market, argued that these misrepresentations had inflated the price at which they purchased their shares.[10] The plaintiffs noted specifically the interconnected nature of the different financial markets on which the issuer's securities traded, stating that "[the issuer's] shares trade in tandem on the world's markets."[11] In their view, then, harm and effect in the different jurisdictions were intertwined, with two particular implications. First, fraudulent statements made outside the United States would affect prices on U.S. exchanges as well, causing harm within the United States. Second, misstatements included in filings with the U.S. Securities and Exchange Commission would affect prices on foreign exchanges, harming investors who purchased the issuer's securities abroad. On the latter basis, plaintiffs forwarded a sort of "fraud on the global market" theory, noting that because the statements in those filings would necessarily have affected the price of shares in the foreign markets, investors should be deemed to have relied on them in purchasing the securities. This case echoes the global cartel cases, and suggests a similar under-deterrence argument: even if corporations that engage in fraudulent behavior are liable for damages in actions brought by U.S. investors, the net effect of insufficient regulation elsewhere is likely to be under-deterrence. It therefore indicates, like the cartel cases, that linked global markets require new solutions to cross-border misconduct.

Both of these cases fit within the traditional jurisdictional narrative, in which states enjoy regulatory authority as a consequence of their sovereignty over territory.[12] On this view, because the cases concern transactions that take place outside the United States, they raise the question whether the legislative acts of the United States were intended to reach conduct or transactions taking place outside the country's borders. That question is typically answered by inquiring whether the connections between the transaction and the regulating country are close enough to justify application of a rule that is not shared by the other jurisdictions involved. And, indeed, that is the narrative the courts used in deciding these cases. In the vitamins case, for instance, the U.S. Supreme Court proceeded from a fairly rigid assumption that the harm the cartel caused in the United States was independent of the harm it caused in foreign countries. It then concluded that if the plaintiffs' claims stemmed from the foreign harm, the United States lacked prescriptive jurisdiction over the conduct.[13] The Court subsequently remanded the case to the Court of Appeals for a determination of whether the local and foreign harms were in fact independent. The appellate court concluded that they were.[14] While recognizing the global nature of the vitamin market, it held that only an indirect connection existed between prices on the U.S. market and the prices at which the plaintiffs had purchased in overseas transactions.[15] It therefore concluded that the United States lacked prescriptive jurisdiction over their claims, thus maintaining an allocation of regulatory authority according to territorial boundaries.

The courts hearing the securities regulation cases likewise depended on traditional, territory-based jurisdictional standards: the "conduct" test, which recognizes a basis for prescriptive jurisdiction if the fraudulent conduct takes place in the United States, and the "effects" test, which recognizes jurisdiction if the effects of that conduct are felt within the United States.[16] Most plaintiffs whose purchases take place on foreign securities exchanges invoke the conduct test, arguing that fraudulent misrepresentations made within the United States led to their damages. Many courts, however, reminiscent of the holding in the vitamins case, have held that the harm to the plaintiffs must be caused *directly* by the fraudulent actions in the United States.[17] On this view, the fact that statements made in the United States affect prices on foreign markets is not sufficient as a basis of jurisdiction; rather, the plaintiffs must show specific reliance on U.S. filings in order to establish their reliance on the fraudulent statements. This approach thus attempts to separate U.S. and foreign markets despite the global nature of securities trading. In cases in which foreign investors have sought the application of U.S. law on the basis of the effects test, courts have similarly looked to territorial borders. These claims suggest that if the same conduct that harms foreign markets also harms U.S. markets, then the effects felt in the United States should be sufficient to confer prescriptive jurisdiction over all claims, including those brought by foreign investors. Such claims generally founder because the courts view the effects caused within the United States as independent of the effects caused abroad.[18] This view is identical to that adopted in the vitamin cartel litigation, a fact noted by one recent court: "While the Supreme Court has not commented on the conduct and effects test in the securities law arena, it recently ruled that under the antitrust laws, federal courts lack subject matter jurisdiction over foreign plaintiffs' claims that are based solely on the foreign effect of the defendant's conduct and independent from any domestic effect caused by the defendant's conduct."[19] It also, as in the global cartel cases, attempts to segregate, on the basis of territory, effects that flow from integrated global misconduct.

It is important to recognize that these cases are quite different from classic extraterritoriality cases. Those caused resentment primarily[20] because the U.S. courts sought to apply rules whose *substance* conflicted with the law of the country in which the conduct occurred. In the transnational cases, however, the plaintiffs seek application of domestic law almost as a stand-in for world law.[21] There is no international antitrust law available to prosecute participants in global cartels – but the substance of U.S. law, prohibiting hard-core pricing-fixing arrangements, is shared across antitrust systems.[22] Similarly, in some of the securities cases, it was alleged that the issuer in question had failed to establish reserves as required not only by U.S. generally accepted accounting principles, but by International Accounting Standards.[23] These cases therefore present no conflict as to the substance of the law being applied. If a regulatory norm is shared across jurisdictions, as in these cases, the more relevant question might be whether its application, even through the vehicle of U.S. law, might not serve to protect the interconnected global markets – particularly when the transactions in question took place in a country that does not or cannot itself regulate the prohibited conduct.

Ultimately, the difficulty with the use of territory-driven jurisdictional analysis in these cases is that such analysis risks foreclosing entirely arguments concerning the substantive regulatory benefit that litigation in national courts might confer. In an era in which unchecked corporate power results in economic misconduct on a global scale, such arguments should be considered. The assistance that could be afforded particularly to developing countries, where the challenges of global economic harm have not yet been adequately addressed, would be significant.[24] In this regard, then, using a different narrative to analyze jurisdiction in such cases – a narrative that looks to the functional role that national judiciaries might play in enhancing cross-border regulation – is necessary to a fair evaluation of the benefits the cases promise.

* * *

Nevertheless, the fact that these cases, involving global harms and shared regulatory norms, can be placed in a different narrative – one that does not take the territorial allocation of jurisdictional power as the starting point for thinking about global jurisdiction – does not mean that prescriptive jurisdiction over all such cases is necessarily justified. In responding to ATCA litigation, foreign governments as well as commentators have articulated various valid objections to the assertion of jurisdiction over transnational claims. Many of those objections apply in the economic context as well. For instance, it is possible that private civil actions in the courts of one country will interfere with mechanisms developed in other countries to regulate the conduct in question.[25] In the vitamin cartel litigation, for example, several governments argued that the availability of private actions in U.S. courts would undermine the effectiveness of local amnesty programs used to enhance domestic regulatory efforts. In addition, litigation in domestic courts necessarily involves the application of the forum's procedural rules, which (particularly in the case of U.S. procedure) may be inconsistent with the procedural law of other jurisdictions involved, or incompatible with foreign public policy.[26]

Indeed, in some respects, the regulatory cases are even more problematic than the transnational public law cases. First of all, because they turn on the application not of international law but of domestic law, they raise the concern that the norms applied are not in fact shared by the international community. If that is the case, then these claims do present a typical extraterritoriality problem: an attempt to apply to foreign-linked transactions a rule of law that differs from the rule in other jurisdictions affected. It is therefore critical in these cases – particularly because regulatory norms lack the claim to universality that can be made for fundamental human rights – to establish that the regulatory standard in question is indeed shared. I do not mean to suggest that there is a large group of shared regulatory norms today, or that identifying those that are shared is a simple task. There is wide divergence in regulatory law and policy internationally, and even countries that agree on basic regulatory principles adopt laws of substantial variety in their detail. Thus, while some starting points can be identified,[27] categorizing the norms that are an appropriate basis for transnational litigation in the sense described will continue to be a challenge.

Second, even when a rule of international acceptance is applied, there remain potential legitimacy questions, as the development of international consensus on regulatory policy plays out against the backdrop of disparate economic power. The political realities of the negotiating process lead to convergence around the policies of the more powerful states, calling into question the international legitimacy of the norms adopted. Finally, because it is to date the American state, in particular, in which transnational litigation takes place,[28] concerns arise about the hegemony of the United States as a global actor. As one commentator has noted, litigation that transcends state boundaries says something "about the social distribution of power within the international community."[29] Against this backdrop, expanding the use of civil litigation in U.S. courts to serve global regulatory goals is highly problematic.

* * *

In considering how to resolve the tension between jurisdictional rules and substantive regulatory goals, it is worth noting one category of domestic claims that were initiated by foreign governments themselves. These cases were brought by foreign governments, including Canada and the European Community, under the Racketeer Influenced and Corrupt Organizations Act (RICO), in order to recover tax revenue lost to cross-border cigarette smuggling.[30] Each of the cases involved allegations that money laundering and wire fraud within the United States had facilitated the tax-evasion schemes. As with the antitrust and securities law cases, the plaintiffs argued not merely that the conduct in question crossed borders, but that the global nature of the money transfer system created a regulatory gap. Some of the corporations and individuals involved in the scheme were prosecuted under domestic criminal statutes; however, the plaintiffs in these cases argued that access to U.S. courts was necessary in order successfully to combat the misconduct involved. The European Community stated in its brief, for instance, that "only the U.S. courts are situated, equipped, and empowered to enjoin" the conduct in question.[31] In the view of the plaintiffs, the shared interest in preventing cross-border tax evasion justified the assistance of U.S. national courts.

The U.S. courts hearing these cases ultimately declined jurisdiction over the claims on the basis of the common-law revenue rule, providing that the courts of one country need not enforce tax claims, or judgments for the payment of taxes, of another sovereign.[32] But what remains particularly interesting about the revenue cases is the way in which the governments initiating them discuss the role of U.S. civil litigation as part of the global regulatory system. The European Community, for instance, noted specifically that RICO – and, more particularly, its private attorney general mechanism – was intended to be used not only domestically but also "to pursue transnational organized crime directed against foreign allies."[33] In support of this suggestion, it cited at length the legislative history of the U.S. Patriot Act, including a statement assuring that "[America's] allies will have access to [U.S.] courts and the use of [U.S.] laws if they are the victims of smuggling, fraud, money laundering, or terrorism."[34] The European Commission thus drew attention not only to the willingness of U.S. legislators to leverage the deterrent function of private actions under U.S. law for the benefit of the global community, but also to its own willingness to accept a role for U.S. national courts in regulating global misconduct.

The revenue cases thus suggest the possibility of dialogue concerning the development of a role for national courts in achieving effective cross-border regulation. Juxtaposed with the regulatory actions initiated in U.S. courts by foreign private plaintiffs, they also indicate the importance of state consent in crafting the tools of global governance. For transnational litigation to become an effective component of global economic regulation, the consent of the other countries involved – an agreement that they too view as desirable the leveraging of additional regulatory resources through U.S. or another nation's courts – is necessary. A judicial role that is accepted as legitimate only in the country whose courts adopt it does little to advance the coordination and cooperation necessary to effective global regulation. The question, ultimately, is whether the case for enhanced substantive regulation of global markets is strong enough to convince the international community that the jurisdictional framework should make room for transnational litigation. Only if transnational regulatory litigation can be integrated with other mechanisms of cooperative cross-border regulation can national courts realize their potential as actors in the transgovernmental process.

## Notes

1 The Alien Tort Claims Act, 28 U.S.C. § 1350 (2005), grants U.S. federal courts jurisdiction over claims by foreign plaintiffs for violations of international law.

2 See Harold Koh's work on "transnational public law litigation," drawing on Abram Chayes' account of

private litigation used to serve public goals, especially Harold Hongju Koh, 'Transnational Public Law Litigation', 100 *Yale L.J.* (1991) p. 2347.

3 Mayo Moran, 'An Uncivil Action: The Tort of Torture and Cosmopolitan Private Law', in Craig Scott, ed., *Torture as Tort* (Oxford, Hart 2001) p. 661 at p. 683.

4 *Sosa* v. *Alvarez-Machain*, 542 U.S. 692 (2004), Brief Amicus Curiae for the European Commission in Support of Neither Party, available at 2004 WL 177036.

5 With some exceptions, including the cases brought in Belgium under that country's war crimes statute and the Pinochet litigation in Britain, transnational litigation has taken place almost exclusively in U.S. courts. See Beth Stephens, 'Translating Filártiga: A Comparative and International Law Analysis of Domestic Remedies for International Human Rights Violations', 27 *Yale J. Int'l L.* (2002) p. 1 (discussing functional equivalents in other systems).

6 *F. Hoffman-LaRoche Ltd.* v. *Empagran S.A.*, 542 U.S. 155, 124 S.Ct. 2359, 159 L.Ed.2d 226 (2004). For further discussion of this case, see Hannah L. Buxbaum, 'National Courts, Global Cartels', 5 *German L.J.* (2004) p. 1095.

7 See *Den Norske Stats Oljeselskap A.S.* v. *Heeremac V.O.F.*, 241 F.3d 420 (5th Cir. 2001) (case brought by a Norwegian oil company against the providers of heavy-lift barge services, based on transactions occurring in the North Sea); *Kruman* v. *Christie's Int'l PLC*, 284 F.3d 384 (2d Cir. 2002) (case brought by purchasers and sellers of art against two major auction houses, based on transactions occurring in England); *Empagran S.A.* v. *F. Hoffman-LaRoche Ltd.*, 315 F.3d 338 (D.C. Cir. 2003) (case brought by purchasers of vitamins against a consortium of pharmaceutical manufacturers, based on transactions occurring in Ecuador, the Ukraine, Australia and Panama).

8 The potential for insufficient regulation is of course most pronounced in the case of developing countries, which often lack either the legal infrastructure or adequate resources to pursue cartels.

9 In *re Baan Co. Securities Litigation*, 103 F.Supp.2d 1 (D.D.C. 2000).

10 Id. at 9.

11 Id. at 10.

12 See F.A. Mann, 'The Doctrine of Jurisdiction in International Law', 111 *Recueil des Cours* (1964) p. 1 at pp. 30-31 (describing the roots of jurisdictional law in territorial sovereignty).

13 *F.Hoffman-LaRoche Ltd.* v. *Empagran S.A.*, 542 U.S. 155, 124 S.Ct. 2359.

14 *Empagran, S.A.* v. *F. Hoffman-LaRoche, Ltd.*, _ F.3d _, 2005 WL 1512951 (D.C. Cir. 2005).

15 Id. at 3.

16 See *Leasco Data Processing Equip. Corp.* v. *Maxwell*, 468 F.2d 1326 (2d. Cir. 1972) (conduct) and *Schoenbaum* v. *Firstbrook*, 405 F.2d 200 (2d. Cir. 1968) (effects).

17 See, e.g., *McNamara* v. *Bre-X Minerals Ltd.*, 32 F.Supp.2d 920, 923 (E.D.Tex. 1999) ("In order to satisfy the conduct test, the Canadian Plaintiffs must demonstrate that domestic conduct *directly caused* the alleged fraud." [emphasis in original]).

18 In *re Baan*, for instance, the court recognized that the fact of global trading might mean that foreign-based fraud created "greater and more pervasive generalized effects" in the United States, but held that no link had been established between those effects and the claims of the foreign plaintiffs. Baan at 11.

19 See *re Royal Ahold N.V. Securities & ERISA Litigation*, 351 F.Supp.2d 334, 356 (D.Md. 2004) (citing *Empagran* at 124 S.Ct. 2363 but then distinguishing it from the case at bar)).

20 Not exclusively: as noted below, conflict also results from the application of local procedural and remedial law.

21 See Ralf Michaels & Daniel Zimmer, *US-Gerichte als Weltkartellgerichte?*, IPRax 2004.

22 See *infra* n. 27.

23 See, e.g., in *re Bayer AG Securities Litigation*, not reported in F.Supp.2d, 2004 WL 2190357 (S.D.N.Y. 2004).

24 See e.g. see also Eleanor M. Fox, 'Global Problems in a World of National Law', 34 *New Eng. L.Rev.* (1999) p. 11 (identifying improvements in less developed and developing countries as a benefit of a more cosmopolitan approach to international antitrust).

25 In the human rights context, for instance, foreign governments often argued that private litigation in the United States would undermine local transitional justice programs.

26 In addition, the availability in U.S. regulatory actions of multiple damages awards continues to generate criticism in other countries. This may change as other systems move toward a similar regulatory approach; see e.g. Jürgen Basedow, 'Private Enforcement of Article 81 EC: A German View', in *European Competition Law Annual 2001: Effective Private Enforcement of EC Antitrust Law* (2003) p. 143 (discussing the possible adoption in the European Union of a U.S.-style private attorney general approach).

[27] In the area of securities regulation, for instance, while there remains substantial diversity across jurisdictions, much progress has been made toward the adoption of International Disclosure Standards and International Accounting Standards. As countries adopt those systems, and as private securities claims are brought alleging violations of those rules, they would fall into the category of shared norms. Similarly, in the antitrust context, national laws reflect a wide variety of regulatory approaches and there are many issues on which there is no discernible consensus. On the question of hard-core price-fixing, however, a shared view emerges. It is reflected in the Organisation for Economic Cooperation Development's platform against hard-core cartels, for instance, and in the nearly universal prohibition against such conduct across national systems. Thus, while it is unlikely that every jurisdiction will share a regulatory approach to the letter, it is fair to conclude that some basics have the agreement of all regulating jurisdictions.

[28] There are some exceptions: on the human rights side, see *supra* n. 5; with respect to regulatory law, see *Provimi Ltd.* v. *Aventis Animal Nutrition SA.* [2003] EWHC 961 (Comm) (UK case relating to the vitamins cartel).

[29] M.O. Chibundu, 'Making Customary International Law Through Municipal Adjudication: A Structural Inquiry', 39 *Va. J. Int'l L.* (1998) p. 1069 at p. 1147.

[30] *Attorney General of Canada* v. *R.J. Reynolds Tobacco Holdings, Inc. et al.*, 268 F.3d 103 (2d Cir. 2001); *European Community* v. *RJR Nabisco, Inc. et al.*, 355 F.3d 123 (2d Cir. 2004), vacated and remanded, 125 S.Ct. 1968 (2005); *European Community* v. *Japan Tobacco, Inc.*, 186 F.Supp.2d 231 (E.D.N.Y. 2002), vacated and remanded, 125 S.Ct. 1968 (2005); *Republic of Ecuador* v. *Philip Morris*, 188 F.Supp.2d 1359 (S.D.Fla. 2002); *Republic of Honduras* v. *Philip Morris*, 341 F.3d 1253 (11th Cir. 2003).

[31] Brief for Plaintiffs-Appellants in 02-7330, 02-7325, 2002 WL 32463410, at p. 9.

[32] Two of the cases have recently been remanded, however, and the application of the revenue rule will be reconsidered. See 125 S.Ct. 1968 (2005), vacating and remanding the cases brought by the European Commission against RJR Nabisco and Japan Tobacco.

[33] Brief for Plaintiffs-Appellants, *supra* n. 31, at p. 46.

[34] Id. at pp. 30-32 (citing statement of Senator Kerry). See also id. at p. 43, citing a related statement noting that "Since some of the money-laundering in the world today also defrauds foreign governments, it would be hostile to the intent of [the Patriot Act] for us to interject into the statute any rule of construction of legislative language which would in any way limit our foreign allies access to our courts to battle against money laundering."

# REMARKS BY WILLIAM W. BURKE-WHITE*

## DOUBLE-EDGED TRIBUNALS: DOMESTIC POLITICS AND THE RELATIONSHIPS AMONG NATIONAL AND INTERNATIONAL COURTS

Over the past decade, the number of international courts and tribunals has expanded dramatically. In a range of substantive fields of international law, new judicial mechanisms have emerged at the national, regional, and supranational levels. These include the International Criminal Tribunal for the Former Yugoslavia (ICTY), the International Criminal Tribunal for Rwanda, the International Tribunal on the Law of the Sea (ITLOS), the World Trade Organization dispute settlement mechanisms, the International Criminal Court, the dispute settlement mechanisms of the North American Free Trade Agreement, and the African Court on Human and People's Rights, just to name a few. Scholars have noted the proliferation of international courts with both acclaim and alarm.

* Assistant Professor of Law, University of Pennsylvania School of Law.

Such tribunals have largely arisen in response to functional needs. In the past decade, the processes of globalization have created new challenges that often require transnational solutions. In a number of circumstances, states have chosen to legalize their relationships with one another and to delegate authority to courts and tribunals in an attempt to provide order by depoliticizing complex issues and subjecting them to legal process. It is not, therefore, surprising that scholarly attention to such tribunals has focused largely on their legal impact. Much has been written on the developing bodies of jurisprudence in substantive fields ranging from international trade to international criminal law. Similarly, scholars have examined the impact of the decisions of these tribunals, asking under what conditions such decisions are likely to be implemented in domestic law.

By focusing on the legal impact of international courts, states and scholars alike have largely neglected the fact that such courts remain political institutions and have political, as well as legal, effects. This essay argues that, even if international courts are created in an attempt to move issues from the realm of the political to that of the legal, they will continue to have tangible political effects on the countries over which they exercise jurisdiction. Such effects can alter the incentives and preferences of key actors in target states and may result in changes to state behavior outside of the court's direct legal impact.

The political influence of international courts can be of sufficient magnitude to have a major influence on a tribunal's ability to ensure state compliance with underlying substantive legal obligations. Some political influences may hinder a court's work, but, if used properly, many can significantly enhance the effectiveness of international courts. At its core, this essay suggests that to grapple with the interplay between national, regional, and international courts, we must understand these institutions to be 'double-edged' – they influence states both legally and politically. Rather than ignoring the political effects of international courts or further trying to insulate them from politics, the political impact of courts on target states should often be embraced as an integral element of the court's operation. Recognizing the political effects of international courts and tribunals requires a rethinking of the way international courts are viewed and view themselves. It transforms courts from purely legal actors, constrained by their statutes, into autonomous political agents in the international system. Such a view of courts recognizes that they will make choices with independent political impact, not directly governed by law. While this may be a dangerous proposition and one with potentially troubling implications for the legitimacy of international tribunals, the political impact of courts must be addressed head-on by the designers and officers of international judicial institutions as well as by scholars seeking to understand their influences.

The first part of this essay offers a brief theoretical account of the political effects of international courts and tribunals. The second part draws on examples from a range of international courts and tribunals – particularly in the subfield of international criminal law – to identify the ways in which international courts influence target states through political processes. The third section briefly offers some proscriptive advice for the designers of international courts and considers how recognition of the political effects of international courts and tribunals alters our understanding of the interplay between national, regional and international courts.

## 1. Toward a Theoretical Account of Political Effect

It has long been understood that international courts and tribunals can have an impact on legal outcomes in domestic courts. Nowhere is this more evident than in the context of the European Union, where such decisions may, at times, have a direct effect on the national judiciaries of Member States. Even where international courts do not create binding precedent for domestic judiciaries, the stature, respect, and esteem of tribunals such as the International Court of Justice, lead other courts to consider – and often follow – their judgments. In his Hague Lectures, Jonathan Charney demonstrated that the views of the ICJ are 'given considerable weight' by other tribunals. The cross-citation by domestic constitutional courts to one another and to international tribunals is nothing new. Even the United States Supreme Court has recently cited to the European Court of Justice in considering the legality of a state anti-sodomy statute.

This essay suggests a far deeper and potentially more powerful set of connections between national and international courts that operates not through the law itself but rather through layers of political influence created by the structure of the international legal system. Although the focus of theoretical inquiry on the effects of international courts and tribunals has been on their legal effects, international law and courts have long been understood to be part of a larger political system. E.H. Carr reminds us: 'politics and law are indissolubly intertwined .... Law, like politics, is a meeting place for ethics and power.' In order to examine the political effects of international courts and tribunals, it is necessary to distinguish such influences from a court's purely legal effects.

More specifically, here 'political effect' refers to *the influences of international courts on target states and interest groups within those states that result not from ultimate decisions on the law, but from the threat of adjudication, embedded incentives for state actors, or the use of a court's non-legal powers.* The critical distinction between such political effects and the traditional legal effects of an international court is that political effects may occur without any final decision by the court based on the applicable law and without the resolution of the substantive claims before the court. In effect, 'political' is used to encompass the full range of non-legal effects an international tribunal may have on those states whose cases it adjudicates or on whom it may focus attention in the near future.

The theoretical explanation for the political effect of international tribunals offered here is deeply rooted in domestic politics and draws largely on liberal theories of international affairs. It begins from two basic propositions about the nature of the international system. First, it presupposes that states are in fact disaggregated and that their constituent entities can operate in a quasi-autonomous fashion in international affairs. This means that courts, legislatures, and various departments of the government may be influenced directly by events on the international stage and, similarly, may have an independent influence on international events. Hence, states relate to the international system not as unified 'billiard balls', but as permeable conglomerations of actors and institutions.

The second basic proposition of this theoretical account is that domestic political interactions are central to a state's policies on the international level. This approach assumes that the preferences of individuals within a state and the governmental structure that determines which preferences are represented by that government are causal determinants of state behavior. This is a 'bottom-up' theory in which individuals hold preferences, some of which are then articulated in state policy, and some of which interact across borders to result in international outcomes.

These two propositions – the disaggregation of the state and the centrality of domestic politics – offer the outline of a theoretical account of how international courts can have political effects on target states. The existence of an international tribunal or its focus on a particular state can apply pressure at three leverage points identified by liberal theory as critical to state policy and international outcomes. First, the tribunal's existence can change how individuals formulate or calculate their own interests. These shifts in the perceived interests of individual actors will then percolate through governmental institutions, ultimately leading to changes in state behavior. Second, an international tribunal can have a political effect is by empowering or disempowering particular groups, agencies, or governmental entities within a target state. Third, the existence or attention of an international court may alter the calculation of costs and benefits of a particular policy for the target state and for other states in the system, making the pursuit of particular preferences more or less desirable for the target state. Each of these three points of potential political effect gives international courts the ability to sway the policies of target states even without issuing a formally binding legal decision.

## 2. Political Effects of International Courts and Tribunals

The leverage points through which political effects can change the behavior of target states result in a number of distinct categories of political influences. Among these are the externalization of the costs of domestic enforcement, the creation of an abdication hazard, the legitimation or deligitimation of particular individuals, and the catalyzation of national judicial institutions. Each will be explored in turn.

The cost-externalization effect recognizes that international courts can allow national governments to externalize the political costs of domestic action onto international courts and tribunals. Many states – particularly weak states – are often unable to undertake domestic judicial action because the political costs to interest groups within the state or the costs imposed on third states are too high for the national government to bear. The cost-externalization effect shifts the political costs of national action onto an international body. States with limited capacity, fragile institutions, and vulnerable governments may be unable to take domestic actions that would jeopardize their domestic constituencies or result in retaliation from more powerful neighbors. This is often the case when states are recovering from governmental collapse, civil war, ethnic strife or other conflict. In these circumstances, the international court may buttress the national government and allow it to take otherwise impossible actions.

When states use an international court to externalize the *political* costs of domestic action, they effectively blame the international entity for what would otherwise be politically costly domestic policy. This, in turn, expands the win-sets available to national governments. Where domestic interest groups within the state are opposed to the proposed action, the national government may be able to convince that audience that the actions were required by the international court or were even taken by it.

Where a target state seeks to act but is blocked by pressure from a powerful neighboring state, the target state's government may seek to convince the neighboring state that it is acting because of an international requirement or that the international court is in fact the relevant actor. Either way, the political effect of cost externalization expands the options available to the domestic government, making action by the national government possible.

A prime example of cost externalization is the Special Panels established by the United Nations Transitional Administration in East Timor (UNTAET) to prosecute international crimes during the 1999 conflict. Upon the conclusion of UN Administration of East Timor, the Constituent Assembly of East Timor embedded the Special Panels into the new Constitution. Even though now part of the East Timorese government, the Special Panels continue to operate as a hybrid international court. By applying international, as well as domestic, law and relying on both national and international judges, the Special Panels retain their quasi-international character, with their decisions not directly attributable to the newly independent East Timorese government.

One effect of the continued operation of the East Timorese Special Panels has been to externalize the costs of prosecution of the perpetrators of the 1999 violence onto the international community. Indonesia is a powerful neighboring state, and the former occupying authority of East Timor, and has expressed a clear policy preference against the prosecution of crimes committed during the conflict. While the decision to continue operations of the Special Panels is within East Timor's control, the East Timorese government has cited strong international pressure as the driving force behind prosecution. Moreover, by having two international judges on each panel and applying international law, East Timor has 'blamed the internationals' and distanced itself from these decisions in its relations with Indonesia.

The second effect, the abdication hazard, refers to the tendency of an international court to change the incentive structure for a domestic government by providing an alternative forum for action. Whereby, before the existence of the international tribunal, the only means of resolution of a dispute may have been the use of domestic courts, an international tribunal may present an abdication hazard by giving a national government a second, though arguably sub-optimum, policy option. Rather than acting domestically, the state may defer the case to the international court. While the ultimate resolution of the case by any court may be a net positive, in many circumstances the use of domestic institutions might be more cost-efficient, legitimate and, ultimately, enforceable. In many cases, this new incentive structure will result in a failure to act at the national level and a deferral of the situation to international adjudication.

A clear example of the abdication hazard problem is evidenced by the International Criminal Court investigation in Uganda. In January 2004, the President of Uganda referred the situation in the northern portion of the country – particularly the crimes committed by the Lord's Resistance Army – to the ICC, pursuant to Article 14 of the Rome Statute. This move came as a surprise to many observers who had expected referrals to come from third states, rather than from the state where the crimes in question occurred. While the specifics of the Uganda case are beyond the scope of this inquiry, there is significant evidence that the Ugandan government is capable of bringing key members of the LRA to justice through the use of domestic institutions if it chose to do so. Despite some shortcomings, if the Ugandan government wanted to, it could probably bring much of the Lord's Resistance Army to justice through military, police, and judicial means.

The ICC, however, creates an abdication hazard by giving President Museveni a second option, namely referring the case to the International Criminal Court. The existence of the ICC may well have changed Museveni's calculation of interests. Before the court, he could either absorb the costs of acting against the LRA more forcefully or face international and domestic pressure for allowing the LRA impunity. By referring the case to the ICC, he has been able to garner international commendation for bringing the ICC to Uganda and to offer a legitimate response to domestic critics by citing the court's involvement in the country. As one Ugandan legal expert put it, the Ugandan government 'tries to hide behind organizations and other entities' rather than taking serious action at home. While this policy has offered Museveni a win-win situation, it has failed to promote domestic judicial reform and has not fully taken into account the actual domestic costs and benefits of prosecution.

A third political effect of international courts and tribunals is the legitimation or delegitimation of sub-state actors and institutions. Early examples of such delegitimation are the lustration policies adopted after World War II era and again after the fall of Communist regimes in Eastern Europe. More recently, international courts – particularly international criminal tribunals – have had powerful effects at delegitimizing particular officials and expediting their exit from the political scene. Either through the indictment of government officials or by drawing attention to international crimes in which such officials may be involved, international criminal tribunals can undermine the legitimacy of even the most senior officials and cause shifts in domestic political alignments that may remove them from power.

International courts achieve this delegitimation by altering the way representation occurs within the target state. In this model, the state is conceived of as a conglomeration of individuals and groups with particular interests, all of whom seek to control the government and to have their interests reflected in state policy. Those interests with the most influence and power are also most likely to hold positions in the government or, at least, to have their preferences articulated as state policy. An international court can facilitate power shifts among coalitions of domestic interest groups. Stinging statements by international prosecutors or indictments by international courts can provide new leverage for interest groups opposed to a current regime, buttressing their claims for control of the government or reducing support for an incumbent leader. An indictment can also alter the attitudes of third states, giving them concrete grounds to oppose a particular official. In cases where governance is hotly contested, the political impact of such international moves may be sufficient to facilitate regime change.

On 22 May 1999 Louise Arbour, then the prosecutor of the Yugoslav War Crimes Tribunal, indicted Slobodan Milosevic for crimes against humanity and war crimes. Far more significant than the indictment's asserted role in ending the Kosovo conflict was its delegitimizing effect on Milosevic's government. After Milosevic's multi-decade long reign of power and influence in the Balkans, in 1999 a powerful opposition group called Optor – the Serbian word for Resistance – emerged in Belgrade. Its operative slogan was 'He [Milosevic] is finished'. By the 25 September 2000 elections Milosevic lost the popular vote to Vojislav Kostunica 52 per cent–35 per cent and was removed from office. The degree to which the indictment of Milosevic aided Optor and the resistance is disputable. But there is evidence to suggest the indictment at least played a part, including Optor's use of graffiti campaigns that mentioned the indictment. Other examples of the delegitimation effect include the March 2003 indictment by the Special Court for Sierra Leone of then Liberian President Charles Taylor for crimes against humanity and war crimes and the impact of the Spanish and British proceedings against Agusto Pinochet on his status in Chile.

A fourth category of political effect is the ability of an international tribunal to catalyze the activation of domestic courts by altering the incentives facing domestic actors. An inverse twin of the abdication hazard, this effect most often occurs when there is a domestic legal or political process that could be utilized should the domestic government decide to do so, but the costs of domestic action are deemed by the state to outweigh the benefits thereof. The existence of an international tribunal, however, can provide structural incentives that shift the cost-benefit calculation and result in the utilization of a domestic process that would have otherwise been neglected.

International tribunals thus catalyze national action by altering incentives for national governments to use their own institutions. The legal structure serving as a catalytic device is most often a restriction on the ability of the international court to exercise jurisdiction unless there has been a failure of the national government to use its own internal processes. The basic assumption at work here is that states will prefer to adjudicate matters domestically, rather than give the situation to an international tribunal over which they have little or no control. By utilizing a domestic institution – even an independent judiciary – national governments are generally better able to influence the process, or at least moderate the repercussions, of any adverse decision. Where this assumption fails, the result may instead be the abdication hazard effect discussed above. The fact that action by the international court is conditioned on domestic inaction gives national courts the first mover advantage and the option of acting themselves. A national government's perceived costs of inaction will be increased by the knowledge that the international court may intervene if it does not act. In many cases, this will provide sufficient incentive for states to activate or, if necessary, create their own domestic judicial processes.

The clearest example of this catalytic effect is the complementarity provision of the Rome Statute of the International Criminal Court, which embeds a preference for prosecution by national authorities. The ICC's first case in the Democratic Republic of Congo provides early evidence that the court is, in fact, having a catalytic effect on the use and operation of national institutions. In an ideal case of catalysm, the initiation of an investigation by an international court would spur the domestic judiciary into action, resulting in an effective domestic prosecution. The ICC case in Congo has not had such a dramatic effect, in part because the Congolese domestic judiciary was largely destroyed by a ten-year civil war. As anticipated by the theoretical analysis, in the wake of the Prosecutor's 2003 announcement of an investigation in Congo, a range of efforts were initiated by certain elements within the Congolese government to reform the Congolese judiciary so as to be able to assert primacy over the ICC and undertake national proceedings. In late September 2003, a series of senior Congolese officials appeared on local TV and radio arguing 'Congo is competent to try these cases'. The Congolese Minister of Justice has asserted 'for crimes committed by Congolese, we will hold them accountable in national courts.'[1] Reform efforts to date have included attempts to reunify the divided judiciary through nation-wide judicial conferences, commissions on legislative reform, and a Truth and Reconciliation Commission. Though these may be relatively small first steps, there is significant evidence that these judicial reform efforts have been facilitated by the initiation of an investigation by the ICC.

Each of these categories of political effect – cost externalization, abdication hazard, legitimation/delegitimation, and courts as catalysts – offers a means whereby international courts and tribunals can have a direct and often powerful influence on outcomes at the national level, without reaching a binding legal decision. As such, they represent both the under-used political power of international courts and yet another complex element in the interplay between national, regional, and international courts.

## 3. Political Effects and the Structure of the International Legal System

The analysis and discussion in Parts 1 and 2 result in two basic propositions about the relationships between international and domestic courts and tribunals. *First, international legal institutions are as much political actors in target states as they are instruments of international law. Second, the design and operation of international courts can enhance their effectiveness by maximizing beneficial political effects.* These propositions, in turn, yield both proscriptive recommendations for the design and operation of international courts and tribunals and some potential grounds for concern about the politicization of international courts.

Through political and diplomatic processes, states create courts and make key decisions about the nature, powers, and scope of these institutions. In this process, diplomats, lawyers, and institutional designers have the option of creating institutions that either maximize or minimize political effects. By making broad choices about the institution, its legal mandate, structure, jurisdiction, and access, the states creating international courts set the parameters of a court's political effect. Within these parameters, courts as independent actors then have a second order choice as to the strategies to employ to take advantage of the political effects embedded in their legal framework.

The designers of international courts need to be aware that many of the political effects of international tribunals will be context specific and depend on particular factors of the case and target state in question. Too often judges, court personnel, and prosecutors (in the case of criminal courts) are unaware of or refuse to accept the political context in which they operate. If courts are to take maximum advantage of their political effects or even if institutional designers seek to create courts that avoid political effects, the information and knowledge of the court's staff will be critical. When establishing the criteria for selecting judges, prosecutors, or other officials, drafters might consider including some political expertise, either through staff selection or the establishment of an office of the political advisor within the court itself.

Whether or not a tribunal seeks to use its political power, the key judicial officers of international courts must be aware that their actions cast political shadows on target states. Taken to an extreme, this implies a transformation in the self-conception of judges, prosecutors, and other officials of international courts from purely legal actors to dual legal and political identities. The mere awareness and recognition among court officers of their dual identity can go far to empower courts to use their political effects.

Even if they seek strategies that minimize those effects, awareness and recognition will be critical.

While institutional designers and judicial officials have the potential to enhance the effectiveness of the political effects of international courts and tribunals, such political effects also give reason for pause and potential concern. If courts are seen as explicitly seeking to impact the politics of a target state they may sacrifice their legitimacy or even undermine the willingness of states to create such courts in the first place. If courts are viewed as political, rather than legal, institutions the 'compliance pull' of the law might be lost. If their jurisprudence were to become overtly politicized, it is unlikely states would follow their decisions or choose judicial recourse at all. Even when courts try to use their political influence, they may fail. After all, they are neither generally designed for nor have experience with domestic politics. The use of a court's political power will often involve an intricate balancing game. Mistakes will be made. Extreme caution is called for.

These dangers are real, but the fact remains that international courts have political impacts. This influence points toward deep questions about the legitimacy, appropriateness, and capacity of courts to act as autonomous political agents. When courts move beyond the law how should they be held accountable? Will states accept courts that they recognize as political? Are courts well positioned or well designed to make tough political decisions? What principles ought to guide a court's action when making political determinations? These are tough questions and they will require serious thought. As the number and scope of international tribunals continues to increase, these questions have become ever more salient.

For scholars and practitioners examining the interaction between national, regional and international courts, the political effects of international courts and tribunals provide an important new line of inquiry into the already dense relationships between such courts. International and domestic courts and tribunals influence one another not only through standard legal relationships, but also through more subtle political channels. Multiple layers of legal and political relationships exist that may, at times, be complementary or, at other times, operate to at cross purposes. No strict formulas for analysis exist. International courts may enhance the effective operation of their domestic counterparts or may undermine their ability and desire to adjudicate efficiently. What is clear, however, is that the political influences of international courts and tribunals can not be overlooked. An important new research agenda in both comparative politics and international law is emerging to examine the actual effects of these courts on target states.

This is not to say that there is no rhyme or reason to the emerging relationships among these institutions. Rather, there is evidence to suggest that international and domestic courts are, in fact, moving toward a common system. It is, however, far from a classic domestic legal system. Relationships among these courts may be best described as a system of multi-level global governance, in which international and domestic governance structures (such as courts) are engaged in deeply interconnected governance efforts, whereby each level of authority continuously cross influences, reshapes, and, ideally, reinforces activities at other levels of governance. The challenge ahead for institutional designers, judicial officials, and scholars alike is to ensure that these influences enhance the effectiveness of the transnational legal system without undermining the unique attributes of judicial process.

NOTE

1 Personal Interview Mr. Honorius Kisimba-Ngoy, Minister of Justice, Kinshasa, 29 October 2003 (interview conducted by Yuriko Kuga, Leslie Medema and Adrian Alvarez).

## DISCUSSION

KATHLEEN PAISLEY:* began the question and answer session by stating that she had two questions, both of which relate to the issue of antitrust/competition. First, for Professor Buxbaum, Ms. Paisley queried what were the arguments made by the plaintiffs and the US Supreme Court's response to them in the *Vitamins* case as to why the United States should exert jurisdiction over the case rather than a European court? If the US rules are essentially equivalent to the European rules, would not this provide stronger support for sending the case to Europe? Where the actual harm occurred? Second, for Mr. Davies, with respect to the modification to the European Union antitrust rules, Ms. Paisley questioned whether in the context of his talk, he had given any thought to how the points he made relate to the changes to the procedural rules applicable to competition cases? In addition, Ms. Paisley stated that if the best argument that can be made as to why appeals should not be taken from national courts is because they would not like it – so what? Ms. Paisley expressed that in her view, in the post-treaty world, the more interesting point is not so much that national courts would not like it, but that it is politically very difficult today to essentially create a 'super court' over national courts no matter how good it would be.

HANNAH BUXBAUM responded with regard to the *Vitamins* case by first noting that the plaintiffs were really arguing that the harm occurred everywhere; that the harm to the US markets was an integral part of the successful 'cartelization' because without the harm in the United States, the whole thing would not have worked. Second, not all of the plaintiffs came from European countries and some came from countries whose governments were not addressing the price-fixing at all. Third, Professor Buxbaum noted that it is still the case that a plaintiff is much more likely to obtain an award for treble damages by suing in a US court. While that situation is changing rapidly in Europe, as it presently stands, the US court was a more promising avenue for the plaintiffs in the *Vitamins* case in that regard. Professor Buxbaum stressed that in her presentation she was not suggesting that jurisdiction in US courts in all such cases is necessarily appropriate. Rather, the way in which one thinks of the traditional territorial allocation of jurisdiction merits re-inspection.

GARETH DAVIES then replied to Ms. Paisley's remaining questions by stating that while he does not know much about antitrust, he has been aware that it is an area where it is often asked whether a particular agreement is a restriction on competition or a particular measure is justified by other purposes such as in the interests of the advancement of society. In other words, the question often arises whether a particular matter is one of Community law to be referred to the ECJ or is a question for a national judge. What is distinctive about antitrust, particularly in the European Com-

* Paisley & Kruithof, Brussels.

munity context, is that from early on, the ECJ has accepted that these are real questions that must be decided with reference to the real world – i.e., with regard to economic analyses. Thus, consideration of antitrust issues involves a slightly more objective procedure and to some extent neutralizes the problem of 'who gets to decide' because the issues are essentially decided by economists. What is distinctive about free movement law is that you have the same kinds of questions arising requiring facts or factual analysis – i.e., questions as to how much a regulation obstructs movement and is it genuinely necessary for protecting the consumer or the environment – but the ECJ refuses to engage in it and decides whether a measure is necessary or not without any idea of what it is talking about, often getting it wrong.

With regard to the issue of national supreme courts not liking being subjugated to the ECJ as a reason for not having an appeals system, Mr. Davies stated that he noted this in his discussion merely as an indication of the powerful domestic lobbies that do not want such hierarchy. This is a legitimate lobby because it is about who is the ultimate court in one's country, which is a reasonable democratic question.

BLANCA MONTEJO:* addressed her first question generally to the panel in reference to Mr. Burke-White's presentation. She noted that while Mr. Burke-White focused on the question of political effects resulting from interactions between national and international courts and tribunals, what are the implications for increased interactions between international courts with competing jurisdictions? Specifically, Ms. Montejo pointed to the *Swordfish* case involving Chile and the European Community. Chile took the case to the International Tribunal on the Law of the Sea while the European Community went before the WTO. Two totally different areas of international law were implicated – the law of the sea and WTO law protecting the opening up of markets. While noting that in the end, that particular case was settled, Ms. Montejo queried as to what should be the appropriate procedure for choosing which international tribunal should hear the matter in a similar context?

As to her second question, Ms. Montejo directed it to Professor Buxbaum with regard to the *Microsoft Windows* case. If the European Commission were to decide something contrary to what the US courts have been holding against Microsoft, what would be the result? In other words, is it only the centre and not the periphery that is able to dictate the rules for addressing global harms? What about extraterritorial application in the opposite direction?

Ms. Montejo's third question was put to Mr. Goodman. With regard to the Argentine cases before ICSID, what would be the result if there were completely different outcomes from the tribunals hearing arbitrations against Argentina? How would that impact ICSID's legitimacy as an institution? How would Argentina deal with potentially conflicting decisions, for example, on the question of the 'state of necessity'? Ms. Montejo posited that the potential for conflicting outcomes in these cases is a risk for ICSID as an institution and for the BITs themselves.

Finally, with regard to Mr. Davies' presentation on the system of referral to the ECJ, Ms. Montejo queried whether it was really as bad as he had presented it to be.

GARETH DAVIES first responded by stating that in his view, yes, the system of referral to the ECJ was as bad as he had stated. This is so because of the length of time which it takes at present for a reference to be answered – about two or two and a half

* Freshfields, Bruckhaus, Deringer, Paris.

years – and this is increasing. All of the judges forecast it will only get worse with no end in sight because they simply cannot cope with the workload. The reason they have this impossible workload is because they continue to apply a concrete approach in determining their jurisdiction, which means they have huge numbers of references.

RONALD GOODMAN responded next by suggesting that instead of asking 'what if' questions, one should look at what has happened in reality thus far. There have been 7 ICSID decisions concerning Argentina on jurisdiction so far, all of which are remarkably the same, if not identical, in their outcomes. A year ago, in a conference in New York, an arbitrator who sat on several of these Argentine cases was asked what would be the effect on her if 4 other cases addressing a particular matter were going one way before she issued her decision on that same matter. She responded that those other cases would be overwhelmingly persuasive and that it would be extremely difficult for later tribunals to go in a different direction. Mr. Goodman also pointed out that the system now relies a lot on avoiding conflicts through their choice of arbitrators. There is also a tendency towards consolidation of similar cases for similar industries by similar claimants. Thus, although the possibility of completely different outcomes is a risk, Mr. Goodman stated that in his own view, it was more of a hypothesis than reality.

HANNAH BUXBAUM then addressed Ms. Montejo's question on the *Microsoft Windows* case. She stated that what interested her about the kinds of cases she raised in her discussion was that the substantive norms could not be different. In other words, they involved situations where although a national court was being utilized, the actual substance of the rule was agreed upon by the States involved. However, she noted that if you are considering a situation where the substantive outcome would be different in two national courts, then this is a classic extraterritoriality type of case where there is a collision between the norms.

With regard to the question raised on a possible conflict between the International Law of the Sea Tribunal and the WTO in dealing with a case, Professor Buxbaum noted that it leads to a question raised to some degree by all of the presentations on the panel. That issue is whether hierarchy is necessary in thinking about a re-shuffling of judicial resources. Professor Buxbaum stated that with regard to her own presentation, one of the major arguments to the use of US courts is that even where the norms are shared internationally, US courts appear to be setting themselves up as the 'first among equals' capable of dispensing justice globally. With regard to the potential conflicts from international tribunals, Professor Buxbaum opined that it is hard to see how there could be a solution without an 'order'.

Following up on Professor Buxbaum's remarks on this issue, WILLIAM BURKE-WHITE highlighted two points. He noted that many of the international tribunals still refer with deference to the jurisprudence of the International Court of Justice (ICJ), even though it is not hierarchically superior, as giving guidance. In addition, most of the specialized international regimes still have recourse to public international law and general principles of international law as their fall back after applying the *lex specialis* within the regime itself. These general principles can give some guidance for reconciling conflicting obligations and results from international tribunals, which will inevitably arise.

BERT BARNHOORN:* posed a question for Mr. Goodman noting that in his presentation, Mr. Goodman raised a number of traditional remedies for dealing with the sit-

* TMC Asser Institute, The Hague.

uation of competing jurisdiction between national courts and international arbitral tribunals. However, in that list of remedies, Mr. Goodman did not refer to the concept of 'comity' although he had previously mentioned that in the *KBC* v. *Pertamina* and *SGS* v. *Pakistan* cases, the jurisdictional question was decided with a reference to comity. Mr. Barnhoorn wondered whether comity could also be explicitly mentioned as a solution or general rule for deciding jurisdiction in competing cases where nothing has been arranged in relation to a treaty or other national or international 'hard rules'.

RONALD GOODMAN replied by stating that if he had suggested that comity was at stake in the *SGS* v. *Pakistan* case, he should have not. In that case, there was a war of injunctions and in the end, ICSID issued a recommendation that there be a suspension of the Pakistan cases while the ICSID proceeding was ongoing. Thus, the dispute was resolved in a more forceful way. However, in the *KBC* v. *Pertamina* case, the US Circuit Court of Appeals, in disposing of an appeal before it on the injunction issued by the Texas District Court, did say that the injunction should not have been issued for reasons of comity. Comity is often used in dealing with the enforcement of foreign civil judgments in the United States because the United States does not have treaties on the recognition and enforcement of foreign civil judgments, at least not yet. Is comity a solution? Mr. Goodman stated that in his view, comity is an argument one can make to courts. It is *a* solution and it is one that a practitioner should always plead, but he was not sure that it would always resolve the incredible 'jealous' assertions of jurisdiction by courts that have the view that their jurisdiction extends worldwide.

REBECCA HAMILTON:* directed her question to Mr. Burke-White and queried as to what were his suggestions for the way forward for the Prosecutor at the ICC for navigating the political arena of prosecutorial discretion. In other words, how does the Prosecutor maintain distance as a legal actor while simultaneously recognizing that he or she is a political agent, particularly when issuing indictments whilst a conflict is ongoing, with the ability to hold off a prosecution 'in the interests of justice'?

WILLIAM BURKE-WHITE recognized that this is certainly a big debate with serious questions. In his opinion, what is done behind closed doors in The Hague is one thing and what is said on the street in Kinshasa or Kampala is another. While there is a fundamental tension there, the ICC must maintain its sense of legitimacy and to do so, it should not necessarily say openly in a particular country that it is taking certain political factors into account, but it should recognize that it has several tools at its disposal for doing so. While some of these tools may not be readily apparent from the Rome Statute, the concept of 'interests of justice' is one that is beginning to have a lot more meaning than initially intended for it at Rome. The Prosecution and the ICC have difficult political decisions to make. For example, with regard to timing in terms of when prosecutions should be brought and indictments handed down. In designing international institutions that have to make those kinds of decisions, the international community must do its utmost to make sure that they are prepared to make the best ones possible with full awareness of their political effects. This requires that they have much more local knowledge than the ICTY and the ICC had in their earliest days and possibly have an office of the political advisor sitting in the Prosecutor's office giving guidance on potential political outcomes. In other words, Mr. Burke-White noted that international tribunals should confront the reality of political effects head-on by

* Harvard Law School and Kennedy School of Government.

obtaining as much information as possible in facing difficult choices with the hope that the right decisions will be made as much as possible while recognizing that some mistakes will inevitably be made along the way.

GLIDEN HERNANDEZ:* posed the final questions to the panel, specifically to Mr. Burke-White. Mr. Hernandez stated that while he agreed that political effects are apparent in the practice of international courts and tribunals, the legitimation of those effects and their practice, or a normative recognition of them, raises two concerns. The first is with regard to the effect of this legitimation on an international court's consciousness, i.e., whether a court in recognizing a role for itself as a political actor and taking on that role, might be anxious to preserve its own legitimacy and arrogate to itself the power to make itself more indispensable within the system. Mr. Hernandez expressed his view that this legitimation, instead of furthering the rule of law or leading to beneficial political effects, might pander to more powerful political actors and entrench the system in order to enhance its own legitimacy within that system.

The second concern noted by Mr. Hernandez is that the marshalling of judicial resources towards the legitimation of political effects presupposes the notion of progress in international law. That the international legal order is moving, or should be moved, towards a specific idea of what is the appropriate legal order. In light of the considerable influence of the United States and Europe in the development of international law, is there no danger that instead of actually working towards a better international legal order, we are instead pushing for a more Western-oriented, or even more American, international legal order?

WILLIAM BURKE-WHITE noted that Mr. Hernandez had raised tough questions with good theoretical issues. He responded that with regard to the effect of legitimation of political effects on an international court's consciousness, it had to be recognized that any time an international institution is created, there is a kind of momentum that develops and a sense of self-preservation. What he was arguing in his presentation is that international courts should be 'called' on their political effects and that this should be brought out into the open a bit more recognizing the effects and that these courts think as political institutions. While these international courts may seek to preserve there own power, there is nothing new about this activity and there may not be anything particularly problematic about it. Mr. Burke-White clarified that he was not proposing that an international court should say that a particular situation does not constitute a crime against humanity because, if it did, this would have a negative political effect. However, he did think that a lot more could be built into the office of the Prosecutor as a gatekeeper in the choices its making that does not lead to problematic jurisprudential decisions pandering to a national authority.

In terms of the issue of working towards an international legal system that reflects the United States or Europe, Mr. Burke-White clarified that this was not his position. The model he proposes is a pluralist one because it is a view recognizing that there are many voices and institutions in the global arena and they can all be different. He was not of the view that international courts and tribunals ought to be policing in order to come to a particular, exact standard from the United States or Europe for the development of the international legal order. Rather, there should be a 'margin of appreciation' of acceptable kinds of domestic jurisprudence and judicial institutions that

* University of Oxford.

should be activated. The question is how to create and structure the incentives to activate them, recognizing that there are a variety of legitimate forms of justice that still conform to a minimal set of legal principles deemed acceptable globally.

Closing Remarks

Professor Buxbaum concluded the panel by thanking her co-panellists, the committee organizing the conference, and the rapporteur as well as the audience for their kind attention.

*Rapporteur:* Hannah Garry*

* International Criminal Tribunal for the Former Yugoslavia (ICTY).

# Institutional Challenges Facing Regional Human Rights Courts

The panel was convened by its Chair, Judge T. Buergenthal*

## Introductory Remarks by Judge T. Buergenthal

As you know the title of our panel is 'The challenges facing regional human rights courts'. But as you will see, once you hear what our panellists have to say, the challenge this panel faces is that each of the three regional courts we will examine faces very different challenges and problems. Not surprisingly, these challenges are largely directly related to the stages of their institutional development and to some extent, of course, also to the political environment in which they operate. Given the differences that exist between Europe, the Americas and Africa, it is of course not surprising, that each of these tribunals faces a very different challenge. At the same time though, looking at each of the three courts at their current stage of development and the problems they confront, may tell us a lot about the problems other regional human rights tribunals might face if new ones should be established. Incidentally, some of you know, I am a great supporter of the establishment of other regional human rights tribunals in other regions of the world or sub-regions of the world, and I hope that one of these days we will see not only three such regional courts but one in each region or appropriate sub-regions. [...]

## Remarks by Wilhelmina Thomassen**

### Historical Background and Organisation

The Convention for the Protection of Human Rights and Fundamental Freedoms was drawn-up within the Council of Europe. It was opened for signature in Rome on 4 November 1950 and entered into force in September 1953.

In addition to laying down a catalogue of civil and political rights and freedoms, the Convention set-up a mechanism for the enforcement of the obligations entered into by Contracting States. Three institutions were entrusted with this responsibility: the European Commission of Human Rights (set-up in 1954), the European Court of

* Judge, International Court of Justice.

** Judge, Netherlands Supreme Court, former Judge, European Court of Human Rights.

Human Rights (set-up in 1959) and the Committee of Ministers of the Council of Europe, the latter organ being composed of the Ministers of Foreign Affairs of the Member States or their representatives.

Complaints could be brought against Contracting States either by other Contracting States or by individual applicants. Recognition of the right of individual application was, however, optional and it could therefore be exercised only against those States which had accepted it (Protocol No. 11 to the Convention was subsequently to make its acceptance compulsory).

The complaints were first the subject of a preliminary examination by the Commission, which determined their admissibility. Where an application was declared admissible, the Commission placed itself at the parties' disposal with a view to brokering a friendly settlement. If no settlement was forthcoming, it drew-up a report establishing the facts and expressing an opinion on the merits of the case. The report was transmitted to the Committee of Ministers.

Where the respondent State had accepted the compulsory jurisdiction of the Court, the Commission and/or any Contracting State concerned had a period of three months following the transmission of the report to the Committee of Ministers within which to bring the case before the Court for a final, binding adjudication. Individuals were not entitled to bring their cases before the Court.

If a case was not referred to the Court, the Committee of Ministers decided whether there had been a violation of the Convention and, if appropriate, awarded 'just satisfaction' to the victim. The Committee of Ministers also had responsibility for supervising the execution of the Court's judgments.

From 1980 onwards, the steady growth in the number of cases brought before the Convention institutions made it increasingly difficult to keep the length of proceedings within acceptable limits. The problem was aggravated by the accession of new Contracting States from 1990. The number of applications registered annually with the Commission increased from 404 in 1981 to 4.750 in 1997. The Court's statistics reflected a similar story, with the number of cases referred annually rising from 7 in 1981 to 119 in 1997.

## Protocol No. 11

The increasing case-load prompted a lengthy debate on the necessity for a reform of the Convention supervisory machinery, resulting in the adoption of Protocol No. 11 to the Convention. The aim was to simplify the structure with a view to shortening the length of proceedings while strengthening the judicial character of the system by making it fully compulsory and abolishing the Committee of Ministers' adjudicative role.

Protocol No. 11, which came into force on 1 November 1998, replaced the existing, part-time Court and Commission by a single, full-time Court.

## Workload and Jurisdiction

The full-time European Court of Human Rights is now the biggest international Court that has ever existed. It is composed of a number of judges equal to that of the, now 46, Contracting States.

With the sole exception of Belarus, all European States are today members of the Council of Europe. Of these all but Monaco, which was recently admitted, have ratified the European Convention on Human Rights, whose protection now stretches from Iceland to Turkey, from Lisbon to Vladivostock, from Riga to Malta, but also from Chechnya to the Basque region, from Northern Ireland to Cyprus and Nagornon-Karabach. This means that some 800 million people fall under the 'jurisdiction' of the Court. Whereas the official languages of the Court are English and French, applications may be drafted in any one of the official languages of the Contracting States, and there are at present 41 official languages in these States.

The Court receives around 900 letters per day and some 250 international telephone calls a day. Its internet site was visited by 45 million hits in 2003. In the past five years, the number of applications has increased by about 15 per cent in comparison with each preceding year. At November 2004 the Court had 78,300 pending applications before it. In the year of 2004, close to 45,000 applications were received. Some 17,300 decisions were issued and 700 judgments on the merits. The highest number of cases have come from Russia, Poland, Turkey and Romania (the so-called big four: Russia 14 per cent, Poland 14 per cent, Turkey 12 per cent, Romania 12 per cent), followed by Ukraine, France, Italy and Germany. These 'big eight' countries account for some 75 per cent of all applications that have reached the Court. Some 63 per cent of all cases have come from the 21 new Member States of Central and Eastern Europe, 12 per cent from Turkey and only some 25 per cent from the traditional Western European States.

## Expansion and Success

It is obvious that the history of the European Court of Human Rights has been a story of expansion and success: a compulsory right of individual petition to an independent Court, shorn of its earlier optional features; a geographical expansion, across Western Europe to central and eastern, Baltic and Caucasian Europe and Turkey; a widening of the safeguards of the ECHR through an evolutive case law and additional Protocols.

It is a logical consequence of such developments, that the Court's caseload has increased hugely, so much that today the system's effectiveness is seriously jeopardised, despite the remarkable progress which the Court had achieved in its output. Between 1999 (the first full year of activity of the new Court) and 2004, while the Court's budget increased by roughly 54 per cent and the complement of Registry staff by roughly 80 per cent, the productivity in terms of terminated applications rose by some 470 per cent, thanks largely to streamlining of working methods and internal organisation. The different internal measures taken during the first three years are summarized in the Courts' Working Party on Working Methods of January 2002 'three years work for the future'.

However, even the increases in productivity proved insufficient to keep pace with the constant rise in the number of cases and the resultant growing backlog. A rough estimate shows that the Court can expect 52, 000 applications in 2005, 60,000 in 2006 and 69,000 in 2007.

## Protocol No. 14

In response to this problem, the Committee of Ministers of the Council of Europe adopted Protocol No. 14 to the ECHR in May 2004, together with a number of recommendations and resolutions designed to increase its effectiveness. The aim of this reform is to allow the Court to devote more attention to meritorious applications, in particular those disclosing serious human rights violations, by increasing its filtering capacity and improving the implementation of the ECHR at national level.

Some of the most important changes of Protocol No. 14 concern the following.

The Court will be competent to sit in a single judge formation to declare cases inadmissible or strike out of the Court's list of cases, where such a decision can be taken without further examination (Arts. 4 and 5).

In principle the decisions on admissibility and the merits will be taken at the same time (Art. 9).

The competence of the Committee of three judges is enlarged. It can declare admissible and render at the same time a judgment on the merits, if the underlining question in the case, concerning the interpretation or the application of the Convention or the Protocols thereto, is already the subject of well-established case-law of the Court (Art. 8).

At the request of the plenary Court, the Committee of Ministers may, by unanimous decision, and for a fixed period, reduce to five the number of judges of the Chambers (Art. 5).

A new admissibility criteria is added (Art. 12), changing Article 35, paragraph 3, in that a case is declared inadmissible if the applicant had not suffered a significant disadvantage, unless respect for human rights as defined in the Convention and the Protocols thereto requires an examination of the application on the merits and provided that no case may be rejected on this ground which has not been duly considered by a domestic tribunal.

Furthermore, a number of Recommendations to the Member States have been adopted by the Committee of Ministers on 12 May 2004, to ensure an effective human rights protection system on the national level, including education and training, and to enforce the execution of judgments.

## Long-term Changes Needed

Despite of all the efforts to rationalise the Courts' proceedings and to make the organisation more efficient, the last forecast show that the potentially substantial increases in judicial productivity which may ultimately be achieved by Protocol No. 14, will not on their own be sufficient to close the gap between the level of incoming cases and the Court's output capacity.

According to these forecasts, by 2007 the caseload could require staff numbers to be doubled, leaving aside the additional resources that would be necessary to eliminate the backlog and the practical question of the Registry's ability to absorb increases on this scale of a short time-span. Only in order to eliminate the backlog, an external audit report estimates that the theoretical additional workforce, over one year, is 1.035 additional staff members: 407 lawyers, 271 assistants and 357 support staff.

In a memorandum to the Third Summit of the Council of Europe in Warsaw the European Court of Human Rights expresses its view that further measures, going beyond a constant search for improvements in working methods and internal organisation, are likely to be necessary if the human rights protection system set-up by the ECHR is to remain effective over the long-term. In addition to a rapid ratification of Protocol No.14, the Governments therefore need to start reflecting on the long-term options available for further action capable of ensuring a stable, practicable system providing the highest possible effective protection, while preserving the basic philosophy underlying the ECHR. Fundamentally, the Governments are faced with a choice about the nature of the international protection machinery which must be provided to individuals in the Europe of the 21st century.

## Warsaw Summit

For that reason the Court recommended to the third summit of the Council of Europe to launch an in-depth discussion of the future of the ECHR and its Court in the 21st century, taking into account the new challenges resulting from the pan-European dimension which the system has now acquired. This could be done, in the view of the Court, by giving an independent group of eminent and experienced national and international judges and other experts the task of considering these issues and identifying possible scenarios for the long-term future of the ECHR system, together with their various benefits and costs, and by inviting governments to take-up the matter in the light of their findings.

In the meantime, the heads of State and Government, at their meeting in Warsaw on 16-17 May 2005, did accept the latter proposal by announcing that a group of wise persons will be set-up to draw-up a comprehensive strategy to secure the effectiveness of the system in the longer term.

## What Can Be Done?

Certainly, more lawyers and more money will help. But simply putting more resources into the system with every increase in business will not be enough on its own. The system as it is presently organised is likely sooner or later to reach a saturation point. The Court's statistics show that about 90 per cent of all applications to the Court are declared inadmissible. Most of these cases are declared inadmissible by a committee of three judges. There is no indication that these trends will change. The overwhelming problem is therefore to introduce a system which can deal with these cases in an efficient way while maintaining the Court's important task to deal mainly with new issues under the Conventions.

The problem of these Committee cases is not that they are complicated or time consuming per case, it is the huge number of them. Someone has to read each application, to assess whether the admissibility conditions have been complied with and to prepare the file for adjudication. Thus, the organisation as a whole is completely focused on the inadmissible cases.

## Pick and Choose Substantial Issues

A possible solution could be that the Court should choose its own cases and a limited number per year, like in the certiorari system of the US Supreme Court. This approach, also known as the 'pick and choose' system, has given rise to passionate debates.

The different approaches for and against 'pick and choose' became visible during the preparatory proceedings of the 14th Protocol when the proposal was made that the Court should be empowered to decline to examine in detail applications raising no substantial issue under the Convention. The objection to this proposal was that from a practical point there would be serious difficulties to decide how the criteria for 'a substantial issue' should be defined. In an international court dealing with cases from 46 countries a substantial issue may mean one thing in a country and another in another country. Or, for instance, are all Article 2 and 3 cases of substantial issues? And what would happen to all those cases which are not chosen by the Court? The Court would risk being politicised and criticised what ever decisions it would take. The fear was that such a 'pick and choose' system might lead to a system which could eventually discourage ordinary people from having recourse to it.

## Individual Right of Petition

An approach opposite to the 'pick and choose' solution maintains that each application submitted to the Court should be examined. Opposition against the 'pick and choose' option in itself is not so difficult to understand since stopping the influx of applications is not only an obvious possible solution but also fit to put the individual right of petition at risk. The right of individual petition which forms the essence of the human rights protection system in Europe. A right which has proved to be a democratic instrument which gives the European citizens the possibility to participate in the debate on fundamental values in nowadays societies whenever they feel unrepresented in their societies decision-making process.

## The Court's Dual Mission

Despite of these two different approaches there seems to be a common understanding that the Court should concentrate on the truly important cases.

So why, instead of limiting the Courts tasks in one way or another, couldn't we accept the dual mission of the Court, namely the duty to give a response to every application received and the duty to produce convincing adjudications in meritious applications?

If we accept this dual mission, we could also accept two kind of procedures. One would concern examining applications on receipt in order to identify the few applications that do merit a full judicial consideration, and the second would ensure such full judicial consideration in appropriate conditions.

## A Separate Filtering Mechanism

One way to do this would be to introduce a separate filtering mechanism physically separating initial filtering from adjudicating on the meritorious applications that do raise an arguable human rights issue. Such a separate body or tribunal could handle for itself the clearly inadmissible cases and those cases where the Court already has a firm and clear case-law, i.e., 'clone' cases as for instance length of proceedings and other repetitive cases, where the Court has delivered judgment in a 'pilot' case. If the tribunal would decide that it had no competence to deal with the case, the case should then be transmitted to the Strasbourg Court. A decision to refer a case from the tribunal to the Strasbourg Court could take form of a simple letter without any reasoning. It would thus not amount to restoring the former system where, *inter alia*, time-consuming Article 31 reports by the Commission had to be drafted. Such a restoration should be avoided since the effectiveness of the human rights protection system runs the risk of being seriously jeopardised if too many consecutive rulings were to be obtained before justice is done. This becomes even more true since already two Courts at the European level deal with human rights protection and will continue to do so in the future.

## Human Rights Tribunal(s)

The filtering mechanism could take form of a tribunal in Strasbourg, separate from the Courts' organisation or regional human rights tribunals could be introduced. In both models the involvement of Strasbourg judges and staff members should make sure that the selection of cases takes place under the strict scrutiny of the Court.

The tribunal(s) should not create case-law, including case law on admissibility conditions, it (they) should follow the Courts' case law. The tribunal(s) could be composed of Strasbourg judges on a rotation basis and judges of highest national courts. One could also envisage appointing some 'stand by judges' and temporary lawyers, who could be called in to sit in these kind of cases or to deal with backlog. Regional tribunals could meet on part time basis and decisions could be taken in chambers of 3, 5 or 7, with in each composition at least one Strasbourg judge. The tribunals could also be given the tasks of fact findings, friendly settlements and art 41 issues after referral by the Strasbourg Court.

One could expect that a filtering mechanism, as proposed in this paper, would indeed permit the Court to treat mainly new issues under the Convention and within a reasonable time. And while maintaining of the 'basic philosophy' underlying the ECHR, as the Court put it in its last memorandum.

## European Court of Justice of the European Communities

Any future scenario for the European Court of Human Rights should pay great attention to the relation of the Court and the European Court of Justice of the European Communities in Luxembourg. These two Courts have much in common which justifies a close cooperation.

Both Courts embody the novelty of their judicial models, which do not correspond to any traditional model, such as their subsidiarity and cooperation with the national jurisdictions and the legal remedies to which individuals have access before the two Courts are generally recognised as constituting ground-breaking developments in the history of legal protection. Both Courts equally have the ECHR as a legal source for their adjudication.

This calls for a structural cooperation in order to guarantee effective legal protection. Furthermore both unnecessary lengthy proceedings should be avoided, as divergence in the jurisprudence on fundamental rights and different standards in the human rights protection in Europe.

Finally, in searching for an effective human rights protection system, any future scenario and any cooperation between the two European Courts should uphold, in essence, the basic philosophy underlining the European Convention of Human Rights, namely the individual right of petition.

## Sources

1. 'The European Court of Human Rights, historical background, organisation and procedure'. Information issued by the Registrar of the European Court of Human Rights on the Courts' web site.
2. Memorandum by the European Court of Human Rights to the Third Summit of the Council of Europe, unpublished.
3. The European Court of Human Rights: The Past, The Present, The Future, by Luzius Wildhaber, President of the European Court of Human Rights, Conference given at the University of Ottawa on 5 April 2005, unpublished.
4. Proposals for changes in the European Convention on Human Rights and measures to be taken within the present framework to guarantee the effectiveness of the Court, internal paper by judges Elisabeth Palm and Wilhelmina Thomassen, 2002, unpublished.

# Remarks by Claudia Martin*

## The Reform Debate in the Inter-American Human Rights System Ten Years after: Successes and Failures

### 1. Introduction

In 1995, at the same time the European Human Rights System was imbued in discussions regarding the scope of the then-recently adopted Protocol 11 to the European Convention for the Protection of Human Rights and Fundamental Freedoms, several Member States of the Organization of American States ('OAS' or 'Organization') triggered a debate as to the need to reform the structure and functioning of the inter-American human rights system. A new Secretary-General of the OAS, Mr. César Gaviria, had recently been elected under the promise to revamp the Organization, and the inter-American human rights system was one of the areas that he considered needed perfecting. The most relevant argument advanced in support of reforming the system was that all the States of the Hemisphere, with the exception of Cuba, enjoyed democratically-elected governments, thereby making a complete overhaul of the system necessary to adapt it to the new political environment.

Though the debate was framed in terms of the need to 'evaluate and perfect' the work of both organs of the system – the Inter-American Commission ('Commission') and the Inter-American Court of Human Rights ('Court') – the subsequent discussions about the reform process showed that the target of the proposed changes was mainly the Commission. It is clear from the Commission's annual reports and the discussions advanced by representatives of civil society and policy-makers that, by the time the reform debate started, this body had already decided to concentrate its resources on strengthening the individual petition system. This decision was evidence of the improvement in the general human rights situation of the Hemisphere; however, it was not well received by certain States which remained sensitive to criticisms of their human rights records. This political context, together with a genuine interest from different sectors of civil society involved with the inter-American system, spearheaded a debate regarding the need to improve the functioning of this regional system. The so-called 'reform debate' has extended for the last ten years and has achieved some positive results, such as the amendments to the Regulations of the Commission and the Court adopted in 2000.

With few exceptions, the reform debate has stalled and consequently has failed to advance new proposals. Moreover, the increasing lack of funds to support the activities of the Commission and the Court – which in the last few years have had to resort to external cooperation funding to be able to function – has impeded the implementation of new ideas and the development of better practices in the individual complaint system.

* Co-Director, Academy on Human Rights and Humanitarian Law and Professorial Lecturer in Residence, American University, Washington College of Law.

This paper intends to describe the different stages in the reform debate and identify the proposals that have been implemented in practice and those which still remain pending as of today.

## 2. The First Stage of the Process: 1995-2000

The '*Declaration of Montrouis*' adopted during the OAS General Assembly in 1995 proposed the need to evaluate the functioning of the human rights system and suggested that, if necessary, the inter-American human rights treaties, particularly the American Convention on Human Rights ('American Convention' or 'Convention') should undergo reforms. This debate was institutionalized with Resolution 1404, adopted by the OAS General Assembly in 1996, in which States requested the Permanent Council – the Organization's permanent political body – to assess the functioning of the human rights system in order to initiate a reform process that would improve the existing human rights treaties as well as the practices and proceedings of the Commission. The discussions centered mainly on the timeliness and appropriateness of amending the American Convention, and on the role that the Commission should play in a Hemisphere where almost all the Governments were democratically and freely elected. Reform proposals that were mentioned in the initial debates included increasing the number of members of the Commission and judges of the Court to alleviate the backlog of cases submitted to the system, and merging the Commission and the Court to make the processing of individual petitions more expeditious, along the lines of Protocol 11 to the European Convention on Human Rights.

To contribute to the debate, in November 1996 the Secretary-General of the OAS issued '*Toward a New Vision of the Inter-American Human Rights System*', a document in which he stated his recommendations regarding the aspects of the human rights system that required improvement or reform.[1] The report analyzed three issues considered pivotal for the proper functioning of the system, namely: the procedures regarding the case system; the strengthening of the structure and function of the system; and the strengthening of the administration of the system. In regard to the first issue, the report identified the need to develop guidelines on the admissibility of petitions, reduce the existing fact-finding duplication with the Court, set out criteria for referring a case to the Court, and address the problem of the dual role of the Commission as a quasi-adjudicator with respect to cases before it and an advocate for the petitioner once the case was submitted to the Court.

With respect to the strengthening of the structure and function of the system, the report pointed, *inter alia*, to the need to: seek complete and universal accession to the American Convention and acceptance of the compulsory jurisdiction of the Court by all OAS Member States; provide an institutional role to the political bodies of the OAS to supervise enforcement of the human rights system's decisions; encourage States to adopt implementing legislation to enable enforcement before domestic courts of the judgments of the Court; and study the possibility of transforming the Commission and/or the Court into full-time bodies.

On the strengthening of the administration of the system, the report proposed the creation of a Directorate for the Promotion of Human Rights, which would perform non-adjudicatory functions such as advisory, promotional and political functions. The Commission would continue to carry out its reporting and case systems independently of this new entity. Finally, the report neither opposed the introduction of amendments to the inter-American human rights treaties nor the enhancement of the promotional functions of the system.

Also, in December 1996 the Commission organized an international seminar to debate in an open forum and with representatives from governments, civil society, academia and international organizations the issues related to the reform process that were, until that moment, only discussed by States in the OAS Permanent Council without the participation of other interested actors. Similarly to the recommendations issued by Secretary-General Gaviria, the Commission concluded in the final report of the seminar that improvements to the Commission's processing of individual complaints were essential for the perfecting of the system.[2]

In particular, the Commission highlighted the need to set out clear guidelines regarding the admissibility stage of the proceedings and to separate the decisions on admissibility and merits. Moreover, the Commission's report criticized the rules of confidentiality used in the final stages of the Commission's proceedings, impeding this body from transmitting the preliminary report issued under Article 50 of the American Convention to the petitioners. Next, the report recognized the importance of developing a follow-up procedure to the Commission's recommendations to be implemented by the OAS Permanent Council or the Commission itself. Also, the Commission concluded that there was a need to avoid duplicative fact-finding by the Court when processing complaints submitted by the Commission. Additionally, it noted the importance of establishing criteria to refer cases to the Court. Finally, it concluded that the Commission's participation in the Court's proceedings as an advocate for the victims must be de-emphasized by warranting individual victims an autonomous status in all the stages of the cases brought before this tribunal.

The Commission's report rejected the proposals to amend the American Convention and indicated that the suggested procedural reforms could be made through changes to the Regulations of the Commission and the Court. Moreover, it supported the actual two-tier system in which cases are processed first by the Commission and later by the Court, thereby rejecting the proposal to merge both bodies into one. Finally, the report stated that an increase in the number of members of the Commission and the Court would not improve the efficiency of the overall system.

The Court organized an international seminar in November 1999 and held four meetings of experts to discuss the aspects of the inter-American human rights system that needed reform in September and November 1999, and in February 2000.[3] Also, an *ad hoc* working group on human rights created by the Ministers of Foreign Affairs of the OAS Member States met on two occasions to debate concrete measures to improve and perfect the functioning of the human rights system. The *ad hoc* working group recommended a substantial increase of the resources allocated to the Commission and the Court; the ratification or accession of the inter-American human rights treaties and the acceptance of the contentious jurisdiction of the Court by all the OAS Member States; the development of national plans to incorporate international human rights obligations into the domestic legislation and practice of States; the participation of the General Assembly and the Permanent Council in enforcing the recommendations of the Commission and the decisions of the Court; and the amendment of the

Regulations of the Commission and the Court to improve procedural aspects of the individual complaint system.[4]

These recommendations were reproduced and enhanced in Resolution 1701, adopted by the OAS General Assembly in 2000. This resolution constituted a critical point in the reform debate because, for the first time, it identified and recommended the adoption of concrete measures to the Commission and the Court. First, the resolution recommends that the Commission make concrete improvements in the processing of individual petitions, including: defining the criteria followed for the registration of petitions; opening a separate and mandatory admissibility procedure and issuing the findings in concise resolutions; making all necessary efforts to ensure that individual cases are processed expeditiously and that each procedural stage, in particular the admissibility phase, is governed by reasonable deadlines; continuing to promote the friendly settlement procedure as a suitable mechanism for the successful resolution of individual cases; and defining criteria to refer cases to the Court. Finally, the resolution recommends that the Court allow autonomous participation by the victim in all stages of its proceedings and develop procedural rules to prevent fact-finding duplication with the Commission's findings in cases submitted to its jurisdiction.

In sum, the outcome of this first stage of the reform debate shows that there was no consensus among Member States to introduce changes to the American Convention, to merge the Commission and the Court into one organ, or to increase the number of their members. Furthermore, Resolution 1071 suggests that States reached an agreement that the recommended measures had to be implemented through amendments to the Regulations of the Commission and the Court. As the following section will indicate, some of the issues debated in the first stage of the reform process were later incorporated in the new Regulations adopted by the Commission and the Court in 2000, while many others continue to be pending of implementation as of today.

## 3. The Second Stage of the Process: the Amendment of the Commission's and Court's Regulations and the Debate as to the Adoption of an Additional Protocol to the American Convention

As a result of the initial reform debate and consultations with States, non-governmental organizations and other independent experts, the Commission and the Court amended their Regulations in 2000. The changes to the Regulations of both organs reflected in great measure the recommendations made by the OAS General Assembly in Resolution 1071. The new Regulations of the Commission came into force on 1 May 2001 and the Regulations of the Court entered into effect on 1 June 2001.

The Commission's Regulations incorporated important changes in the processing of individual petitions as well as in the procedure that this organ follows when deciding when to refer a case to the Court. In regard to the processing of individual petitions, the Regulations first clarified the procedure to register a petition and the role of the Commission's Executive Secretary in the initial handling of a complaint. Second, it established a separate phase for reviewing and deciding on the admissibility of a petition, and provided for the publication of the admissibility reports in the Commission's annual report. Third, the Regulations shortened the deadlines in the admissibility and merits phases of the petition process. Next, it improved the manner in which hearings were conducted by introducing, *inter alia*, new procedural guarantees, such as a witness's duty to take an oath or make a solemn promise to tell the truth before testifying.

The Regulations also greatly improved the procedure to decide on whether or not to refer a case to the Court. First, the Regulations provided for petitioner's notification upon the Commission's approval of the preliminary report and transmittal to the accused State. Petitioners will have a month from notification to present their views as to whether or not the petition should be submitted to the Court and present supporting information. Next, the Regulations introduced a presumption in favor of submitting a case to the Court whenever the accused State has not complied with the recommendations of the preliminary report, unless there is a reasoned decision by an absolute majority of the members of the Commission to the contrary.

The Court's Regulations included several changes to speed up the processing of individual cases. However, the most relevant amendments were the authorization for individual victims to participate autonomously in all stages of the proceedings before the Court and the adoption of a procedural rule establishing *de novo* review of evidence only in exceptional circumstances. In regard to the independent participation of victims, the Regulations provide that, once the Commission or a State refers a case to the Court, the victim will be notified and authorized to present his or her pleadings, motions and evidence autonomously. Later case law has clarified this rule by establishing that in their pleadings, petitioners may allege the violation of rights not argued by the Commission – or the State – in its submission, but must respect the facts included in that submission.[5]

In regard to the procedural rule on *de novo* evidentiary review, the Court's Regulations introduced a presumption in favor of the Commission's findings, provided that the evidence was produced respecting the adversarial principle. The presumption applies unless the Court considers it essential to request the production of such evidence again. Notwithstanding this rule, it is not clear whether the Court has been applying that presumption in practice. Most recently, however, the Court has granted certain deference to the Commission's findings on the admissibility of a complaint, particularly in regard to the application of the rule on exhaustion of domestic remedies.[6]

After the adoption of the Regulations of the Commission and the Court, a new debate was initiated with respect to the possibility of adopting an additional Protocol to the American Convention. This proposal was initially advanced by the then-President of the Court, Judge Antônio A. Cançado Trindade, who presented several reports to the political bodies of the OAS recommending the adoption of such a Protocol.[7] The proposal by Judge Cançado Trindade recommended, in following with the trend set by Protocol 9 to the European Convention on Human Rights, that Article 61 of the Convention be modified to grant individuals the right to refer a case to the Court.

Judge Cançado Trindade's proposal was adopted by the Government of Costa Rica, which submitted a 'Draft Optional Protocol to the American Convention on Human Rights' for consideration of the OAS General Assembly in 2001. Though the proposal was considered in Resolutions 1833 and 1895 – adopted in 2001 and 2002 respectively – and the General Assembly requested the Permanent Council to analyze granting direct access to individuals to the Court, the issue was never seriously treated in subsequent years. The reasons for this outcome could be found in the negative reaction of other interested actors, including the Commission and States, which considered that the time was not ripe to grant individuals direct access to the Court. Moreover, the amendments introduced to both Regulations of the Commission and the Court may have had an impact as well. The presumption that every case should be referred to the Court unless good reasons justified otherwise has been successfully implemented by the Commission, thereby granting access to this tribunal to almost all the victims. This 'automatic access', coupled with the independent participation of victims in the proceedings before the Court, may have in practice deprived the proposal of its initial appeal.

## 4. The Final Stage of the Process: Current Status of the Debate and Pending Issues

The Declaration of Quebec and the Plan of Action of the Third Summit of the Americas held in April 2001 pledged the support of the Heads of State and Government to strengthen and enhance the effectiveness of the inter-American human rights system.

In 2004, the General Assembly requested that the Permanent Council engage in a broad process of reflection on the inter-American system for the promotion and protection of human rights, in consultation with Member States, specialized agencies of the inter-American human rights system, non-governmental organizations, national human rights institutes, academic institutions, and experts in the field. In 2005, the General Assembly adopted a similar Resolution and requested the Permanent Council to continue with the process of reflection.

In compliance with the General Assembly request, the Permanent Council started a process of reflection on the inter-American human rights system. For that purpose it asked the Member States, the Commission and the Court to submit their views on the challenges faced by the human rights system and the actions that should be implemented to strengthen and perfect it. There is no information available on the responses submitted by Member States, the Commission and the Court, but it appears that the process is currently on-going.

In addition to the process initiated by the Permanent Council, the Commission and the Court also started a process of reflection on the challenges faced by the human rights system launched in Mexico City on 19-20 July 2004. The agenda of the meeting as well as the conclusions reached in this event have not been made public; therefore, it is not clear what the current status of this debate is or the outcome of any recommendations adopted in that meeting.

Finally, it is worth noting that, on 15 September 2004, Secretary-General Miguel Angel Rodríguez E. issued Executive Order 04-01 reorganizing the General Secretariat of the OAS. The Executive Order created a Department of Human Rights to coordinate all the political, technical and administrative matters of the OAS General Secretariat in relation to human rights issues. Also, it placed the Executive Secretary of the Commission under the supervision of the Department of Human Rights, which retained the power to hire the Commission's personnel and determine its budget. The Commission considered that the new structure proposed by the Secretary-General curtailed its independence and autonomy.[8] Moreover, it called for the amendment of its Statute to ensure respect for that independence and autonomy. With the resignation of Secretary-General Rodríguez because of a pending criminal investigation in his country of origin, the Executive Order was left without effect and replaced with Executive Order 05-03 issued on 1 January 2005.[9] The new Executive Order maintained the Executive Secretariat of the Commission as the only body with human rights functions in the new structure of the OAS.

The decision of Secretary-General Rodríguez to create a Department of Human Rights generated a broad debate and split the human rights community as to the proper role that the Commission should play in a Hemisphere plagued with political instability and rampant poverty. The adoption of a new Executive Order did not close the debate and this continues to be a pending issue that requires further discussion.

A recapitulation of the debate that has taken place in the last few years indicates that many issues remain to be addressed in the process of strengthening the inter-American human rights system. First, there is a need to increase funding to support the work of the Commission and the Court. Despite the continuous pledges of the OAS Member States to support a substantial increase of the budgets of the Commission and the Court, both organs continue to face ongoing financial crises. In recent years, the OAS General Assembly has favored requesting external funding from cooperation donors and other financial institutions. Additionally it has created a voluntary fund to which OAS Member States and other donors can contribute to support activities carried out by the Commission and the Court.

Second, the failure by some OAS Member States to ratify the human rights treaties and accept the jurisdiction of the Court remains an issue for which there is no solution in the near future. Though on several occasions Canada has indicated its willingness to accede to the American Convention, domestic political problems have impeded ratification as of today. The situation of the United States is even more complicated, given the position of the current administration in regard to international law and the international obligations binding upon this State. Likewise, the relationship of several Caribbean States with the inter-American system – particularly with respect to the application of the death penalty – does not offer much hope as to future ratification or accession from these countries.

Third, enforcement of the decisions issued by the organs of the inter-American human rights system continues to be an issue that requires specific attention. Though all the interested actors participating in the system, including Member States, have advocated for the creation of a body within the Permanent Council to supervise enforcement of the judgments of the Court and the recommendations of the Commission, the political bodies of the OAS remain disengaged from this process. To alleviate the lack of involvement from the political bodies, the Commission introduced a follow-up mechanism to monitor compliance with its recommendations into its Regulations and has published annually the status of enforcement of those recommendations. On the other hand, the Court in a recent decision reaffirmed its jurisdiction to monitor enforcement of its judgments through a written procedure and by issuing resolutions on the status of compliance of each case decided by this tribunal.[10]

Next, there is a need to define the proper role of the Commission. As reflected in the discussions that followed the adoption of Executive Order 04-01 reorganizing the General Secretariat of the OAS, a debate exists as to the role that the Commission must play in protecting human rights in the Western Hemisphere. Even though the Commission has powers to adopt reports on the general human rights conditions of specific countries and to carry out on-site visits, some actors participating in the system consider that the current political situation of the Hemisphere warrants the creation of another organ within the OAS to deal with political crisis and to advise the political bodies and the Secretary-General on human rights issues. Suggestions include the creation of a Directorate of Human Rights, a Department of Human Rights or a High Commissioner for Human Rights. Since this approach is supported by a wide array of actors that enlist representatives from governments, non-governmental organizations, and policy-makers, it is expected that this debate will continue in the near future.

Other issues that remain pending and require further attention include the need to ensure transparency in the selection of new Commissioners and Judges of the Court. In 2005, the OAS General Assembly adopted Resolution 2120 inviting Member States to implement a consultation process with civil society organizations to identify and nominate candidates to the Commission and Court. Finally, the amendments to the Regulations of the Commission and the Court, though crucial for improving the processing of individual petitions, have not resolved the backlog of petitions that remain to be decided by the inter-American system. Therefore, it is possible that in the future the Commission may have to entertain the possibility of implementing mechanisms to restrict access to the individual complaint procedure.

## 5. Conclusions

The debate on the need to strengthen and perfect the inter-American human rights system has extended for ten years now. Though the process was initially triggered by States, mainly for political reasons, an open and participatory debate with all the actors interested in the system has contributed to the identification and debate of the aspects of the system that were in need of reform. As a result of this debate, the Commission and the Court amended their Regulations in 2000, reinvigorating the individual complaint mechanism by making it more transparent and inclusive.

Unfortunately, many of the issues that remain to be reformed, such as the universal ratification of the human rights treaties, the involvement of the political bodies of the OAS in monitoring enforcement of the decisions of the system, and the substantial increase of funds to support the work of the Commission and the Court, depend heavily upon the political will of the OAS Member States. For many reasons these States are not engaged in strengthening the human rights system, thereby making the task of improving the functioning of this system very complicated at this point.

## Notes

1 OEA/Ser.G CP/doc.2828/96, adopted on 26 November 1996.

2 Seminario sobre 'El Sistema Interamericano de Promoción y Protección de los Derechos Humanos', 2 al 4 de diciembre de 1996, 'Conclusiones de la Comisión Interamericana de Derechos Humanos', in Juan E. Méndez and Francisco Cox (eds.), *Editores El Futuro del Sistema Interamericano de Protección de los Derechos Humanos.*

3 See Informe: 'Bases para un Proyecto de Protocolo a la Convención Americana sobre Derechos Humanos para Fortalecer su Mecanismo de Protección', in *El Sistema Interamericano de Protección de los Derechos*

*Humanos en el Umbral del Siglo XXI, Corte Interamericana de Derechos Humanos*, Tomo II, Relator Judge Antônio A. Cançado (Trindade, Mayo 2001).

4 OEA/Ser.G CP/CAJP-1620/00, 1 March 2000.

5 See I/A Court H.R., '*Five Pensioners*' v. *Peru*, Judgment of 28 February 2003, Series C No. 98, para. 155.

6 I/A Court H.R., *Tibi* v. *Ecuador*, Judgment of 7 September 2004, Series C No. 114, para. 54-55.

7 See *supra* n. 3.

8 See Press Release 21/04 of the Inter-American Commission on Human Rights, 21 October 2004.

9 General Secretariat, Executive Order 05-03, Reorganization of the General Secretariat, adopted on 25 January 2005.

10 I/A Court H.R., *Baena, Ricardo et al.* v. *Panama*, Judgment of 28 November 2003, Series C No. 104.

## Remarks by Fatsah Ouguergouz*

### The Ongoing Metamorphosis of The African System of Human Protection – A Focus on The African Court of Human And Peoples' Rights

Before turning to the African Court of Human and Peoples' Rights proper, I deem it necessary to say a few words on the African System of Human Rights protection in general; some of you might indeed not be very familiar with this system.

To make it simple, I would say that this African system rests on four major pillars. I must add two things: first that these pillars are of unequal solidity, and second, that some of these pillars have been strengthened over the years.

From a chronological point of view, the first pillar is the one erected in 1963 at Addis-Ababa (Ethiopia); it is the Constitutive Charter of the Organization of African Unity which devoted relatively little attention to the question of human rights compared to the Charter of the United Nations, the Charter of the Organization of American States of 1948 or the Statute of the Council of Europe of 1950. The OAU Charter indeed made two brief references to the Charter of the United Nations and the Universal Declaration of Human Rights.[1] It was, beyond any doubt, the weakest pillar of the whole system, and it badly needed to be reinforced or rebuilt. As shown later, this pillar has ultimately been replaced by a more solid one. The second pillar of the African system is the Convention governing the Specific Aspects of Refugee Problems in Africa signed on 10 September 1969.[2] This is an important and generous Convention since it enlarges the definition of the refugee, which was provided for in the 1951 United Nations Geneva Convention on the Status of Refugees. The third and strongest pillar is found in the African Charter on Human and Peoples' Rights adopted on 27 June 1981.[3] The fourth pillar is the African Charter on the Rights and Welfare of the Child which has been adopted in July 1990.[4]

* Secretary of the Court, International Court of Justice (The Hague) and Associate Editor of the African Yearbook of International Law. The opinions expressed in this contribution are strictly personal to the author and do not necessarily reflect those of the International Court of Justice.

As noted above, the first pillar of this system, and also the weakest, was the OAU Charter, that is the constitutional legal instrument *par excellence* of the African continent. On 26 May 2001, this old pillar has however been demolished and replaced by a much stronger one, namely the Constitutive Act of the African Union.[5] This instrument grants a much more important place to respect for human rights, the rule of law and good governance than its predecessor of 1963. Indeed, according to its Article 3, two of the objectives of the Union are to 'promote democratic principles and institutions, popular participation and good governance' and to 'promote and protect human and peoples' rights in accordance with the African Charter on Human and Peoples' Rights and other relevant human rights instruments'; its Article 4, moreover, provides that the Union shall function in accordance with, *inter alia*, the principles of

> '(m) respect for democratic principles, human rights, the rule of law and good governance; (n) promotion of social justice to ensure balanced economic development; (o) respect for the sanctity of human life, condemnation and rejection of impunity and political assassination, acts of terrorism and subversive activities; (p) condemnation and rejection of unconstitutional changes of governments.'[6]

Even more remarkable is the fact that subparagraph (h) of that Article 4 recognizes a genuine right of humanitarian intervention in certain circumstances; it lays down, 'the right of the Union to intervene in a Member State pursuant to a decision of the Assembly in respect of grave circumstances, namely war crimes, genocide and crimes against humanity.'[7] In this connection, it should also be mentioned that the Constitutive Act of the African Union makes provision for a whole range of sanctions for States parties in the event of their failure to comply with the decisions and policies of the Union.[8]

The third pillar of the African system of human rights protection, that is the African Charter on Human and Peoples' Rights, has also been strengthened. It has indeed been reinforced twice by way of protocols: first in 1998 with the adoption of the Protocol establishing the African Court of Human and People's Rights,[9] and more recently in July 2003 with the adoption of the Protocol on the Rights of Women in Africa.[10] This third pillar is so far the strongest pillar of the whole system, and is, in my view, the core of the system of human rights protection in Africa.

As far as its substantive content is concerned, the more striking feature of the African Charter is that it incorporates two different categories of individual rights in a single instrument, namely the civil and political rights or the first generation of human rights, the economic, cultural and social rights or the second generation of human rights. The African Charter is the only international agreement to do so. A different solution has indeed been chosen at the universal level with the two 1966 Covenants, at the European level (European Convention of 1950 and European social Charter of 1961) and at the Inter-American level (American Convention of 1969 and Protocol of San Salvador of 1988).

The African Charter also provides for the rights of solidarity or the third generation of human rights; it is also the first and only international binding agreement to do so. As a matter of fact, the African Charter provides for the right of peoples to their economic, social and cultural development, the right of peoples to the equal enjoyment of the common heritage of mankind, the right of peoples to international peace and security and the right of peoples to a general satisfactory environment favourable to their development.[11]

The third and most striking feature of the African Charter which is its consecration of the duties of the individuals. It is not the first legally binding instrument which incorporates the duties of the individual. Indeed, the two United Nations Covenants of 1966 (last paragraph of their preamble and Art. 19 of the second Covenant, freedom of expression), the European (freedom of expression, Art. 10) and the American (chapter V, Art. 32) Conventions also provide for the duties of the individual though admittedly with less emphasis and in a less detailed manner. The African Charter, for its part, devotes no less than a whole chapter and eleven paragraphs to these duties. It provides for the duties of the individual towards his family, towards the society, towards the State and towards the international community. The American Declaration of the Rights and Duties of Man of 1948 also provided for a whole range of duties, but it was not an instrument with the same legal value as the African Charter, it was a declaration, not an international treaty.

The institutional content of the African Charter is far less original as its substantive content. Indeed, as initially conceived, the safeguard mechanism provided for by the African Charter consisted of a binary yet hierarchical structure:

- the African Commission of Human and Peoples' Rights: a conciliation and investigation body entrusted with the task of promoting and protecting human and peoples' rights in Africa, which has been set-up in 1987.
- the Assembly of African Heads of State and Government: the supreme political organ of the Organization of African Unity, now the African Union, which is assigned major prerogatives in the operation of the safeguard system.

The African Charter proper may therefore be clearly distinguished from its two regional counterparts – the European and the American Conventions – since its text does not provide for the establishment of a judicial body.

Since its inception in 1981, this safeguard mechanism has however undergone a slow but noticeable metamorphosis. This metamorphosis is threefold:

This metamorphosis consists firstly in the strengthening of the African Commission itself which has progressively broadened its powers under the African Charter on Human and Peoples' Rights.

This metamorphosis consists secondly, as mentioned above, in the evolution of the political and legal environment in which the safeguard mechanism is rooted. Indeed, the question of the protection of human rights now occupies an important place among the objectives and the principles of the fledgling African Union and the Assembly of the Heads of State and Government of the Union will necessarily have to incorporate these major changes into its policy and take account of them in its deliberations and decisions.

This metamorphosis consists thirdly in the recent creation of a judicial body designed to complement the protection activities of the African Commission.

I will focus here on the first and third stages of this metamorphosis, namely the evolution of the African Commission and the creation of the African Court.

1) The African Commission of Human and Peoples' Rights, originally conceived as a weak body, has indeed progressively broadened its powers under the African

Charter, in so doing eroding certain major prerogatives of the Assembly of Heads of State and Government. The Commission has slowly strengthened its powers and is now carrying quasi-judicial and quasi-legislative functions. This metamorphosis of the African Commission itself actually started in 1988 with the adoption of its Rules of Procedure, and it continued thanks to the Commission's practice. The Commission has not only liberally interpreted its powers under the African Charter, but has sometimes arrogated to itself certain powers it does not possess under that instrument.

As regards its consideration of non-State communications, the Commission has succeeded in creating its 'jurisdiction' in this field out of nothing. The Commission has thus interpreted the expression 'other communications' as being communications from individuals, from their representatives or from NGOs. It has even interpreted this expression as authorizing it to deal not only with flagrant and massive human rights violations, but also with isolated human rights violations.

The Commission has also gradually emptied the obligation of confidentiality laid down in Article 59 of the African Charter of all content, since it has developed the habit of publishing summary information on communications considered, without waiting for authorization from the Assembly of Heads of State and Government.

In the area of procedure, the Commission has also made a broad interpretation of the condition for the exhaustion of local remedies, thus demonstrating a great deal of flexibility in its interpretation of a condition of admissibility. This progressive interpretation by the Commission of the condition of exhaustion of local remedies should be likened to that made of the same condition by the Inter-American Court of Human Rights, at the request of the Inter-American Commission, in its eleventh advisory opinion of 10 August 1990.[12]

The Commission has exploited its prerogatives in the field of the promotion of human rights to the maximum, by the regular adoption of resolutions stigmatizing the conduct of one State party to the African Charter or another.[13] Although the African Charter and the Rules of the Commission are silent on this issue, the Commission has also appointed six Special Rapporteurs to deal with questions of particular interest to its activities.[14] It has recently decided to send a fact-finding mission to investigate the violations of human rights which occurred on the territory of a State party to the African Charter.[15]

In short, the African Commission appears to be following a similar pattern of development to that of the Inter-American Commission on Human Rights. Originally conceived as a simple organ for the promotion of human rights, as defined by the American Declaration of the Rights and Duties of Man of 1948,[16] the Inter-American Commission has gradually evolved into a true organ for the protection of human rights, broadening its powers by a courageous interpretation of its Statute.

During its eighteen years of existence, the African Commission has been much criticized for its weakness. As far as I am concerned, I would not be too critical towards this body which has so far worked with a chronic lack of staffing and financial resources. In this regard, I invite you to a quick look to the Greek mythology and to Sisyphus in particular. Indeed, as one enlightened French thinker has put it so well: 'There is no such thing as useless effort: Sisyphus was developing his muscles'. I know that some would still argue that after eighteen years of warming up and training, it is now time for action. I would simply reply that the situation might change with the establishment of the African Court, which is the topic turned to now.

2) The last step of the metamorphosis consists of the recent reinforcement of the whole system by the creation of an African Court of Human and Peoples' Rights. While the purpose of this panel is indeed to discuss, 'the similar difficulties' that the three regional human rights courts are facing, 'in particular how to cope with (potentially) very large numbers of complaints' and 'to compare the institutional solutions envisaged for these three courts', it is difficult to talk about the institutional challenges the African Court of Human and Peoples' Rights is facing, mainly for two reasons.

Firstly, the African Court has not yet been established; so far, it exists only on paper. Therefore, it has not so far faced any difficulties or challenges.

Secondly, and more important, the African Court is somehow a still born judicial institution. Put in other words, the only challenge the African Court is now facing is simply to stay alive! It is indeed its very existence which is the actual challenge. This warrants a brief explanation.

In June 1998, the States parties to the African Charter on Human and Peoples' Rights adopted a Protocol establishing an African Court of Human and Peoples' Rights.

This protocol entered into force recently, on 24 January 2004, only one year and half ago.

The election of the judges should have taken place in July 2004 during the Third Ordinary Session of the Assembly of Heads of State and Government of the African Union.

Ultimately, these elections did not take place for reasons which remain unclear. Instead, the Assembly of the African Union decided that 'the African Court on Human and Peoples' Rights and the African Court should be integrated into one Court'.[17]

The 'African Court' referred to in this decision is the Court of Justice of the African Union has been created by the Protocol of the Court of Justice adopted on 29 July 2003, but still not yet in force.[18] This Court, which is conceived as the 'principal judicial organ of the Union',[19] would, *inter alia*, have jurisdiction over disputes relating to the interpretation or application of the Constitutive Act of the African Union and other treaties and legal instruments adopted within the framework of the Union. The missions of the two Courts are thus clearly distinct: the African Court of Human Rights has a specialized material jurisdiction (*ratione materiae*), whereas the Court of Justice of the African Union has a much broader one; their personal jurisdiction (*ratione personae*) is also different.

If taken earlier, this decision of merger would certainly have been understandable given, *inter alia*, the chronic lack of financial resources of the African Union. The issue was actually raised in 2003, during the *travaux préparatoires* of the Protocol establishing the African Court of Justice. The draft protocol was providing for the merger of the two courts. The Executive Council of the African Union, composed of the Ministers for foreign affairs of the Member States, however decided that 'the African Court of Human and Peoples' Rights shall remain a separate and distinct institution from the Court of Justice of the African Union.'[20] This decision has been endorsed by the Assembly of the African Union, which ultimately adopted the Protocol as it stands today.

In January 2005, the Commission of the African Union has recommended to the Executive Council that the necessary amendments should be made to both the Protocol of the Court of Justice and the Protocol on the Establishment of an African Court of Human and Peoples' Rights, and that these amendments should be incorporated in a third protocol which could be ratified by Members States of the African Union.[21]

In short, the merger of the two African Courts is not yet effective and creates lots of legal issues which solutions are far from being clear (e.g., the two courts do not have the same jurisdiction *ratione materiae* and *ratione personae*; some African States might decide to become party to the African Human Rights Court and not to the Court of Justice of the African Union, and vice versa).

Today, Saturday, 2 July 2005, at this very moment, the Executive Council of the African Union is meeting in Libya and might take a decision on this issue. This decision should then normally be endorsed by the Assembly of Heads of State and Government which will meet early next week.

It is therefore still difficult to predict if there will be one merged African Court, two African Courts, one dealing with human rights issues, the other one with general legal issues, or no court at all. It should be stressed that for the merged court to come to existence, not one, not two but three international treaties need to be into force: the Protocol establishing an African Court of Human and Peoples' Rights, the Protocol of the Court of Justice of the African Union, and the third protocol providing for the merger. The Protocol of the Court of Justice of the African Union is still far from entering into force;[22] the same goes *a fortiori* for the would be Protocol relating to the merger.

***

My knowledge of the two other regional courts is rather limited but I know, for example, and Judge Thomassen can correct me if I am mistaken, that the main problem that the European system was facing in the past and is now facing again is its overloading. The volume of applications filed with the European Court is indeed raising very quickly, about 500 per cent between 1993 and 2000. The paper of Judge Thomassen shows that in November 2004, that is last year, there were about 80 000 applications pending before the European Court of Human Rights. At this stage, it is difficult to predict what could be the workload of the future African Court, but if I take for reference the current number of applications considered by the African Commission in Banjul, I would not be worrying too much as far as the near future of the African Court is concerned. There are unfortunately no statistics concerning the number of applications actually filed with the Commission during its eighteen years of existence but there are some about the number of communications examined: the African Commission has examined only 440 communications and has given about 120 decisions on the merits.

I will therefore forget about the potential overloading of the African Court and focus on some other sensitive issues which are raised by the Protocol. I was intending to consider in turn the composition of the Court, its operation and its contentious function.

### 1) Budget

The money issue is certainly the most critical one that the African Court will have to face. The question here is not a question of possible reform. It is simply a question of implementation of the Protocol. According to the Protocol, the expenses of the Court, emoluments for judges as well as the budget of its registry, shall be borne by the African Union. States parties to the Protocol and Member States of the African Union must therefore respect their commitments and provide the Court with the human and financial resources it needs. It should be noted at this point that since its establishment in 1987, the African Commission has not obtained from the Organization of African Unity, and now the African Union, all the assistance needed. Still today, the Commission continues to solicit for financial and material assistance from foreign partners such as, for example, the Government of the Netherlands, which is supporting the Documentation Centre, the Press and Information Section and has recently granted a subvention to finance the positions of the two Legal Officers. As a judicial, and therefore independent body, the African Court ought to have an adequate budget with a view to both its efficacy and its credibility.

### 2) Procedure before the Court

The main singularity of the Protocol in that respect lies in the third paragraph of its Article 6, which states that '[t]he Court may consider cases or transfer them to the Commission'. Indeed, it may be wondered whether this provision does not concern the examination of the petitions on the merits. In this case, it would entail recognizing that the Court could decline to rule on a case submitted to it, thus opening up the possibility of a genuine denial of justice. The referral of a case by the Court to the Commission, which possibility does not exist in the European and Inter-American systems, is not sufficient to prevent such a denial of justice as only the Court has judicial powers. On the other hand, Article 6 of the Protocol could be interpreted as authorizing the Court and the Commission to exercise their contentious jurisdiction with regards to different types of cases. The Court could thus refer to the Commission all cases involving minor violations of individual rights and keep for itself cases involving major questions of principles or serious or massive violations of human rights. By so doing, the African Court would adopt the 'pick and choose' system mentioned by Judge Thomassen in her very enlightening paper on the European Court.

## Conclusion

Would an African Court, specialized in human rights or integrated, bring any added value to the African System? My answer is definitely '*yes*' in terms of:
- independence and impartiality of its members,
- legal value and authority of its decisions,
- and implementation of its decisions.

## Notes

[1] See Preamble, para. 9, and Art. II, para. 1.

[2] Entered into force on 20 June 1974; as of 6 June 2005, 45 African States were parties thereto, see the web site of the African Union: <http://www.africa-union.org>.

[3] Entered into force on 21 October 1986; as of 6 June 2005, 53 African States were parties thereto. The only African State which is still not party to the African Charter is Morocco; it has suspended its participation in the O.A.U. in 1983 and is not member of the African Union.

[4] Entered into force on 29 November 1999; as of 6 June 2005, 35 African States were parties thereto.

[5] The Constitutive Act of the African Union was adopted on 11 July 2000 at Lomé (Togo) and entered into force on 26 May 2001. Text of the Constitutive Act of the African Union in (2000), 8 *African Yearbook of International Law* (2000), at pp. 479-502.

[6] See also para. 9 of the Preamble of the Constitutive Act, which provides that the 'Heads of State and Government of the Member States of the Organization of African Unity' are 'determined to promote and protect human and peoples' rights, consolidate democratic institutions and culture, and to ensure good governance and the rule of law.'

[7] This provision has been expanded by the Protocol of 2003 on Amendments to the Constitutive Act of the African Union, to read: '[...] as well as a serious threat to legitimate order to restore peace and stability to the Member State of the Union upon the recommendation of the Peace and Security Council'; the Protocol is not yet in force. See also Art. 4(j) of the Constitutive Act, which provides for 'the right of Member States to request intervention from the Union in order to restore peace and security'.

[8] See Art. 30 and Art. 23(2) of the Constitutive Act.

[9] Entered into force on 25 January 2004; as of 6 June 2005, 20 African States were parties thereto.

[10] As of 6 June 2005, only 10 African States had ratified it: Comoros, Djibouti, Lesotho, Libya, Mali, Namibia, Nigeria, Rwanda, Senegal, South Africa. 15 ratifications are required for the entry into force of this Protocol.

[11] In *Historia Naturalis* (II, Viii, 42), a vast encyclopaedia of knowledge of its time, Pliny the Eldest (23-79) wrote '*Ex Africa semper aliquid* novi' [Out of Africa, there is always something new]. I must say that African States have certainly been true to this Roman naturalist deceased nearly 2000 years ago.

[12] 'Exceptions to the Exhaustion of Domestic Remedies', Advisory Opinion No. 11 of 10 August 1990, Inter-American Court of Human Rights, *Series A: Judgments and Opinions No. 11*.

[13] See for instance, *Resolution on the Human Rights Situation in Darfur, Sudan*, adopted at the 37th Ordinary Session of the African Commission, held in Banjul (The Gambia), from 27th April to 11th May 2005.

[14] Special Rapporteurs on Extra-Judicial, Summary or Arbitrary Executions in Africa, on Prisons and Detention Conditions in Africa, on the Rights of Women in Africa. on Refugees, Asylum Seekers and Internally Displaced Persons in Africa, on Human Rights Defenders, and on the Right to Freedom of Expression in Africa.

[15] *Resolution on the Human Rights Situation in Togo*, adopted at the 37th Ordinary Session of the African Commission (27th April/11th May 2005).

[16] Statute of the Inter-American Commission on Human Rights, Arts. 1 and 2.

[17] *Decision on the seats of the African Union*, Doc Assembly/AU/Dec. 45 (III), para. 4.

[18] Fifteen (15) ratifications are indeed required; as of 6 June 2005, only eight (8) States have ratified this protocol.

[19] Art. 2 of the Protocol on the Court of Justice of the Union.

[20] *Decision on the Draft Protocol of the Court of Justice*, African Union, Doc. EX/CL/58 (III).

[21] *Report on the Decision of the Assembly of the Union to merge the African Court on Human and Peoples' Rights and the Court of Justice of the African Union.*

[22] As of 6 June 2005, seven (7) ratifications are still missing, see *supra*, n. 18.

## Discussion

Professor Henry Schermers* started the discussion by questioning the notion of duties under the African Charter of Human and Peoples' Rights. He asked whether there

* Leiden University.

was any case law of the African Commission regarding that notion, and especially whether a link between the fulfilment of duties and guaranteeing of the rights had ever been made by the Commission or pleaded before it. He thought that the notion might be potentially dangerous to individuals as the governments may deny them rights justifying the denial by non-fulfilment of the individual's duties.

In FATSAH OUGUERGOUZ's opinion, the issue of duties has proved not to be a problem. He pointed out that duties exist in any national constitutional system, as well as in human rights systems other than the African one. There is no case law of the African Commission which would make a link between fulfilling the duties and guaranteeing the rights. What is more, the issue of duties has not given rise to any complaints by individuals. Instead, the notion has been creatively used by the African Commission in order to qualify the limitation clauses of the African Charter, which are very vague: under the Charter the rights can be limited only by reference to national laws, unlike in the European system where the limitation clauses are more elaborate.

ELLEN HEY* posed the second question to Judge THOMASSEN, which concerned the cooperation between the European Court of Human Rights and the European Court of Justice in Luxembourg, especially the desirable forms of that cooperation in light of insufficient reforms of the Strasbourg Court by Protocol 14 to the ECHR and the crisis in the ratification of the Constitutional Treaty for the EU.

In JUDGE THOMASSEN's opinion, the cooperation between the two Courts is an extremely important question, which so far has not received enough attention. At the moment the forms of cooperation which do exist, i.e., periodic summaries of case law on the European Convention questions provided by the respective Courts to their counterpart, are not sufficient. The cooperation should be more structured. One could imagine that as soon as the issue under the ECHR is at stake the Luxembourg Court could ask a preliminary question to the Strasbourg Court to avoid possible divergences in the case law. One could imagine even closer cooperation in the future, for example in the form of human rights chambers in the Luxembourg Court linked with the Strasbourg Court. According to Judge Thomassen, one should experiment with various possible forms of cooperation, as it has happened in national legal systems with two highest courts, for example in the Netherlands between the Council of State and the Supreme Court. In any case, the individual should never be a victim of the fact that two highest courts exist in Europe, and situations whereby he or she has to go through 14 years of proceedings as it sometimes happens, should never take place.

Following-up on the answer of Judge Thomassen, JUDGE BUERGENTHAL was reminded of an event illustrative of the different challenges facing two regional human rights courts. When the judges of the first Inter-American Court of Human Rights were elected in 1979, they decided almost immediately to establish relations with the European Court of Human Rights. This was based on two reasons. First, in a region ruled mostly by dictatorships, as the American region then was, the Court would have been totally disregarded unless it was seen to have international legitimacy. Having the European Court demonstrate an interest in the work of the Inter-American Court served that purpose to some extent. Second, being 'neophytes', the judges of the Inter-American Court wanted to learn from the experience of their European colleagues. To

* Erasmus University Rotterdam.

that end a system of mutual periodic visits was developed. On one such visit to Strasbourg by the judges of the Inter-American Court, the European Court was hearing the *Campbell* case on corporal punishment in Britain. Listening to the argument, one of his Latin American colleagues turned to Judge Buergenthal and whispered: 'If we ever have that kind of cases in our Court we will have solved all human rights problems in our region'.

The next question, asked by ELENI CHAITIDOU,* concerned the participation of NGOs in the proceedings of the different courts and in the enforcement of their judgments. She was particularly interested in whether there was more space for greater involvement of NGOs, whether such involvement could help reduce the workload of the courts, and whether that issue was being discussed in the current reform undertakings.

CLAUDIA MARTIN replied that the participation of NGOs had always been a very important feature of the Inter-American system. Although initially the NGOs were not involved in the recent reform project, they eventually got involved and have been very active in questioning and challenging various reform proposals. Participation of NGOs in the proceedings is in fact quite essential. In the new Rules of Court victims have an autonomous status in the proceedings before the Court, during which they are usually represented by NGOs, which provide them also with resources to litigate their case. Concerning the enforcement of the Commission's recommendations, the NGOs are very active in requesting the Commission to institute follow up procedures, and in keeping an eye on what states do with the cases. As for the enforcement of the judgments of the Court, there is a written procedure, and whenever the state presents a written report on a case that report then proceeds to the petitioner who can challenge it. It is also in these kinds of proceedings that NGOs are constantly present.

JUDGE THOMASSEN pointed out that in the Strasbourg system, with the permission of the Court, the NGOs have a possibility to file observations and they do make use of that possibility. Such observations are often of a very high quality and they form a part of the case file. The NGOs cannot file applications themselves; there is no possibility of a class action in the European system, since only the victims of a violation of the Convention may bring cases to the Court. Although, according to Judge Thomassen, the class action would probably not help much in reducing the workload of the Court, filing a case by an NGO may be desirable in situations when it is dangerous for individuals to file their applications themselves, for example in current Chechen cases.

In the case of the African system, as stressed by Dr OUGUERGOUZ, the role of the NGOs is extremely important. This was already evident in the process of drafting the African Charter and it continues to be so. The African Charter as interpreted by the African Commission does not require the complainant to be a victim of a violation and most applications are filed or reviewed by NGOs. By now some three hundred African and non-African NGOs have obtained the observer status before the African Commission. The role of NGOs was equally prominent in the 1994 decision to establish the African Court of Human Rights, taken in the aftermath of the genocide in Rwanda. Currently, there is a coalition of African NGOs for the African Court, pushing for the effective human rights Court for Africa. Another aspect of NGO contribu-

* International Criminal Court.

tion is their help in financing the activities of the Commission, e.g., by providing funds for establishing posts of legal officers, as well as organizing seminars together with the Commission. Finally, NGOs can have *locus standi* before the Court. Under Article 5 of the Protocol, individuals and NGOs have access to the Court if a state party makes a specific declaration to that effect.

DINAH SHELTON* asked Prof. MARTIN about whether any discussions were being held on improving the system of elections of members of the American Commission and judges to the Inter-American Court, whose qualifications to hold their positions are often shaky at best. She was interested if anything similar to the European solution of reviewing qualifications of prospective judges by the Parliamentary Assembly of the Council of Europe had been considered.

In her reply, MARTIN expressed her personal view that the composition of the Commission has not been very good lately. There were some concerns about the recent elections that took place a month before and there are concerns about the election of future members of the Court, which will take place next year. Bearing that in mind, some NGOs started an initiative to lobby the Organization and the governments to develop a more transparent process for the nomination of members of the Commission and judges to the Court. They have been quite successful and managed to obtain a resolution from the General Assembly of the Organization of American States in June 2005, which requests the states to adopt a more transparent procedure. The issue is especially important in the case of the Court, as it is a judicial body whose decisions are followed by national courts. The NGOs continue to push for that kind of more transparent procedures.

Considering that all speakers had mentioned material and personnel shortages in the different institutions as a serious problem, SHELTON directed the final question to all the panellists concerning the extent to which it would be possible to look for other sources of funding, such as foundation money, contributions in kind, unpaid interns provided by universities, etc. She asked whether it was appropriate to do so and whether there were any legal problems with doing so.

MARTIN remarked that some ten years ago she had been horrified by the African Commission's practice of looking for various cooperation and NGO funds. Now it is a practice also in the American system, and several European governments also provide funds to the Commission and the Court to finance some of their activities. She does not believe, however, that this is appropriate, as the states should finance the system they created. The problem is that if they do not fund it then the organs of the system need to look for additional money to perform their functions, which is why it is difficult to criticize such a practice. The question of whether or not such a practice is legal is a very interesting one. The resolutions of the General Assembly of the OAS have recently started to encourage both the Commission and the Court to look for alternative sources of funding, so at least they do not see that practice as illegal.

In that context JUDGE BUERGENTHAL recalled that when the Inter-American Court was first established, the annual meeting of the General Assembly of the Organization of American States failed to give the Court a budget. This experience was among the reasons that prompted the judges of the Court to establish the Inter-American Insti-

* George Washington University Law School.

tute of Human Rights, which could go out and raise money from various foundations and governments. It enabled the Institute in the early years to support the work of the Court. Thus, for example, when the Court lacked funds for additional sessions, the Institute would convene a meeting and, since all the judges were on the Council of the Institute, their trips to Costa Rica were paid for by the Institute. A large part of the Court's library was funded in the same way. Moreover, other activities which the Court could not engage in directly, such as promotion of the Court's work, was performed by the Institute. Other regional courts might in the future find this approach a useful precedent.

JUDGE THOMASSEN mentioned that there had been a discussion on the alternative sources of the European Court's funding when the new Court was being established, but such an option was rejected. Personally, she is against having an alternative system of resources, since the essence of the human rights system is that it is very much concerned with the national states, and that it is very important that there is democratic legitimation of the judicial power of the Court. Of course states tend to contribute inadequate resources as human rights are not always their highest priority, but they can be controlled, for example, by national parliaments. States should fund the system they established. One possible exception to that rule could be for projects the financing of which does not threaten the independence of the Court, such as having a good library, and maybe even translation of judgments. The latter is a grave problem in the Strasbourg system. Indeed, it is sad and unfortunate that owing to the lack of resources, judgments in cases against Russia are not translated into Russian, which means that the Russian judges and members of the legislature who have to implement them cannot read them.

OUGUERGOUZ pointed out that in the African system the alternative sources of funding had been explored since its inception. A true alternative to the present situation would be if the African Union actually started complying with its obligation to finance the Court. The African Union has established the African Fund for Human Rights, but the Fund is still empty. Additionally, there is an idea which is already working within the ECOWAS (Economic Community of Western African States), in the form of the apportionment of a very small part of the external flux diverted to a fund managed by the central banks of the member states and used to finance various activities. This results in a system (now the African system) that is very much dependent on the funding coming from outside Africa.

*Reporter:* Michael Gondek*

* LL.M., Junior researcher, Faculty of Law, Maastricht University.

# Specialized and Niche International Institutions: Special Issues of Reform

The panel was convened by its Chair, Susan Karamanian*

## Remarks by Laurent Grosse**

### Reform Issues for Interpol: the financing and budgetary perspective

#### Introduction

The ICPO-Interpol was created in 1923, and is one of the longest-standing international organizations.

It is easy to imagine that such an organization has had to adapt over the years to become what it is today. At first, it had very few members (representatives of 24 countries attended the initial conference in 1914, and only 17 attended the 1923 conference at which the Organization was formally constituted), and the criminological environment was very different (these were early days in the internationalization of crime). Interpol is now an organization with 182 member countries, an essential player in the fight against international crime, and a valuable partner for other organizations involved in dealing with these problems (United Nations, UNESCO, ICC, WHO, etc.).

Much could be said about the successive reforms Interpol has undergone and, above all, the challenges it currently faces.

It would be interesting, however, in the context of the present conference, to focus on a particular issue which might be considered unexpected, given that we are talking about an international criminal police organization. That issue is the financial perspective.

The issue is all the more topical as it comes at the end of a transition period which, in a few months' time, will see the full implementation of a new system of statutory contributions first introduced at the beginning of 2002.

#### Context and Prospects

Let us go back a few years in order to grasp the full significance of this issue.

* George Washington University Law School.

** Director, Management & Budget and former General Counsel (2001-2004) of the ICPO-Interpol. This article reflects the personal views of the author.

In 1997, after a number of years of informal discussions, the Organization's General Assembly decided to tackle the question of how to finance its activities, by asking the Executive Committee 'to submit to the General Assembly, at its 1998 session, a comprehensive report updating and modernizing the whole system of member countries' statutory contributions' (Resolution AGN/66/RES/13).

This decision came as no surprise. The Organization's finances had previously been assured by means of a system of 'budget units' (ranging from 2 to 100 budget units, based on a model similar to the one used in the Universal Postal Union, for example) paid by its member countries on an essentially voluntary basis, even though in the past, and in 1990 in particular, attempts had been made to find a better balance so that some countries would agree to pay more units. It is interesting to see how the subject was summarized in 1997 in a report submitted to the General Assembly:

> 'It was based on the principle of solidarity, in that the most highly industrialized countries *were asked* to make a major effort, and the principle [of] fairness, *in that an attempt was made* to correct various disparities that had come to light over the years.' (Report AGN/66/RAP. No. 16, submitted by the Executive Committee)

This shows that, in 1997, although participation in the Organization's budget was not based solely on voluntary contributions, it was at least the result of negotiations conducted when countries joined the Organization, and there was hardly any means of changing things subsequently.

The main focus of the study which the General Assembly requested was therefore financial, and the aim was to redistribute member countries' financial contributions. The same report stated that 'It would appear that the economic situation in some member countries has changed since the conclusions of the former study were implemented in 1990'.

But another factor came into play as soon as discussions on the study had begun and, although it was not actually spelt out in Report AGN/66/RAP. No. 16, it was quite clear to the informed reader. The report also considered the question of funding the Sub-Regional Bureaus – decentralized structures of the General Secretariat; at the time, and only shortly after the first of these Bureaus had been opened, the funding aspect posed particular problems. Resolution AGN/66/RES/13 therefore asked the Executive Committee to propose 'new ways of funding the Sub-Regional Bureaus'.

To understand the reasons behind this, we need to refer to Report AGN/66/RAP. No. 17, which was also discussed in 1997. The report said that:

> 'However, these resolutions do not impose any binding financial obligations on the countries covered by the Sub-Regional Bureaus and their wording suggests that financial participation would be voluntary. The General Assembly resolutions which call on the countries covered by Sub-Regional Bureaus to contribute voluntarily to their functioning are merely recommendations for those countries, whereas they impose obligations on the General Secretariat.'

Clearly, in those conditions, any overhaul of the system of financial participation in the Organization could not avoid the basic question of the legal nature of the contributions paid by member countries. Indeed, this question was magnified by the fact that the Organization's very existence was not based on a formal convention.

LEGAL APPROACHES

The Organization's General Assembly eventually adopted the revised system of statutory contributions during its 70th session in 2001. This system is fundamentally different from the previous one, which was based on a system of budget units, where the country would negotiate with the Executive Committee the number of units it would pay on joining the Organization.

Two resolutions adopted in 2001 (AG-2001-RES-01 and AG-2001-RES-02) established a contributions system based on a percentage of the budget.

This system helps to redress the economic balance regarding member countries' financial contributions by distinguishing three basic groups:

In the first group, six countries (the United States, Japan, Germany, the United Kingdom, France and Italy) account for a little over 52 per cent of the total amount called up in statutory contributions.

In the second group, the number of budget units paid by OECD member countries not among the six countries already mentioned was assessed as a percentage of the budget, and that percentage was maintained, at least during the transition period. Finally, for the third group, the percentage of the budget paid by the remaining countries was calculated on a *pro rata* basis according to the contributions scale used for the United Nations' budget.

Furthermore, thanks to this new contributions system, the General Assembly has recovered all its financial powers: it is now the Assembly which decides, in full sovereignty, the level of contribution for all member countries, thus bringing an end to a system in which the funding for the Organization was based on voluntary participation.

Curiously, this change gave rise to practically no objections in principle or, above all, to any legal objections, despite the fact that it clearly established the mandatory nature of statutory contributions: 'Members' statutory contributions are due annually and are compulsory' (Art. 3.1 of the version of the Financial Regulations adopted in 2001).[1]

There are a number of possible explanations for this. First, although it was based on voluntary contributions, the previous system had another side to it, since penalties existed if the contributions were not paid (Art. 52 of the Organization's General Regulations). Second, the new system merely reflects well-established international practice based on international case law (see ICJ, *Certain expenses of the United Nations*, 20 July 1962). In fact, the question of contributions being compulsory only arose in the context of the expert group set-up to develop this new system of financing.

That did not settle everything, however, and it took a resolution adopted in 2004 (Resolution AG-2004-RES-03) to show clearly and unambiguously the compulsory nature of the contributions intended to finance the functioning of the Sub-Regional Bureaus: 'The statutory contributions paid by member countries to the specific budgets for Sub-Regional Bureaus are due annually and are compulsory' (Art. 3.5 of the Financial Regulations).

Nevertheless, the Organization's budget is still particularly small, given the number of its member countries (182) and missions.

Consequently, it is hardly surprising that Interpol should look for financial support outside the system of statutory contributions paid by its member countries. However, before elaborating on this particular aspect, we should look at the effects of this new system on the Organization's institutions.

## The Institutional Aspect

The most immediate effect, as stated above, is that the General Assembly has recovered all its financial powers, and is less dependent on the good will of the Organization's member countries. It is therefore able (in application of Art. 8(g) of Interpol's Constitution) to 'determine the financial policy of the Organization' with far fewer constraints.

Member countries – especially the main contributors – have certainly understood the institutional and policy implications of this change and know where they now stand. This is why they decided to react even before the new system of statutory contributions was formally adopted by the General Assembly. Urged on by the Group of Experts, in which these countries were represented, the General Assembly adopted Resolution AGN/69/RES/12,[2] asking the Executive Committee

> 'to further consider the recommendations of the Group of Experts and examine the conditions under which a group of financial experts could be set up to be responsible for aiding the Executive Committee in examining financial matters, as well as the composition of such a group.'

Reference should be made at this point to the meetings of the Group of Experts, during which the future main contributors – well aware of the potential impact of the reforms being proposed – had discussed ways of compensating for the loss of the 'voluntary' element by an increase in their power. In this connection, two proposals in particular were put forward, before the creation of a group of financial experts was finally envisaged.

In the first instance, taking into account their agreement to cover over 50 per cent of the Organization's budget, the six main contributors asked to have permanent seats on the Executive Committee. This proposal was, however, quickly ruled out given the political implications. In addition, it would have required a modification to the Organization's Constitution, which can only be done with the agreement of two thirds of the member countries[3] which would not only have to be won over, but also encouraged to attend the General Assembly session – a practical difficulty given the usual attendance figures at such sessions.

Secondly, the six main contributors put forward the idea of being granted the right of veto when the General Assembly came to vote on the budget. Once again, such a proposal could only be taken up by amending the Organization's basic texts, since it would have undermined the 'one country, one vote' principle set out in Article 13 of Interpol's Constitution ('Only one delegate from each country shall have the right to vote in the General Assembly'), and in Article 18 of the General Regulations ('[...] each country represented has one vote'). Consequently, in the absence of any specific provision introducing a weighting factor, these provisions establish the principle of equal voting power. The introduction of a veto would therefore have necessarily led to a revision of this basic principle. This proposal was also ruled out.

The countries concerned nevertheless had a strong argument in their favour. Indeed, it has been emphasized by commentators that

> 'The interest between equality of voting-strength and inequality of the interests involved is a handicap for many international organizations. Under the system of equal voting power, member states which pay the bill for almost all an organization's expenses often possess so little voting strength that they are unable to prevent it from taking new obligations.'[4]

The approach taken by the main contributors was therefore, on the face of things, fully justified and perfectly legitimate. It was nonetheless apparent that such a proposal would have seriously called into question the principle of equality among the Organization's member countries which not only derives from the official texts – as mentioned above – but also from well-established practice.

It was in this context that the idea arose of setting-up a group of financial experts to be responsible, under the terms of Resolution AGN/69/RES/12, for 'aiding the Executive Committee in examining financial matters'.

It may seem rather surprising that a group of countries which had made such strong demands as asking for a permanent seat on the Organization's select policy-making body, or for the right to veto the budget, should be satisfied with the creation of an apparently purely technical body composed of 'financial experts'.

But since this group of experts includes, at the very least, the main contributing countries (which – in a rather subtle fashion – were given the right to sit on the group[5]), it is obvious that the group has considerable indirect policy-making and financial power because its members represent over half the contributions paid to the Organization's budget.

Furthermore, although the original idea expressed by the General Assembly had been to set up a group of 'financial experts', the Executive Committee eventually modified this approach and, with reference to the composition of the Advisory Group on Financial Matters, spoke of 'countries represented', thereby combining a strictly technical approach with a more political approach. For instance, in the terms of reference, paragraph 1 of the section on 'Composition of the Advisory Group on Financial Matters' states:

> 'The number of countries represented on the Advisory Group on Financial Matters shall be determined by the Executive Committee which shall, in this connection, take account of the fact that an upper limit of 20 members should not be exceeded unless justified by circumstances.'

Paragraph 3 of the same section gives another example: 'The representatives on the Advisory Group on Financial Matters should preferably be experts on the budgets and finances of international organizations'.

The Advisory Group on Financial Matters is, in fact, a subsidiary body of the Executive Committee, set-up in application of Article 4.2 of the latter's Rules of Procedure.[6] In addition to the Executive Committee's decision creating the Advisory Group on Financial Matters, a formal link was established via the Finance Sub-Committee, which is composed of three members of the Executive Committee and whose role is to prepare the Executive Committee's decisions on financial matters. In application of the terms of reference of the Advisory Group on Financial Matters, 'At least one member of the Finance Sub-Committee will attend the meetings of the Advisory Group as an observer' (para. 7 of the section on 'Composition of the Advisory Group on Financial Matters').

The establishment of the Advisory Group on Financial Matters therefore supplements the Organization's institutional financial framework, while preserving the general principle of equality discussed earlier.

Although most of the decision-making power regarding financial issues rests with the General Assembly, most of the discussions take place at Executive Committee level (with the Finance Sub-Committee and the Advisory Group on Financial Matters) and the main contributing countries bring most of their influence to bear within the Advisory Group on Financial Matters.

This structure may seem to be unbalanced and unrepresentative of the distribution of powers that was intended in the Organization's Constitution; indeed, we might well ask whether the General Assembly really does have a leading part to play in this respect, even though, in the end, it is the General Assembly which approves – or otherwise – the budget.

It is also worth mentioning that the Finance Committee, which previously met during General Assembly sessions in application of Article 11.1 of the Constitution[7] was, in practice, abolished in 1998.

There are definitely important questions to be answered here and serious consideration will have to be given this issue which directly involves the institutional balance of the Organization.

## Outlook

The private sector, including the business, academic and professional components has, on many occasions, requested Interpol's support and assistance. For example, since the beginning of 1999, Interpol has signed agreements with the most important players in the payment card industry for close cooperation in the fight against payment fraud.[8]

In April 1998, during the First International Conference on Corruption-Related Crimes, Interpol also established a Group of Experts on Corruption (IGEC) that comprises a representative from the Financial Services Community.[9]

Numerous other examples could also be given to demonstrate the value to the private sector of cooperating with Interpol.

What is interesting is the way in which Interpol has also sought the assistance of the private sector.

Indeed, for a number of years now, the Organization has been cautiously looking to national administrations, and even private or semi-private entities, for direct funding, as permitted by Interpol's Constitution which states that

> 'The Organization's resources shall be provided by: (a) The financial contributions from Members; (b) Gifts, bequests, subsidies, grants and other resources after these have been accepted or approved by the Executive Committee.' (see Art. 38)

The conditions governing this have been set out in the Financial Regulations, Article 15.7 of which provides that: 'Prior authorization from the Executive Committee is required for the acceptance of all donations to the Organization such as funds from foundations, subsidies, gifts and bequests [...]' (the non-exclusive nature of this provision should be noted).

This provision is supplemented by implementing rules which specify the conditions. Therefore,

> 'Any gifts, bequests, subsidies or voluntary contributions paid to the Organization are subject to the following conditions: – The donation must be intended for purposes compatible with the principles, aims and activities of the Organization; – The activities of the donor must be compatible with the principles, aims and activities of the Organization.' (Financial Regulations Implementing Rule 115.7(d))

Despite all this and despite the existence of a legal context approved by the General Assembly, the issue of private financial assistance is the subject of ongoing discussion within the Organization. Indeed, in certain member countries, the very nature of police work means that such financing is quite inconceivable. It is therefore with due caution that the Organization has embarked on this course of action.

With due caution, but also with a certain degree of success. To date, more than 27.3 per cent of the Organization's projects (projects funded outside the regular budget) have been funded, to a greater or lesser extent, by the private sector. However, this only amounts to 40,1 per cent of total outside funding, which also includes public institutions (such as the European Commission).

Given that this approach is relatively new, and the fact that the Organization does not yet have sufficient hindsight, it is still difficult to determine any real trend. However, it can be seen that recent funding has been on a larger scale. In this respect, it is worth mentioning the donation of almost USD 1 million over two years given by a foundation to launch the Organization's bio-terrorism programme.

Also worthy of mention is the recent signature of an agreement setting out arrangements for a private company to make a contribution in kind towards the Organization's Disaster Victim Identification activities. The company in question has offered Interpol free use, for five years, of its specialized software which is used for comparing *ante-mortem* and *post-mortem* data.[10] The value of this arrangement is estimated at two million Euros.

In a resolution adopted in 1998 (Resolution AGN/67/RES/5), Interpol's General Assembly had noted

> 'that the public or private resources which could be collected in addition to Member States' statutory or voluntary contributions to be used for a project of international public utility launched by Interpol are limited, *inter alia*, by the fact that there is no suitable structure (foundation or similar body) to prevent the rare subsidies received by the Organization from being included in the mass of income, rather than being specifically allocated, making it impossible for the donors to exercise any form of control.'

The General Assembly's observation came following a request from Interpol's Executive Committee in 1993, 'to seek sources of finance in addition to the Organization's normal income, i.e. income from statutory or voluntary contributions paid by member countries' (see Report AGN/67/RAP/8 submitted to the General Assembly at its 67th session in 1998).

The General Assembly consequently decided, in 1998, on the principle of setting-up one or more foundations intended to manage outside funding (Resolution AGN/67/RES/5).

However, it has to be said that this idea has never actually been put into practice since, to date, no foundation has been set-up on the basis of the General Assembly's 1998 resolution.

Recent discussions have taken place about establishing a legal framework which would be better suited to receiving external contributions and the idea of developing trust funds was put forward. However, this has not gained full acceptance mainly because such a system does not appear to be worthwhile given the current financial system and its related rules.

We have in fact seen that, even without any purpose-built mechanisms, the Organization has been able – and is still able – to attract substantial external funding by guaranteeing the use of the funds made available.

The underlying question is to determine which activities should, or should not, be funded out of the Organization's ordinary budget. The activities currently funded – in whole or in part – by external sources (that is, not out of statutory contributions), come mainly within the scope of the Organization's core business. The necessity, or even the advisability, of separating such funding from the general budget has not become apparent, and would require much more in-depth study from an institutional perspective if it is to come to anything. In this respect, the strictly legal considerations – important though they may be – are purely accessory.

Other leads could probably be pursued by taking advantage of existing arrangements. For instance, a document published by the United Nations Information Department in 1998 reported that, in March of that year, Luxembourg had paid the UNDCP over USD 1.7 million, taken from assets confiscated from drug traffickers.

In this connection, it is worth drawing attention to Article 5(5, b) of the 1988 Vienna Convention, which provides that

> 'When acting on the request of another Party in accordance with this article, a Party may give special consideration to concluding agreements on: (i) Contributing the value of such proceeds and property, or funds derived from the sale of such proceeds or property, or a substantial part thereof, to *intergovernmental bodies* specializing in the fight against illicit traffic in and abuse of narcotic drugs and psychotropic substances.'

This is certainly another avenue Interpol could explore, in order to supplement its financial resources within the context of international law.

## Notes

1 This provision has since developed to take account of a 'General Budget' and 'specific budgets' (which are also compulsory), in particular for the Sub-Regional Bureaus.

2 69th General Assembly session, Rhodes, 30 October-4 November 2000.

3 Art. 42 of the Organization's Constitution.

4 In Schermers & Blokker, *International Institutional Law*, 4th edn. (2003).

5 See para. 5 of the section '*Composition of the Advisory Group on Financial Matters*' of the terms of reference adopted by the Executive Committee at its 130th session (June 2001): 'However, as an exception to that rule, the six main contributing countries and any other contributors substantially increasing their contributions shall

be given right of first refusal for seats on the Advisory Group on Financial Matters.'

6 Art. 4.2 of the Executive Committee's Rules of Procedure stipulates that 'The Executive Committee may, within the limits of its powers, set up subsidiary consultative bodies whose composition and terms of reference it shall determine.'

7 Art. 11.1 of Interpol's Constitution: 'The General Assembly may, when in session, set up special committees for dealing with particular matters'; Art. 35.1 of the General Regulations: 'At each session, the Assembly shall form such committees as it deems necessary. On the proposal of the President, it shall allocate work relative to the various items on the agenda to each committee.'

8 See at: <http://www.interpol.int/Public/CreditCards/Default.asp>.

9 See at: <http://www.interpol.int/Public/Corruption/IGEC/Default.asp>.

10 See at: <http://www.interpol.int/Public/ICPO/PressReleases/PR2005/PR200515.asp>.

# Remarks by D. Stephen Mathias*

## Adaptations and Challenges of an Independent International Peacekeeping Organization

Any serious discussion of the role of international institutions in the international system must begin with an acknowledgment of their great diversity. It is a complex diversity that could be plotted along a variety of axes, for example, of number and types of members or parties, of range and subject-matter of functions, of type and status of institutional action. Only if this diversity is fully understood and appreciated can meaningful conclusions about international institutions in general, or, international institutional reform in particular, be derived. Consideration of one of the lesser-studied types of international institution, the specialized and niche international institution, can thus make an appropriate and valuable contribution to the understanding of the subject as a whole.

To understand and appreciate the diversity that exists even among specialized and niche institutions, it is best to proceed by considering individual institutions of this character in their specific and particular contexts, in this case, the Multinational Force and Observers, or MFO, operating in Egypt and Israel, and the 'adaptations and challenges' that it faces. Discussion of the adaptations that the MFO has adopted to discharge its mandate in an effective manner and the challenges the MFO faces as it carries out its work may suggest conclusions of a more general character.

Why consider the MFO? One reason is that it possesses some unusual institutional features that differentiate it from other, more widely known, peacekeeping entities, and it may be of interest to consider whether any of those institutional features, or adaptations, may lend themselves to possible application in other contexts. Another is that the very existence of an 'independent international peacekeeping organization' is somewhat rare and it may be worthwhile to consider the characteristics of such an entity.

To understand the MFO, it is necessary to begin before its beginning. One must note, of course, the important roles and histories of UN-created entities that had func-

* General Counsel, Multinational Force and Observers.

tioned previously or were functioning in the region: the United Nations Truce Supervision Organization, which was created in June 1948 and continues to perform a mission in the area; the first United Nations Emergency Force, which was deployed in the area from November 1956 until June 1967; and the second United Nations Emergency Force, which was deployed in the area from October 1973 until July 1979.[1] Indeed, there are echoes in some of the agreements related to the MFO of provisions regarding these entities.

In a formal sense, an analysis of the MFO must begin with the landmark Treaty of Peace Between the Arab Republic of Egypt and the State of Israel, signed in Washington on 26 March 1979, and witnessed by the United States. In that Treaty, the Parties agreed that security arrangements would be established including 'limited force zones' in Egypt and Israel and the presence of 'United Nations forces and observers'.[2] Annex I to the Treaty of Peace provided that the Parties would 'request the United Nations to provide forces and observers to supervise the implementation of the Annex and to employ their best efforts to prevent any violation of its terms.'[3] Specific arrangements with respect to these United Nations forces and observers were set out in the Annex, including, for example, the operation of check points, reconnaissance patrols, and observation posts in certain areas, periodic verification of the implementation of the Annex not less than twice a month unless otherwise agreed by the Parties, and ensuring freedom of navigation through the Strait of Tiran in accordance with Article V of the Treaty of Peace.[4] Annex I further provided that the Parties would 'agree on the nations from which the United Nations force and observers will be drawn [and that t]hey will be drawn from nations other than those which are permanent members of the UN Security Council.'[5] In an Agreed Minute, the Parties further provided that if no agreement could be reached on composition, they would accept or support a US proposal concerning it.[6]

Significantly for present purposes, in identical, separate letters to President Sadat and Prime Minister Begin dated the same date, US President Carter wrote that:

> 'The United States believes the Treaty provision for permanent stationing of United Nations personnel in the designed limited force zone can and should be implemented by the United Nations Security Council. The United States will exert its utmost efforts to obtain the requisite action by the Security Council. If the Security Council fails to establish and maintain the arrangements called for in the Treaty, the President will be prepared to take those steps necessary to ensure the establishment and maintenance of an acceptable alternative multinational force.'[7]

The Multinational Force and Observers, the MFO, is the alternative that was established, following an indication by the President of the UN Security Council on 18 May 1981, that the Security Council was unable to reach the necessary agreement on the proposal to establish the UN Forces and Observers.[8]

The MFO was established in a Protocol agreed between Egypt and Israel and witnessed by the United States on 3 August 1981. The Protocol provided that the provisions of the Treaty which relate to the establishment, functions, and responsibilities of the UN Forces and Observers shall apply *mutatis mutandis* to the establishment, functions, and responsibilities of the MFO as provided in the Protocol.[9]

The MFO began its work in Egypt and Israel on 25 April 1982.[10] It has carried out its mission, which is fundamentally a mission of observing and reporting to the

Parties, continuously since that time. The peace between Egypt and Israel has been maintained and the MFO continues to enjoy the strong support of both Parties. It must be regarded as an ongoing success story within the specialized niche in which it operates.[11]

This background is of assistance in understanding the adaptations that the MFO incorporates or has adopted, the challenges that it has faced and continues to face, and the ongoing adaptation process that is underway there.

There are a number of noteworthy institutional features of the MFO, some of them 'constitutional', in the sense that they have their origin in the constituent agreements that created the organization, and some that were developed over time in the practice of the organization.

One unusual feature of this peacekeeping organization, already noted, has to do with the manner of its establishment. It was established by Egypt and Israel to carry out a mission in those countries. Their status as the only Parties to the Protocol that created the MFO is significant in two respects.

First, it establishes the clear, direct and fundamental responsibility of the MFO to each of the Parties. This is unusual for a peacekeeping organization and has a defining character in respect of the relationship between the organization and the States in which it operates.

Second, it provides Egypt and Israel with a common role *vis-à-vis* the MFO. Each plays an equal part in overseeing the performance of the MFO, for example, in reviewing its budget and management. Each sits as a member of a 'Board of Directors', providing guidance to the organization. The exercise by each State of this common role itself creates opportunities for interaction between the two States. That interaction, in turn, serves to reinforce the undertakings of each State in the Treaty of Peace.

One of the defining characteristics of an international institution is its 'membership', although it is clear that not all international organizations are membership organizations in the traditional sense. In the case of the MFO, there are several distinct types of State involvement. The status of Egypt and Israel as the sole Parties to the Protocol creating it is one type.

A second type is related to the unusual arrangement established for bearing the expenses of the organization. The Protocol provides that '[t]he expenses of the MFO which are not covered by other sources shall be borne equally by the Parties'.[12] In two exchanges of letters dated the same date as the Protocol between US Secretary of State Haig and Foreign Ministers Ali and Shamir, respectively, Secretary Haig wrote that: 'subject to Congressional authorization and appropriations, ... [t]he United States will contribute one-third of the annual operating expenses of the MFO' (except during the initial period in which there would be exceptional costs connected with the establishment of the MFO, during which the United States agreed to provide three/fifths of the cost).[13] Accordingly, this second type of State involvement, known in MFO parlance as Funds Contributing States, is shared by Egypt, Israel, and the United States.

The 'Funds Contributing States' are not, however, the only States that provide funding to the MFO. There is a third category of States known as 'Donor States', for States that make annual voluntary contributions of lesser amounts than the Funds Contributing States. Germany, Switzerland and Japan are each Donor States at present and have been for a number of years.[14]

Finally, one cannot have a peacekeeping force without peacekeepers. Currently, the 11 troop-contributing countries that provide military contingents that combine to total the 1686 (as of 4 October 2004) military peacekeepers of the MFO are Australia, Canada, Colombia, Fiji, France, Hungary, Italy, New Zealand, Norway, Uruguay, and the United States.[15] The United Kingdom and the Netherlands also provided contingents for a number of years. For the soldiers of the MFO, the peacekeeping experience is truly a multinational one. The soldiers of the MFO eat together in a Multinational Dining Facility, live together at the two main camps, and work together, in some cases in mixed units, In addition to the military component of the MFO, there are 15 civilian observers as well as other civilian employees, including both international and locally-hired staff.[16] There are also Egyptian personnel supplied by an Egyptian contractor. The civilian functions at the MFO are interesting and important, and they are discussed below.

The leadership of the MFO is provided for in the Protocol. The Parties are to appoint a Director-General 'who shall be responsible for the direction of the MFO'.[17] The Director-General 'shall, subject to the approval of the Parties, appoint a Commander, the Force Commander, who shall be responsible for the daily command of the MFO'.[18] The Annex to the Protocol provides that the Director-General 'shall be responsible for the direction of the MFO in the fulfilment of its functions' and authorizes him to take certain actions of a general nature to this end.[19] Subject to the authorization of the Parties, the Director-General is also authorized to negotiate and enter into agreements with troop contributing nations.[20] The Appendix to the Annex contemplates the appointment of a Deputy Director-General.[21]

The Annex expressly provides that the Director-General shall report to the Parties on developments relating to the functioning of the MFO.[22] He may raise with either or both Parties, as appropriate, any matter concerning the functioning of the MFO.[23] The Annex further provides that Egypt and Israel shall designate senior responsible officials as agreed points of contact for the Director-General.[24]

The Exchange of Letters between Secretary of State Haig and Foreign Ministers Ali and Shamir reflects an agreement that the post of Director-General will be held by US nationals suggested by the United States.[25]

The Annex provides that the Force Commander will be an officer of general rank who shall not be of the same nationality as the Director-General.[26] So far, there have been Force Commanders from Australia, Canada, Italy, the Netherlands, New Zealand, and Norway. Subject to the authority of the Director-General, the Force Commander has full command authority over the MFO and is to promulgate the Standing Operating Procedures.[27] The Annex provides that the Force Commander shall establish a chain of command for the MFO linked to the commanders of the national contingents made available by contributing nations. The members of the MFO, although remaining in their national contingents, are, during their period of assignment to the MFO, under the Director-General and subject to the authority of the Force Commander through the chain of command.[28]

The Force Commander has general responsibility for the good order of the MFO and the authority to repatriate any member, including the contingent commander, of any military contingent. The responsibility for conventional disciplinary action in national contingents rests with the commanders of the national contingents.[29] The Director-General and the Force Commander insist on the maintenance of high standards within the national contingents, however, and in an appropriate case will work with the responsible authorities back in the respective country to address the rare systematic or significant discipline issue within a national contingent at the MFO.

The experience of the MFO suggests that the combination of the responsibility for direction of the organization provided by the Director-General and the responsibility for the daily operation provided by the Force Commander provides an effective senior management structure for an independent international peacekeeping operation.

In contrast to the first tier, the second tier of leadership in the MFO has no basis in the various foundational agreements establishing and elaborating on the nature of the MFO, but rather was an innovation in practice. This tier is composed of the Director-General's Representatives – in Cairo and Tel Aviv. The individuals in these positions serve as senior political representatives of the Director-General in the capitals of the Parties.[30] They represent the Director-General in political matters relating to the MFO and advise the Director-General concerning developments in the respective State affecting the MFO. They have additional responsibilities in such areas as security and force protection and administration.[31] They also supervise the local procurement activities in Cairo and Tel Aviv, which are discussed below.

The next point is, strictly speaking, not about the MFO at all but rather about the highly successful manner in which the Party States have chosen to organize themselves to deal with issues relating to the Treaty of Peace and the MFO. Annex I to the Treaty of Peace provides for the establishment of a liaison system between the Parties. According to Annex I, the liaison system

> 'is intended to provide an effective method to assess progress in the implementation of obligations under the present Annex and to resolve any problem that may arise in the course of implementation, and refer other unresolved matters to the higher military authorities of the two countries respectively for consideration. It is also intended to prevent situations resulting from errors or misinterpretation on the part of either Party.'[32]

The Annex to the Protocol defines the function of the liaison system in the context of the operation of the MFO, and provides that the Force Commander and the chiefs of the respective liaison offices will have access to one another in their respective offices.[33]

In practice, the interactions of the Liaison Office of the MFO and the Force Commander with the respective liaison entities of the Parties, the Arab Republic of Egypt's Liaison Agency With International Organizations (LAWIO) and the Israel Defense Forces Liaison and Foreign Relations Division (IDFLFRD), and their chiefs, have been on-going, substantive and constructive. In his 2004 Trilateral Report, the Director-General wrote that one of the key areas for his attention would be 'nurturing the highly effective Liaison System between the Parties, with the MFO at its center using our 'best efforts' to facilitate their work and communications, and helping them to manage and resolve issues that arise.'[34] He noted that he believed that the totality of contacts among the liaison systems and the Force Commander and their Chiefs, 'are key to the success of the MFO mission'.[35]

The MFO puts so much stock in the liaison officers and the liaison system for two reasons. First, because the MFO sees its role as not only to ensure that small problems do not become big, that is, political, problems, but also to create a system in which the small problems will disappear because they will be resolved. Second, because the MFO understands that, while its military deployments and limitations on the Parties keep the two sides apart, its liaison system works to build bridges between the Parties to bring them closer together.

If one were creating anew an independent international peacekeeping organization, one might wish to give careful consideration to establishing a liaison network along the lines of that which has functioned effectively in the context of the MFO.

An additional structural feature of the MFO is the Civilian Observer Unit, which is the 'Observer' component of the Multinational Force and Observers. The original concept of the role of the observers in Annex I to the Treaty of Peace was that the arrangements described for the UN forces and observers for each zone would be implemented in Zones A, B and C (the zones in Egypt) by the United Nations Force and in Zone D (in Israel) by the United Nations Observers.[36] This concept evolved over time, however, and this provision from Annex I was not included in the Protocol or its Annex. As reflected in the 2004 Trilateral Report, the Civilian Observer Unit carries out reconnaissance and verification missions in all four Treaty Zones.[37]

The composition of the Civilian Observer Unit is of interest. The Exchange of Letters between Secretary of State Haig and Foreign Ministers Ali and Shamir states that, 'subject to Congressional authorization and appropriations, ... [t]he United States ... will provide a group of civilian observers to the MFO'.[38] As noted in the 2004 Trilateral Report, in practice, half of the members of the Unit are seconded from the US Department of State, including the Chief; the other half are retired US military personnel recruited directly by the MFO.[39]

The composition of the Civilian Observer Unit is another aspect, in addition to the status of the United States as a non-Party Funds Contributing State and its contribution of the largest national contingent to the Force, of the unique relationship of the United States to the MFO, a relationship that has existed from the organization's outset.

There are a couple of other aspects of the civilian function at the MFO, neither of them 'constitutional', that should be noted.

Certain functions within the MFO, including, for example, the legal and accounting functions, are completely civilianized and operate in accordance with relevant professional standards. The Headquarters staff in Rome is entirely civilian. Other functions, including engineering and contracting in the Sinai, are mixed civilian/military functions, in which the civilian employees, sometimes ex-military, provide both their own expertise and also continuity and institutional memory.

In its support-side functions, including, for example, procurement and contracting for services, the MFO operates, to the extent possible, like a commercial entity. In the procurement area, for example, MFO offices in Cairo and Tel Aviv, as well as those in Rome and the Sinai, seek on an on-going basis to find new and less expensive sources for needed items, including, in particular, in the economies of the Parties. According to the Director-General's 2004 Trilateral Report,

> 'DGR office and Sinai procurement staffs have aggressively gone out to the local market and obtained favorable prices from both established and new vendors for products and services, thus reducing the procurement of offshore products. All procurement is undertaken on an open

competition basis, the objective being to obtain the best possible price with no loss of quality to the Force. The Procurement process is apolitical and market-driven. Because of the fluctuations within the market place and in the economies of both countries, regionally placed business routinely shifts back and forth.'[40]

The Report specifically notes the 'large volume in disbursements in Egypt and Israel, ... includ[ing] official MFO and Morale Support Program spending' and also makes reference to 'the considerable personal spending of the MFO members in both countries'.[41]

The management of the procurement function of the MFO in an apolitical manner that produces cost savings for the MFO while generating revenue for local businesses in the Party States is a significant and effective feature of the organization.

Finally under the heading of noteworthy institutional features of the MFO, it is relevant to note that the observations and reports of the MFO relating to its operations are non-public. While some information about the organization is on its web site and other information can be gleaned from published sources, at the heart of its mission is what its members observe and what they report exclusively to the Parties concerning those observations. Similarly, its interactions with the Parties concerning its operations are not made public.

It is the experience of the MFO that such discretion has enhanced its ability to perform its mission.

Throughout its existence and into the present, the MFO has faced and continues to face a number of challenges.

One challenge that the MFO has in common with virtually all peacekeeping organizations and some other sorts of organizations, for example, *ad hoc* international tribunals, as well, is that they are intended to be temporary. Long-term planning and the adoption of policies that are more costly in the short-term but will pay off in the long-term are inherently difficult when the tenure of the organization is limited and uncertain. In the case of the MFO, the most relevant 'constitutional' provision regarding its duration is the Protocol provision that '[t]he two Parties may consider the possibility of replacing the arrangements hereby established with alternative arrangements by mutual agreement.'[42] At present, support of the Parties for the MFO is strong and there has even been speculation in some quarters concerning the provision of additional functions to the MFO. The point remains, however, that the organization must be assumed, by its nature, to be a temporary one.

A second issue, again shared broadly with other peacekeeping organizations, is the frequent turnover of MFO members, especially military personnel. As a general matter, the military personnel of the Force spend periods of six or twelve months, sometimes fewer, in the Sinai. The entire military component, excluding the Force Commander but including his senior military staff, turns over at least annually. Preserving continuity and ensuring best practices in the face of such turnover is a difficult task, and one to which the MFO devotes a great deal of attention. The use of civilian personnel in appropriate positions, noted above, is one key means of ameliorating the negative aspects of frequent military turnover.

A third challenge for the MFO and for other peacekeeping organizations, related to the problem of frequent turnover, is effective training. For the MFO, training is not a one-time exercise but a process that begins 'pre-deployment', before troops or other personnel are deployed to the Sinai, continues with 'deployment orientation and training' at the time of arrival in the Sinai, and then remains on-going with 'post-deployment skill maintenance' training throughout the period of deployment. This brief description of the general training sequence does not begin to capture the unique and comprehensive training process for the civilian observer unit, which occupies most observers for months after their initial arrival at MFO Sinai.

A fourth challenge, a function of the fact that the MFO is deployed not only at two main base camps in Zone C in the Sinai but also at 28 (as of 11 October 2004)[43] remote sites in Zone C, is the difficult operating and supply environment. It is, for example, a technical challenge to install, operate, maintain and manage a sophisticated telecommunications and computer system among more than twenty sites, many of which are in still relatively undeveloped areas. Phones and computers are not the only issues, of course. Many locations require the delivery of water and food, the use and maintenance of electric power generators, and, in some cases, the presence of MFO personnel and vehicles to clear roads of sand.

A fifth challenge, perhaps related to the previous one, is recruiting qualified individuals for the key civilian positions at the Force, and then retaining them. Most of the positions are unaccompanied, no children are permitted in any case, and the living conditions have been described as primitive and the housing small. Although the Sinai is magnificent and the MFO facilities are excellent, the MFO is not for everybody. It is a tribute to the personnel department that, notwithstanding the main camp's isolated location and other challenges, the MFO has successfully recruited and retained highly professional accountants, communications and computer managers, a force exchange manager, a force counsel, and many others. But here, too, there can be a fair amount of turnover, and, unlike in the case of the military rotations, there is no successor unless the MFO recruits one.

The last challenge, of course, is paying for it all. An independent international peacekeeping organization, especially one that has been at its mission successfully for over twenty years and does not seek publicity, runs the danger of being overlooked or underfunded in favor of more visible alternatives. The MFO has had tremendous and continuing support from many States from its inception: Egypt and Israel, the United States, the Donor States, and the troop-contributing States. This stability of support is one of its greatest strengths. At the same time, the MFO has to continually defend its cost-effectiveness and its needs. For 11 consecutive years, the MFO budget has stayed the same. This is a testament to its strong management as well as the rigorous accountability to which it is subjected.

It is appropriate to consider how the concept of international institutional reform applies in the case of an organization like the MFO.

In the first place, of course, the adaptations noted above are themselves a kind of reform, in that they reflect the creation of new structures and processes, in some cases unique to the MFO, to adapt the MFO to the particular challenges posed by its circumstances and its mandate.[44]

In the second place, the challenges that were noted above over time have led the MFO to undertake 'reforms' in its way of doing business. The challenge of frequent turnover has led to new approaches to training, for example, and the challenge of increasing budgets and stable funding has led to innovations in procurement.

Finally, there is a third kind of reform that can be conceptualized: the on-going process by which the MFO adapts itself to changing circumstances. In some cases, this involves changing the way that it performs its mission, for example, by adjusting the number of remote sites that it operates, or the responsibilities of a particular contingent. In other cases, it involves improving the efficiency of operations, for example, by adopting innovations in the way that it supplies and transports its personnel. In still other cases, it involves adopting new procedures or even taking on new mandates in response to requests from the Parties.

'Reforms' of all these types have been achievable over the history of the MFO, under the direction of the Director-General and the command authority of the Force Commander, and with the support of the Parties and the other Funds Contributing, troop-contributing and Donor States.

My final observation returns to my initial point, concerning the diversity of international institutions. That diversity is, of course, itself a function of the diversity of the international system and, more specifically, in the peacekeeping context, the diversity of the situations in which international peacekeeping forces and observers may be required. It has become increasingly clear over time that peacekeeping is not a one-size-fits-all enterprise. In one particular context, at least, the MFO has been highly successful. It may well be that its adaptations of the sort set forth above may be useful to other States in other contexts, as suggestions of a kind of 'reform' – or as a model of a form of institution – that may be appropriate in those contexts as well.

## Notes

1 See, e.g., United Nations, *The Blue Helmets: A Review of UN Peacekeeping* (1996) at pp. 15-32 (UNTSO), pp. 33-55 (UNEF I), pp. 57-70 (UNEF II). See also D.W. Bowett, *United Nations Forces, A Legal Study* (1964).

2 Treaty of Peace Between the Arab Republic of Egypt and the State of Israel, Art. IV, para. 1.

3 Annex I to the Treaty of Peace, Protocol Concerning Israeli Withdrawal and Security Arrangements, Art. VI, para. 1.

4 Id., Art. VI, para. 2.

5 Id., Art. VI, para. 8.

6 Agreed Minutes to Arts. I, IV, V and VI and Annexes I and III of the Treaty of Peace, provision relating to Annex I.

7 Letters from President Carter to President Sadat and Prime Minister Begin, 26 March 1979.

8 See, e.g., Protocol, 3 August 1981, preamble.

9 Protocol, 3 August 1981, para. 2.

10 See, e.g., Annual Report of the Director-General, Multinational Force and Observers, 25 April 1984, Director-General's Foreward.

11 See generally, Director-General's Report, 2004 Trilateral Meeting, 11 October 2004, hereinafter '2004 Trilateral Report'. For additional information about the MFO, see the MFO's web site: <www.mfo.org>.

12 Protocol, 3 August 1981, para. 7.

13 Exchange of Letters Between Secretary of State Haig and Foreign Ministers Ali and Shamir, 3 August 1981, paras. 3, 3B, hereinafter 'Exchange of Letters'.

14 2004 Trilateral Report at p. 37.

15 Id. at p. 5.

16 See, e.g., Director-General's Report, 2003 Trilateral Meeting, 20 October 2003, at p. 4.

17 Protocol, 3 August 1981, para. 6.

18 Id.

19 Annex to the Protocol, para. 2.

[20] Id., para. 3.
[21] Appendix to the Annex to the Protocol, para. 25.
[22] Annex to the Protocol, para. 4.
[23] Id.
[24] Id.
[25] Exchange of Letters, para. 1.
[26] Annex to the Protocol, para. 5.
[27] Id., para. 6.
[28] Id.
[29] Id., para. 7.
[30] MFO Policy and Administrative Manual, Vol. 2, section 203 (Revised 2004).
[31] Id.
[32] Annex I to the Treaty of Peace, Art. VII, para. 1
[33] Annex to the Protocol, paras. 31, 32.
[34] 2004 Trilateral Report at p. 1.
[35] Id. at p. 14.
[36] Annex I to the Treaty of Peace, Art. VI, para. 3.
[37] 2004 Trilateral Report at p. 8.
[38] Exchange of Letters, paras. 3, 3A.
[39] See *supra* n. 37.
[40] Id., at p. 25.
[41] Id.
[42] Protocol, 3 August 1981, para. 1.
[43] See *supra* n. 37, at p. 9.
[44] See, e.g., Siekmann, 'The Multinational Peace-Keeping Force in the Sinai in the Light of United Nations Practice on Peace-Keeping Forces', 24 *Indian Journal of International Law* (1984), p. 504.

## Remarks by Rebecca Everly*

### Judicial Review[1] of High Representative Decisions by Institutions in Bosnia and Herzegovina

The 'High Representative' is the chief international official responsible for civilian aspects of peacebuilding in post-war Bosnia and Herzegovina (BiH). Deriving his authority from an Annex to the General Framework Agreement for Peace in BiH (the Dayton Agreement)[2] and a Chapter VII Security Council Resolution,[3] the High Representative is formally tasked with monitoring the peacebuilding efforts of domestic authorities and coordinating the activities of other international actors operating in BiH. The institution that has grown around the High Representative, the 'Office of the High Representative' (OHR), was established after the signing of the Dayton Agreement in order to assist with the implementation of the High Representative's mandate.

Unlike the UN Interim Administration Mission in Kosovo and the UN Transitional Administration in East Timor, both of which were established as temporary administrations in their respective host territories, the OHR was not originally intended to play a governmental role in BiH. Rather, the High Representative and his office

* Trinity College, Cambridge University. I wish to thank Chris Harland for his helpful comments on this article.

were simply intended to facilitate and support the post-war transition process, leaving domestic actors with responsibility for exercising public or governmental power. However, over time and in response to perceived intransigence by local actors, the High Representative has interpreted his mandate in an increasingly robust manner and now plays a quasi-governmental role in BiH alongside domestic authorities.

Since late 1997, the High Representative has issued over six hundred decisions with binding legal effect in BiH. These decisions have been used, *inter alia*, to enact legislation and other legal instruments, as well as to amend/repeal legal instruments adopted by domestic authorities. They have also been used to suspend/remove individuals from public office and party positions in BiH, to freeze the financial assets of individuals suspected of aiding persons indicted by the International Criminal Tribunal for the former Yugoslavia, and to reallocate public funds originally intended for political parties. The High Representative's robust interpretation of his mandate has been supported by both the Security Council[4] and by the Peace Implementation Council (PIC), a political body composed of over fifty states and agencies which provides political guidance to the High Representative. In December of 1997, the PIC issued written conclusions to a conference held in Bonn, in which it welcomed the High Representative's intention to make binding decisions as he judges necessary in order to facilitate the resolution of difficulties in BiH.[5] These conclusions are cited by the High Representative in the preamble to both his legislative and non-legislative decisions.

As an international actor performing a quasi-governmental role in BiH, the High Representative presents an interesting problem for international lawyers: whether and to what extent the public/governmental conduct of international actors should be subject to judicial review within their host states. While international actors often operate outside the scrutiny of judicial bodies in host states, it is common for public/governmental institutions to allow their conduct to be reviewed by judicial bodies in the territories where they function (e.g., through administrative disputes, constitutional challenges and actions before human rights institutions). In this respect, the international *status* of the High Representative and his public *function* seem to pull in different directions. The following seeks to contribute to a discussion of this issue by providing an overview of the novel approach that judicial institutions in BiH have taken concerning review of High Representative decisions. It focuses in particular on the jurisprudence of the Constitutional Court of BiH (Court) and the Human Rights Chamber for BiH (Chamber).

Both the Court and the Chamber were established in Annexes to the Dayton Agreement.[6] The former has exclusive jurisdiction to decide any dispute that arises under the Constitution of BiH between the two sub-State Entities in BiH (the Federation of BiH and Republika Srpska); between BiH and an Entity or Entities and between institutions of BiH. The Court also has appellate jurisdiction over constitutional issues arising out of a judgment of any other court in BiH and jurisdiction

> 'over issues referred by any court in Bosnia and Herzegovina concerning whether a law, on whose validity its decision depends, is compatible with (the) Constitution, with the European Convention for Human Rights and Fundamental Freedoms and its Protocols, or with the laws of Bosnia and Herzegovina; or concerning the existence of or the scope of a general rule of public international law pertinent to the court's decision'.[7]

The Court has nine members, six of whom are from Bosnia and Herzegovina. The remaining members are from outside the region, and are selected by the President of the European Court of Human Rights.

The Chamber, which operated until the end of 2003 (when it was succeeded by a Human Rights Commission operating within the Court), had jurisdiction to consider alleged or apparent violations of human rights by the State of BiH, the Federation and Republika Srpska.[8] Like the Court, the Chamber was composed of both local and international members. Of the Chamber's 14 total members, eight individuals were appointed from outside of the region by the Committee of Ministers of the Council of Europe.

## Obstacles to Judicial Review

The High Representative and the OHR are largely insulated from the scrutiny of judicial bodies in BiH by virtue of Annex 10 to the Dayton Agreement, which provides the High Representative and members of his staff with wide immunity.[9] Moreover, both the Court and the Chamber have ruled inadmissible on jurisdictional grounds a number of cases challenging the High Representative's decisions.[10] An example is the Chamber's 1998 decision in *Dragan Čavić against Bosnia and Herzegovina,* which involves a High Representative decision removing an individual from public office.[11] Although the removal decision was not taken in conjunction with local authorities in BiH and did not require further action by such authorities, the applicant argued that BiH should be held responsible for the removal (which he claimed to be in excess of the High Representative's authority and in violation of various human rights guarantees).

The Chamber declared the application inadmissible, deciding that it did not have jurisdiction *ratione personae* over the High Representative and that the removal could not be said to come within the responsibility of BiH for the purpose of invoking the Chamber's jurisdiction. Specifically, the Chamber observed that:

> '(I)t is beyond doubt that the actions of the High Representative are not subject to any review in relation to the carrying out of his functions under the General Framework Agreement. For this to be the case, the General Framework Agreement would have to provide specifically for any such review…
>
> The actions complained of were carried out by the High Representative in the performance of his functions under the General Framework Agreement, as interpreted by the Bonn Peace Implementation Conference. There is no provision for any intervention by the respondent Party (or by any of the other Parties to the General Framework Agreement) in those actions. In addition, the High Representative cannot be said to be acting as, or on behalf of, the State or the Entities when acting in pursuance of his powers.
> As a result, the actions giving rise to the present application cannot be considered to be within the scope of responsibility of the respondent Party.'[12]

The Chamber has been faced with a number of similar cases, in which applicants have variously argued that High Representative removals are in violation of international due process standards,[13] the right to work,[14] the right to an effective remedy for a violation of rights,[15] the right of access to public service,[16] and internal OHR guidance on removals and suspensions.[17] In a case brought by an individual removed by the High Representative from the position of Minister of Finance of the Federation of BiH, the applicant sought to highlight the danger associated with unregulated High Representative power and argued that:

> '... if there is no recourse to the actions of the High Representative for violations of human rights and fundamental freedoms, then the protection of fundamental human tenets, on which a free democratic society is based, is meaningless.'[18]

Nonetheless, in each of these cases, the Chamber has reiterated that it does not have jurisdiction *ratione personae* over the High Representative, and has refused to hold domestic authorities responsible for High Representative-issued removal decisions.

The Constitutional Court has taken a similar approach, and has repeatedly stated that it is not competent to review the international powers of the High Representative or the exercise of those powers.[19] For instance, in March of 2001, several members of the House of Representatives of the Federation Parliament brought a case before the Court concerning the High Representative's removal of an individual from the directorship of a public company in BiH. The applicants challenged the ability of the High Representative to take the removal decision, and argued that the substance of the decision violated the Constitution of BiH and various provisions of the European Convention for the Protection of Human Rights and Fundamental Freedoms incorporated therein. The Court ruled, *inter alia*, that it is not competent to review High Representative decisions removing public officials.[20]

Moreover, the Court's reluctance to review High Representative decisions has not been limited to decisions removing public officials. In 2004, the Court also refused to review the constitutionality of a High Representative decision tying the two sub-State Entities in BiH into final and binding arbitration concerning the delineation of the inter-Entity boundary line.[21]

## Judicial Review of Legislative Decisions

Despite the general reluctance of the Chamber and the Court to review decisions issued by the High Representative, both bodies have carved out an exception with respect to the High Representative's 'legislative' decisions. In other words, where they have been faced with challenges to High Representative decisions enacting legislation/amendments and challenges concerning the implementation by local authorities of High Representative enacted legislation/amendments, the Chamber and the Court have treated these legal instruments as part of the domestic law of BiH and reviewed them accordingly.

The Court first took this position in a case involving a challenge to a High Representative-issued law creating a BiH border service. In deciding to review the law for conformity with the Constitution, the Court noted that the role of the High Representative is characterized by a 'functional duality.[22] That is to say, the High Representative is an international actor who is empowered to substitute for BiH domestic authorities. The Court noted that:

> 'the High Representative – whose powers under Annex 10 to the General Framework Agreement, the relevant resolutions of the Security Council and the Bonn Declaration as well as his exercise of those powers are not subject to review by the Constitutional Court – intervened in the legal order of Bosnia and Herzegovina substituting himself for the national authorities. In this respect, he therefore acted as an authority of Bosnia and Herzegovina and the law which he enacted is in the nature of a national law and must be regarded as a law of Bosnia and Herzegovina.'[23]

Thus, while the Court has not questioned the High Representative's competence to take decisions with the force of law in BiH or the legality of doing so in individual cases, it has attributed High Representative enacted legislation to local authorities for the purpose of reviewing its constitutionality. On this basis, the Court has reviewed a High Representative enacted law creating the State Court of BiH,[24] as well as legislative amendments involving residential property privatization[25] and BiH travel documents.[26] The Court has also reviewed legislation originally enacted by the High Representative but subsequently adopted in identical text by domestic authorities (e.g., public broadcasting legislation[27] and legislation concerning the immunity of public officials).[28] In none of these cases has the Court found legislation/amendments enacted by the High Representative to be in violation of the BiH Constitution.

Similarly, the Chamber has been willing to review actions taken by domestic authorities for the purpose of implementing High Representative enacted legislation/amendments, including amendments to the election law in BiH,[29] amendments to legislation concerning the Commission for Real Property Claims of Displaced Persons and Refugees[30] and amendments concerning repossession of apartments in BiH by former members of the Yugoslav National Army.[31] In some cases, the Chamber has found High Representative enacted legislation/amendments to be consistent with international human rights norms, but has nevertheless found a human rights violation due to the manner in which domestic authorities have implemented such legislation/amendments.[32] However, in at least one instance, the Chamber has found High Representative enacted amendments themselves to be in violation of human rights guarantees and ordered remedial action.[33]

Finally, the High Representative has suggested on several occasions that the European Court of Human Rights may review his legislative decisions once the possibility of local remedies has been exhausted.[34] Any such cases would of course need to be brought against Bosnia and Herzegovina as a party to the European Convention for the Protection of Human Rights and Fundamental Freedoms. Yet, it remains to be seen what the ECHR would do when faced with this question, as it has not yet issued judgment in a case involving a High Representative decision.[35]

## Analysis and Conclusion

An understanding of the peculiar brand of judicial review that has emerged in connection with the High Representative in BiH is important background for anyone seeking to assess the latter's overall accountability. As discussed above, both the Court and the Chamber have developed a mechanism for reviewing certain High Representative decisions despite the fact that their constituent instruments do not explicitly give them competence to do so. Their willingness to creatively interpret their mandates in this regard has softened the potentially blunt impact of the High Representative's immunity within the BiH judicial system.

That said, it is important to be aware of the limits of this novel type of judicial review. As discussed above, neither the Court nor the Chamber has yet questioned the High Representative's interpretation of his powers or his ability to exercise those powers in specific cases. As a result, the High Representative and his office have had broad discretion to determine the nature and scope of actions that they may take in furtherance of the BiH peace implementation process. This is doubly the case given that, to date, no international judicial institution has sought to review the High Representative's interpretation of his mandate. Moreover, as discussed above, neither the Court nor the Chamber has yet directly reviewed non-legislative decisions issued by the High Representative (e.g., decisions removing public officials, decisions freezing financial assets).

These limits on the judicial review of High Representative decisions can be attributed to a variety of factors. First, although the High Representative and the OHR are by no means the first international actors to exercise governmental responsibilities, the relative novelty of international administrations means that there is not yet an established, accepted theory of judicial review in this context. Second, as noted, the High Representative was not originally intended to issue legislation and other binding legal decisions in BiH. It is therefore unsurprising that little thought was given during the Dayton peace talks to circumscribing the High Representative's immunity or granting judicial bodies in BiH a clear mandate to review High Representative decisions. In the absence of such a mandate, the Chamber and the Court have only reviewed High Representative decisions where they have been able to attribute the latter to domestic authorities.

Finally, the High Representative and his office have made clear that they are opposed to more robust judicial review of the High Representative's conduct by judicial bodies in BiH.[36] They have consistently maintained that the High Representative issues certain non-legislative decisions under his 'international powers', and that these decisions are non-justiciable. Indeed, such decisions often contain detailed language to this effect.[37] The High Representative/OHR's position on this issue indicates a concern regarding the possible consequences of allowing judicial bodies in BiH to second-guess international actors. While the desire to avoid the scrutiny of host state judicial bodies is shared by many international institutions, it may be compounded in the OHR context by a fear that judicial review of High Representative decisions could slow or stymie the peace implementation process.

However, acknowledging that there are obstacles to the robust judicial review of international administrations such as the OHR does not lead one to the inexorable conclusion that the limited mechanisms of review that have emerged in BiH are sufficient from an accountability perspective. In particular, there is a conceptual difficulty with using the legislative/non-legislative distinction as a basis for determining whether a particular High Representative decision may be subject to judicial review, given that both types of decisions produce legal effects and have the potential to violate the rights of individuals within BiH. It is also important to recognize the dangers inherent in subjecting only certain categories of international decisions to judicial review while, at the same time, giving the international decision-maker discretion to categorize his own decisions. The type of leeway that the High Representative enjoys in this regard is certainly at odds with the notion of accountability as it has been developed in more traditional governmental contexts.

An extensive discussion of the possible mechanisms for enhancing the judicial review of OHR and other international administrations is well beyond the scope of the present article. Certainly, narrowing the immunity granted to such administrations and formally expanding the jurisdiction of host state judicial bodies is one option that could be pursued in this context. Another option, which could be used alone or in conjunction with expanded host state judicial review, is the establishment of a *sui generis* international judicial institution with competence to review an administration's compliance with its mandate and/or the substance of administration decisions. This option may be preferred by those concerned about the consequences of host state judicial review in the context of international administrations. It could also be useful in cases where functioning judicial bodies do not exist within the host state, perhaps due to a general breakdown in societal institutions. A further possibility is to expand the jurisdiction of existing international judicial bodies, so as to permit them to hear claims against international institutions such as the OHR.

In light of the robust use made of international administrations in recent years and the frequent calls for establishment of such administrations in conflict and post-conflict settings, there is a need for further research on judicial review in this context. Any prescriptions for enhancing judicial review that emerge from such research should take into account the differences among international administrations, including the different legal standards that govern these administrations and the varied contextual circumstances in which they are deployed. Such prescriptions should also take into account the dual (international/domestic) function played by international administrations and the consequent need to provide for their accountability to both the governed population and the wider international community.

## Notes

1 For the purpose of this article, the term 'judicial review' is used in the broad sense to denote the review of legislative and executive acts of the High Representative.

2 Agreement on Civilian Implementation of the Peace Settlement, Annex 10, General Framework Agreement for Peace in Bosnia and Herzegovina (1995) in: Office of the High Representative (2000) Bosnia and Herzegovina: Essential Texts. 3rd edn., pp. 56-57 (Sarajevo). The General Framework Agreement (Dayton Agreement) was initialed in Dayton on 21 November 1995 and signed in Paris on 14 December 1995.

3 UN Security Council, 3607th meeting, Resolution 1031, S/RES/1031. 15 December 1995. Subsequent Security Council Resolutions have agreed the designation of individuals for the position of High Representative. See, e.g., UN Security Council, 3787th meeting, Resolution 1112, S/RES/1112. 12 June 1997, para. 1 and UN Security Council, 4030th meeting, Resolution 1256, S/RES/1256. 3 August 1999, para. 1.

4 See, e.g., UN Security Council, 3892nd meeting, Resolution 1174, S/RES/1174. 15 June 1998, para. 4 and UN Security Council, 4014th meeting, Resolution 1247, S/RES/1247. 18 June 1999, para. 4.

5 Summary of Conclusions, Bonn Peace Implementation Conference, December 10, 1997, Article XI(2) in: Office of the High Representative (2000) Bosnia and Herzegovina: Essential Texts. 3rd edn., pp. 199 (Sarajevo).

6 Respectively, Annexes 4 and 6 to the Agreement.

7 Constitution of Bosnia and Herzegovina, Annex 4, General Framework Agreement for Peace in Bosnia and Herzegovina (1995), Article VI(3) in: Office of the High Representative (2000) Bosnia and Herzegovina: Essential Texts. 3rd edn., pp. 41-46 (Sarajevo).

8 Agreement on Human Rights, Annex 6, General Framework Agreement for Peace in Bosnia and Herzegovina (1995), Chapter Two, Articles II and VIII in: Office of the High Representative (2000) Bosnia and Herzegovina: Essential Texts. 3rd edn., pp. 47-50 (Sarajevo). For a commentary on the Chamber's jurispru-

dence, see Christopher Harland, Ralph Roche, and Ekkehard Strauss (2003) A Commentary to the European Convention on Human Rights as Applied in Bosnia and Herzegovina and at Strasbourg (Sarajevo).

[9] Agreement on Civilian Implementation of the Peace Settlement, Annex 10, General Framework Agreement for Peace in Bosnia and Herzegovina (1995), Article III(4).

[10] The Court and the Chamber have taken a similar hands-off approach to other international institutions and to mixed local/international institutions envisaged in the Dayton Agreement. For relevant Chamber jurisprudence, see, e.g., Human Rights Chamber, Case No CH/98/230, *Adnan Suljanović* and Case No. CH/98/231 *Edita Čišić and Asim Lelić against the State of Bosnia and Herzegovina and Republika Srpska* (decision on admissibility of 14 May 1998) (concerning actions of the Organization for Security and Co-operation in Europe, as well as the actions of bodies directly and indirectly established by this organization). For relevant jurisprudence of the Court, see, e.g., Constitutional Court of BiH, U 32/01, 22 June 2001, website of the Constitutional Court of Bosnia and Herzegovina, Decisions by Year of Adoption, 2001, <http://www.ccbh.ba/?lang=en&page=decisions/byyear/2001>, visited on 1 April 2005 (concerning decisions of the Commission for Real Property Claims of Displaced Persons and Refugees) and Constitutional Court of BiH, U 40/00, 2 February 2001, website of the Constitutional Court of BiH, Decisions by Year of Adoption, 2001, <http://www.ccbh.ba/?lang=en&page=decisions/byyear/2001>, visited on 1 April 2005 (concerning actions of the Provisional Election Commission).

[11] Human Rights Chamber, Case No. CH/98/1266, *Dragan Čavić against Bosnia and Herzegovina* (decision on admissibility of 18 December 1998).

[12] See *supra* n. 11, paras. 18-19.

[13] Human Rights Chamber, Case No. CH/02/12466, *Nikola Grabovac against Bosnia and Herzegovina and the Federation of Bosnia and Herzegovina* (decision on admissibility of 1 April 2003), para. 7.

[14] Human Rights Chamber, Case No. CH/02/12457, *Munir Alibabić against Bosnia and Herzegovina and the High Representative* (decision on admissibility of 2 April 2003), para. 6 and Human Rights Chamber, Cases No. CH/00/4027 and CH/00/4074, *Municipal Council of the Municipality South-West Mostar against the High Representative* (decision on admissibility of 9 March 2000), para. 4.

[15] See *supra* n. 13, para. 9.

[16] *Idem.*

[17] Human Rights Chamber, Case No. CH/02/12457, *Munir Alibabić against Bosnia and Herzegovina and the High Representative* (decision on admissibility of 2 April 2003), para. 2.

[18] See *supra* n. 13, para. 6.

[19] See, e.g., Constitutional Court of BiH, U 9/00, 3 November 2000, para. 5, website of the Constitutional Court of Bosnia and Herzegovina, Decisions by Year of Adoption, 2000, <www.ccbh.ba/?lang=en&page=decisions/byyear/2000>, visited on 30 March 2005 and Constitutional Court of BiH, U 25/00, 23 March 2001, para. 22, website of the Constitutional Court of Bosnia and Herzegovina, Decisions by Year of Adoption, 2001, <www.ccbh.ba/?lang=en&page=decisions/byyear/2001>, visited on 30 March 2005.

[20] Constitutional Court of BiH, U 37/01, 2 November 2001, website of the Constitutional Court of Bosnia and Herzegovina, Decisions by Year of Adoption, 2001, <www.ccbh.ba/?lang=en&page=decisions/byyear/2001>, visited on 30 March 2005. However, the European Commission for Democracy Through Law (Venice Commission) has observed that: 'in a recent decision on admissibility of 29 September 2004 a chamber of the Constitutional Court rejected an application against a dismissal by the High Representative for non-exhaustion of local remedies. This may indicate that judicial control will after all become possible.' Opinion on the Constitutional Situation in Bosnia and Herzegovina and the Powers of the High Representative, European Commission for Democracy Through Law (Venice Commission), 11 March 2005, CDL-AD (2005) 004, FN 23.

[21] Constitutional Court of BiH, U 41/01, 30 January 2004, website of the Constitutional Court of Bosnia and Herzegovina, Decisions by Year of Adoption, 2004, <http://www.ccbh.ba/?lang=en&page=decisions/byyear/2004>, visited on 30 March 2005.

[22] Constitutional Court of BiH, U 9/00, 3 November 2000, para. 5, website of the Constitutional Court of Bosnia and Herzegovina, Decisions by Year of Adoption, 2000, <www.ccbh.ba/?lang=en&page=decisions/byyear/2000>, visited on 30 March 2005. See also the discussion of 'functional duality' in Ralph Wilde, 'The Complex Rule of the Legal Adviser When International Organizations Administer Territory', 95 *Am. Soc'y Int'l L. Proc.* (2001) p. 251.

[23] Constitutional Court of BiH, U 9/00, 3 November 2000, para. 5, website of the Constitutional Court of Bosnia and Herzegovina, Decisions by Year of Adoption, 2000, <www.ccbh.ba/?lang=en&page=decisions/byyear/2000>, visited on 30 March 2005.

[24] Constitutional Court of BiH, U 26/01, 28 September 2001, website of the Constitutional Court of Bosnia and Herzegovina, Decisions by Year of Adoption, 2001, <http://www.ccbh.ba/?lang=en&page=decisions/byyear/2001>, visited on 30 March 2005.

[25] Constitutional Court of BiH, U 16/00, 2 February 2001, website of the Constitutional Court of Bosnia and Herzegovina, Decisions by Year of Adoption, 2001, <www.ccbh.ba/?lang=en&page=decisions/byyear/2001>, visited on 30 March 2005.

[26] Constitutional Court of BiH, U 25/00, 23 March 2001, website of the Constitutional Court of Bosnia and Herzegovina, Decisions by Year of Adoption, 2001, <www.ccbh.ba/?lang=en&page=decisions/byyear/2001>, visited on 30 March 2005.

[27] Constitutional Court of BiH, U 42/03, 17 December 2004, website of the Constitutional Court of Bosnia and Herzegovina, Decisions by Year of Adoption, 2004, <http://www.ccbh.ba/?lang=en&page=decisions/byyear/2004>, visited on 25 March 2005.

[28] Constitutional Court of BiH, U 24/03, 22 September 2004, website of the Constitutional Court of Bosnia and Herzegovina, Decisions by Year of Adoption, 2004, <http://www.ccbh.ba/?lang=en&page=decisions/by>, visited on 30 March 2005.

[29] Human Rights Chamber, Case No. CH/02/12470, *Nedjeljko Obradović against Bosnia and Herzegovina and the Federation of Bosnia and Herzegovina* (decision on admissibility and merits of 10 October 2003).

[30] Human Rights Chamber, Case No. CH/02/9130, *Stana Samardžić against the Republika Srpska* (decision on admissibility and merits of 6 January 2003).

[31] Human Rights Chamber, Case Nos. CH/97/60, CH/98/276, CH/98/287, CH/98/362 and CH/99/1766, *Andrija Miholić and Others against Bosnia and Herzegovina and the Federation of Bosnia and Herzegovina* (decision on admissibility and merits of 9 November 2001).

[32] See *supra* n. 29.

[33] See *supra* n. 31.

[34] See, e.g., M. Bajtarevic, Interview with Paddy Ashdown, the High Representative for BiH, BiH Radio 1, 12 July 2003, website of the Office of the High Representative, Press Office Interviews, <http://www.ohr.int/ohr-dept/presso/pressi/default.asp?content_id=30312>, visited on 13 April 2005.

[35] There are, however, several cases currently pending before the European Court of Human Rights concerning High Representative-issued decisions. See the Opinion on the Constitutional Situation in Bosnia and Herzegovina and the Powers of the High Representative, European Commission for Democracy Through Law (Venice Commission), 11 March 2005, CDL-AD (2005) 004, para. 93.

[36] See, e.g., Speech by the High Representative, Paddy Ashdown, to the Venice Commission, dated 8 October 2004, website of the Office of the High Representative, Press Office, Speeches, <http://www.ohr.int/ohr-dept/presso/presssp/default.asp?content_id=33344>, visited on 5 April 2005.

[37] See, e.g., Order of 9 February 2004 Blocking All Bank Accounts of, held by and/or in the name of Milovan Marijanovic, which states, *inter alia*: 'For the avoidance of doubt, it is hereby specifically declared and provided that the provisions of the Order contained herein are, as to each and every one of them, laid down by the High Representative pursuant to his international mandate and are not therefore justiciable by the Courts of Bosnia and Herzegovina or its Entities or elsewhere whether in respect of the Banking Agencies or otherwise, and no proceedings may be brought in respect of duties carried out thereunder before any court whatsoever at any time hereafter.' Website of the Office of the High Representative, High Representative's Decisions by Topic, Decisions Relating to Individuals Indicted for War Crimes in the Former Yugoslavia, <http://www.ohr.int/decisions/war-crimes-decs/default.asp?content_id=31814>, visited on 15 March 2005.

## Remarks by Federico Castellucci*

No paper received.

## Discussion

The Chair, Susan Karamanian, started the discussion by highlighting the themes of the presentations. She noted that the organisations presented have different mandates ranging from broad to quite narrow in very different areas of responsibility (for example, crime to wine) and have differed in how they adjusted to their mandates. This

* Director General, Organisation Internationale de la Vigne et du Vin.

raises questions of power and accountability. Power in the sense of the role played by States and/or shareholders, staff and employees, experts and observers, and the ever important issue of funding and the ability of non-state actors to have a say in the role of the organisation (e.g., private funding of Interpol). Accountability and openness questions are raised with respect to states and shareholders, founding countries, the institutions and tribunals reviewing the acts of international organisations, and in some cases the interests of the general public or consumers.

LUCY REED:* I have two questions from my perspective as former General Counsel of the Korean Energy Development Organisation, a small, niche international organisation:

1. For the international lawyers on the panel, what is the most interesting issue on which you were asked to advise? In my case, I can think of two – one was being asked whether one of my ambassadors would be personally liable if he voted on a fiscal issue knowing that there were insufficient funds, and the second was advising one of our employees whether he would be criminally liable when he had $25,000 in cash stolen at the JFK airport as the funds had not been declared as many of our operations in Korea had to be done in cash.

STEPHEN MATHIAS: From the MPO perspective, the details are unfortunately all confidential.

LAURENT GROSSE: I agree that every day presents unique challenges. Legal issues have historically not been very interesting to Interpol officials, even though they are police men, and only recently has this become a real question. When I first joined the Interpol legal office I got the impression that we were a glorified registration office and it took time for us to become involved in the decision-making process itself before it was too late to have any influence and we simply had the cleanup job. Now they have started to involve us earlier and this is much easier as the process has become more transparent.

FEDERICO CASTELLUCCI: From the OVV perspective, when I joined there was a tension between geographical references and appellations of origin, but this has changed. What is happening now is that the consumers are letting us know what they need, rather than the wine producers telling the consumers what they should want. As a result in certain regions territories are getting smaller and others are getting bigger, but it all remains interesting.

2. How do you handle the protection of the 'International Organisation' veil, given that the smaller the international organisation the more blatantly nationalistic the Member representatives can be?

There were no specific replies to this question.

I.L. WORIKA:** One would have expected in the sessions of this conference that OPEC would have been discussed in one of them. However, I have attended all relevant sessions and there has been no mention of OPEC, including at this one considering niche international organisations. This raises the question whether this panel considers OPEC to be an international organisation or a specialized international institution or just an intergovernmental organisation as some would say and do you

* Partner specialized in international disputes and international law, Freshfields Bruckhaus Deringer, New York.

** Opec, Vienna, Austria.

consider that the rules applicable to international organisations should apply to OPEC given the role it plays in international law and policy?

SUSAN KARAMANIAN: As a matter of interest, the definition of international organisation from Professor Bradley is a distinct legal personality with a permanent association of States with lawful objects equipped with organs, with a distinction between the organisation and its Member States and the power to act exists on the international plane and not solely within the national state systems. Any comments taking into account this definition?

There were no further comments.

OLIVIER RIBBELINK:* I am interested in the public/private funding of Interpol and in particular the funding by credit card companies in that international payment card fraud is a major issue for Interpol. In general, I would be interested to understand how this is arranged concerning transparency and accountability?

KATHLEEN PAISLEY:** I have a question related to Dr. Ribbelink's question but from a more practical perspective. For example, we all know that there are major events of credit card fraud. Given your relationship to the payment/credit card companies, how are you certain that Interpol entails no liability or the like from its relationship to the credit card companies in this respect?

LAURENT GROSSE: I will respond to these questions together. Arrangements with private companies are quite new to Interpol, and the credit card example in particular is only from 1999. The credit card relationship is a good example of how these private relationships develop in practice. Before this partnership existed Interpol was working on financial crimes in order to provide by our Member States with information about credit card fraud, as we have with counterfeit money since the 1930s.

We therefore sought to create a database accessible through a restricted web site allowing our Member countries to access data re fraudulent credit cards. To obtain the information necessary to create the database we contacted the credit card companies and they gave us both the information necessary to create the data base and the funds required to second police officers to build and maintain this database and train Member country representatives to use it.

We have not looked into the liability issue in depth, as we have always done this within the limits of our rules – and it all goes into our budget. However, as this becomes a more regular aspect of our funding we will need to look into these issues in depth. In general, our rules are very flexible and we have no formal treaty.

SUSAN KARAMANIAN: What I would really like to know Laurent is if I asked who had given how much money to Interpol on what date and for what purpose, would anyone be able and willing to tell me? However, that will have to wait for another day as for now we are out of time and I am only left to thank the panellists and the reporter and I look forward to seeing everyone at later sessions.

*Reporter:* Kathleen Paisley

* TMC Asser Institute, The Hague.

** Session Reporter; Paisley & Kruithof, Brussels, Belgium former partner specialised in EU competition law and international disputes at Morrison & Foerster, Brussels, Belgium; legal advisor to the US arbitrators at the Iran-US Claims Tribunal in the Hague, the Netherlands.

# ICSID and Other Investment Arbitration Tribunals: Is There a Need for Judicial Oversight or Other Reforms?

The panel was convened by its Chair, Andrea K. Bjorklund*

## Introductory Remarks by Andrea K. Bjorklund

Welcome to our panel on potential reforms to the International Centre for Settlement of Investment Disputes, also known as ICSID. ICSID is an arm of the World Bank. It was established in the late 1960s to provide a forum for the neutral arbitration of disputes between investors and host governments. Most early ICSID cases were referred to the Centre by contractual agreements and involved contractual claims.

In spite of ICSID's rather moderate beginnings there has been a staggering rise in the number of claims stemming from alleged breaches of investment treaties, including bilateral investment treaties or BITS and multilateral treaties such as the North American Free Trade Agreement. I want to give you a few numbers just for perspective: at the end of 1994, there had been three treaty-based claims brought to ICSID; as of November 2004, there were 106. More than 30 of those cases have been filed against the government of Argentina in the aftermath of the Argentine fiscal crisis. If you add the more than 50 known cases brought under other investment dispute settlement regimes such as UNCITRAL, you can see the new scale of these cases.

The increase in its caseload has brought renewed scrutiny to its procedures. As a consequence, ICSID itself has published two white papers on potential reforms, which include the idea of increasing transparency in the proceedings and establishing an appellate body to hear appeals from the awards given by *ad hoc* tribunals.

## Remarks by Andrea K. Bjorklund*

### Reform of the International Centre for Settlement of Investment Disputes: an Introduction

Reform – The amendment, or altering for the better, of some faulty state of things
*Oxford English Dictionary* (2nd edn. 1989)

The calls for reform of any institution are loud in the aftermath of crises, whether real

* Professor of Law at the University of California, Davis School of Law.

or merely perceived. Movements for reform sometimes come from within an institution, sometimes from without, and sometimes from both. The impetus for change tends to abate as time lapses. Inertia, forgetfulness, the need to attend to new crises, all attenuate sustained efforts at reform. It is indeed an achievement when an organization such as ICSID proposes reforms to itself, invites suggestions and criticisms from interested parties, and follows through on its ideas.

The idea of reform in the context of the International Centre for Settlement of Investment Disputes (ICSID) arose in the aftermath of the first annulment decisions in the early 1990s, when a few *ad hoc* committees were believed to have overstepped their boundaries by engaging in more wholesale review of tribunal awards than was consistent with their mandate under the ICSID Convention. The annulment process had been designed to guard the integrity of the institution rather than to guarantee the correctness of awards. When the first three cases were not immediately followed by other requests for annulment, concerns that the annulment process was too easily turned into an appellate mechanism diminished.

In late 2004, the idea of ICSID reform again appeared. The ideas were sparked, at least in part, by the perceived threat to the legitimacy of investor-State arbitration posed by ostensibly inconsistent decisions in similar cases. Two of the cases at issue were not even ICSID cases, but brought greater public attention to investor-State arbitration. Other cases in which non-governmental organizations aspired to participate either as parties or as *amici curiae*, also had raised the public profile of investor-State arbitration and of ICSID. Furthermore, the United States had entered free trade agreements containing investment chapters that called for the treaty parties to consider the establishment of an appellate body to hear appeals from tribunal decisions in investor-State disputes.

On 22 October 2004, the ICSID Secretariat issued a White Paper entitled "Possible Improvements of the Framework for ICSID Arbitration." The proposal addressed preliminary procedures, suggesting amendments to the Rules making possible expedited requests to a tribunal for provisional measures in aid of arbitration and expedited consideration by a tribunal of possibly frivolous claims. The proposal also addressed publication of awards and the access of third parties to tribunal proceedings. It called for reforming the rules so that ICSID might promptly publish excerpts of the main holdings, while awaiting party consent to the publication of the full text, in order to facilitate a more timely release of information. It also suggested that consideration be given to permitting the filing of *amicus curiae* submissions in certain circumstances, and to facilitating access to hearings, when appropriate. The paper proposed that disclosure requirements placed on arbitrators be strengthened and that parties be encouraged to avail themselves of the conciliation and mediation facilities of ICSID. Finally, ICSID broached the subject of establishing an appellate mechanism under its auspices.

ICSID sent its proposal to the ICSID Administrative Council and invited commentary from all interested parties, including members of civil society and arbitration experts from around the world. On 12 May 2005, ICSID issued another paper detailing proposed amendments to the ICSID Arbitration Rules and the ICSID (Additional Facility) Arbitration Rules to incorporate those reforms still considered worth pursuing after public comment and after the Administrative Council had considered the proposals. The procedural reforms were accepted, as was the encouragement of conciliation and mediation. The proposal for more open access to hearings and the filing of *amicus curiae* submissions generated more comment and more hesitation; concerns were expressed at the potential for unduly burdening and disrupting the parties to the proceedings. ICSID proposed changes to the rules to permit such participation at the discretion of the tribunal. This second White Paper did not include the establishment of an appellate body. Members of the ICSID Administrative Council agreed that, were an appellate mechanism to be established, ICSID might be an appropriate venue, but that consideration of such an idea was premature.

The panel discussion from which the following papers derived was conceived not long before ICSID issued its first White Paper, and convened not long after it issued its second. During that time, the fervor for reform had abated. ICSID itself had retracted its proposal to establish an appellate mechanism, at least for the foreseeable future. The panelists addressed the need for reform from different perspectives – that of the practitioner, of the State Party, of the academic, and of the ICSID. The panelists were united on the issue of transparency – giving the public greater knowledge of proceedings, access to awards, and the ability to participate in proceedings when appropriate. The panelists diverged, however, on the extent to which the "legitimacy" of investor-State arbitration is threatened. They also disagreed as to what, if any, steps should be taken in response to that threat. Thus, the panelists did not agree on the desirability of and need for establishing an appellate mechanism. One panelist noted that the quest for consistent opinions might be illusory, even with an appellate mechanism in place.

Reform itself is a malleable concept. It can mean anything from tinkering at the margins of institutional structure to wholesale change in the institution itself. Yet whether reforms are big or small, they are meant to alter *for the better* some faulty state of things. Change for the sake of change does not fall within the rubric of reform. Suggesting, weighing, and even rejecting proposed changes are necessary parts of a reform process designed to ensure that any changes made are actually for the better.

## Remarks by Susan D. Franck*

## ICSID Institutional Reform: The Evolution of Dispute Resolution and the Role of Structural Safeguards

### Introduction

No system of dispute resolution – created by flawed human beings – can be perfect.[1] But this should not prevent scholars, lawyers and policy-makers from asking whether micro or macro changes to a system's structure might improve its value and efficacy. During the evolution of a dispute resolution system, there are inevitably challenging

* Professor of Law at the University of Nebraska Law School.

transitional periods which require a re-examination of the bedrock principles upon which a system was founded. As Henry Ward Beecher wrote in 1858, '[l]aws and institutions are constantly tending to gravitate ... [and] [l]ike clocks, they must be occasionally cleansed and wound up, and set to true time.'[2]

After a variety of arbitral tribunals have issued awards during the past decade – developing jurisprudence that is coherent in some areas and less so in others – investment arbitration is now at this critical juncture. This conference's theme of analyzing international institutional reform finds particularly fertile ground in the area of investment arbitration; not only does the World Bank's International Centre for Settlement of Investment Disputes (ICSID) play a major role as a gatekeeper in the evolution of investment treaty arbitration but it has also been engaging in self-reflection about its own role within the system. It is therefore useful to consider whether institutional reform is appropriate in order to promote and retain ICSID's legitimacy and the overall integrity of the system of investment treaty arbitration.

These remarks will provide a basic background on the nature of investment treaties and focus on the evolution of investment treaty arbitration by asking two fundamental issues: (1) whether there is a substantive problem and (2) what, if anything, ICSID should do about. This piece analyzes the various potential approaches to reform, and evaluates ICSID's use of structural safeguards to enhance the efficacy, efficiency and reliability of the dispute resolution process at ICSID. By using such safeguards, ICSID institutional reform can have positive impact on the integrity of the system currently charged with resolving investment treaty disputes.

## The Evolution of Investment Arbitration

In an effort to evolve away from 'gunboat diplomacy', countries have promulgated treaties to promote foreign investment and instill confidence in the stability of the investment environment.[3] These efforts began with Treaties of Friendship, Commerce and Navigation,[4] but soon grew into a system where States[5] agreed to provide foreign investors in their country with a broad set of investment rights.[6] As efforts to create a multilateral investment agreement were unsuccessful, many countries undertook a more modest effort to encourage and promote stable investment climates – they initiated bilateral investment treaty programs to secure substantive and procedural rights for international investors.[7]

There are now over 2,100 investment treaties; given their common roots, they tend to provide investors with similar – although not always textually identical – rights.[8] Their promulgation – primarily on a bilateral level but sometimes in a multilateral context as well[9] – was a seed change in international investment law. These rights were an innovation as they created a new body of substantive standards that provided specific and mutually agreed protection for foreign investors.[10] Likewise the procedural rights were an innovation as they provided a direct enforcement mechanism for the substantive rights. Specifically, they permitted investors to bring a cause of action[11] against a State thereby bypassing two unattractive dispute resolution options: (1) suing a government in its own courts, and (2) by-passing the diplomatic channels required to lobby their home government to espouse a claim on their behalf before the International Court of Justice.[12]

As with any new system which is being tested and evaluated, there is bound to be a teething period. This phenomenon is not new. Let us not forget that when ICSID Convention system of international commercial arbitration was in its infancy, the novel and untested nature of the annulment process created various bumps along the road. As one *ad hoc* committee astutely commented that the growth and interpretation of international dispute resolution treaties can be 'especially delicate because of the absence of any previous interpretation of [a treaty] and the lack of sufficiently clear or consistent indications from prior international practice.'[13] But after the procedural kinks in the system were smoothed out, the work of individual tribunals resolving commercial disputes and *ad hoc* committees evaluating procedural irregularities has been relatively uneventful.[14]

But now we do have something new. Investors now regularly bring investment treaty claims before ICSID.[15] This means ICSID is no longer used simply to resolve disputes related to familiar commercial concepts between foreign investors and host States – it is now resolving disputes related to new and distinctive investment rights provided in investment treaties. As the number of investment treaty claims has exploded during the past decade (particularly at ICSID during the last five years) and as the number of awards has increased, the number of inconsistencies amongst the decisions has also grown. This has caused investment arbitration to experience certain 'growing pains'. Much like a child's growth process, this evolution is inevitable and was even anticipated.

## The Issues

So the questions rightly becomes, has this transformation resulted in problems? If not, then the old adage should apply: 'if it's not broke, don't fix it'. But if there is a problem, then the next question rightly becomes, 'what should we do about it?' This resolution of later question depends largely upon one's perception of what the 'problem' is and the costs and benefits of various approaches to reform.

## The Answers

There is a problem in investment treaty arbitration: the challenge of inconsistency and its detrimental impact upon legitimacy. Inconsistency creates uncertainty and results in a lack of predictability and certainty for both investors and States alike; it also raises other concerns related to the signaling of errors, suggestions of unfairness and systemic inefficiencies.[16] Although there are a variety of sources of multiplicity – as suggested by Mr. Suarez's remarks – these remarks will focus upon inconsistencies caused by divergent outcomes rendered by arbitral tribunals interpreting individual treaties within the investment treaty network. The sources of multiplicity will continue to expand as the number of treaties increase, lawyers actively advise clients to structure transactions to take advantage of multiple treaties, arbitration practitioners make clever arguments to apply rights to an ever expanding range of government conduct,[17] and reasonable arbitrators make reasonable decisions that still differ on fundamental issues.

Inconsistencies in awards generally devolve from varying permutations in commercial situations, government conduct, and the text conveying the right in the applicable treaty. While some divergences can be explained by distinctions in situation, conduct, or text, several cases remain problematic irrespective of whether they are administered through ICSID[18] itself or through ICSID's Additional Facility.[19]

Although outside the ICSID framework, the *Lauder* cases provide a tangible example of the impact of inconsistency. A not inconsiderable amount of ink has been spilled in discussing these two cases where related entities brought related actions against the Czech Republic.[20] The cases involved a US investor and his Dutch investment vehicle. After the Czech investment became worthless, the individual investor initiated a claim under the US/Czech treaty, and his Dutch investment vehicle made a claim under the Dutch/Czech treaty. Although the two treaty claims were based upon a common set of facts and nearly identical treaty rights, on all but one point, the two tribunals came to diametrically opposed results. Both tribunals agreed the investment had been subjected to discrimination but disagreed on all other issues (including whether there had been expropriation, a failure to provide full protection and security, a breach of an obligation to provide fair and equitable treatment, and violations of the minimum standard of treatment required by international law).[21]

These inconsistencies have presented challenges. After the *Lauder* awards, there was speculation that the Czech Republic might pull out of its BITs.[22] Meanwhile, Ronald Lauder was testifying before the US Congress about the unfavorable business environment in the Czech Republic and taking out full-page ads in the *New York Times* telling US investors why they should not invest in the Czech Republic.[23] The *Lauder* cases are not isolated incidents. Argentina is subject to multiple treaty claims related to its recent currency crisis, which may result in different applications of the same (or similar) treaty provisions and different conclusions regarding liability regarding the same government conduct.[24]

As things stand, the problem is likely to grow. Even now, the number of claims under BITs is exploding. Meanwhile, given the broad definition of 'investor' and 'investment' and recent case law,[25] investors have greater incentives to heed the advice of counsel and structure their investments through corporate layers with divergent nationalities. This plants the seeds for 'twin' or 'triplet' cases similar to *Lauder* and creates future opportunities to game the system.

**The implications**

The current system of creating *ad hoc*, disparate decisions on related issues of public international law should be unified to create a coherent, clear and understandable jurisprudence. 'Getting it right' – or at the bare minimum, getting it more reliable – is essential to an area where there is little analogous jurisprudence (whether in the form of decisions or academic literature) and tribunals interpret and apply public rights with public implications. While a minor degree of inconsistency in decisions may actually be useful to help the doctrine develop in a considered manner, it is possible to have too much of a good thing; and the utility of such inconsistency, like many issues in law, is a question of degree.

Tribunals are doing their utmost to review previous decisions, avoid previous mistakes and harmonize their decisions to create a coherent body of law. Nevertheless, the stakes in investment arbitration are too great to sit by idly while issues of public international law are being decided inconsistently, in private, particularly when the dispute resolution mechanism provides few, if any, express structures to create an incentive to promote consistent decision making. While complete consistency is most likely an unattainable holy grail, the question is not whether perfection is possible – but whether we can create structures and incentives to minimize errors, abuses, ambiguities and inconsistencies in a way that promotes legitimacy.[26]

**ICSID's self assessment**

ICSID has long recognized that it experiences difficulties related to inconsistency.[27] As a result of these difficulties and the increased number of cases, ICSID issued a White Paper in October 2004 in an effort to 'encourage discussion of such possible improvements and to invite any further suggestions for change.'[28] ICSID's first Discussion Paper suggested a variety of changes to the ICSID system, some of which address technical related to arbitration procedure – such as improved preliminary procedures[29] or increased use of non-arbitration-related alternative dispute resolution services.[30] In contrast, other reform efforts involved the potential introduction of preventative and corrective measures to directly or indirectly minimize the risk of inconsistent substantive decisions. The reforms in the later category essentially break down into suggestions related to greater transparency,[31] enhanced opportunities for training of officials from developing countries[32] and the establishment of an investment arbitration appellate body at ICSID.[33]

Unfortunately, ICSID has not made the notes and comments it has received publicly available. Nevertheless, certain groups have distributed their comments to ICSID's initial recommendations. Some groups have criticized ICSID and suggested ICSID exceeded its mandate by engaging in *ultra vires* activity and inappropriately failed to consult with developing countries.[34] While there was some mixed reaction to the appropriateness of some suggestions for reform – particularly the participation of *amicus curaie* and the establishment of an appellate body – ICSID's proposals were generally well-received.[35]

In June 2005,[36] as a follow-up to their initial white paper, ICSID published a Working Paper with suggested textual changes to the ICSID Rules.[37] The proposed technical amendments largely proved uncontroversial and were expanded to provide specific textual recommendations.[38] But the more substantive suggestions for reform were addressed in different ways. In particular, while ICSID has forged ahead with procedural mechanisms designed to prevent a democracy deficit – namely those related to transparency. But in other, more challenging areas – such as an appellate body and technical assistance to developing countries – were tabled for future discussion.

**Evaluating the way forward**

There are a variety of changes that could be made to the present system. While some of the suggested modifications are incremental and more 'preventative' (i.e., designed to prevent inconsistencies before they occur), other reform 'corrective' efforts (i.e., designed to correct inconsistencies after the fact) are more substantive and would require institutional adjustments as well as changes to the investor-state dispute mechanisms delineated within the 2,100 BITs themselves.

Nevertheless, in an effort to avoid prescribing a remedy that is more harmful than the malady, it is useful to consider the various approaches to institutional reform prior to undertaking the road to reform. Given the concerns related to inconsistency and legitimacy, there is an emerging literature about the most effective methods for evaluating suggestions for reform and improving the efficiency and consistency of the investment treaty dispute resolution system.[39] Suggestions and efforts for reform generally break down into four categories: (1) the barrier building approach; (2) the arbitration rejecter approach; (3) a legislative approach; and (4) the safeguard builder approach. The 'barrier building' (or gatekeeper) approach focuses on creating hurdles that limit an investor's direct access to arbitration, in certain circumstances preventing the evaluation of the investor's substantive rights. The 'arbitration rejecter' approach posits that arbitration is an inappropriate mechanism, preferring that the substantive rights of parties to an investment treaty dispute return to a public forum. The 'legislative' approach focuses on changing the text of treaties to provide greater clarity about the content and scope of investment rights. Meanwhile, 'safeguard builders' suggest that the structure of investment arbitration can be modified to provide procedural safeguards that enhance the efficiency and reliability of the dispute resolution process.[40] In order to evaluate the utility of these approaches, one must evaluate whether each generates a jurisprudence that is more consistent, predictable, and clear. Providing such predictability and clarity fosters the integrity of the dispute resolution process; likewise, it can create opportunities to enhance the utility of investment treaties.

The recommendations of the barrier builders and arbitration rejecters are unlikely to result in a consistent jurisprudence. Rather, their recommendations are likely to inhibit the development of a consistent and predictable jurisprudence and may, in come circumstances, exacerbate the difficulties caused by inconsistent awards.[41] In contrast, advocates of a legislative approach and safeguard building may have more useful suggestions. While the efforts of legislative reformers may be useful in creating certainty for treaties negotiated in the future,[42] safeguard building reforms are most likely to have an immediate and effective impact in creating consistency and offering enhanced predictability about the meaning of substantive rights in investment treaty arbitration.[43]

## Analysis of ICSID's proposals

ICSID's proposals are designed to safeguard and improve the arbitration process for investment treaty disputes. The areas for potential reform are essentially designed to maximize the integrity of the dispute resolution process. This analysis will focus on those particular reforms which hold may minimize the possibility for inconsistent awards, namely transparency, the promulgation of ICSID training programs and the creation of an appellate body.

ICSID's proposals for transparency reverse arbitration's traditional conception of confidentiality. Nevertheless, transparency is an idea whose time has come for cases involving public parties, rights and implications. Particularly since greater transparency holds the potential to lead indirectly to enhanced consistency and coherence, there has been a consensus that the creation of transparency measures is, generally, of benefit.[44]

ICSID's proposal regarding the publication of excerpts from awards, while a step in the right direction, may not go far enough, however, in its efforts to create consistency. There are three significant challenges in its current proposals. First, preventing access to the full factual context and legal reasoning, which underlies the holding of and rules articulated by the tribunal, decreases the utility of the award. Failure to understand the full context may cause the misinterpretation and misapplication of the award in future cases. Lack of full access also prevents commentators from having an opportunity to appreciate those nuances which may have influenced the tribunal's conclusions; this dearth of information inhibits commentators from offering analysis which might actually reconcile otherwise facially inconsistent decisions. Instead, publishing entire awards (with highly sensitive information redacted) would permit parties and tribunals in future cases to learn from the full analysis of those tribunals who have wrestled with similar issues.

Second, the proposal fails to offer access to underlying pleadings and documents. Such information, which might also shed light on the ratio of the decision, again prevents commentators from analyzing awards and understanding the subtleties of a decision. Particularly as analysis from recognized scholars has precedential weight under the statute of the International Court of Justice,[45] the dearth of public access to these materials may inhibit the creation of scholarship, which can assist in the development of a consistent jurisprudence. Ultimately, having the capacity to subject awards to greater scrutiny provides an opportunity to create considered commentary on the development of the doctrine, to establish and to recognize the unique factual and textual nexus of each case.

Third, publishing excerpts does not prevent the underground trading of awards, which effectively serve as precedent. This permits parties to conceal what might otherwise be adverse authority, prevents those parties lacking access to the arbitration 'club' from gaining access to useful authority and precludes arbitrators from considering potentially relevant analysis. While the internet is a useful equalizer – with no less than three web sites are dedicated to locating and publishing treaty awards[46] – these databases are not complete either in terms of awards, nor underlying pleadings, documents and hearing transcripts.[47] Ultimately, a presumption in favour of public access to primary sources will provide the information necessary for considered, informed and accurate commentary; which, in turn, can provide guidance for the development of consistent and coherent jurisprudence.

ICSID's other transparency recommendations, including permitting public attendance at hearings and third party participation, are also useful safeguards to enhance the possibility that future tribunals will render consistent awards.[48] The capacity for public observance of hearings usefully provides commentators with the ability to hear the evidence and arguments put to the tribunal. Ironically, although access to a transcript would permit commentators to more accurately describe and analyze those hearings, ICSID's proposals do not permit commentators to secure a copy of a verbatim transcript; rather, they must still request the agreement of both parties. As suggested earlier, the inability to access this information freely creates barriers for commentators who desire to accurately analyze and describe the *ratio* of awards. Increasing opportunities for third party participation – particularly in the form of an *amicus* brief – would permit arbitrators to consider alternative considerations and modes of analysis during their deliberations and, hopefully, improve the quality of both the deliberations and the ultimate award. Nevertheless, further transparency related to making transcripts and pleadings publicly available would facilitate effective third-party participation; with this information, *amici* might usefully know what legal arguments and facts were already before the tribunal and could clarify and streamline those areas in which additional analysis might prove useful. Such public access and participation has the potential, in the long-term, to offer greater clarity and certainty to tribunals wrestling with the interpretation of investment treaty claims.

Beyond these specific efforts at transparency, there are two areas which impact consistency that ICSID has tabled for future discussion, namely, the possibility of enhanced training and the creation of an appellate body. There are critical reasons why both of these issues are worthy of serious, ongoing consideration.

Enhanced training about ICSID and investment treaty arbitration provides a useful opportunity to enhance consistency indirectly. By promoting opportunities for equality of arms between the parties, a dispute can be resolved fully and fairly. Parties who have the capacity to participate in a meaningful way will have a better opportunity of to brief and argue cases properly. Within an adversarial system, where the advocates of both parties have minimal competencies and common understandings about basic assumptions, the process of resolving disputes can be more efficient; and where advocates have knowledge and expertise, cases which are fully plead, briefed and argued are likely to lead to considered and consistent jurisprudence. In contrast, lopsided advocacy where parties miss or misunderstand critical issues are unlikely to have the same effect. Training only goes so far, however. ICSID has not yet considered the possibility of an entity, much like the WTO's advisory centre[49] providing more than simple background to the law but providing specific legal advice to developing nations who may be without the financial wherewithal and expertise in this highly specialized area of litigation to fight on a level playing field with multi-national law firms. By promoting the equality of arms, tribunals can deliberate with greater confidence that relevant arguments have been raised and briefed, which better enables them to make reasoned and appropriate decisions.

Although ICSID explained the idea of an appellate body was 'premature ... particularly in view of the difficult technical and policy issues', it promised to 'continue to study such issues to assist member countries when and if it is decided to proceed towards the establishment of an ICSID appeal mechanism.'[50] While it is a more challenging reform to implement, this option should not be discounted, particularly as the international obligations of a variety of countries now require consideration of the creation of an appellate body.[51] A single appellate facility, which can provide a clear line of authority, can correct or explain logical inconsistencies in awards. Such an appellate body would provide a useful opportunity to review fundamental issues, which are common to investment treaties, including disputed legal interpretations and can begin to establish clear margins about the basic meaning of substantive rights. Clarity at this level will promote consistency and enhance certainty about what rights investors have and for which conduct Sovereigns are liable. 'Getting it right' in a 'bet the country' dispute is vital and perhaps, in a novel area of jurisprudence with critical public implications, more important than finality and confidentiality. By establishing such an appellate body and creating a forum where diametrically opposed decisions can be corrected or explained, investment treaty arbitration will adapt to its new reality.

## Conclusion

As investment arbitration is still in its infancy but in the middle of its first 'growing pains', it is appropriate to help the jurisprudence develop, acknowledge the difficulties in the current framework, and find ways to minimize the looming legitimacy crisis. In this manner, investment arbitration will not be thrown out with the proverbial bathwater and international arbitration will be firmly on track to promote international justice and addressing the concerns of investors, States and citizens alike.

## Notes

1 Susan D. Franck, 'The Legitimacy Crisis in Investment Treaty Arbitration: Privatizing Public International Law Through Inconsistent Decisions', 73 *Fordham L. Rev.* (2005), 1521, 1610; see also Constantine N. Katsoris, 'The Resolution of Securities Disputes', 6 *Fordham J. Corp. & Fin. L.* (2001), 307, 368-369 (suggesting that in order to maintain public confidence in a dispute resolution system 'we can never become complacent and feel as though we have achieved the perfect dispute resolution system'); *Hoffman* v. *Cargill, Inc.*, 236 F.3d 458, 462 (8th Cir. 2001) (noting that arbitration is not a perfect system of justice).

2 Henry Ward Beecher, *Life Thoughts* (1858), 129.

3 Franck, *supra* n. 1 at 1525-1526; Kenneth J. Vandevelde, *United States Investment Treaties: Policy And Practice* (1992) 7-22; Jeswald W. Salacuse & Nicholas P. Sullivan, 'Do BITS Really Work?: An Evaluation of Bilateral Investment Treaties and Their Grand Bargain', 46 *Harv. Int'l L.J.* (2005), 67, 111-112; Ray C. Jones, 'NAFTA Chapter 11 *Investor-To-State Dispute Resolution: A Shield To Be Embraced Or A Sword To Be Feared?', 2002 Byu L. Rev.* (2002), 527, 529-531; Jeswald Salacuse, 'BIT by BIT: The Growth of Bilateral Investment Treaties and Their Impact on Foreign Investment in Developing Countries', 24 *Int'l Law.* (1990), 655, 656-658.

4 E.I. Nwogugu, *The Legal Problems Of Foreign Investment In Developing Countries* (1965), 119-122.

5 For the purpose of these remarks, a 'State' is a sovereign national government.

6 David A. Gantz, 'Potential Conflicts Between Investor Rights and Environmental Regulation Under NAFTA's Chapter 11', 33 *Geo. Wash. Int'l L. Rev.* (2001), 719-720; Patricia M. Robin, 'The BIT Won't Bite: The American Bilateral Investment Treaty Program', 33 *Am. U. L. Rev.* (1984), 931, 942-943.

7 M. Sornarajah, *International Law On Foreign Investment* (1994) 231-237; United Nations Conference On Trade And Development, Lessons From The Mai, UNCTAD/ITE/ITT/Misc.22 (1999), at: <http://www.unctad.org/en/docs//psiteiitm22.en.pdf>; Guillermo A. Alvarez & William W. Park, 'The New Face of Investment Arbitration: NAFTA Chapter 11', 28 *Yale J. Int'l L.* (2003), 365, 366-367; Kenneth J. Vandevelde, 'The Bilateral Investment Treaty Program of the United States', 21 *Cornell Int'l L.J.* (1988), 201; Kenneth J. Vandevelde, 'U.S. Bilateral Investment Treaties: The Second Wave', 14 *Mich. J. Int'l L.* (1993), 621

8 Franck, *supra* n. 1 at 1527-1530.

9 Some of the more well-known multilateral efforts include the North American Free Trade Agreement (NAFTA), the Central American Free Trade Agreement (CAFTA) and the Energy Charter Treaty (ECT).

10 Investment treaties typically provide general guarantees related to the protection of their investments including appropriate compensation for expropriation, freedom from unreasonable or discriminatory measures, guarantees of national treatment, fair and equitable treatment of investments, promises of full protection and security, treatment no less favorable than that accorded under international law and an obligation to honor contractual obligations. Franck, *supra* n. 1 at 1529-1532; Salacuse *&* Sullivan, *supra* n. 3, at 83-85.

11 Franck, *supra* n. 1, at 153; see also Tai-Heng Cheng, *Power,* 'Authority and International Investment Law', 20 *Am. U. Int'l L. Rev* (2005), 465, 471.

12 Ian Brownie, *Principles of Public International Law*, 6th edn. (2003) 677-690; Daniel M. Price, 'NAFTA Chapter 11 Investor-State Dispute Settlement: Frankenstein or Safety Valve?', 26 *Can-Us. L.J.* (2001), 107, 112.

13 *Holiday Inn, Klockner, et al.* v. *Cameroon*, ICSID Case No. ARB/81/2, reprinted in 1 ICSID REV.-FILJ 90, (1986) § 118.

14 Christoph H. Schreuer, *The ICSID Convention: A Commentary* (2001).

15 Ninety-two claims have been filed by investors in the past three years. UNCTAD, *Investor-State disputes*

*and policy implications*, TD/B/COM.2/62 (17 January 2005), at: <http://www.unctad.org/sp/docs/c2d62_sp.pdf>.

16 Susan D. Franck, 'The Nature and Enforcement of Investor Rights Under Investment Treaties: Do Investment Treaties Have A Bright Future', [forthcoming *U.C.-Davis J. Int'l L. & Pol'y* 2005] [hereinafter Franck II].

17 Likewise, clever and experienced practitioners can also be enlisted to make arguments to counter what Jan Paulsson has described at 'BIT creep'. To the extent, however, that States (1) cannot afford to hire these practitioners or (2) defend themselves and lack access to case law or basic legal materials, it may be more challenging for a State to assert these arguments.

18 See, e.g., Franck, *supra* n. 1 at 1568-1574 (describing the inconsistencies in the two *SGS* cases where tribunals had radically different conceptions of the existence of an investor's right to bring a claim under an umbrella clause).

19 See, e.g., Franck, *supra* n. 1 at 1574-1581 (describing the trio of cases in which some cases decided that 'fair and equitable' treatment was an additive right that is distinct from the international minimum standard of treatment whereas other tribunals concluded that it was not).

20 Wolfgang Kühn, 'How to Avoid Conflicting Awards: The Lauder and CME Cases', 5 *J. World. Invest. & Trade* (2004), 7; Bohuslav Klein, 'How to Avoid Conflicting Awards: The Lauder and CME Cases', *5 J. World. Invest. & Trade* (2004), 19; Jeremy Carver, 'How to Avoid Conflicting Awards: The Lauder and CME Cases', 5 *J. World. Invest. & Trade* (2004), 23 (2004); Hans Bagner, 'How to Avoid Conflicting Awards: The Lauder and CME Cases', 5 *J. World. Invest. & Trade* (2004), 31.

21 *Lauder* v. *Czech Republic*, UNCITRAL, Final Award (3 September 2001), at: <http://ita.law.uvic.ca/documents/LauderAward.pdf>; *Czech Republic B.V.* v. *Czech Republic*, UNCITRAL, Partial Award (13 September 2000), at: < http://ita.law.uvic.ca/documents/CME-2001PartialAward.pdf>.

22 See Petra Pasternak, 'EU, U.S. Treaty Issues Unresolved', *Prague Post*, 29 May 2003 available on LexisNexis (suggesting that the Czech Republic may have needed to terminate the US/Czech BIT).

23 See Peter S. Green, 'Czech Senate A Safe Haven For Principal In Media War', *N.Y. Times*, 11 November 2002, at A8 (noting that Mr. Lauder responded with full page newspaper advertisements calling the Czech Republic unsafe for foreign investors); Prepared Testimony of Ronald S. Lauder, Chairman Central European Media Enterprises, 28 June 2000, Before the Senate Committee on Foreign Relations European Affairs Subcommittee.

24 There are more than thirty claims brought against Argentina, which involve the same government measure (the devaluation of the peso). While they involve different (and sometimes related) investors, the treaty rights typically involve the same BIT, textually identical treaty rights, or substantially similar substantive rights. See, e.g., Investment Claims, *Orders and Awards*, at: <http://www.investmentclaims.com/oa2a.html>. Nevertheless, these different cases could result in inconsistent substantive determinations as to Argentina's liability.

25 See *Tokios Tokels* v. *Ukraine*, ICSID (W. Bank) Case No. ARB/02/18, Decision on Jurisdiction (29 April 2004), available at: <http://www.worldbank.org/icsid/cases/tokios-decision.pdf> (holding that a local Ukrainian company that had reincorporated itself in Lithuania could qualify as a foreign investor and benefit from the protections afforded by the Ukraine/Lithuania investment treaty).

26 In many respects, the standards articulated by the New York Convention (for setting aside awards) and the ICSID Convention (for annulling awards) provide arbitrators with an incentive to ensure procedural due process and encourage procedural integrity. There is no such incentive within the investment treaty arbitration mechanism itself to promote consistent decision-making. There may be, however, market forces which may foster consistent decision-making. Parties may wish to appoint similar arbitrators in cases where consistency is desirable. Likewise, arbitrators whose professional reputation (and the possibility of future appointments) is staked upon providing clear, thorough and reasoned analysis may also have an incentive to render consistent awards.

27 Antonio Parra, Secretary General of ICSID at the time, has noted that the 'scope for inconsistent decisions in regard to essentially the same issues is obvious'. Antonio R. Parra, 'Provisions on the Settlement of Investment Disputes in Modern Investment Laws, Bilateral Investment Treaties and Multilateral Instruments on Investment', 12 ICSID REV. -F.I.L.J (1997), 287, 352.

28 ICSID Secretariat, 'Possible Improvements of the Framework for ICSID Arbitration', at: <http://www.worldbank.org/icsid/improve-arb.pdf> [last visited 15 July 2005] at § 7.

29 There were three preliminary procedures, which ICSID suggested. The first related to provisional measures and suggested providing for enhanced clarity as to when parties may seek assistance from national courts and facilitating early applications to tribunals for provisional measures. Id. at § 9. Second, ICSID suggested providing a special procedure where dispositive issues can be decided at an early stage. Id. at § 10. Third,

ICSID suggested expanding the disclosure obligations of arbitrators both at outset and throughout the duration of the case. Id. at §§ 16-17.

30 ICSID noted its promotion of conciliation but suggested that mediation may in some cases be more effective for the parties and has begun to consider the sponsoring of a mediation service for investor-State disputes. Id. at § 18.

31 ICSID suggested a variety of modifications to the current structure to address issues related to transparency of the arbitration process. First, ICSID has suggested the mandatory publication of extracts. Id. at § 12. Second, it suggested clarifying to tribunals that they have the authority to accept and consider submissions from third-parties. Id. at § 13. Finally, ICSID suggested that, after an opportunity to consult the parties, the hearings may be opened up to the public. Id. at § 15.

32 ICSID has collaborated with organizations such as the United Nations Conference on Trade and Development to develop training programs related to investment disputes and recommended that ICSID 'consider ways of intensifying and further systematizing such training activities'. Id. at § 19.

33 Noting their objective to foster coherence and consistency in the emerging case law, ICSID suggested that these goals would be best accomplished by having a single appellate mechanism in order to avoid fragmentation of any potential appeals system. Id. at §§ 21-23.

34 South Center, Developments on Discussions for the Improvement of the Framework for ICSID Arbitration and the Participation of Developing Countries, SC-TADP/AN/INV/1 9-11 (February 2005), at: <http://www.southcentre.org/tadp_webpage/research_papers/investment_project/icsid_discpaper_feb05.doc>.

35 Matthew Gearing & Autumn Ellis, 'Reforming ICSID', 20-1 *Mealy's Int'l Arb. Rep.* 14 (January 2005) International Institute for Sustainable Development, Comments on ICSID Discussion Paper, 'Possible Improvements of the Framework for ICSID Arbitration', 15 June 2005, 6, at: <http://www.iisd.org/pdf/2004/investment_icsid_response.pdf>; Organization for Economic Co-operation and Development, Transparency and Third Party Participation in Investor-State Dispute Settlement Procedures: Statement by the OECD Investment Committee, June 2005, at: <http://www.oecd.org/dataoecd/25/3/34786913.pdf>; see also Bretton Woods Project, 'Secretive World Bank tribunal confronts calls to open up', 13 June 2005, at: <http://www.brettonwoodsproject.org/article.shtml?cmd[126]=x-126-236015> [last visited 28 August 2005] (discussing the mixed reaction to ICSID's proposals).

36 ICSID News Release, Suggested Changes to the ICSID Rules and Regulations, 2 June 2005, at: <http://www.worldbank.org/icsid/sug-changes.htm> [last visited July 15, 2005].

37 ICSID, Suggested Changes to the ICSID Rules and Regulations: Working Paper of the ICSID Secretariat, 12 May 2005, at: <http://www.worldbank.org/icsid/052405-sgmanual.pdf> [last visited 15 July 2005] [hereinafter Working Paper].

38 See Working Paper, *supra* n. 37 at 6-8, 12. As regards efforts related to strengthening non-arbitration options, ICSID simply said it would issue a separate paper on this in due course. Id. at § 5.

39 Charles H. Brower II, 'Structure Legitimacy and NAFTA's Investment Chapter', 36 *Vanderbilt J. Trantion'l L.* (2000), 37; Franck, *supra* n. 1; see also Thomas M. Franck, *The Power of Legitimacy Among Nations* (1990); Thomas M. Franck, *Fairness in International Law And Institutions* (1995).

40 Franck, *supra* n. 1, at 1587-1610.

41 See Franck II, *supra* n. 16 (suggesting that (1) inhibiting claims does not provide an opportunity to provide guidance and clarity to the scope of current jurisprudence and (2) various national courts, which may be unfamiliar with complex international law issues or unwilling to follow the rule of law, coming to different conclusions is unlikely to provide a uniform jurisprudence); but see id. (noting that a single, public, permanent body, akin to a mixed-claims commission, would may usefully promote a consistent and considered jurisprudence).

42 For example, legislative reformers can further operationalize (or eliminate) substantive rights within BITs; and they can also change the nature of the dispute resolution mechanism set out in BITs to ensure that they have opportunities – such as including a provision to require consolidation of related disputes – to prevent inconsistent decisions. See Franck II, *supra* n. 16.

43 Safeguard building might, for example, lead to the creation of direct mechanisms to rectify inconsistency, such as an appellate body to correct inconsistencies or a Free Trade Commission to establish standards of interpretation. This approach might also recommend indirect or hybrid measures to create incentives, or provide opportunities for enhanced consistency; these mechanisms tend to be those recommended by ICSID's Working Paper. See Franck II, *supra* n. 16.

44 See Working Paper, *supra* n. 37 at § 6 (suggesting that there were 'generally favorable reactions' to comments related to transparency).

45 Statute of the International Court of Justice, 26 June 1945, Art. 34, 59 Stat. 2055, *UNTS* 993 (not ex-

pressly providing that arbitral decisions are a form of precedent in international law but setting out a hierarchy of other types of precedent, including 'the teachings of the most highly qualified publicists of the various nations').

46 See, e.g., <www.investmentclaims.com, http://ita.law.uvic.ca/> and <http://www.worldbank.org/icsid/cases/awards.htm>. Westlaw also recently launched a new investment treaty arbitration database, called APPLETON-ISR.

47 The one exception to this is NAFTA cases, where the NAFTA signatories and other sources tend to make such documents available. See <www.naftaclaims.org> and <http://www.state.gov/s/l/c3741.htm> [last visited 10 September 2005].

48 ICSID's proposals usefully balance the need for public participation in a process with public implications against the historical needs and concerns of confidentiality. In particular, the Working Paper suggests that proprietary information be safeguarded and that logistical arrangements are appropriate such that hearings are not disrupted. Likewise, the participation of third parties is limited to situations where such parties have significant interest in the proceedings and they would assist in the determination of a factual or legal issue in dispute; in any event, such participation cannot disrupt the proceedings or burden or prejudice either party. Working Paper, *supra* n. 37 at 10-11.

49 See Institute for Sustainable Development, *IISD Model International Agreement on Investment for Sustainable Development: Negotiators Handbook*, 56 (2005), at: <http://www.iisd.org/pdf/2005/investment_model_int_handbook.pdf>; Franck II, *supra* n. 16.

50 Working Paper, *supra* n. 37 at § 4. During a videolink conference with the author, ICSID explained that those countries which had been the subject of investment treaty claims were in favor of an appellate body – while those countries who had not opposed the idea. ICSID representatives suggested there was not a 'North-South' divide but rather a 'have' and 'have not' divide.

51 For example, the Central American Free Trade Agreement, requires the signatories to consider the creation of an appellate body. United States Trade Representative, CAFTA-DR Final Text, available at: <http://www.ustr.gov/Trade_Agreements/Bilateral/CAFTA/CAFTA-DR_Final_Texts/Section_Index.html>. CAFTA involves the United States, the Dominican Republic, Costa Rica, El Salvador, Guatemala, Honduras, and Nicaragua. United States Trade Representative, *CAFTA Briefing Book*, at: <http://www.ustr.gov/Trade_Agreements/Bilateral/CAFTA/Briefing_Book/Section_Index.html>. Other Free Trade Agreements, also require the United States, Chile and Singapore to consider the creation of appellate bodies. United States-Chile Free Trade Agreement, 6 June 2003, US-Chile, at: <http://www.ustr.gov/new/fta/Chile/text/index.html>, Annex 10-H; United States-Singapore Free Trade Agreement, 6 May 2003, US-Sing., at: <http://www.ustr.gov/new/fta/Singapore/final/2004-01-15-final.pdf>.

# Remarks by C. Ignacio Suárez Anzorena*

## Multiplicity of Claims under Bits: Changing Institutions and Proceedings or Changing the Way We Construe the Treaties?

### 1. Introduction

In this short contribution, I will address the problem of growing numbers of cases in the field of investment treaty adjudication in which the respondent States are subject to multiple claims involving common issues of fact and law before different jurisdictions, both arbitral and/or judicial. In particular, I will try to identify the reasons for

* Formerly of the Argentinean Solicitor General's Office ('Procuración del Tesoro de la Nación') where represented the Argentine Government in multiple international arbitrations, Ignacio Suarez Anzorena is a special counsel to Clifford Chance LLP and member of its International Commercial Arbitration and International Law Groups.

this multiplicity and, taking into account the theme of this conference (i.e., reform), I will try to respond to the following threefold question: Do we have to change institutions, investment treaties or the way investment treaties are being applied?

Until not long ago, the problems rising from multiplicity of proceedings in investment disputes were just theoretical. However, circumstances have changed and multiplicity is now a major issue that may well compromise the credibility and the sustainability of investment arbitration, as shown by the situation in Argentina and the well-known Czech cases.

The most famous cases are the ones against Argentina. There are nearly 40 investment arbitrations pending that have been brought by foreign investors against Argentina, alleging that the Governmental emergency measures adopted in early 2002 in response to a severe economic and social crisis were in breach of the obligations assumed by Argentina in several bilateral investment treaties.[1] Moreover, there is already an award against Argentina for over 130 million US dollars,[2] which I consider far from convincing from a legal and analytical point of view.

Another example of multiplicity of proceedings is the situation experienced not long ago by the Czech Republic. Two different arbitration proceedings were submitted against the Czech Republic, both established in accordance with the Arbitration Rules of the United Nations Commission on International Trade Law,[3] and both focused on certain Governmental measures affecting a local company that owned a TV licence.[4] Both claims were submitted almost simultaneously. One claim was submitted by a Dutch company which was a shareholder of the local company under the Netherlands-Czech Republic BIT, and the other claim was forward by an American investor who was the ultimate controlling shareholder of the local company under the US-Czech Republic BIT. Although the Czech Republic succeeded against the American investor, it was ordered to pay a substantial compensation to the Dutch company. At the end of the day, the American investor was compensated although he had lost his case, and two different arbitrations based on the same legal facts and legal issues were submitted against the Czech Republic and decided the opposite way.

But there are other situations that are not as well-known as the ones arising out of the Argentinean crisis and the Czech Republic cases that deserve to be mentioned. Ecuador has also experienced multiplicity of proceedings on identical facts and points of law in two cases concerning the reimbursement of VAT to oil companies.[5] In addition, Argentina experienced this problem before the crisis, in a couple of cases related to oil taxes, which are now settled.[6] Recently, certain measures adopted by Bolivia and Venezuela regarding the oil industry are also likely to trigger several arbitration cases under BITs based on identical facts and points of law.

In the context of the North American Free Trade Agreement,[7] there have been recent developments concerning multiplicity of claims involving common issues of law and fact. Two arbitration proceedings have recently been started by two different American companies against Mexico to challenge an excise tax on soft drinks[8] and three cases were launched against the United States of America by Canadian companies questioning certain duties and antidumping measures affecting Canadian exports of softwood lumber.[9] Both respondent States sought consolidation of the claims invoking the specific provisions set forth in Article 1126 of NAFTA which provides for the possibility of consolidating claims involving common points of law and fact. While the claims against the United States were consolidated and will be decided by the consolidated tribunal,[10] the claims against Mexico have been remanded to the tribunals that were originally constituted to decide the disputes.[11]

There is little debate as to the fact that multiplicity of claims involving common issues of law and fact is undesirable and should be at least minimized, if not eliminated. Numerous arguments concerning efficiency, integrity and fairness point in favour of such a policy. As regards efficiency, multiplicity implies an allocation of resources to settle disputes that are identical or have issues in common that is not optimal. Efficiency would also point against imposing a burden on the States that have to defend themselves in multiple investment disputes. In relation to integrity, the risk of inconsistent awards may create uncertainty in relation to the rule of the law. As to fairness, multiplicity can lead to procedural harassment, including double-dipping and other forms of abuse of process. A recent study by the World Bank on the economic impact of BITs also identifies the risks of non-fiduciary costs resulting from the fact that States may feel discouraged to push through new legislation in the face of threats of having it continuously challenged before different tribunals.

Given the risk of inconsistent decisions, multiplicity creates uncertainty as to the State of the law, which, in turn, makes it more difficult for investors to calculate the price of the assets to be invested and for the States to evaluate the exposure resulting from regulatory behaviour. A recent study by the World Bank on the economic impact of bilateral investment treaties is instructive as to the risks of non-fiduciary costs that may result from the fact that necessary regulation may be discouraged by the threat of an infinite number of challenges before different tribunals.[12]

## 2. The First Source of Multiplicity: Blanket Protection

The first source of multiplicity is of structural nature. It is related to the non-systemic nature of the legal and institutional arrangements governing investment protection adjudication and is linked to the types of the substantive and jurisdictional commitments made by States in BITs.

Investment treaties provide for blanket protection in favour of an undetermined number of persons and entities and, simultaneously, provide access to multiple types of dispute settlement mechanisms, including *ad hoc* decentralized adjudication in the form of international arbitration. In such a scenario, a given governmental act can trigger as many claims as the number of investors affected by it. It is sensible to argue that those claims may be submitted to different tribunals.

The options available to investors for the purposes of settling disputes with States vary from treaty to treaty but, in general, investors can pursue remedies for an alleged breach of a treaty before national courts or international arbitration tribunals. The arbitration rules of ICSID and UNCITRAL are the most commonly used. In fact, under the wording of a typical BIT, one governmental act affecting 10 individuals can hypothetically give rise to two claims before local courts, two claims before UNCITRAL tribunals and 6 claims before ICSID tribunals.

Claims submitted to local courts are likely to be decided together, given that the local rules on procedure usually provide for compulsory consolidation and the decisions of lower local courts can be reviewed by a hierarchical and centralized system of appeal. In contrast, the outcome of claims submitted to international arbitration, whether under the ICSID, UNCITRAL or other rules, may well be inconsistent with the decisions of local courts and of other arbitral tribunals that are dealing with the same points of law and fact. This potential inconsistency derives from the decentralized nature of international arbitration.

Moreover, neither the ICSID Convention[13] nor the UNCITRAL rules provide for consolidation of claims submitted to arbitration. And the same goes for the large majority of investment treaties.[14] Thus, consolidation of claims is contingent upon the agreement of all the claimant(s) and respondents(s) to have their claims consolidated and, where the UNCITRAL rules are the governing rules of the proceedings, one must check whether the law of the seat of the arbitration provides for consolidation of claims.

The majority of the cases against Argentina fall into the category of 'structural multiplicity'. Even though some *de facto* consolidation was achieved in some cases, there are over 30 different arbitrators appointed to decide nearly 40 cases arising out of one and the same exact event: the Argentinean crisis of late 2001 and early 2002.

Is Argentina in such an uncomfortable position because of the shortcomings of the ICSID Convention? Certainly not. The ICSID convention was silent on consolidation long before most of the investment treaties, including the Argentine ones, were signed and ratified. States were aware or should have been aware of this problem and could have provided for consolidation in the treaties, as is the case in NAFTA[15] and in the current US model BIT.[16]

When ICSID was designed in the early sixties, BITs were a German eccentricity and investor-State arbitration was still a chimera. It is important to take into account that ICSID was conceived as a contractual forum rather than a forum to administer offers of jurisdiction to an undetermined number of persons and entities.[17] This explains, probably, the lack of provisions on consolidation.

One may ask why the main body of the investment treaties currently in force does not offer a solution to this problem. There are two possible explanations. The first one is that multiplicity of claims is mostly a defendant's problem, and investment treaties were generally drafted by capital exporting countries that were unlikely to become defendants. The second reason is that States did not anticipate that liability could arise out of general governmental activity. However, this second argument is weakened by the fact that most treaties exclude international responsibility in cases of emergency as long as treatment of investors is not discriminatory.[18] Such a clause would be redundant if general governmental activity could not create international responsibility.

Going back to the question as to what should be changed, it is quite clear, from my perspective, that, in this case, it is the treaties and not the institutions that are the source of multiplicity of proceedings. However, it is surprising that none of the recent ICSID working papers refer to the possibility of providing for consolidation as a means to minimizing multiplicity. I am aware that under most BITs this would not prevent inconsistencies in non-ICSID cases, but it would certainly be a start.

## 3. The Second Source of Multiplicity: Indirect Claims

The second source of multiplicity is the trend to admit indirect claims or claims for reflective losses, also called derivative claims, especially from direct or indirect investors in equity participations. These kinds of claims are not based upon a wrongdoing affecting the investor directly, but on a wrongdoing affecting a different entity or person, with the result that the value of the investment is diminished. These cases can lead to horizontal multiplicity and/or vertical multiplicity. Horizontal multiplicity occurs when, for example, different shareholders pursue identical claims in relation to measures affecting a certain company. Vertical multiplicity is exemplified by the Czech cases, where identical claims are launched from different layers of one and the same corporate structure.

Four different situations should be distinguished: (i) claims by direct controlling shareholders, (ii) claims by direct minority shareholders, (iii) claims by indirect controlling shareholders, and (iv) claims by indirect minority shareholders.

(i) Indirect claims by direct controlling shareholders do not give rise to multiplicity, as there is only one direct controlling shareholder in each company.
(ii) Indirect claims by direct minority shareholders can give rise to as many claims involving common issues of law and fact as there are equity investors. This is a potential source of very significant multiplicity, as companies might have a substantial number of shareholders.
(iii) Indirect claims by investors in indirect equity holdings can give rise to multiplicity because there can be a vertical chain of companies between the affected company and the ultimate controlling shareholder. Therefore different entities can qualify as an indirect controlling shareholder.
(iv) Indirect claims by minority indirect shareholders can give rise to the same situation as indirect claims by minority direct shareholders, although the former can be aggravated by the fact that the claimants can belong to different layers of the corporate chain.

The difference between this source of multiplicity and the one considered previously is that, in the present case, a particular governmental measure affecting only one entity can give rise to multiple claims. Besides, claims by indirect shareholders can give rise to issues of double dipping and double recovery, given the potential overlap of beneficiaries in the different claims.

What are the problems caused by this situation?[19] The first is that litigation can continue *ad infinitum* given that there can be as many claims as shareholders. Secondly, the creditors' rights may be adversely affected because the investor could be stripping away corporate assets by means of an indirect claim. Thirdly, there are problems of causation, as the existence of the alleged damage to the shareholder claiming a loss may depend (partially or entirely) on the company's reaction to the governmental measure. Finally, a central problem is the destruction of the corporate vehicle, one of the greatest inventions of modern legal theory, due to prohibitive transaction costs resulting from the fragmentation of the company's interests.

What is causing this situation? At the core of the problem is customary international law as reflected in the *Barcelona Traction* case and the fierce reaction this decision has caused in some quarters. It is true that many investment treaties have attempted to get around the *Barcelona Traction* case by, for example, allowing locally controlled companies to qualify as investors and in some cases, like the UK Model BIT, by providing for express protection against expropriation for investors with equity participations.

Tribunals are failing to distinguish properly between the protection of shareholders as direct shareholders and the protection of shareholders against reflective or indirect losses. The arguments that are being used do not support their conclusions in this regard and are not persuasive in my view. Tribunals refer to *ELSI*,[20] to the Iran–US tribunals,[21] and to other decisions that have dealt with the protection of shareholders as such but not with the particular problem of derivative claims.

Shares are investments, it is said. But, to outline a parallelism, the definition of *investment* is like the definition of *property* under national systems and encompasses virtually every right or asset on the market. However, in national systems, it does not follow from the fact that a specific measure has had a negative impact on the value of a certain right or property that the affected party can act as if the owner of the affected asset did not exist.

Subject to very limited exceptions, an investor owns a claim as long as it results from an adverse impact on the rights he has as the owner of a specific investment. The claim does not extend to the reflective losses that he might have suffered as a result of measures affecting third parties that do not qualify as investors and whose assets do not qualify as an investment pursuant to the definitions of the relevant treaty. Otherwise, international tribunals would end up deciding issues that concern the rights of third parties to the proceedings and that are beyond the scope of application and protection under the relevant treaty.

In national systems, this is an issue of standing. It is true that some BITs provide for access to international remedies in the case of disputes related to investments, and shares are investments. But even assuming that jurisdictional barriers can be overcome, what about causation? If the local company has remedies or is pursuing other remedies, it will be quite difficult in most cases to establish a causal link between the damage allegedly suffered by the shareholder and the act of the defendant State. The problem is especially acute in the case of minority shareholders who do not control the local company. The tribunal acting in *Gami* v. *Mexico*[22] seemed to be aware of this and used this argument as one of the grounds to reject the claim.

The recent decision in the *CMS* case overlooked this issue altogether. The tribunal awarded damages to a shareholder who, in principle, was keeping the shares on the basis of the expected future income flows of the company. But if the local company obtains damages for the same loss pursuant to the remedies available to it, CMS will then get double compensation.

Thus, as regards this type of multiplicity, I am inclined to conclude that it can be reduced to some extent by modifying the way treaties are being construed and thus tribunals, and not institutions, are the ones to be blamed for this problem.

## 4. The Third Source of Multiplicity: Availability of Local and International Remedies

The third source of multiplicity concerns the relationship between the international remedies available to investors under investment treaties and the other jurisdictional remedies, whether contractual or not, whether of judicial or arbitral nature, that either the investor or the entity to which the investment is related might pursue. For example, an investor may pursue local remedies and international remedies simultaneously, under different causes of action, but involving the same facts and identical issues under local law. Apart from the risk of inconsistent outcomes, there are clear issues of potential double dipping and double recovery.

Some tribunals have adopted a formalistic approach to deciding whether claims are precluded from being heard on the basis that investors have made a definitive decision between international remedies and local remedies (the so-called 'fork in the road' provision), as provided by some investment treaties. There is a trend to require identity *rationae personae* and *rationae materiae*, including identical causes of action.[23] Such a trend, combined with the practice of allowing indirect claims by shareholders and the practice of distinguishing treaty claims from contractual claims on the basis of how the claims have been labelled by the claimants instead of applying a more substantive test, constitutes a significant source of multiplicity. In this context a claimant can (i) simultaneously pursue remedies under local law and under certain treaties to seek the same relief (i.e., damages) and/or (ii) use a corporate vehicle to bring a treaty claim before local jurisdictions and another corporate vehicle to bring a treaty claim before an international arbitral tribunal.

NAFTA's chapter 11, for example, has a 'no U-turn clause' that requires waiving local remedies as a pre-requisite to pursuing international remedies.[24] Thus multiplicity between local and international remedies and all the dangers associated with it are ruled out. But a significant number of BITs are either silent or unclear on the subject or, even when providing that the investor has to choose between international and domestic remedies, only refer to this option as 'disputes concerning the application of the investment treaty'.

In summary, the problem is again mostly a problem of drafting of the investment treaties. No institution to be reformed, but treaties to be overhauled if multiplicity arising from this source is to be reduced. It should be noted, however, that a greater willingness to grant requests to stay proceedings pending decisions of other tribunals, and to consider allegations of abuse of process when claimants engage in procedural harassment and/or excessive speculation to the detriment of good faith and good administration of justice would reduce the possibility of multiplicity arising from this source in some cases. Such a change of attitude would also contribute to preserving the reputation and the sustainability of investment protection adjudication.

## 5. Final Considerations

It is quite clear that most of the problems related to multiplicity were created by the States that put themselves in awkward positions as potential respondents when drafting investment treaties. While it is reasonable to assume that, as a general rule, they did not intend to create such multiplicity, the structure and the wording of most bilateral investment treaties leave little space for interpretation to prevent this undesirable effect.

It is worth mentioning, however, that certain institutional reforms might be helpful in correcting this problem, at least to some extent. Given that there are nearly 2000 treaties in force, an institutional solution might be more efficient than renegotiating each and every treaty.

Creating an appellate system or a permanent tribunal to replace the current structure of *ad hoc* panels, whether in the context of ICSID, which has recently promoted such a possibility,[25] or in a different context, might lead to greater uniformity and certainty. However, such a system would not eliminate multiplicity arising from claims submitted to local jurisdictions or, if such a system was created within ICSID, multiplicity arising from claims brought under other arbitrations rules. Moreover, this type of solution is highly unlikely at a global level, in the medium term, if ever. Certain recent treaties, such as CAFTA or the US Model BIT, provide for the possibility of incorporating an appellate system to complement the dispute settlement mechanism set forth in the relevant treaty, but, of course, such an addition would only have effect among the parties to that treaty.

Another possibility is to promote a system of *stare decisis* or at least a greater authoritativeness of precedent. However, such a philosophy conflicts with the most basic principles underlying *ad hoc* adjudication and the right of the parties to participate in the constitution of the tribunal.[26] It is submitted, however, that it is desirable that tribunals pay proper attention to the body of jurisprudence that is being created. This should be seen as an opportunity to reflect rather than an opportunity to repeat and 'free ride' on other tribunal's conclusions.

To conclude, if the equation of greater substantive and jurisdictional protection for investors in exchange for a greater volume of investment and/or lower cost of capital is to be sustainable, investors need certainty to price their assets and States need certainty to know how to deal with price regulation. Multiplicity is a major problem in this regard, and every effort to minimize its undesirable effects should be made. This would contribute to preserve the noble aims that inspired bilateral investment treaties from disrepute.

## Notes

1 Hereinafter BIT or BITs.

2 *CMS Gas Transmission Company* v. *Argentine Republic* – International Centre for the Settlement of Investment Disputes (hereinafter ICSID) case No. ARB/01/8 (hereinafter the *CMS* case).

3 Hereinafter UNCITRAL.

4 *Lauder* v. *Czech Republic* (UNCITRAL arbitration under the USA/Czech Republic BIT) and *CME Czech Republic B.V.* v. *Czech Republic* (UNCITRAL arbitration under the Netherlands/Czech Republic BIT).

5 *Occidental* v. *Republic of Ecuador* (LCIA case No. UN3667) and *Encana* v. *Republic of Ecuador* (UNCITRAL arbitration under the Canada/Ecuador BIT).

6 *Mobil Exploration and Development Inc. Suc. Argentina and Mobil Argentina, S.A.* v. *Argentine Republic* (*ICSID* case No. ARB/04/16) and *Enersis, S.A. et al* v. *Argentine Republic* (ICSID case No. ARB/03/21).

7 Hereinafter NAFTA.

8 *Corn Products International, Inc.* v. *United Mexican States* (ICSID case No. ARB (AF)/04/01) and *Archer Daniels Midland Company and Tate & Lyle Ingredients Americas, Inc.* v. *United Mexican States* (ICSID case No. ARB (AF)/04/05).

9 *Canfor Corp.* v. *United States of America, Tembec, Inc. et al.* v. *United States of America* and *Terminal Forest Products, Ltd.* v. *United States of America.*

10 *See Canfor Corp.* v. *United States of America, Tembec, Inc. et al.* v. *United States of America* and *Terminal Forest Products, Ltd.* v. *United States of America,* Order of the Consolidation Tribunal of 7/09/2005.

11 *See Corn Products International, Inc.* v. *United Mexican States* (ICSID case No. ARB (AF)/04/01) and *Archer Daniels Midland Company and Tate & Lyle Ingredients Americas, Inc.* v. *United Mexican States* (ICSID case No. ARB (AF)/04/05), Order of the Consolidation Tribunal of 20/05/2006.

12 Mary Hallward-Dreimeier, 'Do Bilateral Investment Treaties Attract FDI? Only a bit ... and it might bite', *World Bank Policy Research Working Paper Series,* Number 3121, Washington, World Bank.

[13] The Convention on the Settlement of Investment Disputes between States and Nationals of other States, which was signed in Washington D.C. and entered into force on 14 October 1966 (hereinafter the ICSID Convention).

[14] See, however, Art. 33 of the 2004 US Model BIT and the investment chapters of the Free Trade Agreements entered by the United States of America.

[15] Art. 1125 (consolidation) of NAFTA, which reads as follows:

'1. A Tribunal established under this Article shall be established under the UNCITRAL Arbitration Rules, and shall conduct its proceedings in accordance with those Rules, except as modified by this Subchapter.

2. Where a Tribunal established under this Article is satisfied that claims have been submitted to arbitration under Article 1120 that have a question of law or fact in common, the Tribunal may, in the interests of fair and efficient resolution of the claims, and after hearing the disputing parties, order that the Tribunal:

(a) shall assume jurisdiction over, and hear and determine together, all or part of the claims; or

(b) shall assume jurisdiction over, and hear and determine one or more of the claims, the determination of which it believes would assist in the resolution of the others.

3. A disputing party that seeks an order under paragraph 2 shall request the Secretary-General of ICSID to establish a Tribunal and shall specify in the request:

(a) the name of the disputing Party or disputing parties against which the order is sought;

(b) the nature of the order sought; and

(c) the grounds on which the order is sought.

4. The disputing party shall give to the disputing Party or disputing parties against which the order is sought a copy of the request.

5. Within 60 days of receipt of the request, the Secretary- General of ICSID shall establish a Tribunal consisting of three arbitrators. The Secretary-General shall appoint the presiding arbitrator from the roster described in paragraph 4 of Article 1124. In the event that no such presiding arbitrator is available to serve, the Secretary-General shall appoint a presiding arbitrator, who is not a national of any of the Parties, from the ICSID Panel of Arbitrators. The Secretary-General shall appoint the two other members from the roster described in paragraph 4 of Article 1124, and to the extent not available from that roster, from the ICSID Panel of Arbitrators, and to the extent not available from that panel, in the discretion of the Secretary-General. One member shall be a national of the disputing Party and one member shall be a national of the Party of the disputing investors.

6. Where a Tribunal has been established under this Article, a disputing party that has not been named in a request made under paragraph 3 may make a written request to the Tribunal that it be included in an order made under paragraph 2, and shall specify in the request:

(a) the party's name and address;

(b) the nature of the order sought; and

(c) the grounds on which the order is sought.

7. A disputing party described in paragraph 6 shall give a copy of its request to the parties named in a request made under paragraph 3.

8. A Tribunal established under Article 1120 shall not have jurisdiction to decide a claim, or a part of a claim, over which a Tribunal established under this Article has assumed jurisdiction.

9. A disputing Party shall give to the Secretariat of the Commission, within 15 days of receipt by the disputing Party, a copy of:

(a) a request for arbitration made under paragraph 1 of Article 36 of the ICSID Convention;

(b) a notice for arbitration made under Article 2 of the Additional Facility Rules; or

(c) a notice of arbitration given under the UNCITRAL Arbitration Rules.

10. A disputing Party shall give to the Secretariat of the Commission a copy of a request made under paragraph 3 of this Article:

(a) within 15 days of receipt of the request, in the case of a request made by a disputing investor;

(b) within 15 days of making the request, in the case of a request made by the disputing Party.

11. A disputing Party shall give to the Secretariat of the Commission a copy of a request made under paragraph 6 of this Article within 15 days of receipt of the request.

12. The Secretariat of the Commission shall maintain a public register consisting of the documents referred to in paragraphs 9, 10 and 11.'

[16] See Art. 33 (consolidation) of the US model BIT, which reads as follows:

'1. Where two or more claims have been submitted separately to arbitration under Article 24(1) and the claims have a question of law or fact in common and arise out of the same events or circumstances, any disputing party may seek a consolidation order in accordance with the agreement of all the disputing parties sought to be covered by the order or the terms of paragraphs 2 through 10.

2. A disputing party that seeks a consolidation order under this Article shall deliver, in writing, a request to the Secretary-General and to all the disputing parties sought to be covered by the order and shall specify in the request:

(a) the names and addresses of all the disputing parties sought to be covered by the order;

(b) the nature of the order sought; and

(c) the grounds on which the order is sought.

3. Unless the Secretary-General finds within 30 days after receiving a request under paragraph 2 that the request is manifestly unfounded, a tribunal shall be established under this Article.

4. Unless all the disputing parties sought to be covered by the order otherwise agree, a tribunal established under this Article shall comprise three arbitrators:

(a) one arbitrator appointed by agreement of the claimants;

(b) one arbitrator appointed by the respondent; and

(c) the presiding arbitrator appointed by the Secretary-General, provided, however, that the presiding arbitrator shall not be a national of either Party.

5. If, within 60 days after the Secretary-General receives a request made under paragraph 2, the respondent fails or the claimants fail to appoint an arbitrator in accordance with paragraph 4, the Secretary-General, on the request of any disputing party sought to be covered by the order, shall appoint the arbitrator or arbitrators not yet appointed. If the respondent fails to appoint an arbitrator, the Secretary-General shall appoint a national of the disputing Party, and if the claimants fail to appoint an arbitrator, the Secretary-General shall appoint a national of the non-disputing Party.

6. Where a tribunal established under this Article is satisfied that two or more claims that have been submitted to arbitration under Article 24(1) have a question of law or fact in common, and arise out of the same events or circumstances, the tribunal may, in the interest of fair and efficient resolution of the claims, and after hearing the disputing parties, by order: – 32 –

(a) assume jurisdiction over, and hear and determine together, all or part of the claims;

(b) assume jurisdiction over, and hear and determine one or more of the claims, the determination of which it believes would assist in the resolution of the others; or

(c) instruct a tribunal previously established under Article 27 [Selection of Arbitrators] to assume jurisdiction over, and hear and determine together, all or part of the claims, provided that

(i) that tribunal, at the request of any claimant not previously a disputing party before that tribunal, shall be reconstituted with its original members, except that the arbitrator for the claimants shall be appointed pursuant to paragraphs 4(a) and 5; and

(ii) that tribunal shall decide whether any prior hearing shall be repeated.

7. Where a tribunal has been established under this Article, a claimant that has submitted a claim to arbitration under Article 24(1) and that has not been named in a request made under paragraph 2 may make a written request to the tribunal that it be included in any order made under paragraph 6, and shall specify in the request:

(a) the name and address of the claimant;

(b) the nature of the order sought; and

(c) the grounds on which the order is sought.

The claimant shall deliver a copy of its request to the Secretary-General.

8. A tribunal established under this Article shall conduct its proceedings in accordance with the UNCITRAL Arbitration Rules, except as modified by this Section.

9. A tribunal established under Article 27 [Selection of Arbitrators] shall not have jurisdiction to decide a claim, or a part of a claim, over which a tribunal established or instructed under this Article has assumed jurisdiction.

10. On application of a disputing party, a tribunal established under this Article, pending its decision under paragraph 6, may order that the proceedings of a tribunal established under Article 27 [Selection of Arbitrators] be stayed, unless the latter tribunal has already adjourned its proceedings.'

[17] It should be noted, however, that the Report of the Executive Directors refers also to jurisdictional offers in local legislation.

[18] See for example, Art. IV.3 of the US-Argentina BIT, which reads as follows:

'3. Nationals or companies of either Party whose investments suffer losses in the territory of the other Party owing to war or other armed conflict, revolution, state of national emergency, insurrection, civil disturbance or other similar events shall be accorded treatment by such other Party no less favorable than that accorded to its own nationals or companies or to nationals or companies of any third country, whichever is the more favorable treatment, as regards any measures it adopts in relation to such losses.'

19 See the United States of America 'Article 1128 Submission on Jurisdiction' of 30/06/2003 in the NAFTA case *GAMI Investment, Inc.* v. *The United Mexican States* <www.naftaclaims.com>.
20 *Elettronica Sicula, S.p.A.* (ELSI), *United States of America* v. *Republic of Italy* (International Court of Justice – 1987/1989).
21 *Amoco International Finance Corporation* v. *Iran* (1987) 15 Iran-US CTR 189.
22 Award of 15 November 2004 <www.naftaclaims.com>.
23 See, for example, the decisions on jurisdiction in the following cases: *CMS Gas Transmission Company* v. *Argentine Republic* (ICSID case No. ARB/01/8), decision on jurisdiction of 2/05/2005; *Enron and Ponderosa Assets* v. *Argentine Republic* (ICSID case No. ARB/01/3), decision on jurisdiction of 14/01/2004; *LG&E Energy Corp., LG&E Capital Corp. and LG&E International Inc.* v. *Argentine Republic* (ICSID case No. ARB/02/1), decision on jurisdiction of 30/04/2004; and *Azurix Corp.* v. *Argentina Republic* (ICSID case No. ARB/01/12), decision on jurisdiction of 08/12/2003. It must be noted that in those decisions the tribunals tried to apply the US–Argentina BIT and if a BIT with a different wording was applicable the decision on jurisdiction would probably not be the same. See for example, *Vivendi Universal & Compañía de Aguas del Aconquija* v. *Argentine Republic* (ICSID case No. ARB/97/3), decision on annulment of 03/07/2002, interpreting the text of the France–Argentina BIT, and *Waste Management* v. *United Mexican States I* (ICSID case No. ARB(AF)/98/2), decision on jurisdiction of 30/04/2004, interpreting NAFTA's Chapter 11.
24 Art. 1121.2 NAFTA, which reads as follows:
'2. A disputing investor may submit a claim under Article 1117 to arbitration only if both the investor and the enterprise:

(a) consent to arbitration in accordance with the provisions of this Subchapter; and

(b) waive their right to initiate or continue before any administrative tribunal or court under the domestic law of any Party any proceedings with respect to the measure of the disputing Party that is alleged to be a breach of Subchapter A of this Chapter, Article 1502(3)(a) (Monopolies and State Enterprises) or Article 1503(2) (State Enterprises), except for proceedings for injunctive, declaratory or other extraordinary relief, not involving the payment of damages, before an administrative tribunal or court under the domestic law of the disputing Party.

3. A consent and waiver required by this Article shall be in writing, shall be given to the disputing Party, and shall be included in the submission of a claim to arbitration.'
25 See the working paper released by the ICSID Secretariat on Suggested Changes to the ICSID Rules and Regulations <http://www.worldbank.org/icsid>.
26 For an interesting discussion on the subject see *SGS Société Générale de Surveillance S.A.* v. *Republic of the Philippines* (ICSID case No. ARB/02/6), decision on jurisdiction of 29/01/2004, and *AES Corporation* v. *Argentine Republic* (case No. ARB/02/17).

## Remarks by Jan Paulsson*

### The practitioner's perspective on the need for reform: '*Hâtez-vous lentement*'

It seems that what was a hot topic when the organizers of the session thought it up has turned into something rather more lukewarm. The topic has to do – if I focus exactly on what I was intending to speak on – with the need or not to have an appellate review of the decisions of investment tribunals, whether or not their decisions can be final, or whether they need to be corrected. Last year, I suppose, when this conference was planned, this was very much in the foreground of a number of discussions as it was one of the conceivable elements for a possible reform of ICSID arbitration that as you have heard, has now been put off, happily I would suggest, to another day.

* Partner and Head of the International Arbitration and Public International Law Groups at Freshfields Bruckhaus Deringer in Paris. The original manuscript of this contribution was not received. The following text has been derived from the tapes on which the conference sessions were recorded.

When the end of the world is nigh and all of our existence is about to be rubbed out, we will do drastic things because anything is better than the end of the world, and to some extent I had the feeling that some of the apocalyptic motivations a couple of years ago of this thrust towards appealing investment awards had to do with perceptions that the end of the world was nigh, and there one wanted to change everything without really giving much thought to what it was one was proposing to put in its stead. I think prudence has come to the fore as people have thought about what we have today and the difficulties of putting something else in place. I do not know what the end of the world was conceived to be, perhaps depending on which your favourite country is, the end of the world might be the conceivable outcome that the United States might be held liable for violation of international law, and then I guess you would want reviews until somebody says that that is not true, and then I suppose the system would be sufficient, and perhaps there is still some sort of a motivation in that direction and people who want to sign treaties with the United States, like the Dominican Republic might go along with this, and so we continue to have some impetus in this direction. The United States, of course, has yet to lose a single dollar in an investment arbitration. My tea-leaves tell me that before the end of the summer we will read the Methanex award and see if this string continues unabated. My tea-leaves tell me nothing about what we will read in that award, but that is where we stand today.

I am speaking apparently as a representative of practitioners. Ignacio Suarez Anzorena was speaking as a representative of States. That suggests to me an unfortunate dichotomy. That apprehension I had was also accentuated when I read a line in Susan Francks's paper which said 'arbitration practitioners make clever arguments to apply rights to an ever-expanding range of government conduct', and I wish to protest that some arbitration practitioners just conceivably might make clever arguments about how to restrict BIT creep and that some of us are sometimes in that position. Speaking personally, I have been involved in 13 ICSID arbitrations as counsel and as it happens, 7 times on the side of States and 6 times on the side of investors. This makes me a specialist, not an expert. Experts are people who have known one case and therefore know everything and have no doubts whatsoever.

So, who wants review? Be careful, Cameroon certainly did not want an appellate review in what was the first ICSID decision ever to be taken to the *ad hoc* committees of ICSID. I happened to be the loser on that appeal and found a very irate client thinking that they had won a conclusive victory then finding out that for the first time ever someone tries the annulment proceeding, and for the first time ever it has to be Cameroon that has its victory taken away from it. I suppose today, as we sit here in the specific context of investment decisions, that the United Arab Emirates and Algeria feel the same way at having won jurisdictional decisions and then finding themselves before *ad hoc* committees. No one is questioning at this point the role of *ad hoc* committees. The question is whether we go further and have appellate review.

When I mentioned that the hot topic has become lukewarm, you will see that the way it has gone into this happy lukewarm solution where everyone can agree is that we seem to be agreeing on one thing, which is transparency, and with this I too agree.

Transparency is something that will improve the process and it is not unrelated to the idea of getting a correct, meaningful, predictable, and consistent decision. It has something to do with the quality of awards. We learned this when we were 4 years old. We do behave a little bit differently if someone is looking at us. Indeed, those of us who are trying very hard to produce good awards – human nature is what it is – we do not mind too much if somebody actually is looking to see that the work we did was actually good. So transparency, I think, is a good thing indeed.

As for consistency and predictability and the idea that its absence in investment arbitration is proof that the world is coming to an end, let me suggest to you that legal systems in which justice comes quickly and perfectly at no cost to the deserving party is something which is unknown in any human system, and if we have been paying attention to the things that we have heard in the couple of days of this conference, you will have heard of the imperfections of the struggling judicial system of East Timor for instance.

But let me tell you that if you go to the courthouse steps of any city in France, you will see a number of people coming out of the courtroom saying 'this legal system of our country is just awful! What they have done to me, and let me tell you…' And you will find people in every town who will complain about what has happened to them and how it is inconsistent and unfair. And sometimes they do have a point.

One of my favourite legal systems is the Swiss one and whenever I have the audacity to tell a Swiss colleague that I admire their legal system, they start rolling their eyes and say 'you should have heard what happened in the canton of such-and-such not so long ago, and some crazy decision came down against my client, which I absolutely don't agree with.'

Sweden, I think, is also a jurisdiction which has a good judicial system with very little corruption but there are challenges there as well as budgetary restraints and the prosperity of the legal profession in the private sphere makes us ask questions whether or not the best legal minds are still attracted to the judicial profession.

So imperfections exist everywhere, and I now wish to make the additional point that I said I wanted to add to the six or seven points that I made in my contribution in writing. It is this: I am in sharp disagreement with Susan Franck, I must say, but that will at least enliven our debate on that point, with regard to what one is to make of the Czech cases. Why do we care about inconsistency if we are not involved in the case? We care only if it makes it more difficult for us as advisers or as parties to predict what will happen in future cases.

On that score, there was no meaningful inconsistency in these two decisions. Two tribunals held that the Czech Republic had violated the relevant BIT – two BITs involved as you heard – but the operative language was the same. Each tribunal held that there had been a violation, and the violation was that if you give a licence to somebody under certain conditions and that party then invests in reliance on an understanding as to the basis of which that licence is given, you cannot jerk the investor around by changing the rules of the game. That is unfair, and unfairness is proscribed in each of the relevant BITs. The tribunals then went on, as a matter of fact in each of those cases, to find that factually there was a difficulty of causation, and to understand what the grounds were and to decide which case you prefer, you really have to go into the facts of those cases, and I do not think for any advisor that it is necessary at all to worry about any normative inconsistency in those two decisions.

The outcome was indeed different in monetary terms but of course the Czech Republic brought that upon itself by making a tactical error when rejecting the consolidation of the two cases before one single tribunal. In the end, it was not a spectacular tactical error, it was hedging your bets, and so sometimes when I hear complaints from the lawyers of the Czech Republic, I say to myself 'so you really think the end of the world is nigh because of this lack of consistency? You really wanted to lose twice, is that right?'

By contrast, let's take cases where we have heard about inconsistencies that are of a normative nature. SGS versus Philippines, SGS versus Pakistan. Same type of contract. SGS is a service company that inspects goods which are then sent on to Pakistan and the Philippines. Each contract called for a local – in one case, arbitration, in another case, court – dispute resolution method.

In each BIT there was something called an umbrella clause, an umbrella clause which provides that each party to the BIT – the two States – undertakes to respect their international obligations. As a result, these contracts contained 'internationalised' obligations, i.e., a 'mere' contractual breach was suddenly elevated to an international forum. The investor is thereby entitled to choose not to use the contractually stipulated dispute resolution mechanism and use instead the BIT. In each case, the foreigner – SGS – preferred that its contract not be dealt with in local arbitration or in a local court.

In the Pakistan case, the ICSID tribunal said it had no jurisdiction because this type of claim is not suitable for ICSID arbitration and an investor would have to go to local arbitration in Pakistan. In the Philippines case, the tribunal did not hold that it was without jurisdiction, but it said that the claim was not admissible. The investor must first go to the Philippine courts and if any part of its claim still remained, then it could eventually come back. The two tribunals decided in opposite directions: roughly one rejected jurisdiction and the other accepted it. So, what are we to make of this?

In terms of what the outcome was, the daily newspapers of Pakistan, which I consulted on the Internet the day after the decision, claimed victory. The newspapers in Pakistan trumpeted 'We won. Pakistan obtained what it wanted. This case is not going to be heard in ICSID, it's going to be heard in accordance with the contractual dispute resolution system.' And what did the newspapers in the Philippines say? 'We won. This dispute will not be heard in ICSID, it will be heard in accordance with the contractual dispute resolution system.' Now we hear that these cases are intolerably inconsistent and make it difficult to make predictions for the future.

While agreeing that, unlike the Czech cases, there is a normative distinction in these two cases, I am not quite sure how that makes it difficult to predict the future.

We might want to clear this up, but surely that would be a matter – if we were going to get into it at all – for a type of cassation system where principles of true law are going to be adjusted and not where factual matters determined by tribunals are to be revised. Before we get to that point, we are going to have a debate as to whether the inherent legitimacy of tribunals composed in accordance with the agreement of the parties, the investment tribunal, have something about them which makes them less worthy than whatever appellate body you have in mind. But that is a long discussion and much beyond what we can do today.

## Conclusions*

My conclusion is that it is urgent to go slowly: *speude bradeôs, festina lente.* The system of investment arbitration is not in a crisis. It has taken many years to create an immensely valuable mechanism which enables states to give internationally meaningful promises. No one is saying that improvements are unwelcome. But dispassionate consideration of possible ameliorations should not be distorted by the fervour with which some disappointed litigants insist on blaming everyone but themselves, and would like to convince the world that the whole system is fundamentally deficient.

Once the following truths set in, the impulse for radical change should abate:

1. The interest in finality is likely to be shared by states as well as investors. The first ICSID award to be annulled was one in which Cameroon had entirely prevailed. The government was disappointed to find that its victory could be snatched away by a procedure which opened the way for half a decade of more litigation, at great cost and little improvement in quality of decision-making.
2. No investor has ever drafted an investment treaty. Investors are not to be blamed for defective drafting. States wanting to limit the scope of such treaties can do so by providing that investors can invoke them only with respect to investments that are specifically approved in accordance with a defined process. States wanting to avoid a multiplicity of international proceedings arising out of the same measure can provide for consolidation – as the NAFTA does.
3. An international consensus seems to be emerging that transparency is important in investment arbitration. This is a good development. Its welcome effects will undoubtedly include an amelioration in the quality of awards. It is not sound policy to change everything at once. Let us see how investment arbitration works with transparency.
4. 'Consistency' is a mirage. It should be pursued, but it will not be attained – at least not with respect to the truly difficult and irremediably open-textured issues. And will most certainly not be achieved by creating appellate bodies. The proof: generations of experience with national supreme courts.
5. The practical realities of creating appellate bodies in this field are daunting, and there is no basis on which to assume that the appellate bodies being proposed would in fact have greater claims to legitimacy than the traditional tribunals set up in accordance with traditional mechanisms.

* As submitted by the author for the purposes of the Conference.

## Remarks by Alejandro A. Escobar*

### Procedural Issues Raised by Treaty Interpretation in ICSID Proceedings

#### 1. Introduction

The 1965 ICSID or Washington Convention[1] is the international treaty that governs arbitration proceedings between each of its Contracting States and nationals of other Contracting States. It establishes ICSID as the intergovernmental organization responsible for administering those proceedings through its Secretariat.

Under the Convention, ICSID has a set of Conciliation Rules, Arbitration Rules, Rules for Institution of Proceedings and a set of Administrative and Financial Regulations. These rules were adopted in 1967, revised somewhat in 1984, and harmonized in 2002.[2] ICSID Convention proceedings have been described as self-contained, since they operate regardless of national procedural rules and without the intervention of national courts. They do indeed constitute a system.

Article 42(1) of the ICSID Convention provides that, in the absence of agreement by the disputing parties, the arbitration tribunal shall apply international law together with the law of the disputing Contracting Party to decide the dispute.[3] The rules of public international law referred to are understood to be those found in Article 38 of the ICJ Statute.[4]

ICSID arbitration tribunals have therefore normally had to deal with the application of international law sources, not least the application of the ICSID Convention itself.

Recently, however, ICSID tribunals have been facing a number of issues that arise from the interpretation of investment treaties. Those treaties serve, in the great majority of proceedings currently pending at ICSID, both as the basis of consent for the proceeding as well as the principal source of substantive rules for deciding the dispute. In a 22 October 2004 discussion paper on possible improvements of ICSID arbitration procedures, the ICSID Secretariat noted that there are more than 1,500 investment treaties, including some multilateral treaties, with consent provisions for ICSID arbitration.[5] The paper notes a resulting dramatic growth in the number of arbitration proceedings: 73 new cases from the beginning of 2002 to October 2004, compared to 95 cases through 2001. A tally today of the number of ICSID registered cases, both concluded and pending, comparing those registered before and after the year 2000, provides an even more dramatic contrast.[6] From 1966 through 1999, ICSID registered a total of 69 cases, of which three were conciliation proceedings, 66 arbitrations. From 2000 to date (11 September 2005), ICSID has registered 132 cases, of which two have been conciliation proceedings, 130 arbitrations (i.e., nearly twice as many arbitrations as in the preceding 33 years). There are 96 pending arbitration proceedings.

* Associate in Latham & Watkins, London. The author was Senior Counsel at ICSID through July 2002. He did not take part in the preparation of the 22 October 2004 ICSID discussion paper or in the 12 May 2005 working paper referred to below.

ICSID now has a set of proposed changes to the ICSID arbitration rules.[7] They are an attempt to provide tools for coping with some of the new procedural issues that face ICSID tribunals and the Secretariat as a consequence of the general consents of ICSID member and other States in their treaties providing for the legal protection of foreign investment. This paper will attempt to outline the type of procedural issues that have been raised by investment treaty cases at ICSID, discuss some of the current set of proposed changes to the ICSID rules, and offer some general conclusions about possible future developments in the ICSIS system.

## 2. The Impact of Investment Treaties on ICSID's Management of Proceedings

The ICSID Secretariat has had to deal with the procedural dimensions of arbitration pursuant to investment treaties since the first case under such a treaty was registered on 20 July 1987.[8]

The Secretariat no doubt had to consider how it might deal with potential issues of this kind since the registration on 28 August 1984 of the first case in which a claimant investor invoked a State's general offer of arbitration contained in its domestic investment law.[9] The second investment treaty arbitration before ICSID was registered on 2 February 1993.[10] In each subsequent year through 1996, ICSID registered about two cases in which investment treaty issues arose. In 1997, ICSID registered its first two investor-State proceedings under the North American Free Trade Agreement and its first case against Argentina. Since then, the number of investment treaty arbitrations at ICSID has grown almost exponentially.

The developments just described have in turn led to developments in how the ICSID Secretariat deals both with the parties and with the various arbitral tribunals established to hear and decide investment treaty cases. This is of course not the place to enter into a detailed examination of ICSID's practice in this respect.[11] A first approach, however, at a description those issues could consider the various stages of the arbitration proceeding in which investment treaty issues have arisen.

### A. Registration of the request for arbitration

The institution of proceedings on the basis of investment treaties has highlighted the ICSID Secretary-General's role as the 'gatekeeper' of ICSID arbitration. Article 36 of the ICSID Convention call for the Secretary-General to register a request for arbitration 'unless he finds, on the basis of the information contained in the request, that the dispute is manifestly outside the jurisdiction of the Centre'.

Although this seems like a straightforward provision, it may not be a simple matter for a request for arbitration to account for all the jurisdictional requirements under both the ICSID Convention and the relevant investment treaty (the latter being the source of the terms of consent to arbitration). The claimant, for example, may be concerned that jurisdictional or substantive issues may be flagged and raised unnecessarily if the request is too detailed. The ICSID Secretariat, on its part, may harbour the concern that registration may (erroneously) be seen to influence a future decision on jurisdiction or the merits;[12] or that rejection of registration may be seen as too restrictive at a time when treaty provisions have not been fully tested.[13] There is also the simple reality that the ICSID Secretariat is exposed to the criticism of the respondent party. Those criticisms either might too easily overlook the limitations imposed by Article 36 of the ICSID Convention or might simply consider it to be a shortcoming of the Convention.

It is in this context that ICSID has been careful to ensure that requests for arbitration do address all the jurisdictional requirements that arise from investment treaties as a basis of consent, in combination with the ICSID Convention.[14] Only when such requirements are addressed would the Secretary-General be in a position to determine whether the dispute is, according to the information contained in the request, manifestly outside the jurisdiction of the Centre. It is said in common parlance about investment treaty arbitration before ICSID that claimants have to 'fit into two treaties, not just one'.[15]

## B. The appointment of arbitrators

The importance of the appointment of arbitrators in investment treaty arbitration proceedings cannot be understated. Accordingly, ICSID's role in this respect is crucial.

Over the years, ICSID has faced significant logistical challenges that derive from a combination of (a) an almost exponential increase in the number of cases initiated on the basis of investment treaties; and (b) the fact that Articles 38 and 40 of the Convention require ICSID's appointments to be made by the President of ICSID's Administrative Council from the ICSID Panel of Arbitrators,[16] unless the parties agree on an arrangement outside the scope of these provisions.

Given that designations to the ICSID Panel depend largely on member governments, a sufficiently large pool of appropriate candidates is not always available. ICSID has been proactive in this respect, and has now embraced the practice of proposing to the parties that they designate the ICSID Secretary-General as an appointing authority, thus precisely taking the appointing procedure outside the scope of Articles 38 and 40 of the Convention. On occasion, even without such prior designation, ICSID has directly proposed names of arbitrator appointees to the parties from outside the Panel. Such proposals come with the implied proviso that agreement of the parties is needed in order to make ICSID's appointment consistent with the Convention. Nonetheless, this practice is a noteworthy example of the Secretariat's involved handling of the process.

## C. Objections to jurisdiction and preliminary phase of proceedings

A respondent could raise questions, such as attribution, cause of action or standing, that go to issues of interpretation of the relevant treaty. Those questions may concern the ICSID Secretariat if only because some respondent States have on occasion sought to reverse the registration of a request.[17]

There could be additional questions of jurisdiction in terms of the scope of application of the treaty. Although those questions, if they concern the scope of the relevant obligations assumed by the respondent State, might readily be framed as issues going to the merits of a dispute, tribunals will often be faced with having to decide questions preliminarily if they can be treated as discrete issues. If this decision is not always an easy one for an ICSID tribunal, the difficulty is not aided by the requirement that proceedings on the merits are automatically suspended upon the raising of an objection to jurisdiction. The ICSID Secretariat is being gently proactive by proposing a procedural amendment[18] that would leave suspension to the discretion of the tribunal and thus instil agility in handling this sort of issues.

The role of ICSID here could also be a passive one: a tribunal could want to know how other ICSID tribunals have dealt with similar questions and they may consult ICSID awards and other publications.

## D. Procedures for taking into account the views of non-disputing State Parties to an investment treaty for the purpose of its interpretation

Investment treaties that provide for investor-State arbitration also provide for State-State procedures for settling questions of interpretation of the treaty. For example, NAFTA provides that the Free Trade Commission of the three NAFTA Parties may agree on interpretations of the NAFTA investment provisions that will be binding on arbitral tribunals.

BITs normally provide for State-State arbitration or sometimes submission to the ICJ. At least on one occasion the State-State procedure was put in motion alongside the ICSID procedure. This led to a request for suspension by the Respondent State, but the tribunal held that 'the conditions for a suspension of the proceedings were not met'.[19] Could or should there be a 'preventive' or 'precautionary' role for ICSID in this type of situation?

It is a well-known feature of investor-State proceedings under the North American Free Trade Agreement ('NAFTA') that non-disputing States may make submissions on questions of interpretation of relevant NAFTA provisions to the investor-State arbitral tribunals. ICSID has accommodated these provisions well in the management of NAFTA proceedings conducted under the ICSID Additional Facility Rules.

This feature is absent from investment treaties concluded among non-NAFTA States. In a non-ICSID case, the respondent State approached the non-disputing State to attempt an agreed interpretation of the applicable bilateral investment treaty.[20] In an ICSID case where the scope of a particular provision raised questions of jurisdiction, the non-disputing State objected to the interpretation reached by the tribunal.[21]

Investment treaty arbitration can thus raise the question of how to take into account the views of a non-disputing State that is a Contracting Party to the treaty. Those views, in particular if they have been express prior to the emergence of the dispute, could be a crucial factor to determine the meaning of a particular provision of the treaty. The relation between the treaty Parties and the parties to the investor-State proceeding is possibly one of the most perplexing aspects of investment treaty arbitration. Undoubtedly this question can be an important one for ICSID. Among other things, it may affect stakeholders' perceptions of the fairness of proceedings or of the quality of the tribunals' decisions. The question of a possible a 'preventive' or 'precautionary' role for ICSID again arises.

This concern has also been expressed in ICSID's recent proposals for amendment of the Arbitration Rules and will be examined below.

## 3. The Changes that ICSID is Proposing to Make to its Procedural Rules

I would like to mention five of the amendments being proposed. They concern provisional measures, attendance by third parties at hearings, submissions by third parties, preliminary objections, and the publication of excerpts of awards.

### A. **Rule 39: provisional measures**

The central aspect of this proposed change is to add the following paragraph:

> '(5) If a party makes a request pursuant to paragraph (1) before the constitution of the Tribunal, the Secretary-General shall, on the application of either party, fix time limits for the parties to present observations on the request, so that the request and observations may be considered by the Tribunal upon its constitution.'

This proposal leaves unaltered, and indeed presupposes, the underlying principle concerning the availability of provisional measures in proceedings under the ICSID Convention. That is to say, provisional measures are only available from the Arbitral Tribunal, unless the parties have agreed that they may seek such measures from 'a judicial or other authority', prior to or during a proceeding. Article 39(5) of the Arbitration Rule, added in the 1984 amendment to the ICSID rules, states this principle expressly. In the absence of agreement, the parties must await the constitution of the Arbitral Tribunal before provisional measure can be obtained. In this context, the proposed amendment is designed to improve efficiency and is eminently sensible.

### B. **Rule 32: attendance of hearings by third parties**

In essence, the proposal concerning Arbitration Rule 32 eliminates the requirement of the consent of the parties for the tribunal to decide which persons other that those directly involved in the proceeding (namely, 'the parties, their agents, counsel and advocates, witnesses and experts during their testimony, and officers of the Tribunal') may attend hearings. The proposal specifies that such other persons may be allowed to 'observe' rather than attend a hearing. When making such a decision, a tribunal shall establish procedures for the protection of proprietary information and for making 'appropriate logistical arrangements'.

At first glance, it might seem far-reaching to do away with the requirement of the parties' consent for attendance of third parties at hearings. The amendment should be understood, however, in the light of ICSID's existing practice of implementing access of third parties in NAFTA proceedings with minimal (if any) disruption to the parties. Largely, this type of arrangements have so far been made at ICSID's seat, within the World Bank building complexes in Washington, D.C. As with the normal holding of hearings outside the seat of the Centre, the proposal envisages the requirement that the tribunal is to consult the Secretary-General (who may raise questions of how this could be done outside the seat) prior to deciding these questions.

## C. Rule 37: submissions to the Tribunal by third parties

The essence of this proposal is to add the following additional paragraph to Rule 37:

> '(2) After consulting both parties as far as possible, the Tribunal may allow a person or a State that is not a party to the dispute (hereafter called the "non-disputing party") to file a written submission with the Tribunal. In determining whether to allow such a filing, the Tribunal shall consider, among others things, the extent to which:
> (a) the non-disputing party submission would assist the Tribunal in the determination of a factual or legal issue related to the proceeding by bringing a perspective, particular knowledge or insight that is different from that of the disputing parties;
> (b) the non-disputing party submission would address a matter within the scope of the dispute;
> (c) the non-disputing party has a significant interest in the proceeding.
> The Tribunal shall ensure that the non-disputing party submission does not disrupt the proceeding, unduly burden or unfairly prejudice either party, and that both parties are given an opportunity of presenting their observations on the non-disputing party submission.'

This proposal echoes similar arrangements implemented in the context of non-ICSID investor-State proceedings under NAFTA, and in the recent adoption of procedural arrangements in an ICSID proceeding. It represents a significant development in the conduct of investor-State, and particularly investment treaty, arbitration. In the light of the balance of the arbitration system under the ICSID Convention forged by its framers, an essential aspect of any proposal of this kind will be its appropriate implementation by tribunals and the ICSID Secretariat.

One of the guiding principles that derives from the ICSID Convention (as well as other systems of arbitration) is that the tribunal's duty is first and foremost to the parties in dispute, who by their consent have conferred jurisdiction and competence on the tribunal to resolve the dispute. By definition, therefore, no ICSID tribunal could ever work procedural injustice with respect to a third party, who is not a disputing party. Such procedural injustice could affect only the disputing parties, who are the parties to the proceeding.

A terminological consequence of the above is that what the proposal refers to as a 'non-disputing party' is not in any sense a party to the proceeding. The envisaged non-disputing parties, it would appear, have none of the obligations of a party and they certainly are not bound by the outcome of the proceeding. Thus, it would seem, the proposal makes an appropriate distinction between a 'non-disputing party' (*passim*) and the procedural safeguards to be afforded to 'either party' and 'both parties', in the last sentence of the proposed second paragraph of Rule 37.

An additional consequence would be that the nationality requirements (or the membership requirement in the case of a non-disputing State) of the ICSID Convention will not apply to the participation of a 'non-disputing party' in an ICSID Convention proceeding. This would be logical since such non-disputing parties are not legally connected to the proceeding. Nationality may of course be a factor that a tribunal in a given instance may take into account when eventually applying a new provision of this kind.

As noted above, this proposal may be a useful 'case management' tool with respect to substantive questions, specifically, in order to take into account the views of a non-disputing State that is a Contracting Party to an investment treaty being applied in a proceeding. The following remarks on this aspect of the proposal do not aspire to be comprehensive, but only to suggest that certain principles of international law may be important in giving effect to the role that a non-disputing State could have in an ICSID proceeding.

a. The non-disputing State would not, as noted, be a party to the proceedings. It would have none of the obligations of a party and is not bound by the outcome. In addition, it would seem that Article 27 of the ICSID Convention, and the provisions of many BITs, rule out the possibility that a non-disputing State whose national is a claimant may take a position on the ultimate merits of the claim.
b. Arbitration tribunals have invariably acknowledged that the 1969 Vienna Convention on the Law of Treaties contains the relevant rules for the interpretation of investment treaties in investor-State proceedings. The fundamental rule of Article 31(1) of the Vienna Convention calls for interpretation of treaty provisions in good faith in accordance with the ordinary meaning to be given to the terms of the treaty in their context and in the light of its object and purpose.
c. All the other elements of interpretation in Article 31 (subsequent agreement between the parties on the interpretation of the treaty; subsequent practice in the application of the treaty which establishes the agreement of the parties; and relevant rules of international law applicable in the relations between the parties) and Article 32 (supplementary means of interpretation) of the Vienna Convention are objective in character. The views of the non-disputing State would therefore not necessarily be dispositive even if they coincide with those of the respondent State.
d. 'The Tribunal may not bring in a finding of *non liquet* on the ground of silence or obscurity of the law.'[22] This provision of the Convention is binding on tribunals and may not be avoided even if the States parties to an investment treaty hold widely divergent opinions.

## D. Rule 41: preliminary objection that 'a claim is manifestly without merit'

This proposed amendment would introduce a specific preliminary procedure governed by the following two new paragraphs:

> '(5) A party may, no later than 30 days after the constitution of the Tribunal, and in any event before the first session of the Tribunal, file an objection that a claim is manifestly without merit. The party shall specify as precisely as possible the basis for the objection. The Tribunal, after giving the parties an opportunity to present their observations shall, at its first session or promptly thereafter, notify the parties of its decision on the objection. The decision of the Tribunal shall be without prejudice to its authority to decide on other objections that the parties may make in the course of the proceeding.
>
> (6) If the Tribunal decides that the dispute is not within the jurisdiction of the Centre or not within its own competence, or that all claims are manifestly without merit, it shall render an award to that effect.' (underlining and strikeout in original)

ICSID's note to this proposal recalls that

> 'the Secretary-General's power to screen requests for arbitration does not extend to the merits of the dispute or to cases where jurisdiction is merely doubtful but not manifestly lacking. In such cases, the request for arbitration must be registered and the parties invited to proceed to constitute the arbitral tribunal.'[23]

Thus, the new proposal seems to address the situations where the ICSID Secretary-General must register, but where on the facts as stated the 'claim is manifestly without merit'. The proposal may have originally been meant to add a means of screening disputes which is supplemental to the Secretary-General's powers.[24] If so, it would have implied that requests for arbitration would have needed to be even more carefully presented in order to make out a *prima facie* case that, on the facts as stated, there was a plausible argument for a meritorious claim (particularly if brought under an investment treaty).

The use of the term 'claim' (as opposed to dispute) in the proposal, however, gives rise to some doubt. Is the dispute to be decided summarily on the merits with *res judicata* effect? Or may the dispute be resubmitted with a fresh statement of facts and law to overcome the objection (as would be allowed in the case of a refusal to register a request for arbitration)? Perhaps it is best to proceed on the former assumption, since it would be more in keeping with the effect of comparable preliminary procedures in certain recent investment treaties which may have inspired this proposal.[25]

If this is the case, however, then in order for the proposed amendment to be effective it would seem that requests for arbitration will need to be much more substantive submissions that as currently envisaged by the ICSID Institution Rules. Institution Rule 2(1)(e) requires a request for arbitration to contain only 'information concerning the issues in dispute indicating that there is, between the parties, a legal dispute arising directly out of an investment.' By contrast, the investment treaties that envisage similar procedures also provide for substantial notices to initiate arbitration setting forth the 'legal and factual basis for each claim'. Without this fuller statement of a claim (comparable perhaps to the Statement of Claim required by Art. 18 of the UNCITRAL Arbitration Rules[26]) there would not be much point for the respondent to raise a detailed objection within 30 days and for the parties merely to exchange observations prior to a ruling by the tribunal. The claimant could all too easily argue that it has not stated 'the claim' and will do so in the memorial on the merits.

A procedural safeguard of the ICSID Convention might become relevant at this point. Article 45(2) of the Convention provides that, if a party fails to appear or to present his case at any stage of the proceedings the other party may request the tribunal 'to deal with the questions submitted to it and to render an award'. The tribunal must first, however, notify the party in default and grant it a period of grace, unless the tribunal is satisfied that the defaulting party has no intention to appear or present its case. This has been identified as a mandatory provision of the ICSID Convention.[27] If a tribunal were to apply Article 45(2) in the scenario envisaged by the proposal in order to safeguard the integrity of the proceeding, the expected result might be a telescoping of the claimant's memorial into an early phase of the proceeding. This might not necessarily ensure greater efficiency in the handling of unmeritorious claims. Nor does it compel a requirement to make the objection within the short time frame envisaged in the current proposal.

It would seem that the balance of this proposal needs to be carefully examined. It might be already be very useful for the ICSID Arbitration Rules to restate a tribunal's inherent power to deal summarily with unmeritorious claims, as noted by the ICSID Discussion Paper.[28]

## E. Rule 48: publication of excerpts

This proposal calls for relatively minor yet subtly very important adjustment to Rule 48:

> '(4) The Centre shall not publish the award without the consent of the parties. The Centre shall, however, promptly include in its publications excerpts of the conclusions of the Tribunal.' (underlining and strikeout in original)

Investment arbitration awards are now usually made public through informal channels and find their way quickly on to dedicated web sites and sometimes to specialist publications. Even before the current on-line case-watch for investment treaty decisions, ICSID regularly asked parties to consent to the publication of awards and decisions, stating that this would ensure a neutral medium. The current provision that allows the Secretary-General to publish excerpts of awards dates from the 1984 amendments to the rules. Due to ICSID's solicitude in seeking consent, the power has been used rarely.

With the increase in ICSID's caseload, the number of decisions and awards is also increasing and they are appearing with greater frequency. Because the great majority of cases concern the provisions of investment treaties, it is understandable that a number of cases will involve the analysis by different tribunals of overlapping or cognate issues. In addition to the commentary by the legal community, which might be disparate and not readily digestible by a tribunal in the midst of its task, this proposal will have the salutary effect of making visible to tribunals and parties alike the kernel of the latest ICSID awards, including those applying the provisions of investment treaties. The proposal is to make this task mandatory for the ICSID Secretariat, rather than discretional, thus also ensuring an even result and consequently the real and apparent neutrality of the Centre.

## 4. Conclusions

The combination of ICSID's unique responsibilities in the management of investor-State proceedings and the novel questions of interpretation posed by treaty-based investor claims have focused attention on how ICSID, both as an institution and as a service-provider, should react to those novel questions.

The reaction is to what in the end is the use of ICSID by its Member States. It is crucial that this reaction should not compromise ICSID's balance. Otherwise there are likely be even more serious issues to which ICSID its Member States will need to react in the future. Given ICSID's successful record and its balanced structure, it would seem that what is called for is fine-tuning rather than overhaul. ICSID has distinguished itself by the management of its cases and the careful approach it takes to that task. The proposed changes themselves will require continued careful management by

ICSID. Not all arbitrators will be in a position to apply the changes effectively. Like all human beings, many arbitrators must learn from what has been done before.

The current innovative formulation of proposals for specific amendments to its Arbitration Rules are themselves an important measure of self-reflection on the part of ICSID. The current set of proposals, for example, in and of itself sheds considerable light on the inherent powers of tribunals under Article 44 of the ICSID Convention. It might form the basis of a newly annotated set of arbitration rules that could provide guidance to tribunals. In addition, there is probably a significant contribution that ICSID can make in a 'passive' manner through the publication of decisions and awards and ideally their indexation by subject or arrangement in some form of digest. It is ideally placed for this by being the repository of experience in investment arbitration.

In sum, ICSID should change organically, consistently with its foundational principles (especially due process of law). Even more than managed, those principles must be cultivated and nurtured. It is probably beyond doubt, for example, that the ICSID Secretariat should in no way involve itself (or be seen to involve itself) in the substance of a particular tribunal's decisions. Being a creature of international law, ICSID is likely to find renewal within the most fundamental principles of that legal order, including those inspired by fairness and 'natural justice'.

## Notes

1 Convention on the Settlement of Investment Disputes between States and Nationals of Other States, submitted for signature and ratification, 18 March 1965, entered into force 14 October 1966, Doc. ICSID/15/Rev. 1, January 2003.

2 ICSID also has a set of Additional Facility Rules which operate outside the scope of the Convention, Doc. ICSID/11/Rev. 1.

3 Art. 42(1) of the ICSID Convention provides: 'The Tribunal shall decide a dispute in accordance with such rules of law as may be agreed by the parties. In the absence of such agreement, the Tribunal shall apply the law of the Contracting State party to the dispute (including its rules on the conflict of laws) and such rules of international law as may be applicable.'

4 'The term "international law" as used in this context should be understood in the sense given to it by Article 38(1) of the Statute of the International Court of Justice, allowance being made for the fact that Article 38 was designed to apply to inter-State disputes.' Report of the Executive Directors on the Convention on the Settlement of Investment Disputes between States and Nationals of Other States, International Bank for Reconstruction and Development, 18 March 965. Para. 40, Doc. ICSID\15\Rev. 1, January 2003, at p. 47.

5 ICSID Secretariat, 'Possible Improvements of the Framework for ICSID Arbitration', Discussion Paper, 22 October 2004, at para. 5, available at <http://www.worldbank.org/icsid/improve-arb.htm>.

6 Ibid., para. 4. See <http://www.worldbank.org/icsid/cases/cases.htm>.

7 ICSID Secretariat, 'Suggested Changes to the ICSID Rules and Regulations', Working Paper, 12 May 2005, <http://www.worldbank.org/icsid/sug-changes.htm>.

8 *Asian Agricultural Products Ltd.* v. *Republic of Sri Lanka* (ICSID Case No. ARB/87/3). The Tribunal's award was rendered on 27 June 1990, 6 ICSID Review – FILJ 526 (1991 No. 2).

9 *Southern Pacific Properties (Middle East) Limited* v. *Arab Republic of Egypt* (ICSID Case No. ARB/84/3). See J. Paulsson, 'Arbitration without Privity', 10 ICSID Review – FILJ 232 (1995 No. 2).

10 *American Manufacturing and Trading, Inc.* v. *Democratic Republic of Congo* (ICSID Case No. ARB/93/1), Award rendered on 21 February 1997, 36 *ILM* (1997) 1534.

11 See in this respect, I.F.I. Shihata and A.R. Parra, 'The Experience of the International Centre for Settlement of Investment Disputes', 14 ICSID Review – FILJ 299 (1999 No. 2).

12 Rule 7(e) of the ICSID Rules of Procedure for the Institution of Conciliation and Arbitration Proceedings currently provides that the notice of registration of a request shall 'remind the parties that the registration of a request is without prejudice to the powers and functions of the ... Arbitral Tribunal in regard to jurisdic-

tion, competence and the merits'. This provision was added in the 2002 harmonisation of the ICSID rules to reflect a long-standing practice of the Secretariat.

13 For an account of an attempt to argue that a request for arbitration had been improperly registered because it did not meet the criteria of Art. 36 of the ICSID Convention, see: *Compañía de Aguas del Aconquija S.A. & Compagnie Générale des Eaux (now Vivendi Universal)* v. *Argentine Republic* (ICSID Case No. ARB/97/3), Award of 21 November 2000, paras. 12 and 13, 16 ICSID Review – FILJ 651 (2001 No. 2).

14 See, e.g., the description in *Emilio Agustín Mafezzini* v. *Kingdom of Spain* (ICSID Case No. ARB/97/7), Decision on Objections to Jurisdiction dated 25 January 2000, para. 2.

15 See the sophisticated discussion in *Tokios Tokels* v. *Ukraine* (ICSID Case No. ARB/02/18), Dissenting Opinion of Professor Proper Weil dated 29 April 2004, paras. 1-13, in connection with the Decision on Jurisdiction of the same date, paras. 14-20.

16 See ICSID, Members of the Panels of Conciliators and of Arbitrators (periodic updates, current July 2005), at: <http://www.worldbank.org/icsid/pubs/icsid-10/icsid-10.htm>.

17 See the reference above to *Compañía de Aguas del Aconquija S.A. & Compagnie Générale des Eaux (now Vivendi Universal)* v. *Argentine Republic* (ICSID Case No. ARB/97/3), Award of 21 November 2000, paras. 12 and 13, 16 ICSID Review – FILJ 651 (2001 No. 2).

18 See ICSID Working Paper, 12 May 2005, suggested changes to Arbitration Rule 39.

19 *Empresas Lucchetti S.A. & Lucchetti Perú S.A.* v. *Republic of Peru* (ICSID Case No. ARB/03/4), Award of 7 February 2005.

20 See *CME Czech Republic (The Netherlands) B.V.* v. *The Czech Republic*, Final Award, 14 March 2003, paras. 87-93.

21 *SGS Societé Générale de Surveillance S.A.* v. *Islamic Republic of Pakistan* (ICSID Case No. ARB/ 01/13).

22 ICSID Convention, Art. 42(2).

23 ICSID Working Paper, 12 May 2005, at p. 7.

24 Thus the Working Paper adds, ibid.:

'It is suggested to make it clear, by the introduction of a new paragraph (5), that the tribunal may at an early stage of the proceeding be asked on an expedited basis to dismiss all or part of a claim on the merits. The change would be helpful in addressing any concerns about the limited screening power of the Secretary-General.'

25 See, e.g., United States-Uruguay bilateral investment treaty; Chile-United States Free Trade Agreement; and Central American (DR) Free Trade Agreement.

26 UN General Assembly Resolution 31/98. Art. 18(2) provide in part:

'The statement of claim shall include the following particulars:

*(a)* The names and addresses of the parties;

*(b)* A statement of the facts supporting the claim;

*(c)* The points at issue;

*(d)* The relief or remedy sought.'

27 See A.R. Parra, 'The Limits of Party Autonomy in Arbitration Proceedings under the ICSID Convention', *ICC International Court of Arbitration Bulletin* Vol. 10/No. 1 – Spring 1999, p. 27 at p. 31.

28 See ICSID Discussion Paper, 22 October 2004, para. 10.

## Discussion

Kathleen Paisley:* I have a theoretical and a practical question. Following on Jan Paulsson remarks, I would be interested in Susan Franck and Ignacio Suárez Anzorena views as to whether bilateral treaty cases inherently require more consistency than do other complex cross-border commercial and investment disputes involving state parties.

It seems inherent in such cases that they pose a risk of overlapping jurisdictions that can lead to inconsistent results. Query whether it is necessary to create procedures geared at eliminating this risk in bilateral treaty cases, which exist in other for deciding such cases.

* Brussels.

And for Alejandro Escobar, from your current position or from the perspective of an ICSID Senior Counsel turned into practitioner, what is your view as to how ICSID should streamline the registration process without calling into question its legitimacy as an organisation and how can we as practitioners facilitate such a process.

SUSAN FRANCK: I think that you are quite right to point out that there is always the possibility for conflict.

The question is however (a) how do we minimize it, and (b) once we acknowledge it exists, how do we deal with it and why should we distinguish it.

What makes investment arbitration distinguishable is that we deal with a public right not a private right, with public parties and not with wholly private parties. Unlike the commercial context, the law is evolving here. Thus, the nature of the right is very different and this is why I would proceed in a slightly different manner.

IGNACIO SUAREZ ANZORENA: From my perspective, the issue is not ICSID arbitration but bilateral investment treaty arbitration. In most of these cases, what is at stake is the State acting as a sovereign dealing with general government issues where public values are at stake.

Predictability is certainly desirable given that on the one hand investors should know which is the level of protection they can count on and the function of BITs and ICSID would be better served. On the other hand, if the States also know better what is the framework of their duties, they could do better damage control.

ALEJANDRO ESCOBAR: Regarding registration, there are two elements to it.

First, the reason registration is longer than expected is related to the complex issues of jurisdiction to be taken into account (the more detailed the treaty the more attention that has to be paid to the request). Hence, perhaps reaching some sort of implicit understanding with Member States as to the speed at which this will occur could help in this regard.

IGNACIO SUAREZ ANZORENA: One last thing that I would like to add is related to a paper by the World Bank published a year and a half ago concerning multiplicity and BITs.

There was something interesting with regard to the issue of predictability and multiplicity. The paper addressed the possibility of investors launching hundreds of claims to challenge a certain measure. The lack of consistency in this regard could lead to a sort of *ad infinitum* challenge of regulatory actions which might create what is called non-fiduciary costs. That could eventually prevent regulation which is fair and needed. By this sort of harassment *ad infinitum* by launching a thousand claims by shareholders or ten claims from different layers of the corporation against particular measures, sometimes a needed and good regulation might be prevented.

In my view, this is an important factor to take into account in this context.

BETTE SHIFMAN:* My question was just touched upon I think by Ignacio Suarez Anzorena – it is maybe more of a comment but I would like to have the panel's views on it.

The problem is not ICSID, but I think most of you know that. Many – if not most – bilateral investment treaties give the investor an option of dispute resolution mechanisms and one that we have not really touched upon very much are the UNCI-

* Permanent Court of Arbitration.

TRAL Rules. These rules raise many of the same problems we discussed today: the lack of transparency.

The UNCITRAL Rules were designed for contract disputes. The very first paragraph of the first article refers to the parties to a contract. They do not provide for the kind of transparency that I think most of the panellists agreed is necessary.

My question is really whether do we ask UNCITRAL to develop rules that are more flexible for different types of disputes? Or do we encourage contracting States to no longer include UNCITRAL clauses in their bilateral investment treaties? Or do we ask UNCITRAL or some other entity to come up with a flexible set of rules?

Jan Paulsson: I do not wish to sound unkind but I think it is true to say that sometimes UNCITRAL is engaged in relatively esoteric activities. Whereas one thing that they have given to the world is the 1976 UNCITRAL Arbitration Rules which are surpassingly important they now look a bit threadbare.

At the time, the International Chamber of Commerce was operating under the 1955 Rules. These rules have been modified 3 times since then. The LCIA Rules have been modified several times; WIPO has come up with a very modern set of arbitration rules, and in all that time the 1976 UNCITRAL Arbitration Rules stay unchanged, particularly given UNCITRAL's role in bilateral treaties but independently of that, only in the commercial field itself it is high time, in my opinion, for UNCITRAL to have a look at those 1976 rules.

It seems that finally UNCITRAL is going to hold a meeting next year in April and start thinking about this. There will be a good occasion to think not only of reforming the UNCITRAL Rules under their current compass but think about the implications of the fact that states have chosen to point to UNCITRAL for a function which was not originally contemplated in the 1970s.

Susan Franck: I would like to add that it is important to remember the distinction between public and private and the hybrid nature of different types of arbitration. The need for transparency in investment arbitration is – I think – quite different in an international commercial context between private trading parties. Hence, I am not sure we would want to import everything we are talking about within the context of ICSID into the UNCITRAL system. I would want to analyze first such an initiative on a functional basis. Thus, is there a reason for making the change? And, does it apply in this context? In any event, it is an interesting question.

Hans Kurell:* My question concerns the utility of the BITs. I saw a thesis on the issue to what extent BITs actually contribute to investments being made and in that case where are they being made, and my question is do you think that the BITs are an ever growing phenomenon or have they come to stay?

Ignacio Suarez Anzorena: At least six or seven economic studies published during the last year and a half have reached contradictory conclusions as to whether BITs promote or not international flows of investment.

What I can say in that regard is that among all elements determining foreign investment, the BITs are probably one in fifteen or twenty. This would explain for example why Brazil can get away with an extraordinary level of investment (which increases over time) in spite of having signed only 14 BITs and never having ratified any of them.

* Former Legal Counsel of the United Nations.

Hence, it seems clear that for the time being, BITs are only one among many factors motivating investors' decision to invest.

ANDREA BJORKLUND: Invoking the Chair's privilege, I would add a few words on this. Some of you may be aware of many studies about whether BITs actually increase the flow of foreign investment into developing countries. As is often the nature in the area of economic studies, the result of those studies vary across the board, from some researchers at the London School of Economics finding that yes they do have some effect, to somebody at the World Bank finding that there is no effect, and some others in Yale finding that there is probably some effect probably in the riskiest countries, but little effect otherwise.

At this stage, it seems to me that the jury is at best out about whether bilateral investment treaties really in themselves dramatically affect the flow of foreign investment. I think Ignacio is right in that it is one factor among many and that it is hard to distinguish.

JAN PAULSSON: On the general point of BITs I could do a Donald Rumsfeld imitation: are BITs a good thing? Yes. Have there been unintended consequences? Certainly. Is it the greatest thing ever to happen to the rule of law in the world? No, not at all. Have we fully understood the interplay between contracts and treaty? No, not all. etc., etc.

But I would make the point that what impact this has on investment is inconclusive, even though the last World Bank study purports to conclude that there is something positive derived from the treaties.

The most interesting feature of the impact of BITs is the so-called 'compliance pull', i.e. the existence of BITs has had an effect on the conduct of public officials. And that is perhaps the most interesting phenomenon that comes out of the BITs.

*Reporter:* Blanca Montejo*

* Freshfields Bruckhaus Deringer, Paris, France.

# Alternative Paths to International Institutional Reform

The panel was convened by its Chair, Charlotte Ku*

## Remarks by Laura Dickinson**

### Privatization and Alternative Modes of Accountability Under International Law

This paper identifies the growing trend towards privatization in foreign affairs, particularly with regard to military and foreign aid activities. This trend poses accountability problems for many traditional international law doctrines, which are (at least historically) premised on state action. I therefore suggest the potential for alternative modes of accountability. In particular, I discuss ways in which accountability mechanisms can be contractually mandated and ways in which the institutional cultures of various private contractors can be harnessed or changed to increase compliance with international legal norms.

In the United States, privatization has long been the subject of scholarly and policy debate. Indeed, over the past twenty years, the US government has increasingly farmed out a variety of domestic functions – from health care, to welfare, to prison management – to private for-profit and non-profit organizations. And, as a result, a rich body of scholarly discourse has developed concerning privatization and how best to insure that public law values are maintained even absent direct governmental action.

In recent years, however, privatization has extended to the international sphere. Not only are states such as the United States exporting the ideology of privatization to developing countries, but the United States, other states, and international organizations are increasingly privatizing foreign affairs functions themselves. For example, states are increasingly turning to private actors to perform military functions. The issue hit the media recently when private contractors working as interrogators and translators for the United States government abused detainees at Abu Ghraib prison. But this kind of military privatization is only the tip of the iceberg. In the United States, although our government still does not contract out direct combat functions, we are increasingly turning to private actors to provide logistical support to those in combat on the battlefield as well as to aid in strategic planning and tactical advice.[1]

* Executive Director, American Society of International Law.
** Associate Professor, University of Connecticut School of Law.

Other states such as Sierra Leone have used private contractors to engage in direct combat,[2] and international organizations have weighed the possibilities of using private contractors to perform peacekeeping functions.[3]

In the foreign aid context, states and international organizations are increasingly turning to private non-profit and for-profit entities to deliver all forms of aid, including humanitarian relief, development assistance, and post-conflict reconstruction.[4] Even diplomatic tasks such as peacekeeping negotiations are increasingly being undertaken by private actors in relationship with governments and international organizations.[5]

The rise of non-state actors in the international sphere raises concerns about accountability of these various private actors under international law norms. International law norms traditionally apply primarily to states. The Convention Against Torture, for example, prohibits primarily only official misconduct.[6] As more and more non-state actors emerge on the international scene, many have speculated that these individuals and groups will fall through the cracks of international law. This trend thus raises the question, is the sky falling on international law?

My answer to the question is 'no', and I argue that the domestic US literature on privatization may provide a useful set of responses to privatization that has been largely overlooked by international law scholars, policy-makers, and activists. To begin with, in considering the question of accountability under international law, we need to recognize that it is not as if *state* actors are always held accountable under international law. Indeed, international law has often been criticized as having relatively weak enforcement mechanisms. While this fact may not be cause for celebration, it does serve to remind us that we do not quite lose as much with respect to accountability when we privatize in the international sphere as we do when, for example, we privatize domestically. But more importantly, we should understand that there are forms of accountability that inhere in the privatized relationship itself. In other words, there are what might be called alternative accountability mechanisms contained in the relationship between governments (and international organizations) and private contractors, and it is important for us to examine and consider these mechanisms.

International law scholars have not, to date, focused extensively on such alternative mechanisms. Rather, the response to the problem of privatization has usually been normative. With each wave of non-state actors – such as guerrilla movements,[7] terrorists,[8] non-governmental organizations,[9] and corporations[10] – international law practitioners and scholars have advocated an expansion of the international law norms to apply to each group. Thus, scholars and practitioners have argued either that states should (by treaty or customary international law) develop new norms that apply directly to these categories of non-state actors, or that any 'state action' requirements contained in existing norms (again either in treaties or customary international law) should be interpreted expansively to apply to non-state actors in a broad range of contexts. At the same time, these scholars and practitioners have tended to focus on the need for courts and tribunals – in many cases new ones – to apply and interpret these norms.

While this approach is important and useful because it results in the articulation of norms in the international sphere, ultimately it can only have a limited effect. After all, even if the proposed courts and tribunals are established and fully functioning, and even if they expand the norms of international law to apply to the broad range of privatized action, these tribunals will never have the capacity to hold more than a limited number of individuals (and groups) accountable. A corresponding focus on alternative modes of accountability is thus essential.

International law scholars and practitioners have not generally focused on these alternative modes of accountability in part because they tend to frame the issue of privatization quite broadly. Accordingly, they have usually framed the question as one concerning the rise of 'non-state actors' more generally rather than 'privatization' specifically. This is a crucial point, because it has meant that less attention has been paid to a key facet of privatization that makes it different from, say, the rise of guerrilla movements. Privatization as a specific phenomenon involves an increasing contractual relationship between governments (or international organizations) and private actors. Thus, as US administrative law scholars have suggested, there may be alternative modes of accountability that inhere in the privatized relationship itself. [11] These domestic scholars have not, however, considered the privatization of foreign affairs functions. Accordingly, my projects aims to open a dialogue between international law scholars and domestic administrative law scholars concerning privatization and public law accountability.

So, what are some of the alternative mechanisms for holding private actors accountable in the international sphere, beyond applying expanded international law norms in international courts and tribunals? First, we could think more about the contracts hat are the very engine of privatization and the extent to which these contracts could be used as a mode of accountability. Second, we could look at the ways in which internal institutional cultures might affect the willingness and ability of private organizations to follow international law and ways we might change and affect those cultures over time to enhance accountability.

## A. Contract

First, turning to contract, there are a number of different mechanisms that could be used to ensure that privatized activities are carried out in accord with international norms. I have used as a case study all of the publicly available contracts that the US government has negotiated in Iraq, but the principles would apply to other types of contracts negotiated by states or international organizations with contractors providing a variety of foreign affairs functions.

1. The contracts themselves could explicitly require that the contractors obey international human rights and humanitarian law. This may seem like an obvious point, but in the contracts that I have examined, none contained specific provisions requiring contractors to obey international human rights and humanitarian law.
2. The contracts could explicitly require the contractors to receive training in international human rights and humanitarian law. Again, none of the publicly available Iraq contracts appear to require such training.
3. Provisions could be made for increased monitoring of the contracts, both by government monitors – the contract officers and ombudspersons within the government – and outside for-profit and non-profit organizations who could be empow-

ered under the contracts to provide monitoring.

4. The contracts could include more concrete performance benchmarks. This is probably particularly useful in the foreign aid context and has to some degree been implemented, particularly with regard to development aid.
5. The contracts could require self-evaluation by contractors. Contractors could thus be required to assess their own performance as a way of enhancing accountability.
6. Contracts could include terms allowing the government (or international organization) to take over the contract by degrees and ultimately terminate the contract for failure to observe international human rights and humanitarian law norms. Many of the US Iraq contracts do have termination provisions but they are very rarely exercised. Indeed, in the Abu Ghraib context, the relevant contractor not only did not face termination after its employees were implicated in the abuse, but the contract was actually expanded. It is important that the governments (and international organizations) are encouraged to invoke termination provisions when contractors fall short. But even without full termination of the contractors, graduated government (or international organization) takeover could provide an added incentive for contractors to obey international human rights and humanitarian law norms.
7. The contracts could provide for enhanced whistleblower protections and third-party beneficiary suit provisions. For instance, those who are receiving aid or those who are subject to contractor security action might be able to make claims under the contracts for non-compliance with international human rights and humanitarian law norms.

Of course, these compliance mechanisms are necessarily only as good as the quality of the monitoring in question and, perhaps more to the point, the willingness of domestic or international actors to seek judicial enforcement at the back end if these norms are not observed. But, significantly, these contract-based mechanisms are no weaker than the existing formal transnational/international court system, and at least they have the benefit of opening up the possibility of legal enforcement regardless of whether or not there is state action and to provide the foundation for legal action in domestic, as well as international, fora.

### B. Internal Institutional Accountability

Internal institutional accountability is another under-explored mode of accountability that can be used to promote the implementation of international law norms in an increasingly privatized world.

1. Contracts could seek to harness the distinctive institutional cultures of various forms of contracting parties. For example, non-profit organizations, for-profit corporations, religious organizations, and governmental organizations each has specific institutional norms and cultures that make them more likely to obey certain norms and less likely to obey others. Such institutional cultures could be considered in the contracting process.

2. Professional standardization and accreditation could be encouraged. Accreditation of contractors, for example, could encourage an ethic of professionalism within the industry. Contracts and the courts could then use professional standards as benchmarks for interpreting compliance.
3. Internal institutional sanctions could be harnessed and used more effectively. Demotion, firing, and other forms of shaming or non-legal sanctions that have social meaning within institutions could be brought to bear on individual actors to a greater degree. For example, within the military, a hierarchical organization in which rank and status are important, demotion and firing are sanctions that are very strongly felt. These kinds of sanctions could be used more effectively.

### C. Other Issues – Democratic Accountability

In addition to both contractual and institutional forms of accountability, we might also want to think more about the feedback loop between the populations affected by privatization and the governmental activity in question: what we might call democratic accountability. In the domestic context, there has long been a worry that privatization removes a crucial democratic check on government because the link between those affected by government action and the government actors is attenuated when that activity is farmed out first from legislatures to agencies, and then from agencies to private contractors. Scholars and policy-makers worry that this form of delegation reduces transparency, which in turn reduces the ability of those affected to vote their preferences when things are not going well.

Internationally, however, the problem is even more complicated because many of the people affected by the activities in question do not belong to a democratic polity at all. In order to ensure the type of democratic feedback loop that is arguably necessary to serve as an effective check on governmental activity, we thus might want to think about ways that members of the affected population could be involved in the policies that affect them. Perhaps foreign aid recipients might participate in the design of aid contracts, for example. Indeed, such aid recipients might be allowed to evaluate those contracts and, through third-party beneficiary suit provisions, enforce their terms. In the development aid context, governments such as the United States have in fact allowed some participation of aid recipients in the design of contracts. And the United Nations High Commissioner for Refugees has begun to explore the possibility of refugee and IDP evaluation of humanitarian aid.

Of course there may well be resistance to the proposals that I have suggested. Indeed, even if all of them are implemented fully and successfully, one might argue that such reforms would remove some of the purported efficiency gains that privatization arguably provides. It should be noted, however, that the jury is still out on whether or not privatization does in fact result in efficiency gains. In addition, some might suggest that governments are pursuing privatization precisely to *avoid* the type of accountability mechanisms I am suggesting and would therefore never be effective monitors of contract compliance. However, governments are not monolithic entities, and it is important to develop proposals that will empower those within government bureaucracies who are interested in compliance with international norms. Moreover, governments often respond to pressure from international organizations, other governments, or NGOs, and so these entities should at least consider advocating the alternative accountability mechanisms I suggest here.

In the end, my most important point is that international law scholars, advocates, and policy-makers, rather than focusing primarily on expanding norms to private actors and extending the formal court-like mechanisms for holding such actors accountable under those norms, should spend at least as much time advocating for ways to use alternative accountability mechanisms that derive specifically from the fact of privatization itself.

## Notes

1 See generally P.W. Singer, *Corporate Warriors: The Rise of the Privatized Military Industry* (2003).

2 See Abraham McLaughlin, *Guns for Hire Thrive in Africa*, Christian Sci. Mon., 15 March 2004, at 6.

3 See, e.g., Singer, *supra* n. 1, at 182-186.

4 See, e.g., 'Beyond UN Subcontracting: Task-Sharing with Regional Security Arrangements and Service-Providing NGOs' (Thomas G. Weiss (ed.) 1998) [hereinafter UN Subcontracting]; Ian Smillie, 'At Sea in a Sieve? Trends and Issues in the Relationship Between Northern NGOs and Northern Governments', in *Stakeholders: Government-NGO Partnerships for International Development*, at 7 (Ian Smillie & Henny Helmich (eds.) 1999).

5 See, e.g., James L. Taulbee & Marion V. Creekmore, 'NGO Mediation: The Carter Center', in *Mitigating Conflict: The Role of NGOs*, at 156 (Henry F. Carey & Oliver P. Richmond (eds.) 2003).

6 Convention Against Torture and Other Cruel, Inhuman or Degrading Treatment or Punishment, opened for signature 10 December 1984, Art. 1, 1465 *UNTS* 85, 116, 23 *ILM* 1027, 1030 (defining torture as certain activities designed to inflict pain or suffering when such 'pain or suffering is inflicted by or at the instigation of or with the consent or acquiescence of a public official or other person acting in an official capacity').

7 See, e.g., Sylvie Junod, 'Additional Protocol II: History and Scope', 33 *Am.U.L.Rev.* 29, 30-33 (1984).

8 See, e.g., Rosa Ehrenreich Brooks, 'War Everywhere: Rights, National Security Law, and the Law of Armed Conflict in the Age of Terror', 153 *U.Pa.L.Rev.* 675, 756-57 (2004).

9 See, e.g., Math Noortman, *Non-State Actors in International Law, in Non-State Actors in International Relations*, at 71, 72 (Bas Arts, Math Noortmann & Bob Reinalda (eds.) 2001).

10 See, e.g., Steven R. Ratner, 'Corporations and Human Rights: A Theory of Legal Responsibility', 111 *Yale L.J.* 443, 526-30 (2001); see also David Weissbrodt & Muria Kruger, 'Norms on the Responsibilities of Transnational Corporations and Other Business Enterprises with Regard to Human Rights', 97 *AJIL* 901 (2003).

11 See, e.g., Jody Freeman, 'The Private Role in Public Governance', 75 *NYU L.Rev.* 543 (2000).

## Remarks by John King Gamble* and Joshua L. Wilczynski**

## Definition, Perspective, Caution: The View through a Wide Angle Treaty Lens

### 1. Introduction

No one can doubt that the organizers of this conference have identified a vitally-important topic the resolution of which is essential to the development of international law through international organizations. But, like most important topics, this one is subject to dramatically different interpretations. Even the wording of the conference theme can elicit controversy. Was the intention to favor a particular type of reform by the wording chosen for the title? The differences between 'International Institutional Reform' and 'Reform of International Institutions' can be huge.

Reform in intergovernmental organizations (IGOs) has attracted considerable attention especially over the last decade, but institutional reform is neither a new idea nor easily defined. In fact, it can be one of those slippery concepts such as freedom, federalism, or subsidiarity that mean very different things to different people. While everyone favours reform in the abstract, agreement often evaporates when concrete actions are proposed. And we must realize that reform, to be effective and sustainable, must have broad support from IGOs themselves, foreign ministries, and the general public.

Those of us who discuss institutional reform should exercise caution and remember the admonition of British poet Alexander Pope who wrote:

> 'For forms of government let fools contest; Whate'er is best administer'd is best. For modes of faith let graceless zealots fight; His can't be wrong whose life is in the right.'[1]

Many facile, quick-fix analyses of reform would do well to heed Pope's warning. If an effective strategy for reform could be developed for a particular IGO, is there any assurance the strategy could be generalizable? For example, reforming the FAO presumably would involve

> 'raising levels of nutrition and standards of living of the peoples under their respective jurisdictions; securing improvements in the efficiency of the production and distribution of all food and agricultural products; bettering the condition of rural populations; and thus contributing towards an expanding world economy and ensuring humanity's freedom from hunger.'[2]

This might be expensive and administratively difficult, yet not an impossible task. Contrast this to problems attendant with reforming the United Nations itself relative to its mission 'to maintain international peace and security' and

* Distinguished Professor of Political Science and International Law,The Behrend College, The Pennsylvania State University, Erie.

** Research Associate, CSDMT Project, The Behrend College, Pennsylvania State University Erie.

> 'to take effective collective measures for the prevention and removal of threats to the peace, and for the suppression of acts of aggression or other breaches of the peace, and to bring about by peaceful means, and in conformity with the principles of justice and international law, adjustment or settlement of international disputes or situations which might lead to a breach of the peace.'[3]

It is clear that, due to huge differences in mandate and scope, reform of the UN will be a much taller order.

Before turning to the oft-ignored matter of defining reform, an unpleasant reality must be acknowledged. How does one deal with instances where an individual or a state is so fundamentally opposed to an organization that proposals for reform become a contradiction in terms unless one accepts the premise that destruction of an organization can be the ultimate reform? During his second term, 1985-1989, President Reagan appointed William J. Bennett to be Secretary of Education. Bennett had said creating of the department was an:

> '... historic blunder, a combination of overweening federal ambition and pandering to interest groups. Still the department exists. The question now becomes: How can it be turned into an agency of minimum nuisance? ... A suitably reformed Department of Education would resemble a three-room schoolhouse.'[4]

Would it be appropriate to consider the actions of Mr. Bennett to be 'reform'? A much more recent example, painfully salient to those who believe in international law, is President G.W. Bush's decision to nominate John Bolton to be US Ambassador to the UN. Secretary of State Rice described Bolton as one of 'our most skilled and experienced diplomats' and Bolton spoke of 'American leadership to achieve successful reform'.[5] But Bolton must be judged by his *résumé* that includes saying 'it is a big mistake to grant any validity to international law' and advocating 'halting U.S. contributions to the UN altogether'.[6]

The Reagan and Thatcher 'revolutions' of the 1980s had profound implications for IGOs the effects of which continue to this day and will affect reform efforts. Conservative governments following in the philosophical wake of leaders such as Prime-Ministers Thatcher and Mulroney and President Reagan found governmental organizations – local, national, or international – had become bloated, inefficient, and ineffective. IGOs were especially likely to be criticized because they threatened the sovereignty so cherished by neoconservative leaders. The feeling of neoconservative leaders today tends to be that that the marketplace is the best remedy for problems facing IGOs. This means the 'reforms' they propose will rely on Adam Smith's invisible hand as the primary means of reform.

## 2. Definitions and Approaches

There is ample reason to believe that 'reform' may be too slippery, too much of an 'in the eye of the beholder' concept. This conference will spend considerable time analyzing the Report of the High-level Panel on Threats, Challenges and Change accepted by Secretary-General Annan on 2 December 2004.[7] One of the more remarkable things about the Report is how seldom the word 'reform' is used – only about 30 times. Perhaps panel members understood the problematic nature of the concept.

Of course some definitions of 'institutional reform' are so platitudinous to be worthless. They are not wrong *per se*, but have little chance of encouraging movement towards desired policy outcomes. For example, the Embassy of the Republic of Uganda in Washington discusses the government's successful efforts in the area of institutional reforms describing 'reducing corruption in public administration, improving the public procurement system, simplifying administrative procedures, and improving tax administration.'[8]

Another approach to institutional reform is a reaction to a problem perceived to be inadequately dealt with within the existing institutional framework and suggests creating a new organization. This is understandable; in fact, this process spawned many of the IGOs that exist today, e.g., UNIDO, WIPO, and the ICC. This urge to create a new organization, called 'institutionalization',[9] is understandable but it would lead to a separate IGO for every possible sphere of international activity. One fascinating article advocating forcefully for a world environmental organization made the *naïve* assertion that such an organization could be 'non-sovereignty-impairing'.[10]

Although often implicit, a key aspect of a definition of institutional reform is to harmonize structure with mission. This has been a constant theme as the EU has broadened and deepened, i.e., a 'continuous expansion of EU legislative activity ... accompanied by periodic changes of the EU's institutional framework.'[11] A thoughtful and more explicit definition of institutional reform was provided by the Crisis States Research Centre:

> 'We are particularly interested in understanding the conditions that lead some systems to engage in processes of reform, restructuring, reshaping or 'mutation', whereby aspects of the system are modified to enable it to adapt to the new conditions and deal with the new challenge.'[12]

Many efforts at reform are narrowly focused and piecemeal; all such efforts should be required to ask what principles have been discovered about how and when reforms are likely to be effective.

It is desirable to have some agreement on a definition of 'institutional reform' lest we engage in discussions where syntactic ambiguity obscures real problems. Once this minimum level of definitional clarity is reached, it is vital to acknowledge how difficult and complex institutional reform can be. Better analyses of institutional reform acknowledge a delicate trade-off among conflicting values all of which, when viewed in isolation, may be positive. For example, the WTO must balance 'efficiency in decision-making and universal participation'.[13] Efficiency, while important, is not everything; in fact members of the EU 'are willing to tolerate a decrease in decision-making efficiency in order to achieve other goals, such as reducing the EU's "democratic deficit".'[14]

Another important conclusion seems to be that institutional reform, even if it appears to be working, may be difficult to sustain. There must be broad-based support for reforms in order 'to increase the legitimacy of . . . institutions and rules in the public eye.'[15] Further, success might have come from 'fortuitous circumstances' and 'might well be reversed by a different alignment of interests and party constituencies in the future.'[16] Any reform will produce losers along with winners and will have unintended and perhaps completely unforeseen consequences.[17]

An excellent approach to institutional reform was developed as part of an undergraduate course entitle 'Political Systems', taught at Southeast Missouri State University.[18] On one level, Professor Hanebrink's suggestions might seem self evident, but often they have been ignored. Generally, institutions are biased against change and will try to avoid it. All reform is difficult which makes it essential to weigh 'reform proposals carefully for the soundness of their political logic'.[19]

It is possible to adopt a workable definition for institutional reform as described above. However, we should not lose sight of the fact there is a system of international institutional reform embedded in multilateral treaties that has been operating for more than a century.

## 3. Through a Long-Range Treaty Lens

When discussing reform of international institutions, we should remember reform is not something discovered in the 1990s with the growing pains of the European Union. Virtually all IGOs can be reformed by protocols, amendments and other actions to the treaties that created them in the first place. Of course, certain treaties have explicit provisions on amendments, review conferences, etc. The Comprehensive Statistical Database of Multilateral Treaties (CSDMT),[20] a project begun at Pennsylvania State University (Erie) in 1998, contains basic information about all multilateral treaties signed from 1648 to1995. About 15 per cent of these treaties bear directly on IGOs and do so in two principal ways: creating those IGOs or actions relevant to them, e.g., amendments, protocols. Figure I provides a very broad picture of these IGO-related treaties from the end of World War I through 1995. The left most bars for each time period show the total number of new IGOs created; the numbers are fairly consistent. IGOs, by definition, are continuing phenomena; a few fade away or are replaced by others but most continue for many decades. The next figures (second from the left) are estimates of the total number of IGOs operating at each point in time. Even with correcting for expirations and a decline in the number of new IGOs created after 1975, the total number of IGOs operating increased steadily and certainly exceeds 300 today.

The right two bars for each epoch show actions concerning existing IGOs. Two figures are given, the number of actions occurring during the period (3rd from the left) and total cumulative effect (rightmost bar) reflecting the fact most of these create permanent changes – reforms – to IGOs. The overall, cumulative effect of 'IGO Actions (Cumulative)' appears to be substantial although it peaks about 1975 and declines thereafter. Perhaps this method of reform is becoming less effective.

Figure 2 shows patterns of amendments, protocols, etc., to six important IGOs. Again, the assumption is that these represent a reform mechanism that is available. Except for the UPU, there has been markedly less activity since about 1970. This is consistent with the pattern seen in Figure 1 when all multilateral IGO-related treaties were considered.

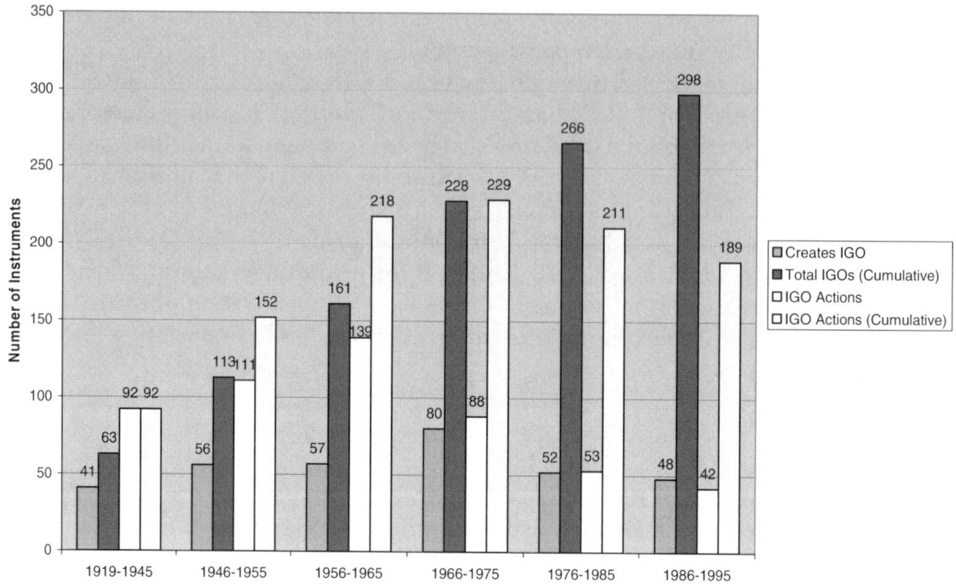


*Figure 1.* IGO Activity Since 1918 – Cumulative Effect

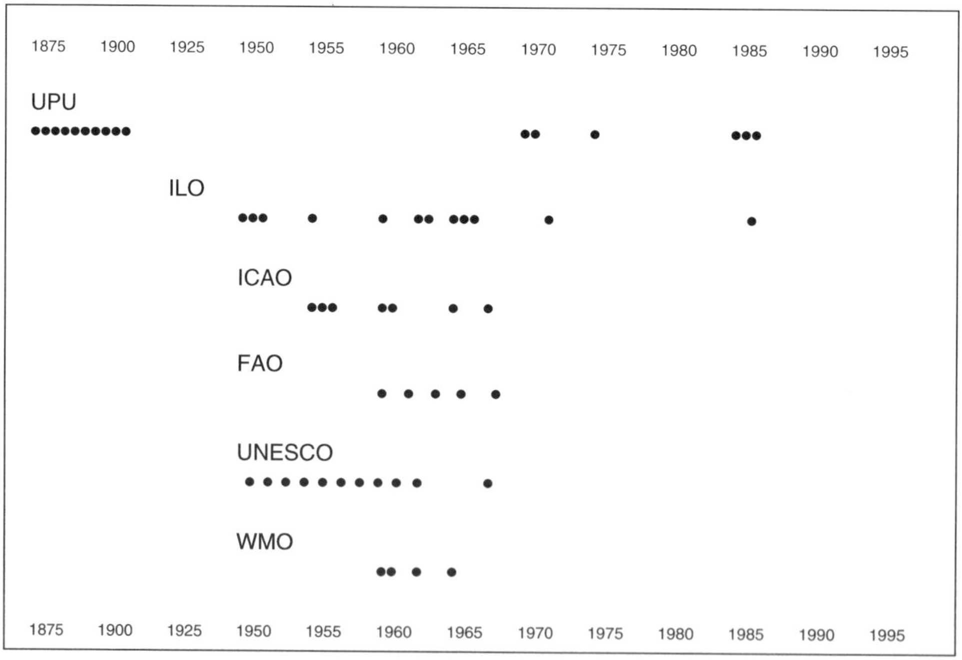


*Figure 2.* Derivative Instrument Patterns of Selected IGOs

## 4. Conclusions

Reform of international institutions is of paramount importance but the gap between rhetoric and success is large, perhaps unbridgeable. Treaty data from the CSDMT show the existing reform process that is in place. It might not please everyone, but it does work and, by definition, is consensual; but it has been used less since 1975 suggesting the need to reinvigorate these modes or to find new ones.

There may be consensus on what reform is. It is remarkably similar to the concept of good governance. The ILA Committee on the Accountability of International Organisations wrote that good governance included 'transparency ... a large degree of democracy in the decision-making process; access to information open to all ... well-functioning of the international civil service; sound financial management; and appropriate reporting and evaluation mechanisms.'[21] The goal is clear, but how do we achieve it? Mr. Pope seems ever wiser 'Whate'er is best administer'd is best'.[22]

Instead should efforts be directed towards a massive global public education program to build support for international institutions? Perhaps this is prerequisite for reforms to succeed. There is a lot of evidence this is lacking not only in the United States (Bolton nomination, UN dues) but in Europe (rejection of the EU Constitution). Is this talk about reform just another example of intelligentsia losing contact with the person in the street in New Delhi, Peoria, or Utrecht.

Should reform be attempted even when failure is virtually assured? Prudence is in order. Unintended consequence will occur. Will loose talk create the illusion of reform and remove pressure for real reform. Labelling something 'reform' does not make it so. Witness 'let a thousands flowers bloom' and 'no child left behind'. Reform of international institutions is essential, but achieving it is difficult, maintaining it problematic, and reconciling it with other positive values may be impossible. Success requires ideas and creativity bolstered by an ethos of internationalism, an ethos that extends to and is supported by the average citizen.

## Notes

1 Alexander Pope, *The Works*, Vol. II, Containing the Epistles and the Satires, 'An Essay on Man', Epistle iii, p. 42, lines 301-304 (1736).

2 See Constitution of the Food and Agriculture Organisation of the United Nations (Quebec, 16 October 1945), at 'preamble'. Also, see discussion in 'Harvesting Votes', *The Economist* (15 May 1999) at p. 49.

3 Charter of the UN, Art. 1.1.

4 Philip Burch, *Reagan, Bush, and Right-Wing Politics: Elites, Think Tanks, Power, and Policy* (1997), pp. 307-309.

5 Secretary Rice's Announcement of Nomination of John Bolton, US Dept. of State, 7 March 2005, <www.state.gov/secretary/rm/2005/43062.htm>.

6 'Questions for John Bolton at his Confirmation Hearing', Peace and Justice Center, 4 April 2005, <peaceandjustice.org/article.php?story=20050406201627741>.

7 Report of the High-level Panel on Threats, Challenges and Change, with letter from S-G dated 2 December 2004, A/59/565.

8 Uganda web site (Washington Embassy), 'The Economy', <www.ugandaembassy.com/index.html>.

9 Frank Biermann, Udo Simonis, 'Institutional Reform of International Environmental Policy', Science Center Berlin, *Discussion Papers* FS II 00-401 (2000) at p. 5.

10 Id. at p. 9.

11 Heiner Schulz, Thomas Konig, 'Institutional Reform and Decision-Making in the European Union', 44 *Amer. J. of Pol. Sci.*, (2000), p. 653.
12 Crisis States Research Centre, LSE, 'What do we means by crisis and breakdown', 18 March. 2004 at p. 2, <www.crisisstates.com/Research/intro.htm>.
13 Jacob Werksman, Oxfam GB Discussion Paper, 'Institutional Reform of the WTO', (March 2000) at p. 4, <www.Oxfam.org.uk/what we do/issues/trade/wto reform.htm>.
14 See *supra* n. 11, at p. 665.
15 See *supra* n. 13, at p. 18.
16 Michael Hiscox, 'The Magic Bullet? The RTAA, Institutional Reform and Trade Liberalization', 53 *International Organization* (1999), p. 691.
17 See *supra* n. 12, at pp. 3-4.
18 Bruce Hanebrink, PS 103, Political Systems Home Page, spg. Semester, 2005, Southeast Missouri State Univ. – section in institutional reform: <www2.semo.edu/vending/PS103/>.
19 Id. at 'The Tricky Business of Institutional Reform'.
20 The CSDMT is a project of the Honors Programs at Pennsylvania State University. It originated in 1998 with a review by John Gamble of Christian L. Wiktor, *Multilateral Treaty Calendar*, 1648-1995 (1998) prepared for the *AJIL* (v. 93, pp. 565-566, 2000). Since then, Wiktor and other sources have been used to collect basic information about all multilateral treaties from 1648-1995.
21 The ILA Committee on the Accountability of International Organisations, 2002 New Delhi Conference, <http://www.ila-hq.org/html/layout_committee.htm> at p. 2.
22 See *supra* n. 1.

# Remarks by J. Math Noortmann*

## The Role of Civil Society in International Institutional Reform: Decreasing the Private by Increasing the Private

### Introduction

When one is ask to shed some 'alternative' light on 'international institutional reform' it is difficult to disregard Luck's observation with respect to UN reform that:

> 'Through the years, scores of independent commissions, governmental studies and individual scholars have put forward literally hundreds of proposals aimed at making the world body work better, decide more fairly, modify its mandate or operate more efficiently. Not to be left behind by the reform bandwagon, successive Secretaries-General and units of the Secretariat have engaged in frequent, if episodic bouts of self-examination and self-criticisms, offering their own reform agendas.'[1]

While it is a comfortable thought to be on the reform bandwagon, with so many others, the idea that one might forward just another alternative reform proposal which is as good or as bad as the 'hundreds of proposals' before and the probably thousand of proposals after is slightly discouraging. However, since I take 'alternative' as 'being different from what is usual or traditional' or as 'not accepting or demonstrating conventional' rather then just 'being able to be used instead of something else', I have taken

* Associate Professor in International Law, Erasmus University, Rotterdam.

this opportunity to engage in an academic, practically irrelevant exercise of alternative 'path finding'

International institutional designs cannot cover all future developments and contingencies. Every act of creation triggers – rather sooner then later – its own future demands for institutional improvement. Clever institutional designs anticipate such demands and incorporate bureaucratic and/or institutional reform mechanisms. International institutional reform, therefore, does not necessarily require unanimous intergovernmental approval. On the contrary, most international institutional reform is the result of bureaucratic and institutional practice and policy.

In terms of institutional theory, institutional reform is either inherent in the modern 'rational-legal type of organizational structure', which automatically leads to more efficiency (Weber) or is the result of external pressures, which does not necessarily improve the institutional setting (DiMagio and Powel).[2] In terms of results then, institutional reform can be characterized as an 'adaptive response' or a 'creative innovation', depending on whether the reform process resembles 'design conformism' and as such 'stays within the range of current practice, custom and procedures' or not.[3]

There is little doubt that international organizations increasingly encroach upon the rights and interests of individuals, which in the current state of international institutional design seem have no alternative except for voting NO or participating in peaceful and less peaceful actions against hermetically closed international institutions. The 'international institutional reform' discourse tends to neglect the necessity to include the pure private interest of the individual citizen, in international institutions. The 'natural' hesitation against introducing 'direct citizens' representation' in the reformation discourse, is understandable as such 'alternative' proposals are easily discarded as unrealistic, idealistic or utopian.

The increasing emancipation of the masses and the increasing awareness and the position of individual, unrepresented citizens in international affairs has been neglected in bureaucratic and institutional 'design conform' reforms. The academic international institutional reform discourse should not make the same mistake.

'International institutional design conformism' inherently neglects the individual citizen, a flaw in international institutional reform which can only be remedied by international institutional transformation and redesign. Contemporary international institutions bear the very birthmarks of the international legal system, which is essentially a private law system. The reform of international institutions should therefore concentrate on the 'de-privatization' of these institutions. My argument will be that the introduction of the 'pure' private element into international organizations ultimately reinforces the public element.

The introduction of the private is not achieved by creating and reforming the formal participation of the private/civil society sector, but by allowing them to actually influence decision and law-making and not only to 'participate' in decision and law-making processes. Where private actors are actually allowed to bring private claims against international organizations, the public dimension of international institutions will benefit. The main question is whether the gatekeepers of international institutions allow the introduction of such a role of civil society and how civil society or public concern and interest can be effectively voiced and guarded. Alternative solutions can be found in the introduction of formal procedures where civil society groups can effectively challenge decisions through independent institutional channels.

For illustrative purposes I will sketch the position of the individual in three different organizations: The UN, World Bank and EC.

1) The UN is that classical institution, which were the role of and relationship with civil society perfectly reflects the intergovernmental nature. Contemporary developments within the UN will be criticized as lip service to the idea of the existence of a public interest within the organization.
2) The World Bank stands out for introducing a complaint or grievances procedure. which introduces an element of public accountability by inviting civil society representation and individual citizens to voice their concern in an intergovernmental context. The inspection panel procedure holds the middle between legitimation and innovation.
3) The European Community has introduced from the very beginning the possibility for the private sector to challenge Community decisions. In combination with the judicial activism of the EC Court, this incorporation of the private interest has taken the EC on a reform trip beyond its original design.

## Reforming the International Institutional Design

Design conform reforms find their limitations in the very institutional design they seek to improve. The current international institutional design is predominantly a socio-legal construction designed to operate in a 'society of states'. As such international organizations bear all the characteristics of the legal order of that society. While we euphemistically refer to the legal order of the 'society of states' as *public* international law, the legal format of that 'society' resembles all the characteristics of Roman private law. State consent, which still is the paradigmatic corner-stone of intergovernmental institutional design, can only be understood in its historical, Westphalian and especially Grotian construction of the legal order of the 'society of states'.

One does not have to be a critical or non-conformist scholar to observe that the international institutional reform discourse is blinkered in this respect. The parameters for the international institutional reform are set and the framework for the discourse is determined by the positivistic design of the international legal order. In this respect, many, neo-liberal, institutionalist and reformist approaches and proposals do not provide alternatives with a capital A, as they stay within the dominant realist and positivist state oriented perspective. That perspective excludes direct citizen's participation. The lack of a *direct* relationship between the people and international organizations is an inherent result of the traditional notion of inter*nation*al law as the law of and between states. States can be called 'societies' as these constitute 'the collective self-creating of human beings'.[4] However, their international co-existence and cooperation does *not* constitute a 'collective self-creating of human beings'. The mandate, which is given to governments and national parliamentarians by their constituencies to govern the state, cannot be extrapolated to the international level. International law is not (yet) the 'law of international society'.

Therefore,

> 'The international "community" established by the constitutive documents of international organizations ... is not a "civil society" consisting of peoples and individuals, but an exclusive community of political and diplomatic representatives of states and governments. For international organizations the "consent" or concurrence of those representatives is much more important then the views of individuals.'[5]

International organizations can hardly be called 'societies' in the social theoretical sense of the word.[6] They are not 'a collective self-constituting of human beings'. On the contrary, most international organizations must be characterized as 'exclusive' with respect to 'people'. At most an international organization can be defined as 'society of societies'. In its basis, international organizations are legal rather then social constructs. The power relationship between the members and the institution is based on an explicit legal contract rather then an extended 'social contract'. Not only are international organizations characterized by their exclusive state membership, but also the closed decision-making system. International organizations do not allow individuals to participate and/or intervene. At most international organizations are willing to accept 'consultative processes'.

However, it must be questioned whether 'the consultative process approach ... brings the organization closer to the "people" [and whether] consultative procedures evolve into a modus operandi ... the consequence [of which] will be that they tend to strengthen the organizations' functional independence from state and governments, on whose political will and formal consent they are based.[7] Consultative processes are based on the involvement of international non-governmental organizations, the majority of which do not represent an individual's interest.

Consultative processes involving IGO and INGOs should not be confused with the participatory processes of civil society organizations and individuals. Rajagopal, considers the 'NGOization' of the notion of 'civil society' as 'problematic'.[8] If this 'NGOization, misses the radical potential of a social movement perspective to transform international law'[9] as Rajagopal contends, one might very well ask whether the international institutional elites promote the 'NGOization' of the consultative process and the notion of civil society in order prevent the 'deprivatization' of international law and its institutions.

The term 'civil society' denotes various ideas on the relationship between the individual and suprastructural manifestations like the state. In neo-Marxist terms it has been defined as 'the area of social life which appears as the realm of the private citizen and individual consent'.[10]

The very idea of a 'civil society' is add odds with representation. The state may reflect such realm, but it does not represent it. As the individual state cannot be the representative agency of a given civil society neither can the international community of states claim such representative status? International organizations can therefore only reflect an international civil society if and to the extent that they reflect the 'area of social life which appears as the international realm of the private citizen and individual consent'.

THE UNITED NATIONS AND THE EXCLUSION OF THE INDIVIDUAL'S INTEREST

Reform at the UN could – if we cut and paste in the citations of UN Secretary-General Kofi Anan – be characterized as follows:

> 'Reshaping the organization in ways not previously imagined, while purposes should be firm and principles constant, practice and organization should move with the times. The United Nations is a work in progress [but] reform must be rooted in a new consensus among governments.'

With respect to the UN and civil-society relation, the Secretary-General's 'reform' report on the 'Strengthening of the United Nations' concludes that:

> '1)Interaction between Un and civil society has grown significantly
> 2) Thousand of NGOs now have formal consultative status and
> 3) Their contribution has enriched the debates and influenced the outcome of many intergovernmental deliberations.
> There have been problems along the way [which justify]:
> 1) To take stock and find better ways of organizing the relationship and
> 2) To establish a high level panel to make recommendations in this regard.'[11]

A school example of the 'NGOization of civil society'. The UN's frame of reference for civil society is Article 71, which I characterized two years ago as a 'symbol rather the a vehicle of progress'. Perhaps, it was never designed as a 'vehicle of progress.' The embedded participation of non-governmental organizations was not meant to gradually transform the UN into a public interest organization. Whether the current UN's interest in 'civil society' and 'private (read: business) interest' is likely to alter the UN's closed organizational structure must be doubted. The UN's public interest goes as far as the cumulated (private) interests of a majority of 191 Member States.

The UN Secretary-General's 'agenda for further change' comes nowhere near a proposal for an enhanced involvement of the people in the decision-making process of the UN.[12] In 'promoting partnerships' the report is traditionally exclusive with respect to the role and position of the people in the UN.

The report of the Panel of Eminent Persons on United nations-Civil Society Relations equally misses the opportunity to give 'civil society a (individual) human face'.[13] While the panel recognizes that 'citizens increasingly act politically by participating directly, through civil society mechanisms', the report almost exclusively deals with and assesses the relationship between the UN and civil society organizations or other forms of indirect institutionalized representation like NGOs and parliamentarians. However, neither CSOs, NGOs, the 'private' sector nor parliamentarians constitute the civil society.

The reason for the UN 'for reaching out beyond its constituency of the central Governments and enhancing dialogue and cooperation with civil society' is a means to become 'more effective' reaching out to people is not in itself a reform objective. The opinion of the panel that 'the unique role of the United Nations as an intergovernmental forum is vitally important [which] must be protected as all costs', rests my case.[14] The UN reform process is managed within the framework of the traditional intergovernmental design; it is not going to neglect the major paradigm of contemporary international law, i.e., the consent of the state and develop a new constituency. 'Reaching out to the people' is the UN's reform credo with respect to civil society, instead of opening up for the people.

The majority of UN reform proposals ignore the representation of the 'real' private interest in the UN. Where international economic and financial organizations have been successfully criticized by the civil society for the lack of private interest representation, the UN has never been the subject of such criticism. The 'battle of Seattle' is not taken to New York or Geneva. Article 71 has functioned and is still functioning as a political lightning conductor. Major publications on the reform of the UN system focus on the reform of Article 71 rather then the introduction of non-organized private interest.

Sohn and Clark's understood as early as 1958 that the development of 'a spirit of world citizenship' would be not only be crucial for the position of the United Nations in international affairs but for the very maintenance of 'World Peace through World Law'.[15] Clark and Sohn sought to facilitate the development of such a spirit by: (1) creating UN citizenship and (2) introducing 'a more' direct representation in the General Assembly and the Security Council.[16] Considering Sohn and Clarks preoccupation with the position of the citizen within the UN, their rather uncritical acceptance of Article 71 as it stands is remarkable. Should they not have concluded as Childers and Urquhart did in their 1994 publication titled 'renewing the United Nations System' that 'NGOs cannot, in their nature, fully and adequately represent "we the peoples of the United Nations".'[17] In the latter author perception, such a role should be entrusted to a 'United Nations Parliamentary Assembly'. In order to avoid a pure symbolic exercise, the authors suggest that such an organ should be given 'serious work and real oversight functions on behalf of all citizens'.[18]

While it is unlikely that 'direct representation' is going to enter the reform agenda of international institutions in the near future, other possibilities for public participation have been or could have been the subject of experience. In 2002, the UN appointed an Ombudsman who could 'address employment related problems of staff-members' investigate private complaints against A civil society oriented UN could have established an Ombudsman for problems of individuals with the UN, UN organs and personal or it could have created a complaint or grievances procedure following the Inspection panel example of the World Bank.

## The World Bank and the Complaining Citizen

Recently the World Bank issued a report the tile of which makes clear that the Bank's predominantly focuses on the relationship with Civil Society *Organizations*.[19] While the Bank's civil society 'partners' and civil society 'baffles' are very often organizations, the Bank's 'civil society protest' however is assessed in terms of 'individuals'.[20] Here again the question is not so much how the World Bank can 'reach out' but how it can open up to the individual interest and concern, i.e., how the individual can 'reach in'. The recognition that '[p]lacing emphasis on more *upstream engagement* ... in the design and pre-approval stages can improve the quality of the Bank' should not be limited to CSOs.[21] In such an upstream engagement, special attention should be paid to 'the role of various grievances mechanisms such as the bank's Inspection Panel and the

IFC/MIGA's Compliance Advisor Ombudsman (CAO)' according to the Bank's report.[22]

It is probably this *upstream engagement, which* has led scholars to characterize the World Bank's Inspection Panel as an 'experiment in institutional reform'.[23] The Inspection Panel procedure enables 'a directly affected person' to file a request and entitles him or her to direct representation. The right to file a complaint is not limited to 'entities',[24] thus the World Bank Inspection Panel should therefore not be defined as a 'institutional reform' paradigm case ... of the influence of transnational advocacy networks over international norms and policies',[25] But as a paradigm case for the direct representation an inclusion of individual private interest in the norm-setting and policy adjustment within international organizations.

The creation of the Inspection Panel in 1993 can be explained both in terms of an 'adaptive response' to civil society protests, as well as in terms of 'creative innovation'. The 'adaptive response' theory would focus on the impulse which induced the World Bank to establish 'an independent forum to private citizens who believe that they or their interests have been or could be directly harmed by a project financed by the World Bank' and would consider this 'reform' to fit within the current institutional design. The creative innovation theory would highlight the uniqueness of the Inspection Panel as a formal 'body to give voice to private citizens in an international context'. According to Chinkin, it 'it shifts the focus of discussion in two ways: first the complaint is against the institution itself and secondly it is initiated by non-state actors, that are by definition, non-parties to the institutional regime.'[26]

The individuals and CSOs which are invited in by the World Bank in the framework of the Inspection Panel procedure, must be distinguished from the Individuals and CSO which can generally be grouped in the WB/CSO categories of activity: facilitation, dialogue and consultation, and partnership. The individuals and CSOs which seek the World Bank's attention are affected locals and involved community based and grass-root organizations. These individuals and organizations do not represent civil society; they are civil society.

## The European Union and the Private NO

With the 'European Single Act' in 1986 the European Community started a 'reformation' process, which was recently halted by the popular vote of the 'Citizens of the Union' in France and the Netherlands. The fact that some of the European Governments did not dare to take the institutional reform process of the European Union beyond Nice without formally consulting its constituency, indicates that the European Union has progressed beyond a mere 'society of states'.

From the very beginning and through various institutional and intergovernmental reforms, the European Community has created political and legal mechanisms for citizen's participation.

The original design already provided for (1) the possibility for individuals and companies to institute proceedings which allowed for a 'review of the Community's regulatory machine' and (2) a Parliament, which consist of the 'representatives of the peoples of the States brought together in the Community.'[27] In 1992 the 'Citizenship of the Union' was introduced and in 1994 the European Ombudsman.

According to Alter, 'the *transformation* of the European legal system was orchestrated by the ECJ through bold legal interpretations.'[28] She identifies private litigation and not state litigation as one of the 'central' factors in this process. She assumes a direct link between 'cases private litigants raised' and the 'advancement of the agenda of the European integration'. Private litigants provided a context for European judicial activism, which contributed to the European institutional reform in the following manners:

1) national policies and law that violated European law was challenged,
2) the European system [was used] as a venue were deals made at the national or European level can be reopened
3) individual constitutional complaints against issues of European integration were filed.[29]

Alter considers the 'harnessing of private litigants', as the basis of the paradigmatic transformation process of the European system from a political to a legal system.[30]

Whether that transformation was a successful one from the perspective of the European citizens must be doubted. The European Court, which has the used the position it was put in by private litigants to engage in judicial activism seems to have made the European transformation process the victim of its own success; the reform dialectics of progress.

The European Court has sought to transform the European Community beyond its original international institutional design. Such transformation process is doomed to fail as it progress beyond what is 'usual or acceptable'; it is too an alternative.

## Conclusion

International institutional reform may take various shapes, depending on the impulse for institutional improvement and change. International institutional reform demands may come from stakeholders within the institution or stakeholders outside the institution or result from an unintended alliance such as in the European Union case. Institutional bureaucracy, governments and judiciaries are the stakeholders within whereas civil society, non-governmental organizations and business organizations are the main stakeholders outside the international institution.

Traditional international institutions cannot be transformed into public interest organizations without the parallel development of an international civil society. International institutions must be (pre)designed or reformed in this direction to allow the international citizen to participate in that ultimate transformation.

International institutions ego-perspective as intergovernmental organizations and their notion of civil society as being able to be represented has a confining impact upon the International institutional capability to reform from a private interest organization into a public interest organization.

International institutional reform, which would aim at the incorporation of public participation within the organization, in order to transform the original design of the intergovernmental organizations would be alternative with a capital A. However as this is unlikely to happen in the near future, maybe as a first step we could stop labelling each and every international institutional upgrade as an international institutional reform.

## NOTES

1 E.C. Luck, 'Reforming the United nations: Lessons from a History in progress', *International Relations Studies and United Nations Occasional papers 2003* (Academic Council on the United Nations System (ACUNS) No. 1 at p. 1.

2 D.S. Pugh & D.J. Hickson, *Writers on Organizations*, 5th edn. (London, Penguin Books, 1996) at p. 188.

3 Idem p. 24.

4 P. Allot, *Eunemia* (Oxford, Oxford University Press 1990) at p. 1.

5 V. Heiskanen, 'Introduction' in *The Legitimacy of International Organizations*, Coicaud & Heiskanen (eds.), (Tokyo, UN University Press 2001) at p. 6.

6 See *supra* n. 4, at p. 53.

7 See *supra* n. 5, at p. 10.

8 B. Rajagopal, *International Law from Below; Developments, Social Movements and Third World Resistance* (Cambridge, Cambridge University Press 2003) at p. 258.

9 Idem.

10 See the *Penguin Dictionary of Sociology*, 4th edn. (Penguin Books 2000) at p. 49.

11 UN Doc. A/57/387.

12 See Report of the Secretary-General of the UN, Strengthening of the United Nations: an agenda for further change, UN Doc. A/57/387 (9 September 2002).

13 We the people: civil society, the United Nations and global governance. UN Doc. A/58/517.

14 Idem at p. 8.

15 G. Clark and L.B. Sohn, *World Peace through World Peace* (Harvard, Harvard University Press 1960) at p. 82.

16 Idem at p. 14 and p. 82.

17 E. Childers and B. Urquhart, *Renewing the United Nations System* (Uppsale, Dagmar Hammerskold Foundation 1994) at p. 212.

18 Idem at p. 213.

19 *Issues and Options for Improving Engagement between the World Bank and Civil Society Organizations*, The World Bank, March 2005.

20 Idem at pp. 22-23.

21 Idem at p. 34.

22 Idem. The Inspection Panel should indeed be characterized as a 'grievances' and 'complaint' procedure rather then a 'dispute settlement procedure.' See C. Chinkin, *Third Parties in International Law* (Oxford, Clarendon Press 1993), pp. 512-514; J. Collier and V. Lowe, *The Settlement of International Disputes* (Oxford, Oxford University Press 1999), pp. 119-121.

23 J.A. Fox, 'The World Bank Inspection Panel and the Limits of Accountability', in Pincus & Winters (eds.), *Reinventing the World Bank* (London, Cornell University Press 2002) p. 131 at p. 163.

24 See *supra* nn. 19 and 22.

25 See *supra* n. 23, at p. 163.

26 See C. Chinkin, *supra* n. 22 at p. 513.

27 Both mechanisms have been changed and adapted through jurisprudence and the 1976 decision of the Council based on former Art. 190 to introduce 'direct and universal suffrage'.

28 K.J. Alter establishing the Supremacy of European Law; *The Making of an International Rule of Law in Europe* (Oxford, Oxford University Press 2001) at p. 1.

29 Idem at p. 14, 70, 110.

30 Idem at p. 4.

## Remarks by Dinah Shelton*

No paper received.

## Discussion

Chris Harmann:** Professor Gamble could you explain what an IGO activity is? If it is not a treaty how did you find it? How do you predict the climbing rate of new activities of both IGOs and the activities that are predicted continuing to decrease?

John Gamble: Gives a quick and dirty explanation of the figures. He looks only at actual treaties that have entered into force – although he looks them over in a 500-year period. So he could pick-up the constituent document that created an IGO and subsequent protocols and amendments, although they are not always called protocols and amendments. What can be seen is a flurry of activity. The number of newly created IGOs does decline as the number of actions declines. The most difficult points are the methodological questions. At the moment there is a mathematician working on how to accommodate the fact that in most instances a treaty creates an IGO and that IGO exists and effects the international system for decades or in some cases fore centuries or more, although fewer come up from a century. For now there is no answer yet on how to accommodate this.

Chris Harmann: Professor Shelton, is there any evidence that MOUs are, or soft law in general is, better respected than treaties? Following on recent studies with respect to how well respected treaties have been in human rights context, I am wondering if soft law is only a partial answer because people feel closer somehow to the decisions that they take.

Dinah Shelton: This is the hardest question that could be asked in this matter and it was actually the origin of this study. I tried to find out what type of compliance there is with soft law. At one point it was even questioned why it should be expected that any compliance should be found with soft law if it is not legally binding. At the end of the study she got converted to soft law because a number of things were found when looking at case studies across four areas of international law: human rights, environment, trade and finance and multilateral arms control. In general, law does matter. Compliance with the recommendation of the inter-American commission of human rights was compared with compliance of judgments of the European Court or the inter-American court and a clear difference was found. In case of binding judgments large states do feel they have to comply with them, but on the other hand when something is a recommendation states do not necessary feel they have to comply.

A number of factors that went into making certain kinds of soft law institutions are highly effective, perhaps even more than an equivalent treaty law basis might have been. If you are looking at the Helsinki process in the OSCE, and you are saying: "Is this as effective as a treaty would have been?" then that would probably be the wrong comparison because you would never have gotten a treaty. So in short it is OSCE versus nothing as opposed to OSCE versus a treaty.

* George Washington University Law School.

** International Committee of the Red Cross.

One of the things that made it so effective was the issue linkage that went on in that process as well as the ongoing monitoring. In the environmental field one of the interesting aspects that we looked at is that if the issue is in compliance with the norm than you will probably get less compliance with soft law than with hard law. If the issue is environmental protection than probably it is better to use soft law. When you are writing non-binding instruments states are willing to go much further in terms of the normative obligations that they will put in there, because they know they are not legally bound. So, better norms that need less compliance will achieve the same end. It is a very complex interplay between the state behaviour in the soft law and the hard law.

Other findings were that across all of these areas you will almost never find free standing soft law. It is always linked to hard law or hard institutions in some way that enhances its effectiveness.

CHRIS HARMANN: Is there anything that we can see in terms of the effect of the soft law and the custom, Professor Dickinson? I am wondering if there is anything that we can see in terms of the effect of soft law and custom. Normally you would not expect it but if there is such a volume you might find it at some point. Could you, through some means of getting soft law build into custom or getting this custom better respected, develop this custom so it actually becomes hard law?

LAURA DICKINSON: I would add to what I described in my paper by noting that treaty obligations on states can be extended to non-state actors through contractual terms in agreements between states and non-state actors. If such terms become commonplace, they may then lay the groundwork for new treaty language that would explicitly bind non-state actors. Thus, the 'soft' law of contract might be seen as a means to develop new 'hard' treaty law. At the same time, even if you have a 'hard' law treaty regime in place – for example a treaty regime that explicitly binds non-state actors – the 'soft' law of contract is still useful to help put that treaty regime in place and make it effective. Either way the process of using the contract as a tool is very important.

SUSAN BREAU:* Professor Noortmann could you expand upon the role of civil society in the international society? Can you explain why civil society may not be a method for individual participation?

MATH NOORTMANN: The basis component of every civil society is the individual. The basic component of the UN's idea of 'civil society' is an organisation (whether NGO or business). The Article 71 arrangement does not provide for true civil society representation. Except for the UN human rights mechanisms, the pure individual interest is not represented in the UN. It is the 'NGOisation' of civil society in the UN what I object.

PETER BAEHR:** When you give the OSCE as an example of a successful case of soft law, would you agree with me on the fact that the Helsinki agreements were picked up by all kinds of non-governmental organisations, committees and what have you in Eastern Europe helped to make it such a success. The Western European governments and the Western nations did not really consider the effect that the healthy Helsinki conference was seen as a victory for the Soviet Union. Only thanks to the fact that this was picked up, the human rights aspect got so much attention.

* British Institute of International and Comparative Law.

** Utrecht University.

DINAH SHELTON: There was a tremendous criticism at the end of the Helsinki conference, particularly in the US congress, that this was a total sell out to the Soviet Union. At the same time the national commissions were picking up the commitments. The creation of the national commissions was allowing them to function and was also one of the commitments written in the agreement. The commitment in the Helsinki process has allowed the national organisations to function and pick up the other commitments and make them effective. So I think it really worked both ways.

PETER BAEHR: Dealing with the IGOs. Does this mean that you deal with them all on the same level? I mean creating UN of legal nations there is a little difference, I wonder if you could say a few things on this matter.

JOHN GAMBLE: Professor Manley O. Hudson once said: 'Count, by all means count but count what counts'. I would supplement that and say count accurately and understand the things that you are counting.

One of the next stages to the database project is to find a way to accommodate the vast difference in quality and importance of the 7000 treaties. For example there is a trilateral agreement of a one year duration on the importation on zipper chain. At present, that is counted as one multilateral treaty on equal footing with the treaty alone or the UN charter. There obviously needs to be a way to accommodate the vast difference in the quality and importance of the duration of treaties. There are mathematical ways to accommodate this far better than assuming all to be equal.

PETER BAEHR: The following comments are for Professor Noortmann and Professor Dickinson. For Professor Noortmann: I appreciate very much that you put some doubts on the use of the word international community. It is very dear to me. I heard in this conference several times 'the international community does this and the international community does that' and it does not exist and I fully share the points that you have quoted.

For Professor Dickinson: You already made the point during the presentation on the fact that in history there have been more cases. Certainly in the Netherlands we used to say 'no money no Swiss', so we could not hire any Swiss soldiers to fight our wars for us. I would appreciate in the paper you would might to put it stronger.

PELT:* This is a follow-up of Mr. Baehr's question about Professor Shelton's study on compliance. Pelt wonders whether the dichotomy is not so much between hard law and soft law as between law in the books and law in action. Soft law seems less likely to be law in the books than hard law. Could Professor Gamble also comment on this?

DINAH SHELTON: The Helsinki commitments did get into the books in a number of states in terms of national law. In different kinds of ways it effected compliance and linked most favoured nation status to compliance with parts of the Helsinki commitments. That part of Helsinki got into the law books in the United States. It is very difficult to distinguish soft law and hard law, because they interplay in so many different ways. One of the things that became clear is the difficulty of clearly classifying something as soft or hard.

AUKJE VAN HOEK:** I had a question about the privatisation of government functions. The system, where you have a contract asking the private party to comply with

* Open University.

** University of Tilburg.

international norms, seems to be a way where the state can comply with the state's responsibility under the same convention, especially if you contract out internal tasks like the prison system. I wonder if that is the same in the international level. Is it always one state carrying responsibility and the contract being a way of carrying that responsibility or are there also cases where the privatisation actually takes place in a situation where the state responsibilities are unclear?

LAURA DICKINSON: My research has focused primarily on privatisation of U.S. foreign affairs functions, but it is a very important point that different problems arise when international organisations privatise their activities. For example, one set of enforcement issues arises when the international organisation contracts directly with a non-profit or for-profit organisation. A different set of issues arises when the contract is between a Member State and a non-profit or for-profit organisation to provide aid or other services on behalf of the international organisation. In some ways the latter situation provides more opportunities for incorporating public law values in the terms of contracts and the enforcement of contractual terms.

JEFF DUNHOFF:* I want to extend on a question about NGOs and civil society. It strikes me that most of the conversation took a view of civil society as other pressure groups or interacting states with IOs, taking on traditional governmental functions. I am just wondering if there might be another way to think about civil society in creating somewhat alternative forms of government outside the state system. Think of private labelling schemes, maybe consumer boycotts, monitoring programmes, private codes of conduct, etc. The question would be whether the problem or the issues of accountability are more or less important and in that context what kind of tools might be appropriate or do we need to think about alternative tools.

MATH NOORTMANN: The subtitle of my paper was 'Decreasing the private by increasing the private'. International organisations are private institutions as they represent the private interest of their constituent members. At the International plane, states have a private interest and not a global public interest. It is necessary to decrease the private interest of international organisations in order to reform them into public organisations. This can be done in different ways. One would be to increase the individual interest in the organisation.

LAURA DICKINSON: I am reminded in this debate of the position that is taken by a U.S. scholar Kenneth Anderson. He argues that the participation of NGOs and other private actors is fundamentally illegitimate and undemocratic, because these are mediating actors. He argues that the appropriate relationship is between international organisations and state representatives. Individuals should participate in international organisations through their state representatives. I disagree with this view because, first of all, many states are not democratic, which leaves few options for individuals from those state. Influencing the international organisation through the state representative is not really a viable option. In any event, having NGOs involved in international organisation is an important way in which, although mediated, individuals can have more of a voice.

MATH NOORTMANN: The whole discourse on civil society of course depends on what we mean by civil society. I would like to recall the part of my paper that defines

* Temple Lawschool.

civil society as a relationship between the individual en supra-structural manifestation: 'It is the area of life which appears at the realm of the private citizen and the individual consent.' In order to create an international civil society, the individual consent and the private citizen has to be included in the intergovernmental supranational structure.

DINAH SHELTON: I would like to take your question in respect to one specific type of problem that has been under discussion in recent years and that is corporate social responsibility. If one thinks of multinational corporations as sort of another centre of governance with all the problems that it raises in a privatised, globalised world, there are several types of responses that could be taken to this question. One is business as usual; the only business of corporations is making a profit. One could make some kind of treaty directly relating to corporate behaviour. One can have national regulations of very diverse characters in one country or another. Or one could have self-regulation through industry and corporate codes of conduct which goes directly to your question. If you have those, do you then just simply leave it alone, or does there have to be some transparent verification system for accountability similar to what would happen to other types of institutional arrangements? I think the answer is yes, you would have to have some sort of monitoring verification system if you are going to allow these powerful actors to self-regulate.

JOHN GAMBLE: A point that was made in a paper that Professor Ku and Professor Gamble wrote is that there are so many NGOs or civil society organisations representing so many interests, often claiming to represent interest with no way to track when interests are really represented or not. The academic community has an overwhelmingly positive attitude towards these organisations just as I have. There is an enormous possibility for new NGOs to enter. No one has a clue how many NGOs there are. So we have the issue of organisations clamouring for a seat at the table with people like Math Noortmann advocating giving them a seat at the table, but we have to ask whom they do represent. At some point we are spending so much time providing seats for so many entities. This is not cost free. At some point the organisations have to get something done and not just worry about how many of thousands of IGOs, NGOs, civil, society organisations there are participating. We want participation but we also have to remember that presumably the reason why the organisations were created in the first place was there was some specific task for them to accomplish and that can get lost in the shuffle.

BARBARA RUIS:* I would like to know what the opinion of Professor Shelton is on the difficulties regarding the fact that a large part of soft law is not publicly known in the environmental field. There is no body of soft law as compared to a body of treaty law. Of course declarations are well known in the public domain but there has been an enormous proliferation of MOUs. How to it find out?

DINAH SHELTON: I agree with you. Once I asked someone in the legal office whether the government considers MOUs as legally binding or not and the answer was some are and some are not. It does not help with research if you do not know which ones can be found in the code and which ones not. This gets back to the definition of what is meant by soft law. Major declarations are published and MOUs do not because they are considered as informal agreements.

* United Nations Environment Programme Nairobi, Kenya.

ANDEM:* In the first place I want to say that we need the UN and the UN system. I am looking back at the history of the US, before it became what it is today. In the legal system itself you would not see soft law inside there. In this aspect in the field of public international law it is very clear. And if you refer back to Article 38 of the statute of the court, it is very clear. I think American international lawyers have contributed to the development of this area of law. I would like to say that we all need the UN, whether you like it or not. Without the UN I do not think most of us would be free to move around in the world today. Without those institutions created, we would not be seeing what is going on in the world. A society can never be a subject of public international law. The state is there to enforce the law. You can enforce the law, soft law or whatever you call it. A contract can be taken as a social public international law. I think that if one stands here to criticise the UN system he makes a mistake. President Roosevelt, Stalin, Churchill, they had something in mind. They had a vision. Can one person stand up and criticise an institution that people have so far made it to exist today. We have to be more positive, more realistic.

DINAH SHELTON: I agree with what you say but I just do have to correct it. We do have soft law in domestic law as well. We have things like opinions of the attorneys general, we have professional standards, we have the resolutions of the congress, the Olympic rules, there are a number of examples that could be given, so soft law is something that is known in domestic law as well as in international law.

MATH NOORTMANN: I tend to disagree with you. First of all, never say never I am not so sure whether we need the UN from now until eternity, or whether the UN as we know it today will survive future developments. Organisations might be transformed, redesigned or reformed in such a way that comparison with the original design is useless. Anywhere in the future the need for completely different organisations may arise.

JOHN GAMBLE: The comment about the support for the UN I think is important. At conferences representatives from governments usually say something like: 'My remarks not necessarily represent the department of state of the US'. These days professors from the United States should have a variation, an assumption that we do not always agree with what our government is doing at this time. On a far more serious level a lot of us who are professors spend an enormous amount of time trying to explain the subtleties, nuances and contributions of the UN in the hope that the view of the average educated citizen will be more enlightened and will drive policies of the government. We are perhaps at a low point right now in respect for the UN but things will change and will improve so I disagree with Math Noortmann and I think the organisation will exist for a century longer at least.

CHARLOTTE KU: To close the session out: Some of you may have come across studies of how international organisations in fact spawn other international organisations. So a certain family tree is beginning to develop. When looking at the importance of treaties, there may be additional weighting factors required. Sometimes, activities the parent gives rise to, are perhaps more important than the parent. This is a phenomenon that is also occurring institutionally so one should not just look at actions on the surface but should also look beneath the surface. The issue of interplay is

* University of Lapland.

very interesting. The American Society has done a lot of work to bring international law awareness to the work of the US judiciary both at the federal level as well as our sub-national level and the state area. What we discover in this is that we are talking in fact about interplay of legal systems. It is not even so much bringing in something that is taken as a whole package and then implemented, but in fact there is an interaction and what results is not entirely the same as the elements that went through the process. That will also come back to address some of what John Gamble and Math Noortmann are pushing us towards, which is to remember that broad popular understanding and support for institutions, whether it is the UN or other international institutions, ultimately is crucial to the success of any reform projects. I think that capacity is really the leitmotiv of our discussion whether it is the capacity of the institutions or the capacities of states to carry out the tasks required by virtue of membership in these institutions.

*Reporter:* Marlies Vreeswijk*

* Erasmus University, Rotterdam.

# Plenary Lunch Session

## The Hague as Leading Host of International Organizations: The Historical Perspective

The panel was convened by its Chairs, Lucy Reed* and James Carter**

Report of the Plenary lunch session

The session opened with the Co-Chairs welcoming the panel. L. Reed noted the The Hague's history of promoting international organizations, made references to the Peace conferences, and mentioned that 32 international organizations are currently based there. She expressed the regrets of the Deputy Mayor of The Hague, Peter van Woensel, for being unable to attend. In his stead, she noted the point in his submitted paper that international organizations and businesses bring large numbers of visitors, knowledge and employment to host cities. L. Reed added that with the good comes the not-so-good, and there are always complications for the hosts of international organizations, and so the panel would also address the rare disputes that arise in The Hague.

## Remarks by Charles N. Brower***

## The Hague as Leading Host of International Organizations

Hear these words of Socrates:

> "Regard your good name as the richest jewel you can possibly be possessed of – for credit is like fire; when once you have kindled it you may easily preserve it, but if you once extinguish it, you will find it an arduous task to rekindle it again."

Hear, too, these more trenchant words of Benjamin Franklin, that great and most literate of early American diplomats, who served as Minister to France at the same time

* Vice-President, American Society of International Law; Freshfields Bruckhaus Deringer, New York.

** President, American Society of International Law; Sullivan & Cromwell, New York.

*** Judge of the Iran-United States Claims Tribunal.

that our later President, John Adams, was resident here as Minister Plenipotentiary to The Netherlands:

> "Glass, china and reputation are easily cracked, and never well mended."

In case my point has escaped you, it is that The Netherlands, having over more than a century built a glistening reputation of The Hague as "The Legal Capital of the World," in recent years has begun to tarnish it; this reputation has become cracked, a process which, if not soon reversed, may, as Franklin noted, never be "well mended." I wish to tell you why this is the case, and to urge one thing that must be done, and done soon, if the course is to be reversed.

I should tell you that with the exception of one fellow Judge of the Iran-United States Claims Tribunal and its Secretary-General, I am almost certainly the longest serving principal in an international organization in The Hague, having first been appointed in 1983. I like The Hague. I have actually resided here for years. I am a genuine friend of The Netherlands. I experienced the effusive appreciation which enveloped my Tribunal when it was established here in the early 1980s, the first such arrival since that of the International Court of Justice 35 years before. Hence it grieves me all the more to see this country impair its reputation as a friendly host to international organizations, especially courts and tribunals.

But that is exactly what has happened. I should note at this point that this has occurred notwithstanding what I know to be the great efforts in the other direction of the Ministry of Foreign Affairs, in particular those of my colleague on this panel, Mr. de Savornin Lohman, and his staff, which are known to, and have been deeply appreciated by, my Tribunal as well as all the other international organizations resident in The Netherlands. And I am aware that just this past Monday the Secretary-General of the Ministry presented all international organizations with a series of proposals now in the process of evaluation. I do believe in giving credit where credit is due.

The few minutes allotted me are far too short to list the many reasons why The Hague's historic reputation has become cracked. I may say, however, that they fall into three categories: (1) matters beyond the immediate influence of the Government, such as availability of adequate medical services and the capacity of international schools, but as to which matters I must note the Government has made distinct efforts to improve the situation; (2) the fiscal and tax exemptions granted, and more recently withdrawn, by the Government, and other matters which obviously are entirely within its and the Parliament's control; and (3) the means of resolving disputes with international organizations of a legal character, such as asserted violations of headquarters agreements, also a matter entirely within governmental and parliamentary control.

What most greatly has caused The Hague's reputation to crack is the progressive reduction of previously granted, and in some cases previously agreed, financial incentives with which international organizations were, at least in part, persuaded to settle here. That cracking is compounded by the repeated, adamant refusal of the Government to do what The Netherlands have urged others to come to this city to do since the first Hague Convention of 1899, namely to engage in the peaceful settlement of legal disputes with international organizations through arbitration. In the case of my own Tribunal, notwithstanding two meetings of our President with successive Foreign Ministers, separated by extensive written diplomatic exchanges, including a formal demand for arbitration, all attempts at arbitration, and even conciliation or mediation, have been rejected by the Government. The reasons have ranged from frank oral admission of fear of losing such a proceeding, and the effect that such a loss might have in respect of other international organizations, to stating in formal diplomatic correspondence that "the relative importance and the nature and the substance of the [Dutch Government's] measures [subject of the Tribunal's Request for Arbitration] do not justify arbitration proceedings" and that the Government regards its own arguments as "sufficiently convincing that arbitration would not be appropriate."

But lest you think that what I have said regarding the cracking of The Hague's reputation is simply the plaint of a rejected suitor, listen to what the relevant Dutch authorities and the local press have to say:

– Item: When the International Criminal Court was established here the Dutch Government understandably assumed that there should be no trouble in having its candidate elected as its Registrar, as indeed happened at the International Criminal Tribunal for the Former Yugoslavia. To its stunned surprise, however, a competing candidate was fielded by France, and in fact was elected, a result publicly attributed to a spreading perception that The Netherlands is no longer such a friendly host government to international organizations.

– Item: In a much reported interview program on Radio 1 on 22 February of this year the Mayor of The Hague, the Director of the newest international organization to settle in The Hague (Mr. Sam Mulder of the Institute for the Internationalization of Law), and Mr. Tjaco van den Hout, a senior Dutch diplomat who is Secretary-General of the oldest international organization here, the Permanent Court of Arbitration, sounded the alarm. Thus the Mayor of The Hague, whom you heard yesterday evening at the Peace Palace, himself a former Minister: "I don't understand the attitude of some government members. We surely want to be a pleasant host." And listen to Secretary-General van den Hout: "The Netherlands is not a good host country for international organizations." He noted that The Hague is in danger of losing its status as "The Legal Capital of the World." He added that international organizations here increasingly meet with resistance from the various Ministries, which he described as "unnecessarily formalistic" and "calvinistically parsimonious."

– Item: The largest international organization in The Hague, the European Patent Office, which employs approximately 2,700 individuals, publicly threatened to move out of The Netherlands, its own staff having picketed it and demonstrated to express their extreme dissatisfaction with conditions here.

As I have noted, I personally have every reason to want The Hague to continue succeeding as "The Legal Capital of the World." You might say I have a vested interest in it doing so. Thus it is as a friend that I must emphasize how short time is for The Netherlands to turn the situation around. I suggest the Government begin by, as we say in my country, "putting its money where its mouth is," and agreeing to arbitration, or at least conciliation or mediation, of the rare legal disputes that arise between it and an international organization, processes which heretofore were synonymous with The Hague.

In closing, let me add one more pertinent quotation, this time from perhaps the most significant American industrialist of the 20th century, Henry Ford, who in his characteristically pithy style said: "You can't build a reputation on what you are going to do."

## Remarks by Bette Shifman*

### International Institutional Reform

#### Introduction

Having requested a representative of the Permanent Court of Arbitration (PCA) to survey the history of how The Hague came to host such a panoply of international organizations, you will not – I think – be surprised, if I devote particular attention to the Hague Peace conferences, particularly the first Peace Conference in 1899, as this not only marks the genesis of my own organization, the PCA, but also the watershed for The Hague's position as a capital of peace and international justice. But for the establishment of the PCA at the 1899 Peace Conference, there would be no Peace Palace in The Hague and, most probably, no Hague Academy of International Law or International Court of Justice. It is difficult to imagine that the various international tribunals and institutions that came to be headquartered in The Hague in subsequent years would have done so in their absence. In keeping with the theme of this joint conference, if the 1899 Peace Conference indeed heralded, as some commentators have suggested 'the Dawn of a New – International – Era', one can only speculate whether, had it never taken place, there would even be international institutions as we know them today. As Professor Robin Sharwood has posited, '[b]oth the League of Nations and the United Nations can be regarded ... as standing "peace conferences" along lines inaugurated at The Hague in 1899.'

This is not to say that The Hague was totally lacking in international legal or pacifist credentials prior to 1898, and these no doubt influenced, at least in part, its selection as venue of the Peace Conferences. The Netherlands was the historical venue for the signing of several major peace treaties, including the Treaty of Utrecht in 1713. Due in large part to the work of Hugo Grotius, who also spent part of his career in The Hague, the Netherlands was considered 'the cradle of the science of international law'. In 1893, the first Hague Conference on Private International Law was convened, at the initiative of the prominent Dutch international jurist and later Nobel laureate, Tobias Asser, who also played a major role in the Hague Peace Conferences.

But nothing could prepare the sleepy Dutch seat of government for the diplomatic and media frenzy that surrounded the 1899 Peace Conference. It is difficult for us – over 100 years later – to get a feel for the atmosphere and spirit of that time. For those who are interested in more detail than I have time to provide today, I can highly recommend Barbara Tuchman's, 'The Proud Tower', a brilliant portrait of the world in the years preceding the First World War, and Arthur Eyffinger's 1999 book celebrating the centennial of the First Peace Conference.

#### Origins of the Peace Conference

In August 1898, at his regular weekly reception for the diplomatic corps in St. Petersburg, the Russian Foreign Minister communicated to those gathered an unprecedent-

* Deputy Secretary-General, Permanent Court of Arbitration, The Hague.

ed and startling proposal by Czar Nicholas II for the organization of a peace conference, aimed at discussing "the most effectual means of ensuring to all peoples the benefits of a real and durable peace, and, above all, of putting an end to the progressive development of the present armaments ... ." While there was, at the end of the 19$^{th}$ century, a strong pacifist movement, inspired by the likes of Ivan Bloch, Frédéric Passy, and Countess Bertha von Suttner (who, incidentally, became the only woman to attend the first Peace Conference), Russia was a major military power, and the Czar's proposal met with a great deal of cynicism. This cynicism is clearly reflected in the composition of the delegations that States ultimately dispatched to The Hague the following year: nearly every one included a fairly high-ranking military officer. Historians believe that despite Russia's military might, it was having trouble keeping up with the arms race, and the Czar's hidden agenda was to persuade Germany in particular to agree to disarmament.

## Selection of The Hague as Venue

For our purposes here today, it is most important to ascertain why The Hague was chosen as the venue of the first Peace Conference. It appears that the Russians felt the conference could best be held outside the spheres of influence of the great powers of the time, and proposed Copenhagen, Berne, Brussels or The Hague. The Czar had stated that he 'considers it advisable that the Conference should not sit in the capital of one of the Great Powers, where so many political interests are centred which might, perhaps, impede the progress of a work in which all the countries of the universe are equally interested.' The Netherlands was a neutral country at the time (remaining neutral even through the First World War), and while small, it had an excellent infrastructure and was easily accessible by train and ship. Queen Wilhelmina, grandmother of the present queen, had just been crowned, upon reaching the age of 18. Her grandmother, Anna Pavlovna, had been a Romanov and a member of the Russian imperial family, and Wilhelmina offered her cousin, Czar Nicholas, the use of her summer palace, Huis Ten Bosch [*The House in the Woods*] as the Conference venue. You will no doubt be hearing today from representatives of the Netherlands Ministry of Foreign Affairs and the municipality of The Hague about recent and ongoing efforts to attract international organizations to The Hague, so it may well come as something of a surprise to learn that the Dutch Minister of Foreign Affairs at the time, de Beaufort, was less than enthusiastic, and unlike the Belgians, refused to lobby for holding the conference in The Hague. 'Personally', he later wrote in his diary, 'I was not exactly looking forward to the conference assembling in The Hague, well aware as I was of the fact that . . . it would . . . be a heavy burden which might well cause all sorts of problems As a rule, a small Power does well to keep out of the throng and crush.'

And throng and crush it was, as the international press descended on The Hague in May 1899 – on the Czar's birthday – for the opening of the conference. The scope of the press coverage, and the superlatives used in describing the conference played an important role in bolstering the prestige of The Hague. The media heralded the 'Dawn of a New Age', with the conference that they dubbed 'The Parliament of Man, the Federation of the World'. But these superlatives sound a but less so when one considers how little there was in the way of multilateral diplomacy at the turn of the last century, and how few international – or intergovernmental – organizations were in existence at the time. States were jealous of their sovereignty – not surprising, as most were governed by sovereigns at the time (most of whom were related to each other through Queen Victoria). Their reluctance to sacrifice any of this sovereignty was crucial to the establishment, and subsequent development, of the Permanent Court of Arbitration.

## Establishment of the PCA

As I mentioned, the Czar's original 1898 proposal for a peace conference referred only to disarmament. But by the time the conference opened in May 1899, it was subdivided by topic into three commissions, dealing with disarmament, humanitarian aspects of war, and peaceful settlement of disputes. It is, of course, this last topic that was to have a lasting effect on international law and diplomacy, and on the status of The Hague as host to international tribunals and other legal and peace-related institutions. While Germany refused to budge on disarmament in the first commission, and the second commission adopted declarations prohibiting such things as the lancing of projectiles from balloons, the third commission managed – with quite some difficulty – to hammer out a Convention on the Pacific Settlement of International Disputes (the '1899 Convention'), which established the Permanent Court of Arbitration. At the inception of the conference, a group of delegates led by Sir Julian Pauncefote, the British representative, argued that to advance the cause of arbitration, the conference ought to establish a permanent institution that could settle disputes between consenting nations. Opposing them was a group of countries, led by Germany, that had serious reservations about relinquishing sovereignty to a supra-national body of any kind, and that did its best to limit the powers and status of the organization. The institution described in the 1899 Convention diverges, however, from our usual image of a court. Its peculiarities reflect the difficulties that the delegates encountered as they struggled towards a compromise. Nevertheless, the 1899 Convention establishing the PCA, is generally seen as the crowning – and most lasting – achievement of the First Hague Peace Conference.

## Construction of the Peace Palace

The subsequent construction of the Peace Palace further illustrates the optimism engendered by the Peace Conference and the establishment of the PCA. There was a strong sense that this new entity should have a fitting headquarters in a 'Palace of Peace'. Funding – to the tune of US $1.5 million – was sought and obtained from the Scottish-American industrialist, Andrew Carnegie, and an international architectural competition was held, with the winning design submitted by a Frenchman, Louis Cordonnier. On the occasion of the opening of the Second Hague Peace Conference in 1907, Andrew Carnegie laid the cornerstone of the Peace Palace building, construction of which was completed in 1913.

## World Wars

While the Netherlands was able to remain neutral in the First World War, the failure of the PCA and the Peace Conferences to avert such a bloody conflict could not go unnoticed. By the 1920s, the world was ready to acknowledge the need for more permanent, and powerful, intergovernmental organizations. One may well wonder why – in the aftermath of the Peace Conferences – The Hague was not considered the obvious venue for locating the headquarters of the new League of Nations. One historical explanation involves British and American dismay at the Netherlands' decision to grant refuge and asylum to the German Kaiser after the war. Yet there is little indication that the Dutch even lobbied for the League to be established here – perhaps out of the same reluctance shown by de Beaufort with respect to the Peace Conference in 1899. Luckily for The Hague, the League of Nations elected to establish the first true international court, the Permanent Court of International Justice, not at the League's Geneva headquarters, but at the Peace Palace in The Hague, paving the way for the fledgling United Nations to do the same in 1946.

## The Decade of International Law; The Decade of The Hague

Despite this illustrious past, the true explosion in the establishment of international organization headquarters in The Hague – particularly those of a legal or judicial character – did not in fact take place until the last decade of the 20th century. It was only in the 1990s that then UN Secretary-General Boutros Boutros-Ghali coined the phrase 'legal capital of the world' in reference to The Hague. By then, the Iran-United States Claims Tribunal had been operating in The Hague for over a decade, but such organizations as the OPCW, International Criminal Tribunal for the Former Yugoslavia, and the International Criminal Court, all set-up operation in The Hague after 1990.

There are currently said to be over thirty intergovernmental organizations headquartered in the Netherlands. By now, the Dutch government and the municipality of The Hague appear to have dropped whatever compunction there might have been against actively lobbying for IGO headquarters. Nowhere is this more obvious than in the massive offensive launched in order to ensure that the International Criminal Court would be headquartered in here. This, I understand, is the topic on which some of my fellow panellists have come prepared to address you, so this seems the appropriate time to look forward instead of back and turn the floor over to them.

**Sources**

Eyffinger, Arthur, *The 1899 Hague Peace Conference: The Parliament of Man, the Federation of the World* (1999)

Jonkman, Hans, 'The Role of the Permanent Court of Arbitration in International Dispute Resolution', in 279 *Recueil de Cours* 13 (1999).

Sharwood, Robin, 'Princes and Peacemakers: The Story of the Hague Peace Conference of 1899' in *A Century of War and Peace: Asia-Pacific Perspectives on the Centenary of the 1899 Hague Peace Conference 3* (McCormack, Tilbury & Triggs (eds.) 2001).

Tuchman, Barbara, *The Proud Tower*, 1966.

van Krieken, Peter J. and McKay, David (eds.), *The Hague – Legal Capital of the World* (2005).

P. DE SAVORIN LOHMAN*

P. de Savorin Lohman opened with a reference to The Netherlands' long-running connections with international law and pointed to the inclusion of a clause in the Dutch constitution obliging the Government to promote the development of the international legal order. Being host to a number of international courts and organizations is in line with this constitutional obligation. P. de Savorin Lohman noted that the number of organizations has steadily increased, particularly during the 1990s, due largely to the efforts of the Dutch government to attract them. The Dutch cabinet, however, has recently updated its policy for attracting international organizations to bring it into line with current needs. He reported the breaking news that, as set out in a policy paper sent to the Parliament only in June, the government would require future bids for international organizations to be made only with the relevant ministries acting in concert, and based on plans for the fair provision of housing, security arrangements, medical facilities, international schools, and conference facilities. He emphasized that the government also plans to streamline and harmonize the privileges and immunities offered to staff of international organizations in the Netherlands. The highest-ranking staff of international organizations will be granted the same status as diplomats of equivalent rank at embassies, while other staff will be granted the same status as administrative and technical staff of embassies, without exception.

P. de Savorin Lohman also addressed the concerns and complaints of some international organizations concerning unequal treatment, communication and information. There will now be systematic liaison with organizations both on the policies that will affect them and the intended changes to legislation.

PANEL DISCUSSION

There followed a lively discussion between C. Brower and P. de Savorin Lohman, in which the latter emphasized the new policy of the Dutch government to harmonize fiscal and other privileges and immunities to avoid perceptions of inequality or unfair treatment.

*Reporter:* Kate Annand**

* Director of the Protocol Department for the Ministry of Foreign Affairs, the Netherlands. The original manuscript of this contribution was not received. The following text has been derived from the tapes on which the conference sessions were recorded.

** King's College London.

# FINAL SESSION

## CONCLUSIONS AND RECOMMENDATIONS

The panel was convened by its Co-chairs, Lucy Reed* and Menno Kamminga**

The Final Session focused on drawing out common themes and highlights from the 14 sessions and workshops which took place during the course of this two day conference. To draw out these highlights, the organizing committee had invited two distinguished guests, Ms. Judy Freedberg and Professor Peter Baehr, to attend the various sessions with an eye towards identifying common premises, unique challenges, and parallel issues.

Co-Chair Professor Kamminga opened this discussion with a question to both panellists: 'what are the main nuggets you take away with you from this conference?'

MS. FREEDBERG observed that recurring themes did not materialized in the sessions she attended; however, she noted a few pleasant surprises:

- The presenters did not hide behind an 'it all depends' deflection. The speakers were straight forward in their comments without any 'flip-flopping or waffling'.
- Freedberg remarked positively on the contribution of young scholars who made outstanding presentations in many sessions. This should encourage future organizing committees to consider an expanded role for young scholars to present papers at future conference, in particular young scholars from less wealthy countries, supported by scholarships and funding if necessary. The importance of contributing papers from scholars in Asia, Africa, and non-Western European countries was also later emphasized by Professor Baehr at the close of the session.
- It was surprising that the subject of religion had not been mentioned in these sessions because, in Freedberg's opinion, religion is a contemporary element in the life and function of international organisations.
- At the close of the session, Freedberg offered a final point on the distinction between long-term and short-term international organisation which, in her opinion, had not been clearly flushed out by the program. The evaluation of short-term international organisations was that they were pragmatic, flexible, and focused on the mission. Although they were created in haste, this turned to their advantage because their constituting documents did not defining their mandate in too constricting of a manner which allowed them flexibility in interpreting their mission and achieving their goals.

* Freshfields Bruckhaus Deringer, New York.

** Maastricht University.

Professor Baehr responded to the Chair's question with the following points:

- Although the term 'international community' is in vogue, Baehr cautioned against its use because of its vagueness. If it is used, it should be made clear what is meant by it.
- On the debate about the democratic nature of the UN Security Council or General Assembly, Baehr opined that neither is particularly democratic.
- The majority of speakers favoured amending the UN Charter. Some suggested the possibility of change in the UN without changes at the constitutional level. In Baehr's opinion, effective reform would have been at the constitutional level. He later also noted his surprise at how readily lawyers would amend themselves to a 'soft-law' approach.
- Regarding the proposal for a Human Rights Council to replace the Human Rights Committee, Baehr challenged the suggestion that such a change in structure and institutional organisation would have any real effect in removing the problems of politicalization which have hampered effective protection of human rights.
- It was surprising that the United States was not mentioned for the most part in most panels. It is after-all the world's only remaining super-power and one of the world's largest economies.
- It is still questionable whether an African court for human rights will materialize.
- The role of NGO was generally presented as positive with focus on its positive contributions and consequences. Baehr noted that we should also explore the possible downside of NGO participation.
- There was a lack of critical questioning, of raising doubts and probing behind the presented facts. Matters were presented as 'this is how it is'.
- There was also a lack of historical perspective.

The Chair then opened the discussion to the participants and invited interventions from the audience.

Unknown speaker from George Washington University (USA) noted how often 'law' was not mentioned and that the discussions frequently looked at the central issues from a political perspective.

Unknown speaker from Heidelberg University (Germany) lamented the missed opportunity for more courageous proposals for change (with the expect of two proposals for a war damage claims court). The Chair invited the intervener to offer any such proposals she may have. The intervener offered two proposals for change in connection with the European Court of Human Rights: (1) the creation of a fact-finding organ within the Court and (2) on the issue of reparations, Article 46 should be reformed. Where a violation is found, the Court should be allowed to direct states as to what should be done in order to comply with the Convention. This would in turn help reduce the Court's heavy caseload.

Both panellists concurred on the point of missed opportunity for more courageous proposals. Freedberg noted however that this may be a matter of perspective baring in mind that proposals for change may be in the form of 'evolution' or 'revolution'. The emphasis at this conference was on an 'evolution' approach to change. Moreover, she remarked that from the perspective of a specialist in the field a suggested change may seem like a 'revolution' because those very close to the subject matter are particularly alert to how change to a particular pillar, feature, organ of an international institution may have far-reaching effects in the functioning of that organisation. However, from the perspective of a non-specialist, all this may seem like small tinkering.

The Chair next raised the 'now or never' issue. Noting that it has been remarked that 'if we desire reform to the United Nations, we must do so now', the Chair invited the audience to offer their reactions on this point. Is this so? Are we at a time of unique opportunity to make reforms to the UN and if we do not do so now, does that mean the door to change will close for a long period to come?

PROF. NICO SCHRIJVER, Leiden University (Netherlands) replied that to some extent one can say that the 'now or never' hype around the UN is to some extent self-induced. Nevertheless, Professor Schrijver emphasized that we are at an important moment in time, not just in light of outer formal time indicators such as 'the new millennium' and '60 year anniversary', but more significantly in light of the implications arising from recent behaviour of States. In his opinion, recent events, such as the process leading up the invasion of Iraq, have had the effect of marginalizing the United Nations. Therefore, there is added pressure to make the United Nations a more genuine player and to give it a more genuine role as an international organisation representing more genuinely the international community and not just an inter-state organisation to function as a formal meeting place between governments.

The session and the conference was closed with an exchange of gifts, recognition of the numerous individuals at various levels who had devoted themselves to the preparation of the conference, and last but not least, acknowledgement of the excellent work and vision of the organizing committing in selecting a timely subject and collecting an impressive range of speakers.

*Reporter:* Dana Shahram*

* Maastricht University, the Netherlands.

# Program Committee

The American Society of International Law

Lucy Reed, Chair
Hannah Buxbaum
Susan Karamanian
Ralph Wilde

Nederlandse Vereniging voor Internationaal Recht

Menno Kamminga, Chair
Niels Blokker
Ellen Hey
Susan Karamanian
Olivier Ribbelink
Erika de Wet
Ralph Wilde

Conference Secretariat

T.M.C. Asser Instituut
R.J. Schimmelpennincklaan 20-22
2517 JN The Hague
The Neteherlands

The American Society of International Law

2223 Massachusetts Avenue
NW Washington DC 20008
U.S.A.
Tel.: 1-202-939-6000
Fax: 1-202-797-7133

Nederlandse Vereniging voor Internationaal Recht

Steenschuur 25
2311 ES Leiden
The Netherlands
Tel.: 31-71-527-7748
Fax: 31-71-527-8794

# Officers

The American Society of International Law

Honorary President:
Judge Thomas Buergenthal

President:
James H. Carter

Vice Presidents:
David Caron,
Lucy Reed
Ruth Wedgwood

Executive Vice President and Executive Director:
Charlotte Ku

Secretary:
Frederic L. Kirgis

Treasurer:
Nancy Perkins

Executive Council:
Adeno Addis, Roger Alford, José E. Alvarez, James Bacchus, Stewart Baker, Rosemary Barkett, Peter E. Bass, Karima Bennoune, Franklin Berman, Daniel Bethlehem, Daniel Bodansky, Kent Bressie, Rosa E. Brooks, Charles H. Brower II, Charles N. Brower, Ian Brownlie, Hannah Buxbaum, Lan Cao, Douglass Cassel, Hilary Charlesworth, Allison M. Danner, Eliana Davidson, Pierre-Marie Dupuy, Tom J. Farer, Thomas M. Franck, John King Gamble, Jamie Gorelick, Conrad

Nederlandse Vereniging voor Internationaal Recht

President:
Nico Schrijver

Secretary:
Marcel Brus

Treasurer:
Mieke Boersma

Board member (esp. for ILA matters):
Jacomijn van Haersolte-van Hof

Executive Council:
Katharina Boele-Woelki
Niels Blokker
Ige Dekker
Astrid Delissen
Ellen Hey
Carla Joustra
Marielle Koppenol-Laforce
Hans Lammers
Frans Nelissen
Fons Orie
Bart Punt
Sierd Schaafsma
Bette Shifman
Guus Stille
Frans van der Velden
Elisabeth de Vos
Jan Wouters
Paul Vlas

# List of Abbreviations

| | |
|---|---|
| ACP | African, Caribbean and Pacific states |
| AJCompLaw | American Journal of Comparative Law |
| AJIL | American Journal of International Law |
| Amer. J. of Pol. Sci | American Journal of Political Science |
| Am. Soc'y Int'l L. Proc. | American Society of International Law and Procedure |
| Am. U. L. Rev | American University Law Review |
| APC | All People's Congress |
| ATCA | Alien Tort Claims Act |
| BiH | Bosnia and Herzogovina |
| BITs | Bilateral investment treaties |
| BWC | Biological Weapons Convention |
| BYU L. Rev. | Brigham Young University Law Review |
| CAFTA | Central America Free Trade Agreement |
| CAN-US L.J. | Canada-US Law Journal |
| CAO | Compliance Advisor Ombudsman |
| CCP | Common Commercial Policy |
| CFSP | Common Foreign and Security Policy |
| CMLRev. | Common Market Law Review |
| Cornell Int'l L.J | Cornell International Law Journal |
| CSDMT | Comprehensive Statistical Database of Multilateral Treaties |
| CSO | Civil Society Organizations |
| CWC | Chemical Weapons Convention |
| Davis J. Int'l L. & Pol.'Y | Davis Journal of International Law and Politics Yearbook |
| DRC | Democratic Republic Congo |
| ECHR | European Convention on Human Rights |
| ECJ | European Court of Justice |
| ECOWAS | Economic Community of Western African States |
| ECT | Energy Charter Treaty |
| EEAS | European External Action Service |
| EJIL | European Journal of International Law |
| EP | European Parliament |
| ESDP | European Security and Defence Policy |
| FAO | Food and Agriculture Organisation |
| Fordham L. Rev. | Fordham Law Review |
| FRY | Federal Republic of Yugoslavia |

| | |
|---|---|
| GATT | General Agreement on Tariffs and Trade |
| GAVI | Global Alliance on Vaccine and Immunization |
| GDP | Gross Domestic Product |
| Geo. Wash. Int'l L.Rev. | George Washington International Law Review |
| GOARN | Global Outbreak Alert and Response Network |
| GPHIN | Global Public Health Intelligence Network |
| GYIL | German Yearbook of International Law |
| | |
| Harv. Int'L L.J. | Harvard International Law Journal |
| | |
| IAEA | International Atomic Energy Agency |
| ICANN | Internet Corporation for Assigned Names and Numbers |
| ICAO | International Civil Aviation Organization |
| ICC | International Criminal Court |
| ICJ | International Court of Justice |
| ICPO | International Criminal Police Organization |
| ICTY | International Criminal Tribunal for the former Yugoslavia |
| ICSID | International Centre for Settlement of Investment Disputes |
| IGC | Intergovernmental Conference |
| IGO | Intergovernmental organizations |
| IHR | International Health Regulations |
| ILA | International Law Association |
| ILM | International Legal Materials |
| ILO | International Labour Organization |
| IMF | International Monetary Fund |
| INGO | International Non-Governmental Organization |
| ITLOS | International Tribunal on the Law of the Sea |
| | |
| JCMS | Journal of Common Market Studies |
| J. World. Invest. & Trade | Journal of World Investment & Trade |
| | |
| LJIL | Leiden Journal of International Law |
| LRA | Lord's Resistance Army |
| | |
| Mealy's Int'l Arb. Rep. | Mealy's International Arbitration Report |
| MFO | Multinational Force and Observers |
| Mich. J. Int.'l L | Michigan Journal of International Law |
| MMV | Medicines for Malaria Venture |
| | |
| NAFTA | North American Free Trade Agreement |
| NATO | North Atlantic Treaty Organisation |
| NGO | Non-governmental organization |
| NPT | Nuclear Non-Proliferation Treaty |

| | |
|---|---|
| OAS | Organization of American States |
| OAU | Organization of African Unity |
| OSCE | Organization for Security and Co-operation in Europe |
| OECD | Organisation for Economic Co-operation and Development |
| OHR | Office of the High Representative |
| OJ | Official Journal of the European Communities |
| OPCW | Organisation for the Prohibition of Chemical Weapons |
| PCA | Permanent Court of Arbitration |
| PIC | Peace Implementation Council |
| PLO | Palestinian Liberation Organization |
| QMV | Qualified majority voting |
| RUF | Revolutionary United Front |
| SC | Security Council |
| TEU | Treaty on European Union |
| TRC | Truth and Reconciliation Commission |
| TRIPS | Trade Related Aspects of International Property Rights |
| UDRP | Uniform Domain Name Dispute Resolution Policy |
| UMFA | Union Minister for Foreign Affairs |
| UNDP | United Nations Development Programme |
| UNESCO | United Nations Educational, Scientific and Cultural Organization |
| UNFPA | United Nations Fund for Population Activities |
| UNGA | United Nations General Assembly |
| UN GAOR | United Nations General Assembly Official Records |
| UNFPA | United Nations Fund for Population Activities |
| UNICEF | United Nations (International) Children's (Emergency) Fund |
| UNIDO | United Nations Industrial Development Organisation |
| UNCITRAL | United Nations Commission on International Trade Law |
| UNSC | United Nations Security Council |
| UNSCR | United Nations Security Council Resolution |
| UNTAET | United Nations Transitional Administration in East Timor |
| UNTS | United Nations Treaty Series |
| WB | World Bank |
| WEOG | Western European and Others Group |
| WHO | World Health Organization |
| WIPO | World Intellectual Property Organization |

| | |
|---|---|
| WMO | World Meteorological Organization |
| WTO | World Trade Organization |
| WMD | Weapons of Mass Destruction |
| Yale J. Int'l L. | Yale Journal of International Law |
| YEL | Yearbook of European Law |
| ZaöRV | Zeitschrift für ausländisches öffentliches Recht und Völkerrecht |

# Index of Names